MACROECONOMICS

For our other contributions to
the next generation:
Catherine, Nicholas and Peter;
and Benjamin, Oliver and Harriet

MICROECONOMICS

N. Gregory Mankiw and Mark P. Taylor

SOUTH-WESTERN
CENGAGE Learning

Australia • Brazil • Japan • Korea • Mexico • Singapore • Spain • United Kingdom • United States

SOUTH-WESTERN
CENGAGE Learning

Microeconomics
Second Edition
N. Gregory Mankiw and Mark P. Taylor

Publishing Director: Linden Harris

Publisher: Brendan George

Development Editor: Annabel Ainscow

Editorial Assistant: Helen Green

Content Project Editor: Lucy Arthy

Production Controller: Eyvett Davis

Marketing Manager: Amanda Cheung

Typesetter: MPS Limited, a Macmillan Company

Cover design: Adam Renvoize

Text design: Design Deluxe

This work is adapted from *Economics*, 1st Edition, published by South-Western, a division of Cengage Learning, Inc. © 2008.

British Library Cataloguing-in-Publication Data
A catalogue record for this book is available from the British Library.

ISBN: 13: 978-1-4080-1791-3

Cengage Learning EMEA
Cheriton House, North Way, Andover, Hampshire SP10 5BE
United Kingdom

Cengage Learning products are represented in Canada by Nelson Education Ltd.

For your lifelong learning solutions, visit
www.cengage.co.uk

Purchase your next print book, e-book or e-chapter at
www.cengagebrain.com

For product information and technology assistance,
contact **emea.info@cengage.com**

For permission to use material from this text or product,
and for permission queries,
email **emea.permissions@cengage.com**

Printed in Singapore by Seng Lee Press
2 3 4 5 6 7 8 9 10 – 14 13 12

BRIEF CONTENTS

CONTENTS

INTRODUCTION   1

SUPPLY AND DEMAND I: HOW MARKETS WORK   67

PART 3

SUPPLY AND DEMAND II: MARKETS AND WELFARE   137

PART 4

THE ECONOMICS OF THE PUBLIC SECTOR   197

PART 5

FIRM BEHAVIOUR AND THE ORGANIZATION OF INDUSTRY 263

PART 6

THE ECONOMICS OF LABOUR MARKETS 381

TOPICS FOR FURTHER STUDY   437

21 The Theory of Consumer Choice   438

AUTHORS:

N. GREGORY MANKIW is Professor of Economics at Harvard University. As a student, he studied economics at Princeton University and the Massachusetts Institute of Technology. As a teacher he has taught macroeconomics, microeconomics, statistics and principles of economics. Professor Mankiw is a prolific writer and a regular participant in academic and policy debates. In addition to his teaching, research and writing, Professor Mankiw has been a research associate of the National Bureau of Economic Research, an advisor to the Federal Reserve Bank of Boston and the Congressional Budget Office. From 2003 to 2005, he served as chairman of the US President's Council of Economic Advisors. Professor Mankiw lives in Wellesley, Massachusetts, with his wife Deborah, their three children and their border terrier Tobin.

MARK P. TAYLOR is Dean of Warwick Business School at the University of Warwick and Professor of International Finance. He obtained his first degree in philosophy, politics and economics from Oxford University and his master's degree in economics from London University, from where he also holds a doctorate in economics and international finance. Professor Taylor has taught economics and finance at various universities (including Oxford, Warwick and New York) and at various levels (including principles courses, advanced undergraduate and advanced postgraduate courses). He has also worked as a senior economist at the International Monetary Fund and at the Bank of England and, before becoming Dean of Warwick Business School, was a managing director at BlackRock, the world's largest financial asset manager, where he worked on international asset allocation based on macroeconomic analysis. His research has been extensively published in scholarly journals and he is today one of the most highly cited economists in the world. Professor Taylor lives with his family in a 15th century farmhouse near Stratford upon Avon, Warwickshire, where he collects clocks and keeps bees.

CONTRIBUTOR:

ANDREW ASHWIN has over 20 years experience as a teacher of economics. He has an MBA and is currently researching for a Ph.D. investigating assessment and the notion of threshold concepts in economics. Andrew is an experienced author writing a number of texts for students at different levels, journal publications related to his Ph.D. research and is currently working on a text on the business environment for undergraduates. Andrew is Chair of Examiners for a major awarding body for business and economics and is Editor of the Economics, Business and Enterprise Association (EBEA) journal. As one of the content editors for Biz/ed (http://www.bized.co.uk), Andrew writes articles and resources on business studies and economics for the website. Andrew lives in Rutland with his wife Sue and their twin sons Alex and Johnny.

'Economics is a study of mankind in the ordinary business of life.' So wrote Alfred Marshall, the great 19th-century British economist, in his textbook, *Principles of Economics*. Although we have learned much about the economy since Marshall's time, this definition of economics is as true today as it was in 1890, when the first edition of his text was published.

Why should you, as a student of the 21st century, embark on the study of economics? Here are three good reasons. The first reason to study economics is that it will help you understand the world in which you live. There are many questions about the economy that might spark your curiosity. Why do airlines charge less for a return ticket if the traveller stays over a Saturday night? Why is Julia Roberts paid so much to star in films? Why are living standards so meagre in many African countries? Why do some countries have high rates of inflation while others have stable prices? Why have some European countries adopted a common currency? These are just a few of the questions that a course in economics will help you answer.

The second reason to study economics is that it will make you a more astute participant in the economy As you go about your life, you make many economic decisions. While you are a student, you decide how many years to stay in full-time education. Once you take a job, you decide how much of your income to spend, how much to save and how to invest your savings. One day you may find yourself running a small business or a large firm, and you will decide what prices to charge for your products. The insights developed in the coming chapters will give you a new perspective on how best to make these decisions. Studying economics will not by itself make you rich, but it will give you some tools that may help in that endeavour if that is what you desire.

The third reason to study economics is that it will give you a better understanding of the potential and limits of economic policy. As a voter, you help choose the policies that guide the allocation of society's resources. When deciding which policies to support, you may find yourself asking various questions about economics. What are the burdens associated with alternative forms of taxation? What are the effects of free trade with other countries? What is the best way to protect the environment? How does the government budget deficit affect the economy? These and similar questions are always on the minds of policy makers.

Thus the principles of economics can be applied in many of life's situations. Whether the future finds you reading the newspaper, running a business or running the country, you will be glad that you studied economics.

FOR WHOM IS THIS BOOK WRITTEN?

It is tempting for professional economists writing a textbook to take the economist's point of view and to emphasize those topics that fascinate them and other economists. We have done our best to avoid that temptation. We have tried to put ourselves in the position of someone seeing economics for the first time. Our goal has been to emphasize the material that *students* should and do find interesting about the study of the economy.

One result is that this book is briefer than many books used to introduce students to economics. Another is that more of this book is devoted to applications and policy – and less to formal economic theory – than is the case with many other books written for an introductory course. Throughout this book we have tried to return to applications and policy questions as often as possible. All the chapters include case studies illustrating how the principles of economics are applied. In addition, 'In the News' boxes offer highlights from news events showing how economic ideas shed light on current issues facing society. After students finish their first course in economics, they should think about news stories from a new perspective and with greater insight.

Something else worth pointing out is that the book has a distinctively European focus. This is not to say that it is an introduction to the economics of the European economy – it is not. Nor does the book ignore the importance of the US economy and the rest of the world – to do so would give a very lopsided view. But what it does attempt to do is to relate economic concepts to an environment that will be familiar and interesting to a European student, and we do examine some important issues relevant specifically to the European economy, such as the single European currency. The case studies and 'In the News' boxes also draw on European material. Since this is a book designed to teach students how to think about the world like an economist, analyses of particular institutional details are necessary primarily in order to illustrate the underlying economic principles, but we have used European institutional examples wherever possible. In some instances we have chosen to focus on a particular economy for reasons of space or clarity of exposition but in this Second Edition we have been able to introduce analysis of other economies as well, for example, in our discussion of the tax system we have covered the UK, South Africa and Germany.

HOW IS THIS BOOK ORGANIZED?

To write a brief and student-friendly book, we had to consider new ways to organize familiar material. What follows is a whirlwind tour of this text. With any textbook, instructors can choose to cover material in different orders; each section in the book does contain chapters that build on previous ones, although but each section can be tackled independently of the others if desired. The tour will, we hope, give instructors some sense of how the pieces fit together.

Introductory Material

Chapter 1, 'Ten Principles of Economics', introduces students to the economists' view of the world. It previews some of the big ideas that recur throughout economics, such as opportunity cost, marginal decision-making, the role of incentives, the gains from trade, and the efficiency of market allocations. Throughout the book, we refer regularly to the *Ten Principles of Economics* introduced in Chapter 1 to remind students that these ideas are the foundation for all economics. An icon in the margin calls attention to these key, interconnected principles.

Chapter 2, 'Thinking Like an Economist', examines how economists approach their field of study. It discusses the role of assumptions in developing a theory and introduces the concept of an economic model. It also discusses the role of economists in making policy. The appendix to this chapter offers a brief refresher course on how graphs are used and how they can be abused.

Chapter 3, 'Interdependence and the Gains from Trade', presents the theory of comparative advantage. This theory explains why individuals trade with their neighbours, as well as why nations trade with other nations. Much of economics is about how market forces coordinate many individual production and consumption decisions. As a starting point for this analysis, students see in this chapter why specialization, interdependence and trade can benefit everyone.

The Fundamental Tools of Supply and Demand

The next three chapters introduce the basic tools of supply and demand. Chapter 4, 'The Market Forces of Supply and Demand', develops the supply curve, the demand curve and the notion of market equilibrium. Chapter 5, 'Elasticity and its Application', introduces the concept of elasticity and uses it to analyse events in three different markets. Chapter 6, 'Supply, Demand and Government Policies', uses these tools to examine price controls, such as rent control, minimum wage laws, and tax incidence.

Chapter 7, 'Consumers, Producers and the Efficiency of Markets', extends the analysis of supply and demand using the concepts of consumer surplus and producer surplus. It begins by developing the link between consumers' willingness to pay and the demand curve, and the link between producers' costs of production and the supply curve. It then shows that the market equilibrium maximizes the sum of the producer and consumer surplus. Thus, students learn early about the efficiency of market allocations.

The next two chapters apply the concepts of producer and consumer surplus to questions of policy. Chapter 8, 'Application: The Costs of Taxation', shows why taxation results in deadweight losses and what determines the size of those losses. Chapter 9, 'Application: International Trade', considers who wins and who loses from international trade and presents the debate over protectionist trade policies.

More Microeconomics

Having examined why market allocations are often desirable, the book then considers how the government can sometimes improve on them. Chapter 10, 'Externalities', explains how external effects such as pollution can render market outcomes inefficient and discusses the possible public and private solutions to those inefficiencies. Chapter 11, 'Public Goods and Common Resources', considers the problems that arise when goods, such as national defence, have no market price. Chapter 12, 'The Design of the Tax System', describes how the government raises the revenue necessary to pay for public goods. It presents some institutional background about the UK tax system and an outline of the system in Germany and South Africa for comparison, and then discusses how the goals of efficiency and equity come into play when designing a tax system.

The next five chapters examine firm behaviour and industrial organization. Chapter 13, 'The Costs of Production', discusses what to include in a firm's costs, and it introduces cost curves. Chapter 14, 'Firms in Competitive Markets', analyses the behaviour of price-taking firms and derives the market supply curve. Chapter 15, 'Monopoly', discusses the behaviour of a firm that is the sole seller in its market. It discusses the inefficiency of monopoly pricing, the possible policy responses, and the attempts by monopolies to price discriminate. Chapter 16, 'Monopolistic Competition', looks at behaviour in a market in which many sellers offer similar but differentiated products. It also discusses the debate over the effects of advertising. Chapter 17, 'Oligopoly', covers markets in which there are only a few sellers, using the prisoner's dilemma as the model for examining strategic interaction.

The next three chapters present issues related to labour markets. Chapter 18, 'The Markets for the Factors of Production', emphasizes the link between factor prices and marginal productivity. Chapter 19, 'Earnings and Discrimination', discusses the determinants of equilibrium wages, including compensating differentials, human capital and discrimination. Chapter 20, 'Income Inequality and Poverty', examines the degree of inequality in UK society, alternative views about the government's role in changing the distribution of income and various policies aimed at helping society's poorest members.

The next two chapters present optional material. Chapter 21, 'The Theory of Consumer Choice', analyses individual decision-making using budget constraints and indifference curves. Chapter 22, 'Frontiers of Microeconomics', introduces the topics of asymmetric information, political economy and behavioural economics.

Many instructors may choose to omit all or some of this material. Instructors who do cover these topics may choose to assign these chapters earlier than they are presented in the book, and we have written them to give instructors flexibility.

LEARNING TOOLS

The purpose of this book is to help students learn the fundamental lessons of economics and to show how such lessons can be applied to the world in which they live. Towards that end, we have used various learning tools that recur throughout the book.

- *Case studies*. Economic theory is useful and interesting only if it can be applied to understanding actual events and policies. This book, therefore, contains numerous case studies that apply the theory that has just been developed.
- *'In the News' boxes*. One benefit that students gain from studying economics is a new perspective and greater understanding about news from around the world. To highlight this benefit, we have incorporated discussions of news events including excerpts from newspaper articles. These articles, together with our brief introductions, show how basic economic theory can be applied and raise important questions for discussion.
- *'FYI' boxes*. These boxes provide additional material 'for your information'. Some of them offer a glimpse into the history of economic thought. Others clarify technical issues. Still others discuss supplementary topics that instructors might choose either to discuss or skip in their lectures.
- *Definitions of key concepts*. When key concepts are introduced in the chapter, they are presented in **bold** typeface. In addition, their definitions are placed in the margins. This treatment should aid students in learning and reviewing the material.
- *Quick quizzes*. After most major sections, students are offered a 'quick quiz' to check their comprehension of what they have just learned. If students cannot readily answer these quizzes, they should stop and reread material before continuing.
- *Chapter summaries*. Each chapter ends with a brief summary that reminds students of the most important lessons that they have just learned. Later in their study it offers an efficient way to revise for exams.
- *List of key concepts*. A list of key concepts at the end of each chapter offers students a way to test their understanding of the new terms that have been introduced. Page references are included so that students can review the terms they do not understand. All key terms can also be found in the glossary at the end of the book.
- *Questions for review*. At the end of each chapter are questions for review that cover the chapter's primary lessons. Students can use these questions to check their comprehension and to prepare for exams.
- *Problems and applications*. Each chapter also contains a variety of problems and applications that ask students to apply the material they have learned. Some professors may use these questions for homework assignments. Others may use them as a starting point for classroom discussions.

WHAT'S NEW IN THE SECOND EDITION?

One of the most interesting things about economics is that though a science, it is built on shifting sands – dynamic and forever changing. What we understand about human behaviour and the way in which the economy works is constantly being updated to take account of new data and new events. The Second Edition brings you some new, and not so new, thinking to help you understand the debates and dilemmas facing economists and policy makers in making sense of the world. The financial crisis which began to gather pace in 2007 and the subsequent recession have led to a major rethink about some fundamental assumptions in economic theory. The consequences of the crisis have raised new questions for economists as well as challenging some widely held assumptions and beliefs. These topical issues are introduced throughout the book where appropriate to highlight the dynamic nature of the discipline. All chapters have been thoroughly revised and updated with the latest data at the time of writing. The growing influence of behavioural economics is acknowledged throughout the book and attempts have been made to use new case studies and 'In the News' articles to reflect the European focus of the book and the importance of business economics. Together the new and revised chapters provide a range of fascinating new topics to explore. All the issues and economic concepts covered will be familiar to students and provide them with further food for thought in their quest to 'think like an economist'.

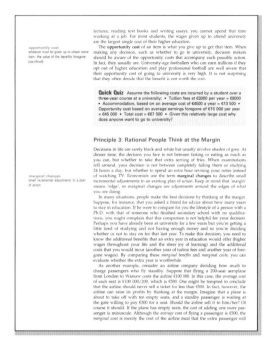

Quick quizzes are provided at the end of each section and allow students to check their comprehension of what they have just learned.

Summaries at the end of each chapter remind students of what they have learned so far, offering a useful way to review for exams.

Problems and applications allow students to apply the material they have learned within the chapter. These can also be used for classroom discussions or homework assignments.

Questions for review cover each chapter's primary lessons. These can be used to check comprehension and to prepare for exams.

FYI provides additional material 'for your information'; the boxes offer a range of supplementary material, such as a glimpse into the history of economic thought, technical issues and current topics that can be discussed in lectures.

Case studies are provided throughout the text that apply the theory that has been developed to understanding events and policies.

Ten Principles of Economics references within the text are marked by a coin icon in the margin.

'In the News' articles relate key ideas covered in the chapter to topical news events to highlight the application of economic ideas and introduce new angles to consider in topical debates.

SUPPLEMENTS

Cengage Learning offers various supplements for instructors and students who use this book. These resources are designed to make teaching the principles of economics easy for the instructor and learning them easy for the student.

ABOUT THE WEBSITE

Please visit the *Economics* Second Edition website for all the following material at: www.cengage.co.uk/mankiw_taylor2

For Instructors

Teaching the principles of economics can be a demanding job. The supplements designed for the instructor make the job less difficult. The instructor's supplements have been written by Chris Downs of University College, Chichester and Andrew Ashwin.

- **Instructor's Manual** – a detailed outline of each chapter of the text that provides learning objectives, identifies stumbling blocks that students may face, offers helpful teaching tips and provides suggested in-classroom activities for a more cooperative learning experience. The Instructor's Manual also includes solutions to all of the end-of-chapter exercises, Quick Quizzes, Questions for Review, and Problems and Applications found in the text.
- **PowerPoint Lecture Slides and Exhibit Slides** – instructors can save valuable time as they prepare for classes using these fully adaptable comprehensive lecture presentations with integrated graphs, tables, lists and concepts. A separate exhibit presentation provides instructors with all of the tables and graphs from the main text.
- **ExamView Testbank** – with test generator software included, allows lecturers to create online, paper and local area network (LAN) tests specifically for this book.

For Students

The supplements designed for the student enrich and support the learning experience, providing excellent revision tools and further study opportunities.

- **Learning Objectives** – listed for each chapter, they help the student to monitor their understanding and progress through the book.
- **Exhibit Slides** – provided in PowerPoint, the exhibit presentations provide students with animated figures from the main text.
- **Glossary** – the full glossary of key terms that appears at the end of the book in a downloadable PDF file.
- **Multiple Choice Questions** – test yourself, chapter by chapter.
- **Advanced Critical Thinking Questions** – short scenario-related questions and answers.
- **Discussion Questions** – these can be used to practise and improve your essay-writing skills.

- **Short-answer-questions** – a series of questions requiring some thorough and some more extended writing to assess understanding and application skills.
- **Case studies** – a case study will be available for each chapter focusing on some aspect of the content in the chapter and developing the theory covered, introducing new and relevant research material along with a series of questions to promote thinking and develop writing skills.
- **Practice Questions** – test yourself on a set of questions for each chapter, with the chance to check your answers once you have finished.
- **Internet Activities** – interesting and practical tasks for the student to undertake using internet research linked to the content of each chapter.
- **Maths Workout** – introductory guide and questions on the use of maths in economics related to appropriate topics in relevant chapters.

OTHER SUPPLEMENTARY RESOURCES

Global Economic Watch   Cengage Learning's Global Economic Watch is a powerful, continuously updated online resource which stimulates discussion and understanding of the global downturn through articles from leading publications, a real-time database of videos, podcasts and much more.

Aplia   Cengage Learning's Aplia is an online homework solution, is dedicated to improving learning by increasing student effort and engagement. Aplia has been used by more than 1 million students at over 1,200 institutions. It offers chapter assignments, tutorials, news analyses, and experiments to make economics relevant and engaging. All assignments are automatically graded, and there are detailed explanations for every question to help students stay focused, alert, and thinking critically.

CourseMate   Cengage Learning's CourseMate brings course concepts to life with interactive learning, study and exam preparation tools that support the printed textbook. Watch student comprehension soar as your class works with the printed textbook and the textbook-specific website. CourseMate includes: an interactive eBook; interactive teaching and learning tools including videos, games, quizzes and flashcards (resources are mapped to specific disciplines so the range of resources will vary with each text); Engagement Tracker, a first-of-its-kind tool that monitors student engagement in the course.

For more information about these digital resources, please contact your local Cengage Learning representative.

Virtual Learning Environment   All of the web material is available in a format that is compatible with virtual learning environments such as Moodle, Blackboard and WebCT.

TextChoice   The home of Cengage Learning's online digital content. It provides the fastest, easiest way for you to create your own learning materials. You may select content from hundreds of our best selling titles to make a custom text.

ACKNOWLEDGEMENTS

The authors would like to thank the following reviewers for their comments.

Robert Ackrill – Nottingham Trent University
Sverrir Arngrimsson – Iceland Engineering College
Michael Artis – European University Institute, Florence
Snæfríður Baldvinsdóttir – Bifrost School of Business, Iceland
Dr John Ball – University of Swansea
Jürgen Bitzer – Free University Berlin
Randy Bootland – Webster University
Phil Bowers – University of Edinburgh
Peter Clarke – University of Lincoln
Paul de Grauwe – Catholic University, Leuven
Julia Darby – University of Strathclyde
Kevin Denny – University College Dublin
Michael Devereux – University of Warwick
Sebastian Dullien – HTW Berlin, University of Applied Sciences
James Duncan – Robert Gordon University
Robert Eastwood – University of Sussex
Peter Else – University of Sheffield
Kirstín Flygenring – Reykjavik University – Iceland
Vanina Farber – Webster University, Geneva Campus
Michael Funke – University of Hamburg – Germany
Heather Gage – University of Surrey
Erich Gundlach – Kiel Institute for World Economics/Helmut-Schmidt University Hamburg
Bjarni Már Gylfason – Commercial College of Iceland
Heinz-Deiter Hardes – University of Trier
Philippe Gugler – University of Fribourg, Switzerland
Bolli Héðinsson – Reykjavik University, Iceland
Andrew Henley – Swansea University
David Higgins – University of York
Hilary Ingham – Lancaster University
Ian Jackson – Staffordshire University
Colin Jennings – University of Strathclyde
Brendan Kennelly – NUI Galway
Xander Koolman – Erasmus University Medical Centre
Richard Ledward – Staffordshire University
Oliver Marnet – University of Aberystwyth
Michael J. McCrostie – University of Buckingham
Lukas Menkhoff – University of Hannover
Jonathan Michie – Director of the Oxford University Department for Continuing Education
Kerry Patterson – University of Reading
Martin Peiz – International University in Germany
Odile Poulsen – University of East Anglia
Tom Segers – Group T Leuven Engineering School
Frank Seitz – Amberg-Weiden University of Applied Sciences
Kunal Sen – University of East Anglia
Lorena Škuflic – University of Zagreb
Tilman Slembeck – University of St. Gallen and Zurich University of Applied Sciences
Ian Smith – University of St. Andrews
Remigiusz Smolinski – Leipzig Graduate School of Management
Frank H. Stephen – Manchester School of Law
Kristian Sund – University of Applied Sciences, Chur
Benjamin Swalens – Vrije Universiteit Brussels
Oliver Taylor – University of Cambridge
Karen Thomas – University of the Free State, South Africa
Elsie Tosi – EAI CERAM, Sophia Antipolis
Jan Janse van Rensburg – University of Pretoria, South Africa
Rolf Weder – University of Basel
Linda Yueh – University of Oxford

1

INTRODUCTION

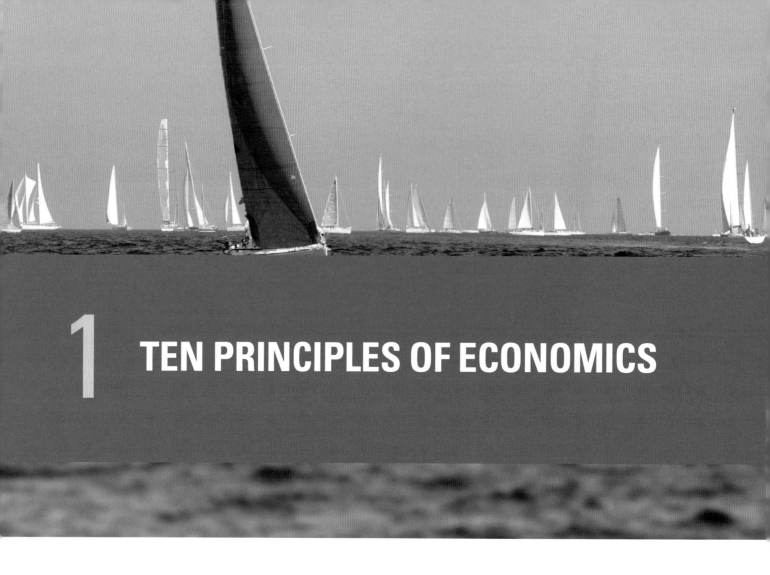

1 TEN PRINCIPLES OF ECONOMICS

The word *economy* comes from the Greek word *oikonomos,* which means 'one who manages a household'. At first, this origin might seem peculiar. But, in fact, households and economies have much in common.

A household faces many decisions. It must decide which members of the household do which tasks and what each member gets in return: Who cooks dinner? Who does the laundry? Who gets the extra slice of cake at tea time? Who chooses what TV programme to watch? In short, the household must allocate its scarce resources among its various members, taking into account each member's abilities, efforts and desires.

Like a household, a society faces many decisions. A society must decide what jobs will be done and who will do them. It needs some people to grow food, other people to make clothing and still others to design computer software. Once society has allocated people (as well as land, buildings and machines) to various jobs, it must also allocate the output of goods and services that they produce. It must decide who will eat caviar and who will eat potatoes. It must decide who will drive a Jaguar and who will take the bus.

The management of society's resources is important because resources are scarce. **Scarcity** means that society has limited resources and therefore cannot produce all the goods and services people wish to have. Just as a household cannot give every member everything he or she wants, a society cannot give every individual the highest standard of living to which he or she might aspire.

Economics is the study of how society manages its scarce resources. In most societies, resources are allocated not by a single central planner but through the

scarcity
the limited nature of society's resources

economics
the study of how society manages its scarce resources

© MONIKA LEWANDOWSKA / ISTOCK

combined actions of millions of households and firms. Economists therefore study how people make decisions: how much they work, what they buy, how much they save and how they invest their savings. Economists also study how people interact with one another. For instance, they examine how the multitude of buyers and sellers of a good together determine the price at which the good is sold and the quantity that is sold. Finally, economists analyse forces and trends that affect the economy as a whole, including the growth in average income, the fraction of the population that cannot find work and the rate at which prices are rising.

Although the study of economics has many facets, the field is unified by several central ideas. In the rest of this chapter we look at *Ten Principles of Economics*. Don't worry if you don't understand them all at first, or if you don't find them completely convincing. In the coming chapters we will explore these ideas more fully. The ten principles are introduced here just to give you an overview of what economics is all about. You can think of this chapter as a 'preview of coming attractions'.

HOW PEOPLE MAKE DECISIONS

There is no mystery to what an 'economy' is. Whether we are talking about the economy of a group of countries such as the European Union, or the economy of one particular country, such as the United Kingdom, or of the whole world, an economy is just a group of people interacting with one another as they go about their lives. Because the behaviour of an economy reflects the behaviour of the individuals who make up the economy, we start our study of economics with four principles of individual decision-making.

CASE STUDY

A Decision of Life and Death

Millions of people every day use medicinal drugs for a variety of reasons but mostly because taking them brings some benefit. In some cases, the use of medicinal drugs helps to alleviate relatively mild conditions but for a large number of patients, for example, those suffering from different types of cancer, such drugs can literally mean the difference between life and death. In recent years there have been a large number of drugs developed by companies to help cancer sufferers. The complexity of the illness, however, means that the cost of developing such drugs can be extremely high. In Europe, the European Medicines Agency (EMA) evaluates and supervises medicines for human and animal use. In the UK, the National Institute for Health and Clinical Excellence (NICE) carries out a similar role and licenses drugs for use within the National Health Service (NHS). It has to decide whether to recommend drugs for use within the NHS. It balances out the costs of using a drug against the benefits to patients. It also considers the wider costs and benefits as well. If the costs outweigh the benefits then it may reject the use of the drug under the NHS.

One example of such a rejection occurred in November 2009. The drug in question was called sorafenib or, to give it its brand name, Nexavar. The drug is produced by German pharmaceutical company Bayer and is for treatment of hepatocellular carcinoma (HCC). This is a cancer of the liver, a disease which affects around 3000 people in the UK every year. Of these, around

600–700 would benefit from the drug; it is not a cure but extends the life of patients for up to six months. Given the life expectancy of patients with this illness, this can be a significant benefit. The prognosis for liver cancer sufferers is poor; 80 per cent die within a year of diagnosis and 95 per cent die within five years.

Despite the benefits, NICE rejected the use of the drug on the NHS because the cost of licensing greatly outweighed the benefits. This was not simply the financial cost of administering the drug, estimated at £3000 per month, but the wider costs in terms of the benefits to other patients with other illnesses that would have to be foregone. The NHS budget, like most other health budgets across Europe, is limited. Decisions have to be made on who to treat and who not to because resources are scarce in relation to demand. NICE decided that the money that could be spent on sorafenib could be better spent on treating other patients; the value of the benefits to those patients would outweigh the value of the benefits to liver cancer sufferers. Andrew Dillon, chief executive of NICE, said: 'The price being asked by Bayer is simply too high to justify using NHS money which could be spent on better value cancer treatments.'

For liver cancer sufferers the decision by NICE was a major blow. The decision means that some will be deprived of additional months of good quality life which they could have had if they had access to the drug. For other cancer patients, the decision might be good news – it may mean there is more money available to treat them and that money may result in a longer period of good quality life. The decision may seem like a cold and calculating one, but in simple economics terms it makes sense.

Principle 1: People Face Trade-offs

The first lesson about making decisions is summarized in an adage popular with economists: 'There is no such thing as a free lunch'. To get one thing that we like, we usually have to give up another thing that we also like. Making decisions requires trading off one goal against another.

Consider a student who must decide how to allocate her most valuable resource – her time. She can spend all of her time studying economics; she can spend all of her time studying psychology; or she can divide her time between the two fields. For every hour she studies one subject, she gives up an hour she could have used studying the other. And for every hour she spends studying, she gives up an hour that she could have spent in the gym, riding a bicycle, watching TV, napping or working at her part-time job for some extra spending money.

Or consider parents deciding how to spend their family income. They can buy food, clothing or a family holiday. Or they can save some of the family income for retirement or perhaps to help the children buy a house or a flat when they are grown up. When they choose to spend an extra euro on one of these goods, they have one less euro to spend on some other good.

When people are grouped into societies, they face different kinds of trade-offs. The classic trade-off is between 'guns and butter'. The more we spend on national defence (guns) to protect our country from foreign aggressors, the less we can spend on consumer goods (butter) to raise our standard of living at home. Also important in modern society is the trade-off between a clean environment and a high level of income. Laws that require firms to reduce pollution raise the cost of producing goods and services. Because of the higher costs, these firms end up earning smaller profits, paying lower wages, charging higher prices, or some combination of these three. Thus, while pollution regulations give us the benefit of a cleaner environment and the improved levels of health that come with it, they have the cost of reducing the incomes of the firms' owners, workers and customers.

Another trade-off society faces is between efficiency and equity. Efficiency means that society is getting the most it can from its scarce resources. **Equity** means that the benefits of those resources are distributed fairly among society's members. In other words, efficiency refers to the size of the economic cake, and equity refers to how the cake is divided. Often, when government policies are being designed, these two goals conflict.

equity
the property of distributing economic prosperity fairly among the members of society

Consider, for instance, policies aimed at achieving a more equal distribution of economic well-being. Some of these policies, such as the social security system or unemployment insurance, try to help those members of society who are most in need. Others, such as the individual income tax, ask the financially successful to contribute more than others to support the government. Although these policies have the benefit of achieving greater equity, they have a cost in terms of reduced efficiency. When the government redistributes income from the rich to the poor, it reduces the reward for working hard; as a result, people work less and produce fewer goods and services. In other words, when the government tries to cut the economic cake into more equal slices, the cake gets smaller.

Recognizing that people face trade-offs does not by itself tell us what decisions they will or should make. A student should not abandon the study of psychology just because doing so would increase the time available for the study of economics. Society should not stop protecting the environment just because environmental regulations reduce our material standard of living. The poor should not be ignored just because helping them distorts work incentives. Nevertheless, acknowledging life's trade-offs is important because people are likely to make good decisions only if they understand the options that they have available.

Quick Quiz   Does the adage 'there is no such thing as a free lunch' simply refer to the fact that someone has to have paid for the lunch to be provided and served? Or does the recipient of the 'free lunch' also incur a cost?

Principle 2: The Cost of Something is What You Give Up to Get It

Because people face trade-offs, making decisions requires comparing the costs and benefits of alternative courses of action. In many cases, however, the cost of some action is not as obvious as it might first appear.

Consider, for example, the decision whether to go to university. The benefit is intellectual enrichment and a lifetime of better job opportunities. But what is the cost? To answer this question, you might be tempted to add up the money you spend on tuition fees, books, room and board. Yet this total does not truly represent what you give up to spend a year at university.

The first problem with this answer is that it includes some things that are not really costs of going to university. Even if you decided to leave full-time education, you would still need a place to sleep and food to eat. Room and board are part of the costs of higher education only to the extent that they are more expensive at university than elsewhere. Indeed, the cost of room and board at your university might be less than the rent and food expenses that you would pay living on your own. In this case, the savings on room and board are actually a benefit of going to university.

The second problem with this calculation of costs is that it ignores the largest cost of a university education – your time. When you spend a year listening to lectures, reading textbooks and writing essays, you cannot spend that time working at a job. For most students, the wages given up to attend university are the largest single cost of their higher education.

opportunity cost
whatever must be given up to obtain some item – the value of the benefits foregone (sacrificed)

The **opportunity cost** of an item is what you give up to get that item. When making any decision, such as whether to go to university, decision makers should be aware of the opportunity costs that accompany each possible action. In fact, they usually are. University-age footballers who can earn millions if they opt out of higher education and play professional football are well aware that their opportunity cost of going to university is very high. It is not surprising that they often decide that the benefit is not worth the cost.

> **Quick Quiz** Assume the following costs are incurred by a student over a three-year course at a university: • Tuition fees at €3 000 per year = €9 000 • Accommodation, based on an average cost of €4 500 a year = €13 500 • Opportunity cost based on average earnings foregone of €15 000 per year = €45 000 • Total cost = €67 500 • Given this relatively large cost why does anyone want to go to university?

Principle 3: Rational People Think at the Margin

Decisions in life are rarely black and white but usually involve shades of grey. At dinner time, the decision you face is not between fasting or eating as much as you can, but whether to take that extra serving of fries. When examinations roll around, your decision is not between completely failing them or studying 24 hours a day, but whether to spend an extra hour revising your notes instead of watching TV. Economists use the term **marginal changes** to describe small incremental adjustments to an existing plan of action. Keep in mind that 'margin' means 'edge', so marginal changes are adjustments around the edges of what you are doing.

marginal changes
small incremental adjustments to a plan of action

In many situations, people make the best decisions by thinking at the margin. Suppose, for instance, that you asked a friend for advice about how many years to stay in education. If he were to compare for you the lifestyle of a person with a Ph.D. with that of someone who finished secondary school with no qualifications, you might complain that this comparison is not helpful for your decision. Perhaps you have already been at university for a few years but you're getting a little tired of studying and not having enough money and so you're deciding whether or not to stay on for that last year. To make this decision, you need to know the additional benefits that an extra year in education would offer (higher wages throughout your life and the sheer joy of learning) and the additional costs that you would incur (another year of tuition fees and another year of foregone wages). By comparing these *marginal benefits* and *marginal costs*, you can evaluate whether the extra year is worthwhile.

As another example, consider an airline company deciding how much to charge passengers who fly standby. Suppose that flying a 200-seat aeroplane from London to Warsaw costs the airline €100 000. In this case, the average cost of each seat is €100 000/200, which is €500. One might be tempted to conclude that the airline should never sell a ticket for less than €500. In fact, however, the airline can raise its profits by thinking at the margin. Imagine that a plane is about to take off with ten empty seats, and a standby passenger is waiting at the gate willing to pay €300 for a seat. Should the airline sell it to him/her? Of course it should. If the plane has empty seats, the cost of adding one more passenger is minuscule. Although the *average* cost of flying a passenger is €500, the *marginal* cost is merely the cost of the airline meal that the extra passenger will consume (which may have gone to waste in any case) and possibly an extremely slight increase in the amount of aircraft fuel used. As long as the standby passenger pays more than the marginal cost, selling him or her a ticket is profitable.

As these examples show, individuals and firms can make better decisions by thinking at the margin. A rational decision maker takes an action if and only if the marginal benefit of the action exceeds the marginal cost.

Principle 4: People Respond to Incentives

Because people make decisions by comparing costs and benefits, their behaviour may change when the costs or benefits change. That is, people respond to incentives. When the price of an apple rises, for instance, people decide to eat more pears and fewer apples because the cost of buying an apple is higher. At the same time, apple orchards decide to hire more workers and harvest more apples, because the benefit of selling an apple is also higher. As we shall see, the effect of price on the behaviour of buyers and sellers in a market – in this case, the market for apples – is crucial for understanding how the economy works.

Public policy makers should never forget about incentives, because many policies change the costs or benefits that people face and, therefore, alter behaviour. A tax on petrol, for instance, encourages people to drive smaller, more fuel-efficient cars. It also encourages people to use public transport rather than drive and to live closer to where they work. If the tax were large enough, people would start driving electric cars.

When policy makers fail to consider how their policies affect incentives, they often end up with results they did not intend. For example, consider public policy regarding motor vehicle safety. Today all cars sold in the European Union have to have seat belts fitted by law (although actual seat belt use – especially by rear-seat passengers – varies widely, with official estimates ranging from about 30 per cent of car occupants in some member states to around 90 per cent in others, notably Sweden).

How does a seat belt law affect car safety? The direct effect is obvious: when a person wears a seat belt, the probability of surviving a major car accident rises. But that's not the end of the story, for the law also affects behaviour by altering incentives. The relevant behaviour here is the speed and care with which drivers operate their cars. Driving slowly and carefully is costly because it uses the driver's time and energy. When deciding how safely to drive, rational people compare the marginal benefit from safer driving to the marginal cost. They drive more slowly and carefully when the benefit of increased safety is high. It is no surprise, for instance, that people drive more slowly and carefully when roads are icy than when roads are clear.

Quick Quiz The emphasis on road safety throughout Europe has increased over the last 25 years. Not only are cars packed with safety technology and devices but roads are also designed to be safer with the use of safety barriers and better road surfaces, for example. Is there a case, therefore, for believing that if people feel that they are safer in their cars there is an incentive to drive faster because the marginal cost is now outweighed by the marginal benefit?

Consider how a seat belt law alters a motorist's cost–benefit calculation. Seat belts make accidents less costly because they reduce the likelihood of injury or death. In other words, seat belts reduce the benefits of slow and careful driving. People respond to seat belts as they would to an improvement in road

Music, TV and television producer and executive Simon Cowell understood opportunity cost and incentives. He decided to leave school before completing his post-16 education and is reported to earn in excess of £50 million a year!

conditions – by faster and less careful driving. The end result of a seat belt law, therefore, is a larger number of accidents and so it will affect both motorists and pedestrians. The decline in safe driving has a clear, adverse impact on pedestrians, who are more likely to find themselves in an accident but (unlike the motorists) don't have the benefit of added protection.

At first, this discussion of incentives and seat belts might seem like idle speculation. Yet a 1981 study of seat belt laws in eight European countries commissioned by the UK Department of Transport showed that the laws did appear to have had many of these effects. Similar evidence was also presented in a 1975 study of US seat belt laws by the American economist Sam Peltzman. It does indeed seem that seat belt laws produce both fewer deaths per accident and more accidents. The net result is little change in the number of motorist deaths and an increase in the number of pedestrian deaths.

This is an example of the general principle that people respond to incentives. Many incentives that economists study are more straightforward than those of the car-safety laws. No one is surprised that people drive smaller cars in Europe, where petrol taxes are relatively high, than in the United States, where petrol taxes are lower. Yet, as the seat belt example shows, policies can have effects that are not obvious in advance. When analysing any policy, we must consider not only the direct effects but also the indirect effects that work through incentives. If the policy changes incentives, it will cause people to alter their behaviour.

Quick Quiz List and briefly explain the four principles of individual decision-making.

HOW PEOPLE INTERACT

The first four principles discussed how individuals make decisions. As we go about our lives, many of our decisions affect not only ourselves but other people as well. The next three principles concern how people interact with one another.

Principle 5: Trade Can Make Everyone Better Off

The Americans and the Japanese are often mentioned in the news as being competitors to Europeans in the world economy. In some ways this is true, because American and Japanese firms do produce many of the same goods as European firms. Airbus and Boeing compete for the same customers in the market for aircraft. Toyota and Citroën compete for the same customers in the market for cars.

Yet it is easy to be misled when thinking about competition among countries. Trade between Europe and the United States or between Europe and Japan is not like a sports contest, where one side wins and the other side loses (a zero-sum game). In fact, the opposite is true: trade between two economies can make each economy better off.

To see why, consider how trade affects your family. When a member of your family looks for a job, he or she competes against members of other families who are looking for jobs. Families also compete against one another when they go shopping, because each family wants to buy the best goods at the lowest prices. So, in a sense, each family in the economy is competing with all other families.

Despite this competition, your family would not be better off isolating itself from all other families. If it did, your family would need to grow its own food,

"You'll have to look harder than that to find a job, son."

make its own clothes and build its own home. Clearly, your family gains much from its ability to trade with others. Trade allows each person to specialize in the activities he or she does best, whether it is farming, sewing or home building. By trading with others, people can buy a greater variety of goods and services at lower cost.

Countries as well as families benefit from the ability to trade with one another. Trade allows countries to specialize in what they do best and to enjoy a greater variety of goods and services. The Japanese and the Americans, as well as the Egyptians and the Brazilians, are as much our partners in the world economy as they are our competitors.

Principle 6: Markets Are Usually a Good Way to Organize Economic Activity

The collapse of communism in the Soviet Union and Eastern Europe in the 1980s may be the most important change in the world during the past half century. Communist countries worked on the premise that central planners in the government were in the best position to guide economic activity. These planners decided what goods and services were produced, how much was produced, and who produced and consumed these goods and services. The theory behind central planning was that only the government could organize economic activity in a way that promoted economic well-being for the country as a whole.

Today, most countries that once had centrally planned economies have abandoned this system and are trying to develop market economies. In a **market economy**, the decisions of a central planner are replaced by the decisions of millions of firms and households. Firms decide whom to hire and what to make. Households decide which firms to work for and what to buy with their incomes. These firms and households interact in the marketplace, where prices and self-interest guide their decisions.

At first glance, the success of market economies is puzzling. After all, in a market economy, no one is considering the economic well-being of society as a

market economy
an economy that allocates resources through the decentralized decisions of many firms and households as they interact in markets for goods and services

Adam Smith and the Invisible Hand

Adam Smith's great work *An Inquiry into the Nature and Causes of The Wealth of Nations* was published in 1776 and is a landmark in economics. In its emphasis on the invisible hand of the market economy, it reflected a point of view that was typical of so-called 'enlightenment' writers at the end of the 18th century – that individuals are usually best left to their own devices, without the heavy hand of government guiding their actions. This political philosophy provides the intellectual basis for the market economy.

Why do decentralized market economies work so well? Is it because people can be counted on to treat one another with love and kindness? Not at all. Here is Adam Smith's description of how people interact in a market economy:

Man has almost constant occasion for the help of his brethren, and it is vain for him to expect it from their benevolence only. He will be more likely to prevail if he can interest their self-love in his favour, and show them that it is for their own advantage to do for him what he requires of them. . . . It is not from the benevolence of the butcher, the brewer, or the baker that we expect our dinner, but from their regard to their own interest. . . .

Every individual . . . neither intends to promote the public interest, nor knows how much he is promoting it. . . . He intends only his own gain, and he is in this, as in many other cases, led by an invisible hand to promote an end which was no part of his intention. Nor is it always the worse for the society that it was no part of it. By pursuing his own interest he frequently promotes that of the society more effectually than when he really intends to promote it.

Smith is saying that participants in the economy are motivated by self-interest

Adam Smith

and that the 'invisible hand' of the marketplace guides this self-interest into promoting general economic well-being.

Many of Smith's insights remain at the centre of modern economics. Our analysis in the coming chapters will allow us to express Smith's conclusions more precisely and to analyse fully the strengths and weaknesses of the market's invisible hand.

whole. Free markets contain many buyers and sellers of numerous goods and services, and all of them are interested primarily in their own well-being. Yet, despite decentralized decision-making and self-interested decision makers, market economies have proven remarkably successful in organizing economic activity in a way that promotes overall economic well-being.

In his 1776 book *An Inquiry Into the Nature and Causes of the Wealth of Nations,* the British economist Adam Smith made the most famous observation in all of economics: households and firms interacting in markets act as if they are guided by an 'invisible hand' that leads them to desirable market outcomes. One of our goals in this book is to understand how this invisible hand works its magic. As you study economics, you will learn that prices are the instrument with which the invisible hand directs economic activity. Prices reflect both the value of a good to society and the cost to society of making the good. Because households and firms look at prices when deciding what to buy and sell, they unknowingly take into account the social benefits and costs of their actions. As a result, prices guide these individual decision makers to reach outcomes that, in many cases, maximize the welfare of society as a whole.

There is an important corollary to the skill of the invisible hand in guiding economic activity: when the government prevents prices from adjusting naturally to supply and demand, it impedes the invisible hand's ability to coordinate the millions of households and firms that make up the economy. This corollary explains why taxes adversely affect the allocation of resources: taxes distort prices and thus the decisions of households and firms. It also explains the even greater harm caused by policies that directly control prices, such as rent control. And it also explains the failure of communism. In communist countries, prices were not determined in the marketplace but were dictated by central planners. These planners lacked the information that gets reflected in prices when prices are free to respond to market forces. Central planners failed because they tried to run the economy with one hand tied behind their backs – the invisible hand of the marketplace.

Principle 7: Governments Can Sometimes Improve Market Outcomes

If the invisible hand of the market is so wonderful, why do we need government? One answer is that the invisible hand needs government to protect it. Markets work only if property rights are enforced. A farmer won't grow food if he expects his crop to be stolen, and a restaurant won't serve meals unless it is assured that customers will pay before they leave. We all rely on government-provided police and courts to enforce our rights over the things we produce.

Yet there is another answer to why we need government: although markets are usually a good way to organize economic activity, this rule has some important exceptions. There are two broad reasons for a government to intervene in the economy – to promote efficiency and to promote equity. That is, most policies aim either to enlarge the economic cake or to change the way in which the cake is divided.

Although the invisible hand usually leads markets to allocate resources efficiently, that is not always the case. Economists use the term **market failure** to refer to a situation in which the market on its own fails to produce an efficient allocation of resources. One possible cause of market failure is an **externality**, which is the uncompensated impact of one person's actions on the well-being of a bystander (a third party). For instance, the classic example of an external cost is pollution. Another possible cause of market failure is **market power**, which refers to the ability of a single person (or small group) to unduly influence market prices. For example, if everyone in a remote village in the Scottish Highlands needs water but there is only one well, the owner of the well is not subject to the rigorous competition with which the invisible hand normally keeps self-interest in check. In the presence of externalities or market power, well designed public policy can enhance economic efficiency.

The invisible hand may also fail to ensure that economic prosperity is distributed equitably. A market economy rewards people according to their ability to produce things for which other people are willing to pay. The world's best footballer earns more than the world's best chess player simply because people are willing to pay more to watch football than chess. The invisible hand does not ensure that everyone has sufficient food, decent clothing and adequate health care. Many public policies, such as income tax and the social security system, aim to achieve a more equitable distribution of economic well-being.

To say that the government *can* improve on market outcomes at times does not mean that it always *will*. Public policy is made not by angels but by a political process that is far from perfect. Sometimes policies are designed simply to reward the politically powerful. Sometimes they are made by well intentioned leaders who are not fully informed. One goal of the study of economics is to help you judge when a government policy is justifiable to promote efficiency or equity, and when it is not.

market failure
a situation where scarce resources are not allocated to their most efficient use

externality
the uncompensated impact of one person's actions on the well-being of a bystander (a third party)

market power
the ability of a single economic agent (or small group of agents) to have a substantial influence on market prices

Quick Quiz   List and briefly explain the three principles concerning economic interactions.

HOW THE ECONOMY AS A WHOLE WORKS

We started by discussing how individuals make decisions and then looked at how people interact with one another. All these decisions and interactions together make up 'the economy'. The last three principles concern the workings of the economy as a whole. A key concept in this section is **economic growth** – the percentage increase in the number of goods and services produced in an economy over a period of time usually expressed over a quarter and annually.

economic growth
the increase in the amount of goods and services in an economy over a period of time

Principle 8: An Economy's Standard of Living Depends on its Ability to Produce Goods and Services

gross domestic product per head
the market value of all final goods and services produced within a country in a given period of time divided by the population of a country to give a per capita figure

Table 1.1 shows **gross domestic product per head** of the population in a number of selected countries. It is clear that many of the advanced economies have a relatively high income per capita; in the UK it is $35 728 whilst in Germany and France it is $39 442 and $42 092 respectively. In Spain average income is a little lower at $31 142, somewhat higher in Ireland at $51 128, higher still in Switzerland at $66 127 and an enviable $94 418 in Luxembourg. These figures compare with an income per person of about $39 000 in Canada and $46 500 in the United States. But once we move away from the prosperous economies of Western Europe, North America and parts of Asia, we begin to see differences in income and living standards around the world that are quite staggering. For example, in the same year, 2009, average income in Poland was $11 098 almost a third of the level in Spain, while in Argentina it was just $7 508, in India $1 033 and in Ethiopia just $418 – less than one half of a per cent of the annual income per person in Luxembourg. Not surprisingly, this large variation in average income is reflected in various other measures of the quality of life and **standard of living**. Citizens of high-income countries have better nutrition, better health care and longer life expectancy than citizens of low-income countries, as well as more TV sets, more DVD players and more cars.

standard of living
refers to the amount of goods and services that can be purchased by the population of a country. Usually measured by the inflation-adjusted (real) income per head of the population

Changes in the standard of living over time are also large. Over the last 50 years, average incomes in Western Europe and North America have grown at about 2 per cent per year (after adjusting for changes in the cost of living). At this rate, average income doubles every 35 years, and over the last half-century average income in many of these prosperous economies has risen approximately three-fold. On the other hand, average income in Ethiopia rose by only a third over this period – an average annual growth rate of around only 0.5 per cent.

What explains these large differences in living standards among countries and over time? The answer is surprisingly simple. Almost all variation in living standards is attributable to differences in countries' **productivity** – that is, the amount of goods and services produced from each hour of a worker's time. In nations where workers can produce a large quantity of goods and services per unit of time, most people enjoy a high standard of living; in nations where workers are less productive, most people must endure a more meagre existence. Similarly, the growth rate of a nation's productivity determines the growth rate of its average income.

productivity
the quantity of goods and services produced from each hour of a worker's time

The fundamental relationship between productivity and living standards is simple, but its implications are far-reaching. If productivity is the primary determinant of living standards, other explanations must be of secondary importance. For example, it might be tempting to credit trades unions or minimum wage laws for the rise in living standards of European workers over the past 50 years. Yet the real hero of European workers is their rising productivity.

TABLE 1.1

Gross Domestic Product Per Capita, Current Prices, US dollars 2009

Country	GDP per capita
Albania	3 681
Argentina	7 508
Australia	41 982
Azerbaijan	4 864
Bangladesh	559
Belarus	5 122
Brazil	7 737
Canada	39 217
China	3 566
Ethiopia	418
France	42 092
Germany	39 442
Haiti	772
Iceland	36 873
India	1 033
Ireland	51 128
Japan	39 573
Kazakhstan	6 875
Luxembourg	94 418
Mexico	8 040
Norway	76 692
Pakistan	1 017
Paraguay	2 169
Peru	4 377
Poland	11 098
Portugal	20 655
Romania	7 503
Russia	8 874
Saudi Arabia	14 871
South Africa	5 635
Spain	31 142
Sweden	43 147
Switzerland	66 127
Syrian Arab Republic	2 669
Tajikistan	705
Thailand	3 973
United Arab Emirates	46 584
United Kingdom	35 728
United States	46 443
Zimbabwe	303

Source: International Monetary Fund, World Economic Outlook Database, October 2009.

The relationship between productivity and living standards also has profound implications for public policy. When thinking about how any policy will affect living standards, the key question is how it will affect our ability to produce goods and services. To boost living standards, policy makers need to raise productivity by ensuring that workers are well educated, have the tools needed to produce goods and services, and have access to the best available technology.

Principle 9: Prices Rise When the Government Prints Too Much Money

In Germany in January 1921, a daily newspaper was priced at 0.30 marks. Less than two years later, in November 1922, the same newspaper was priced at 70 000 000 marks. All other prices in the economy rose by similar amounts. This episode is one of history's most spectacular examples of **inflation**, an increase in the overall level of prices in the economy.

While inflation in Western Europe and North America has been much lower over the last 50 years than that experienced in Germany in the 1920s, inflation has at times been an economic problem. During the 1970s, for instance, the overall level of prices in the UK more than tripled. By contrast, UK inflation from 2000 to 2008 was about 3 per cent per year; at this rate it would take more than 20 years for prices to double. In more recent times, Zimbabwe has experienced German-like hyperinflation. In March 2007 inflation in the African state was reported to be running at 2 200 per cent. That meant that a good priced at the equivalent of €2.99 in March 2006 would be priced at €65.78 just a year later. In July 2008 the government issued a Z$100 billion note. At that time it was just about enough to buy a loaf of bread. Estimates for inflation in Zimbabwe in July 2008 put the rate of growth of prices at 231 000 000 per cent. In January 2009, the

inflation
an increase in the overall level of prices in the economy

"… but if daddy increased your allowance he'd be hurting the economy by stimulating inflation. You wouldn't want him to do that, would you?"

government issued Z$10, 20, 50 and 100 trillion dollar notes – 100 trillion is 100 followed by 12 zeros. Because high inflation imposes various costs on society, keeping inflation at a low level is a goal of economic policy makers around the world.

What causes inflation? In almost all cases of high or persistent inflation, the culprit turns out to be the same – growth in the quantity of money. When a government creates large quantities of the nation's money, the value of the money falls. In Germany in the early 1920s, when prices were on average tripling every month, the quantity of money was also tripling every month. Although less dramatic, the economic history of other European and North American countries points to a similar conclusion: the high inflation of the 1970s was associated with rapid growth in the quantity of money and the low inflation of the 2000s was associated with slow growth in the quantity of money.

Principle 10: Society Faces a Short-run Trade-off Between Inflation and Unemployment

When the government increases the amount of money in the economy, one result is inflation. Another result, at least in the short run, is a lower level of unemployment. The curve that illustrates this short-run trade-off between inflation and unemployment is called the **Phillips curve**, after the economist who first examined this relationship while working at the London School of Economics.

Phillips curve
a curve that shows the short-run trade-off between inflation and unemployment

The Phillips curve remains a controversial topic among economists, but most economists today accept the idea that society faces a short-run trade-off between inflation and unemployment. This simply means that, over a period of a year or two, many economic policies push inflation and unemployment in opposite directions. Policy makers face this trade-off regardless of whether inflation and unemployment both start out at high levels (as they were in the early 1980s), at low levels (as they were in the late 1990s) or somewhere in between.

The trade-off between inflation and unemployment is only temporary, but it can last for several years. The Phillips curve is, therefore, crucial for understanding many developments in the economy. In particular, it is important for understanding the **business cycle** – the irregular and largely unpredictable fluctuations in economic activity, as measured by the number of people employed or the production of goods and services.

business cycle
fluctuations in economic activity, such as employment and production

---

TABLE 1.2

Ten Principles of Economics

How people make decisions	1. People face trade-offs
	2. The cost of something is what you give up to get it
	3. Rational people think at the margin
	4. People respond to incentives
How people interact	5. Trade can make everyone better off
	6. Markets are usually a good way to organize economic activity
	7. Governments can sometimes improve market outcomes
How the economy as a whole works	8. A country's standard of living depends on its ability to produce goods and services
	9. Prices rise when the government prints too much money
	10. Society faces a short-run trade-off between inflation and unemployment

Policy makers can exploit the short-run trade-off between inflation and unemployment using various policy instruments. By changing the amount that the government spends, the amount it taxes and the amount of money it prints, policy makers can influence the combination of inflation and unemployment that the economy experiences. Because these instruments of monetary and fiscal policy are potentially so powerful, how policy makers should use these instruments to control the economy, if at all, is a subject of continuing debate.

Quick Quiz List and briefly explain the three principles that describe how the economy as a whole works.

IN THE NEWS

Using Incentives

Policy makers are well aware of the importance of incentives in changing behaviour. The concern over carbon emissions and global warming (despite some questioning the validity of the economics behind some of the predictions that have been made) has meant that governments and the European Union are looking at ways to reduce the reliance on carbon-based energies. In order to change behaviour various policies are adopted to change incentives to achieve the desired outcome. The example in this article highlights a number of the principles referred to in this chapter.

In November 2009, the European Union (EU) issued notice of a new directive in relation to the energy efficiency of newly constructed buildings. The Directive requires member states to plan ahead for the introduction of near zero energy buildings which make use of renewable energy from 2020. The Directive also requires member states to implement targets to the public sector to only use (whether owned or rented) buildings that adhere to near zero energy standards. This means that all members must find ways of converting or refurbishing existing buildings to comply with this standard by the end of 2018.

Such a Directive presents major challenges not only to the public sector in member states but also to the private sector. There are trade-offs in putting in place such plans. It has been reported that around 40 per cent of all energy use is attributable to buildings and that they are responsible for over a third of Europe's CO_2 emissions. Whilst the Direc-

tive will cost millions to implement, the trade-off is that savings of €300 [per building] each year in energy bills could result (Principle 1). In addition, the EU says that there will be a boost to the construction and building renovation industry throughout the continent (Principle 5).

After 2020, any new building will have to meet energy efficiency standards set by Brussels. If left to the market, the sort of work envisaged by the EU may not happen – the cost of doing this in relation to the benefits accruing to private individuals would likely be insufficient to encourage individuals to act on their own. So in this case the 'invisible hand' needs some assistance (Principle 7). EU governments are being encouraged to provide a list of incentives which include technical assistance, subsidies, loan schemes, low interest rate deals and other financial assistance to help change the relative costs and benefits (Principle 4). Part of the reason for this was that following the original

2002 Energy Performance of Buildings Directive, progress towards improving standards had been limited largely due to a lack of inspectors qualified to issue certificates, a qualified workforce and ambition. The market, in the eyes of the EU, had failed to bring about the resource allocation they desired.

As a result the introduction of incentives and a restatement of the Directive are designed to bring about that desired resource allocation. Incentives such as subsidies, for example, help reduce the cost to the producer (the building owner in this example) of carrying out the work required to comply with the standards. In diverting resources to this desired outcome the EU believe that it represents a more efficient allocation of resources and therefore has benefits which are wider than just those to the building owner but to society at large. Diverting resources by subsidy has a cost, however. Someone has to pay for the subsidy and this is the EU taxpayer.

The use of taxes for this purpose has an opportunity cost – the value of the benefits that could have accrued from the tax money that could have been used for the next best alternative (Principle 2).

Whenever government intervenes in the market resource allocation is distorted. We saw in Principle 3 that rational people think at the margin and that this margin is associated with the costs and benefits of additional (or fewer) units.

When governments intervene in the market with incentives such as those in this example, those marginal costs and benefits are changed and hence rational people respond to those changes and alter their behaviour as a result.

One issue to consider here is the value of the outcomes as a result of these changed behaviours. The EU has stated clearly that it believes there are significant cost savings to be made for

all buildings as exemplified above. However, it is sometimes difficult to measure the value of the outcomes of the next best alternative and in addition if the decision to encourage this sort of behaviour is based on inaccurate or inappropriate assumptions, then the outcome may actually lead to an overall cost to society as a whole as opposed to the overall benefit envisaged by the EU.

FYI

How To Read This Book

Economics is fun, but it can also be hard to learn. Our aim in writing this text has been to make it as easy and as much fun as possible. But you, the student, also have a role to play. Experience shows that if you are actively involved as you study this book, you will enjoy a better outcome, both in your exams and in the years that follow. Here are a few tips about how best to read this book.

1. *Summarize, don't highlight.* Running a yellow marker over the text is too passive an activity to keep your mind engaged. Instead, when you come to the end of a section, take a minute and summarize what you have just learnt in your own words, writing your summary in the wide margins we've provided. When you've finished the chapter, compare your summary with the one at the end of the chapter. Did you pick up the main points?

2. *Test yourself.* Throughout the book, Quick Quizzes offer instant feedback to find out if you've learned what you are supposed to. Take the opportunity. Write your answer in the book's margin. The quizzes are meant to test your basic comprehension. If you aren't sure your answer is right, you probably need to review the section.

3. *Practise, practise, practise.* At the end of each chapter, Questions for Review test your understanding, and Problems and Applications ask you to apply and extend the material. Perhaps your lecturer will assign some of these exercises as course-work. If so, do them. If not, do them anyway. The more you use your new knowledge, the more solid it becomes.

4. *Study in groups.* After you've read the book and worked through the problems on your own, get together with other students to discuss the material. You will learn from each other – an example of the gains from trade.

5. *Don't forget the real world.* In the midst of all the numbers, graphs and strange new words, it is easy to lose sight of what economics is all about. The Case Studies and In the News boxes sprinkled throughout this book should help remind you. Don't skip them. They show how the theory is tied to events happening in all of our lives. If your study is successful, you won't be able to read a newspaper again without thinking about supply, demand and the wonderful world of economics.

CONCLUSION

You now have a taste of what economics is all about. In the coming chapters we will develop many specific insights about people, markets and economies. Mastering these insights will take some effort, but it is not an overwhelming task.

The field of economics is based on a few basic ideas that can be applied in many different situations.

Throughout this book we will refer back to the *Ten Principles of Economics* highlighted in this chapter and summarized in Table 1.2. Whenever we do so, an icon will be displayed in the margin, as it is now. But even when that icon is absent, you should keep these building blocks in mind. Even the most sophisticated economic analysis is built using the ten principles introduced here.

SUMMARY

- The fundamental lessons about individual decision-making are that people face trade-offs among alternative goals, that the cost of any action is measured in terms of foregone opportunities, that rational people make decisions by comparing marginal costs and marginal benefits, and that people change their behaviour in response to the incentives they face.

- The fundamental lessons about interactions among people are that trade can be mutually beneficial, that markets are

usually a good way of coordinating trade among people, and that the government can potentially improve market outcomes if there is some market failure or if the market outcome is inequitable.

- The fundamental lessons about the economy as a whole are that productivity is the ultimate source of living standards, that money growth is the ultimate source of inflation, and that society faces a short-run trade-off between inflation and unemployment.

KEY CONCEPTS

scarcity, p. 2
economics, p. 2
equity, p. 5
opportunity cost, p. 6
marginal changes, p. 6
market economy, p. 9

market failure, p. 11
externality, p. 11
market power, p. 11
economic growth, p. 12
gross domestic product per head, p. 12
standard of living, p. 12

productivity, p. 12
inflation, p. 14
Phillips curve, p. 15
business cycle, p. 15

QUESTIONS FOR REVIEW

1. Give three examples of important trade-offs that you face in your life.

2. What is the opportunity cost of going to the cinema to see a film?

3. Water is necessary for life. Is the marginal benefit of a glass of water large or small?

4. Why should policy makers think about incentives?

5. Why isn't trade among countries like a game, with some winners and some losers?

6. What does the 'invisible hand' of the marketplace do?

7. Explain the two main causes of market failure and give an example of each.

8. Why is productivity important?

9. What is inflation, and what causes it?

10. How are inflation and unemployment related in the short run?

PROBLEMS AND APPLICATIONS

1. Describe some of the trade-offs faced by each of the following.
   a. A family deciding whether to buy a new car.
   b. A member of the government deciding how much to spend on building a new national football stadium.
   c. A company chief executive officer deciding whether to open a new factory.
   d. A university lecturer deciding how much to prepare for her lecture.

2. You are trying to decide whether to take a holiday. Most of the costs of the holiday (airfare, hotel, foregone wages) are measured in euros, but the benefits of the holiday are psychological. How can you compare the benefits to the costs?

3. You were planning to spend Saturday working at your part-time job, but a friend asks you to go to a football match. What is the true cost of going to the football match? Now suppose that you had been planning to spend the day studying in the library. What is the cost of going to the football match in this case? Explain.

4. You win €1 000 in the EuroMillions Lottery. You have a choice between spending the money now or putting it away for a year in a bank account that pays 5 per cent interest. What is the opportunity cost of spending the €1 000 now?

5. The company that you manage has invested €5 million in developing a new product, but the development is not quite finished. At a recent meeting, your sales people report that the introduction of competing products has reduced the expected sales of your new product to €3 million. If it would cost €1 million to finish development and make the product, should you go ahead and do so? What is the most that you should pay to complete development?

6. Three managers of the Hubble Bubble Magic Potion Company are discussing a possible increase in production. Each suggests a way to make this decision.
   FIRST WITCH: When shall we three meet again? We need to decide how much Magic Potion to produce. Personally, I think we should examine whether our company's productivity – litres of potion per worker per hour – would rise or fall if we increased output.

   SECOND WITCH: We should examine whether our average cost – cost per worker – would rise or fall.

   THIRD WITCH: We should examine whether the extra revenue from selling the additional potion would be greater or smaller than the extra costs.
   Who do you think is right? Why?

7. The social security system provides income for people over the age of 65. If a recipient of social security decides to work and earn some income, the amount he or she receives in social security benefits is typically reduced.
   a. How does the provision of social security affect people's incentive to save while working?
   b. How does the reduction in benefits associated with higher earnings affect people's incentive to work past age 65?

8. Your flatmate is a better cook than you are, but you can clean more quickly than your flatmate can. If your flatmate did all of the cooking and you did all of the cleaning, would your household chores take you more or less time than if you divided each task evenly? Give a similar example of how specialization and trade can make two countries both better off.

9. Suppose the European Union adopted central planning for its economy, and you became the Chief Planner. Among the millions of decisions that you need to make for next year are how many DVDs to produce, what films to record and who should receive the DVDs.
   a. To make these decisions intelligently, what information would you need about the DVD industry? What information would you need about each of the people in the countries making up the European Union?
   b. How would your decisions about DVDs affect some of your other decisions, such as how many DVD players to make or Blu-ray discs to produce? How might some of your other decisions about the economy change your views about DVDs?

10. Explain whether each of the following government activities is motivated by a concern about equity or a concern about efficiency. In the case of efficiency, discuss the type of market failure involved.
    a. Regulating water prices.
    b. Regulating electricity prices.
    c. Providing some poor people with vouchers that can be used to buy food.
    d. Prohibiting smoking in public places.
    e. Imposing higher personal income tax rates on people with higher incomes.
    f. Instituting laws against driving whilst under the influence of alcohol.

11. Discuss each of the following statements from the standpoints of equity and efficiency.
    a. 'Everyone in society should be guaranteed the best health care possible.'

b. 'When workers are laid off, they should be able to collect unemployment benefits until they find a new job.'

12. In what ways is your standard of living different from that of your parents or grandparents when they were your age? Why have these changes occurred?

13. Suppose Europeans decide to save more of their incomes. If banks lend this extra saving to European businesses, which use the funds to build new European factories, how might this lead to faster growth in European productivity? Who do you suppose benefits from the higher productivity? Is society getting a free lunch?

14. Imagine that you are a policy maker trying to decide whether to reduce the rate of inflation in your country. To make an intelligent decision, what would you need to know about inflation, unemployment and the trade-off between them?

15. Look at a newspaper or at the website http://www. economist.com to find three stories about the economy that have been in the news lately. For each story, identify one (or more) of the *Ten Principles of Economics* discussed in this chapter that is relevant, and explain how it is relevant. Also, for each story, look through this book's table of contents and try to find a chapter that might shed light on the news event.

For further resources, visit
www.cengage.com/mankiw_taylor2

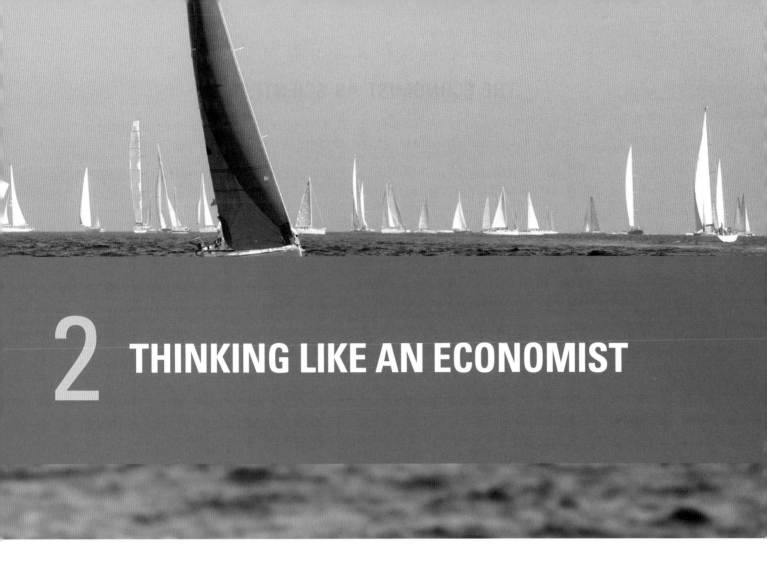

2 THINKING LIKE AN ECONOMIST

Every field of study has its own language and its own way of thinking. Mathematicians talk about axioms, integrals and vector spaces. Psychologists talk about ego, id and cognitive dissonance. Medics talk about dyspnoea, claudication and myocardial infarction. Lawyers talk about venue, torts and promissory estoppel.

Economics is no different. Supply, demand, elasticity, comparative advantage, consumer surplus, deadweight loss – these terms are part of the economist's language. In the coming chapters, you will encounter many new terms and some familiar words that economists use in specialised ways. At first, this new language may seem needlessly arcane. But, as you will see, its value lies in its ability to provide you with a new and useful way of thinking about the world in which you live.

The single most important purpose of this book is to help you learn the economist's way of thinking. Of course, just as you cannot become a mathematician, psychologist, medical doctor or lawyer overnight, learning to think like an economist will take some time. Yet with a combination of theory, case studies and examples of economics in the news, this book will give you ample opportunity to develop and practise this skill.

Before delving into the substance and details of economics, it is helpful to have an overview of how economists approach the world. This chapter, therefore, discusses the field's methodology. What is distinctive about how economists confront a question? What does it mean to think like an economist?

THE ECONOMIST AS SCIENTIST

Economists try to address their subject with a scientist's objectivity. They approach the study of the economy in much the same way as a physicist approaches the study of matter and a biologist approaches the study of life: they devise theories, collect data, and then analyse these data in an attempt to verify or refute their theories.

To beginners, it can seem odd to claim that economics is a science. After all, economists do not work with test tubes or telescopes. The essence of science, however, is the *scientific method* – the dispassionate development and testing of theories about how the world works. This method of inquiry is as applicable to studying a nation's economy as it is to studying the earth's gravity or a species' evolution. As Albert Einstein once put it, 'The whole of science is nothing more than the refinement of everyday thinking.'

Although Einstein's comment is as true for social sciences such as economics as it is for natural sciences such as physics, most people are not accustomed to looking at society through the eyes of a scientist. Let's therefore discuss some of the ways in which economists apply the logic of science to examine how an economy works.

The Scientific Method: Observation, Theory and More Observation

Isaac Newton, the famous English 17th century scientist and mathematician, allegedly became intrigued one day when he saw an apple fall from a tree. This observation motivated Newton to develop a theory of gravity that applies not only to an apple falling to the earth but to any two objects in the universe. Subsequent testing of Newton's theory has shown that it works well in many circumstances (although, as Einstein would later emphasize, not in all circumstances). Because Newton's theory has been so successful at explaining observation, it is still taught today in undergraduate physics courses around the world.

This interplay between theory and observation also occurs in the field of economics. An economist might live in a country experiencing rapid increases in prices and be moved by this observation to develop a theory of inflation. The theory might assert that high inflation arises when the government prints too much money. (As you may recall, this was one of the *Ten Principles of Economics* in Chapter 1.) To test this theory, the economist could collect and analyse data on prices and money from many different countries. If growth in the quantity of money were not at all related to the rate at which prices are rising, the economist would start to doubt the validity of his theory of inflation. If money growth and inflation were strongly correlated in international data, as in fact they are, the economist would become more confident in his theory.

Although economists use theory and observation like other scientists, they do face an obstacle that makes their task especially challenging: experiments are often difficult in economics. Physicists studying gravity can drop many objects in their laboratories to generate data to test their theories. By contrast, economists studying inflation are not allowed to manipulate a nation's monetary policy simply to generate useful data. Economists, like astronomers and evolutionary biologists, usually have to make do with whatever data the world happens to give them.

To find a substitute for laboratory experiments, economists pay close attention to the natural experiments offered by history. When a war in the Middle East interrupts the flow of crude oil, for instance, oil prices shoot up around the world. For consumers of oil and oil products, such an event depresses living standards. For economic policy makers, it poses a difficult choice about how best to respond. But for economic scientists, it provides an opportunity to study the effects of a key natural resource on the world's economies, and this opportunity persists long after the wartime increase in oil prices is over. Throughout this book, therefore, we consider many historical episodes. These episodes are valuable to study because they give us insight into the economy of the past and, more important, because they allow us to illustrate and evaluate economic theories of the present. The study of events and outcomes at different periods of time is called 'intertemporal study'.

The Role of Assumptions

If you ask a physicist how long it would take for a cannonball to fall from the top of the Leaning Tower of Pisa, she will probably answer the question by assuming that the cannonball falls in a vacuum. Of course, this assumption is false. In fact, the building is surrounded by air, which exerts friction on the falling cannonball and slows it down. Yet the physicist will correctly point out that friction on the cannonball is so small in relation to its weight that its effect is negligible. Assuming the cannonball falls in a vacuum greatly simplifies the problem without substantially affecting the answer.

Economists make assumptions for the same reason: assumptions can simplify the complex world and make it easier to understand. To study the effects of international trade, for example, we may assume that the world consists of only two countries and that each country produces only two goods. Of course, the real world consists of dozens of countries, each of which produces thousands of different types of goods. But by assuming two countries and two goods, we can focus our thinking. Once we understand international trade in an imaginary world with two countries and two goods, we are in a better position to understand international trade in the more complex world in which we live.

The art in scientific thinking – whether in physics, biology or economics – is deciding which assumptions to make. Suppose, for instance, that we were dropping a beach ball rather than a cannonball from the top of the building. Our physicist would realize that the assumption of no friction is far less accurate in this case: friction exerts a greater force on a beach ball than on a cannonball because a beach ball is much larger and, moreover, the effects of air friction may not be negligible relative to the weight of the ball because it is so light. The assumption that gravity works in a vacuum may, therefore, be reasonable for studying a falling cannonball but not for studying a falling beach ball.

Similarly, economists use different assumptions to answer different questions. Suppose that we want to study what happens to the economy when the government changes the amount of money in circulation. An important piece of this analysis, it turns out, is how prices respond. Many prices in the economy change infrequently; the prices of magazines and newspapers, for instance, are changed only every few years. Knowing this fact may lead us to make different assumptions when studying the effects of the policy change over different time horizons. For studying the short-run effects of the policy, we may assume that prices do not change much. We may even make the extreme and artificial assumption that all prices are completely fixed. For studying the long-run effects of the policy, however, we may assume that all prices are completely flexible. Just as a physicist uses different assumptions when studying falling cannonballs and falling beach balls, economists use different assumptions when studying the short-run and long-run effects of a change in the quantity of money.

CASE STUDY

Developing Theories in Economics

As in physical sciences, theories are developed in economics to help make predictions. The ways in which these theories develop evolve over time as the scientific method of theory, observation and refinement of the theory continues. As with any science, economics does not have definitive answers to any question, only theories that are developed on the basis of currently known information. In physics, Newtonian laws explained a great deal but were improved by Einstein who opened up new avenues of investigation and challenged existing orthodoxies. Physicists know that Einstein's theories, as remarkable and good as they are, do not represent the whole 'truth' and that if anything his theories raise even more questions than they provide answers. Experiments using the Large Hadron Collider (LHC) are expected to shed more light on our understanding of physics but the cost of finding out this information has not come cheap; estimations put the cost of building the LHC and carrying out the experiments at nearly €4 billion.

In economics the development of theories is no different, but rather than creating new data as is the case with the LHC, we have to rely on observation. Many economic theories are relatively simple in nature but this can hide a number of complexities which may influence outcome and thus the power of the theory to predict and help in the generation of economic policy. Later in this book you will learn about economic growth. Economic growth is the change in the value of output in a country or region over a period of time. At its simplest it measures the amount of goods and services produced in a time period multiplied by the price of those goods and services. Economic growth, as you will see, is crucial to improvements in standards of living around the world. A fundamental question in economics, therefore, is what determines economic growth?

There have been different theories of economic growth put forward over time, one of the most popular has been that advanced by Robert. M. Solow and Trevor Swan in 1956. They identified the rate of human and physical capital and population growth as being key determinants of economic growth. Over the years, economists have looked at other factors that may influence economic growth including the level of macroeconomic stability in an economy, the type of trade policy that exists in a country (is the country outward looking or does it tend to be insular), the nature and quality of institutions and governance (i.e. how effectively the rule of law operates and how well governments are able to control corruption) in the country concerned, the extent to which violence, war and conflict exist in a country, regional characteristics such as whether the country is part of Europe, North America, Asia or sub-Saharan Africa, geographical factors such as physical resource endowments and climate, the extent to which the country is competitive in international markets and internal factors such as the amount of productive land available.

These could all be represented as a simple equation which might look like the following.

$$E = f(SS_1, \text{ Me, Tp, G, St, R, Gf, P, Ic, } \gamma)$$

This simply states that economic growth (E) is dependent on (is a function of) a range of possible factors which are given symbols or letters corresponding to the list given above. In order to influence economic growth, therefore, policy makers would have to find ways of influencing one or more of the factors in the equation to boost economic growth. The problem is, which factors should they focus on? This will depend on a variety of effects, including the resources policy makers have at their disposal, but will also be heavily dependent on which of the factors exerts the most powerful effects. Different economists may place a different reliance on the importance of one or more of these factors and this can significantly influence the outcome.

For example, assume that one economist places a value against each of the factors in the equation as follows:

$$E = f\,(0.5SS_1, \; 0.03Me, \; 0.01Tp, \; 0.1G, \; 0.15St, \; 0.03R, \; 0.024Gf, \; 0.06P, \; 0.08Ic, \; 0.115\;\gamma)$$

This tells us that the most important factor influencing economic growth is SS_1 the Solow-Swan human/physical capital, population growth. The value assigned to it means that it accounts for half of the determinants of economic growth. This would imply that emphasis might be placed on this factor if policy makers are interested in increasing economic growth. However, the assumptions made in deriving such an equation are varied. Economists will use sophisticated statistical and mathematical techniques in interpreting data to derive such equations and these can all influence the nature of the equation and the value of the theory as a predictor or basis of policy making.

Alin Mirestean and Charalambos Tsangarides[1] looked at the way in which these factors are assessed and arrived at some interesting conclusions which highlight the way in which economists think and work. They applied a different mathematical method of analysing data and found that this method cast doubt on some of the accepted assumptions about the relative value of each factor. Whilst they pointed out that all the factors were clearly important in economic growth, their analysis suggested some had a less important role. They identified four key factors – initial income, investment, population growth and life expectancy – as having the strongest evidence for being important whilst inflation, debt and trade openness were 'strong' factors. They pointed out, however, that their findings did depend to an extent on the type of data set used for the analysis. If 5-year averaged data are used it might give different outcomes to those based on 8-year average data. They conclude that different mathematical methods may give more robust data and may, therefore, be more appropriate in looking at theories of the determinants of economic growth.

[1]Mirestean, A. & Tsangarides, C. (2009) *Growth Determinants Revisited*, IMF Research Department Working Paper: http://www.imf.org/external/pubs/ft/wp/2009/wp09268.pdf accessed 10 December 2009.

Economic Models

Secondary school biology teachers often teach basic anatomy with plastic replicas of the human body. These models have all the major organs – the heart, the liver, the kidneys and so on. The models allow teachers to show their students in a simple way how the important parts of the body fit together. Of course, these plastic models are not actual human bodies, and no one would mistake the model for a real person. These models are stylised, and they omit many details. Yet despite this lack of realism – indeed, because of this lack of realism – studying these models is useful for learning how the human body works.

Economists also use models to learn about the world, but instead of being made of plastic, they are most often composed of diagrams and equations. Like a biology teacher's plastic model, economic models omit many details to allow us to see what is truly important. Just as the biology teacher's model does not include all of the body's muscles and capillaries, an economist's model does not include every feature of the economy.

As we use models to examine various economic issues throughout this book, you will see that all the models are built with assumptions. Just as a physicist begins the analysis of a falling cannonball by assuming away the existence of friction, economists assume away many of the details of the economy that are irrelevant for studying the question at hand. All models – in physics, biology or economics – simplify reality in order to improve our understanding of it.

Another analogy that is useful in thinking about the role of assumptions in economic models has to do with maps. Maps are scaled-down representations of the world, but every map leaves out some features of the real world. Imagine what a map would look like that tried to describe every feature of the area it was supposed to represent: as well as standard features like roads and parks, it would, for example, have to represent all of the buildings, the rooms within the buildings, the furniture within each room, and so on. There would be so much detail that the scale would have to be very large and the map would be very hard to read. Of course, you might say that it would be ridiculous to have so much detail in a map, and you would be right. But how do you decide what details to leave out and what details to leave in? The answer depends on what you plan to do with the map.

Suppose a friend knocks on your door one day and asks whether you can lend her a map of Berlin. In fact, you have three maps that would answer this general description: a road map showing the motorways and main roads going around and through the Berlin area, an A-to-Z street map of Berlin city centre and a U-Bahn metro map showing all of the lines and stations of the metro system. Which should you give her? It all depends on the use to which your friend wants to put the map. If she is planning to travel around Berlin on the metro, a metro map is indispensable. But if she wants to walk from Kurfürstendamm to see the Reichstag building, the metro map will be completely useless – it doesn't have a single street on it (unless the street name happens to coincide with a metro station) and she will need the A-to-Z. On the other hand, if she just wants to drive around the greater Berlin area avoiding the city centre she will need the road map: the other two maps – since they do not show any major roads outside of Berlin city centre – will not help her. Now, each of the maps leaves out certain features of the real world and, as a result, each of them is indispensable for a particular purpose and useless for other purposes.

The same is true of economic models. Becoming a skilled economic modeller involves deciding what features of the real world to try to capture in the model and what features are just so much unnecessary detail. The decision as to which details are necessary to leave in and which details should be left out will depend crucially on the purpose for which you wish to use the model. In our first model of the economy, we shall try to understand in very general terms how the economy works and we shall therefore not try to explain within the model, for example, how firms decide exactly how many workers to employ or households decide how much milk to buy.

Our First Model: The Circular-flow Diagram

The economy consists of millions of people engaged in many activities – buying, selling, working, hiring, manufacturing and so on. To understand how the economy works, we must find some way to simplify our thinking about all these activities. In other words, we need a model that explains, in general terms, how the economy is organised and how participants in the economy interact with one another.

FIGURE 2.1

The Circular Flow

This diagram is a schematic representation of the organization of the economy. Decisions are made by households and firms. Households and firms interact in the markets for goods and services (where households are buyers and firms are sellers) and in the markets for the factors of production (where firms are buyers and households are sellers). The outer set of arrows shows the flow of money, and the inner set of arrows shows the corresponding flow of inputs and outputs.

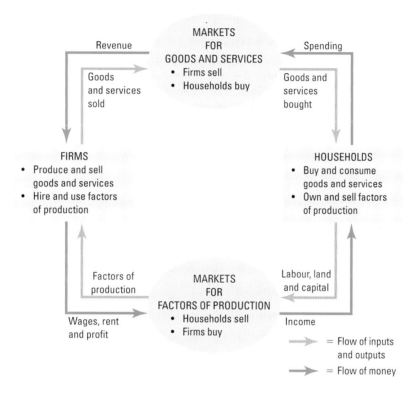

Figure 2.1 presents a visual model of the economy, called a **circular-flow diagram**. In this model, the economy is simplified to include only two types of decision makers – households and firms. Firms produce goods and services using inputs, such as labour, land and capital (buildings and machines). These inputs are called the *factors of production*. Households own the factors of production and consume all the goods and services that the firms produce. (Readers of this book are owners of the factor of production 'labour'. If you are a student then you are seeking to improve the value of this factor so that you can sell it for a higher price!)

Households and firms interact in two types of markets. In the *markets for goods and services*, households are buyers and firms are sellers. In particular, households buy the output of goods and services that firms produce. In the *markets for the factors of production,* households are sellers and firms are buyers. In these markets, households provide the inputs that the firms use to produce goods and services. The circular-flow diagram offers a simple way of organizing all of the economic transactions that occur between households and firms in the **economy**.

The inner loop of the circular-flow diagram represents the flows of inputs and outputs. The households sell the use of their labour, land and capital to the firms in the markets for the factors of production. The firms then use these factors to

circular-flow diagram
a visual model of the economy that shows how money and production inputs and outputs flow through markets among households and firms

economy
a word to describe all the economic activity (buying and selling or transactions) that take place in a country or region

produce goods and services, which in turn are sold to households in the markets for goods and services. Hence, the factors of production flow from households to firms, and goods and services flow from firms to households.

The outer loop of the circular-flow diagram represents the corresponding flows of money. The households spend money to buy goods and services from the firms. The firms use some of the revenue from these sales to pay for the factors of production, such as the wages of their workers. What's left is the profit of the firm's owners, who themselves are members of households. Hence, spending on goods and services flows from households to firms, and income in the form of wages, rent and profit flows from firms to households.

Let's take a tour of the circular flow by following a one euro coin as it makes its way from person to person through the economy. Imagine that the euro begins at a household, sitting in, say, your pocket. If you want to buy a cup of coffee, you take the euro to one of the economy's markets for goods and services, such as your local café. There you spend it on your favourite drink: a double espresso. When the euro moves into the café cash register, it becomes revenue for the owner of the café. The euro doesn't stay with the café owner for long, however, because he uses it to buy inputs in the markets for the factors of production. For instance, the café owner might use the euro to pay rent to the owner of the building that the café occupies or to pay the wages of its workers. In either case, the euro enters the income of some household and, once again, is back in someone's pocket. At that point, the story of the economy's circular flow starts once again.

The circular-flow diagram in Figure 2.1 is one simple model of the economy. As such, it is useful for developing some basic ideas as to how the economy works, but at the same time dispenses with details that, for some purposes, might be significant. A more complex and realistic circular-flow model would include, for instance, the roles of government and international trade. Yet these details are not crucial for a basic understanding of how the economy is organised. Because of its simplicity, this circular-flow diagram is useful to keep in mind when thinking about how the pieces of the economy fit together.

Our Second Model: The Production Possibilities Frontier

Most economic models, unlike the purely visual circular-flow diagram, are built using the tools of mathematics. Here we consider one of the simplest such models, called the production possibilities frontier, and see how this model illustrates some basic economic ideas.

Although real economies produce thousands of goods and services, let's imagine an economy that produces only two goods – cars and computers. (Note, as outlined on page 23, we are making an assumption to help simplify the complexity of real economies, just like physicists make assumptions in order to simplify the complex world.) Together the car industry and the computer industry use all of the economy's factors of production. The **production possibilities frontier** is a graph that shows the various combinations of output – in this case, cars and computers – that the economy can possibly produce given the available factors of production and the available production technology that firms can use to turn these factors into output.

Figure 2.2 is an example of a production possibilities frontier. In this economy, if all resources were used in the car industry, the economy would produce 1 000 cars and no computers. If all resources were used in the computer industry, the economy would produce 3 000 computers and no cars. The two end points of the production possibilities frontier represent these extreme possibilities. If the economy were to divide its resources between the two industries, it could produce

production possibilities frontier a graph that shows the combinations of output that the economy can possibly produce given the available factors of production and the available production technology

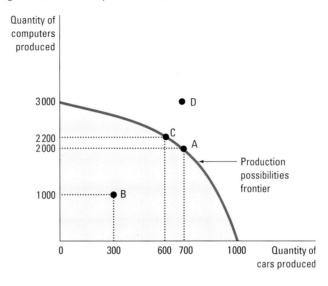

FIGURE 2.2

The Production Possibilities Frontier

The production possibilities frontier shows the combinations of output – in this case, cars and computers – that the economy can possibly produce. The economy can produce any combination on or inside the frontier. Points outside the frontier are not feasible given the economy's resources.

700 cars and 2000 computers, shown in the figure by point A. By contrast, the outcome at point D is not possible because resources are scarce: the economy does not have enough of the factors of production to support that level of output. In other words, the economy can produce at any point on or inside the production possibilities frontier, but it cannot produce at points outside the frontier.

An outcome is said to be *efficient* if the economy is getting all it can from the scarce resources it has available. Points on (rather than inside) the production possibilities frontier represent efficient levels of production. When the economy is producing at such a point, say point A, there is no way to produce more of one good without producing less of the other. Point B represents an *inefficient* outcome. For some reason, perhaps widespread unemployment, the economy is producing less than it could from the resources it has available: it is producing only 300 cars and 1000 computers. If the source of the inefficiency were eliminated, the economy could move from point B to point A, increasing production of both cars (to 700) and computers (to 2000).

One of the *Ten Principles of Economics* discussed in Chapter 1 is that people face trade-offs. The production possibilities frontier shows one trade-off that society faces. Once we have reached the efficient points on the frontier, the only way of getting more of one good is to get less of the other. When the economy moves from point A to point C, for instance, society produces more computers but at the expense of producing fewer cars.

Another of the *Ten Principles of Economics* is that the cost of something is what you give up to get it. This is called the opportunity cost. The production possibilities frontier shows the opportunity cost of one good as measured in terms of the other good. When society reallocates some of the factors of production from the car industry to the computer industry, moving the economy from point A to point C, it gives up 100 cars to get 200 additional computers. In other words, when the economy is at point A, the opportunity cost of 200 computers is 100 cars.

Notice that the production possibilities frontier in Figure 2.2 is bowed outward. This means that the opportunity cost of cars in terms of computers depends on how much of each good the economy is producing. When the economy is using most of its resources to make cars, the production possibilities frontier is quite steep. Because even workers and machines best suited to making computers are being used to make cars, the economy gets a substantial increase in the number of computers for each car it gives up. By contrast, when the economy is using most of its resources to make computers, the production possibilities frontier is quite flat. In this case, the resources best suited to making computers are already in the computer industry, and each car the economy gives up yields only a small increase in the number of computers.

The production possibilities frontier shows the trade-off between the production of different goods at a given time, but the trade-off can change over time. For example, if a technological advance in the computer industry raises the number of computers that a worker can produce per week, the economy can make more computers for any given number of cars. As a result, the production possibilities frontier shifts outward, as in Figure 2.3. Because of this economic growth, society might move production from point A to point E, enjoying more computers and more cars.

The production possibilities frontier simplifies a complex economy to highlight and clarify some basic ideas. We have used it to illustrate some of the concepts mentioned briefly in Chapter 1: scarcity, efficiency, trade-offs, opportunity cost and economic growth. As you study economics, these ideas will recur in various forms. The production possibilities frontier – our second economic model – offers one simple way of thinking about them.

FIGURE 2.3

A Shift in the Production Possibilities Frontier

An economic advance in the computer industry shifts the production possibilities frontier outward, increasing the number of cars and computers the economy can produce.

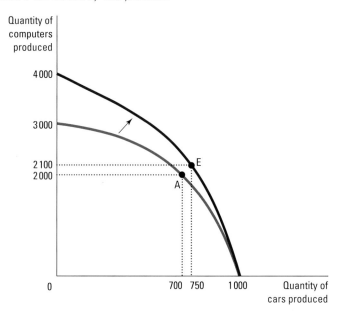

Microeconomics and Macroeconomics

Many subjects are studied on various levels. Consider biology, for example. Molecular biologists study the chemical compounds that make up living things. Cellular biologists study cells, which are made up of many chemical compounds and, at the same time, are themselves the building blocks of living organisms. Evolutionary biologists study the many varieties of animals and plants and how species change gradually over the centuries.

Economics is also studied on various levels. We can study the decisions of individual households and firms. Or we can study the interaction of households and firms in markets for specific goods and services. Or we can study the operation of the economy as a whole, which is just the sum of the activities of all these decision-makers in all these markets.

Since roughly the 1930s, the field of economics has traditionally been divided into two broad subfields. **Microeconomics** is the study of how households and firms make decisions and how they interact in specific markets. **Macroeconomics** is the study of economy-wide phenomena. A microeconomist might study the effects of a congestion tax on the use of cars in central London, the impact of foreign competition on the European car industry or the effects of attending university on a person's lifetime earnings. A macroeconomist might study the effects of borrowing by national governments, the changes over time in an economy's rate of unemployment or alternative policies to raise growth in national living standards.

microeconomics
the study of how households and firms make decisions and how they interact in markets

macroeconomics
the study of economy-wide phenomena, including inflation, unemployment and economic growth

Microeconomics and macroeconomics are closely intertwined. Because changes in the overall economy arise from the decisions of millions of individuals, it is impossible to understand macroeconomic developments without considering the associated microeconomic decisions. For example, a macroeconomist might study the effect of a cut in income tax on the overall production of goods and services in an economy. To analyse this issue, he or she must consider how the tax cut affects the decisions of households concerning how much to spend on goods and services.

Despite the inherent link between microeconomics and macroeconomics, the two fields are distinct. In economics, as in biology, it may seem natural to begin with the smallest unit and build up. Yet doing so is neither necessary nor always the best way to proceed. Evolutionary biology is, in a sense, built upon molecular biology, since species are made up of molecules. Yet molecular biology and evolutionary biology are separate fields, each with its own questions and its own methods. Similarly, because microeconomics and macroeconomics address different questions, they sometimes take quite different approaches and are often taught in separate courses.

Quick Quiz In what sense is economics like a science? • Draw a production possibilities frontier for a society that produces food and clothing. Show an efficient point, an inefficient point and an unfeasible point. Show the effects of a drought. • Define *microeconomics* and *macroeconomics*.

THE ECONOMIST AS POLICY ADVISOR

Often economists are asked to explain the causes of economic events. Why, for example, is unemployment higher for teenagers than for older workers? Sometimes economists are asked to recommend policies to improve economic outcomes. What, for instance, should the government do to improve the economic well-being of teenagers? Can economics shed any light on the problem of non-medicinal drug use? How might economics help in finding solutions to the problems associated with global warming? When economists are trying to explain the world, they are scientists. When they are trying to help improve it, they are policy advisors.

Positive versus Normative Analysis

To help clarify the two roles that economists play, we begin by examining the use of language. Because scientists and policy advisors have different goals, they use language in different ways.

For example, suppose that two people are discussing minimum wage laws. Here are two statements you might hear:

PASCALE: Minimum wage laws cause unemployment.
SOPHIE: The government should raise the minimum wage.

Ignoring for now whether you agree with these statements, notice that Pascale and Sophie differ in what they are trying to do. Pascale is speaking like a scientist: she is making a claim about how the world works. Sophie is speaking like a policy advisor: she is making a claim about how she would like to change the world.

In general, statements about the world are of two types. One type, such as Pascale's, is positive. **Positive statements** are descriptive. They make a claim about how the world *is*. A second type of statement, such as Sophie's, is normative. **Normative statements** are prescriptive. They make a claim about how the world *ought to be*.

positive statements
claims that attempt to describe the world as it is

normative statements
claims that attempt to prescribe how the world should be

A key difference between positive and normative statements is how we judge their validity. We can, in principle, confirm or refute positive statements by examining evidence. An economist might evaluate Pascale's statement by analysing data on changes in minimum wages and changes in unemployment over time. By contrast, evaluating normative statements involves values as well as facts. Sophie's statement cannot be judged using data alone. Deciding what is good or bad policy is not merely a matter of science; it also involves our views on ethics, religion and political philosophy.

Of course, positive and normative statements may be related. Our positive views about how the world works affect our normative views about what policies are desirable. Pascale's claim that the minimum wage causes unemployment, if true, might lead us to reject Sophie's conclusion that the government should raise the minimum wage. Yet our normative conclusions cannot come from positive analysis alone; they involve value judgements as well.

As you study economics, keep in mind the distinction between positive and normative statements. Much of economics just tries to explain how the economy works. Yet often the goal of economics is to improve how the economy works. When you hear economists making normative statements, you know they have crossed the line from scientist to policy advisor.

Economists in Governmental and Supra-governmental Institutions

An old joke about economists concerns the politician who one day said that she would only employ economists with one hand: she was tired of receiving advice of the form, 'On the one hand,...On the other hand....'

Throughout Europe, North America and the world more generally, many government ministries dealing with economic issues – such as a country's finance ministry or Treasury – have large numbers of economists working for them, providing advice on alternative policy measures or forecasts of the economy. In the UK, the Government Economic Service is the biggest single employer of economists, with about 1 000 of them working in 30 government departments and agencies.

The joke about one-handed economists does reflect an element of truth concerning the nature of economic advice – namely that good economic advice is not always straightforward. This tendency is rooted in one of the *Ten Principles of Economics* in Chapter 1: people face trade-offs. Economists are aware that trade-offs are involved in most policy decisions. For example, a policy might, on the one hand, increase efficiency but, on the other hand, reduce equity. It might help future generations but hurt current generations. An economist who says that all policy decisions are easy is an economist not to be trusted.

Economists are also found outside the administrative branch of government. The Bank of England, the institution that implements the UK's monetary policy, employs a large staff of economists to analyse economic developments in the United Kingdom and throughout the world. At the time of writing this chapter, both the Governor and Deputy Governor of the Bank of England were former professors of the London School of Economics, while the President of the German central bank, the Bundesbank, and of the US central bank, the Federal Reserve, were also former professors of economics. Most of the central banks of other European countries also have economic research departments, as do the European Central Bank in Frankfurt and the US Federal Reserve in Washington.

WE HAVE TO MAKE MASSIVE CUTS SO WE CAN REDUCE DEBT... WHICH WILL CUT INTO GROWTH WHICH IS NEEDED SO WE CAN MAKE MASSIVE CUTS....

Economists are also employed to provide advice at the supra-governmental level. The International Monetary Fund, which was created in 1945 to help promote the health of the world economy, employs at its headquarters in Washington DC probably the largest number of economics Ph.D.s based at a single location anywhere in the world, originating from a very large proportion of the 185 countries that make up the IMF's near-global membership. Table 2.1 lists the websites of some of these agencies.

The influence of economists on policy goes beyond their role as advisors: their research and writings often affect policy indirectly. The great British economist John Maynard Keynes offered this observation:

> The ideas of economists and political philosophers, both when they are right and when they are wrong, are more powerful than is commonly understood. Indeed, the world is ruled by little else. Practical men, who believe themselves to be quite exempt from intellectual influences, are usually the slaves of some defunct economist. Madmen in authority, who hear voices in the air, are distilling their frenzy from some academic scribbler of a few years back.

Although these words were written in 1935, they remain true today. Indeed, the 'academic scribbler of a few years back' now influencing public policy is often Keynes himself.

Quick Quiz   Give an example of a positive statement and an example of a normative statement. • Name four government departments that regularly rely on advice from economists.

TABLE 2.1

Websites

Here are the websites for a few of the government and supra-governmental agencies that are responsible for collecting economic data and making or advising on economic policy.

European Central Bank	http://www.ecb.int
Organization for Economic Cooperation and Development	http://www.oecd.org
International Monetary Fund	http://www.imf.org
Bank of England	http://www.bankofengland.co.uk
UK Treasury	http://www.hm-treasury.gov.uk
UK Office for National Statistics	http://www.ons.gov.uk
US Federal Reserve Board	http://www.federalreserve.gov

CASE STUDY

Professor Mankiw Goes to Washington

Both of the authors of the textbook you are now reading are university professors. But in the past few years, each of us has had the opportunity to leave the ivory tower and put our economics to the test. One of us, Professor Taylor, went into the world of global finance, while the other, Professor Mankiw, had the opportunity to become the chairman of the US Council of Economic Advisors (CEA) and the US President's chief economist from 2003 to 2005. Here, Professor Mankiw describes what it was like to be the chief economic advisor in one of the world's most powerful economies.

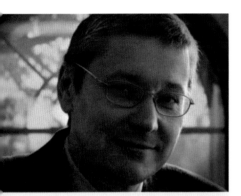

Professor Mankiw

As chair of the CEA, I met with the President about twice a week. Some of these meetings were briefings on the state of the economy; most were discussions of current issues in economic policy. I worked closely with other members of the White House staff to analyse policy options and brief the President on a wide range of topics, such as tax policy, the federal budget, social security and international trade. I also met regularly with economic officials outside the White House, such as the Secretary of the Treasury (the head of the US finance ministry) and the Federal Reserve Chairman (the head of the US central bank) and with leaders of the business community.

For anyone used to the measured pace and quiet reflection of university life, taking such a job is exhilarating. Sitting with the President in his famous Oval Office in the White House, flying on *Air Force One,* and spending the weekend with the President and his aides at his country retreat, Camp David, are unforgettable experiences. Testifying as the President's representative before congressional committees, which include politicians who are usually partisan and sometimes hostile, is also an experience a person does not easily forget – no matter how hard one might try.

During my two years in Washington, I learned a lot about the process by which economic policy is made. It differs in many ways from the idealised policy process assumed in economics textbooks.

Throughout this text, whenever we discuss economic policy, we often focus on one question: What is the best policy for the government to pursue? We act as if policy were set by a benevolent king. Once the king figures out the right policy, he has no trouble putting his ideas into action.

In the real world, figuring out the right policy is only part of a leader's job, sometimes the easiest part. After the President hears from his economic advisers about what policy is best from their perspective, he turns to other advisors for related input. His communications advisors will tell him how best to explain the proposed policy to the public, and they will try to anticipate any misunderstandings that might arise to make the challenge more difficult. His press advisors will tell him how the news media will report on his proposal and what opinions will likely be expressed on the nation's editorial pages. His legislative affairs advisors will tell him how Congress will view the proposal, what amendments members of Congress will suggest, and the likelihood that Congress will pass some version of the President's proposal into law. His political advisors will tell him which groups will organize to support or oppose the proposed policy, how this proposal will affect his standing among different groups in the electorate, and whether it will affect support for any of the President's other policy initiatives. After hearing and weighing all this advice, the President then decides how to proceed.

My two years in Washington were a vivid reminder of an important lesson: making economic policy in a representative democracy is a messy affair – and there are often good reasons presidents (and other politicians) do not advance the policies that economists advocate. Economists offer crucial input into the policy process, but their advice is only one ingredient of a complex recipe.

WHY ECONOMISTS DISAGREE

'If all economists were laid end to end, they would not reach a conclusion.' This witticism from George Bernard Shaw is revealing. Economists as a group are often criticised for giving conflicting advice to policy makers. There are two basic reasons:

- Economists may disagree about the validity of alternative positive theories about how the world works.
- Economists may have different values and, therefore, different normative views about what policy should try to accomplish.

Let's discuss each of these reasons.

Differences in Scientific Judgements

Several centuries ago, astronomers debated whether the earth or the sun was at the centre of the solar system. More recently, meteorologists have debated whether the earth is experiencing global warming and, if so, why. Science is a search for understanding about the world around us. It is not surprising that as the search continues, scientists can disagree about the direction in which truth lies.

Economists often disagree for the same reason. Economics is a young science, and there is still much to be learned. Economists sometimes disagree because they have different beliefs about the validity of alternative theories or about the size of important parameters.

For example, economists disagree about whether the government should levy taxes based on a household's income or based on its consumption (spending). Advocates of a switch from an income tax to a consumption tax believe that the change would encourage households to save more, because income that is saved would not be taxed. Higher saving, in turn, would lead to more rapid growth in productivity and living standards. Advocates of an income tax system believe that household saving would not respond much to a change in the tax laws. These two groups of economists hold different normative views about the tax system because they have different positive views about the responsiveness of saving to tax incentives.

Differences in Values

Suppose that Henrik and Carlos both take the same amount of water from the town well. To pay for maintaining the well, the town imposes a property tax on its residents. Henrik lives in a large house worth €2 million and pays a property tax of €10 000 a year. Carlos owns a small cottage worth €20 000 and pays a property tax of €1 000 a year.

Is this policy fair? If not, who pays too much and who pays too little? Would it be better to replace the tax based on the value of the property with a tax that was just a single payment from everyone living in the town (a poll tax) in return for using the well – say, €1 000 a year? After all, Henrik lives on his own and actually uses much less water than Carlos and the other four alpine pipe players in Carlos's band who live with him and bathe regularly before and after a gig. Would that be a fairer policy?

In the 1980s, when the UK government attempted to replace the system of property tax in the UK with a poll tax, it resulted in riots in Trafalgar Square – many people clearly thought that it was indeed very unfair. There were also a large number of people who thought it a much fairer system than the one which existed at the time. This raises two interesting questions in economics – how do we define words like 'fair' and 'unfair' and who holds the power to influence and make decisions? If the power is in the hands of the anti-poll tax lobby then the policy may be dropped even if it is a much 'fairer' system!

What about replacing the property tax not with a poll tax but with an income tax? Henrik has an income of €100 000 a year so that a 5 per cent income tax would present him with a tax bill of €5 000. Carlos, on the other hand, has an income of only €10 000 a year and so would pay only €500 a year in tax (although his four tenants, who earn about the same, would also have to pay a similar tax bill). Does it matter whether Carlos's low income is due to his decision to pursue a career as an alpine horn player? Would it matter if it were due to a physical disability? Does it matter whether Henrik's high income is due to a large inheritance from his uncle? What if it were due to his willingness to work long hours at a dreary job?

These are difficult questions on which people are likely to disagree. If the town hired two experts to study how the town should tax its residents to pay for the well, we should not be surprised if they offered conflicting advice.

This simple example shows why economists sometimes disagree about public policy. As we learned earlier in our discussion of normative and positive analysis, policies cannot be judged on scientific grounds alone. Economists give conflicting advice sometimes because they have different values. Perfecting the science of economics will not tell us whether it is Henrik or Carlos who pays too much.

Perception versus Reality

Because of differences in scientific judgements and differences in values, some disagreement among economists is inevitable. Yet one should not overstate the amount of disagreement. In many cases, economists do offer a united view.

Table 2.2 contains ten propositions about economic policy. In a survey of economists in business, government and academia, these propositions were endorsed by an overwhelming majority of respondents. Most of these propositions would fail to command a similar consensus among the general public.

TABLE 2.2

Proposition (and Percentage of Economists Who Agree)

Ten propositions about which most economists agree

1. A ceiling on rents reduces the quantity and quality of housing available. (93%)
2. Tariffs and import quotas usually reduce general economic welfare. (93%)
3. Flexible and floating exchange rates offer an effective international monetary arrangement. (90%)
4. Fiscal policy (e.g., tax cut and/or government expenditure increase) has a significant stimulative impact on a less than fully employed economy. (90%)
5. If the government budget is to be balanced, it should be done over the business cycle rather than yearly. (85%)
6. Cash payments increase the welfare of recipients to a greater degree than do transfers-in-kind of equal cash value. (84%)
7. A large government budget deficit has an adverse effect on the economy. (83%)
8. A minimum wage increases unemployment among young and unskilled workers. (79%)
9. The government should restructure the welfare system along the lines of a 'negative income tax'. (79%)
10. Effluent taxes and marketable pollution permits represent a better approach to pollution control than imposition of pollution ceilings. (78%)

Source: Adapted from Richard M. Alston, J.R. Kearl and Michael B. Vaughn, 'Is There Consensus Among Economists in the 1990s?' *American Economic Review* (May 1992): 203–209. Used by permission.

One of the propositions in the table concerns tariffs and import quotas, two policies that restrict trade among nations. For reasons we will discuss more fully in later chapters, almost all economists oppose such barriers to free trade. This, in fact, is one of the major reasons why the European Union was set up and why countries are queuing up to join it: tariffs and quotas are not imposed on trade between EU member countries. Tariffs and quotas *are*, however, often imposed by EU countries on goods coming from outside of the European Union. In the USA, the President and Congress have, over the years, often chosen to restrict the import of certain goods. In 2002, for example, the Bush administration imposed large tariffs on steel to protect domestic steel producers from foreign competition – although they later had to drop the policy when the European Union threatened to retaliate by increasing the tariffs on US goods imported into EU countries from the US. In this case, economists did offer united advice, but policy makers chose to ignore it.

Another of the propositions concerns the imposition of a legal minimum wage – nearly 80 per cent of economists surveyed said that they thought that a minimum wage increases unemployment among unskilled and young workers. Nevertheless, the US and nine European Union countries, including the UK, now have a statutory minimum wage. Of course, these economists were not necessarily *against* the imposition of a minimum wage. Some of them might argue, for example, that while, on the one hand, introducing a minimum wage above a certain level may affect unemployment, on the other hand it may increase the average quality of goods and services produced in the economy by making it harder for producers of low-quality goods and services to compete by keeping wages and prices low, and this may lead to a net benefit to the economy overall. Remember: people face trade-offs.

Table 2.3 shows another aspect of this same idea. This is based on a paper written by Alan Budd, a former Chief Economic Advisor to HM Treasury in the UK and Provost of The Queen's College, Oxford University. The paper appeared in the journal *World Economics* in 2004. This table shows a list of things that Sir Alan thinks that economists know and therefore agree on. Most of these things

TABLE 2.3

What Economists Know

- **Economists know that demand curves slope downwards from left to right.**
  - This suggests that when prices rise, the quantity demanded of a product (under normal circumstances) will fall, and vice versa.
- **Economists know that supply curves slope upwards from left to right.**
  - This suggests that when prices rise, the quantity supplied by producers will also rise and vice versa.
- **Economists know that the proportion of income spent on food falls as income rises.**
  - This is what is referred to as Engel's Law, after the German statistician Ernst Engel. Budd points out that this law applies not only to studies of the differences in the proportion of income spent on food by the rich and the poor, but also over time. When nations go through economic development and become richer, the proportion of national income spent on food falls.
- **Economists know that there are gains from trade to be had when countries or individuals have comparative advantage.**
  - What this means is that one country might be better at producing a number of goods than another. However, if it focuses its attention on producing the good in which it has a comparative advantage, both countries can gain from trade and the world economy will be in a better state. By focusing on production of one good at the expense of others, countries move resources from the production of one good to another. By doing so, the country sacrifices the output of this other good that it could have produced. However, the gains made from shifting resources into production of products in which they are more efficient in production helps to raise total output. A mutually beneficial rate of exchange between the two countries means they both are better off than before.
- **Economists tend to think in terms of general rather than partial equilibrium.**
  - Economies are made up of millions of interrelated markets. Non-economists, argues Budd, tend to see things from a partial equilibrium point of view. In many cases, this view is based around a zero-sum outcome – the benefit received by one party to an economic decision is offset by a negative impact on someone else. Looking at the big picture gives a more accurate understanding of how economies work and what the consequences of economic policy can be.
- **Economists know that sunk costs should not affect pricing decisions.**
  - Sunk costs are those costs have been spent and cannot be recovered or affected by future economic activity. What this means is that the spending on projects like the Olympic Games site in east London and the associated infrastructure will be largely academic. Arguments about how much it will cost to build a new rail link from London to the Channel coast to support the staging of the Games are simply not relevant. What will be important are the ongoing costs of actually running the line and the infrastructure that is built when the Games go ahead, as well as the cost of running the legacy that the Games will leave.
- **There is a difference between what economists know and what non-economists know.**
  - This can be summarized under the heading 'folk economics'. Folk economics is the intuitive understanding that untrained people have about how the economy operates. If you like, this can be seen as being a novice perspective as opposed to an expert one.

    Budd makes an interesting observation here. If you (as a non-physicist) were engaged in conversation with a physicist who tells you about string theory, you are unlikely to interrupt him or her and disagree with what they were telling you. An economist engaged in a discussion about obesity, for example, with a non economist would be far more likely to be questioned about the views being put forward. If I, as an economist, told you, a non-economist, that obesity was caused by the rise in poverty levels in countries, it is likely that there would be some disagreement with my view. In short, economists think in the subject, whereas non-economists do not!

are based on hypotheses that have been tested and observed and which appear to explain key behaviours. It is worth bearing the information in these two tables in mind as you read through the book.

Quick Quiz Why might economic advisors to the government disagree about a question of policy?

Economists as Decision Makers

It could be said that economics is the science of decision-making. The way that economists go about making decisions is a specific one. They will initially try to identify the problem or issue related to the decision, for example, will measures to cut greenhouse gas emissions be efficient or is it worth my while travelling 50 kilometres to redeem a voucher for €50 at a particular store?

The next stage is to look at the costs and benefits involved in the decision. These costs and benefits are not just the private costs and benefits to the individual concerned, however, they will also include the costs and benefits to third parties who are not directly involved in the actual decision. For example, cutting greenhouse gas emissions means that resources will have to be diverted to new ways of production or different ways of producing energy. The private costs will be those borne by the businesses that will have to implement measures to adhere to the limits placed upon them. The social costs might include the impact on local people of the construction of wind farms or new nuclear power stations. If I chose to make the 50-kilometre journey then I would incur travelling costs – petrol, vehicle depreciation and so on as well as the cost in terms of the time I have to give to make the journey. The social costs include the addition to possible road congestion that I add as well as the potential danger to other road users that my being on the road presents.

Having identified the costs and benefits, the economist then seeks to place a value on them in order to get some idea of the relationship between the costs and benefits of making the decision. In some cases, valuing costs and benefits can be easy; in the case of my shopping trip, the benefit is the €50 saved; the costs of petrol used on the journey are easy to calculate. Some costs and benefits are much more difficult to value. The loss of visual amenity for a resident living near a wind turbine or the value of the possible loss of life from a nuclear catastrophe at a power plant may be very difficult to value. Economists have devised ways in which these values can be estimated.

Once the sum of the costs and benefits are calculated, the decision then becomes clearer. If the cost outweighs the benefit then making the decision may be unwise but if the costs are less than the benefits then it may mean the decision is warranted. Policy makers may want to look at the extent to which the costs outweigh the benefit or the benefit outweighs the cost, however. If the benefit to me of going to redeem the voucher is €50 but the cost of making the trip to do so is valued at €49 then it may not be worth my while going, but if the cost were valued at just €10 then my decision may be more obvious.

Every day millions of decisions are made by individuals, businesses and governments. Whilst not every one of these decisions will be made using the exact processes outlined above, economists do make assumptions that humans do behave in a rational way and part of this rational behaviour involves weighing up the costs and benefits of an action.

The Economist as Mathematician

As your course in economics progresses you will have to develop skills in mathematics to help you understand some of the key concepts and methods that economists adopt. If you read academic economics journals you will see examples of how mathematics is used as a tool to help frame and explain hypotheses and theories. The appendix to this chapter provides a brief outline of some important points to learn about graphing. The website will provide more detailed information on the relevance of mathematics to key concepts you will encounter in this book.

LET'S GET GOING

The first two chapters of this book have introduced you to the ideas and methods of economics. We are now ready to get to work. In the next chapter we start learning in more detail the principles of economic behaviour and economic policy.

As you proceed through this book, you will be asked to draw on many of your intellectual skills. You might find it helpful to keep in mind some advice from the great John Maynard Keynes:

> The study of economics does not seem to require any specialised gifts of an unusually high order. Is it not…a very easy subject compared with the higher branches of philosophy or pure science? An easy subject, at which very few excel! The paradox finds its explanation, perhaps, in that the master-economist must possess a rare *combination* of gifts. He must be mathematician, historian, statesman, philosopher – in some degree. He must understand symbols and speak in words. He must contemplate the particular in terms of the general, and touch abstract and concrete in the same flight of thought. He must study the present in the light of the past for the purposes of the future. No part of man's nature or his institutions must lie entirely outside his regard. He must be purposeful and disinterested in a simultaneous mood; as aloof and incorruptible as an artist, yet sometimes as near the earth as a politician.

It is a tall order. But with practice you will become more and more accustomed to thinking like an economist.

SUMMARY

- Economists try to address their subject with a scientist's objectivity. Like all scientists, they make appropriate assumptions and build simplified models in order to understand the world around them. Two simple economic models are the circular-flow diagram and the production possibilities frontier.

- The field of economics is divided into two subfields: microeconomics and macroeconomics. Microeconomists study decision-making by households and firms and the interaction among households and firms in the marketplace. Macroeconomists study the forces and trends that affect the economy as a whole.

- A positive statement is an assertion about how the world *is*. A normative statement is an assertion about how the world *ought to be*. When economists make normative statements, they are acting more as policy advisors than scientists.

- Economists who advise policy makers offer conflicting advice either because of differences in scientific judgements or because of differences in values. At other times, economists are united in the advice they offer, but policy makers may choose to ignore it.

KEY CONCEPTS

circular-flow diagram, p. 27
economy, p. 27
production possibilities frontier, p. 28

microeconomics, p. 31
macroeconomics, p. 31
positive statements, p. 32

normative statements, p. 32

QUESTIONS FOR REVIEW

1. How is economics like a science?

2. Why do economists make assumptions?

3. Should an economic model describe reality exactly?

4. Draw and explain a production possibilities frontier for an economy that produces olive oil and milk. What happens to this frontier if disease kills half of the economy's cow population?

5. Use a production possibilities frontier to describe the idea of 'efficiency'.

6. What are the two subfields into which economics is divided? Explain what each subfield studies.

7. What is the difference between a positive and a normative statement? Give an example of each.

8. Why do economists sometimes offer conflicting advice to policy makers?

PROBLEMS AND APPLICATIONS

1. Describe some unusual language used in one of the other fields that you are studying or have studied besides economics. Why are these special terms useful?

2. One common assumption in economics is that the products of different firms in the same industry are indistinguishable. For each of the following industries, discuss whether this is a reasonable assumption.
   a. steel
   b. novels
   c. wheat
   d. fast food.

3. Draw a circular-flow diagram. Identify the parts of the model that correspond to the flow of goods and services and the flow of euros for each of the following activities.
   a. Sam pays a shopkeeper €1 for a litre of milk.
   b. Georgia earns €4.50 per hour working at a fast food restaurant.
   c. Millie spends €7 to see a film.
   d. Owen earns €10 000 from his 10 per cent ownership of Pan-European Industrial.

4. Imagine a society that produces military goods and consumer goods, which we'll call 'guns' and 'butter'.
   a. Draw a production possibilities frontier for guns and butter. Explain why it most likely has a bowed-out shape.
   b. Show a point that is impossible for the economy to achieve. Show a point that is feasible but inefficient.
   c. Imagine that the society has two political parties, called the Hawks (who want a strong military) and the Doves (who want a smaller military sector). Show a point on your production possibilities frontier that the

   Hawks might choose and a point the Doves might choose.
   d. Imagine that an aggressive neighbouring country reduces the size of its military sector. As a result, both the Hawks and the Doves reduce their desired production of guns by the same amount. Which party would get the bigger 'peace dividend', measured by the increase in butter production? Explain.

5. The first principle of economics discussed in Chapter 1 is that people face trade-offs. Use a production possibilities frontier to illustrate society's trade-off between a clean environment and the quantity of industrial output. What do you suppose determines the shape and position of the frontier? Show what happens to the frontier if engineers develop an automobile engine with almost no emissions.

6. Classify the following topics as relating to microeconomics or macroeconomics.
   a. A family's decision about how much income to save.
   b. The effect of government regulations on car emissions.
   c. The impact of higher national saving on economic growth.
   d. A firm's decision about how many workers to recruit.
   e. The relationship between the inflation rate and changes in the quantity of money.

7. Classify each of the following statements as positive or normative. Explain.
   a. Society faces a short-run trade-off between inflation and unemployment.
   b. A reduction in the rate of growth of money will reduce the rate of inflation.

c. The European Central Bank should reduce the rate of growth of money.

d. Society ought to require welfare recipients to look for jobs.

e. Lower tax rates encourage more work and more saving.

8. Classify each of the statements in Table 2.2 as positive, normative or ambiguous. Explain.

9. If you were prime minister, would you be more interested in your economic advisors' positive views or their normative views? Why?

10. The *Bank of England Quarterly Bulletin* contains statistical information about the UK economy as well as analysis of current policy issues by the Bank's economic staff. Find a recent copy of this bulletin and read a chapter about an issue that interests you. Summarize the issue discussed and describe the Bank's recommended policy.

11. Who is the current President of the European Central Bank? Who is the current Governor of the Bank of England? Who is the current UK Chancellor of the Exchequer?

12. Would you expect economists to disagree less about public policy as time goes on? Why or why not? Can their differences be completely eliminated? Why or why not?

13. Look up one of the websites listed in Table 2.1. What recent economic trends or issues are addressed there? For further resources, visit www.cengage.co.uk/mankiw_taylor_second

For further resources, visit
www.cengage.com/mankiw_taylor2

APPENDIX Graphing: A Brief Review

Many of the concepts that economists study can be expressed with numbers – the price of bananas, the quantity of bananas sold, the cost of growing bananas and so on. Often these economic variables are related to one another. When the price of bananas rises, people buy fewer bananas. One way of expressing the relationships among variables is with graphs.

Graphs serve two purposes. First, when developing economic theories, graphs offer a way to express visually ideas that might be less clear if described with equations or words. Secondly, when analysing economic data, graphs provide a way of finding how variables are in fact related in the world. Whether we are working with theory or with data, graphs provide a lens through which a recognizable forest emerges from a multitude of trees.

Numerical information can be expressed graphically in many ways, just as a thought can be expressed in words in many ways. A good writer chooses words that will make an argument clear, a description pleasing or a scene dramatic. An effective economist chooses the type of graph that best suits the purpose at hand.

In this appendix we discuss how economists use graphs to study the mathematical relationships among variables. We also discuss some of the pitfalls that can arise in the use of graphical methods.

FIGURE 2A.1

Types of Graph

The pie chart in panel (a) shows how UK government expenditure was divided between the major spending categories in 2008 to 2009. The bar graph in panel (b) compares the average income in four countries in 2007. The time-series graph in panel (c) shows the EU unemployment rate for all 27 countries from November 2008 to October 2009.

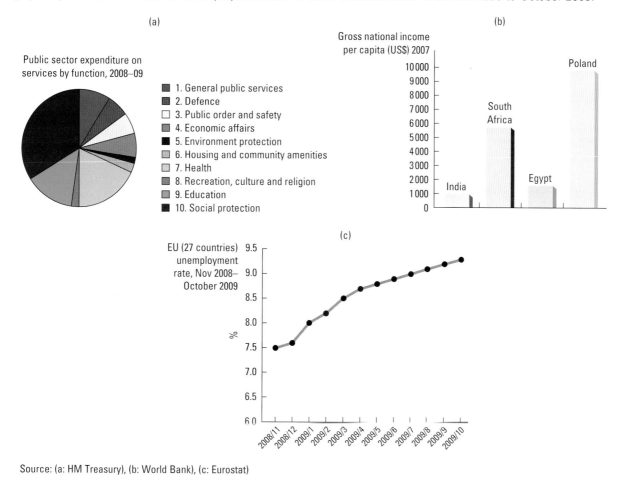

Source: (a: HM Treasury), (b: World Bank), (c: Eurostat)

Graphs of a Single Variable

Three common graphs are shown in Figure 2A.1. The *pie chart* in panel (a) shows how total government expenditure in the UK in 2008–2009 was divided among the major categories such as social protection the National Health Service, education, defence and so on. A slice of the pie represents each category's share of total government expenditure. The *bar graph* in panel (b) compares income per person for four countries in 2007, each expressed in US dollars. The height of each bar represents the average income in each country. The *time-series graph* in panel (c) traces the course of unemployment in the 27 countries of the EU over a year. The height of the line shows the percentage of the workforce that was out of work in each year. You have probably seen similar graphs presented in newspapers and magazines.

Graphs of Two Variables: The Coordinate System

Although the three graphs in Figure 2A.1 are useful in showing how a variable changes over time or across individuals, such graphs are limited in how much

Using the Coordinate System

Final examination mark is measured on the vertical axis and study time on the horizontal axis. Albert E., Alfred E. and the other students on their course are represented by various points. We can see from the graph that students who study more tend to get higher marks.

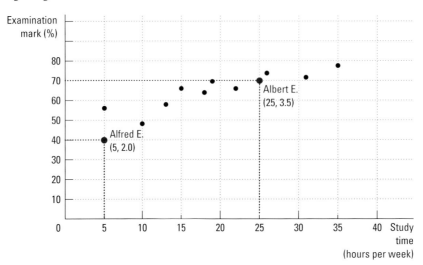

they can tell us. These graphs display information only on a single variable. Economists are often concerned with the relationships between variables. Thus, they need to be able to display two variables on a single graph. The *coordinate system* makes this possible.

Suppose you want to examine the relationship between study time and examination marks. For each student attending your economics lectures, you could record a pair of numbers: hours per week spent studying and marks obtained in the final course examination. These numbers could then be placed in parentheses as an *ordered pair* and appear as a single point on the graph. Albert E. ('Young Einstein'), for instance, is represented by the ordered pair (25 hours/week, 70 per cent examination mark), while his classmate Alfred E. ('What, me worry?') is represented by the ordered pair (5 hours/week, 40 per cent examination mark).

We can graph these ordered pairs on a two-dimensional grid. The first number in each ordered pair, called the *x-coordinate*, tells us the horizontal location of the point. The second number, called the *y-coordinate*, tells us the vertical location of the point. The point with both an *x*-coordinate and a *y*-coordinate of zero is known as the *origin*. The two coordinates in the ordered pair tell us where the point is located in relation to the origin: *x* units to the right of the origin and *y* units above it.

Figure 2A.2 graphs examination marks against study time for Albert E., Alfred E. and the rest of the students who attended the course. This type of graph is called a *scatterplot* because it plots scattered points. Looking at this graph, we immediately notice that points farther to the right (indicating more study time) also tend to be higher (indicating a better examination result). Because study time and examination mark typically move in the same direction, we say that these two variables have a *positive correlation*. By contrast, if we were to graph time spent partying per week and examination marks, we would probably find that higher party time is associated with lower marks; because these variables typically move in opposite directions, we would call this a *negative correlation*. In either case, the coordinate system makes the correlation between the two variables easy to see.

Curves in the Coordinate System

Students who study more do tend to get higher marks, but other factors also influence a student's marks. Previous preparation is an important factor, for instance, as are talent, attention from teachers and even eating a good breakfast. A scatterplot like Figure 2A.2 does not attempt to isolate the effect that study has on grades from the effects of other variables. Often, however, economists prefer looking at how one variable affects another while holding everything else constant.

To see how this is done, let's consider one of the most important graphs in economics – the *demand curve*. The demand curve traces out the effect of a good's price on the quantity of the good consumers want to buy. Before showing a demand curve, however, consider Table 2A.1, which shows how the number of novels that Pascale buys depends on her income and on the price of novels. When novels are cheap, Pascale buys them in large quantities. As they become more expensive, she borrows books from the library instead of buying them or chooses to go to the cinema instead of reading. Similarly, at any given price, Pascale buys more novels when she has a higher income. That is, when her income increases, she spends part of the additional income on novels and part on other goods.

We now have three variables – the price of novels, income and the number of novels purchased – which is more than we can represent in two dimensions. To put the information from Table 2A.1 in graphical form, we need to hold one of the three variables constant and trace out the relationship between the other two. Because the demand curve represents the relationship between price and quantity demanded, we hold Pascale's income constant and show how the number of novels she buys varies with the price of novels.

Suppose that Pascale's income is €30 000 per year. If we place the number of novels Pascale purchases on the x-axis and the price of novels on they y-axis, we can graphically represent the middle column of Table 2A.1. When the points that represent these entries from the table – (5 novels, €10), (9 novels, €9) and so

TABLE 2A.1

Novels Purchased by Pascale

This table shows the number of novels Pascale buys at various incomes and prices. For any given level of income, the data on price and quantity demanded can be graphed to produce Pascale's demand curve for novels, as shown in Figures 2A.3 and 2A.4.

Price	Income		
	€20 000	€30 000	€40 000
€10	2 novels	5 novels	8 novels
€9	6	9	12
€8	10	13	16
€7	14	17	20
€6	18	21	24
€5	22	25	28
	Demand curve, D_3	Demand curve, D_1	Demand curve, D_2

FIGURE 2A.3

Demand Curve

The line **D₁** *shows how Pascale's purchases of novels depend on the price of novels when her income is held constant. Because the price and the quantity demanded are negatively related, the demand curve slopes downward.*

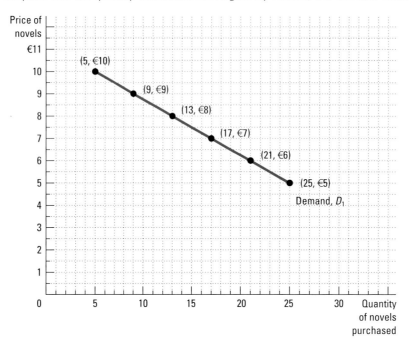

on – are connected, they form a line. This line, pictured in Figure 2A.3, is known as Pascale's demand curve for novels; it tells us how many novels Pascale purchases at any given price. The demand curve is downward sloping, indicating that a higher price reduces the quantity of novels demanded. Because the quantity of novels demanded and the price move in opposite directions, we say that the two variables are *negatively or inversely related*. (Conversely, when two variables move in the same direction, the curve relating them is upward sloping, and we say the variables are *positively related*.)

Now suppose that Pascale's income rises to €40 000 per year. At any given price, Pascale will purchase more novels than she did at her previous level of income. Just as earlier we drew Pascale's demand curve for novels using the entries from the middle column of Table 2A.1, we now draw a new demand curve using the entries from the right-hand column of the table. This new demand curve (curve D_2) is pictured alongside the old one (curve D_1) in Figure 2A.4; the new curve is a similar line drawn farther to the right. We therefore say that Pascale's demand curve for novels *shifts* to the right when her income increases. Likewise, if Pascale's income were to fall to €20 000 per year, she would buy fewer novels at any given price and her demand curve would shift to the left (to curve D_3).

In economics, it is important to distinguish between *movements along a curve* and *shifts of a curve*. As we can see from Figure 2A.3, if Pascale earns €30 000 per year and novels are priced at €8 apiece, she will purchase 13 novels per year. If the price of novels falls to €7, Pascale will increase her purchases of novels to 17 per year. The demand curve, however, stays fixed in the same

FIGURE 2A.4

Shifting Demand Curves

The location of Pascale's demand curve for novels depends on how much income she earns. The more she earns, the more novels she will purchase at any given price, and the further to the right her demand curve will lie. Curve **D₁** *represents Pascale's original demand curve when her income is €30 000 per year. If her income rises to €40 000 per year, her demand curve shifts to* **D₂**. *If her income falls to €20 000 per year, her demand curve shifts to* **D₃**.

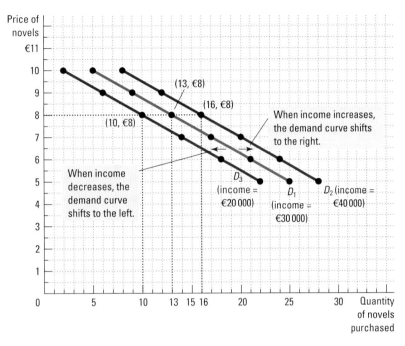

place. Pascale still buys the same number of novels *at each price,* but as the price falls she moves along her demand curve from left to right. By contrast, if the price of novels remains fixed at €8 but her income rises to €40 000, Pascale increases her purchases of novels from 13 to 16 per year. Because Pascale buys more novels *at each price,* her demand curve shifts out, as shown in Figure 2A.4.

There is a simple way to tell when it is necessary to shift a curve. When a variable that is not named on either axis changes, the curve shifts. Income is on neither the *x*-axis nor the *y*-axis of the graph, so when Pascale's income changes, her demand curve must shift. Any change that affects Pascale's purchasing habits, besides a change in the price of novels, will result in a shift in her demand curve. If, for instance, the public library closes and Pascale must buy all the books she wants to read, she will demand more novels at each price, and her demand curve will shift to the right. Or, if the price of going to the cinema falls and Pascale spends more time at the movies and less time reading, she will demand fewer novels at each price, and her demand curve will shift to the left. By contrast, when a variable on an axis of the graph changes, the curve does not shift. We read the change as a movement along the curve.

Slope

One question we might want to ask about Pascale is how much her purchasing habits respond to price. Look at the demand curve pictured in Figure 2A.5. If this curve is very steep, Pascale purchases nearly the same number of novels regardless of whether they are cheap or expensive. If this curve is much flatter, Pascale

FIGURE 2A.5

Calculating the Slope of a Line

To calculate the slope of the demand curve, we can look at the changes in the x- and y-coordinates as we move from the point (21 novels, €6) to the point (13 novels, €8). The slope of the line is the ratio of the change in the y-coordinate (−2) to the change in the x-coordinate (+8), which equals −1/4.

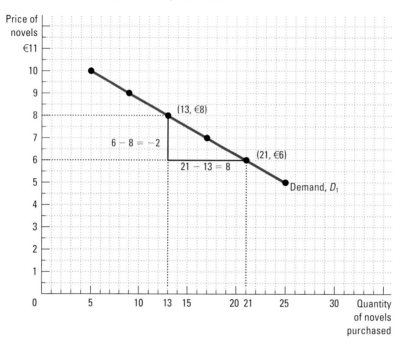

purchases many fewer novels when the price rises. To answer questions about how much one variable responds to changes in another variable, we can use the concept of *slope.*

The slope of a line is the ratio of the vertical distance covered to the horizontal distance covered as we move along the line. This definition is usually written out in mathematical symbols as follows:

$$\text{slope} = \frac{\Delta y}{\Delta x}$$

where the Greek letter Δ (delta) stands for the change in a variable. In other words, the slope of a line is equal to the 'rise' (change in y) divided by the 'run' (change in x). The slope will be a small positive number for a fairly flat upward sloping line, a large positive number for a steep upward sloping line and a negative number for a downward sloping line. A horizontal line has a slope of zero because in this case the y-variable never changes; a vertical line is said to have an infinite slope because the y-variable can take any value without the x-variable changing at all.

What is the slope of Pascale's demand curve for novels? First of all, because the curve slopes down, we know the slope will be negative. To calculate a numerical value for the slope, we must choose two points on the line. With Pascale's income at €30 000, she will purchase 21 novels at a price of €6 or 13 novels at a price of €8. When we apply the slope formula, we are concerned with the change between these two points; in other words, we are concerned with the difference between them, which lets us know that we will have to sub-tract one set of values from the other, as follows:

$$\text{Slope} = \frac{\Delta y}{\Delta x} = \frac{\text{first } y\text{-coordinate} - \text{second } y\text{-coordinate}}{\text{first } x\text{-coordinate} - \text{second } x\text{-coordinate}} = \frac{6 - 8}{21 - 13} = -\frac{2}{8} = -\frac{1}{4}$$

Figure 2A.5 shows graphically how this calculation works. Try computing the slope of Pascale's demand curve using two different points. You should get exactly the same result, –1/4. One of the properties of a straight line is that it has the same slope everywhere. This is not true of other types of curves, which are steeper in some places than in others.

The slope of Pascale's demand curve tells us something about how responsive her purchases are to changes in the price. A small slope (a number close to zero) means that Pascale's demand curve is relatively flat; in this case, she adjusts the number of novels she buys substantially in response to a price change. A larger slope (a number further from zero) means that Pascale's demand curve is rela-tively steep; in this case, she adjusts the number of novels she buys only slightly in response to a price change.

Cause and Effect

Economists often use graphs to advance an argument about how the economy works. In other words, they use graphs to argue about how one set of events *causes* another set of events. With a graph like the demand curve, there is no doubt about cause and effect. Because we are varying price and holding all other variables constant, we know that changes in the price of novels cause changes in the quantity Pascale demands. Remember, however, that our demand curve came from a hypothetical example. When graphing data from the real world, it is often more difficult to establish how one variable affects another.

The first problem is that it is difficult to hold everything else constant when measuring how one variable affects another. If we are not able to hold variables constant, we might decide that one variable on our graph is causing changes in the other variable when actually those changes are caused by a third *omitted variable* not pictured on the graph. Even if we have identified the correct two variables to look at, we might run into a second problem – *reverse causality*. In other words, we might decide that A causes B when in fact B causes A. The omit-ted variable and reverse causality traps require us to proceed with caution when using graphs to draw conclusions about causes and effects.

Omitted Variables To see how omitting a variable can lead to a deceptive graph, let's consider an example. Imagine that the government, spurred by public concern about the large number of deaths from cancer, commissions an exhaus-tive study from Big Brother Statistical Services. Big Brother examines many of the items found in people's homes to see which of them are associated with the risk of cancer. Big Brother reports a strong relationship between two variables: the number of cigarette lighters that a household owns and the probability that someone in the household will develop cancer. Figure 2A.6 shows this relationship.

What should we make of this result? Big Brother advises a quick policy response. It recommends that the government discourages the ownership of ciga-rette lighters by taxing their sale. It also recommends that the government requires warning labels: 'Big Brother has determined that this lighter is danger-ous to your health.'

In judging the validity of Big Brother's analysis, one question is paramount: has Big Brother held constant every relevant variable except the one under

Graph With an Omitted Variable

The upward sloping curve shows that members of households with more cigarette lighters are more likely to develop cancer. Yet we should not conclude that ownership of lighters causes cancer, because the graph does not take into account the number of cigarettes smoked.

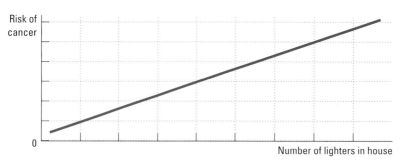

consideration? If the answer is no, the results are suspect. An easy explanation for Figure 2A.6 is that people who own more cigarette lighters are more likely to smoke cigarettes and that cigarettes, not lighters, cause cancer. If Figure 2A.6 does not hold constant the amount of smoking, it does not tell us the true effect of owning a cigarette lighter.

This story illustrates an important principle: when you see a graph being used to support an argument about cause and effect, it is important to ask whether the movements of an omitted variable could explain the results you see.

Reverse Causality Economists can also make mistakes about causality by misreading its direction. To see how this is possible, suppose the Association of European Anarchists commissions a study of crime in Eurovia and arrives at Figure 2A.7, which plots the number of violent crimes per 1000 people in major Eurovian cities against the number of police officers per 1000 people. The anarchists note the curve's upward slope and argue that because police increase rather than decrease the amount of urban violence, law enforcement should be abolished.

If we could run a controlled experiment, we would avoid the danger of reverse causality. To run an experiment, we would set the number of police officers in different cities randomly and then examine the correlation between police and crime. Figure 2A.7, however, is not based on such an experiment. We simply observe that more dangerous cities have more police officers. The explanation for this may be that more dangerous cities hire more police. In other words, rather than police causing crime, crime may cause police. Nothing in the graph itself allows us to establish the direction of causality.

It might seem that an easy way to determine the direction of causality is to examine which variable moves first. If we see crime increase and then the police force expand, we reach one conclusion. If we see the police force expand and then crime increase, we reach the other. Yet there is also a flaw with this approach: often people change their behaviour not in response to a change in their present conditions but in response to a change in their *expectations* of future conditions. A city that expects a major crime wave in the future, for instance, might well hire more police now. This problem is even easier to see in the case

FIGURE 2A.7

Graph Suggesting Reverse Causality

The upward sloping curve shows that Eurovian cities with a higher concentration of police are more dangerous. Yet the graph does not tell us whether police cause crime or crime-plagued cities hire more police.

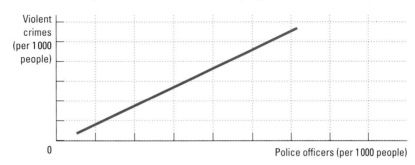

of babies and baby cots. Couples often buy a baby cot in anticipation of the birth of a child. The cot comes before the baby, but we wouldn't want to conclude that the sale of cots causes the population to grow!

There is no complete set of rules that says when it is appropriate to draw causal conclusions from graphs. Yet just keeping in mind that cigarette lighters don't cause cancer (omitted variable) and baby cots do not cause larger families (reverse causality) will keep you from falling for many faulty economic arguments.

3 INTERDEPENDENCE AND THE GAINS FROM TRADE

Consider your typical day. You wake up in the morning and you make yourself some coffee from beans grown in Brazil, or tea from leaves grown in Sri Lanka. Over breakfast, you listen to a radio programme on your radio set made in Japan. You get dressed in clothes manufactured in Thailand. You drive to the university in a car made of parts manufactured in more than a dozen countries around the world. Then you open up your economics textbook written by two authors of whom one lives in the USA and the other lives in England, published by a company located in Hampshire and printed on paper made from trees grown in Finland.

Every day you rely on many people from around the world, most of whom you do not know, to provide you with the goods and services that you enjoy. Such interdependence is possible because people trade with one another. Those people who provide you with goods and services are not acting out of generosity or concern for your welfare. Nor is some government or supra-governmental agency directing them to make products you want and to give them to you. Instead, people provide you and other consumers with the goods and services they produce because they get something in return.

In subsequent chapters we will examine how our economy coordinates the activities of millions of people with varying tastes and abilities. As a starting point for this analysis, here we consider the reasons for economic interdependence. One of the *Ten Principles of Economics* highlighted in Chapter 1 is that trade can make everyone better off. This principle explains why people trade with their neighbours and why nations trade with other nations. In this chapter we examine this principle more closely. What exactly do people gain when they trade with one another? Why do people choose to become interdependent?

A PARABLE FOR THE MODERN ECONOMY

To understand why people choose to depend on others for goods and services and how this choice improves their lives, let's look at a simple economy. Imagine that there are two goods in the world – beef and potatoes. And there are two people in the world – a cattle farmer named Fabia and a market gardener named Marius – each of whom would like to eat both beef and potatoes.

The gains from trade are most obvious if the cattle farmer can produce only meat and the market gardener can produce only potatoes. In one scenario, the farmer and the gardener could choose to have nothing to do with each other. But after several months of eating beef roasted, boiled, fried and grilled, the cattle farmer might decide that self-sufficiency is not all he expected. The market gardener, who has been eating potatoes mashed, fried and baked, would most likely agree. It is easy to see that trade would allow them to enjoy greater variety: each could then have steak and chips.

Although this scene illustrates most simply how everyone can benefit from trade, the gains would be similar if the farmer and the gardener were each capable of producing the other good, but only at great cost. Suppose, for example, that the market gardener is able to rear cattle and produce meat, but that he is not very good at it. Similarly, suppose that the cattle farmer is able to grow potatoes, but that her land is not very well suited for it. In this case, it is easy to see that the gardener and the farmer can each benefit by specializing in what he or she does best and then trading with the other.

The gains from trade are less obvious, however, when one person is better at producing *every* good. For example, suppose that the cattle farmer is better at rearing cattle *and* better at growing potatoes than the market gardener. In this case, should the farmer or gardener choose to remain self-sufficient, or is there still reason for them to trade with each other? To answer this question, we need to look more closely at the factors that affect such a decision.

Production Possibilities

Suppose that the gardener and the farmer each work eight hours a day six days a week (a working week of 48 hours) and take Sunday off. They can spend their time growing potatoes, rearing cattle, or a combination of the two. Table 3.1 shows the amount of time each person takes to produce 1 kilogram of each good. The gardener can produce 1 kilogram of meat in 6 hours and 1 kilogram of potatoes in an hour and a half. The farmer, who is more productive in both

TABLE 3.1

The Production Opportunities of the Gardener and the Farmer

	Time needed to make 1 kg of:		Amount of meat or potatoes produced in 48 hours	
	Meat	Potatoes	Meat	Potatoes
Gardener	6 hrs/kg	1.5 hrs/kg	8 kg	32 kg
Farmer	2 hrs/kg	1 hr/kg	24 kg	48 kg

FIGURE 3.1

The Production Possibilities Frontier

Panel (a) shows the combinations of meat and potatoes that the gardener can produce. Panel (b) shows the combinations of meat and potatoes that the farmer can produce. Both production possibilities frontiers are derived from Table 3.1 and the assumption that the gardener and farmer each work 8 hours a day.

activities, can produce a kilogram of meat in 2 hours and a kilogram of potatoes in 1 hour. The last columns in Table 3.1 show the amounts of meat or potatoes the gardener and farmer can produce in a 48-hour working week, producing only that good.

Panel (a) of Figure 3.1 illustrates the amounts of meat and potatoes that the gardener can produce. If the gardener devotes all 48 hours of his time to potatoes, he produces 32 kilograms of potatoes (measured on the horizontal axis) and no meat. If he devotes all his time to meat, he produces 8 kilograms of meat (measured on the vertical axis) and no potatoes. If the gardener divides his time equally between the two activities, spending 24 hours a week on each, he produces 16 kilograms of potatoes and 4 kilograms of meat. The figure shows these three possible outcomes and all others in between.

This graph is the gardener's production possibilities frontier. As we discussed in Chapter 2, a production possibilities frontier shows the various mixes of output that an economy, or in this case an individual, can produce given existing resources. It illustrates one of the *Ten Principles of Economics* in Chapter 1: people face trade-offs. Here the gardener faces a trade-off between producing meat and producing potatoes. You may recall that the production possibilities frontier in Chapter 2 was drawn bowed out; in that case, the trade-off between the two goods depended on the amounts being produced. Here, however, the gardener's technology for producing meat and potatoes (as summarized in Table 3.1) allows him to switch between one good and the other at a constant rate. If the gardener devotes an extra hour to producing meat he sacrifices potato production. In Chapter 2 we looked at how to calculate the slope of a straight line. In this case increasing meat production by 1 kilogram leads to a sacrifice of 4 kilograms of potatoes. The Δy is 1 kilogram and the Δx is 4 units. The slope is 0.25 which indicates the rate at which potatoes are sacrificed for more meat as more time is devoted to meat production. In this case, the production possibilities frontier is a straight line and so the trade-off is a constant rate. Every extra kilogram of meat produced results in a sacrifice of 4 kilograms of potatoes. The converse of this is that if the gardener switched from meat production to potato production, then every additional 1 kilogram of potatoes produced would involve a trade-off of ¼ kilogram of meat.

Panel (b) of Figure 3.1 shows the production possibilities frontier for the farmer. If the farmer devotes all 48 hours of her working week to potatoes, she produces 48 kilograms of potatoes and no meat. If she devotes all of her time to meat production, she produces 24 kilograms of meat and no potatoes. If the farmer divides her time equally, spending 24 hours a week on each activity, she produces 24 kilograms of potatoes and 12 kilograms of meat. Once again, the production possibilities frontier shows all the possible outcomes. In this case, reducing meat production by one unit means that potato production can increase by 2 units. The slope of this production possibilities frontier is, therefore, 0.5. Conversely, if she devotes more time to producing potatoes then the rate of sacrifice of meat will be 2 kilograms of meat for every 1 kilogram of potatoes.

If the gardener and farmer choose to be self-sufficient, rather than trade with each other, then each consumes exactly what he or she produces. In this case, the production possibilities frontier is also the consumption possibilities frontier. That is, without trade, Figure 3.1 shows the possible combinations of meat and potatoes that the gardener and farmer can each consume.

Although these production possibilities frontiers are useful in showing the trade-offs that the gardener and farmer face, they do not tell us what the gardener and farmer will actually choose to do. To determine their choices, we need to know the tastes of the gardener and the farmer. Let's suppose they choose the combinations identified by points A and B in Figure 3.1: the gardener produces and consumes 16 kilograms of potatoes and 4 kilograms of meat, while the farmer produces and consumes 24 kilograms of potatoes and 12 kilograms of meat.

Specialization and Trade

After several years of feeding her family on combination B, the farmer gets an idea and she goes to talk to the gardener:

FARMER: Marius, have I got a deal for you! I know how to improve life for both of us. I think you should stop producing meat altogether and devote all your time to growing potatoes. According to my calculations, if you devote all of your working week to growing potatoes, you'll produce 32 kilograms of potatoes. If you give me 15 of those 32 kilograms, I'll give you 5 kilograms of meat in return. You will have 17 kilograms of potatoes left to enjoy and also 5 kilograms of meat every week, instead of the
16 kilograms of potatoes and 4 kilograms of meat you now make do with. If you go along with my plan, you'll have more of *both* foods. [To illustrate her point, the farmer shows the gardener panel (a) of Figure 3.2.]

GARDENER: *(sounding sceptical)* That seems like a good deal for me, Fabia, but I don't understand why you are offering it. If the deal is so good for me, it can't be good for you too.

FARMER: Oh, but it is, Marius! Suppose I spend 12 hours a week growing potatoes and 36 hours rearing cattle. Then I can produce 12 kilograms of potatoes and 18 kilograms of meat. You will give me 15 kilograms of your potatoes in exchange for the 5 kilograms of my meat. This means I end up with 27 kilograms of potatoes and 13 kilograms of meat. So I will also be able to consume more of both foods than I do now. [She points out panel (b) of Figure 3.2.]

FIGURE 3.2

How Trade Expands the Set of Consumption Opportunities

The proposed trade between the gardener and the farmer offers each of them a combination of meat and potatoes that would be impossible in the absence of trade. In panel (a), the gardener consumes at point A* rather than point A. In panel (b), the farmer consumes at point B* rather than point B. Trade allows each to consume more meat and more potatoes.

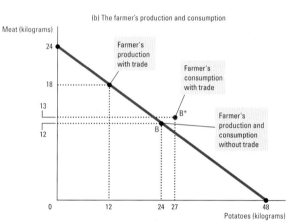

TABLE 3.2

The Gains from Trade: A Summary

	Gardener		Farmer	
	Meat	**Potatoes**	**Meat**	**Potatoes**
Without trade:				
Production and consumption	4 kg	16 kg	12 kg	24 kg
With trade:				
Production	0 kg	32 kg	18 kg	12 kg
Trade	Gets 5 kg	Gives 15 kg	Gives 5 kg	Gets 15 kg
Consumption	5 kg	17 kg	13 kg	27 kg
Gains from trade:				
Increase in consumption	+1 kg	+1 kg	+1 kg	+3 kg

GARDENER: I don't know, Fabia…. This sounds too good to be true.

FARMER: It's really not as complicated as it seems at first. Here – I've summarized my proposal for you in a simple table. [The farmer hands the gardener a copy of Table 3.2.]

GARDENER: *(after pausing to study the table)* These calculations seem correct, but I am puzzled. How can this deal make us both better off?

FARMER: We can both benefit because trade allows each of us to specialize in doing what we do best. You will spend more time growing potatoes and less time rearing cattle. I will spend more time rearing cattle and less time growing potatoes. As a result of specialization and trade, each of us can consume more meat and more potatoes without working any more hours.

Quick Quiz Draw an example of a production possibilities frontier for Hasani, who is stranded on an island after a shipwreck and spends his time gathering coconuts and catching fish. Does this frontier limit Hasani's consumption of coconuts and fish if he lives by himself? Does he face the same limits if he can trade with natives on the island?

THE PRINCIPLE OF COMPARATIVE ADVANTAGE

The farmer's explanation of the gains from trade, though correct, poses a puzzle: if the farmer is better at both rearing cattle and growing potatoes, how can the gardener ever specialize in doing what he does best? The gardener doesn't seem to do anything best. To solve this puzzle, we need to look at the principle of *comparative advantage*.

As a first step in developing this principle, consider the following question: in our example, who can produce potatoes at lower cost – the gardener or the farmer? There are two possible answers, and in these two answers lie the solution to our puzzle and the key to understanding the gains from trade. The slope of the production possibilities frontier discussed above will help us to solve the puzzle.

Absolute Advantage

One way to answer the question about the cost of producing potatoes is to compare the inputs required by the two producers. Economists use the term **absolute advantage** when comparing the productivity of one person, firm or nation to that of another. The producer that requires a smaller quantity of inputs to produce a good is said to have an absolute advantage in producing that good.

In our example, the farmer has an absolute advantage both in producing meat and in producing potatoes, because she requires less time than the gardener to produce a unit of either good. The farmer needs to input only 2 hours in order to produce a kilogram of meat, whereas the gardener needs 6 hours. Similarly, the farmer needs only 1 hour to produce a kilogram of potatoes, whereas the gardener needs 1.5 hours. Based on this information, we can conclude that the farmer has the lower cost of producing potatoes, if we measure cost in terms of the quantity of inputs.

absolute advantage
the comparison among producers of a good according to their productivity

Opportunity Cost and Comparative Advantage

There is another way to look at the cost of producing potatoes. Rather than comparing inputs required, we can compare the opportunity costs. Recall from Chapter 1 that the opportunity cost of some item is what we give up to get that item. In our example, we assumed that the gardener and the farmer each spend 48 hours a week working. Time spent producing potatoes, therefore, takes away from time available for producing meat. As the farmer and gardener reallocate time between producing the two goods, they move along their production possibility frontiers; they give up units of one good to produce units of the other. The

TABLE 3.3

The Opportunity Cost of Meat and Potatoes

	Opportunity cost of:	
	1 kilogram of meat	**1 kilogram of potatoes**
Gardener	4 kg potatoes	0.25 kg meat
Farmer	2 kg potatoes	0.5 kg meat

opportunity cost measures the trade-off between the two goods that each producer faces.

Let's first consider the farmer's opportunity cost. The following analysis confirms our discussion about the slope of the production possibilities frontiers above. According to Table 3.1, producing 1 kilogram of potatoes takes her 1 hour of work. When the farmer spends that 1 hour producing potatoes, she spends 1 hour less producing meat. Because the farmer needs 2 hours to produce 1 kilogram of meat, 1 hour of work would yield ½ kilogram of meat. Hence, the farmer's opportunity cost of producing 1 kilogram of potatoes is ½ kilogram of meat.

Now consider the gardener's opportunity cost. Producing 1 kilogram of potatoes takes him 1½ hours. Because he needs 6 hours to produce 1 kilogram of meat, 1½ hours of work would yield ¼ kilogram of meat. Hence, the gardener's opportunity cost of 1 kilogram of potatoes is ¼ kilogram of meat.

Table 3.3 shows the opportunity costs of meat and potatoes for the two producers. Notice that the opportunity cost of meat is the inverse of the opportunity cost of potatoes. Because 1 kilogram of potatoes costs the farmer ½ kilogram of meat, 1 kilogram of meat costs the farmer 2 kilograms of potatoes. Similarly, because 1 kilogram of potatoes costs the gardener ¼ kilogram of meat, 1 kilogram of meat costs the gardener 4 kilograms of potatoes.

comparative advantage
the comparison among producers of a good according to their opportunity cost

Economists use the term **comparative advantage** when describing the opportunity cost of two producers. The producer who gives up less of other goods to produce good X has the smaller opportunity cost of producing good X and is said to have a comparative advantage in producing it. In our example, the gardener has a lower opportunity cost of producing potatoes than does the farmer: a kilogram of potatoes costs the gardener only ¼ kilogram of meat, while it costs the farmer ½ kilogram of meat. Conversely, the farmer has a lower opportunity cost of producing meat than does the gardener: a kilogram of meat costs the farmer 2 kilograms of potatoes, while it costs the gardener 4 kilograms of potatoes. Thus, the gardener has a comparative advantage in growing potatoes, and the farmer has a comparative advantage in producing meat.

Although it is possible for one person to have an absolute advantage in both goods (as the farmer does in our example), it is impossible for one person to have a comparative advantage in both goods. Because the opportunity cost of one good is the inverse of the opportunity cost of the other, if a person's opportunity cost of one good is relatively high, his opportunity cost of the other good must be relatively low. Comparative advantage reflects the relative opportunity cost. Unless two people have exactly the same opportunity cost, one person will have a comparative advantage in one good, and the other person will have a comparative advantage in the other good.

FYI

The Legacy of Adam Smith and David Ricardo

Economists have long understood the principle of comparative advantage. Here is how the great economist Adam Smith put the argument:

It is a maxim of every prudent master of a family, never to attempt to make at home what it will cost him more to make than to buy. The tailor does not attempt to make his own shoes, but buys them of the shoemaker. The shoemaker does not attempt to make his own clothes but employs a tailor. The gardener attempts to make neither the one nor the other, but employs those different artificers. All of them find it for their interest to employ their whole industry in a way in which they have some advantage over their neighbours, and to purchase with a part of its produce, or what is the same thing, with the price of part of it, whatever else they have occasion for.

This quotation is from Smith's 1776 book *An Inquiry into the Nature and*

Causes of the Wealth of Nations, which was a landmark in the analysis of trade and economic interdependence.

Smith's book inspired David Ricardo – an Englishman born of Dutch parents – to become an economist, having already made his fortune as a stockbroker in the City of London. In his 1817 book *Principles of Political Economy and Taxation,* Ricardo developed the principle of comparative advantage, originally put forward by Robert Torrens, a British Army officer and owner of the *Globe* newspaper in 1815, as we know it today. His defence of free trade was not a mere academic exercise. Ricardo put his economic beliefs to work as a member of the British parliament, where he opposed the Corn Laws, which restricted the import of grain.

The conclusions of Adam Smith and David Ricardo on the gains from trade have held up well over time. Although economists often disagree on questions of policy, they are united in their sup-

David Ricardo

port of free trade. Moreover, the central argument for free trade has not changed much in the past two centuries. Even though the field of economics has broadened its scope and refined its theories since the time of Smith and Ricardo, economists' opposition to trade restrictions is still based largely on the principle of comparative advantage.

CASE STUDY

Afghanistan and the Opium Trade

In the first decade of the 21st century, troops from a number of nations have been in Afghanistan supporting the government, helping rebuild infrastructure, training Afghan police and troops, and fighting Taliban and insurgent groups who pose a perceived threat to security in the country and beyond. One of the regions where problems have been most acute is Helmand province in the south of the country. There have been considerable losses of civilian and military life in this region and the military struggle has been made all the more difficult by some very real economic issues that have militated against lasting peace in the region.

One of these economic issues relates to the growing of opium poppies. Some 70 per cent of all the opium grown in Afghanistan comes from this province. With opium comes all manner of other problems that have a far reaching impact in many other countries. Opium is the raw material used for heroin and the poppy which produces opium represents a lucrative business for many farmers in the region. There is a very good reason why farmers grow opium – it generates financial returns that are greater than any legal crop. Helmand has a comparative advantage in the production of opium; yields per acre are higher than in other parts of Afghanistan and there is a plentiful supply of relatively cheap labour to help produce and harvest the crop – important given that this is a relatively labour intensive crop to grow.

For farmers in the region, decisions about how to use their land are determined in part by the returns they expect to get from alternative crops that could be grown. Different crops will yield a different value of benefits. The opportunity cost of growing opium is relatively low in that the sacrifice of the value of the benefits foregone of alternatives is low. The sacrifice involved in terms of lost benefits from the movement of resources from producing a legal crop such as wheat, for example, is negligible and so there is a real incentive to produce opium which has high rewards. If the return per acre for growing opium is €150, for example, and that for growing wheat is €25, it does not take an economist to point out that the incentive for growing opium is strong.

It can be argued that growing an illegal crop such as opium also brings with it high risks which would increase the opportunity cost. However, in Helmand this is distorted by the fact that the problems enforcing the rule of law means that the power of the authorities to intervene and punish farmers for growing opium is extremely limited. The protection afforded to farmers by warlords and the network of gangs who stand to benefit from the lucrative trade in opium means that the chances of getting caught and punished are negligible. Only if the law can be enforced and there are real and visible risks to growing an illegal crop will the opportunity cost start to increase and incentives to grow a legal crop start to appear.

This means finding ways of encouraging the growth of legal crops and giving farmers adequate returns that increase the opportunity cost of growing opium. This may be achieved through providing subsidies to farmers to produce legal crops. Subsidies do have to be paid for and the Afghan government would need considerable help to be able to put in place such a solution. One other option that has been suggested involves direct intervention in the market for opium. Under such a scheme the US government, for example, could spend around $2.5 billion in purchasing the opium crop from farmers. Such a price might have to be paid each year but in comparison to the $1 billion it currently pays in trying to eradicate the crop and the $200 billion it has paid out in military operations in Afghanistan, the cost may well be offset by the benefits. There is a trade-off and the trade-off might be worth making! In buying the crop those who rely on it to finance their activities through imposing protection money, taking 'taxes' and so on would be sidelined and the corruption in the Afghan government that has been blamed for being part of the problem would also be marginalized.

Comparative Advantage and Trade

Differences in opportunity cost and comparative advantage create the gains from trade. When each person specializes in producing the good for which he or she has a comparative advantage, total production in the economy rises, and this increase in the size of the economic cake can be used to make everyone better off. In other words, as long as two people have different opportunity costs, each can benefit from trade by obtaining a good at a price that is lower than his or her opportunity cost of that good.

Consider the proposed deal from the viewpoint of the gardener. The gardener gets 5 kilograms of meat in exchange for 15 kilograms of potatoes. In other words, the gardener buys each kilogram of meat for a price of 3 kilograms of potatoes. This price of meat is lower than his opportunity cost for 1 kilogram of meat, which is 4 kilograms of potatoes. Thus, the gardener benefits from the deal because he gets to buy meat at a good price.

Now consider the deal from the farmer's viewpoint. The farmer buys 15 kilograms of potatoes for a price of 5 kilograms of meat. That is, the price of potatoes is ⅓ kilogram of meat. This price of potatoes is lower than her opportunity cost of 1 kilogram of potatoes, which is ½ kilogram of meat. The farmer benefits because she is able to buy potatoes at a good price.

These benefits arise because each person concentrates on the activity for which he or she has the lower opportunity cost: the gardener spends more time growing potatoes, and the farmer spends more time producing meat. As a result, the total production of potatoes and the total production of meat both rise. In our example, potato production rises from 40 to 44 kilograms, and meat production rises from 16 to 18 kilograms. The gardener and farmer share the benefits of this increased production. The moral of the story of the gardener and the farmer should now be clear: *trade can benefit everyone in society because it allows people to specialize in activities in which they have a comparative advantage.*

> **Quick Quiz** Hasani can gather 10 coconuts or catch 1 fish per hour. His new friend, Jacek, can gather 30 coconuts or catch 2 fish per hour. What is Hasani's opportunity cost of catching one fish? What is Jacek's? Who has an absolute advantage in catching fish? Who has a comparative advantage in catching fish?

APPLICATIONS OF COMPARATIVE ADVANTAGE

The principle of comparative advantage explains interdependence and the gains from trade. Because interdependence is so prevalent in the modern world, the principle of comparative advantage has many applications. Here are two examples, one fanciful and one of great practical importance.

Should Ingvar Kamprad Mow his own Lawn?

Ingvar Kamprad is the founder of the retail chain IKEA. He began by selling matches, then fish, Christmas tree decorations, ballpoint pens, pencils and more before establishing IKEA as a global retail business. His talents as an entrepreneur have resulted in a personal fortune estimated at €19 billion. Since 1976 he has lived in a villa in Switzerland. Most likely, he is talented at other activities too. For example, let's imagine that Ingvar Kamprad can mow his lawn faster than anyone else. But just because he *can* mow his lawn fast, does this mean he *should?*

To answer this question, we can use the concepts of opportunity cost and comparative advantage. Let's say that Ingvar Kamprad can mow his lawn in 2 hours. In that same 2 hours he could design a new piece of furniture and earn, say, €10 000. By contrast, Alberto, the boy next door, can mow Ingvar's lawn in 4 hours. In that same 4 hours, he could work at the local McDonald's and earn €20.

In this example, Ingvar's opportunity cost of mowing the lawn is €10 000 and Alberto's opportunity cost is €20. Ingvar has an absolute advantage in mowing lawns because he can do the work in less time. Yet Alberto has a comparative advantage in mowing lawns because he has the lower opportunity cost.

The gains from trade in this example are tremendous. Rather than mowing his own lawn, Ingvar should design the furniture and hire Alberto to mow the lawn. As long as Ingvar pays Alberto more than €20 and less than €10 000, both of them are better off.

Should Countries in Europe Trade with other Countries?

imports
goods produced abroad and purchased for use in the domestic economy

exports
goods produced domestically and sold abroad

Just as individuals can benefit from specialization and trade with one another, as the gardener and farmer did, so can populations of people in different countries. Many of the goods that Europeans enjoy are produced abroad, and many of the goods produced in Europe are sold abroad. Goods produced abroad and purchased for use in the domestic economy are called **imports**. Goods produced domestically and sold abroad are called **exports**.

To see how countries can benefit from trade, suppose there are two countries, Germany and Japan, and two goods, food and cars. Imagine that the two countries produce cars equally well: a German worker and a Japanese worker can each produce 1 car per month. By contrast, because Germany has more land suitable for cultivation, it is better at producing food: a German worker can produce 2 tonnes of food per month, whereas a Japanese worker can produce only 1 tonne of food per month.

The principle of comparative advantage states that each good should be produced by the country that has the smaller opportunity cost of producing that good. Because the opportunity cost of a car is 2 tonnes of food in Germany but only 1 tonne of food in Japan, Japan has a comparative advantage in producing cars. Japan should produce more cars than it wants for its own use and export some of them to Germany. Similarly, because the opportunity cost of a tonne of food is 1 car in Japan but only ½ a car in Germany, Germany has a comparative advantage in producing food. Germany should produce more food than it wants to consume and export some of it to Japan. Through specialization and trade, both countries can have more food and more cars.

In reality, of course, the issues involved in trade among nations are more complex than this simple example suggests, as we will see later in the text. Most important among these issues is that each country has many citizens with different interests. International trade can make some individuals worse off, even as it makes the country as a whole better off. When Germany exports food and imports cars, the impact on a German farmer is not the same as the impact on a German car worker. Yet, contrary to the opinions sometimes voiced by politicians and political commentators, international trade is not like war, in which some countries win and others lose. Trade allows all countries to achieve greater prosperity.

Quick Quiz Suppose that the world's fastest typist happens to be trained in brain surgery. Should he do his own typing or hire a secretary? Explain.

IN THE NEWS

Changing Comparative Advantage

We have seen how economics uses simple examples to highlight key concepts and principles in the subject. The principle of comparative advantage is one such concept. Reality, of course, is quite different not least because the opportunity cost of producing goods and services can change over time and as a result the comparative advantage can also change. This In the News article highlights one example of how this can happen.

The basic principle of the theory of comparative advantage is that a country should focus its resources on production of goods in which the relative opportunity cost is lowest. It means that it is likely to be inefficient for a country like England to devote resources to the production of a good which other countries could produce more efficiently. This might be because the natural climate is more conducive to the production of a particular product.

In the UK, the production of salad crops such as tomatoes, cucumbers and peppers requires certain amounts of light and heat as well as nutrients to produce crops of the right quantity and quality. These crops can be grown in the summer months but in the winter the resources needed to continue production might be seen as too costly. As a result, production of these crops has tended to be seasonal and large quantities of salad crops are imported to maintain year-round supply. Other countries have a comparative advantage in the production of salad crops. It makes sense for them to specialize in production of these crops whilst the UK focuses production on crops in which it has a comparative advantage.

Changes in technology and economies of scale can change the opportunity cost ratios, however, which might make it worthwhile for the UK to devote resources to the production of salad

crops. That is exactly what is happening in the south-east corner of England in Kent. Thanet Earth is a development in Birchington, in the east of the county. The development has converted a redundant 91-hectare cauliflower farm into the largest glasshouse complex in the UK. There are seven greenhouses covering an area equivalent to 39 football pitches and a power generation plant that will generate enough electricity to power 50 000 homes. Seven reservoirs have been built to capture the rain from the roofs of the glasshouses, which can store around 65 million gallons of water and over 2 km of new roads have been built.

The Thanet Earth project cost an estimated £80 million and will add 15 per cent to the UK's total salad crop production when it is fully completed. It has been estimated that one of the greenhouses devoted to tomato production will produce 2.5 million tomatoes a week. To get some idea of the scale of production it has been estimated that the new Terminal 5 building at Heathrow would fit twice into one of the greenhouses that has been built! The site is able to generate its own power and the design has focused on ensuring that the green credentials of the site are of the highest standards. The new development shows that the principles of comparative advantage are not set in stone. If technology advances then the relative

opportunity costs can be altered. Such changes may warrant resources being transferred to the production of goods that used to be considered economically inefficient. The sheer scale of production will also bring its own benefits in terms of the lower unit costs of production.

There has been an increasing focus on the production of renewable energy in recent years. One common factor in most countries is the existence of wind which can be used to generate energy. However, whilst many countries could think about renewable energy production, some countries are more efficient in the production of such energy than others and as such have a comparative advantage in the production of renewable energy.

One such country is Scotland. It has two features that mark it out as a country that can produce renewable energy: its geographical location and its natural resources. In December 2009, a report, commissioned by the Scottish government and carried out by energy and mining consultants Wood Mackenzie, was published which investigated the possibilities of renewable energy production for the country[1].

The Report identified a number of factors that could encourage the government to shift resources into renewable energy. These included wind, water, the sea and bio-energies as a result of the particular geological features of the country. Scotland also has the potential to store large amounts of carbon dioxide (CO_2) and could utilize the North Sea for a CO_2 infrastructure network. These natural advantages are complemented by the existence of technology and skills developed as a result of the offshore gas and oil industry over the previous 40 years. These technologies and skills could be transferred, says the report, to help develop fledgling renewable energy industries and allow the country to diversify and expand employment opportunities. The report concludes that Scotland has a comparative advantage in a number of renewable energy technologies that it can look to exploit in the coming years.

[1]http://www.scotland.gov.uk/Publications/2009/12/10134807/0 accessed 15 December 2009.

CONCLUSION

The principle of comparative advantage shows that trade can make everyone better off. You should now understand more fully the benefits of living in an interdependent economy. But having seen why interdependence is desirable, you might naturally ask how it is possible. How do free societies coordinate the diverse activities of all the people involved in their economies? What ensures that goods and services will get from those who should be producing them to those who should be consuming them?

In a world with only two people, such as the farmer and the gardener, the answer is simple: these two people can directly bargain and allocate resources between themselves. In the real world with billions of people, the answer is less obvious. We take up this issue in the next chapter, where we see that free societies allocate resources through the market forces of supply and demand.

SUMMARY

- Each person consumes goods and services produced by many other people both in their country and around the world. Interdependence and trade are desirable because they allow everyone to enjoy a greater quantity and variety of goods and services.

- There are two ways to compare the ability of two people in producing a good. The person who can produce the good with the smaller quantity of inputs is said to have an *absolute advantage* in producing the good. The person who has the smaller opportunity cost of producing the good is said to have a *comparative advantage*. The gains from trade are based on comparative advantage, not absolute advantage.

- Trade makes everyone better off because it allows people to specialize in those activities in which they have a comparative advantage.

- The principle of comparative advantage applies to countries as well as to people. Economists use the principle of comparative advantage to advocate free trade among countries.

KEY CONCEPTS

absolute advantage, p. 57
comparative advantage, p. 58

imports, p. 62
exports, p. 62

QUESTIONS FOR REVIEW

1. Explain how absolute advantage and comparative advantage differ.

2. Give an example in which one person has an absolute advantage in doing something but another person has a comparative advantage.

3. Is absolute advantage or comparative advantage more important for trade? Explain your reasoning using the example in your answer to Question 2.

4. Will a nation tend to export or import goods for which it has a comparative advantage? Explain.

5. Why do economists oppose policies that restrict trade among nations?

PROBLEMS AND APPLICATIONS

1. Consider the gardener and the farmer from our example in this chapter. Explain why the gardener's opportunity cost of producing 1 kilogram of meat is 4 kilograms of potatoes. Explain why the farmer's opportunity cost of producing 1 kilogram of meat is 2 kilograms of potatoes.

2. Manuela can read 20 pages of economics in an hour. She can also read 50 pages of sociology in an hour. She spends 5 hours per day studying.
   a. Draw Manuela's production possibilities frontier for reading economics and sociology.
   b. What is Manuela's opportunity cost of reading 100 pages of sociology?

3. UK and Japanese workers can each produce 4 cars a year. A UK worker can produce 10 tonnes of grain a year, whereas a Japanese worker can produce 5 tonnes of grain a year. To keep things simple, assume that each country has 100 million workers.
   a. For this situation, construct a table analogous to Table 3.1.
   b. Graph the production possibilities frontier of the UK and Japanese economies.
   c. For the UK, what is the opportunity cost of a car? Of grain? For Japan, what is the opportunity cost of a car? Of grain? Put this information in a table analogous to Table 3.3.
   d. Which country has an absolute advantage in producing cars? In producing grain?
   e. Which country has a comparative advantage in producing cars? In producing grain?
   f. Without trade, half of each country's workers produce cars and half produce grain. What quantities of cars and grain does each country produce?
   g. Starting from a position without trade, give an example in which trade makes each country better off.

4. Victoria and David share a flat. They spend most of their time studying (of course), but they leave some time for their favourite activities: cooking pizza and making home-brew beer. Victoria takes 4 hours to produce 1 barrel of home-brew and 2 hours to make a pizza. David takes 6 hours to brew 1 barrel of beer and 4 hours to make a pizza.
   a. What is each flatmate's opportunity cost of making a pizza? Who has the absolute advantage in making pizza? Who has the comparative advantage in making pizza?
   b. If Victoria and David trade foods with each other, who will trade away pizza in exchange for home-brew?
   c. The price of pizza can be expressed in terms of barrels of home-brew. What is the highest price at which pizza can be traded that would make both flatmates better off? What is the lowest price? Explain.

5. Suppose that there are 10 million workers in Belgium, and that each of these workers can produce either 2 cars or 30 tonnes of wheat in a year.
   a. What is the opportunity cost of producing a car in Belgium? What is the opportunity cost of producing a tonne of wheat in Belgium? Explain the relationship between the opportunity costs of the two goods.
   b. Draw Belgium's production possibilities frontier. If Belgium chooses to consume 10 million cars, how much wheat can it consume without trade? Label this point on the production possibilities frontier.
   c. Now suppose that the United Kingdom offers to buy 10 million cars from Belgium in exchange for 20 tonnes of wheat per car. If Belgium continues to consume 10 million cars, how much wheat does this deal allow Belgium to consume? Label this point on your diagram. Should Belgium accept the deal?

6. Consider a lecturer who is writing a book. The lecturer can both write the chapters and gather the needed data faster than anyone else at his university. Still, he pays a student to collect data at the library. Is this sensible? Explain.

7. England and Scotland both produce scones and pullovers. Suppose that an English worker can produce 50 scones per hour or 1 pullover per hour. Suppose that a Scottish worker can produce 40 scones per hour or 2 pullovers per hour.
   a. Which country has the absolute advantage in the production of each good? Which country has the comparative advantage?
   b. If England and Scotland decide to trade, which commodity will Scotland trade to England? Explain.
   c. If a Scottish worker could produce only 1 pullover per hour, would Scotland still gain from trade? Would England still gain from trade? Explain.

8. The following table describes the production possibilities of two cities in the country of Footballia:

	Pairs of red socks per worker per hour	Pairs of blue socks per worker per hour
Manchester	3	3
Chelsea	2	1

   a. Without trade, what is the price of blue socks (in terms of red socks) in Manchester? What is the price in Chelsea?

   b. Which city has an absolute advantage in the production of each colour sock? Which city has a comparative advantage in the production of each colour sock?
   c. If the cities trade with each other, which colour sock will each export?
   d. What is the range of prices at which trade can occur?

9. Suppose that all goods can be produced with fewer worker hours in Germany than in Belgium.
   a. In what sense is the cost of all goods lower in Germany than in Belgium?
   b. In what sense is the cost of some goods lower in Belgium?
   c. If Germany and Belgium traded with each other, would both countries be better off as a result? Explain in the context of your answers to parts (a) and (b).

10. Are the following statements true or false? Explain in each case.
    a. 'Two countries can achieve gains from trade even if one of the countries has an absolute advantage in the production of all goods.'
    b. 'Certain very talented people have a comparative advantage in everything they do.'
    c. 'If a certain trade is good for one person, it can't be good for the other one.'

For further resources, visit
www.cengage.com/mankiw_taylor2

2

SUPPLY AND DEMAND I: HOW MARKETS WORK

4 THE MARKET FORCES OF SUPPLY AND DEMAND

When there is a drought in southern Europe, the price of olive oil rises in supermarkets throughout Europe. It is anticipated that the price of hotel accommodation in London and the South East will rise significantly when London hosts the Olympic Games in 2012. When a war breaks out in the Middle East, the price of petrol in Europe rises and the price of a used Mercedes falls. A poor durum wheat harvest leads to a rise in the price of pasta in Italy. What do these events have in common? They all show the workings of supply and demand.

Supply and *demand* are the two words that economists use most often – and for good reason. Supply and demand are the forces that make market economies work. They determine the quantity of each good produced and the price at which it is sold. If you want to know how any event or policy will affect the economy, you must think first about how it will affect supply and demand.

This chapter introduces the theory of supply and demand. It considers how buyers and sellers behave and how they interact with one another. It shows how supply and demand determine prices in a market economy and how prices, in turn, allocate the economy's scarce resources.

MARKETS AND COMPETITION

market
a group of buyers and sellers of a particular good or service

The terms *supply* and *demand* refer to the behaviour of people as they interact with one another in markets. A **market** is a group of buyers and sellers of a particular good or service. The buyers as a group determine the demand for the product, and the sellers as a group determine the supply of the product. Before discussing how buyers and sellers behave, let's first consider more fully what we mean by a 'market' and the various types of markets we observe in the economy.

Competitive Markets

Markets take many forms. Sometimes markets are highly organized, such as the markets for many agricultural commodities and for metals. In these markets, buyers and sellers meet at a specific time and place, where an auctioneer helps set prices and arrange sales.

More often, markets are less organized. For example, consider the market for ice cream in a particular town. Buyers of ice cream do not meet together at any one time. The sellers of ice cream are in different locations and offer somewhat different products. There is no auctioneer calling out the price of ice cream. Each seller posts a price for a cornet of ice cream in their shop, and each buyer decides how much ice cream to buy at each shop.

Even though it is not organized, the group of ice cream buyers and ice cream sellers forms a market. Each buyer knows that there are several sellers from which to choose, and each seller is aware that his product is similar to that offered by other sellers. The price of ice cream and the quantity of ice cream sold are not determined by any single buyer or seller. Rather, price and quantity are determined by all buyers and sellers as they interact in the marketplace.

The market for ice cream, like most markets in the economy, is highly competitive. Competition exists when two or more firms are rivals for customers. Each firm strives to gain the attention and custom of buyers in the market. A **competitive market** is a market in which there are many buyers and many sellers so that each has a negligible impact on the market price. Each seller of ice cream has limited control over the price because other sellers are offering similar products. A seller has little reason to charge less than the going price, and if he or she charges more, buyers will make their purchases elsewhere. Similarly, no single buyer of ice cream can influence the price of ice cream because each buyer purchases only a small amount.

In this chapter we examine how buyers and sellers interact in competitive markets. We see how the forces of supply and demand determine both the quantity of the good sold and its price.

competitive market
a market in which there are many buyers and many sellers so that each has a negligible impact on the market price

Competition: Perfect and Otherwise

We assume in this chapter that markets are *perfectly competitive*. Perfectly competitive markets are defined by two main characteristics: (1) the goods being offered for sale are all the same (homogenous) and as a result buyers have no preference between one seller or another, and (2) the buyers and sellers are so numerous that no single buyer or seller can influence the market price. Because buyers and sellers in perfectly competitive markets must accept the price the market determines, they are said to be *price takers*.

There are some markets in which the assumption of perfect competition applies to a very large degree. In the wheat market, for example, there are thousands of farmers who sell wheat and millions of consumers who use wheat and wheat products. Because no single buyer or seller can influence the price of wheat, each takes the price as given.

Not all goods and services, however, are sold in perfectly competitive markets. Some markets have only one seller, and this seller sets the price. Such a seller is called a *monopoly*. Your local water company, for instance, may be a monopoly. Residents in your area probably have only one water company from which to buy this service.

Some markets fall between the extremes of perfect competition and monopoly. One such market, called an *oligopoly*, has a few sellers that do not always compete aggressively. Airline routes are an example. If a route between two cities is serviced by only two or three carriers, the carriers may avoid rigorous competition so they can keep prices high. Another type of market is *monopolistically or imperfectly competitive*; it contains many sellers but each offers a slightly different product. Because the products are not exactly the same, each seller has some ability to set the price for its own product. An example is the market for magazines. Magazines compete with one another for readers and anyone can enter the market by starting a new one, but each magazine offers different articles and can set its own price.

Despite the diversity of market types we find in the world, we begin by studying perfect competition. Perfectly competitive markets are the easiest to analyse. Moreover, because some degree of competition is present in most markets, many of the lessons that we learn by studying supply and demand under perfect competition apply in more complicated markets as well.

Quick Quiz What is a market? • What are the characteristics of a competitive market?

DEMAND

We begin our study of markets by examining the behaviour of buyers. To focus our thinking, let's keep in mind a particular good ice cream.

The Demand Curve: The Relationship Between Price and Quantity Demanded

quantity demanded
the amount of a good that buyers are willing and able to purchase

The **quantity demanded** of any good is the amount of the good that buyers are willing and able to purchase. As we shall see, many things determine the quantity demanded of any good, but when analysing how markets work, one determinant plays a central role – the price of the good. If the price of ice cream rose to €20 per scoop, you would buy less ice cream. You might buy a frozen ice lolly instead. If the price of ice cream fell to €0.20 per scoop, you would buy more. Because the quantity demanded falls as the price rises and rises as the price falls, we say that the quantity demanded is *negatively related* to the price. This relationship between price and quantity demanded is true for most goods in the economy and, in fact, is so pervasive that economists call it the **law of demand**: other things equal, when the price of a good rises, the quantity demanded of the good falls, and when the price falls, the quantity demanded rises.

law of demand
the claim that, other things equal, the quantity demanded of a good falls when the price of the good rises

The table in Figure 4.1 shows how many cornets of ice cream Sabine is willing and able to buy each month at different prices of ice cream. If ice cream is free, Sabine would be willing to eat 12 cornets. At €0.50 per cornet, Sabine would be willing to buy 10 cornets. As the price rises further, she is willing to buy fewer and fewer cornets. When the price reaches €3.00, Sabine would not be prepared to buy any ice cream at all. This table is a **demand schedule**, a table that shows the relationship between the price of a good and the quantity demanded, holding constant everything else that influences how much consumers of the good want to buy.

demand schedule
a table that shows the relationship between the price of a good and the quantity demanded

The graph in Figure 4.1 uses the numbers from the table to illustrate the law of demand. By convention, the price of ice cream is on the vertical axis, and the

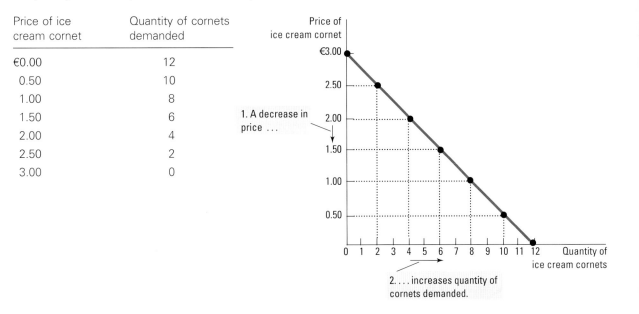

FIGURE 4.1

Sabine's Demand Schedule and Demand Curve

The demand schedule shows the quantity demanded at each price. The demand curve, which graphs the demand schedule, shows how the quantity demanded of the good changes as its price varies. Because a lower price increases the quantity demanded, the demand curve slopes downward.

Price of ice cream cornet	Quantity of cornets demanded
€0.00	12
0.50	10
1.00	8
1.50	6
2.00	4
2.50	2
3.00	0

quantity of ice cream demanded is on the horizontal axis. The downward sloping line relating price and quantity demanded is called the **demand curve**.

demand curve
a graph of the relationship between the price of a good and the quantity demanded

Market Demand versus Individual Demand

The demand curve in Figure 4.1 shows an individual's demand for a product. To analyse how markets work, we need to determine the *market demand,* which is the sum of all the individual demands for a particular good or service.

The table in Figure 4.2 shows the demand schedules for ice cream of two individuals – Sabine and Jan. At any price, Sabine's demand schedule tells us how much ice cream she would be willing and able to buy at different prices, and Jan's demand schedule tells us how much ice cream he is willing and able to buy. The market demand at each price is the sum of the two individual demands.

The graph in Figure 4.2 shows the demand curves that correspond to these demand schedules. Notice that we sum the individual demand curves *horizontally* to obtain the market demand curve. That is, to find the total quantity demanded at any price, we add the individual quantities found on the horizontal axis of the individual demand curves. Because we are interested in analysing how markets work, we shall work most often with the market demand curve. The market demand curve shows how the total quantity demanded of a good varies as the price of the good varies, while all the other factors that affect how much consumers want to buy, such as incomes and taste, amongst other things, are held constant.

FIGURE 4.2

Market Demand as the Sum of Individual Demands

The quantity demanded in a market is the sum of the quantities demanded by all the buyers at each price. Thus, the market demand curve is found by adding horizontally the individual demand curves. At a price of €2, Sabine would like to buy 4 ice cream cornets but Jan would only be prepared to buy 3 ice cream cornets. The quantity demanded in the market at this price, therefore, is 7 cornets.

Price of ice cream cornet	Sabine		Jan		Market
€0.00	12	+	7	=	19
0.50	10		6		16
1.00	8		5		13
1.50	6		4		10
2.00	4		3		7
2.50	2		2		4
3.00	0		1		1

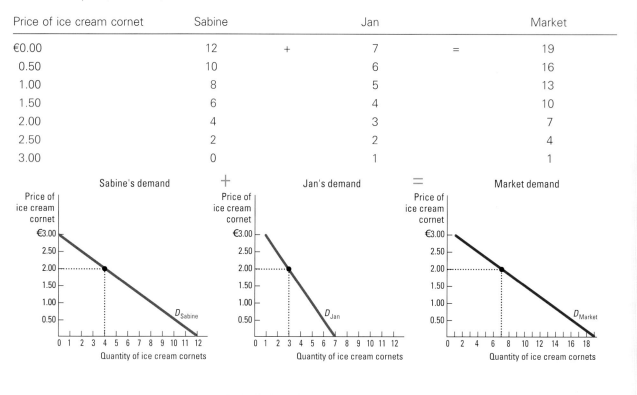

Shifts versus Movements along the Demand Curve

One important distinction that must be made is between a shift of the demand curve and a movement along the demand curve. A shift in the demand curve is caused by a factor affecting demand other than a change in price. The factors affecting demand are outlined below. If any of these factors change then the amount consumers wish to purchase changes whatever the price. The shift in the demand curve is referred to as an *increase or decrease in demand*. A movement along the demand curve occurs when there is a change in price. This may occur because of a change in supply conditions. The factors affecting demand are assumed to be held constant. A change in price leads to a movement along the demand curve and is referred to as a *change in quantity demanded*.

Shifts in the Demand Curve

The demand curve for ice cream shows how much ice cream people are willing to buy at any given price, holding constant the many other factors beyond price that influence consumers' buying decisions. As a result, this demand curve need not be stable over time. If something happens to alter the quantity demanded at any given price, the demand curve shifts. For example, suppose European health

Shifts in the Demand Curve

Any change that raises the quantity that buyers wish to purchase at a given price shifts the demand curve to the right. Any change that lowers the quantity that buyers wish to purchase at a given price shifts the demand curve to the left.

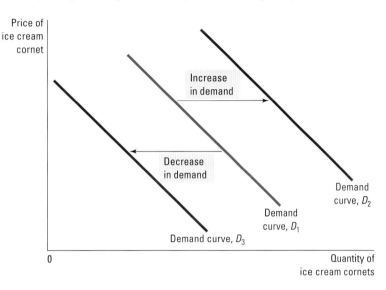

authorities discovered that people who regularly eat ice cream live longer, healthier lives. The discovery would raise the demand for ice cream. At any given price, buyers would now want to purchase a larger quantity of ice cream and the demand curve for ice cream would shift.

Figure 4.3 illustrates shifts in demand. Any change that increases the quantity demanded at every price, such as our imaginary discovery by the European health authorities, shifts the demand curve to the right and is called *an increase in demand*. Any change that reduces the quantity demanded at every price shifts the demand curve to the left and is called *a decrease in demand*.

There are many variables that can shift the demand curve. Here are the most important.

Income What would happen to the demand for ice cream if unemployment increases? Most likely, it would fall because of lower incomes. Lower incomes mean that people have less to spend in total, so they are likely to spend less on some – and probably most – goods. If the demand for a good falls when income falls, the good is called a **normal good**.

Not all goods are normal goods. If the demand for a good rises when income falls, the good is called an **inferior good**. An example of an inferior good might be bus rides. As income falls, people are less likely to buy a car or take a taxi and more likely to take the bus. As income falls, therefore, demand for bus rides tends to increase.

Prices of Related Goods Suppose that the price of ice lollies falls. The law of demand says that people will buy more ice lollies. At the same time, people will probably buy less ice cream. Because ice cream and ice lollies are both frozen, sweet confectionary, they satisfy similar desires. When a fall in the price of one good reduces the demand for another good, the two goods are called **substitutes**. Substitutes are often pairs of goods that are used in place of each

normal good
a good for which, other things equal, an increase in income leads to an increase in demand (and vice versa)

inferior good
a good for which, other things equal, an increase in income leads to a decrease in demand (and vice versa)

substitutes
two goods for which an increase in the price of one leads to an increase in the demand for the other

other, such as beef steak and Wiener schnitzel, pullovers and sweatshirts, and cinema tickets and DVD rentals. The more closely related substitute products are the more effect we might see on demand if the price of one of the substitutes changes.

Now suppose that the price of chocolate flake bars falls. According to the law of demand, people will buy more chocolate flake bars. Yet, in this case, people will buy more ice cream as well, because ice cream and chocolate flake bars are often used together. When a fall in the price of one good raises the demand for another good, the two goods are called **complements**. Complements are often pairs of goods that are used together, such as petrol and cars, computers and software, bread and cheese, strawberries and cream, and bacon and eggs.

complements
two goods for which an increase in the price of one leads to a decrease in the demand for the other (and vice versa).

Tastes The most obvious determinant of demand are tastes and fashions. If people like ice cream, they buy more of it. Economists are increasingly interested in explaining people's tastes. The developments in neuroscience mean that we now have an increasing understanding of why people make decisions and this has come into the realm of economics. This helps economists examine why and what happens when tastes change.

Expectations People's expectations about the future may affect their demand for a good or service today. For example, if people expect to earn a higher income next month, they may be more willing to spend some of their current savings buying ice cream. As another example, if people expect the price of ice cream to fall tomorrow, they may be less willing to buy an ice cream cornet at today's price.

The Size and Structure of the Population A larger population, other things being equal, will mean a higher demand for all goods and services. Changes in the way the population is structured also influences demand. Many European countries have an ageing population and this leads to a change in the demand. Goods and services required by the elderly increase in demand as a result. The demand for retirement homes, insurance policies suitable for elderly drivers and smaller cars may increase as a result.

Summary The demand curve shows what happens to the *quantity demanded* of a good when its price varies, holding constant all the other variables that influence buyers. When one or more of these other variables changes, the demand curve shifts leading to an *increase or decrease in demand*. Table 4.1 lists all the variables that influence how much consumers choose to buy of a good.

TABLE 4.1

Variables That Influence Buyers

This table lists the variables that affect how much consumers choose to buy of any good. Notice the special role that the price of the good plays: a change in the good's price represents a movement along the demand curve, whereas a change in one of the other variables shifts the demand curve.

Variable	A change in this variable . . .
Price	Represents a movement along the demand curve
Income	Shifts the demand curve
Prices of related goods	Shifts the demand curve
Tastes	Shifts the demand curve
Expectations	Shifts the demand curve
Number of buyers	Shifts the demand curve

FIGURE 4.4

Shifts in the Demand Curve versus Movements Along the Demand Curve

If health warnings on cigarette packets convince smokers to smoke less, the demand curve for cigarettes shifts to the left. In panel (a), the demand curve shifts from D_1 to D_2. At a price of €2 per pack, the quantity demanded falls from 20 to 10 cigarettes per day, as reflected by the shift from point A to point B. By contrast, if a tax raises the price of cigarettes, the demand curve does not shift. Instead, we observe a movement to a different point on the demand curve. In panel (b), when the price rises from €2 to €4, the quantity demanded falls from 20 to 12 cigarettes per day, as reflected by the movement from point A to point C.

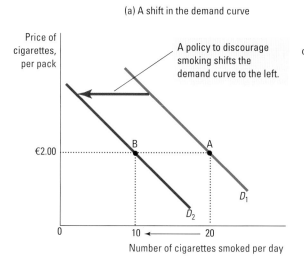

(a) A shift in the demand curve

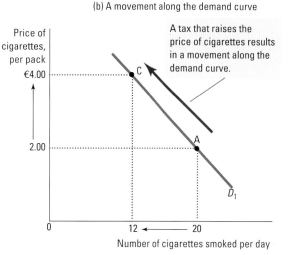

(b) A movement along the demand curve

CASE STUDY

Two Ways to Reduce the Quantity of Smoking Demanded

Public policy makers often want to reduce the amount that people smoke. There are two ways that policy can attempt to achieve this goal.

One way to reduce smoking is to shift the demand curve for cigarettes and other tobacco products. Anti-smoking campaigns on television, mandatory health warnings on cigarette packages and the prohibition of cigarette advertising are all policies aimed at reducing the quantity of cigarettes demanded at any given price. If successful, these policies shift the demand curve for cigarettes to the left, as in panel (a) of Figure 4.4.

Alternatively, policy makers can try to raise the price of cigarettes. If the government taxes the manufacture of cigarettes, for example, cigarette companies pass much of this tax on to consumers in the form of higher prices. A higher price encourages smokers to reduce the numbers of cigarettes they smoke. In this case, the reduced amount of smoking does not represent a shift in the demand curve. Instead, it represents a movement along the same demand curve to a point with a higher price and lower quantity, as in panel (b) of Figure 4.4.

How much does the amount of smoking respond to changes in the price of cigarettes? Economists have attempted to answer this question by studying what happens when the tax on cigarettes changes. They have found that a 10 per cent increase in the price causes about a 4 per cent reduction in the

What is the best way to reduce smoking?

quantity demanded. Teenagers are found to be especially sensitive to the price of cigarettes: a 10 per cent increase in the price causes about a 12 per cent drop in teenage smoking.

A related question is how the price of cigarettes affects the demand for illicit drugs, such as marijuana. Opponents of cigarette taxes often argue that tobacco and marijuana are substitutes, so that high cigarette prices encourage marijuana use. By contrast, many experts on substance abuse view tobacco as a 'gateway drug' leading the young to experiment with other harmful substances. Most studies of the data are consistent with this view: they find that lower cigarette prices are associated with greater use of marijuana. In other words, tobacco and marijuana appear to be complements rather than substitutes.

Quick Quiz Make up an example of a demand schedule for pizza, and graph the implied demand curve • Give an example of something that would shift this demand curve • Would a change in the price of pizza shift this demand curve?

SUPPLY

We now turn to the other side of the market and examine the behaviour of sellers. Once again, to focus our thinking, let's consider the market for ice cream.

The Supply Curve: The Relationship Between Price and Quantity Supplied

quantity supplied
the amount of a good that sellers are willing and able to sell

The **quantity supplied** of any good or service is the amount that sellers are willing and able to sell. There are many determinants of quantity supplied, but once again price plays a special role in our analysis. When the price of ice cream is high, selling ice cream is profitable, and so the sellers are willing to supply more. Sellers of ice cream work longer hours, buy more ice cream machines and hire extra workers in order to ensure supplies to the market rise. By contrast, when the price of ice cream is low, the business is less profitable, and so sellers are willing to produce less ice cream. At a low price, some sellers may even choose to shut down, and their quantity supplied falls to zero. Because the quantity supplied rises as the price rises and falls as the price falls, we say that the quantity supplied is *positively related* to the price of the good. This relationship between price and quantity supplied is called the **law of supply**: other things equal, when the price of a good rises, the quantity supplied of the good also rises, and when the price falls, the quantity supplied falls as well.

law of supply
the claim that, other things equal, the quantity supplied of a good rises when the price of the good rises

The table in Figure 4.5 shows the quantity, Häagen, an ice cream seller, is willing to supply, at various prices of ice cream. At a price below €1.00 per cornet of ice cream, Häagen does not supply any ice cream at all. As the price rises, he is willing to supply a greater and greater quantity. This is the **supply schedule**, a table that shows the relationship between the price of a good and the quantity supplied, holding constant everything else that influences how much producers of the good want to sell.

supply schedule
a table that shows the relationship between the price of a good and the quantity supplied

The graph in Figure 4.5 uses the numbers from the table to illustrate the law of supply. The curve relating price and quantity supplied is called the **supply curve**. The supply curve slopes upward because, other things equal, a higher price means a greater quantity supplied.

supply curve
a graph of the relationship between the price of a good and the quantity supplied

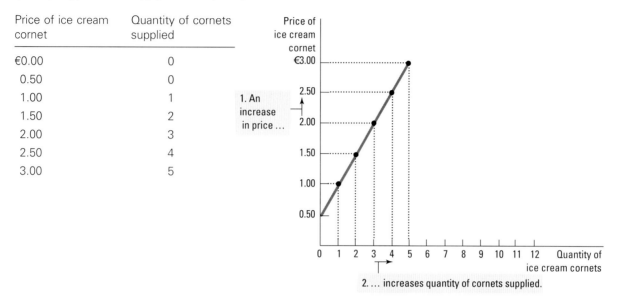

FIGURE 4.5

Häagen's Supply Schedule and Supply Curve

The supply schedule shows the quantity supplied at each price. This supply curve, which graphs the supply schedule, shows how the quantity supplied of the good changes as its price varies. Because a higher price increases the quantity supplied, the supply curve slopes upward.

Price of ice cream cornet	Quantity of cornets supplied
€0.00	0
0.50	0
1.00	1
1.50	2
2.00	3
2.50	4
3.00	5

Market Supply versus Individual Supply

Just as market demand is the sum of the demands of all buyers, market supply is the sum of the supplies of all sellers. The table in Figure 4.6 shows the supply schedules for two ice cream producers – Häagen and Dazs. At any price, Häagen's supply schedule tells us the quantity of ice cream Häagen is willing to supply, and Dazs's supply schedule tells us the quantity of ice cream Dazs is willing to supply. The market supply is the sum of the two individual supplies.

The graph in Figure 4.6 shows the supply curves that correspond to the supply schedules. As with demand curves, we sum the individual supply curves *horizontally* to obtain the market supply curve. That is, to find the total quantity supplied at any price, we add the individual quantities found on the horizontal axis of the individual supply curves. The market supply curve shows how the total quantity supplied varies as the price of the good varies.

Shifts versus Movements along the Supply Curve

As noted in our discussion of demand, a distinction that must be made is between a shift in the supply curve and a movement along the supply curve. A shift in the supply curve is caused by a factor affecting supply other than a change in price. The factors affecting supply are outlined below. If any of these factors change then the amount sellers are willing to offer for sale changes whatever the price. The shift in the supply curve is referred to as an *increase or decrease in supply*. A movement along the supply curve occurs when there is a change in price. This may occur because of a change in demand conditions. The factors

FIGURE 4.6

Market Supply as the Sum of Individual Supplies

The quantity supplied in a market is the sum of the quantities supplied by all the sellers at each price. Thus, the market supply curve is found by adding horizontally the individual supply curves. At a price of €2, Häagen is willing to supply 3 ice cream cornets, and Dazs is willing to supply 4 ice cream cornets. The quantity supplied in the market at this price is 7 cornets.

Price of ice cream cornet	Häagen		Dazs		Market
€0.00	0	+	0	=	0
0.50	0		0		0
1.00	1		0		1
1.50	2		2		4
2.00	3		4		7
2.50	4		6		10
3.00	5		8		13

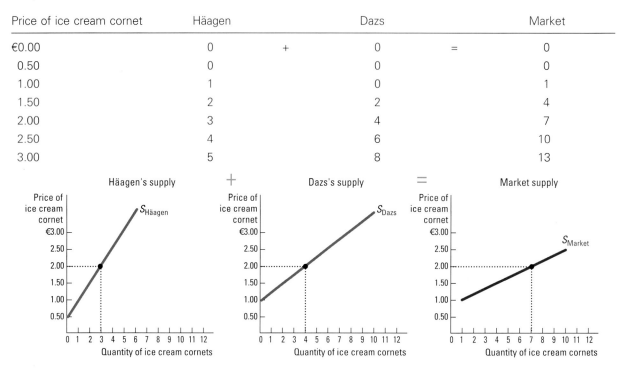

affecting supply are assumed to be held constant. A change in price leads to a movement along the supply curve and is referred to as a *change in quantity supplied*.

Shifts in the Supply Curve

The supply curve for ice cream shows how much ice cream producers are willing to offer for sale at any given price, holding constant all the other factors beyond price that influence producers' decisions about how much to sell. This relationship can change over time, which is represented by a shift in the supply curve. For example, suppose the price of sugar falls. Because sugar is an input into producing ice cream, the fall in the price of sugar makes selling ice cream more profitable. This raises the supply of ice cream: at any given price, sellers are now willing to produce a larger quantity. Thus, the supply curve for ice cream shifts to the right.

Figure 4.7 illustrates shifts in supply. Any change that raises quantity supplied at every price, such as a fall in the price of sugar, shifts the supply curve to the right and is called *an increase in supply*. Similarly, any change that reduces the quantity supplied at every price shifts the supply curve to the left and is called *a decrease in supply*.

FIGURE 4.7

Shifts in the Supply Curve

Any change that raises the quantity that sellers wish to produce at a given price shifts the supply curve to the right. Any change that lowers the quantity that sellers wish to produce at a given price shifts the supply curve to the left.

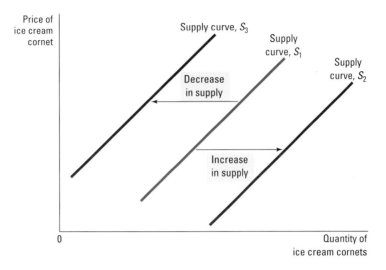

There are many variables that can shift the supply curve. Here are some of the most important.

Input Prices   To produce their output of ice cream, sellers use various inputs: cream, sugar, flavouring, ice cream machines, the buildings in which the ice cream is made, and the labour of workers to mix the ingredients and operate the machines. When the price of one or more of these inputs rises, producing ice cream is less profitable and firms supply less ice cream. If input prices rise substantially, some firms might shut down and supply no ice cream at all. If input prices fall for some reason, then production may be more profitable and there is an incentive to supply more at each price. Thus, the supply of a good is negatively related to the price of the inputs used to make the good.

Technology   The technology for turning the inputs into ice cream is yet another determinant of supply. Advances in technology increase productivity allowing more to be produced using fewer factor inputs. As a result costs, both total and unit, may fall and supply increases. The invention of the mechanized ice cream machine, for example, reduced the amount of labour necessary to make ice cream. By reducing firms' costs, the advance in technology raised the supply of ice cream.

Expectations   The amount of ice cream firms supply today may depend on their expectations of the future. For example, if sellers expect the price of ice cream to rise in the future, they will put some of their current production into storage and supply less to the market today. If there is an expectation of a spell of hot weather then supply may be increased to cater for the expected increase in sales.

TABLE 4.2

Variables That Influence Sellers

This table lists the variables that affect how much producers choose to sell of any good. Notice the special role that the price of the good plays: a change in the good's price represents a movement along the supply curve, whereas a change in one of the other variables shifts the supply curve.

Variable	A change in this variable . . .
Price	Represents a movement along the supply curve
Input prices	Shifts the supply curve
Technology	Shifts the supply curve
Expectations	Shifts the supply curve
Number of sellers	Shifts the supply curve

Number of Sellers   Market supply will be affected by the number of firms in the industry. In the 27 EU countries the number of dairy farmers has fallen in the last five years from over 1.56 million to 1.33 million. Output of milk was around 135 million litres in 2010. Unless existing producers are able to expand production, the supply of milk will fall with fewer producers.

Natural/Social Factors   There are often many natural or social factors that affect supply. These include such things as the weather affecting crops, natural disasters, pestilence and disease, changing attitudes and social expectations (for example over the production of organic food, the disposal of waste, reducing carbon emissions, ethical supply sourcing and so on) all of which can have an influence on production decisions. Some or all of these may have an influence on the cost of inputs into production.

Summary   The supply curve shows what happens to the quantity supplied of a good when its price varies, holding constant all the other variables that influence sellers. When one of these other variables changes, the supply curve shifts. Table 4.2 lists all the variables that influence how much producers choose to sell of a good.

Quick Quiz   Make up an example of a supply schedule for pizza, and graph the implied supply curve • Give an example of something that would shift this supply curve • Would a change in the price of pizza shift this supply curve?

SUPPLY AND DEMAND TOGETHER

Having analysed supply and demand separately, we now combine them to see how they determine the quantity of a good sold in a market and its price.

Equilibrium

Figure 4.8 shows the market supply curve and market demand curve together. Equilibrium is defined as a state of rest, a point where there is no force acting for change. Economists refer to supply and demand as being *market forces*. In

The Equilibrium of Supply and Demand

The equilibrium is found where the supply and demand curves intersect. At the equilibrium price, the quantity supplied equals the quantity demanded. Here the equilibrium price is €2: at this price, 7 ice cream cornets are supplied and 7 ice cream cornets are demanded.

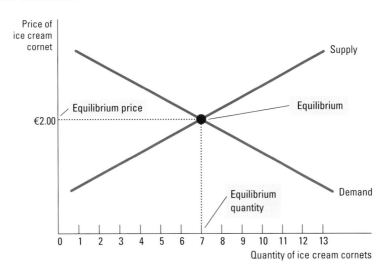

any market the relationship between supply and demand exerts force on price. If supply is greater than demand or vice versa, then there is pressure on price to change. Notice, however, that there is one point at which the supply and demand curves intersect. This point is called the market's **equilibrium**. The price at this intersection is called the **equilibrium price,** and the quantity is called the **equilibrium quantity**. Here the equilibrium price is €2.00 per cornet, and the equilibrium quantity is 7 ice cream cornets.

At the equilibrium price, the quantity of the good that buyers are willing and able to buy exactly balances the quantity that sellers are willing and able to sell. The equilibrium price is sometimes called the *market-clearing price* because, at this price, everyone in the market has been satisfied: buyers have bought all they want to buy, and sellers have sold all they want to sell.

The actions of buyers and sellers naturally move markets towards the equilibrium of supply and demand. To see why, consider what happens when the market price is not equal to the equilibrium price.

Suppose first that the market price is above the equilibrium price, as in panel (a) of Figure 4.9. At a price of €2.50 per cornet, the quantity suppliers would like to sell at this price (10 cornets) exceeds the quantity which buyers are willing to purchase (4 cornets). There is a **surplus** of the good: suppliers are unable to sell all they want at the going price. A surplus is sometimes called a situation of *excess supply.* When there is a surplus in the ice cream market, sellers of ice cream find their freezers increasingly full of ice cream they would like to sell but cannot. They respond to the surplus by cutting their prices. Falling prices, in turn, increase the quantity demanded and decrease the quantity supplied. Prices continue to fall until the market reaches the equilibrium.

Suppose now that the market price is below the equilibrium price, as in panel (b) of Figure 4.9. In this case, the price is €1.50 per cornet, and the quantity of the good demanded exceeds the quantity supplied. There is a **shortage** of the good: demanders are unable to buy all they want at the going price. A shortage is

equilibrium
a situation in which the price has reached the level where quantity supplied equals quantity demanded

equilibrium price
the price that balances quantity supplied and quantity demanded

equilibrium quantity
the quantity supplied and the quantity demanded at the equilibrium price

surplus
a situation in which quantity supplied is greater than quantity demanded

shortage
a situation in which quantity demanded is greater than quantity supplied

FIGURE 4.9

Markets Not in Equilibrium

In panel (a), there is a surplus. Because the market price of €2.50 is above the equilibrium price, the quantity supplied (10 cornets) exceeds the quantity demanded (4 cornets). Suppliers try to increase sales by cutting the price of a cornet, and this moves the price toward its equilibrium level. In panel (b), there is a shortage. Because the market price of €1.50 is below the equilibrium price, the quantity demanded (10 cornets) exceeds the quantity supplied (4 cornets). With too many buyers chasing too few goods, suppliers can take advantage of the shortage by raising the price. Hence, in both cases, the price adjustment moves the market towards the equilibrium of supply and demand.

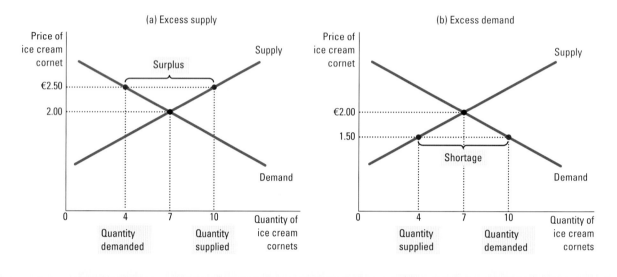

sometimes called a situation of *excess demand*. When a shortage occurs in the ice cream market, buyers have to wait in long queues for a chance to buy one of the few cornets that are available. With too many buyers chasing too few goods, sellers can respond to the shortage by raising their prices without losing sales. As the price rises, quantity demanded falls, quantity supplied rises and the market once again moves toward the equilibrium.

Thus, the activities of the many buyers and sellers automatically push the market price towards the equilibrium price. Once the market reaches its equilibrium, all buyers and sellers are satisfied, and there is no upward or downward pressure on the price. How quickly equilibrium is reached varies from market to market, depending on how quickly prices adjust. In most free markets, surpluses and shortages are only temporary because prices eventually move towards their equilibrium levels (we will see the significance of the word 'free' later in the book). Indeed, this phenomenon is so pervasive that it is called the **law of supply and demand**: the price of any good adjusts to bring the quantity supplied and quantity demanded for that good into balance.

law of supply and demand
the claim that the price of any good adjusts to bring the quantity supplied and the quantity demanded for that good into balance

Three Steps to Analyzing Changes in Equilibrium

So far we have seen how supply and demand together determine a market's equilibrium, which in turn determines the price of the good and the amount of the good that buyers purchase and sellers produce. Of course, the equilibrium price and quantity depend on the position of the supply and demand curves. When some event shifts one of these curves, the equilibrium in the market

F Y I

Prices as Signals

Our analysis so far has only brushed the surface of the way markets operate. Economists have conducted extensive research into the nature and determinants of both demand and supply. It is beyond the scope of this book to go into too much detail on these issues but it is useful to have a little bit of background knowledge on this to help understand markets more effectively.

At the heart of research into demand and supply is why buyers and sellers behave as they do. The development of magnetic resonance imaging (MRI) techniques has allowed researchers to investigate how the brain responds to different stimuli when making purchasing decisions (referred to as *neuroeconomics*). As time goes by our understanding of buyer and seller behaviour will improve and theories will have to be adapted to accommodate this new understanding.

However, much of the theory behind how markets work relies on the assumption of rational behaviour defined in terms of humans preferring more to less. The main function of price in a free market is to act as a signal to both buyers and sellers.

For buyers, price tells them something about what they have to give up

to acquire the benefits that having the good will confer on them. These benefits are referred to as the *utility* (satisfaction) derived from consumption. If I am willing to pay €10 to go and watch a movie then economists will assume that the value of the benefits I gain from watching the movie is greater than the next best alternative – what else I could have spent my €10 on. Principles 1 and 2 of the *Ten Principles of Economics* state that people face trade-offs and that the cost of something is what you have to give up to acquire it. This is fundamental to the law of demand. At higher prices, the sacrifice being made in terms of the value of the benefits gained from alternatives is greater and so we may be less willing to do so as a result. If the price of a ticket for the movie was €20 then it might have to be a very good movie to persuade us that giving up what else €20 could buy is worth it.

For sellers price acts as a signal in relation to the profitability of production. For most sellers, increasing the amount of a good produced will incur some additional input costs. A higher price is required in order to compensate for the additional cost and to also enable the producer to gain

some reward from the risk they are taking in production. That reward is termed *profit*.

If prices are rising in a free market then this acts as a different but related signal to buyers and sellers. Rising prices to a seller means that there is a shortage and thus there is an incentive to expand production because the seller knows that she will be able to sell what she produces. For buyers, a rising price changes the nature of the trade-off they have to face. They will now have to give up more in order to acquire the good and they will have to decide whether the value of the benefits they will gain from acquiring the good is worth the extra price they have to pay.

What we do know is that for both buyers and sellers, there are many complex processes that occur in decision-making. Whilst we do not fully understand all these processes yet, economists are constantly searching for new insights that might help them understand the workings of markets more fully. All of us go through these complex processes every time we make a purchasing decision – although we may not realize it! Having some appreciation of these processes is fundamental to thinking like an economist.

changes. The analysis of such a change is called *comparative statics* because it involves comparing two unchanging situations – an initial and a new equilibrium.

When analysing how some event affects a market, we proceed in three steps. First, we decide whether the event shifts the supply curve, the demand curve or, in some cases, both curves. Secondly, we decide whether the curve shifts to the right or to the left. Thirdly, we use the supply and demand diagram to compare the initial and the new equilibrium, which shows how the shift affects the equilibrium price and quantity. It is important in the analysis that the process by which equilibrium changes is understood and that the changes involved are not instantaneous – some markets will take longer to adjust to changes than others.

Table 4.3 summarizes the three steps. To see how this recipe is used, let's consider various events that might affect the market for ice cream.

Example: A Change in Demand Suppose that one summer the weather is very hot. How does this event affect the market for ice cream? To answer this question, let's follow our three steps.

1. The hot weather affects the demand curve by changing people's taste for ice cream. That is, the weather changes the amount of ice cream that people want to buy at any given price.
2. Because hot weather makes people want to eat more ice cream, the demand curve shifts to the right. Figure 4.10 shows this increase in demand as the shift in the demand curve from D_1 to D_2. This shift indicates that the quantity of ice cream demanded is higher at every price. The shift in demand has led to a shortage of ice creams in the market. At a price of €2.00 buyers now want

FIGURE 4.10

How an Increase in Demand Affects the Equilibrium

An event that raises quantity demanded at any given price shifts the demand curve to the right. The equilibrium price and the equilibrium quantity both rise. Here, an abnormally hot summer causes buyers to demand more ice cream. The demand curve shifts from D_1 to D_2, which causes the equilibrium price to rise from €2.00 to €2.50 and the equilibrium quantity to rise from 7 to 10 cornets.

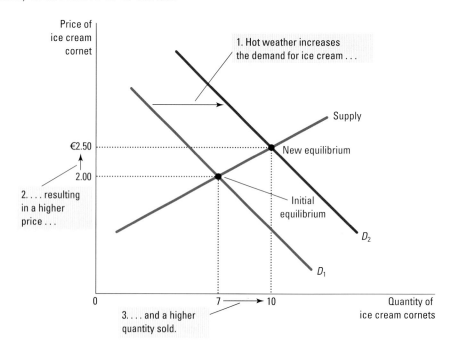

to buy 15 ice creams but sellers are only offering 7 ice creams for sale at this price.

3. As Figure 4.10 shows, the shortage encourages producers to increase the output of ice creams. The additional production incurs extra costs and so a higher price is required to compensate sellers. This raises the equilibrium price from €2.00 to €2.50 and the equilibrium quantity from 7 to 10 cornets. In other words, the hot weather increases the price of ice cream and the quantity of ice cream bought and sold.

"We work on the law of 'supply and demand' - we demand and you supply."

Shifts in Curves versus Movements along Curves   Notice that when hot weather drives up the price of ice cream, the quantity of ice cream that firms supply rises, even though the supply curve remains the same. In this case, economists say there has been an increase in 'quantity supplied' but no change in 'supply'.

'Supply' refers to the position of the supply curve, whereas the 'quantity supplied' refers to the amount suppliers wish to sell. In this example, we assumed supply does not change. Instead, the hot weather alters consumers' desire to buy at any given price and thereby shifts the demand curve. The increase in demand causes the equilibrium price to rise. When the price rises, the quantity supplied rises. This increase in quantity supplied is represented by the movement along the supply curve.

To summarize, a shift *in* the supply curve is called a 'change in supply', and a shift *in* the demand curve is called a 'change in demand'. A movement *along* a fixed supply curve is called a 'change in the quantity supplied', and a movement *along* a fixed demand curve is called a 'change in the quantity demanded'.

Example: A Change in Supply   Suppose that, during another summer, a hurricane destroys part of the South American sugar cane crop and drives up the world price of sugar. How does this event affect the market for ice cream? Once again, to answer this question, we follow our three steps.

1. The change in the price of sugar, an input into making ice cream, affects the supply curve. By raising the costs of production, it reduces the amount of ice cream that firms produce and sell at any given price. The demand curve does not change because the higher cost of inputs does not directly affect the amount of ice cream households wish to buy.
2. The supply curve shifts to the left because, at every price, the total amount that firms are willing and able to sell is reduced. Figure 4.11 illustrates this decrease in supply as a shift in the supply curve from S_1 to S_2. At a price of €2.00 sellers are now only able to offer 2 ice creams for sale but demand is still 7 ice creams. The shift in supply to the left has created a shortage in the market. Once again, the shortage will create pressure on price to rise as buyers look to purchase ice creams.
3. As Figure 4.11 shows, the shortage raises the equilibrium price from €2.00 to €2.50 and lowers the equilibrium quantity from 7 to 4 cornets. As a result of the sugar price increase, the price of ice cream rises, and the quantity of ice cream bought and sold falls.

Example: A Change in Both Supply and Demand (i)   Now suppose that the heat wave and the hurricane occur during the same summer. To analyse this combination of events, we again follow our three steps.

1. We determine that both curves must shift. The hot weather affects the demand curve because it alters the amount of ice cream that households want to buy at any given price. At the same time, when the hurricane drives up sugar prices, it alters the supply curve for ice cream because it changes the amount of ice cream that firms want to sell at any given price.

FIGURE 4.11

How a Decrease in Supply Affects the Equilibrium

An event that reduces quantity supplied at any given price shifts the supply curve to the left. The equilibrium price rises, and the equilibrium quantity falls. Here, an increase in the price of sugar (an input) causes sellers to supply less ice cream. The supply curve shifts from S₁ to S₂, which causes the equilibrium price of ice cream to rise from €2.00 to €2.50 and the equilibrium quantity to fall from 7 to 4 cornets.

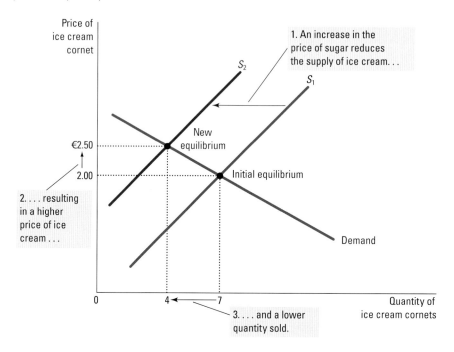

2. The curves shift in the same directions as they did in our previous analysis: the demand curve shifts to the right, and the supply curve shifts to the left. Figure 4.12 illustrates these shifts.

3. As Figure 4.12 shows, there are two possible outcomes that might result, depending on the relative size of the demand and supply shifts. In both cases, the equilibrium price rises. In panel (a), where demand increases substantially while supply falls just a little, the equilibrium quantity also rises. By contrast, in panel (b), where supply falls substantially while demand rises just a little, the equilibrium quantity falls. Thus, these events certainly raise the price of ice cream, but their impact on the amount of ice cream bought and sold is ambiguous (that is, it could go either way).

Example: A Change in Both Supply and Demand (ii) We are now going to look at a slightly different scenario but with both supply and demand increasing together. Assume that forecasters have predicted a heatwave for some weeks. We know that the hot weather is likely to increase demand for ice creams and so the demand curve will shift to the right. However, sellers' expectations that sales of ice creams will increase as a result of the forecasts mean that they take steps to expand production of ice creams. This would lead to a shift of the supply curve

FIGURE 4.12

A Shift in Both Supply and Demand (i)

Here we observe a simultaneous increase in demand and decrease in supply. Two outcomes are possible. In panel (a), the equilibrium price rises from P_1 to P_2, and the equilibrium quantity rises from Q_1 to Q_2. In panel (b), the equilibrium price again rises from P_1 to P_2, but the equilibrium quantity falls from Q_1 to Q_2.

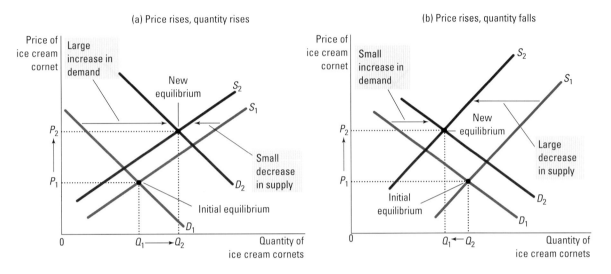

to the right – more ice creams are now offered for sale at every price. To analyse this particular combination of events, we again follow our three steps.

1. We determine that both curves must shift. The hot weather affects the demand curve because it alters the amount of ice cream that households want to buy at any given price. At the same time, the expectations of producers alter the supply curve for ice cream because they change the amount of ice cream that firms want to sell at any given price.
2. Both demand and supply curves shift to the right: Figure 4.13 illustrates these shifts.
3. As Figure 4.13 shows, there are three possible outcomes that might result, depending on the relative size of the demand and supply shifts. In panel (a), where demand increases substantially while supply rises just a little, the equilibrium price and quantity rises. By contrast, in panel (b), where supply rises substantially while demand rises just a little, the equilibrium price falls but the equilibrium quantity rises. In panel (c) the increase in demand and supply are identical and so equilibrium price does not change. Equilibrium quantity will increase, however. Thus, these events have different effects on the price of ice cream although the amount of ice cream bought and sold in each case is higher. In this instance the effect on price is ambiguous.

Summary   We have just seen four examples of how to use supply and demand curves to analyse a change in equilibrium. Whenever an event shifts the supply curve, the demand curve, or perhaps both curves, you can use these tools to predict how the event will alter the amount bought and sold in equilibrium and the price at which the good is bought and sold. Table 4.4 shows the predicted outcome for any combination of shifts in the two curves. To make sure you understand how to use the tools of supply and demand, pick a few

FIGURE 4.13

A Shift in both Supply and Demand (ii)

Here, again, we observe a simultaneous increase in demand and supply. Here, three outcomes are possible. In panel (a) the equilibrium price rises from P_1 to P_2 and the equilibrium quantity rises from Q_1 to Q_2. In panel (b), the equilibrium price falls from P_1 to P_2 but the equilibrium quantity rises from Q_1 to Q_2. In panel (c), there is no change to the equilibrium price but the equilibrium quantity rises from Q_1 to Q_2.

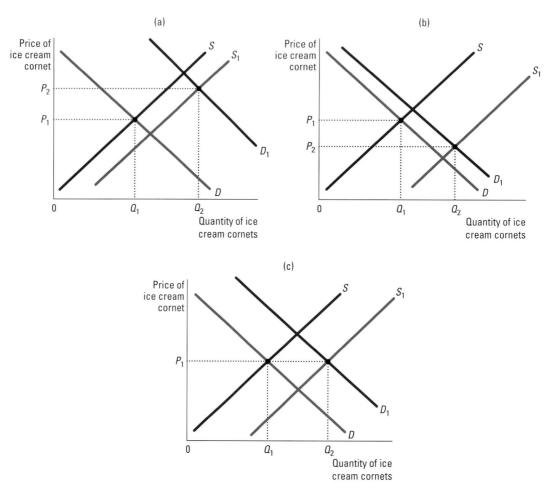

TABLE 4.4

What Happens to Price and Quantity When Supply or Demand Shifts?

As a quick quiz, make sure you can explain each of the entries in this table using a supply and demand diagram.

	No change in supply	An increase in supply	A decrease in supply
No change in demand	P same Q same	P down Q up	P up Q down
An increase in demand	P up Q up	P ambiguous Q up	P up Q ambiguous
A decrease in demand	P down Q down	P down Q ambiguous	P ambiguous Q down

IN THE NEWS

Markets in Action

We have seen how we can use supply and demand analysis to begin to understand markets. The real world has examples of markets in action every day. This article highlights some examples from early 2010.

Winter 2009–2010 in Europe was a cold one. Large parts of northern Europe 'enjoyed' a white Christmas and extremely low temperatures well into the New Year. In the United States, the east coast suffered heavy snow falls and sub-zero temperatures even reached parts of Florida. The effects on demand and supply of various goods were noticeable.

In the UK, the demand for salt for the roads rose significantly. Local councils found that they ran down supplies as the sub-zero temperatures persisted night after night. The sharp increase in demand for salt led to prices in both Europe and the US rising. One of the major suppliers of rock salt for gritting roads in the UK, Salt Union, for example, worked round the clock to try and meet the demand for salt. The additional cost of the inputs required to work 24 hours a day had to be reflected in the price the company received for its product. The significant rise in demand meant that prices rose. A local government association, the UK

Roads Liaison Group, estimated that prices for rock salt were normally between £30 and £40 per ton. As the cold weather continued and the shortage of rock salt got worse, prices rose to between £150 and £200 per ton.

Other businesses also saw changes in demand as a result of the weather. Demand for winter clothing and footwear increased significantly, gas and electricity companies saw demand for energy rising as houses and businesses turned up the thermostats to keep warm and online businesses reported a rise in demand. The explanation was that people were not able to get into work and so tended to sit at home surfing the web and buying goods online! One of the ironic things about this was that sellers had to advise buyers that deliveries of goods might be delayed because of the bad weather.

In many parts of Europe, unseasonably bad weather hit farmers. Parts of southern Europe, normally used to balmy winter weather, suffered snow,

ice and frosts which hit crops susceptible to the cold. Analysts were predicting that the bad weather might affect harvests of delicate crops such as soft fruit, citrus fruits and so on and as a result supply would fall. The fall in supply was likely to increase the price of fruit juice by around 2–3 cents a gallon.

In the US, commodity market traders were anticipating that the bad weather would affect the harvest of grain and soya beans. The expectations of a shortage initially drove the price up but a report on harvest levels by the United States Department of Agriculture (USDA) wrong-footed the market. The USDA estimated, in its report published in January 2010, that corn production would rise to 13.151 million bushels (a bushel is around 60 lbs or 27.2 kg), a rise of 230 million bushels on previous estimates. Meanwhile, soya bean output was estimated to rise by 42 million bushels to 3.361 million bushels. The effect of the report was to push soya bean prices down by between 3 and 6 per cent.

entries in this table and make sure you can explain to yourself why the table contains the prediction it does.

Quick Quiz Analyze what happens to the market for pizza if the price of tomatoes rises. • Analyze what happens to the market for pasta if the price of potatoes falls.

CONCLUSION: HOW PRICES ALLOCATE RESOURCES

This chapter has analysed supply and demand in a single market. Although our discussion has centred around the market for ice cream, the lessons learned here apply in most other markets as well. Whenever you go to a shop to buy something, you are contributing to the demand for that item. Whenever you look for a job, you are contributing to the supply of labour services. Because supply and demand are such pervasive economic phenomena, the model of supply and demand is a powerful tool for analysis. We shall be using this model repeatedly in the following chapters.

One of the *Ten Principles of Economics* discussed in Chapter 1 is that markets are usually a good way to organize economic activity. Although it is still too early to judge whether market outcomes are good or bad, in this chapter we have begun to see how markets work. In any economic system, scarce resources have to be allocated among competing uses. Market economies harness the forces of supply and demand to serve that end. Supply and demand together determine the prices of the economy's many different goods and services; prices in turn are the signals that guide the allocation of resources.

For example, consider the allocation of property on the seafront in a seaside resort. Because the amount of this property is limited, not everyone can enjoy the luxury of living by the beach. Who gets this resource? The answer is: whoever is willing and able to pay the price. The price of seafront property adjusts until the quantity of property demanded exactly balances the quantity supplied. Thus, in market economies, prices are the mechanism for rationing scarce resources.

Similarly, prices determine who produces each good and how much is produced. For instance, consider farming. Because we need food to survive, it is crucial that some people work on farms. What determines who is a farmer and who is not? In a free society, there is no government planning agency making this decision and ensuring an adequate supply of food. Instead, the allocation of workers to farms is based on the job decisions of millions of workers. This decentralized system works well because these decisions depend on prices. The prices of food and the wages of farm workers (the price of their labour) adjust to ensure that enough people choose to be farmers.

If a person had never seen a market economy in action, the whole idea might seem preposterous. Economies are large groups of people engaged in many interdependent activities. What prevents decentralized decision-making from degenerating into chaos? What coordinates the actions of the millions of people with their varying abilities and desires? What ensures that what needs to get done does in fact get done? The answer, in a word, is *prices*. If market economies are guided by an invisible hand, as Adam Smith famously suggested, then prices are the baton that the invisible hand uses to conduct the economic orchestra.

SUMMARY

- Economists use the model of supply and demand to analyse competitive markets. In a competitive market, there are many buyers and sellers, each of whom has little or no influence on the market price.

- The demand curve shows how the quantity of a good demanded depends on the price. According to the law of demand, as the price of a good falls, the quantity demanded rises. Therefore, the demand curve slopes downward.

- In addition to price, other determinants of how much consumers want to buy include income, the prices of substitutes and complements, tastes, expectations and the number of buyers. If one of these factors changes, the demand curve shifts.

- The supply curve shows how the quantity of a good supplied depends on the price. According to the law of supply, as the price of a good rises, the quantity supplied rises. Therefore, the supply curve slopes upward.

- In addition to price, other determinants of how much producers want to sell include input prices, technology, expectations, the number of sellers, and natural and social factors. If one of these factors changes, the supply curve shifts.

- The intersection of the supply and demand curves determines the market equilibrium. At the equilibrium price, the quantity demanded equals the quantity supplied.

- The behaviour of buyers and sellers naturally drives markets toward their equilibrium. When the market price is above the equilibrium price, there is a surplus of the good, which causes the market price to fall. When the market price is below the equilibrium price, there is a shortage, which causes the market price to rise.

- To analyse how any event influences a market, we use the supply and demand diagram to examine how the event affects the equilibrium price and quantity. To do this we follow three steps. First, we decide whether the event shifts the supply curve or the demand curve (or both). Secondly, we decide which direction the curve shifts. Thirdly, we compare the new equilibrium with the initial equilibrium.

- In market economies, prices are the signals that guide economic decisions and thereby allocate scarce resources. For every good in the economy, the price ensures that supply and demand are in balance. The equilibrium price then determines how much of the good buyers choose to purchase and how much sellers choose to produce.

KEY CONCEPTS

market, p. 68
competitive market, p. 69
quantity demanded, p. 70
law of demand, p. 70
demand schedule, p. 70
demand curve, p. 71
normal good, p. 73

inferior good, p. 73
substitutes, p. 73
complements, p. 74
quantity supplied, p. 76
law of supply, p. 76
supply schedule, p. 76
supply curve, p. 76

equilibrium, p. 81
equilibrium price,, p. 81
equilibrium quantity, p. 81
surplus, p. 81
shortage, p. 81
law of supply and demand, p. 82

QUESTIONS FOR REVIEW

1. What is a competitive market? Briefly describe the types of markets other than perfectly competitive markets.

2. What determines the quantity of a good that buyers demand?

3. What are the demand schedule and the demand curve, and how are they related? Why does the demand curve slope downward?

4. Does a change in consumers' tastes lead to a movement along the demand curve or a shift in the demand curve? Does a change in price lead to a movement along the demand curve or a shift in the demand curve?

5. Carlos prefers asparagus to spinach. His income declines and as a result he buys more spinach. Is spinach an inferior or a normal good to Carlos? Explain your answer.

6. What determines the quantity of a good that sellers supply?

7. What are the supply schedule and the supply curve, and how are they related? Why does the supply curve slope upward?

8. Does a change in producers' technology lead to a movement along the supply curve or a shift in the supply curve? Does a change in price lead to a movement along the supply curve or a shift in the supply curve?

9. Define the equilibrium of a market. Describe the forces that move a market toward its equilibrium.

10. Cheese and wine are complements because they are often enjoyed together. When the price of wine rises, what happens to the supply, demand, quantity supplied, quantity demanded and the price in the market for cheese?

11. Describe the role of prices in market economies.

PROBLEMS AND APPLICATIONS

1. Explain each of the following statements using supply and demand diagrams.
   a. When there is a drought in southern Europe, the price of olive oil rises in supermarkets throughout Europe.
   b. When the Olympic Games were held in Greece in 2004, the price of hotel rooms in Athens rocketed.
   c. When a war breaks out in the Middle East, the price of petrol in Europe rises and the price of a used Mercedes falls.

2. 'An increase in the demand for mozzarella cheese raises the quantity of mozzarella demanded, but not the quantity supplied.' Is this statement true or false? Explain.

3. Consider the market for large family saloon cars. For each of the events listed here, identify which of the determinants of demand or supply are affected. Also indicate whether demand or supply is increased or decreased. Then show the effect on the price and quantity of large family saloon cars.
   a. People decide to have more children.
   b. A strike by steel workers raises steel prices.
   c. Engineers develop new automated machinery for the production of cars.
   d. The price of estate cars rises.
   e. A stock market crash lowers people's wealth.

4. During the 1990s, technological advances reduced the cost of computer chips. How do you think this affected the market for computers? For computer software? For typewriters?

5. Using supply and demand diagrams, show the effect of the following events on the market for sweatshirts.
   a. A drought in Egypt damages the cotton crop.
   b. The price of leather jackets falls.
   c. All universities require students to attend morning exercise classes in appropriate attire.
   d. New knitting machines are invented.

6. Suppose that in the year 2005 the number of births is temporarily high. How might this baby boom affect the price of baby-sitting services in 2010 and 2020? (Hint: 5-year-olds need babysitters, whereas 15-year-olds can be babysitters.)

7. Vinegar is a complement (as well as a condiment) for chips (at least in the UK and Ireland). If the price of chips rises, what happens to the market for vinegar? For ketchup? For fish? For orange juice?

8. The case study presented in the chapter discussed cigarette taxes as a way to reduce smoking. Now think about the market for cigars.
   a. Are cigars substitutes or complements for cigarettes?

   b. Using a supply and demand diagram, show what happens in the markets for cigars if the tax on cigarettes is increased.
   c. If policy makers wanted to reduce total tobacco consumption, what policies could they combine with the cigarette tax?

9. The market for pizza has the following demand and supply schedules:

Price	Quantity demanded	Quantity supplied
€4	135	26
5	104	53
6	81	81
7	68	98
8	53	110
9	39	121

   Graph the demand and supply curves. What is the equilibrium price and quantity in this market? If the actual price in this market were *above* the equilibrium price, what would drive the market towards the equilibrium? If the actual price in this market were *below* the equilibrium price, what would drive the market towards the equilibrium?

10. Because bacon and eggs are often eaten together, they are complements.
    a. We observe that both the equilibrium price of eggs and the equilibrium quantity of bacon have risen. What could be responsible for this pattern – a fall in the price of chicken feed or a fall in the price of pig feed? Illustrate and explain your answer.
    b. Suppose instead that the equilibrium price of bacon has risen but the equilibrium quantity of eggs has fallen. What could be responsible for this pattern – a rise in the price of chicken feed or a rise in the price of pig feed? Illustrate and explain your answer.

11. Suppose that the price of tickets to see your local football team play at home is determined by market forces. Currently, the demand and supply schedules are as follows:

Price	Quantity demanded	Quantity supplied
€10	50 000	30 000
20	40 000	30 000
30	30 000	30 000
40	20 000	30 000
50	10 000	30 000

    a. Draw the demand and supply curves. What is unusual about this supply curve? Why might this be true?
    b. What are the equilibrium price and quantity of tickets?

c. Your team plans to increase total capacity in its stadium by 5000 seats next season. What admission price should it charge?

12. An article in *The New York Times* described a successful marketing campaign by the French champagne industry. The article noted that 'many executives felt giddy about the stratospheric champagne prices. But they also feared that such sharp price increases would cause demand to decline, which would then cause prices to plunge.' What mistake are the executives making in their analysis of the situation? Illustrate your answer with a graph.

13. Market research has revealed the following information about the market for chocolate bars: the demand schedule can be represented by the equation QD = 1600 − 300P, where QD is the quantity demanded and P is the price. The supply schedule can be represented by the equation QS = 1400 + 700P, where QS is the quantity supplied. Calculate the equilibrium price and quantity in the market for chocolate bars.

14. What do we mean by a perfectly competitive market? Do you think that the example of ice cream used in this chapter fits this description? Is there another type of market that better characterizes the market for ice cream?

For further resources, visit
www.cengage.com/mankiw_taylor2

5 ELASTICITY AND ITS APPLICATION

Imagine yourself as a producer of silicon chips for use in personal computers, laptops and a variety of other electronic devices. Because you earn all your income from selling silicon chips, you devote much effort to making your factory as productive as it can be. You monitor how production is organized, staff recruitment and motivation levels, check suppliers for cost effectiveness and quality, and study the latest advances in technology. You know that the more chips you manufacture, the more you will have to sell, and the higher will be your income and your standard of living.

One day a local university announces a major discovery. Scientists have devised a new material to produce chips which would help to increase computing power by 50 per cent. How should you react to this news? Should you use the new material? Does this discovery make you better off or worse off than you were before? In this chapter we will see that these questions can have surprising answers. The surprise will come from applying the most basic tools of economics – supply and demand – to the market for computer chips.

The previous chapter introduced supply and demand. In any competitive market, such as the market for computer chips, the upward sloping supply curve represents the behaviour of sellers, and the downward sloping demand curve represents the behaviour of buyers. The price of the good adjusts to bring the quantity supplied and quantity demanded of the good into balance. To apply this basic analysis to understand the impact of the scientists' discovery, we must first develop one more tool: the concept of *elasticity*. We know from Chapter 4 that when price rises, demand falls and supply rises. What we did not discuss in the chapter was *how far* demand and supply change in response to changes in price. When studying how some event or policy affects a market, we can discuss not only the direction of the effects but their magnitude as well. Elasticity, a measure of how much buyers and sellers respond to changes in market conditions, allows us to analyse supply and demand with greater precision.

THE ELASTICITY OF DEMAND

When we introduced demand in Chapter 4, we noted that consumers usually buy more of a good when its price is lower, when their incomes are higher, when the prices of substitutes for the good are higher or when the prices of complements of the good are lower. Our discussion of demand was qualitative, not quantitative. That is, we discussed the direction in which quantity demanded moves, but not the size of the change. To measure how much consumers respond to changes in these variables, economists use the concept of **elasticity**.

elasticity
a measure of the responsiveness of quantity demanded or quantity supplied to one of its determinants

The Price Elasticity of Demand and its Determinants

The law of demand states that a fall in the price of a good raises the quantity demanded. The **price elasticity of demand** measures how much the quantity demanded responds to a change in price. Demand for a good is said to be *elastic* if the quantity demanded responds substantially to changes in the price. Demand is said to be *inelastic* if the quantity demanded responds only slightly to changes in the price.

The price elasticity of demand for any good measures how willing consumers are to move away from the good as its price rises. Thus, the elasticity reflects the many economic, social and psychological forces that influence consumer tastes. Based on experience, however, we can state some general rules about what determines the price elasticity of demand.

price elasticity of demand
a measure of how much the quantity demanded of a good responds to a change in the price of that good, computed as the percentage change in quantity demanded divided by the percentage change in price

Availability of Close Substitutes   Goods with close substitutes tend to have more elastic demand because it is easier for consumers to switch from that good to others. For example, butter and margarine are easily substitutable. A small increase in the price of butter, assuming the price of margarine is held fixed, causes the quantity of butter sold to fall by a relatively large amount. By contrast, because eggs are a food without a close substitute, the demand for eggs is less elastic than the demand for butter.

Necessities versus Luxuries   Necessities tend to have inelastic demands, whereas luxuries have elastic demands. People use gas and electricity to heat their homes and cook their food. If the price of gas and electricity rose together, people would not demand dramatically less of them. They might try and be more energy-efficient and reduce their demand a little, but they would still need hot food and warm homes. By contrast, when the price of sailing dinghies rises, the quantity of sailing dinghies demanded falls substantially. The reason is that most people view hot food and warm homes as necessities and a sailing dinghy as a luxury. Of course, whether a good is a necessity or a luxury depends not on the intrinsic properties of the good but on the preferences of the buyer. For an avid sailor with little concern over her health, sailing dinghies might be a necessity with inelastic demand and hot food and a warm place to sleep a luxury with elastic demand.

Definition of the Market   The elasticity of demand in any market depends on how we draw the boundaries of the market. Narrowly defined markets tend to have more elastic demand than broadly defined markets, because it is easier to find close substitutes for narrowly defined goods. For example, food, a broad category, has a fairly inelastic demand because there are no good substitutes for food. Ice cream, a narrower category, has a more elastic demand because it is easy to substitute other desserts for ice cream. Vanilla ice cream, a very narrow category, has a very elastic demand because other flavours of ice cream are almost perfect substitutes for vanilla.

Proportion of Income Devoted to the Product Some products have a relatively high price and take a larger proportion of income than others. Buying a new suite of furniture for a lounge, for example, tends to take up a large amount of income whereas buying an ice cream might account for only a tiny proportion of income. If the price of a three-piece suite rises by 10 per cent, therefore, this is likely to have a greater effect on demand for this furniture than a similar 10 per cent increase in the price of an ice cream. The higher the proportion of income devoted to the product the greater the elasticity is likely to be.

Time Horizon Goods tend to have more elastic demand over longer time horizons. When the price of petrol rises, the quantity of petrol demanded falls only slightly in the first few months. Over time, however, people buy more fuel-efficient cars, switch to public transport and move closer to where they work. Within several years, the quantity of petrol demanded falls more substantially. Similarly, if the price of a unit of electricity rises much above an equivalent energy unit of gas, demand may fall only slightly in the short run because many people already have electric cookers or electric heating appliances installed in their homes and cannot easily switch. If the price difference persists over several years, however, people may find it worth their while to replace their old electric heating and cooking appliances with new gas appliances and the demand for electricity will fall.

Computing the Price Elasticity of Demand

Now that we have discussed the price elasticity of demand in general terms, let's be more precise about how it is measured. Economists compute the price elasticity of demand as the percentage change in the quantity demanded divided by the percentage change in the price. That is:

$$\text{Price elasticity of demand} = \frac{\text{Percentage change in quantity demanded}}{\text{Percentage change in price}}$$

For example, suppose that a 10 per cent increase in the price of an ice cream cornet causes the amount of ice cream you buy to fall by 20 per cent. We calculate your elasticity of demand as:

$$\text{Price elasticity of demand} = \frac{20\%}{10\%} = 2$$

In this example, the elasticity is 2, reflecting that the change in the quantity demanded is proportionately twice as large as the change in the price.

Because the quantity demanded of a good is negatively related to its price, the percentage change in quantity will always have the opposite sign to the percentage change in price. In this example, the percentage change in price is a *positive* 10 per cent (reflecting an increase), and the percentage change in quantity demanded is a *negative* 20 per cent (reflecting a decrease). For this reason, price elasticities of demand are sometimes reported as negative numbers. In this book we follow the common practice of dropping the minus sign and reporting all price elasticities as positive numbers. (Mathematicians call this the *absolute value*.) With this convention, a larger price elasticity implies a greater responsiveness of quantity demanded to price.

The Midpoint Method: A Better Way to Calculate Percentage Changes and Elasticities

If you try calculating the price elasticity of demand between two points on a demand curve, you will quickly notice an annoying problem: the elasticity from point A to point B seems different from the elasticity from point B to point A. For example, consider these numbers:

Point A: Price = €4 Quantity = 120
Point B: Price = €6 Quantity = 80

Going from point A to point B, the price rises by 50 per cent, and the quantity falls by 33 per cent, indicating that the price elasticity of demand is 33/50, or 0.66. By contrast, going from point B to point A, the price falls by 33 per cent, and the quantity rises by 50 per cent, indicating that the price elasticity of demand is 50/33, or 1.5.

One way to avoid this problem is to use the *midpoint method* for calculating elasticities. The standard way to compute a percentage change is to divide the change by the initial level and multiply by 100. By contrast, the midpoint method computes a percentage change by dividing the change by the midpoint (or average) of the initial and final levels. For instance, €5 is the midpoint of €4 and €6. Therefore, according to the midpoint method, a change from €4 to €6 is considered a 40 per cent rise, because $(6 - 4)/5 \times 100 = 40$. Similarly, a change from €6 to €4 is considered a 40 per cent fall.

Because the midpoint method gives the same answer regardless of the direction of change, it is often used when calculating the price elasticity of demand between two points. In our example, the midpoint between point A and point B is:

Midpoint: Price = €5   Quantity = 100

According to the midpoint method, when going from point A to point B, the price rises by 40 per cent, and the quantity falls by 40 per cent. Similarly, when going from point B to point A, the price falls by 40 per cent, and the quantity rises by 40 per cent. In both directions, the price elasticity of demand equals 1.

We can express the midpoint method with the following formula for the price elasticity of demand between two points, denoted (Q_1, P_1) and (Q_2, P_2):

$$\text{Price elasticity of demand} = \frac{(Q_2 - Q_1)/[(Q_2 + Q_1)/2]}{(P_2 - P_1)/[(P_2 + P_1)/2]}$$

The numerator is the percentage change in quantity computed using the midpoint method, and the denominator is the percentage change in price computed using the midpoint method. If you ever need to calculate elasticities, you should use this formula.

In this book, however, we rarely perform such calculations. For most of our purposes, what elasticity represents – the responsiveness of quantity demanded to price – is more important than how it is calculated.

The Variety of Demand Curves

Economists classify demand curves according to their elasticity. Demand is *elastic* when the elasticity is greater than 1, so that quantity changes proportionately more than the price. Demand is *inelastic* when the elasticity is less than 1, so that quantity moves proportionately less than the price. If the elasticity is exactly 1, so that quantity moves the same amount proportionately as price, demand is said to have *unit elasticity*.

Because the price elasticity of demand measures how much quantity demanded responds to changes in the price, it is closely related to the slope of the demand curve. The following rule of thumb (assuming we are using comparable scales on the axes) is a useful guide: the flatter the demand curve that passes through a given point, the greater the price elasticity of demand. The steeper the demand curve that passes through a given point, the smaller the price elasticity of demand.

Figure 5.1 shows five cases. In the extreme case of a zero elasticity shown in panel (a), demand is *perfectly inelastic*, and the demand curve is vertical. In this case, regardless of the price, the quantity demanded stays the same. As the elasticity rises, the demand curve gets flatter and flatter, as shown in panels (b), (c) and (d). At the opposite extreme shown in panel (e), demand is *perfectly elastic*. This occurs as the price elasticity of demand approaches infinity and the demand curve becomes horizontal, reflecting the fact that very small changes in the price lead to huge changes in the quantity demanded.

Finally, if you have trouble keeping straight the terms *elastic* and *inelastic*, here's a memory trick for you: *I*nelastic curves, such as in panel (a) of Figure 5.1, look like the letter *I*. Elastic curves, as in panel (e), look like the middle bar of the letter *E*. This is not a deep insight, but it might help in your next economics exam.

Total Expenditure, Total Revenue and the Price Elasticity of Demand

total expenditure
the amount paid by buyers, computed as the price of the good times the quantity purchased

total revenue
the amount received by sellers of a good, computed as the price of the good times the quantity sold

When studying changes in supply or demand in a market, two variables we often want to study are **total expenditure** and **total revenue**, the amount paid by buyers and received by sellers of the good. In any market, total revenue received by sellers is $P \times Q$, the price of the good times the quantity of the good sold. Equally, total expenditure is given by the total amount bought multiplied by the price paid. We can show total expenditure graphically, as in Figure 5.2. The height of the box under the demand curve is P, and the width is Q. The area of this box, $P \times Q$, equals the total expenditure in this market. In Figure 5.2, where $P = €4$ and $Q = 100$, total expenditure is $€4 \times 100$, or $€400$.

How does total expenditure change as one moves along the demand curve? The answer depends on the price elasticity of demand. If demand is inelastic, as in Figure 5.3, then an increase in the price causes an increase in total expenditure. Here an increase in price from €1 to €3 causes the quantity demanded to fall only from 100 to 80, and so total expenditure rises from €100 to €240. An increase in price raises $P \times Q$ because the fall in Q is proportionately smaller than the rise in P.

We obtain the opposite result if demand is elastic: an increase in the price causes a decrease in total expenditure. In Figure 5.4, for instance, when the price rises from €4 to €5, the quantity demanded falls from 50 to 20, and so total expenditure falls from €200 to €100. Because demand is elastic, the reduction in the quantity demanded is so great that it more than offsets the increase in the price. That is, an increase in price reduces $P \times Q$ because the fall in Q is proportionately greater than the rise in P.

Although the examples in these two figures are extreme, they illustrate a general rule:

- When demand is inelastic (a price elasticity less than 1), price and total expenditure move in the same direction.

FIGURE 5.1

The Price Elasticity of Demand

The price elasticity of demand determines whether the demand curve is steep or flat. Note that all percentage changes are calculated using the midpoint method.

(a) Perfectly inelastic demand: Elasticity equals 0

Price

Demand

€5

4

1. An increase in price . . .

0   100   Quantity

2. . . . leaves the quantity demanded unchanged.

(b) Inelastic demand: Elasticity is less than 1

Price

€5

4

1. A 22% increase in price . . .

Demand

0   90 ← 100   Quantity

2. . . . leads to an 11% decrease in quantity demanded.

(c) Unit elastic demand: Elasticity equals 1

Price

€5

4

1. A 22% increase in price . . .

Demand

0   80 ← 100   Quantity

2. . . . leads to a 22% decrease in quantity demanded.

(d) Elastic demand: Elasticity is greater than 1

Price

€5

4

1. A 22% increase in price . . .

Demand

0   50 ← 100   Quantity

2. . . . leads to a 67% decrease in quantity demanded.

(e) Perfectly elastic demand: Elasticity equals infinity

Price

1. At any price above €4, quantity demanded is zero.

€4

Demand

2. At exactly €4, consumers will buy any quantity.

0   Quantity

3. At a price below €4, quantity demanded is infinite.

Elasticity of a Linear Demand Curve

The slope of a linear demand curve is constant, but its elasticity is not. The demand schedule in the table was used to calculate the price elasticity of demand by the midpoint method. At points with a low price and high quantity, the demand curve is inelastic. At points with a high price and low quantity, the demand curve is elastic.

Price	Quantity	Total revenue (Price × Quantity)	Per cent change in price	Per cent change in quantity	Price elasticity	Quantity description
€7	0	€0				
6	2	12	15	200	13.0	Elastic
5	4	20	18	67	3.7	Elastic
4	6	24	22	40	1.8	Elastic
3	8	24	29	29	1.0	Unit elastic
2	10	20	40	22	0.6	Inelastic
1	12	12	67	18	0.3	Inelastic
0	14	0	200	15	0.1	Inelastic

to €2 raises total expenditure. When the price is €5, demand is elastic, and a price increase to €6 reduces total expenditure. Between €3 and €4, demand is exactly unit elastic and total expenditure is the same at these two prices.

CASE STUDY

Putting Bums on Seats!

You are the owner of a coach company running a scheduled bus service between a rural town and surrounding villages. The service runs every two hours between 6am and 8pm. The price passengers pay for a return bus journey is a standard fare priced at €3.00. The maximum capacity of each bus is 80 seats.

You have noticed that the number of passengers on the services is falling and you are considering options to try and increase the demand and fill more seats on each service. You know that price and demand are inversely related and so you are planning on reducing the price to try and encourage more passengers to use your buses. However, a colleague cautions you against doing this until you have thought it through in more detail. She tells you that you need to know a lot more about the price elasticity of demand for the service before making any decision.

You decide to look at the pattern of bus usage throughout the day in a little more detail and also to investigate what substitutes exist for bus travel in the region. Your investigations tell you that the occupancy rate for buses (the proportion of seats taken up by passengers) on buses between the hours of 6am and 8am is around 95 per cent on average. Between 8am and 4pm the occupancy rate falls considerably to only 30 per cent and climbs again to 90 per cent between 4pm and 6pm. After 6pm, the rate falls again to 20 per cent. The substitutes for bus travel in the region are domestic vehicles, taxis and a local train service. The train service, however, would involve most passengers having to make a car journey to the station whereas your bus service does visit more villages and so is more convenient. Taxis are considerably more expensive.

After considering the options open to you and discussing these with your colleague you decide on the following strategy:

- During the hours of 6 am and 8 am and 4 pm and 6.pm, the price of a return ticket will rise by €1.00 to €4.00.
- Between 8 am and 4 pm the price of a return ticket will fall by 50 per cent to €1.50.
- The bus service will stop running after 6.30 pm.

Your colleague advises you to monitor the effect on occupancy rates once the new prices are introduced. After six months you go back to her with your findings. The increase in the ticket price has resulted in a fall in occupancy rates to 90 per cent in the morning and 87 per cent in the afternoon. During the day, the 50 per cent cut in the price has raised the occupancy rate from an average of 30 per cent to 65 per cent. You are very pleased with the results because the total expenditure by passengers on tickets has increased and thus, your total revenue has also risen.

You thank you colleague because without her wisdom you might have made the wrong decision on pricing. You would never have thought that increasing the price could actually be of benefit. Whilst you have fewer bums on seats in the busy period in the morning you have been very successful at increasing occupancy rates during the daytime and the increase in total revenue has been most welcome.

If the price of a bus ticket was higher would the number of passengers decline?

Other Demand Elasticities

In addition to the price elasticity of demand, economists also use other elasticities to describe the behaviour of buyers in a market.

The Income Elasticity of Demand The **income elasticity of demand** measures how the quantity demanded changes as consumer income changes. It is calculated as the percentage change in quantity demanded divided by the percentage change in income. That is,

$$\text{Income elasticity of demand} = \frac{\text{Percentage change in quantity demanded}}{\text{Percentage change in income}}$$

income elasticity of demand
a measure of how much the quantity demanded of a good responds to a change in consumers' income, computed as the percentage change in quantity demanded divided by the percentage change in income

FIGURE 5.6

The Price Elasticity of Supply

The price elasticity of supply determines whether the supply curve is steep or flat. Note that all percentage changes are calculated using the midpoint method.

(a) Perfectly inelastic supply: Elasticity equals 0

(b) Inelastic supply: Elasticity is less than 1

(c) Unit elastic supply: Elasticity equals 1

(d) Elastic supply: Elasticity is greater than 1

(e) Perfectly elastic supply: Elasticity equals infinity

FIGURE 5.7

How the Price Elasticity of Supply Can Vary

Because firms often have a maximum capacity for production, the elasticity of supply may be very high at low levels of quantity supplied and very low at high levels of quantity supplied. Here, an increase in price from €3 to €4 increases the quantity supplied from 100 to 200. Because the increase in quantity supplied of 67 per cent (computed using the midpoint method) is larger than the increase in price of 29 per cent, the supply curve is elastic in this range. By contrast, when the price rises from €12 to €15, the quantity supplied rises only from 500 to 525. Because the increase in quantity supplied of 5 per cent is smaller than the increase in price of 22 per cent, the supply curve is inelastic in this range.

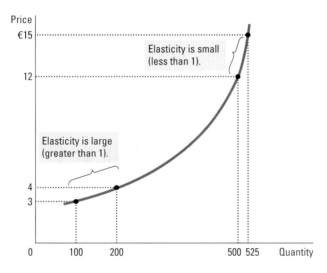

approaches infinity and the supply curve becomes horizontal, meaning that very small changes in the price lead to very large changes in the quantity supplied.

In some markets, the elasticity of supply is not constant but varies over the supply curve. Figure 5.7 shows a typical case for an industry in which firms have factories with a limited capacity for production. For low levels of quantity supplied, the elasticity of supply is high, indicating that firms respond substantially to changes in the price. In this region, firms have capacity for production that is not being used, such as buildings and machinery sitting idle for all or part of the day. Small increases in price make it profitable for firms to begin using this idle capacity. As the quantity supplied rises, firms begin to reach capacity. Once capacity is fully used, increasing production further requires the construction of new factories. To induce firms to incur this extra expense, the price must rise substantially, so supply becomes less elastic.

Figure 5.7 presents a numerical example of this phenomenon. When the price rises from €3 to €4 (a 29 per cent increase, according to the midpoint method), the quantity supplied rises from 100 to 200 (a 67 per cent increase). Because quantity supplied moves proportionately more than the price, the supply curve has elasticity greater than 1. By contrast, when the price rises from €12 to €15 (a 22 per cent increase), the quantity supplied rises from 500 to 525 (a 5 per cent increase). In this case, quantity supplied moves proportionately less than the price, so the elasticity is less than 1.

Quick Quiz Define the price elasticity of supply • Explain why the price elasticity of supply might be different in the long run from in the short run.

Total Revenue and the Price Elasticity of Supply

The principles outlined in the discussion of demand curves and total expenditure by consumers also apply to supply curves. The only difference is that when looked at from the perspective of the seller, changes in sales in relation to changes in price result in changes in total revenue. Total revenue, remember, is calculated by taking the price at which a good is sold and multiplying it by the amount the firm sells. In analysing markets, we will use both demand and supply curves on the same diagram. We will refer to changes in total revenue when looking at the effects of changes in equilibrium conditions but remember that revenue for sellers represents the same identity as expenditure for buyers.

THREE APPLICATIONS OF SUPPLY, DEMAND AND ELASTICITY

Can good news for the computing industry be bad news for computer chip manufacturers? Why do the prices of ski holidays in Europe rise dramatically over public and school holidays? Does drug prohibition increase or decrease drug-related crime? At first, these questions might seem to have little in common. Yet all three questions are about markets and all markets are subject to the forces of supply and demand. Here we apply the versatile tools of supply, demand and elasticity to answer these seemingly complex questions.

Can Good News for the Computer Industry Be Bad News for Chip Makers?

Let's now return to the question posed at the beginning of this chapter: what happens to chip manufacturers and the market for chips when scientists discover a new material for making chips that is more productive than silicon? Recall from Chapter 4 that we answer such questions in three steps. First, we examine whether the supply or demand curve shifts. Secondly, we consider which direction the curve shifts. Thirdly, we use the supply and demand diagram to see how the market equilibrium changes.

This is a situation that is facing chip manufacturers. Scientists are investigating new materials to make computer chips. Such a material may allow the manufacturers to be able to work on building processing power at ever smaller concentrations and increase computing power considerably. In this case, the discovery of the new material affects the supply curve. Because the material increases the amount of computing power that can be produced on each chip, manufacturers are now willing to supply more chips at any given price. In other words, the supply curve for computing power shifts to the right. The demand curve remains the same because consumers' desire to buy chips at any given price is not affected by the introduction of the new material. Figure 5.8 shows an example of such a change. When the supply curve shifts from S_1 to S_2, the quantity of chips sold increases from 100 to 110, and the price of chips falls from €10 per gigabyte to €4 per gigabyte.

FIGURE 5.8

An Increase in Supply in the Market for Computer Chips

When an advance in chip technology increases the supply of chips from **S₁** *to* **S₂**, *the price of chips falls. Because the demand for chips is inelastic, the increase in the quantity sold from 100 to 110 is proportionately smaller than the decrease in the price from €3 to €2. As a result, manufacturers' total revenue falls from €300 (€3 × 100) to €220 (€2 × 110).*

But does this discovery make chip manufacturers better off? As a first stab at answering this question, consider what happens to the total revenue received by chip manufacturers; total revenue is $P \times Q$, the price of each chip times the quantity sold. The discovery affects manufacturers in two conflicting ways. The new material allows manufacturers to produce more chips with greater computing power (Q rises), but now each chip sells for less (P falls).

Whether total revenue rises or falls depends on the elasticity of demand. We can assume that the demand for chips is inelastic, in producing a computer, chips represent a relatively small proportion of the total cost but they also have few good substitutes. When the demand curve is inelastic, as it is in Figure 5.8, a decrease in price causes total revenue to fall. You can see this in the figure: the price of chips falls substantially, whereas the quantity of chips sold rises only slightly. Total revenue falls from €1 000 to €440. Thus, the discovery of the new material lowers the total revenue that chip manufacturers receive for the sale of their products.

If manufacturers are made worse off by the discovery of this new material, why do they adopt it? The answer to this question goes to the heart of how competitive markets work. If each chip manufacturer is a small part of the market for chips, he or she takes the price of chips as given. For any given price of chips, it is better to use the new material in order to produce and sell more chips. Yet when all manufacturers do this, the supply of chips rises, the price falls and manufacturers are worse off.

Although this example is only hypothetical, in fact a new material for making computer chips is being investigated. The material is called hafnium and is used in the nuclear industry. In recent years the manufacture of computer chips has changed dramatically. In the early 1990s, prices per megabyte of DRAM (dynamic random access memory) stood at around $55 but fell to under $1 by the early part of the new century. Manufacturers who were first involved in chip manufacture made high profits but as new firms joined the industry, supply increased and as the technology also spread, supply rose and prices fell. The fall in prices led to a number of firms struggling to stay in business. We assumed above that computer chip manufacturers were price takers but in reality the computer chip market is not perfectly competitive. However, the fact that so many smaller manufacturers struggled to survive as chip technology expanded at such a rapid rate from the early 1990s shows that even markets dominated now by a relatively small number of firms exhibit many of the features we have described so far.

When analysing the effects of technology, it is important to keep in mind that what is bad for manufacturers is not necessarily bad for society as a whole. Improvement in computing power technology can be bad for manufacturers who find it difficult to survive unless they are very large, but it represents good news for consumers of this computing power (ultimately the users of PCs, laptops and so on) who pay less for computing.

"WHY DON'T WE JUST KEEP THE LAW OF DEMAND, AND REPEAL THE SUPPLY PART?"

Why Do Prices of Ski Holidays Differ so Much at Different Times of the Season?

Ski holidays in Europe are becoming ever more popular. There were an estimated 1.3 million people from the UK taking holidays in European ski resorts in 2010. For an increasing number of people the pleasure of a holiday on the slopes is a part of the winter but people also face considerable changes in the prices that they have to pay for their holiday. For example, a quick check of a ski company website for the 2010–11 season revealed the prices shown in Table 5.1 for 7-night ski trips, per person to Austria leaving from London.

There is a considerable variation in the prices that holidaymakers have to pay – £710 being the greatest difference. Prices are particularly high leaving on 26 December and 20 February – why? The reason is that at this time of the season the demand for ski holidays increases dramatically because they coincide with annual holiday periods; 26 December is part of the Christmas holidays and when schoolchildren are also on holiday; 20 February is also a major school holiday for many UK children (although some also have a break which includes or occurs the previous week).

TABLE 5.1

Prices of 7-night Ski holidays in Austria, from London

Departure date	Price per person (£)
5 December 2010	470
26 December 2010	1 000
16 January 2011	650
5 February 2011	670
13 February 2011	720
20 February 2011	1 180
27 February 2011	700

FIGURE 5.9

The Supply of Ski Holidays in Europe

Panel (a) shows the market for ski holidays in off-peak times. The supply curve S₁ is relatively elastic in the short-run. An increase in demand from D₁ to D₂ at this time leads to a relatively small increase in price because the increase can be accommodated by releasing some of the spare capacity that tour operators have. Panel (b) shows the market during peak times. The supply of holidays shown by the curve S₁ is relatively inelastic in the short run. If demand now increases from D₁ to D₂ the result will be a sharp rise in price.

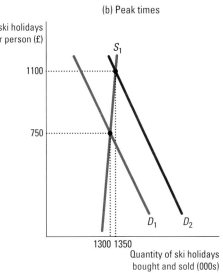

The supply of ski holidays does have a limit – there will be a finite number of accommodation places and passes for ski-lifts and so the elasticity of supply is relatively inelastic (see Figure 5.9). It is difficult for tour operators to increase supply of accommodation or ski-passes easily in the short-run in the face of rising demand at these times. The result is that the increase in demand for ski holidays at these peak times results in prices rising significantly to choke off the excess demand. If holidaymakers are able to be flexible about when they take their holidays then they will be able to benefit from lower prices for the same holiday. Away from these peak periods the demand for ski holidays is lower and so tour operators have spare capacity – the supply curve out of peak times is more elastic in the short run. If there was a sudden increase in demand in early December, for example, then tour operators would have the capacity to accommodate that demand so prices would not rise as much as when that capacity is strictly limited.

Cases for which supply is very inelastic in the short run but more elastic in the long run may see different prices exist in the market. Air and rail travel and the use of electricity may all be examples where prices differ markedly at peak times compared with off peak times because of supply constraints and the ability of firms to be able to discriminate between customers at these times.

Does Drug Prohibition Increase or Decrease Drug-related Crime?

A persistent problem facing society is the use of illegal drugs, such as heroin, cocaine, marijuana and ecstasy. Drug use has several adverse effects. One is that

FIGURE 5.10

Policies to Reduce the Use of Illegal Drugs

Drug prohibition reduces the supply of drugs from S₁ to S₂, as in panel (a). If the demand for drugs is inelastic, then the total amount paid by drug users rises, even as the amount of drug use falls. By contrast, drug education reduces the demand for drugs from D₁ to D₂, as in panel (b). Because both price and quantity fall, the amount paid by drug users falls.

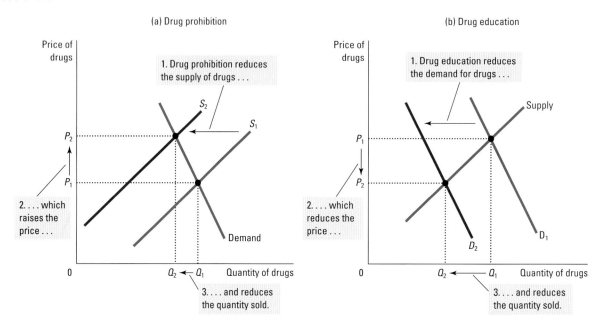

drug dependency can ruin the lives of drug users and their families. Another is that drug addicts often turn to robbery and other violent crimes in order to obtain the money needed to support their habit. To discourage the use of illegal drugs, European governments devote billions of euros each year to reduce the flow of drugs into their countries. Let's use the tools of supply and demand to examine this policy of drug prohibition.

Suppose the government increases the number of undercover police devoted to the war on drugs. What happens in the market for illegal drugs? As is usual, we answer this question in three steps. First, we consider whether the supply or demand curve shifts. Secondly, we consider the direction of the shift. Thirdly, we see how the shift affects the equilibrium price and quantity.

Although the purpose of drug prohibition is to reduce drug use, its direct impact is on the sellers of drugs rather than the buyers. When the government stops some drugs from entering the country and arrests more smugglers, it raises the cost of selling drugs and, therefore, reduces the quantity of drugs supplied at any given price. The demand for drugs – the amount buyers want at any given price – is not changed. As panel (a) of Figure 5.10 shows, prohibition shifts the supply curve to the left from S_1 to S_2 and leaves the demand curve the same. The equilibrium price of drugs rises from P_1 to P_2, and the equilibrium quantity falls from Q_1 to Q_2. The fall in the equilibrium quantity shows that drug prohibition does reduce drug use.

But what about the amount of drug-related crime? To answer this question, consider the total amount that drug users pay for the drugs they buy. Because few drug addicts are likely to break their self-destructive habits in response to a higher price, it is likely that the demand for drugs is inelastic, as it is drawn in the figure. If demand is inelastic, then an increase in price raises total revenue in the drug market. That is, because drug prohibition raises the price of drugs proportionately more than it reduces drug use, it raises the total amount of money that drug users pay for drugs. Addicts who already had to steal to support their habits would have an even greater need for quick cash. Thus, drug prohibition could increase drug-related crime.

Because of this adverse effect of drug prohibition, some analysts argue for alternative approaches to the drug problem. Rather than trying to reduce the supply of drugs, policy makers might try to reduce the demand by pursuing a policy of drug education. Successful drug education has the effects shown in panel (b) of Figure 5.10. The demand curve shifts to the left from D_1 to D_2. As a result, the equilibrium quantity falls from Q_1 to Q_2, and the equilibrium price falls from P_1 to P_2. Total revenue, which is price times quantity, also falls. Thus, in contrast to drug prohibition, drug education can reduce both drug use and drug-related crime.

Advocates of drug prohibition might argue that the effects of this policy are different in the long run from what they are in the short run, because the elasticity of demand may depend on the time horizon. The demand for drugs is probably inelastic over short periods of time because higher prices do not substantially affect drug use by established addicts. But demand may be more elastic over longer periods of time because higher prices would discourage experimentation with drugs among the young and, over time, lead to fewer drug addicts. In this case, drug prohibition would increase drug-related crime in the short run while decreasing it in the long run.

Quick Quiz How might a drought that destroys half of all farm crops be good for farmers? If such a drought is good for farmers, why don't farmers destroy their own crops in the absence of a drought?

IN THE NEWS

Cutting Price in the Console Wars

When firms make pricing decisions, they will have to consider both the short-run and long-run effects, and price elasticity will almost certainly play some part in decision-making. This article looks at pricing of games consoles.

During the summer of 2009 rumours had been circulating suggesting that Sony was planning to cut the price of its PlayStation 3 (PS3) in the face of competition from other games consoles.

The market was in a position where there were no plans by any of the main players in the market to release new consoles. As a result, price was being seen as a way in which games

console manufacturers might be able to compete for sales. Sony's PS3 has not taken off in the same way as the launch of its previous versions and part of the reason has been the existence of cheaper consoles such as Microsoft's Xbox 360, which retailed upwards of £129 (€150) and Nintendo's Wii, which sold at around £169 (€196). The PS3 was retailing at around the £300 (€350) mark but at a press conference ahead of the Game.Com show in Cologne in August, Sony officials announced that the price would be cut. In Europe the PS3 would sell for €299, £249.99 in the UK and $299 in the US.

A new slimmer version of the PS3, which uses 34 per cent less power and is over a third lighter and around a third smaller was to be released in September. Production of existing PS3 consoles would cease and the price reductions would take place immediately. Part of the reason for the price cut is that figures show it is very effective in generating sales. Sony was hoping that the price elasticity of demand in the short run for the PS3 would be sufficiently elastic to generate increased sales and more than cover the lost revenue resulting from the lower price. In considering the price reduction Sony would have had to consider the reaction of its rivals, Nintendo, manufacturer of the Wii, and Microsoft who make the Xbox 360. In addition, it would be looking at the extent to which these rival products were substitutes to a PS3 in consumers' minds and the role of complements – the various games which users can buy for the console. Analysts suggested that any price cut by Sony would be met with similar tactics from Microsoft and Nintendo. The size of those cuts and whether they will indeed follow suit and when, will influence the size of the effect on sales and thus total revenue for Sony.

Reports in early 2010 suggest that the price cut may have had some effect. In the final five weeks of 2009, Sony announced that it had sold 3.8 million consoles worldwide. This represented an increase of 76 per cent on the equivalent period in 2008.

CONCLUSION

According to an old quip, even a parrot can become an economist simply by learning to say 'supply and demand'. These last two chapters should have convinced you that there is much truth in this statement. The tools of supply and demand allow you to analyse many of the most important events and policies that shape the economy. You are now well on your way to becoming an economist (or, at least, a well educated parrot).

SUMMARY

- The price elasticity of demand measures how much the quantity demanded responds to changes in the price. Demand tends to be more elastic if close substitutes are available, if the good is a luxury rather than a necessity, if the market is narrowly defined or if buyers have substantial time to react to a price change.

- The price elasticity of demand is calculated as the percentage change in quantity demanded divided by the percentage change in price. If the elasticity is less than 1, so that quantity demanded moves proportionately less than the price, demand is said to be inelastic. If the elasticity is greater than 1, so that quantity demanded moves proportionately more than the price, demand is said to be elastic.

- Total revenue, the total amount paid for a good, equals the price of the good times the quantity sold. For inelastic demand curves, total revenue rises as price rises. For elastic demand curves, total revenue falls as price rises.

- The income elasticity of demand measures how much the quantity demanded responds to changes in consumers' income. The cross-price elasticity of demand measures how much the quantity demanded of one good responds to changes in the price of another good.

- The price elasticity of supply measures how much the quantity supplied responds to changes in the price. This elasticity often depends on the time horizon under consideration. In most markets, supply is more elastic in the long run than in the short run.

- The price elasticity of supply is calculated as the percentage change in quantity supplied divided by the percentage change in price. If the elasticity is less than 1, so that quantity supplied moves proportionately less than the price, supply is said to be inelastic. If the elasticity is greater than 1, so that quantity supplied moves proportionately more than the price, supply is said to be elastic.

- The tools of supply and demand can be applied in many different kinds of markets. This chapter uses them to analyse the market for computer chips, the market for ski holidays and the market for illegal drugs.

KEY CONCEPTS

elasticity, p. 95
price elasticity of demand, p. 95
total expenditure, p. 98

total revenue, p. 98
income elasticity of demand, p. 103
cross-price elasticity of demand, p. 104

price elasticity of supply, p. 104

QUESTIONS FOR REVIEW

1. Define the price elasticity of demand and the income elasticity of demand.

2. List and explain some of the determinants of the price elasticity of demand.

3. If the elasticity is greater than 1, is demand elastic or inelastic? If the elasticity equals 0, is demand perfectly elastic or perfectly inelastic?

4. On a supply and demand diagram, show equilibrium price, equilibrium quantity and the total revenue received by producers.

5. If demand is elastic, how will an increase in price change total revenue? Explain.

6. What do we call a good whose income elasticity is less than 0?

7. How is the price elasticity of supply calculated? Explain what this measures.

8. What is the price elasticity of supply of Picasso paintings? (Picasso was a renowned artist who died in 1973.)

9. Is the price elasticity of supply usually larger in the short run or in the long run? Why?

10. In the 1970s, OPEC caused a dramatic increase in the price of oil. In the 1980s, the price of oil fell dramatically. What do you think might have prevented it from maintaining a high price through the 1980s?

PROBLEMS AND APPLICATIONS

1. For each of the following pairs of goods, which good would you expect to have more elastic demand and why?
   a. Required textbooks or mystery novels.
   b. Beethoven recordings or classical music recordings in general.
   c. Heating oil during the next six months or heating oil during the next five years.
   d. Lemonade or water.

2. Suppose that business travellers and holidaymakers have the following demand for airline tickets from Birmingham to Naples:

Price	Quantity demanded (business travellers)	Quantity demanded (holidaymakers)
€150	2 100	1 000
200	2 000	800
250	1 900	600
300	1 800	400

a. As the price of tickets rises from €200 to €250, what is the price elasticity of demand for (i) business travellers and (ii) holidaymakers? (Use the midpoint method in your calculations.)
b. Why might holidaymakers have a different elasticity from business travellers?

3. Suppose that your demand schedule for DVDs is as follows:

Price	Quantity demanded (income = €10 000)	Quantity demanded (income = €12 000)
€8	40	50
10	32	45
12	24	30
14	16	20
16	8	12

a. Use the midpoint method to calculate your price elasticity of demand as the price of DVDs increases from €8 to €10 if (i) your income is €10 000, and (ii) your income is €12 000.

b. Calculate your income elasticity of demand as your income increases from €10 000 to €12 000 if (i) the price is €12, and (ii) the price is €16.

4. Xanthe has decided always to spend one-third of her income on clothing.
   a. What is her income elasticity of clothing demand?
   b. What is her price elasticity of clothing demand?
   c. If Xanthe's tastes change and she decides to spend only one-quarter of her income on clothing, how does her demand curve change? What are her income elasticity and price elasticity now?

5. Two drivers – Tom and Jerry – each drive up to a petrol station. Before looking at the price, each places an order. Tom says, 'I'd like 30 litres of petrol.' Jerry says, 'I'd like €30-worth of petrol.' What is each driver's price elasticity of demand?

6. Economists have observed that spending on restaurant meals declines more during economic downturns than does spending on food to be eaten at home. How might the concept of elasticity help to explain this phenomenon?

7. Consider public policy aimed at smoking.
   a. Studies indicate that the price elasticity of demand for cigarettes is about 0.4. If a packet of cigarettes is currently priced at €2 and the government wants to reduce smoking by 20 per cent, by how much should it increase the price?
   b. If the government permanently increases the price of cigarettes, will the policy have a larger effect on smoking one year from now or five years from now?
   c. Studies also find that teenagers have a higher price elasticity than do adults. Why might this be true?

8. Would you expect the price elasticity of *demand* to be larger in the market for all ice cream or the market for vanilla ice cream? Would you expect the price elasticity of *supply* to be larger in the market for all ice cream or the market for vanilla ice cream? Be sure to explain your answers.

9. Pharmaceutical drugs have an inelastic demand, and computers have an elastic demand. Suppose that technological advance doubles the supply of both products (that is, the quantity supplied at each price is twice what it was).
   a. What happens to the equilibrium price and quantity in each market?
   b. Which product experiences a larger change in price?
   c. Which product experiences a larger change in quantity?
   d. What happens to total consumer spending on each product?

10. Seafront properties along the promenade at Brighton on the south coast of England have an inelastic supply, and cars have an elastic supply. Suppose that a rise in population doubles the demand for both products (that is, the quantity demanded at each price is twice what it was).
   a. What happens to the equilibrium price and quantity in each market?
   b. Which product experiences a larger change in price?
   c. Which product experiences a larger change in quantity?
   d. What happens to total consumer spending on each product?

11. Suppose that there is severe flooding in a region in which there is a high concentration of wheat farmers.
   a. Farmers whose crops were destroyed by the floods were much worse off, but farmers whose crops were not destroyed benefited from the floods. Why?
   b. What information would you need about the market for wheat to assess whether farmers as a group were hurt or helped by the floods?

12. Explain why the following might be true: a drought around the world raises the total revenue that farmers receive from the sale of grain, but a drought only in France reduces the total revenue that French farmers receive.

13. Because better weather makes farmland more productive, farmland in regions with good weather conditions is more expensive than farmland in regions with bad weather conditions. Over time, however, as advances in technology have made all farmland more productive, the price of farmland (adjusted for overall inflation) has fallen. Use the concept of elasticity to explain why productivity and farmland prices are positively related across space but negatively related over time.

For further resources, visit
www.cengage.com/mankiw_taylor2

6 SUPPLY, DEMAND AND GOVERNMENT POLICIES

Economists have two roles. As scientists, they develop and test theories to explain the world around them. As policy advisors, they use their theories to help change the world for the better. The focus of the preceding two chapters has been scientific. We have seen how supply and demand determine the price of a good and the quantity of the good sold. We have also seen how various events shift supply and demand and thereby change the equilibrium price and quantity.

This chapter offers our first look at policy. Here we alalyse various types of government policy using only the tools of supply and demand. As you will see, the analysis yields some surprising insights. Policies often have effects that their architects did not intend or anticipate. One of the *Ten Principles of Economics* is that people respond to incentives. When new policies are introduced they may have good intentions to solve particular problems or help groups of people but new policies also generate new incentives and as a result the consequences may go far beyond those envisaged by the policy makers.

We begin by considering policies that directly control prices. For example, some countries have rent-control laws that dictate a maximum rent that landlords may charge tenants or minimum wage laws that dictate the lowest wage that firms may pay workers. Price controls are usually enacted when policy makers believe that the market price of a good or service is unfair to buyers or sellers. Yet, as we will see, these policies can generate inequities of their own.

After our discussion of price controls, we consider the impact of taxes and subsidies. Policy makers use taxes both to influence market outcomes and to raise revenue for public purposes. Although the prevalence of taxes in a

subsidy
payment to buyers and sellers to supplement income or lower costs and which thus encourages consumption or provides an advantage to the recipient

developed economy is obvious, their effects are not. For example, when the government levies a tax on the amount that firms pay their workers, do the firms or the workers bear the burden of the tax? A **subsidy** works almost exactly as the reverse of taxes. They are often used to encourage the supply of a product which is being underproduced and deemed to be in the public interest. In the case of subsidies, someone has to pay for the subsidy, and firms and consumers may benefit in different ways. How taxes and subsidies affect different people and organizations is not at all clear – until we apply the powerful tools of supply and demand.

CONTROLS ON PRICES

To see how price controls affect market outcomes, let's look once again at the market for ice cream. As we saw in Chapter 4, if ice cream is sold in a competitive market free of government regulation, the price of ice cream adjusts to balance supply and demand: at the equilibrium price, the quantity of ice cream that buyers want to buy exactly equals the quantity that sellers want to sell. To be concrete, suppose the equilibrium price is €3 per cornet.

Not everyone may be happy with the outcome of this free market process. Let's say the National Association of Ice Cream Eaters complains that the €3 price is too high for everyone to enjoy a cornet a day (their recommended diet). Meanwhile, the National Organization of Ice Cream Producers complains that the €3 price – the result of 'cut-throat competition' – is too low and is depressing the incomes of its members. Each of these groups lobbies the government to pass laws that alter the market outcome by directly controlling the price of an ice cream cornet.

Of course, because buyers of any good always want a lower price while sellers want a higher price, the interests of the two groups conflict. If the Ice Cream Eaters are successful in their lobbying, the government imposes a legal maximum on the price at which ice cream can be sold. Because the price is not allowed to rise above this level, the legislated maximum is called a **price ceiling** or a price cap. By contrast, if the Ice Cream Makers are successful, the government imposes a legal minimum on the price. Because the price cannot fall below this level, the legislated minimum is called a **price floor**. Let us consider the effects of these policies in turn.

price ceiling
a legal maximum on the price at which a good can be sold

price floor
a legal minimum on the price at which a good can be sold

How Price Ceilings Affect Market Outcomes

When the government, moved by the complaints and campaign contributions of the Ice Cream Eaters, imposes a price ceiling on the market for ice cream, two outcomes are possible. In panel (a) of Figure 6.1, the government imposes a price ceiling of €4 per cornet. In this case, because the price that balances supply and demand (€3) is below the ceiling, the price ceiling is *not binding*. Market forces naturally move the economy to the equilibrium, and the price ceiling has no effect on the price or the quantity sold.

Panel (b) of Figure 6.1 shows the other, more interesting, possibility. In this case, the government imposes a price ceiling of €2 per cornet. Because the equilibrium price of €3 is above the price ceiling, the ceiling is a *binding constraint* on the market. The forces of supply and demand tend to move the price towards the equilibrium price, but when the market price hits the ceiling, it can rise no further. Thus, the market price equals the price ceiling. Given this binding limit on price, incentives change. Some ice cream sellers will not find it profitable to produce ice cream at this price and either cut back production or possibly leave the

FIGURE 6.1

A Market With a Price Ceiling

In panel (a), the government imposes a price ceiling of €4. Because the price ceiling is above the equilibrium price of €3, the price ceiling has no effect, and the market can reach the equilibrium of supply and demand. In this equilibrium, quantity supplied and quantity demanded both equal 100 cornets. In panel (b), the government imposes a price ceiling of €2. Because the price ceiling is below the equilibrium price of €3, the market price equals €2. At this price, 125 cornets are demanded and only 75 are supplied, so there is a shortage of 50 cornets.

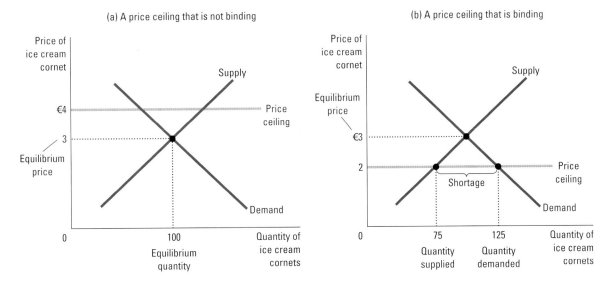

market. Buyers' incentives are different. The lower price means the sacrifice they have to make to buy ice cream is less in terms of alternatives foregone and so are prepared to buy more at the binding price. At this price, the quantity of ice cream demanded (125 cornets in the figure) exceeds the quantity supplied (75 cornets). There is a shortage of ice cream, so some people who want to buy ice cream at the going price are unable to.

When a shortage of ice cream develops because of this price ceiling, some mechanism for rationing ice cream will naturally develop. The mechanism could simply be long queues: buyers who are willing to arrive early and queue get a cornet, while those unwilling to wait do not. Alternatively, sellers could ration ice cream according to their own personal biases, selling it only to friends, relatives, or members of their own racial or ethnic group. Notice that even though the price ceiling was motivated by a desire to help buyers of ice cream, not all buyers benefit from the policy. Some buyers do get to pay a lower price, although they may have to queue a long time to do so, but other buyers cannot get any ice cream at all. In setting policy, the authorities have to consider who gets the benefits and the possible value of these benefits in relation to the cost. The benefit in this case are those buyers who are able to buy ice creams at €2 whereas the cost are those who want to buy ice creams but are unable to do so. There might also be costs in terms of the effect on sellers that has to be taken into consideration. Some sellers may not feel it is worth their while continuing in the market and leave, thus depressing market supply. There will also be the effect on workers and capital which is now taken out of use and will be redundant. To society as a whole there is an opportunity cost of these redundant factor inputs.

FIGURE 6.4

How the Minimum Wage Affects the Labour Market

Panel (a) shows a labour market in which the wage adjusts to balance labour supply and demand. Panel (b) shows the impact of a binding minimum wage. Because the minimum wage is a price floor, it causes a surplus: the quantity of labour supplied exceeds the quantity demanded. The result is unemployment. Panel (c) shows that the more elastic labour demand is, the higher will be ensuing unemployment. In panel (d), because the minimum wage is binding across the whole industry, firms are able to pass a higher proportion of the wage costs onto higher prices without a drastic fall in demand for output, and so the labour demand curve for an individual firm actually shifts to the right at or above the minimum wage, so that the impact on employment is much less.

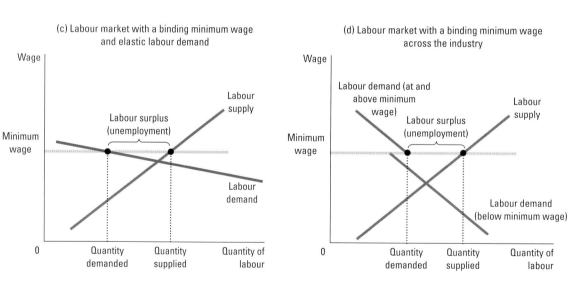

earners, for example, or young people who otherwise would have stayed in full-time education.

Advocates of minimum wage laws view the policy as one way to raise the income of the working poor. They correctly point out that workers who earn the minimum wage can afford only a meagre standard of living. They admit that it may have some adverse effects, including a possible rise in unemployment, but they believe that these effects are small and that, all things considered, a higher minimum wage makes the poor better off. In other words they argue that the value of the benefits of a minimum wage are greater than the value of the costs and so such a policy is worth putting into practice.

Opponents of the minimum wage contend that it is not the best way to combat poverty since it affects only the income of those in employment and may raise unemployment, and because not all minimum wage workers are heads of households trying to help their families escape poverty – some may be second earners or even third earners in relatively well-off households. To decide whether this argument is more powerful than the arguments of the advocates, economists will try and find ways to measure the size of the contrasting effects so that an informed decision can be made with regard to the value of the benefits versus the costs. This is often harder than it may at first appear but is a crucial part of an economist's work.

In short, the effects of the minimum wage on the labour market are complicated. It is one of those cases where there are no clear-cut answers: it all depends on what assumptions you make. At this point you may throw up your hands in despair and ask 'so what's the point of studying economics if it can't tell me one way or the other if introducing a minimum wage benefits the poor or not?' But all our brief economic analysis of the minimum wage has shown is that the issue is very complex: don't shoot the messenger for telling you so. The economist tries to shed light on this complexity so that the costs and benefits of such a policy can be better understood; this is partly why economics is so valuable and so fascinating!

Evaluating Price Controls

One of the *Ten Principles of Economics* discussed in Chapter 1 is that markets are usually a good way to organize economic activity. This principle explains why economists usually oppose price ceilings and price floors. To economists, prices are not the outcome of some haphazard process. Prices, they contend, are the result of the millions of business and consumer decisions that lie behind the supply and demand curves. Prices have the crucial job of balancing supply and demand and, thereby, coordinating economic activity. When policy makers set prices by legal decree, they obscure the signals that normally guide the allocation of society's resources.

Another one of the *Ten Principles of Economics* is that governments can sometimes improve market outcomes. Indeed, policy makers are led to control prices because they view the market's outcome as unfair. Price controls are often aimed at helping the poor. For instance, rent-control laws try to make housing affordable for everyone, and minimum wage laws try to help people escape poverty.

Yet price controls often hurt those they are trying to help. Rent control may keep rents low, but it also discourages landlords from maintaining their buildings and makes housing hard to find in the long run as we have seen. Minimum wage laws may raise the incomes of some workers, but they also cause other workers to be unemployed.

Helping those in need can be accomplished in ways other than controlling prices. For instance, the government can make housing more affordable by paying a fraction of the rent for poor families. Unlike rent control, such rent subsidies do not reduce the quantity of housing supplied and, therefore, do not lead to housing shortages.

Although these alternative policies are often better than price controls, they are not perfect. Rent and wage subsidies cost the government money and, therefore, require higher taxes. As we see in the next section, taxation has costs of its own.

Quick Quiz Define *price ceiling* and *price floor*, and give an example of each. Which leads to a shortage? Which leads to a surplus? Why?

IN THE NEWS

A Price Floor for Alcohol?

Price floors are not only relevant in the case of the labour market. Concerns about the effects of alcohol misuse on health and the economy prompted politicians in Scotland to consider using a price floor as a means of restricting consumption, as highlighted by this article.

Research on industry sales data analysed by the National Health Service in Scotland suggested that adults in the country are drinking the equivalent of 46 bottles of vodka each year. The amount of alcohol consumed by adults has stayed stable since 2005, but at a high level. The findings, published in January 2010 reported that in the year to September 2009 sales averaged 12.2 litres of pure alcohol per person over the age of 18, equivalent to 537 pints or 130 bottles of wine per head of the population. This volume of consumption was above recommended guidelines and amounted to around 25 per cent more than that consumed by individuals in England and Wales.

The report served to highlight the concern that politicians and the health community in Scotland have had over alcohol consumption for some time. The Scottish Health Secretary linked the rise in alcohol consumption with a fall in the real price of alcohol. Sales of alcoholic drinks in pubs, clubs and supermarkets had been subject to price discounting; some pubs and clubs had regular price promotions which offered 'two-for-one' drinks or happy hours. Supermarkets had been accused of selling alcohol at very low prices in order to capture sales and market share and all this had helped to make alcohol not only cheaper but more accessible.

The effects on individual health and the economy in terms of lost output because of employee absenteeism, extra policing and alcohol-related

Would a minimum price on alcohol reduce consumption?

crime and violence, not to mention the cost of treating alcohol-related health problems has spurred politicians to try to consider ways to reduce consumption. The report by the Scottish National Health service put the cost to Scotland's economy at £2.25 billion a year. Alcohol-related deaths accounted for around 1 500 lives a year and there are over 42 000 alcohol related hospital discharges every year. Cheap prices have been targeted as being 'public enemy number one' and so policy measures were focused on introducing a price floor on alcohol amongst other measures to try and cut consumption and improve education.

The price floor would seek to put a minimum price on a unit of alcohol (one unit of alcohol is 10ml (1cl) by volume, or

8g by weight, of pure alcohol) above the market price. The aim would be to exploit the law of demand and cut consumption. The Scottish government has cited evidence for the imposition of a price floor from research carried out by the University of Sheffield, published in December 2008. The research suggested that increasing the price of alcohol would lead to a fall in consumption.

The leader of the research, Dr Petra Meier of the university's School of Health and Related Research (ScHARR), said: 'This is the first study to integrate data on alcohol pricing and purchasing patterns, consumption and harm to answer the question of what would happen if government were to introduce different alcohol pricing policies. The results suggest that policies which increase the price of alcohol can bring significant health and social benefits and lead to considerable financial savings in the NHS, criminal justice system and in the workplace.'

The findings suggested that price increases would have to be implemented 'across the board' otherwise consumers would simply find substitutes of cheaper drinks or different places to buy alcohol. The main target of any price increase should be on cheaper

drinks which the study suggested tended to be bought by those whose drinking caused the most harm whilst only having a limited effect on more moderate drinkers who tended to buy more expensive drinks. In many cases drinkers are paying less than 40p per unit and there was also plenty of evidence that prices of less than 30p per unit were common. Any minimum price, therefore, would have to be above this level. In September 2010, the Scottish

government actually proposed a minimum price of 45p per unit.

The research suggested that as price levels were increased the effect on demand would escalate. At 20p per unit, demand would fall by just 0.1 per cent; at 30p consumption would fall by 0.6 per cent, at 40p demand falls by 2.6 per cent and at 50p, 60p and 70p levels, demand would fall by 6.9 per cent, 12.8 per cent and 18.6 per cent respectively.

TAXES

All governments, whether national or local, use taxes to raise revenue for public projects, such as roads, schools and national defence. Because taxes are such an important policy instrument, and because they affect our lives in many ways, the study of taxes is a topic to which we return several times throughout this book. In this section we begin our study of how taxes affect the economy.

To set the stage for our analysis, imagine that the government decides to hold a national annual ice cream festival – with a parade, fireworks and speeches by leading politicians. To raise revenue to pay for the event, it decides to place a €0.50 tax on the sale of ice cream cornets. When the plan is announced, our two lobbying groups swing into action. The National Organization of Ice Cream Producers claims that its members are struggling to survive in a competitive market, and it argues that *buyers* of ice cream should have to pay the tax. The National Association of Ice Cream Eaters claims that consumers of ice cream are having trouble making ends meet, and it argues that *sellers* of ice cream should pay the tax. The prime minister, hoping to reach a compromise, suggests that half the tax be paid by the buyers and half be paid by the sellers.

To alalyse these proposals, we need to address a simple but subtle question: when the government levies a tax on a good, who bears the burden of the tax – in other words, who actually pays the tax? The people buying the good? The people selling the good? Or, if buyers and sellers share the tax burden, what determines how the burden is divided? Can the government simply legislate the division of the burden, as our prime minister is suggesting, or is the division determined by more fundamental forces in the economy? Economists use the term **tax incidence** to refer to the distribution of a tax burden. As we will see, some surprising lessons about tax incidence arise just by applying the tools of supply and demand.

tax incidence
the manner in which the burden of a tax is shared among participants in a market

How Taxes on Sellers Affect Market Outcomes

Consider a tax levied on sellers of a good. Suppose the government imposes a tax on sellers of ice cream cornets of €0.50 for each cornet they sell. What are the effects of this tax? Again, we apply our three steps.

Step One In this case, the immediate impact of the tax is on the sellers of ice cream. The quantity of ice cream demanded at any given price is the same; thus, the demand curve does not change. By contrast, the tax on sellers makes the ice cream business less profitable at any given price, so it shifts the supply curve.

FIGURE 6.5

A Tax on Sellers

When a tax of €0.50 is levied on sellers, the supply curve shifts up by €0.50 from S₁ to S₂. The equilibrium quantity falls from 100 to 90 cornets. The price that buyers pay rises from €3.00 to €3.30. The price that sellers receive (after paying the tax) falls from €3.00 to €2.80. Even though the tax is levied on sellers, buyers and sellers share the burden of the tax.

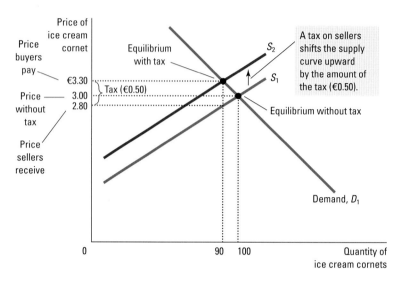

Step Two   Because the tax on sellers raises the cost of producing and selling ice cream, it reduces the quantity supplied at every price. The supply curve shifts to the left (or, equivalently, upward).

Once again, we can be precise about the magnitude of the shift. For any market price of ice cream, the effective price to sellers – the amount they get to keep after paying the tax – is €0.50 lower. For example, if the market price of a cornet happened to be €2.00, the effective price received by sellers would be €1.50. Whatever the market price, sellers will supply a quantity of ice cream as if the price were €0.50 lower than it is. Put differently, to induce sellers to supply any given quantity, the market price must now be €0.50 higher to compensate for the effect of the tax. Thus, as shown in Figure 6.5, the supply curve shifts *upward* from S₁ to S₂ by exactly the size of the tax (€0.50).

Step Three   Having determined how the supply curve shifts, we can now compare the initial and the new equilibrium. The figure shows that the equilibrium price of ice cream rises from €3.00 to €3.30, and the equilibrium quantity falls from 100 to 90 cornets. Once again, the tax reduces the size of the ice cream market. And once again, buyers and sellers share the burden of the tax. Because the market price rises, buyers pay €0.30 more for each cornet of ice cream than they did before the tax was enacted. Sellers receive a higher price than they did without the tax, but the effective price (after paying the tax) falls from €3.00 to €2.80.

Implications   A tax on sellers places a wedge between the price that buyers pay and the price that sellers receive. The wedge between the buyers' price and the sellers' price is the same, and would be the same regardless of whether the tax is levied on buyers or sellers. In reality most governments levy taxes on sellers rather than on buyers, however. The wedge shifts the relative position of the supply and demand curves. In the new equilibrium, buyers and sellers share the burden of the tax.

CASE STUDY

Can the Government Distribute the Burden of a Payroll Tax?

If you have ever received a pay cheque, you probably noticed that taxes were deducted from the amount you earned. In the United Kingdom, one of these taxes is called National Insurance Contributions (NICs). In theory, the UK government uses the revenue from NICs to pay for social security and state pensions (in practice, the money goes into the government coffers without being earmarked for any particular use). NICs are an example of a *payroll tax*, which is a tax on the wages that firms pay their workers. Other European countries have a similar tax with France, Sweden and Slovenia all having a payroll tax.

Who do you think bears the burden of this payroll tax – firms or workers? In fact, if you read official UK government documents, it seems that the burden is split fairly clearly: in 2010–11, for example, average-paid workers paid 11 per cent of their income above a basic level in NICs, while the workers' employer paid 12.8 per cent.

Our analysis of tax incidence, however, shows that politicians cannot so easily dictate the distribution of a tax burden. To illustrate, we can alalyse a payroll tax as merely a tax on a good, where the good is labour and the price is the wage. The key feature of the payroll tax is that it places a wedge between the wage that firms pay and the wage that workers receive. Figure 6.6 shows

FIGURE 6.6

A Payroll Tax

A payroll tax places a wedge between the wage that workers receive and the wage that firms pay. Comparing wages with and without the tax, you can see that workers and firms share the tax burden. This division of the tax burden between workers and firms does not depend on whether the government levies the tax on workers, levies the tax on firms or divides the tax equally between the two groups.

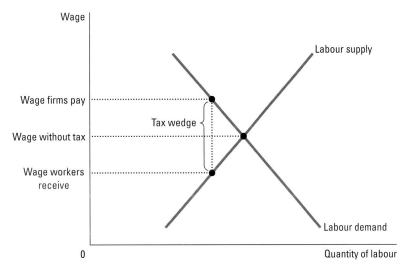

the outcome. When a payroll tax is enacted, the wage received by workers falls, and the wage paid by firms rises. In the end, workers and firms share the burden of the tax, much as the legislation requires. Yet this division of the tax burden between workers and firms has nothing to do with the legislated division. Moreover, the same outcome would prevail if the law levied the entire tax on workers or if it levied the entire tax on firms.

This example shows that the most basic lesson of tax incidence is often overlooked in public debate. Politicians can decide whether a tax comes from the buyer's pocket or from the seller's, but they cannot legislate the true burden of a tax. Rather, tax incidence depends on the forces of supply and demand.

Elasticity and Tax Incidence

When a good is taxed, buyers and sellers of the good share the burden of the tax. But how exactly is the tax burden divided? Only rarely will it be shared equally. To see how the burden is divided, consider the impact of taxation in the two markets in Figure 6.7. In both cases, the figure shows the initial demand curve, the initial supply curve, and a tax that drives a wedge between the amount paid by buyers and the amount received by sellers. (Not drawn in either panel of the figure is the new supply or demand curve. Which curve shifts depends on whether the tax is levied on buyers or sellers. As we have seen, this is irrelevant for the incidence of the tax.) The difference in the two panels is the relative elasticity of supply and demand.

Panel (a) of Figure 6.7 shows a tax in a market with very elastic supply and relatively inelastic demand. That is, sellers are very responsive to changes in the price of the good (so the supply curve is relatively flat), whereas buyers are not very responsive (so the demand curve is relatively steep). When a tax is imposed on a market with these elasticities, the price received by sellers does not fall much, so sellers bear only a small burden. By contrast, the price paid by buyers rises substantially, indicating that buyers bear most of the burden of the tax. Our analysis of elasticity in Chapter 5 should make this something that is not at all surprising. If the price elasticity of demand is low (a steep curve) then demand will fall proportionately less in response to a rise in price – buyers are not very price sensitive. The seller can shift the burden of the tax onto the buyer safe in the knowledge that demand will only fall by a relatively small amount.

Panel (b) of Figure 6.7 shows a tax in a market with relatively inelastic supply and very elastic demand. In this case, sellers are not very responsive to changes in the price (so the supply curve is steeper), while buyers are very responsive (so the demand curve is flatter). The figure shows that when a tax is imposed, the price paid by buyers does not rise much, while the price received by sellers falls substantially. Thus, sellers bear most of the burden of the tax. In this case, sellers know that if they try to pass on the tax to buyers that demand will fall by a relatively large amount.

The two panels of Figure 6.7 show a general lesson about how the burden of a tax is divided: a tax burden falls more heavily on the side of the market that is less elastic. Why is this true? In essence, the elasticity measures the willingness of buyers or sellers to leave the market when conditions become unfavourable. A small elasticity of demand means that buyers do not have good alternatives to consuming this particular good. A small elasticity of supply means that sellers do not have good alternatives to producing this particular good. When the good is taxed, the side of the market with fewer good alternatives cannot easily leave the market and must, therefore, bear more of the burden of the tax.

We can apply this logic to the payroll tax discussed in the previous case study. Most labour economists believe that the supply of labour is much less elastic than the demand. This means that workers, rather than firms, bear most of the burden of any payroll tax, whatever the official split.

FIGURE 6.7

How the Burden of a Tax Is Divided

In panel (a), the supply curve is elastic and the demand curve is inelastic. In this case, the price received by sellers falls only slightly, while the price paid by buyers rises substantially. Thus, buyers bear most of the burden of the tax. In panel (b), the supply curve is inelastic and the demand curve is elastic. In this case, the price received by sellers falls substantially, while the price paid by buyers rises only slightly. Thus, sellers bear most of the burden of the tax.

(a) Elastic supply, inelastic demand

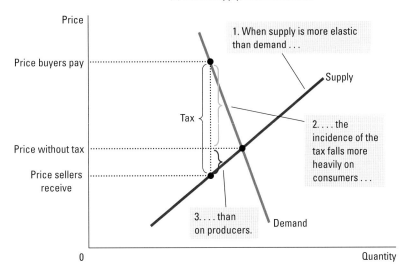

(b) Inelastic supply, elastic demand

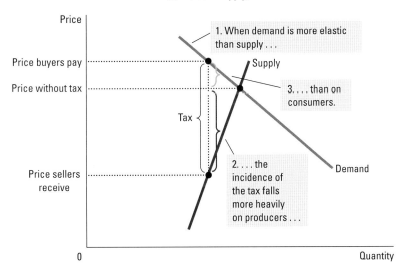

Quick Quiz In a supply and demand diagram, show how a tax on car buyers of €1 000 per car affects the quantity of cars sold and the price of cars. In another diagram, show how a tax on car sellers of €1 000 per car affects the quantity of cars sold and the price of cars. In both of your diagrams, show the change in the price paid by car buyers and the change in price received by car sellers.

How Subsidies Affect Market Outcomes

We mentioned earlier in the chapter that subsidies were the opposite of a tax. Subsidies are levied when governments want to encourage the consumption of a 'good' which they deem is currently underproduced. Subsidies are generally given to sellers and have the effect of reducing the cost of production as opposed to a tax which increases the cost of production. Subsidies exist in a variety of different areas including education, transport, agriculture, regional development, housing and employment.

Subsidies in education help to make the cost of attending college or higher education lower than it would otherwise be; in the UK some students receive an educational maintenance allowance (EMA) which is designed to help them with their travel and subsistence and encourages them to stay on for post-16 education. Most European countries provide subsidies for transport systems and the common agricultural policy oversees subsidies to farmers. In Switzerland some €2.5 billion is spent on subsidies for rail transport, in Germany the figure is nearer to €9 billion whilst in the UK subsidies account for around €3 billion and in France €6.8 billion.

Figure 6.8 shows how a subsidy works using the rail system as an example. In the absence of a subsidy the equilibrium number of journeys bought and sold is Q_e and the equilibrium train ticket for each journey is price P_e.

Step One   If the government gives a subsidy of €20 per journey to train operators, it is the supply curve for journeys which is affected; the demand curve is not affected because the number of train journeys demanded at each price stays the same. The subsidy to train operators reduces the cost of providing a train journey and so the supply curve will shift.

Step Two   Because the subsidy reduces the cost to the train operators, the supply curve shifts to the right by the amount of the subsidy. If the cost of providing

FIGURE 6.8

A Subsidy on Rail Transport

When a subsidy of €20 per journey is given to sellers, the supply curve shifts to the right by €20 from S_1 to S_2. The equilibrium quantity rises from Q_e to Q_1 journeys per year. The price that buyers pay for a journey falls from €75.00 to €60. The subsidy results in lower prices for passengers and an increased number of journeys available. Even though the subsidy is given to sellers, buyers and sellers share the benefits of the subsidy.

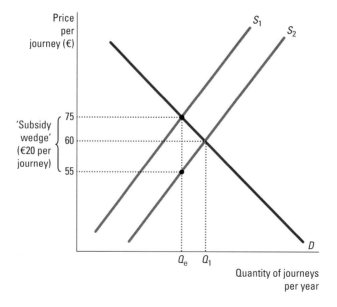

a train journey was an average of €75 and the subsidy was €20 the supply curve would shift so that train operators would now supply train journeys at an effective cost of €20 below the previous cost. They would now be willing to supply more train journeys at every price.

Step Three   Comparing the initial and the new equilibrium we can see that the equilibrium price of each train journey is now lower at €60 and the equilibrium number of journeys travelled increases to Q_1. Passengers and train operators both benefit from the subsidy as passengers can obtain train tickets at a lower price than before the subsidy and have more journeys available and sellers receive more revenue than they did before the subsidy allowing them the potential to invest in the service they provide. The precise division of the benefits between buyers and sellers will depend on the relative elasticities of demand and supply.

Implications   There is a considerable debate surrounding the value of subsidies. We have seen from the example how price and quantity can be affected following the imposition of a subsidy. In the case of transport, it may have the effect of altering the incentives for people to travel on the train rather than on the roads and so have the benefit of reducing congestion on the roads as well as reducing possible pollution that is associated with road use. In the recent recession some countries introduced subsidies to encourage consumers to trade in their old cars for new ones which helped to boost the European motor industry at a time when it was struggling with a downturn in demand. There are also costs associated with subsidies; for one thing someone has to finance the subsidy and it is often the taxpayer. Subsidies may also encourage firms to overproduce which has a wider effect on the market. Subsidies on commodities such as cotton, bananas and sugar distort the workings of the market and change global comparative advantage. Overproduction leads to excess supply on world markets and drives down prices as well as diverting trade to rich countries who can support producers through subsidies at the expense of poor countries whose producers cannot compete because prices are lower than the free market price. Chapter 7 will provide a further example of how subsidies can affect the efficiency of market outcomes.

CONCLUSION

The economy is governed by two kinds of laws: the laws of supply and demand and the laws enacted by governments. In this chapter we have begun to see how these laws interact. Price controls, taxes and subsidies are common in various markets in the economy, and their effects are frequently debated in the press and among policy makers. Even a little bit of economic knowledge can go a long way towards understanding and evaluating these policies.

In subsequent chapters we shall alalyse many government policies in greater detail. We shall examine the effects of taxation more fully, and we shall consider a broader range of policies than we considered here. Yet the basic lessons of this chapter will not change: when alalysing government policies, supply and demand are the first and most useful tools of analysis.

SUMMARY

- A price ceiling is a legal maximum on the price of a good or service. An example is rent control. If the price ceiling is below the equilibrium price, the quantity demanded exceeds the quantity supplied. Because of the resulting shortage, sellers must in some way ration the good or service among buyers.

- A price floor is a legal minimum on the price of a good or service. An example is the minimum wage. If the price floor is above the equilibrium price, the quantity supplied exceeds the quantity demanded. Because of the resulting surplus, buyers' demands for the good or service must in some way be rationed among sellers.

• When the government levies a tax on a good, the equilibrium quantity of the good falls. That is, a tax on a market shrinks the size of the market.

• A tax on a good places a wedge between the price paid by buyers and the price received by sellers. When the market moves to the new equilibrium, buyers pay more for the good and sellers receive less for it. In this sense,

buyers and sellers share the tax burden. The incidence of a tax (that is, the division of the tax burden) does not depend on whether the tax is levied on buyers or sellers.

• A subsidy given to sellers lowers the cost of production and encourages firms to expand output. Buyers benefit from lower prices.

• The incidence of a tax or subsidy depends on the price elasticities of supply and demand. The burden tends to fall on the side of the market that is less elastic because that side of the market can respond less/more easily to the tax/subsidy by changing the quantity bought or sold.

KEY CONCEPTS

subsidy, p. 118
price ceiling, p. 118

price floor, p. 118
tax incidence, p. 127

QUESTIONS FOR REVIEW

1. Give an example of a price ceiling and an example of a price floor.

2. Which causes a shortage of a good – a price ceiling or a price floor? Which causes a surplus?

3. What mechanisms allocate resources when the price of a good is not allowed to bring supply and demand into equilibrium?

4. Explain why economists usually oppose rent controls.

5. How does a tax imposed on a good with a high price elasticity of demand affect the market equilibrium? Who bears most of the burden of the tax in this instance?

6. How does a subsidy on a good affect the price paid by buyers, the price received by sellers and the quantity bought and sold?

7. What determines how the burden of a tax or a subsidy is divided between buyers and sellers? Why?

PROBLEMS AND APPLICATIONS

1. Lovers of classical music persuade the government to impose a price ceiling of €40 per ticket at classical music concerts. Does this policy get more or fewer people to attend?

2. The government has decided that the free market price of cheese is too low.

    a. Suppose the government imposes a binding price floor in the cheese market. Use a supply and demand diagram to show the effect of this policy on the price

    of cheese and the quantity of cheese sold. Is there a shortage or surplus of cheese?

    b. Farmers complain that the price floor has reduced their total revenue. Is this possible? Explain.

    c. In response to farmers' complaints, the government agrees to purchase all of the surplus cheese at the price floor. Compared to the basic price floor, who benefits from this new policy? Who loses?

3. A recent study found that the demand and supply schedules for frisbees are as follows:

Price per frisbee	Quantity demanded	Quantity supplied
€11	1 million frisbees	15 million frisbees
10	2	12
9	4	9
8	6	6
7	8	3
6	10	1

What are the equilibrium price and quantity of frisbees?

a. Frisbee manufacturers persuade the government that frisbee production improves scientists' understanding of aerodynamics and thus is important for national security. The government decides to impose a price floor €2 above the equilibrium price. What is the new market price? How many frisbees are sold?

b. Irate university students march on the government and demand a reduction in the price of frisbees. The government decides to repeal the price floor and impose a price ceiling €1 below the former price floor. What is the new market price? How many frisbees are sold?

4. Suppose that in the absence of any tax whatsoever, the equilibrium price of beer is €1.50 per litre. Now suppose that the government requires beer drinkers to pay a total tax (sales tax plus alcohol duty) of €0.50 on every litre of beer purchased.

a. Draw a supply and demand diagram of the market for beer without the tax. Show the price paid by consumers, the price received by producers and the quantity of beer sold. What is the difference between the price paid by consumers and the price received by producers?

b. Now draw a supply and demand diagram for the beer market with the tax. Show the price paid by consumers, the price received by producers and the quantity of beer sold. What is the difference between the price paid by consumers and the price received by producers? Has the quantity of beer sold increased or decreased?

5. The employment minister wants to raise tax revenue and at the same time make workers better off. A civil servant suggests raising the payroll tax paid by firms and using part of the extra revenue to reduce the payroll tax paid by workers. Would this accomplish the minister's goal?

6. If the government places a €500 tax on luxury cars, will the price paid by consumers rise by more than €500, less than €500 or exactly €500. Explain.

7. The government decides to reduce air pollution by reducing the use of petrol. It imposes €0.50 tax for each litre of petrol sold.

a. Should it impose this tax on petrol companies or motorists? Explain carefully, using a supply and demand diagram.

b. If the demand for petrol were more elastic, would this tax be more effective or less effective in reducing the quantity of petrol consumed? Explain with both words and a diagram.

c. Are consumers of petrol helped or hurt by this tax? Why?

d. Are workers in the oil industry helped or hurt by this tax? Why?

8. A case study in this chapter discusses the minimum wage law.

a. Suppose the minimum wage is above the equilibrium wage in the market for unskilled labour. Using a supply and demand diagram of the market for unskilled labour, show the market wage, the number of workers who are employed and the number of workers who are unemployed. Also show the total wage payments to unskilled workers.

b. Now suppose the minister for employment proposes an increase in the minimum wage. What effect would this increase have on employment? Does the change in employment depend on the elasticity of demand, the elasticity of supply, both elasticities, or neither?

c. What effect would this increase in the minimum wage have on unemployment? Does the change in unemployment depend on the elasticity of demand, the elasticity of supply, both elasticities, or neither?

d. If the demand for unskilled labour were inelastic, would the proposed increase in the minimum wage raise or lower total wage payments to unskilled workers? Would your answer change if the demand for unskilled labour were elastic?

9. A subsidy is the opposite of a tax. With a €0.50 tax on the buyers of ice cream cornets, the government collects €0.50 for each cornet purchased; with a €0.50 subsidy for the buyers of ice cream cornets, the government pays buyers €0.50 for each cornet purchased.

a. Show the effect of a €0.50 per cornet subsidy on the demand curve for ice cream cornets, the effective price paid by consumers, the effective price received by sellers and the quantity of cornets sold.

b. Do consumers gain or lose from this policy? Do producers gain or lose? Does the government gain or lose?

For further resources, visit
www.cengage.com/mankiw_taylor2

3

SUPPLY AND DEMAND II: MARKETS AND WELFARE

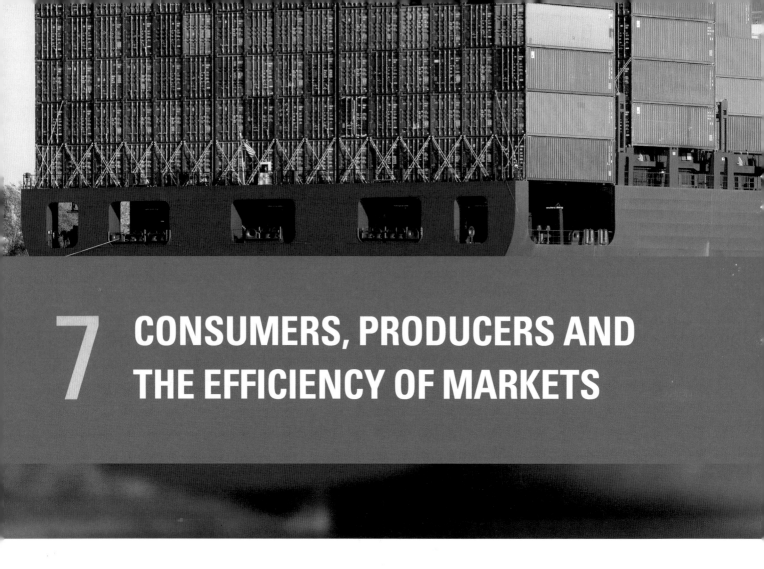

7 CONSUMERS, PRODUCERS AND THE EFFICIENCY OF MARKETS

onsumers celebrating Christian festivals like Christmas go to the butcher's shop or the supermarket to buy their turkeys for dinner, and may be disappointed that the price of turkey is as high as it is. At the same time, when farmers bring to market the turkeys they have reared, they wish the price of turkey was even higher. These views are not surprising: buyers always want to pay less and sellers always want to get paid more. But is there a 'right price' for turkey from the standpoint of society as a whole?

In previous chapters we saw how, in market economies, the forces of supply and demand determine the prices of goods and services and the quantities sold. So far, however, we have described the way markets allocate scarce resources without directly addressing the question of whether these market allocations are desirable. In other words, our analysis has been *positive* (what is) rather than *normative* (what should be). We know that the price of turkey adjusts to ensure that the quantity of turkey supplied equals the quantity of turkey demanded. But, at this equilibrium, is the quantity of turkey produced and consumed too small, too large or just right?

In this chapter we take up the topic of **welfare economics**, the study of how the allocation of resources affects economic **well-being**. Economists use the term well-being a good deal and have taken steps to define the term. A UK Treasury Economic Working Paper published in 2008[1] highlighted two main definitions of

welfare economics
the study of how the allocation of resources affects economic well-being

well-being
happiness or satisfaction with life as reported by individuals

---

[1]Lepper, L. & McAndrew, S. (2008) *Developments in the Economics of Well-being*. Treasury Working Paper number 4. Available at http://www.hm-treasury.gov.uk/d/workingpager4_031108.pdf accessed 21 January 2010.

economic well-being – subjective and objective well-being. Subjective well-being refers to the way in which people evaluate their own happiness. This includes how they feel about work, leisure and their response to the events which occur in their life. Objective well-being refers to measures of the quality of life and uses indicators developed by researchers such as educational attainment, measures of the standard of living, life expectancy and so on. Welfare economics uses some of the microeconomic techniques we have already looked at to estimate **allocative efficiency** – a measure of the utility (satisfaction) derived from the allocation of resources. We have seen how buyers place a value on consumption (which will be discussed in more detail later in the book). Allocative efficiency occurs when the value of the output that firms produce (the benefits to sellers) match the value placed on that output by consumers (the benefit) to buyers.

allocative efficiency
a resource allocation where the value of the output by sellers matches the value placed on that output by buyers

We begin by examining the benefits that buyers and sellers receive from taking part in a market. We then examine how society can make these benefits as large as possible. This analysis leads to a profound conclusion: the equilibrium of supply and demand in a market maximizes the total benefits received by buyers and sellers.

As you may recall from Chapter 1, one of the *Ten Principles of Economics* is that markets are usually a good way to organize economic activity. The study of welfare economics explains this principle more fully. It also answers our question about the right price of turkey: the price that balances the supply and demand for turkey is, in a particular sense, the best one because it maximizes the total welfare of turkey consumers and turkey producers.

CONSUMER SURPLUS

We begin our study of welfare economics by looking at the benefits buyers receive from participating in a market.

Willingness to Pay

Imagine that you own an extremely rare signed copy of Radiohead's album 'The Bends'. Because you are not a Radiohead fan, you decide to sell it. One way to do so is to hold an auction.

Four Radiohead fans show up for your auction: Liam, Paul, Noel and Tony. Each of them would like to own the album, but there is a limit to the amount that each is willing to pay for it. Table 7.1 shows the maximum price that each of the four possible buyers would pay. Each buyer's maximum is called his **willingness to pay**, and it measures how much that buyer values the good. Each buyer would be eager to buy the album at a price less than his willingness to pay, would refuse to buy the album at a price more than his willingness to pay, and would be indifferent about buying the album at a price exactly equal to his willingness to pay.

willingness to pay
the maximum amount that a buyer will pay for a good

TABLE 7.1

Four Possible Buyers' Willingness to Pay

Buyer	Willingness to pay
Liam	€100
Paul	80
Noel	70
Tony	50

To sell your album, you begin the bidding at a low price, say €10. Because all four buyers are willing to pay much more, the price rises quickly. The bidding stops when Liam bids €80 (or slightly more). At this point, Paul, Noel and Tony have dropped out of the bidding because they are unwilling to bid any more than €80. Liam pays you €80 and gets the album. Note that the album has gone to the buyer who values the album most highly.

What benefit does Liam receive from buying the Radiohead album? In a sense, Liam has found a real bargain: he is willing to pay €100 for the album but pays only €80 for it. We say that Liam receives *consumer surplus* of €20. **Consumer surplus** is the amount a buyer is willing to pay for a good minus the amount the buyer actually pays for it. We refer to 'getting a bargain' regularly in everyday language. In economics, a bargain means paying much less for something than we expected or anticipated and as a result we get a greater degree of consumer surplus than we expected.

Consumer surplus measures the benefit to buyers of participating in a market. In this example, Liam receives a €20 benefit from participating in the auction because he pays only €80 for a good he values at €100. Paul, Noel and Tony get no consumer surplus from participating in the auction because they left without the album and without paying anything.

Now consider a somewhat different example. Suppose that you had two identical Radiohead albums to sell. Again, you auction them off to the four possible buyers. To keep things simple, we assume that both albums are to be sold for the same price and that no buyer is interested in buying more than one album. Therefore, the price rises until two buyers are left.

In this case, the bidding stops when Liam and Paul bid €70 (or slightly higher). At this price, Liam and Paul are each happy to buy an album and Noel and Tony are not willing to bid any higher. Liam and Paul each receive consumer surplus equal to his willingness to pay minus the price. Liam's consumer surplus is €30 and Paul's is €10. Liam's consumer surplus is higher now than it was previously, because he gets the same album but pays less for it. The total consumer surplus in the market is €40.

Using the Demand Curve to Measure Consumer Surplus

Consumer surplus is closely related to the demand curve for a product. To see how they are related, let's continue our example and consider the demand curve for this rare Radiohead album.

We begin by using the willingness to pay of the four possible buyers to find the demand schedule for the album. The table in Figure 7.1 shows the demand schedule that corresponds to Table 7.1. If the price is above €100, the quantity demanded in the market is 0, because no buyer is willing to pay that much. If the price is between €80 and €100, the quantity demanded is 1, because only Liam is willing to pay such a high price. If the price is between €70 and €80, the quantity demanded is 2, because both Liam and Paul are willing to pay the price. We can continue this analysis for other prices as well. In this way, the demand schedule is derived from the willingness to pay of the four possible buyers.

The graph in Figure 7.1 shows the demand curve that corresponds to this demand schedule. Note the relationship between the height of the demand curve and the buyers' willingness to pay. At any quantity, the price given by the demand curve shows the willingness to pay of the *marginal buyer*, the buyer who would leave the market first if the price were any higher. At a quantity of 4 albums, for instance, the demand curve has a height of €50, the price that Tony (the marginal buyer) is willing to pay for an album. At a quantity of 3 albums, the demand curve has a height of €70, the price that Noel (who is now the marginal buyer) is willing to pay.

FIGURE 7.1

The Demand Schedule and the Demand Curve

The table shows the demand schedule for the buyers in Table 7.1. The graph shows the corresponding demand curve. Note that the height of the demand curve reflects buyers' willingness to pay.

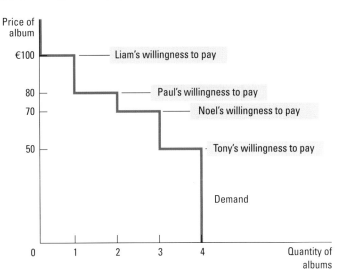

Price	Buyers	Quantity demanded
More than €100	None	0
€80 to €100	Liam	1
€70 to €80	Liam, Paul	2
€50 to €70	Liam, Paul, Noel	3
€50 or less	Liam, Paul, Noel, Tony	4

Because the demand curve reflects buyers' willingness to pay, we can also use it to measure consumer surplus. Figure 7.2 uses the demand curve to compute consumer surplus in our example. In panel (a), the price is €80 (or slightly above) and the quantity demanded is 1. Note that the area above the price and below the demand curve equals €20. This amount is exactly the consumer surplus we computed earlier when only 1 album is sold.

Panel (b) of Figure 7.2 shows consumer surplus when the price is €70 (or slightly above). In this case, the area above the price and below the demand curve equals the total area of the two rectangles: Liam's consumer surplus at this price is €30 and Paul's is €10. This area equals a total of €40. Once again, this amount is the consumer surplus we computed earlier.

The lesson from this example holds for all demand curves: the area below the demand curve and above the price measures the consumer surplus in a market. The reason is that the height of the demand curve measures the value buyers place on the good, as measured by their willingness to pay for it. The difference between this willingness to pay and the market price is each buyer's consumer surplus. Thus, the total area below the demand curve and above the price is the sum of the consumer surplus of all buyers in the market for a good or service.

How a Lower Price Raises Consumer Surplus

Because buyers always want to pay less for the goods they buy, a lower price makes buyers of a good better off. But how much does buyers' well-being rise in response to a lower price? We can use the concept of consumer surplus to answer this question precisely.

FIGURE 7.2

Measuring Consumer Surplus with the Demand Curve

In panel (a) the price of the good is €80 and the consumer surplus is €20. In panel (b) the price of the good is €70 and the consumer surplus is €40.

(a) Price = €80

(b) Price = €70

Figure 7.3 shows a typical downward sloping demand curve. Although this demand curve appears somewhat different in shape from the step-like demand curves in our previous two figures, the ideas we have just developed apply nevertheless: consumer surplus is the area above the price and below the demand curve. In panel (a), consumer surplus at a price of P_1 is the area of triangle ABC.

Now suppose that the price falls from P_1 to P_2, as shown in panel (b). The consumer surplus now equals area ADF. The increase in consumer surplus attributable to the lower price is the area BCFD.

This increase in consumer surplus is composed of two parts. First, those buyers who were already buying Q_1 of the good at the higher price P_1 are better off because they now pay less. The increase in consumer surplus of existing buyers is the reduction in the amount they pay; it equals the area of the rectangle BCED. Secondly, some new buyers enter the market because they are now willing to buy the good at the lower price. As a result, the quantity demanded in the market increases from Q_1 to Q_2. The consumer surplus these newcomers receive is the area of the triangle CEF.

What Does Consumer Surplus Measure?

Our goal in developing the concept of consumer surplus is to make normative judgements about the desirability of market outcomes. Now that you have seen what consumer surplus is, let's consider whether it is a good measure of economic well-being.

Imagine that you are a policy maker trying to design a good economic system. Would you care about the amount of consumer surplus? Consumer surplus, the amount that buyers are willing to pay for a good minus the amount they actually pay for it, measures the benefit that buyers receive from a good *as the buyers*

FIGURE 7.3

How the Price Affects Consumer Surplus

In panel (a) the price is P_1*, the quantity demanded is* Q_1 *and consumer surplus equals the area of the triangle* ABC. *When the price falls from* P_1 *to* P_2*, as in panel (b), the quantity demanded rises from* Q_1 *to* Q_2*, and the consumer surplus rises to the area of the triangle* ADF. *The increase in consumer surplus (area* BCFD*) occurs in part because existing consumers now pay less (area* BCED*) and in part because new consumers enter the market at the lower price (area* CEF*).*

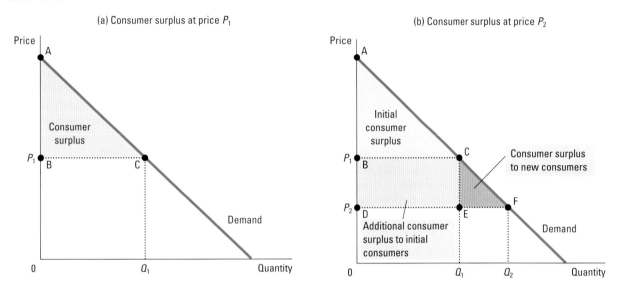

themselves perceive it. Thus, consumer surplus is a good measure of economic well-being if policy makers want to respect the preferences of buyers.

In some circumstances, policy makers might choose not to care about consumer surplus because they do not respect the preferences that drive buyer behaviour. For example, drug addicts are willing to pay a high price for heroin. Yet we would not say that addicts get a large benefit from being able to buy heroin at a low price (even though addicts might say they do). From the standpoint of society, willingness to pay in this instance is not a good measure of the buyers' benefit, and consumer surplus is not a good measure of economic well-being, because addicts are not looking after their own best interests.

In most markets, however, consumer surplus does reflect economic well-being. Economists normally presume that buyers are rational when they make decisions and that their preferences should be respected. In this case, consumers are the best judges of how much benefit they receive from the goods they buy.

Quick Quiz Draw a demand curve for turkey. In your diagram, show a price of turkey and the consumer surplus that results from that price. Explain in words what this consumer surplus measures.

PRODUCER SURPLUS

We now turn to the other side of the market and consider the benefits sellers receive from participating in a market. As you will see, our analysis of sellers' welfare is similar to our analysis of buyers' welfare.

TABLE 7.2

The Costs of Four Possible Sellers

Seller	Cost
Millie	€900
Julie	800
Georgia	600
Nana	500

Cost and the Willingness to Sell

Imagine now that you own a house and you need to get it painted externally. You turn to four sellers of house painting services: Millie, Georgia, Julie and Nana. Each painter is willing to do the work for you if the price is right. You decide to take bids from the four painters and auction off the job to the painter who will do the work for the lowest price.

cost
the value of everything a seller must give up to produce a good

Each painter is willing to take the job if the price she would receive exceeds her **cost** of doing the work. Here the term cost should be interpreted as the painter's opportunity cost: it includes the painter's out-of-pocket expenses (for paint, brushes and so on) as well as the value that the painter places on her own time. Table 7.2 shows each painter's cost. Because a painter's cost is the lowest price she would accept for her work, cost is a measure of her willingness to sell her services. Each painter would be eager to sell her services at a price greater than her cost, would refuse to sell her services at a price less than her cost, and would be indifferent about selling her services at a price exactly equal to her cost.

When you take bids from the painters, the price might start off high, but it quickly falls as the painters compete for the job. Once Nana has bid slightly less than €600 (€599.99), she is the sole remaining bidder. Nana is happy to do the job for this price, because her cost is only €500. Millie, Georgia and Julie are unwilling to do the job for less than €600. Note that the job goes to the painter who can do the work at the lowest cost.

producer surplus
the amount a seller is paid for a good minus the seller's cost

What benefit does Nana receive from getting the job? Because she is willing to do the work for €500 but gets €599.99 for doing it, we say that she receives *producer surplus* of €99.99. **Producer surplus** is the amount a seller is paid minus the cost of production. Producer surplus measures the benefit to sellers of participating in a market.

Now consider a somewhat different example. Suppose that you have two houses that need painting. Again, you auction off the jobs to the four painters. To keep things simple, let's assume that no painter is able to paint both houses and that you will pay the same amount to paint each house. Therefore, the price falls until two painters are left.

In this case, the bidding stops when Georgia and Nana each offer to do the job for a price slightly less than €800 (€799.99). At this price, Georgia and Nana are willing to do the work, and Millie and Julie are not willing to bid a lower price. At a price of €799.99, Nana receives producer surplus of €299.99, and Georgia receives producer surplus of €199.99. The total producer surplus in the market is €499.98.

Using the Supply Curve to Measure Producer Surplus

Just as consumer surplus is closely related to the demand curve, producer surplus is closely related to the supply curve. To see how, let's continue our example.

FIGURE 7.4

The Supply Schedule and the Supply Curve

The table shows the supply schedule for the sellers in Table 7.2. The graph shows the corresponding supply curve. Note that the height of the supply curve reflects sellers' costs.

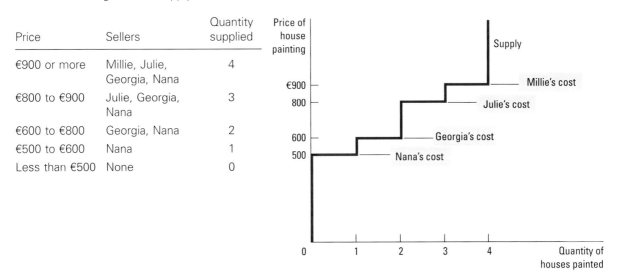

Price	Sellers	Quantity supplied
€900 or more	Millie, Julie, Georgia, Nana	4
€800 to €900	Julie, Georgia, Nana	3
€600 to €800	Georgia, Nana	2
€500 to €600	Nana	1
Less than €500	None	0

We begin by using the costs of the four painters to find the supply schedule for painting services. The table in Figure 7.4 shows the supply schedule that corresponds to the costs in Table 7.2. If the price is below €500, none of the four painters is willing to do the job, so the quantity supplied is zero. If the price is between €500 and €600, only Nana is willing to do the job, so the quantity supplied is 1. If the price is between €600 and €800, Nana and Georgia are willing to do the job, so the quantity supplied is 2, and so on. Thus, the supply schedule is derived from the costs of the four painters.

The graph in Figure 7.4 shows the supply curve that corresponds to this supply schedule. Note that the height of the supply curve is related to the sellers' costs. At any quantity, the price given by the supply curve shows the cost of the *marginal seller*, the seller who would leave the market first if the price were any lower. At a quantity of 4 houses, for instance, the supply curve has a height of €900, the cost that Millie (the marginal seller) incurs to provide her painting services. At a quantity of 3 houses, the supply curve has a height of €800, the cost that Julie (who is now the marginal seller) incurs.

Because the supply curve reflects sellers' costs, we can use it to measure producer surplus. Figure 7.5 uses the supply curve to compute producer surplus in our example. In panel (a) we assume that the price is €600. In this case, the quantity supplied is 1. Note that the area below the price and above the supply curve equals €99.99. This amount is exactly the producer surplus we computed earlier for Nana.

Panel (b) of Figure 7.5 shows producer surplus at a price of €800. In this case, the area below the price and above the supply curve equals the total area of the two rectangles. This area equals €499.99, the producer surplus we computed earlier for Georgia and Nana when two houses needed painting.

The lesson from this example applies to all supply curves: the area below the price and above the supply curve measures the producer surplus in a market.

FIGURE 7.5

Measuring Producer Surplus with the Supply Curve

In panel (a) the price of the good is €600 and the producer surplus is €99.99. In panel (b) the price of the good is €800 and the producer surplus is €499.99.

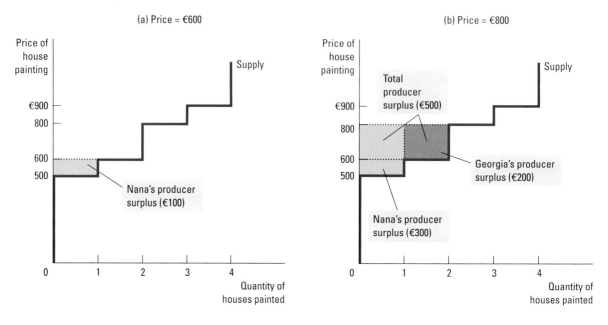

The logic is straightforward: the height of the supply curve measures sellers' costs, and the difference between the price and the cost of production is each seller's producer surplus. Thus, the total area is the sum of the producer surplus of all sellers.

How a Higher Price Raises Producer Surplus

You will not be surprised to hear that sellers always want to receive a higher price for the goods they sell. But how much does sellers' well-being rise in response to a higher price? The concept of producer surplus offers a precise answer to this question.

Figure 7.6 shows a typical upward sloping supply curve. Even though this supply curve differs in shape from the step-like supply curves in the previous figure, we measure producer surplus in the same way: producer surplus is the area below the price and above the supply curve. In panel (a), the price is P_1 and producer surplus is the area of triangle ABC.

Panel (b) shows what happens when the price rises from P_1 to P_2. Producer surplus now equals area ADF. This increase in producer surplus has two parts. First, those sellers who were already selling Q_1 of the good at the lower price P_1 are better off because they now get more for what they sell. The increase in producer surplus for existing sellers equals the area of the rectangle BCED. Secondly, some new sellers enter the market because they are now willing to produce the good at the higher price, resulting in an increase in the quantity supplied from Q_1 to Q_2. The producer surplus of these newcomers is the area of the triangle CEF.

FIGURE 7.6

How the Price Affects Producer Surplus

In panel (a) the price is P_1, the quantity demanded is Q_1 and producer surplus equals the area of the triangle ABC. When the price rises from P_1 to P_2, as in panel (b), the quantity supplied rises from Q_1 to Q_2 and the producer surplus rises to the area of the triangle ADF. The increase in producer surplus (area BCFD) occurs in part because existing producers now receive more (area BCED) and in part because new producers enter the market at the higher price (area CEF).

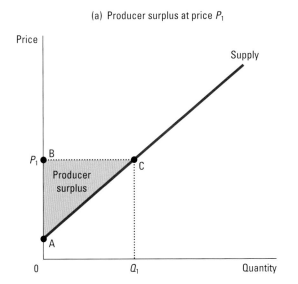

(a) Producer surplus at price P_1

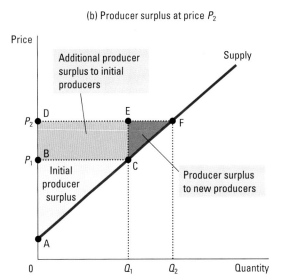

(b) Producer surplus at price P_2

As this analysis shows, we use producer surplus to measure the well-being of sellers in much the same way as we use consumer surplus to measure the well-being of buyers. Because these two measures of economic welfare are so similar, it is natural to use them together. And, indeed, that is exactly what we do in the next section.

Quick Quiz Draw a supply curve for turkey. In your diagram show a price of turkey and the producer surplus that results from that price. Explain in words what this producer surplus measures.

MARKET EFFICIENCY

Consumer surplus and producer surplus are the basic tools that economists use to study the welfare of buyers and sellers in a market. These tools can help us address a fundamental economic question: is the allocation of resources determined by free markets in any way desirable? In other words what evidence is there for allocative efficiency in free markets?

The Benevolent Social Planner

To evaluate market outcomes, we introduce into our analysis a new, hypothetical character, the benevolent social planner – the BSP. The BSP is an omniscient, omnipotent, benign dictator. He wants to maximize the economic well-being of everyone in society. What do you suppose this planner should do? Should he just leave buyers and sellers at the equilibrium that they reach naturally on their own? Or can he increase economic well-being by altering the market outcome in some way?

To answer this question, the planner must first decide how to measure the economic well-being of a society. One possible measure is the sum of consumer and producer surplus, which we call *total surplus*. Consumer surplus is the benefit that buyers receive from participating in a market, and producer surplus is the benefit that sellers receive. It is therefore natural to use total surplus as a measure of society's economic well-being.

To better understand this measure of economic well-being, recall how we measure consumer and producer surplus. We define consumer surplus as:

Consumer surplus = Value to buyers − Amount paid by buyers

Similarly, we define producer surplus as:

Producer surplus = Amount received by sellers − Cost to sellers

When we add consumer and producer surplus together, we obtain:

Total surplus = Value to buyers − Amount paid by buyers + Amount received by sellers − Cost to sellers

The amount paid by buyers equals the amount received by sellers, so the middle two terms in this expression cancel each other. As a result, we can write total surplus as:

Total surplus = Value to buyers − Cost to sellers

Total surplus in a market is the total value to buyers of the goods, as measured by their willingness to pay, minus the total cost to sellers of providing those goods.

efficiency
the property of a resource allocation of maximizing the total surplus received by all members of society

If an allocation of resources maximizes total surplus, we say that the allocation exhibits **efficiency**. If an allocation is not efficient, then some of the gains from trade among buyers and sellers are not being realized. For example, an allocation is inefficient if a good is not being produced by the sellers with lowest cost. In this case, moving production from a high-cost producer to a low-cost producer will lower the total cost to sellers and raise total surplus. Similarly, an allocation is inefficient if a good is not being consumed by the buyers who value it most highly. In this case, moving consumption of the good from a buyer with a low valuation to a buyer with a high valuation will raise total surplus. In Chapter 1, we defined *efficiency* as 'the property of society getting the most it can from its scarce resources'. Now that we have the concept of total surplus, we can be more precise about what we mean by 'getting the most it can'. In this context, society will be getting the most it can from its scarce resources if it allocates them so as to maximize total surplus.

equity
the property of distributing economic prosperity fairly among the members of society

In addition to efficiency, the BSP might also care about **equity** – the property of distributing economic prosperity fairly among the members of society. In essence, the gains from trade in a market are like a cake to be distributed among the market participants. The question of efficiency is whether the cake is as big as possible. The question of equity is whether the cake is divided fairly. Evaluating the equity of a market outcome is more difficult than evaluating the efficiency. Whereas efficiency is an objective goal that can be judged on strictly positive grounds, equity involves normative judgements that go beyond economics and enter into the realm of political philosophy.

In this chapter we concentrate on efficiency as the social planner's goal. Keep in mind, however, that real policy makers often care about equity as well. That is, they care about both the size of the economic cake and how the cake gets sliced and distributed among members of society.

CASE STUDY

Subsidies and Consumer Surplus

In Chapter 6, we introduced the idea of a subsidy. A subsidy is designed to reduce the market price often by giving sellers money which helps to reduce the cost of production. As a result the supply curve shifts to the right and the market equilibrium price will be lower than without the subsidy.

It might be assumed that a lower price would increase the consumer surplus and such an outcome would be desirable for consumers. In the short run this might be the case but markets are dynamic and other factors may affect outcomes and lead to a reduction in the consumer surplus which may bring into question whether the subsidy should be maintained.

To see an example of how this might be the case, we will look at a study carried out by Shahmoradi and Honarvar on the subsidy on gasoline which exists in the Islamic Republic of Iran.[1] The study shows how the existence of a subsidy introduced by the Iranian government on gasoline helps keep the price of driving cars in Iran much lower than the normal free market price. They ask if such a policy increases the welfare of car drivers as measured by consumer surplus.

Figure 7.7 shows how a subsidy would affect the market for gasoline in Iran.

FIGURE 7.7

The Effect of a Subsidy on the Price of Gasoline

In the absence of a subsidy, Iranian drivers would pay the market price of P_{wp} and the quantity Q_1 would be bought and sold. The introduction of a subsidy means that the cost to producers is now lower for each litre of gas they produce and so the supply curve for gas shifts to the right. Car drivers in Iran now pay a price of P_{sub} per litre and the amount bought and sold rises to Q_2. The amount of the subsidy per litre is shown by the vertical distance between the two supply curves.

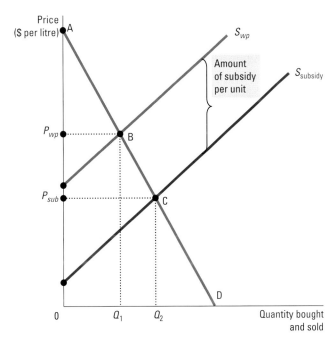

Without the subsidy, car drivers would have to pay the world price for gas, shown as P_{wp} and the amount Q_1 would be purchased. The introduction of the subsidy will shift the supply curve to the right because at each price the cost of producing gas is now cheaper. The result of the subsidy is that car drivers in Iran pay a price of P_{sub} and there is an increase in the amount of gas bought and sold from Q_1 to Q_2.

The welfare benefits to car drivers in Iran is the consumer surplus they gain from the subsidy. Without the subsidy the amount of consumer surplus is given by the area bounded by the triangle $ABP_{wp.}$ After the subsidy is introduced consumer surplus increases as shown by the area bounded by the triangle ACP_{sub}.

The question that Shahmoradi and Honarvar asked was whether the continuation of the policy maintained the level of consumer surplus over time. In the study, the pair identified a number of changes in Iran which have an effect on the success of the policy. Figure 7.7 shows that the quantity demanded of gas increases as a result of the subsidy. But what about the influence of factors affecting demand other than price? Shahmoradi and Honarvar show that the age distribution of the population in Iran is predominantly skewed to the younger end of the population with nearly 50 per cent of the population being 30 years old or younger. This population profile means that the demand for cars has been rising and is likely to continue to rise for some years. In addition, the number of cars available in Iran has increased significantly and so this adds to the demand for gas. As gross domestic product rises and incomes grow, more Iranians can afford cars and so there is a further impetus on demand.

The net result is that these factors combined with the low price of gas has cased demand to rise faster than the capacity of Iran to supply gas for car drivers. Iran is an oil producer but it is increasingly finding it difficult to meet demand (not all oil produced is suitable for gasoline) and so Iran has had to increase imported gas from abroad. Gas consumption has risen by 200 per cent in the last 20 years; in 1986 Iran imported 17 per cent of its gas but by 2005 this had risen to 37 per cent. At the same time, the oil that Iran sells abroad generates export revenue.

For the government the cost of maintaining the subsidy has been rising. Parliament sets the price of gas at the beginning of each year and has been gradually increasing the price but the cost of the subsidy over the ten year period from 1986 is given as \$47.7 billion at current prices. Government spending, in one way or another, accounts for around 80 per cent of Iranian GDP and the maintenance of the subsidy in the wake of increasing demand has put additional pressure on government finances. Export revenue has had to be diverted to paying for the subsidy, which has an opportunity cost.

Shahmoradi and Honarvar further show how changes to the price and income elasticity of demand can affect the picture. They estimate that between the years 1988 and 2005, the income elasticity of demand with respect to gas has been greater than 1 but declining. The average income elasticity of demand over the period is put at 1.15 which means that for every 10 per cent increase in income, demand for gas has increased by 15 per cent. Over the same period, Shahmoradi and Honarvar estimate the price elasticity of demand for gas to be inelastic and decreasing. This means that even if parliament increases the price of gas at its annual review the reduction in demand is limited.

Putting all this together, Shahmoradi and Honarvar suggest that the value of consumer surplus expressed in proportion to GDP per capita was around 10 per cent in the late 1980s and early 1990s rising to 20 per cent by 1994. Since that time it has declined to around 5 per cent and is still declining but positive. Such research allows us to be able to make judgements about the allocation of resources and whether the policy represents an efficient allocation. For the Iranian government the cost of maintaining the subsidy seems to be rising but the welfare benefits in terms of the consumer surplus gained by car drivers is falling. One might ask, therefore, whether the Iranian government might re-think the policy and find other ways to improve the welfare of its population.

[1]Shahmoradi, A. & Honarvar, A. (2008). *Gasoline Subsidy and Consumer Surplus* in the Islamic Republic of Iran. In: *OPEC Energy Review.* 32, **3**. 232–245

Evaluating the Market Equilibrium

Figure 7.8 shows consumer and producer surplus when a market reaches the equilibrium of supply and demand. Recall that consumer surplus equals the area above the price and under the demand curve and producer surplus equals the area below the price and above the supply curve. Thus, the total area between the supply and demand curves up to the point of equilibrium represents the total surplus in this market.

Is this equilibrium allocation of resources efficient? Does it maximize total surplus? To answer these questions, keep in mind that when a market is in equilibrium, the price determines which buyers and sellers participate in the market. Those buyers who value the good more than the price (represented by the segment AE on the demand curve) choose to buy the good; those buyers who value it less than the price (represented by the segment EB) do not. Similarly,

FIGURE 7.8

Consumer and Producer Surplus in the Market Equilibrium

Total surplus – the sum of consumer and producer surplus – is the area between the supply and demand curves up to the equilibrium quantity.

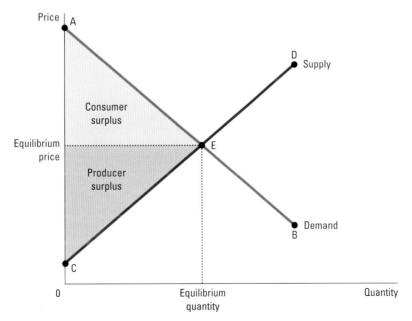

those sellers whose costs are less than the price (represented by the segment CE on the supply curve) choose to produce and sell the good; those sellers whose costs are greater than the price (represented by the segment ED) do not.

These observations lead to two insights about market outcomes:

1. Free markets allocate the supply of goods to the buyers who value them most highly, as measured by their willingness to pay.
2. Free markets allocate the demand for goods to the sellers who can produce them at least cost.

Thus, given the quantity produced and sold in a market equilibrium, the BSP cannot increase economic well-being by changing the allocation of consumption among buyers or the allocation of production among sellers.

But can the BSP raise total economic well-being by increasing or decreasing the quantity of the good? The answer is no, as stated in this third insight about market outcomes:

3. Free markets produce the quantity of goods that maximizes the sum of consumer and producer surplus.

To see why this is true, consider Figure 7.9. Recall that the demand curve reflects the value to buyers and that the supply curve reflects the cost to sellers. At quantities below the equilibrium level, the value to buyers exceeds the cost to sellers. In this region, increasing the quantity raises total surplus, and it continues to do so until the quantity reaches the equilibrium level. Beyond the equilibrium quantity, however, the value to buyers is less than the cost to sellers. Producing more than the equilibrium quantity would, therefore, lower total surplus.

FIGURE 7.9

The Efficiency of the Equilibrium Quantity

At quantities less than the equilibrium quantity, the value to buyers exceeds the cost to sellers. At quantities greater than the equilibrium quantity, the cost to sellers exceeds the value to buyers. Therefore, the market equilibrium maximizes the sum of producer and consumer surplus.

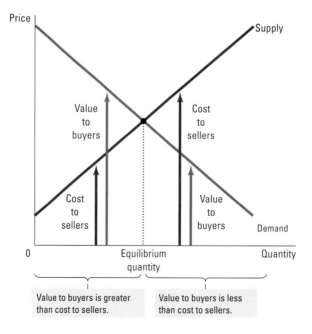

These three insights about market outcomes tell us that the equilibrium of supply and demand maximizes the sum of consumer and producer surplus. In other words, the equilibrium outcome is an efficient allocation of resources. The job of the BSP is, therefore, very easy: he can leave the market outcome just as he finds it. This policy of leaving well enough alone goes by the French expression *laissez-faire,* which literally translated means 'leave them to do'.

We can now better appreciate Adam Smith's invisible hand of the marketplace, which we first discussed in Chapter 1. The BSP doesn't need to alter the market outcome because the invisible hand has already guided buyers and sellers to an allocation of the economy's resources that maximizes total surplus. This conclusion explains why economists often advocate free markets as the best way to organize economic activity.

Quick Quiz Draw the supply and demand for turkey. In the equilibrium, show producer and consumer surplus. Explain why producing more turkey would lower total surplus.

IN THE NEWS

Ticket Touting

To allocate resources efficiently, an economy must get goods to the consumers who value them most highly. Sometimes this job falls to ticket touts.

Ticket Touts – A Much Maligned 'Profession'?

Ticket touts, or scalpers in the United States, are people who try and sell tickets for sporting, public and entertainment events at prices above the face value of the ticket. The issue of ticket touts highlights a number of important points that have been raised in this chapter and in previous chapters where we have been looking at the efficiency of markets. To understand the issues we must look in more detail at what ticket touts do.

There tends to be two distinct groups who may be regarded as touts; one is the individual who may have bought a few tickets to see a concert, for example, but for some reason cannot attend. The individual then makes these tickets available in some way for sale; typically, tickets appear on eBay or other online auction sites. The highest bidder gets the tickets. These people are often not vilified in the same way that 'professional' touts are. This group buy large amounts of tickets when they first go on sale and have no intention of ever going to the event. The purchase they make is simply with the intention of re-selling the tickets to make a profit. This group are often criticized for their mercenary behaviour and are the subject of by-laws, regulation and other regulatory and legal processes.

The next question we have to ask is why ticket touts exist at all? Take the example of a concert tour by the band U2. They announce a gig at the Stade de France in Paris – capacity 80 000; it is their only appearance in France that year. The supply of tickets is perfectly inelastic at 80 000; the promoters know

that demand for tickets is likely to be far in excess of 80 000 but they do not want to set the true market price for the tickets because they do not want to exclude those who may not be able to afford a high price from the chance to see U2. The price of tickets is set at €100 each. At this price demand for tickets far exceeds the available supply – there is a shortage. The concert promoters know that the tickets will have to be rationed in some way, which may be through some sort of first-come-first-served basis. When tickets go on sale they sell out in the first hour.

The market has successfully allocated the tickets but there will be a large number of people who will be left very disappointed by this allocation. Many of these people would have been willing to pay a higher price to get a ticket. In cases of sporting, public and entertainment events, market price is not determined by the actions of millions of buyers and sellers making decisions; promoters of the events will have set a price which may be below the 'natural' equilibrium. Enter the tout. Despite the best efforts of the promoters, touts manage to secure several thousand tickets which they make available for sale. Devoted fans of U2 who were not able to get tickets for whatever reason may be prepared to pay considerably more than €100 to see the band. Most will have some notional upper limit above which they will not be prepared to pay. This may be determined by their income and by their notion of value linked, as we saw in earlier chapters, to the opportunity cost of acquiring the ticket.

Touts will therefore sell tickets to these people at prices in excess of €100. The touts fulfil the function that the market has not done – allocating scarce resources (tickets) according to the value which the buyer places on the ticket. Some fans may pay €200 to get their ticket from a tout and be very happy because they were prepared to pay up to €400 if necessary. They get their ticket and have €200 worth of consumer surplus. The tout gets some producer surplus (€100 assuming they paid the face value for the tickets) and as a result total surplus rises.

The tout does run the risk that they buy a large number of tickets and do not sell them. Outside these sporting and entertainment events one can observe a useful study of markets in action. Two hours before the start of the event touts may be selling tickets

at several times the face value; if all the tickets are sold then they are happy and so, presumably, are buyers because they either pay a price equal to the value they place on the ticket or get a ticket at a price below which they were prepared to pay and so gain some consumer surplus. However, if touts find that tickets are not selling then the closer the time comes to the start of the event, prices will start to fall. The seller may even be prepared to suffer a loss to get rid of any tickets left; getting €50 is better than not getting anything at all!

For both buyer and seller, the whole process represents risk; if the buyer waits too long in the hope that they get lower prices they may miss out on the ticket they desire. Equally, if touts hang on to tickets in the hope of securing higher prices they may find they are left with unsold tickets. Both buyers and sellers have to be careful judges of the market in order to make the right decisions for themselves.

The *Financial Times* columnist and respected economist, Samuel Brittan, referred to research carried out by an American economist, Pascal Courty who wrote an article on touts in the *Journal of Economic Perspectives* in Spring 2003. Courty divides the buyers into two groups – the serious fan and the 'busy professional'. The former will be so dedicated that they know when tickets become available and make sure they get in early to get their tickets. The 'busy professionals' do not like to make up their mind too far in advance. If we assume that the dedicated fan gets their tickets on release at face value, the touts will be selling to the 'busy professionals' at above face value prices.

The view that touts fulfil a valuable market function is not held by everyone. Those that really cannot get tickets on release, because they are at work, away, asleep or whatever reason, feel aggrieved that professional touts use their knowledge to acquire tickets

with the sole intention of selling them on at a profit. By doing so they 'crowd out' the legitimate buyer from the market. Promoters and governments know that touts are seen as being 'bad' and are going to ever greater lengths to try and make the job of being a tout harder and less profitable. Online ticketing is able to introduce a wide range of electronic monitoring and tagging systems to try and make sure that the buyers are genuine fans who get value for money. Tickets for the World Cup in South Africa in 2010, for the reunion concert of Led Zeppelin at London's O$_2$ Arena in November 2007, for the series of Michael Jackson concerts prior to his death in 2009, tickets for the Glastonbury music festival in Somerset in the UK and many more, have all tried to make use of sophisticated ordering, distribution and collection systems to prevent touts from 'exploiting' buyers. Despite these best efforts, touts still exist and many found ways around the systems put in place.

The issue raises important questions about efficiency and equity. The general public may believe that touts are unfair and heap vitriol on them; promoters may despise touts because if they are seen to let them get away with the practice they are being unfair to buyers, but there may also be a sneaking suspicion that promoters are jealous of the fact that touts actually sell tickets at nearer the 'true' market price. Economists may point to the fact that few people are willing to pay a price which does not reflect the value they put on the ticket and that even though they pay a higher price than the face value (which, note, is different to the market value) many get considerable consumer surplus. The simple solution would be for promoters to charge the market price in the first place![1]

[1]'Ticket Touts are Good for Spectators' – http://www.samuelbrittan.co.uk/text162_p.html accessed 22 January 2010.

CONCLUSION: MARKET EFFICIENCY AND MARKET FAILURE

This chapter introduced the basic tools of welfare economics – consumer and producer surplus – and used them to evaluate the efficiency of free markets. We showed that the forces of supply and demand allocate resources efficiently. That is, even though each buyer and seller in a market is concerned only about his or her own welfare, they are together led by an invisible hand to an equilibrium that maximizes the total benefits to buyers and sellers.

A word of warning is in order. To conclude that markets are efficient, we made several assumptions about how markets work. When these assumptions do not hold, our conclusion that the market equilibrium is efficient may no longer be true. As we close this chapter, let's consider briefly two of the most important of these assumptions.

First, our analysis assumed that markets are perfectly competitive. In the real world, however, competition is sometimes far from perfect. In some markets a single buyer or seller (or a small group of them) may be able to control market prices. This ability to influence prices is called *market power.* Market power can cause markets to be inefficient because it keeps the price and quantity away from the equilibrium of supply and demand.

Second, our analysis assumed that the outcome in a market matters only to the buyers and sellers in that market. Yet, in the real world, the decisions of buyers and sellers sometimes affect people who are not participants in the market at all. Pollution is the classic example of a market outcome that affects people not in the market. Such side effects, called *externalities,* cause welfare in a market to depend on more than just the value to the buyers and the cost to the sellers. Because buyers and sellers do not take these side effects into account when deciding how much to consume and produce, the equilibrium in a market can be inefficient from the standpoint of society as a whole.

Market power and externalities are examples of a general phenomenon called market failure – the inability of some unregulated markets to allocate resources efficiently. When markets fail, public policy can potentially remedy the problem and increase economic efficiency. Microeconomists devote much effort to studying when market failure is likely and what sorts of policies are best at correcting market failures. As you continue your study of economics, you will see that the tools of welfare economics developed here are readily adapted to that endeavour.

Despite the possibility of market failure, the invisible hand of the marketplace is extraordinarily important. In many markets, the assumptions we made in this chapter work well, and the conclusion of market efficiency applies directly. Moreover, our analysis of welfare economics and market efficiency can be used to shed light on the effects of various government policies. In the next two chapters we apply the tools we have just developed to study two important policy issues – the welfare effects of taxation and of international trade.

SUMMARY

- Consumer surplus equals buyers' willingness to pay for a good minus the amount they actually pay for it, and it measures the benefit buyers get from participating in a market. Consumer surplus can be computed by finding the area below the demand curve and above the price.

- Producer surplus equals the amount sellers receive for their goods minus their costs of production, and it measures the benefit sellers get from participating in a market. Producer surplus can be computed by finding the area below the price and above the supply curve.

- An allocation of resources that maximizes the sum of consumer and producer surplus is said to be efficient. Policy makers are often concerned with the efficiency, as well as the equity, of economic outcomes.
- The equilibrium of supply and demand maximizes the sum of consumer and producer surplus. That is, the invisible hand of the marketplace leads buyers and sellers to allocate resources efficiently.
- Markets do not allocate resources efficiently in the presence of market failures such as market power or externalities.

KEY CONCEPTS

welfare economics, p. 138
well-being, p. 138
allocative efficiency, p. 139

willingness to pay, p. 139
consumer surplus, p. 140
cost, p. 144

producer surplus, p. 144
efficiency, p. 148
equity, p. 148

QUESTIONS FOR REVIEW

1. Explain how buyers' willingness to pay, consumer surplus and the demand curve are related.

2. Explain how sellers' costs, producer surplus and the supply curve are related.

3. In a supply-and-demand diagram, show producer and consumer surplus in the market equilibrium.

4. What is efficiency? Is it the only goal of economic policy makers?

5. What does the invisible hand do?

6. Explain how charging a higher price for tickets for the Wimbledon tennis championships would not only gets rid of queues but also would be a more efficient market allocation.

7. Name two types of market failure. Explain why each may cause market outcomes to be inefficient.

PROBLEMS AND APPLICATIONS

1. An early freeze in Normandy ruins half of the apple harvest. What happens to consumer surplus in the market for apples? What happens to consumer surplus in the market for cider? Illustrate your answers with diagrams.

2. Suppose the demand for French bread rises. What happens to producer surplus in the market for French bread? What happens to producer surplus in the market for flour? Illustrate your answer with diagrams.

3. It is a hot day, and Oliver is thirsty. Here is the value he places on a bottle of water:

Value of first bottle	€7
Value of second bottle	€5

Value of third bottle	€3
Value of fourth bottle	€1

   a. From this information, derive Oliver's demand schedule. Graph his demand curve for bottled water.

   b. If the price of a bottle of water is €4, how many bottles does Oliver buy? How much consumer surplus does Oliver get from his purchases? Show Oliver's consumer surplus in your graph.

   c. If the price falls to €2, how does quantity demanded change? How does Oliver's consumer surplus change? Show these changes in your graph.

4. Ben owns a water pump. Because pumping large amounts of water is harder than pumping small amounts, the cost of producing a bottle of water rises as he pumps more. Here is the cost he incurs to produce each bottle of water:

Cost of first bottle	€1
Cost of second bottle	€3
Cost of third bottle	€5
Cost of fourth bottle	€7

  a. From this information, derive Ben's supply schedule. Graph his supply curve for bottled water.

  b. If the price of a bottle of water is €4, how many bottles does Ben produce and sell? How much producer surplus does Ben get from these sales? Show Ben's producer surplus in your graph.

  c. If the price rises to €6, how does quantity supplied change? How does Ben's producer surplus change? Show these changes in your graph.

5. Consider a market in which Oliver from Problem 3 is the buyer and Ben from Problem 4 is the seller.

  a. Use Ben's supply schedule and Oliver's demand schedule to find the quantity supplied and quantity demanded at prices of €2, €4 and €6. Which of these prices brings supply and demand into equilibrium?

  b. What are consumer surplus, producer surplus and total surplus in this equilibrium?

  c. If Ben produced and Oliver consumed one fewer bottle of water, what would happen to total surplus?

  d. If Ben produced and Oliver consumed one additional bottle of water, what would happen to total surplus?

6. The cost of producing DVD players has fallen over the past few years. Let's consider some implications of this fact.

  a. Use a supply-and-demand diagram to show the effect of falling production costs on the price and quantity of DVD players sold.

  b. In your diagram, show what happens to consumer surplus and producer surplus.

  c. Suppose the supply of DVD players is very elastic. Who benefits most from falling production costs – consumers or producers of DVD players?

7. There are four consumers willing to pay the following amounts for haircuts:

Roberto: €7   Ronaldo: €2   David: €8   Zinadin: €5

There are four haircutting businesses with the following costs:

Firm A: €3   Firm B: €6   Firm C: €4   Firm D: €2

Each firm has the capacity to produce only one haircut. For efficiency, how many haircuts should be given? Which businesses should cut hair, and which consumers should have their hair cut? How large is the maximum possible total surplus?

8. Suppose a technological advance reduces the cost of making computers.

  a. Use a supply and demand diagram to show what happens to price, quantity, consumer surplus and producer surplus in the market for computers.

  b. Computers and adding machines are substitutes. Use a supply-and-demand diagram to show what happens to price, quantity, consumer surplus and producer surplus in the market for adding machines. Should adding machine producers be happy or sad about the technological advance in computers?

  c. Computers and software are complements. Use a supply-and-demand diagram to show what happens to price, quantity, consumer surplus and producer surplus in the market for software. Should software producers be happy or sad about the technological advance in computers?

  d. Does this analysis help explain why software producer Bill Gates is one of the world's richest men?

For further resources, visit
www.cengage.com/mankiw_taylor2

8 APPLICATION: THE COSTS OF TAXATION

axes have been around a long time. In the Bible, for example, we can read how Jesus's parents had to return to Nazareth to be taxed and how, later, Jesus converted a prominent tax collector to become one of his disciples. In the Koran, there are references to *jizya*, which can be translated as the word 'tax'. In the Ottoman Empire *jizya* was a per-capita tax levied on non-Muslim, able-bodied resident males of military age. Since taxes, by definition, are a means of legally extracting money from individuals or organizations, it is not surprising that they have often been a source of heated political debate throughout history. In 1776 the anger of the American colonies over British taxes sparked the American Revolution. More recently, the issue of whether and how tax systems should be harmonized within the European Union has been the source of much debate.

We began our study of taxes in Chapter 6. There we saw how a tax on a good affects its price and the quantity bought and sold and how the forces of supply and demand divide the burden of a tax between buyers and sellers. In this chapter we extend this analysis and look at how taxes affect welfare, the economic well-being of participants in a market.

The effects of taxes on welfare might at first seem obvious. The government imposes taxes in order to raise revenue, and that revenue must come out of someone's pocket. As we saw in Chapter 6, both buyers and sellers are worse off when a good is taxed: a tax raises the price buyers pay and lowers the price sellers receive. Yet to understand fully how taxes affect economic well-being, we must compare the reduced welfare of buyers and sellers to the amount of revenue the government raises. The tools of consumer and producer surplus allow us to make this comparison. The analysis will show that the costs of taxes to buyers and sellers exceeds the revenue raised by the government.

THE DEADWEIGHT LOSS OF TAXATION

In Chapter 6 we looked at the effect of a tax levied on a seller. The same result would be gained, however, if we had analysed the effect of a tax on a buyer – when a tax is levied on buyers, the demand curve shifts downward by the size of the tax; when it is levied on sellers, the supply curve shifts upward by that amount. In either case, when the tax is imposed, the price paid by buyers rises, and the price received by sellers falls. In the end, buyers and sellers share the burden of the tax, regardless of how it is levied.

" DON'T WORRY! SINCE 28% OF MY SALARY GOES TO THE GOVERNMENT, I'VE DECIDED TO WORK 72% OF THE TIME."

Figure 8.1 shows these effects. To simplify our discussion, this figure does not show a shift in either the supply or demand curve, although one curve must shift. Which curve shifts depends on whether the tax is levied on sellers (the supply curve shifts) or buyers (the demand curve shifts). In this chapter, we can simplify the graphs by not bothering to show the shift. The key result for our purposes here is that the tax places a wedge between the price buyers pay and the price sellers receive. Because of this tax wedge, the quantity sold falls below the level that would be sold without a tax. In other words, a tax on a good causes the size of the market for the good to shrink. These results should be familiar from Chapter 6.

How a Tax Affects Market Participants

Now let's use the tools of welfare economics to measure the gains and losses from a tax on a good. To do this, we must take into account how the tax affects buyers, sellers and the government. The benefit received by buyers in a market is

FIGURE 8.1

The Effects of a Tax

A tax on a good places a wedge between the price that buyers pay and the price that sellers receive. The quantity of the good sold falls.

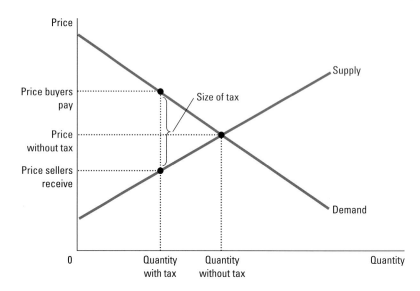

measured by consumer surplus – the amount buyers are willing to pay for the good minus the amount they actually pay for it. The benefit received by sellers in a market is measured by producer surplus – the amount sellers receive for the good minus their costs. These are precisely the measures of economic welfare we used in Chapter 7.

What about the third interested party, the government? If T is the size of the tax and Q is the quantity of the good sold, then the government gets total tax revenue of $T \times Q$. It can use this tax revenue to provide services, such as roads, police and education, or to help the needy. Therefore, to analyse how taxes affect economic well-being, we use tax revenue to measure the government's benefit from the tax. Keep in mind, however, that this benefit actually accrues not to government but to those on whom the revenue is spent.

Figure 8.2 shows that the government's tax revenue is represented by the rectangle between the supply and demand curves. The height of this rectangle is the size of the tax, T, and the width of the rectangle is the quantity of the good sold, Q. Because a rectangle's area is its height times its width, this rectangle's area is $T \times Q$, which equals the tax revenue.

Welfare without a Tax To see how a tax affects welfare, we begin by considering welfare before the government has imposed a tax. Figure 8.3 shows the supply and demand diagram and marks the key areas with the letters A through F.

Without a tax, the price and quantity are found at the intersection of the supply and demand curves. The price is P_1, and the quantity sold is Q_1. Because the demand curve reflects buyers' willingness to pay, consumer surplus is the area between the demand curve and the price, A + B + C. Similarly, because the supply curve reflects sellers' costs, producer surplus is the area between the supply curve and the price, D + E + F. In this case, because there is no tax, tax revenue equals zero.

FIGURE 8.2

Tax Revenue

The tax revenue that the government collects equals T × Q, *the size of the tax* T *times the quantity sold* Q. *Thus, tax revenue equals the area of the rectangle between the supply and demand curves.*

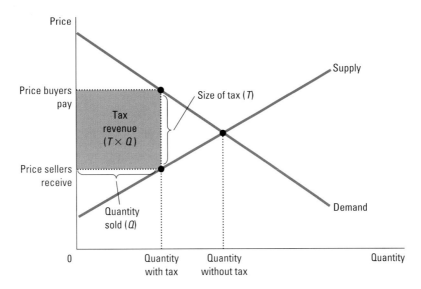

Total surplus – the sum of consumer and producer surplus – equals the area A + B + C + D + E + F. In other words, as we saw in Chapter 7, total surplus is the area between the supply and demand curves up to the equilibrium quantity. The first column of the table in Figure 8.3 summarizes these conclusions.

Welfare with a Tax Now consider welfare after the tax is imposed. The price paid by buyers rises from P_1 to P_B, so consumer surplus now equals only area A (the area below the demand curve and above the buyer's price). The price received by sellers falls from P_1 to P_S, so producer surplus now equals only area F (the area above the supply curve and below the seller's price). The quantity sold falls from Q_1 to Q_2, and the government collects tax revenue equal to the area B + D.

To compute total surplus with the tax, we add consumer surplus producer surplus and tax revenue. Thus, we find that total surplus is area A + B + D + F. The second column of the table provides a summary.

Changes in Welfare We can now see the effects of the tax by comparing welfare before and after the tax is imposed. The third column in the table in Figure 8.3 shows the changes. The tax causes consumer surplus to fall by the area B + C and producer surplus to fall by the area D + E. Tax revenue rises by the area B + D. Not surprisingly, the tax makes buyers and sellers worse off and the government better off.

The change in total welfare includes the change in consumer surplus (which is negative), the change in producer surplus (which is also negative), and the change in tax revenue (which is positive). When we add these three pieces together, we find that total surplus in the market falls by the area C + E. Thus, the losses to buyers and sellers from a tax exceed the revenue raised by the government. The fall in total surplus that results when a tax (or some other policy)

FIGURE 8.3

How a Tax Affects Welfare

A tax on a good reduces consumer surplus (by the area B + C) and producer surplus (by the area D + E). Because the fall in producer and consumer surplus exceeds tax revenue (area B + D), the tax is said to impose a deadweight loss (area C + E).

	Without tax	With tax	Change
Consumer surplus	A + B + C	A	−(B + C)
Producer surplus	D + E + F	F	−(D + E)
Tax revenue	None	B + D	+(B + D)
Total surplus	A + B + C + D + E + F	A + B + D + F	−(C + E)

The area C + E shows the fall in total surplus and is the deadweight loss of the tax.

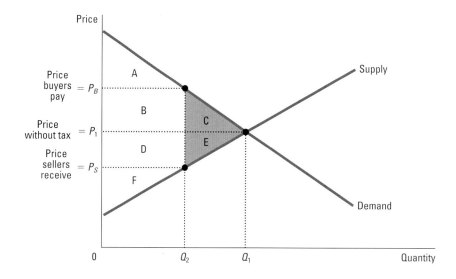

deadweight loss
the fall in total surplus that results from a market distortion, such as a tax

distorts a market outcome is called the **deadweight loss**. The area C + E measures the size of the deadweight loss.

To understand why taxes impose deadweight losses, recall one of the *Ten Principles of Economics* in Chapter 1: people respond to incentives. In Chapter 7 we assumed that markets normally allocate scarce resources efficiently. That is, the equilibrium of supply and demand maximizes the total surplus of buyers and sellers in a market. When a tax raises the price to buyers and lowers the price to sellers, however, it gives buyers an incentive to consume less and sellers an incentive to produce less than they otherwise would. As buyers and sellers respond to these incentives, the size of the market shrinks below its optimum. Thus, because taxes distort incentives, they cause markets to allocate resources inefficiently.

Deadweight Losses and the Gains from Trade

To gain some intuition for why taxes result in deadweight losses, consider an example. Imagine that Carsten cleans Annika's house each week for €100. The opportunity cost of Carsten's time is €80, and the value of a clean house to Annika is €120. Thus, Carsten and Annika each receive a €20 benefit from their deal. The total surplus of €40 measures the gains from trade in this particular transaction.

Now suppose that the government levies a €50 tax on the providers of cleaning services. There is now no price that Annika can pay Carsten that will leave both of them better off after paying the tax. The most Annika would be willing to pay is €120, but then Carsten would be left with only €70 after paying the tax, which is less than his €80 opportunity cost. Conversely, for Carsten to receive his opportunity cost of €80, Annika would need to pay €130, which is above the €120 value she places on a clean house. As a result, Annika and Carsten cancel their arrangement. Carsten goes without the income, and Annika lives in a dirtier house.

The tax has made Carsten and Annika worse off by a total of €40, because they have lost this amount of surplus. At the same time, the government collects no revenue from Carsten and Annika because they decide to cancel their arrangement. The €40 is pure deadweight loss: it is a loss to buyers and sellers in a market not offset by an increase in government revenue. From this example, we can see the ultimate source of deadweight losses: taxes cause deadweight losses because they prevent buyers and sellers from realizing some of the gains from trade.

The area of the triangle between the supply and demand curves (area C + E in Figure 8.3) measures these losses. This loss can be seen most easily in Figure 8.4 by recalling that the demand curve reflects the value of the good to consumers and that the supply curve reflects the costs of producers. When the tax raises the price to buyers to P_B and lowers the price to sellers to P_S, the marginal buyers and sellers leave the market, so the quantity sold falls from Q_1 to Q_2. Yet, as the figure shows, the value of the good to these buyers still exceeds the cost to

FIGURE 8.4

The Deadweight Loss

When the government imposes a tax on a good, the quantity sold falls from Q_1 to Q_2. As a result, some of the potential gains from trade among buyers and sellers do not get realized. These lost gains from trade create the deadweight loss.

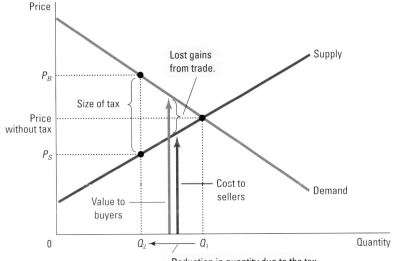

these sellers. As in our example with Carsten and Annika, the gains from trade – the difference between buyers' value and sellers' cost – is less than the tax. Thus, these trades do not get made once the tax is imposed. The deadweight loss is the surplus lost because the tax discourages these mutually advantageous trades.

Quick Quiz Draw the supply and demand curve for ham-and-cheese sandwiches. If the government imposes a tax on sandwiches, show what happens to the quantity sold, the price paid by buyers and the price paid by sellers. In your diagram, show the deadweight loss from the tax. Explain the meaning of the deadweight loss.

THE DETERMINANTS OF THE DEADWEIGHT LOSS

What determines whether the deadweight loss from a tax is large or small? The answer is the price elasticities of supply and demand, which measure how much the quantity supplied and quantity demanded respond to changes in the price.

Let's consider first how the elasticity of supply affects the size of the deadweight loss. In the top two panels of Figure 8.5, the demand curve and the size of the tax are the same. The only difference in these figures is the elasticity of the supply curve. In panel (a), the supply curve is relatively inelastic: quantity supplied responds only slightly to changes in the price. In panel (b), the supply curve is relatively elastic: quantity supplied responds substantially to changes in the price. Notice that the deadweight loss, the area of the triangle between the supply and demand curves, is larger when the supply curve is more elastic.

Similarly, the bottom two panels of Figure 8.5 show how the elasticity of demand affects the size of the deadweight loss. Here the supply curve and the size of the tax are held constant. In panel (c) the demand curve is relatively inelastic, and the deadweight loss is small. In panel (d) the demand curve is more elastic, and the deadweight loss from the tax is larger.

The lesson from this figure is easy to explain. A tax has a deadweight loss because it induces buyers and sellers to change their behaviour. The tax raises the price paid by buyers, so they consume less. At the same time, the tax lowers the price received by sellers, so they produce less. Because of these changes in behaviour, the size of the market shrinks below the optimum. The elasticities of supply and demand measure how much sellers and buyers respond to the changes in the price and, therefore, determine how much the tax distorts the market outcome. Hence, the greater the elasticities of supply and demand, the greater the deadweight loss of a tax.

CASE STUDY

The Deadweight Loss Debate

Supply, demand, elasticity, deadweight loss – all this economic theory is enough to make your head spin. But believe it or not, these ideas go to the heart of a profound political question: how big should the government sector be? The debate hinges on these concepts because the larger the deadweight loss of taxation, the larger the welfare cost of any government expenditure programme such as providing public health services or national defence. If

FIGURE 8.5

Tax Distortions and Elasticities

In panels (a) and (b) the demand curve and the size of the tax are the same, but the price elasticity of supply is different. Notice that the more elastic the supply curve, the larger the deadweight loss of the tax. In panels (c) and (d) the supply curve and the size of the tax are the same, but the price elasticity of demand is different. Notice that the more elastic the demand curve, the larger the deadweight loss of the tax.

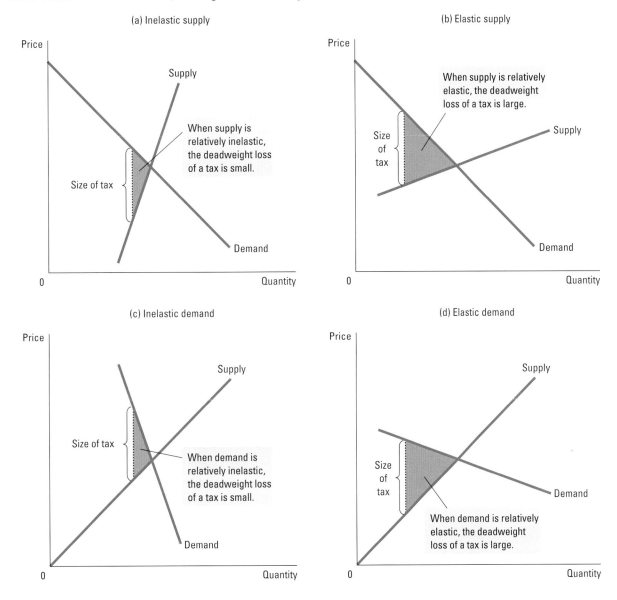

taxation entails large deadweight losses, then these losses are a strong argument for a leaner government that does less and taxes less. But if taxes impose small deadweight losses, then government programmes are less costly than they otherwise might be.

So how big are the deadweight losses of taxation? This is a question about which economists disagree. To see the nature of this disagreement, consider one of the most important taxes in most advanced economies – the tax on labour. In the UK, for example, National Insurance contributions and, to a large extent, income tax are taxes on labour. A labour tax places a wedge between the wage that firms pay and the wage that workers receive. If we add both forms of labour taxes together, the *marginal tax rate* on labour income – the tax on the last pound of earnings – is around 33 per cent for most UK manual workers. In some European countries – particularly Scandinavian countries – the marginal rate is even higher.

Although the size of the labour tax is easy to determine, the deadweight loss of this tax is less straightforward. Economists disagree about whether this 33 per cent labour tax has a small or a large deadweight loss. This disagreement arises because economists hold different views about the elasticity of labour supply.

Economists who argue that labour taxes are not very distorting believe that labour supply is fairly inelastic. Most people, they claim, would work full-time regardless of the wage. If so, the labour supply curve is almost vertical, and a tax on labour has a small deadweight loss.

Economists who argue that labour taxes are highly distorting believe that labour supply is more elastic. They admit that some groups of workers may supply their labour inelastically but claim that many other groups respond more to incentives. Here are some examples:

- Many workers can adjust the number of hours they work – for instance, by working overtime. The higher the wage, the more hours they choose to work.
- Some families have second earners – often married women with children – with some discretion over whether to do unpaid work at home or paid work in the marketplace. When deciding whether to take a job, these second earners compare the benefits of being at home (including savings on the cost of child care) with the wages they could earn.
- Many people can choose when to retire, and their decisions are partly based on the wage. Once they are retired, the wage determines their incentive to work part-time.
- Some people consider engaging in illegal economic activity, such as the drug trade, or working at jobs that pay 'under the table' to evade taxes. Economists call this the *black economy* (or sometimes the underground economy). In deciding whether to work in the black economy or at a legitimate job, these potential criminals compare what they can earn by breaking the law with the wage they can earn legally.

In each of these cases, the quantity of labour supplied responds to the wage (the price of labour). Thus, the decisions of these workers are distorted when their labour earnings are taxed. Labour taxes encourage workers to work fewer hours, second earners to stay at home, the elderly to retire early and the unscrupulous to enter the black economy.

These two views of labour taxation persist to this day. Indeed, whenever you see two political candidates debating whether the government should provide more services or reduce the tax burden, keep in mind that part of the disagreement may rest on different views about the elasticity of labour supply and the deadweight loss of taxation.

Quick Quiz   The demand for beer is more elastic than the demand for milk. Would a tax on beer or a tax on milk have larger deadweight loss? Why?

DEADWEIGHT LOSS AND TAX REVENUE AS TAXES VARY

Taxes rarely stay the same for long periods of time. Policy makers are always considering raising one tax or lowering another. Here we consider what happens to the deadweight loss and tax revenue when the size of a tax changes.

Figure 8.6 shows the effects of a small, medium and large tax, holding constant the market's supply and demand curves. The deadweight loss – the reduction in total surplus that results when the tax reduces the size of a market below the optimum – equals the area of the triangle between the supply and demand curves. For the small tax in panel (a), the area of the deadweight loss triangle is quite small. But as the size of a tax rises in panels (b) and (c), the deadweight loss grows larger and larger.

Indeed, the deadweight loss of a tax rises even more rapidly than the size of the tax. The reason is that the deadweight loss is an area of a triangle, and an area of a triangle depends on the *square* of its size. If we double the size of a tax, for instance, the base and height of the triangle double, so the deadweight loss rises by a factor of 4. If we triple the size of a tax, the base and height triple, so the deadweight loss rises by a factor of 9.

The government's tax revenue is the size of the tax times the amount of the good sold. As Figure 8.6 shows, tax revenue equals the area of the rectangle between the supply and demand curves. For the small tax in panel (a), tax revenue is small. As the size of a tax rises from panel (a) to panel (b), tax revenue grows. But as the size of the tax rises further from panel (b) to panel (c), tax revenue falls because the higher tax drastically reduces the size of the market. For a very large tax, no revenue would be raised, because people would stop buying and selling the good altogether.

FIGURE 8.6

Deadweight Loss and Tax Revenue from Three Taxes of Different Size

The deadweight loss is the reduction in total surplus due to the tax. Tax revenue is the amount of the tax times the amount of the good sold. In panel (a) a small tax has a small deadweight loss and raises a small amount of revenue. In panel (b) a somewhat larger tax has a larger deadweight loss and raises a larger amount of revenue. In panel (c) a very large tax has a very large deadweight loss, but because it has reduced the size of the market so much, the tax raises only a small amount of revenue.

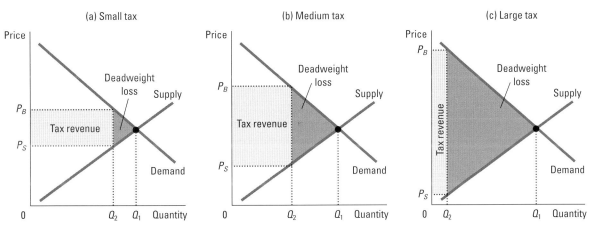

FIGURE 8.7

How Deadweight Loss and Tax Revenue Vary with the Size of a Tax

Panel (a) shows that as the size of a tax grows larger, the deadweight loss grows larger. Panel (b) shows that tax revenue first rises, then falls. This relationship is sometimes called the Laffer curve.

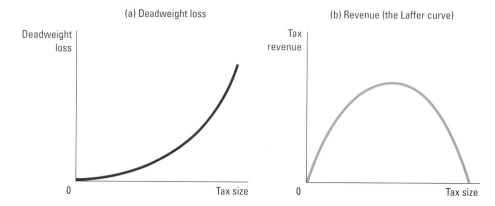

Figure 8.7 summarizes these results. In panel (a) we see that as the size of a tax increases, its deadweight loss quickly gets larger. By contrast, panel (b) shows that tax revenue first rises with the size of the tax; but then, as the tax gets larger, the market shrinks so much that tax revenue starts to fall.

CASE STUDY

The Laffer Curve and Supply-Side Economics

US economist Arthur C. Laffer

One day in 1974, the American economist Arthur Laffer sat in a Washington restaurant with some prominent journalists and politicians. He took out a napkin and drew a figure on it to show how tax rates affect tax revenue. It looked much like panel (b) of our Figure 8.7. Laffer then suggested that the United States was on the downward sloping side of this curve. Tax rates were so high, he argued, that reducing them would actually raise tax revenue.

Most economists were sceptical of Laffer's suggestion. The idea that a cut in tax rates could raise tax revenue was correct as a matter of economic theory, but there was more doubt about whether it would do so in practice. There was little evidence for Laffer's view that tax rates – in the United States or elsewhere – had in fact reached such extreme levels.

Nevertheless, the thinking underlying the *Laffer curve* (as it became known) became very influential in policy circles during the 1980s, particularly in the USA during the years of President Ronald Reagan's administration and in the UK during Prime Minister Margaret Thatcher's government. Tax rates – particularly income tax rates – were cut aggressively in both countries during the 1980s.

In the UK, for example, under Prime Minister Thatcher the top marginal rate of income tax was cut from 83 per cent to 60 per cent in 1980 and then again to 40 per cent in 1988. Economists have, however, found it hard to trace any strong incentive effects of these tax cuts leading to increases in total tax revenue, as the Laffer curve would suggest. A study by the UK Institute for

Fiscal Studies (IFS), for example, concluded that at most about 3 per cent of the increase in tax revenue between 1980 and 1986 could be attributed to the 1980 income tax cut.

In the USA, President Reagan also cut taxes aggressively, but the result was less tax revenue, not more. Revenue from personal income taxes in the United States (per person, adjusted for inflation) fell by 9 per cent from 1980 to 1984, even though average income (per person, adjusted for inflation) grew by 4 per cent over this period. The tax cut, together with policy makers' unwillingness to restrain spending, began a long period during which the US government spent more than it collected in taxes. Throughout Reagan's two terms in office, and for many years thereafter, the US government ran large budget deficits.

Yet Laffer's argument is not completely without merit. Although an overall cut in tax rates normally reduces revenue, some taxpayers at some times may be on the wrong side of the Laffer curve. The idea that cutting taxes can raise revenue may be correct if applied to those taxpayers facing the highest tax rates, but most people face lower marginal rates. Where the *typical* worker is on the top end of the Laffer curve, it may be more appropriate. In Sweden in the early 1980s, for instance, the typical worker faced a marginal tax rate of about 80 per cent. Such a high tax rate provides a substantial disincentive to work. Studies have suggested that Sweden would indeed have raised more tax revenue if it had lowered its tax rates.

Policy makers disagree about these issues in part because they disagree about the size of the relevant elasticities. The more elastic that supply and demand are in any market, the more taxes in that market distort behaviour, and the more likely it is that a tax cut will raise tax revenue. There is no debate, however, about the general lesson: how much revenue the government gains or loses from a tax change cannot be computed just by looking at tax rates. It also depends on how the tax change affects people's behaviour.

Quick Quiz If the government doubles the tax on petrol, can you be sure that revenue from the petrol tax will rise? Can you be sure that the deadweight loss from the petrol tax will rise? Explain.

IN THE NEWS

The Unintended Effects of Taxes

Levying any tax may be done for good reasons but the effects of the tax cannot always be foreseen because it is never easy to predict how incentives will be affected and how behaviour will change as a result. This article highlights such a case.

When the economy is growing strongly governments might want to find ways of making sure that all capacity is fully utilized. One example of such spare capacity is buildings that are lying empty. Having disused shops, offices, industrial or manufacturing facilities is something that the UK government wanted to discourage. In 2006–2007, economic growth was relatively strong, commercial rents were increasing as demand for business property rose. Businesses in the UK have to pay business taxes, specifically a tax on the use of a building for a business. If for some reason the building is not actively being used for business there is some tax relief provided.

In 2007, however, the UK government decided to cut that relief. Prior to the tax change owners of empty business premises paid no tax for the first three months and then 50 per cent thereafter. The aim of this incentive was to give owners of premises the chance to find alternative uses for the building and / or to new tenants. The tax change, which came into effect on 1 April 2008, kept the tax allowance free for the fist three months but thereafter owners were required to pay the full tax. Local government minister Phil Woolas said: 'The reforms will encourage owners of empty properties to bring them back into use, helping to create thriving and vibrant town centres. No-one wants to live or work next to an empty property, and it is frankly daft for the state to subsidize it when commercial rents are so high. That is why a package of reforms that will drive down those rents, encourage business growth, and promote brownfield [former industrial or commercial areas that are not currently being used] development is needed. As well as reforming empty property rates, from last month a new 100% capital allowance is available for the cost of renovating or converting unused businesses in deprived areas.'

The minister was clear on the economic rationale for the tax reforms – provide incentives to get disused buildings back into use, increase the supply of business premises available, drive down rents whilst at the same time giving incentives in the form of capital allowances to encourage renovation. The tax reforms were projected to raise the government around £1.4 billion in tax revenue. Surely a sound policy?

It might have been if economic growth had continued to be strong but the introduction of the tax reforms came at the same time as one of the most severe recessions the UK had witnessed. Bringing disused buildings back into production in a recession was not easy, regardless of the penalty faced for not doing so. The question then arises, how do owners react to the changed circumstances? If they leave their buildings unused then they face a financial penalty in the form of the tax. Trying to bring the building back into use was not an option for many so only one option remained, destroy the building! The cost of demolishing an unused building would have to be factored into the equation but if the cost of demolition was less than the stream of tax payments that have to be made over time then it would be worth doing.

And this is exactly what happened. In Sunderland a business park was demolished after the landlord who owned the land and property, O&H Q7 Ltd., received advice from its agents that the tax liability on the disused buildings was likely to be high. The agents commented: 'The rateable value of the units demolished would have incurred a cost of well over £150 000 per year to our clients, a cost that until then had not been necessary. In demolishing these factory units, we have undoubtedly lost some major assets not just as far as our client is concerned but also as in respect of the City of Sunderland.' This pattern of behaviour was being repeated across many parts of the UK by small and large landlords who owned disused buildings. In addition some construction companies were reported to be leaving sites unfinished rather than incurring the cost of the tax because of the difficulty in the economic climate of the time of letting finished buildings.

The distortions as a result of the policy had some other interesting twists. In the north-east of England, for example, a government agency charged with economic development of the region faced the prospect of having to divert cash it had for regeneration of the area to the Treasury to pay the tax on unused buildings. The buildings concerned were ones that it had taken ownership of and were targeted for regeneration.

The chair of a group representing government backed urban funding councils was quoted as saying: 'There is a lot of pre-emptive demolition going on. This is already having a visual impact – cities are beginning to look like broken teeth.'

CONCLUSION

Taxes, someone once said, are the price we pay for a civilized society. Indeed, our society cannot exist without some form of taxes. We all expect the government to provide us with certain services, such as roads, parks, police and national defence. These public services require tax revenue.

This chapter has shed some light on how high the price of civilized society can be. One of the *Ten Principles of Economics* discussed in Chapter 1 is that markets are usually a good way to organize economic activity. When the government imposes taxes on buyers or sellers of a good, however, society loses some of the benefits of market efficiency. Taxes are costly to market participants not only because taxes transfer resources from those participants to the government, but also because they alter incentives and distort market outcomes. Throughout this chapter we have assumed that the benefit to the government, or more accurately, the third party who receives the benefit of the tax spending, is equal to the tax revenue given by $T \times Q$. This may not always be the case. To get a more accurate analysis of the size of deadweight losses arising from taxes, we may have to find a way to place a value on the benefits of the tax spending. For example, if taxes are spent on improving the road infrastructure there is a benefit to car drivers which may be greater than the tax spending. Calculating the value of these benefits is not easy but has to be carried out to get a more accurate picture of the change in welfare. How the government chooses to spend tax revenue is also a factor to consider. A paper written by Gupta, Verhoeven and Tiongson in 2004[1] entitled 'Public Spending on health care and the Poor' concluded that in 70 developing and transition economies there was evidence to suggest that the impact of public spending on health care on the poor could be substantial in comparison with spending on the non-poor. A 1 per cent increase in public spending on health, for example, reduces child mortality by twice as many deaths amongst the poor as the non-poor and infant mortality rates are similarly affected. This highlights that there are many other factors that may have to be taken into consideration when analysing changes in welfare as a result of taxes.

SUMMARY

- A tax on a good reduces the welfare of buyers and sellers of the good, and the reduction in consumer and producer surplus usually exceeds the revenue raised by the government. The fall in total surplus – the sum of consumer surplus, producer surplus and tax revenue – is called the deadweight loss of the tax.

- Taxes have deadweight losses because they cause buyers to consume less and sellers to produce less, and this change in behaviour shrinks the size of the market

below the level that maximizes total surplus. Because the elasticities of supply and demand measure how much market participants respond to market conditions, larger elasticities imply larger deadweight losses.

- As a tax grows larger, it distorts incentives more, and its deadweight loss grows larger. Tax revenue first rises with the size of a tax. Eventually, however, a larger tax reduces tax revenue because it reduces the size of the market.

KEY CONCEPTS

deadweight loss, p. 162

[1]Gupta, S. Verhoeven, M. & Tiongson, E.R. (2004) 'Public Spending on Health Care and the Poor', in Gupta, S. Clements, B., Inchauste, G. (eds), *Helping Countries Develop: The Role of Fiscal Policy*, Washington DC, IMF.

QUESTIONS FOR REVIEW

1. What happens to consumer and producer surplus when the sale of a good is taxed? How does the change in consumer and producer surplus compare to the tax revenue? Explain.

2. Draw a supply and demand diagram with a tax on the sale of the good. Show the deadweight loss. Show the tax revenue.

3. How do the elasticities of supply and demand affect the deadweight loss of a tax? Why do they have this effect?

4. Why do experts disagree about whether labour taxes have small or large deadweight losses?

5. What happens to the deadweight loss and tax revenue when a tax is increased?

PROBLEMS AND APPLICATIONS

1. The market for pizza is characterized by a downward sloping demand curve and an upward sloping supply curve.
   a. Draw the competitive market equilibrium. Label the price, quantity, consumer surplus and producer surplus. Is there any deadweight loss? Explain.
   b. Suppose that the government forces each pizzeria to pay a €11 tax on each pizza sold. Illustrate the effect of this tax on the pizza market, being sure to label the consumer surplus, producer surplus, government revenue and deadweight loss. How does each area compare to the pre-tax case?
   c. If the tax were removed, pizza eaters and sellers would be better off, but the government would lose tax revenue. Suppose that consumers and producers voluntarily transferred some of their gains to the government. Could all parties (including the government) be better off than they were with a tax? Explain using the labelled areas in your graph.

2. Evaluate the following two statements. Do you agree? Why or why not?
   a. 'If the government taxes land, wealthy landowners will pass the tax on to their poorer renters.'
   b. 'If the government taxes blocks of flats, wealthy landlords will pass the tax on to their poorer renters.'

3. Evaluate the following two statements. Do you agree? Why or why not?
   a. 'A tax that has no deadweight loss cannot raise any revenue for the government.'
   b. 'A tax that raises no revenue for the government cannot have any deadweight loss.'

4. Consider the market for rubber bands.
   a. If this market has very elastic supply and very inelastic demand, how would the burden of a tax on rubber bands be shared between consumers and producers? Use the tools of consumer surplus and producer surplus in your answer.
   b. If this market has very inelastic supply and very elastic demand, how would the burden of a tax on rubber bands be shared between consumers and producers?

   Contrast your answer with your answer to part (a).

5. Suppose that the government imposes a tax on heating oil.
   a. Would the deadweight loss from this tax likely be greater in the first year after it is imposed or in the fifth year? Explain.
   b. Would the revenue collected from this tax likely be greater in the first year after it is imposed or in the fifth year? Explain.

6. After your economics lecture one day, your friend suggests that taxing food would be a good way to raise revenue because the demand for food is quite inelastic. In what sense is taxing food a 'good' way to raise revenue?

   In what sense is it not a 'good' way to raise revenue?

7. The government places a tax on the purchase of socks.
   a. Illustrate the effect of this tax on equilibrium price and quantity in the sock market. Identify the following areas both before and after the imposition of the tax: total spending by consumers; total revenue for producers; and government tax revenue.
   b. Does the price received by producers rise or fall? Can you tell whether total receipts for producers rise or fall? Explain.
   c. Does the price paid by consumers rise or fall? Can you tell whether total spending by consumers rises or falls? Explain carefully. (Hint: think about elasticity.)

If total consumer spending falls, does consumer surplus rise? Explain.

8. Suppose the government currently raises €100 million through a €0.01 tax on widgets, and another €100 million through a €0.10 tax on gadgets. If the government doubled the tax rate on widgets and eliminated the tax on gadgets, would it raise more money than today, less money or the same amount of money? Explain.

9. In the 1980s the UK government imposed a 'poll tax' that required each person to pay a flat amount to the government independent of his or her income or wealth. What is the effect of such a tax on economic efficiency? What is the effect on economic equity? Do you think this was a popular tax? Explain your answer.

10. This chapter analysed the welfare effects of a tax on a good. Consider now the opposite policy. Suppose that the government *subsidizes* a good: for each unit of the good sold, the government pays €2 to the buyer. How does the subsidy affect consumer surplus, producer surplus, tax revenue and total surplus? Does a subsidy lead to a deadweight loss? Explain.

11. (This problem uses some secondary school algebra and is challenging.) Suppose that a market is described by the following supply and demand equations:

$$Q^S = 2P$$
$$Q^D = 300 - P$$

a. Solve for the equilibrium price and the equilibrium quantity.

b. Suppose that a tax of T is placed on buyers, so the new demand equation is:

$$Q^D = 300 - (P + T).$$

Solve for the new equilibrium. What happens to the price received by sellers, the price paid by buyers and the quantity sold?

c. Tax revenue is $T \times Q$. Use your answer to part (b) to solve for tax revenue as a function of T. Graph this relationship for T between 0 and 300.

d. The deadweight loss of a tax is the area of the triangle between the supply and demand curves. Recalling that the area of a triangle is $1/2 \times$ base $\times$ height, solve for deadweight loss as a function of T. Graph this relationship for T between 0 and 300. (Hint: looking sideways, the base of the deadweight loss triangle is T, and the height is the difference between the quantity sold with the tax and the quantity sold without the tax.)

e. The government now levies a tax on this good of €200 per unit. Is this a good policy? Why or why not? Can you propose a better policy?

For further resources, visit
www.cengage.com/mankiw_taylor2

9 APPLICATION: INTERNATIONAL TRADE

If you check the labels on the clothes you are now wearing, you will probably find that some of your clothes were made in another country. A century ago the textiles and clothing industry was a major part of the UK and many other European economies. In fact, when Ricardo first developed his argument about the principle of comparative advantage back in the early 19th century, he used an example of cloth being produced in England and wine in Portugal. Portugal still has a comparative advantage in producing wine relative to many countries in the world, but England no longer has a comparative advantage in producing cloth. Faced with foreign competitors that could produce quality goods at low cost, many European firms have found it increasingly difficult to produce and sell textiles and clothing at a profit. As a result, they have laid off their workers and shut down their factories. Today, much of the textiles and clothing that Europeans consume is imported from outside of Europe.

The story of the textiles industry raises important questions for economic policy: how does international trade affect economic well-being? Who gains and who loses from free trade among countries, and how do the gains compare to the losses?

Chapter 3 introduced the study of international trade by applying the principle of comparative advantage. According to this principle, all countries can benefit from trading with one another because trade allows each country to specialize in doing what it does best. But the analysis in Chapter 3 was incomplete. It did not explain how the international marketplace achieves these gains from trade or how the gains are distributed among various economic actors.

We now return to the study of international trade and take up these questions. Over the past several chapters we have developed many tools for analysing how markets work: supply, demand, equilibrium, consumer surplus, producer surplus and so on. With these tools we can learn more about the effects of international trade on economic well-being.

THE DETERMINANTS OF TRADE

Consider the market for olive oil. The olive oil market is well suited to examining the gains and losses from international trade: olive oil is made in many countries around the world, and there is much world trade in olive oil. Moreover, the olive oil market is one in which policy makers often consider (and sometimes implement) trade restrictions to protect domestic olive oil producers from foreign competitors. We examine here the olive oil market in the imaginary country of Isoland.

The Equilibrium Without Trade

As our story begins, the Isolandian olive oil market is isolated from the rest of the world. By government decree, no one in Isoland is allowed to import or export olive oil, and the penalty for violating the decree is so large that no one dares try.

Because there is no international trade, the market for olive oil in Isoland consists solely of Isolandian buyers and sellers. As Figure 9.1 shows, the domestic price adjusts to balance the quantity supplied by domestic sellers and the quantity demanded by domestic buyers. The figure shows the consumer and producer

FIGURE 9.1

The Equilibrium Without International Trade

When an economy cannot trade in world markets, the price adjusts to balance domestic supply and demand. This figure shows consumer and producer surplus in an equilibrium without international trade for the olive oil market in the imaginary country of Isoland.

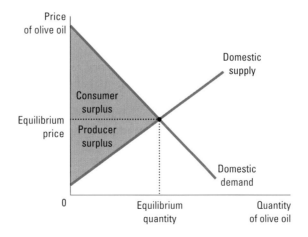

surplus in the equilibrium without trade. The sum of consumer and producer surplus measures the total benefits that buyers and sellers receive from the olive oil market.

Now suppose that, in an election upset, Isoland elects a new president. The president campaigned on a platform of 'change' and promised the voters bold new ideas. Her first act is to assemble a team of economists to evaluate Isolandian trade policy. She asks them to report back on three questions:

- If the government allowed Isolandians to import and export olive oil, what would happen to the price of olive oil and the quantity of olive oil sold in the domestic olive oil market?
- Who would gain from free trade in olive oil and who would lose, and would the gains exceed the losses?
- Should a tariff (a tax on olive oil imports) or an import quota (a limit on olive oil imports) be part of the new trade policy?

After reviewing supply and demand in their favourite textbook (this one, of course), the Isolandian economics team begins its analysis.

The World Price and Comparative Advantage

The first issue our economists take up is whether Isoland is likely to become an olive oil importer or an olive oil exporter. In other words, if free trade were allowed, would Isolandians end up buying or selling olive oil in world markets?

world price
the price of a good that prevails in the world market for that good

To answer this question, the economists compare the current Isolandian price of olive oil with the price of olive oil in other countries. We call the price prevailing in world markets the **world price**. If the world price of olive oil is higher than the domestic price, then Isoland would become an exporter of olive oil once trade is permitted. Isolandian olive oil producers would be eager to receive the higher prices available abroad and would start selling their olive oil to buyers in other countries. Conversely, if the world price of olive oil is lower than the domestic price, then Isoland would become an importer of olive oil. Because foreign sellers offer a better price, Isolandian olive oil consumers would quickly start buying olive oil from other countries.

In essence, comparing the world price and the domestic price before trade indicates whether Isoland has a comparative advantage in producing olive oil. The domestic price reflects the opportunity cost of olive oil: it tells us how much an Isolandian must give up to get one unit of olive oil. If the domestic price is low, the cost of producing olive oil in Isoland is low, suggesting that Isoland has a comparative advantage in producing olive oil relative to the rest of the world. If the domestic price is high, then the cost of producing olive oil in Isoland is high, suggesting that foreign countries have a comparative advantage in producing olive oil.

As we saw in Chapter 3, trade among nations is ultimately based on comparative advantage. That is, trade is beneficial because it allows each nation to specialize in doing what it does best. By comparing the world price and the domestic price before trade, we can determine whether Isoland is better or worse at producing olive oil than the rest of the world.

Quick Quiz The country Autarka does not allow international trade. In Autarka, you can buy a wool suit for 300 grams of gold. Meanwhile, in neighbouring countries, you can buy the same suit for 200 grams of gold. If Autarka were to allow free trade, would it import or export suits? Why?

THE WINNERS AND LOSERS FROM TRADE

To analyse the welfare effects of free trade, the Isolandian economists begin with the assumption that Isoland is a small economy compared with the rest of the world so that its actions have a negligible effect on world markets. The small economy assumption has a specific implication for analysing the olive oil market: if Isoland is a small economy, then the change in Isoland's trade policy will not affect the world price of olive oil. The Isolandians are said to be *price takers* in the world economy. That is, they take the world price of olive oil as given. They can sell olive oil at this price and be exporters, or buy olive oil at this price and be importers.

The small economy assumption is not necessary to analyse the gains and losses from international trade. But the Isolandian economists know from experience (and from reading Chapter 2 of this book) that this assumption greatly simplifies the analysis. They also know that the basic lessons do not change in the more complicated case of a large economy.

The Gains and Losses of an Exporting Country

Figure 9.2 shows the Isolandian olive oil market when the domestic equilibrium price before trade is below the world price. Once free trade is allowed, the domestic price rises to equal the world price. No seller of olive oil would accept less than the world price, and no buyer would pay more than the world price.

With the domestic price now equal to the world price, the domestic quantity supplied differs from the domestic quantity demanded. The supply curve shows the quantity of olive oil supplied by Isolandian sellers. The demand curve shows the quantity of olive oil demanded by Isolandian buyers. Because the domestic quantity supplied is greater than the domestic quantity demanded, Isoland sells olive oil to other countries. Thus, Isoland becomes an olive oil exporter.

FIGURE 9.2

International Trade in an Exporting Country

Once trade is allowed, the domestic price rises to equal the world price. The supply curve shows the quantity of olive oil produced domestically, and the demand curve shows the quantity consumed domestically. Exports from Isoland equal the difference between the domestic quantity supplied and the domestic quantity demanded at the world price.

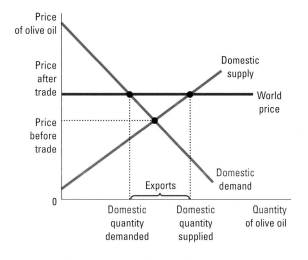

Although domestic quantity supplied and domestic quantity demanded differ, the olive oil market is still in equilibrium because there is now another participant in the market: the rest of the world. One can view the horizontal line at the world price as representing the demand for olive oil from the rest of the world. This demand curve is perfectly elastic because Isoland, as a small economy, can sell as much olive oil as it wants at the world price.

Now consider the gains and losses from opening up trade. Clearly, not everyone benefits. Trade forces the domestic price to rise to the world price. Domestic producers of olive oil are better off because they can now sell olive oil at a higher price, but domestic consumers of olive oil are worse off because they have to buy olive oil at a higher price.

To measure these gains and losses, we look at the changes in consumer and producer surplus, which are shown in the graph and table in Figure 9.3. Before trade is allowed, the price of olive oil adjusts to balance domestic supply and domestic demand. Consumer surplus, the area between the demand curve and the before-trade price, is area A + B. Producer surplus, the area between the supply curve and the before-trade price, is area C. Total surplus before trade, the sum of consumer and producer surplus, is area A + B + C.

After trade is allowed, the domestic price rises to the world price. Consumer surplus is area A (the area between the demand curve and the world price). Producer surplus is area B + C + D (the area between the supply curve and the world price). Thus, total surplus with trade is area A + B + C + D.

FIGURE 9.3

How Free Trade Affects Welfare in an Exporting Country

When the domestic price rises to equal the world price, sellers are better off (producer surplus rises from C to B + C + D), and buyers are worse off (consumer surplus falls from A + B to A). Total surplus rises by an amount equal to area D, indicating that trade raises the economic well-being of the country as a whole.

	Before trade	After trade	Change
Consumer surplus	A + B	A	− B
Producer surplus	C	B + C + D	+(B + D)
Total surplus	A + B + C	A + B + C + D	+D

The area D shows the increase in total surplus and represents the gains from trade.

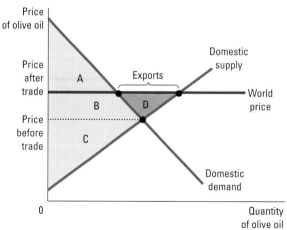

These welfare calculations show who wins and who loses from trade in an exporting country. Sellers benefit because producer surplus increases by the area B + D. Buyers are worse off because consumer surplus decreases by the area B. Because the gains of sellers exceed the losses of buyers by the area D, total surplus in Isoland increases.

This analysis of an exporting country yields two conclusions:

* When a country allows trade and becomes an exporter of a good, domestic producers of the good are better off, and domestic consumers of the good are worse off.
* Trade raises the economic well-being of a nation in the sense that the gains of the winners exceed the losses of the losers.

The Gains and Losses of an Importing Country

Now suppose that the domestic price before trade is above the world price. Once again, after free trade is allowed, the domestic price must equal the world price. As Figure 9.4 shows, the domestic quantity supplied is less than the domestic quantity demanded. The difference between the domestic quantity demanded and the domestic quantity supplied is bought from other countries, and Isoland becomes an olive oil importer.

In this case, the horizontal line at the world price represents the supply of the rest of the world. This supply curve is perfectly elastic because Isoland is a small economy and, therefore, can buy as much olive oil as it wants at the world price.

Now consider the gains and losses from trade. Once again, not everyone benefits. When trade forces the domestic price to fall, domestic consumers are better off (they can now buy olive oil at a lower price), and domestic producers are worse off (they now have to sell olive oil at a lower price). Changes in consumer

FIGURE 9.4

International Trade in an Importing Country

Once trade is allowed, the domestic price falls to equal the world price. The supply curve shows the amount produced domestically, and the demand curve shows the amount consumed domestically. Imports equal the difference between the domestic quantity demanded and the domestic quantity supplied at the world price.

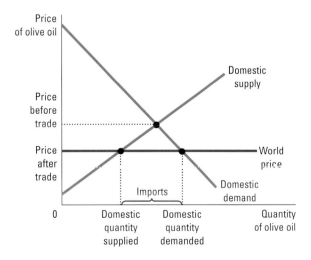

FIGURE 9.5

How Free Trade Affects Welfare in an Importing Country

When the domestic price falls to equal the world price, buyers are better off (consumer surplus rises from A to A + B + D), and sellers are worse off (producer surplus falls from B + C to C). Total surplus rises by an amount equal to area D, indicating that trade raises the economic well-being of the country as a whole.

	Before trade	After trade	Change
Consumer surplus	A	A + B + D	+(B + D)
Producer surplus	B + C	C	− B
Total surplus	A + B + C	A + B + C + D	+D

The area D shows the increase in total surplus and represents the gains from trade.

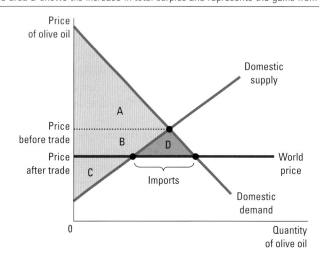

and producer surplus measure the size of the gains and losses, as shown in the graph and table in Figure 9.5. Before trade, consumer surplus is area A, producer surplus is area B + C, and total surplus is area A + B + C. After trade is allowed, consumer surplus is area A + B + D, producer surplus is area C and total surplus is area A + B + C + D.

These welfare calculations show who wins and who loses from trade in an importing country. Buyers benefit because consumer surplus increases by the area B + D. Sellers are worse off because producer surplus falls by the area B. The gains of buyers exceed the losses of sellers, and total surplus increases by the area D.

This analysis of an importing country yields two conclusions parallel to those for an exporting country:

- When a country allows trade and becomes an importer of a good, domestic consumers of the good are better off, and domestic producers of the good are worse off.
- Trade raises the economic well-being of a nation in the sense that the gains of the winners exceed the losses of the losers.

Having completed our analysis of trade, we can better understand one of the *Ten Principles of Economics* in Chapter 1: trade can make everyone better off. If Isoland opens up its olive oil market to international trade the change will create winners and losers, regardless of whether Isoland ends up exporting or importing olive oil.

Notice that in our analysis, we have not made a judgement about the winners and losers – whether the gain to the producers is more valuable than the loss to the consumers. The important issue, from an economic analysis perspective, is the effect on total welfare, which in this case has risen for Isoland. In the real world, policy makers may have to take into consideration the power which resides with different groups. If domestic consumers of olive oil in Isoland had considerable lobbying power compared with olive oil producers then policy decisions may be affected which distort outcomes and reduce total welfare. The effect on consumers, for example, might be limited in comparison with the gains to producers but presenting arguments in this way does not always win political points! This is something that must always be considered because whilst economic analysis may point to a clear policy decision and outcome, there are many other factors that decision makers have to take into account, as exemplified when we look at the arguments for restricting trade on page 189.

In our example, the gains of the winners exceed the losses of the losers, so the winners could compensate the losers and still be better off. In this sense, trade *can* make everyone better off. But *will* trade make everyone better off? Probably not. In practice, compensation for the losers from international trade is rare. Without such compensation, opening up to international trade is a policy that expands the size of the economic cake, whilst perhaps leaving some participants in the economy with a smaller slice.

We can now see why the debate over trade policy is so often contentious. Whenever a policy creates winners and losers, the stage is set for a political battle as outlined above. Nations sometimes fail to enjoy the gains from trade simply because the losers from free trade have more political clout than the winners. The losers lobby for trade restrictions, such as tariffs and import quotas.

The Effects of a Tariff

The Isolandian economists next consider the effects of a **tariff** – a tax on imported goods. The economists quickly realize that a tariff on olive oil will have no effect if Isoland becomes an olive oil exporter. If no one in Isoland is interested in importing olive oil, a tax on olive oil imports is irrelevant. The tariff matters only if Isoland becomes an olive oil importer. Concentrating their attention on this case, the economists compare welfare with and without the tariff.

tariff
a tax on goods produced abroad and sold domestically

The graph in Figure 9.6 shows the Isolandian market for olive oil. Under free trade, the domestic price equals the world price. A tariff raises the price of imported olive oil above the world price by the amount of the tariff. Domestic suppliers of olive oil, who compete with suppliers of imported olive oil, can now sell their olive oil for the world price plus the amount of the tariff. Thus, the price of olive oil – both imported and domestic – rises by the amount of the tariff and is, therefore, closer to the price that would prevail without trade.

The change in price affects the behaviour of domestic buyers and sellers. Because the tariff raises the price of olive oil, it reduces the domestic quantity demanded from Q_1^D to Q_2^D and raises the domestic quantity supplied from Q_1^S to Q_2^S. Thus, the tariff reduces the quantity of imports and moves the domestic market closer to its equilibrium without trade.

Now consider the gains and losses from the tariff. Because the tariff raises the domestic price, domestic sellers are better off, and domestic buyers are worse off. In addition, the government raises revenue. To measure these gains and losses, we look at the changes in consumer surplus, producer surplus and government revenue. These changes are summarized in the table in Figure 9.6.

Before the tariff, the domestic price equals the world price. Consumer surplus, the area between the demand curve and the world price, is area A + B + C + D + E + F. Producer surplus, the area between the supply curve and the world price, is area G. Government revenue equals zero. Total surplus – the sum of consumer

FIGURE 9.6

The Effects of a Tariff

A tariff reduces the quantity of imports and moves a market closer to the equilibrium that would exist without trade. Total surplus falls by an amount equal to area D + F. These two triangles represent the deadweight loss from the tariff.

	Before traiff	After traiff	Change
Consumer surplus	A + B + C + D + E + F	A + B	− (C + D + E +F)
Producer surplus	G	C + G	+ C
Government revenue	None	E	+ E
Total surplus	A + B + C + D + E + F + G	A + B + C + E + G	− (D + F)

The area D + F shows the fall in total surplus and represents the deadweight loss of the tariff.

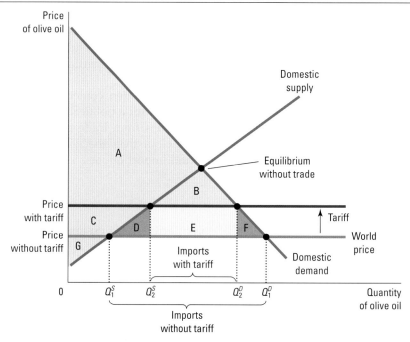

surplus, producer surplus and government revenue – is area A + B + C + D + E + F + G.

Once the government imposes a tariff, the domestic price exceeds the world price by the amount of the tariff. Consumer surplus is now area A + B. Producer surplus is area C + G. Government revenue, which is the quantity of after-tariff imports times the size of the tariff, is the area E. Thus, total surplus with the tariff is area A + B + C + E + G.

To determine the total welfare effects of the tariff, we add the change in consumer surplus (which is negative), the change in producer surplus (positive) and the change in government revenue (positive). We find that total surplus in the market decreases by the area D + F. This fall in total surplus is the *deadweight loss* of the tariff.

A tariff causes a deadweight loss simply because a tariff is a type of tax and follows the same principles as we discussed in Chapter 8. Like most taxes, it distorts incentives and pushes the allocation of scarce resources away from the optimum. In this case, we can identify two effects. First, the tariff on olive oil raises the price of olive oil that domestic producers can charge above the world price and, as a result, encourages them to increase production of olive oil (from Q_1^S to Q_2^S). Second, the tariff raises the price that domestic olive oil buyers have to pay and, therefore, encourages them to reduce consumption of olive oil (from Q_1^D to Q_2^D). Area D represents the deadweight loss from the overproduction of olive oil, and area F represents the deadweight loss from the underconsumption. The total deadweight loss of the tariff is the sum of these two triangles.

The Effects of an Import Quota

The Isolandian economists next consider the effects of an **import quota** – a limit on the quantity of imports. In particular, imagine that the Isolandian government distributes a limited number of import licences. Each licence gives the licence holder the right to import 1 tonne of olive oil into Isoland from abroad. The Isolandian economists want to compare welfare under a policy of free trade and welfare with the addition of this import quota.

The graph and table in Figure 9.7 show how an import quota affects the Isolandian market for olive oil. Because the import quota prevents Isolandians from

import quota
a limit on the quantity of a good that can be produced abroad and sold domestically

FIGURE 9.7

The Effects of an Import Quota

An import quota, like a tariff, reduces the quantity of imports and moves a market closer to the equilibrium that would exist without trade. Total surplus falls by an amount equal to area D + F. These two triangles represent the deadweight loss from the quota. In addition, the import quota transfers E′ + E″ to whoever holds the import licences.

	Before quota	After quota	Change
Consumer surplus	A + B + C + D + E′ + E″ + F	A + B	− (C + D + E′ + E″ + F)
Producer surplus	G	C + G	+ C
Government revenue	None	E′ + E″	+(E′ + E″)
Total surplus	A + B + C + D + E′ + E″ + F + G	A + B + C + E′ + E″ + G	− (D + F)

The area D + F shows the fall in total surplus and represents the deadweight loss of the quota.

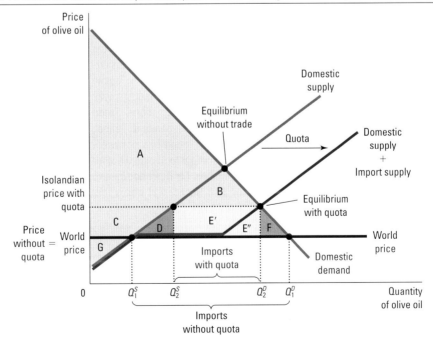

IN THE NEWS

In 2002 economists criticized the US for imposing tariffs on the import of steel, a decision which was later reversed by President Bush in 2003. Whilst Mr Bush was able to show steel producers that he had tried to help them he was also able to claim a victory for free trade in the time it took the World Trade Organization to respond to the accusations that the US move was illegal. So, what lessons have been learned?

Tyred Of Trade?

By succumbing to domestic pressures, America has started an alarming trade row with China.

In raw economic terms Barack Obama's imposition of tariffs on Chinese tyres hardly registers. The number of jobs affected is barely a rounding error in measurements of the mighty American workforce. The cost to consumers is also slight. But in geopolitical terms, it is a whopper. Mr Obama's most overtly protectionist decision so far has triggered a predictably angry reaction from China, which threatened to retaliate against American chickens and car parts and to haul America before the World Trade Organization. The *Global Times*, a newspaper that often reflects the views of hardline nationalists in China, ran a front-page headline saying 'America has erred before the world'.

The decision does come at a risky time. Protectionist actions, in particular against China, have been multiplying in recent years, even within the confines of WTO rules. In November 2008, and April 2009, George Bush and Mr Obama, respectively, on both occasions joined by other leaders of the G20, pledged to 'refrain from raising new barriers to investment or to trade in goods and services'; yet new barriers have steadily increased.

Until now Mr Obama has tried to allay fears that he is a bit of a protectionist by abandoning campaign threats to renegotiate the North American Free-Trade Agreement and to punish China for holding down its currency. He has surrounded himself with mainstream, pro-free-trade economists, watered down (though failed to veto) 'Buy America' provisions in the fiscal stimulus, and opposed carbon tariffs in the cap-and-trade bill now before Congress. Even now Mr Obama insists he is 'committed to pursuing expanded trade and new trade agreements', and this week he defended his action as nothing more than the enforcement of trade laws.

That, however, is a stretch. Mr Obama had no obligation to act. Under the terms of joining the WTO, China gave other countries the right until 2013 to impose temporary 'safeguards' against surges of Chinese imports. In America the relevant law, Section 421 of the Trade Act, does not require proof that China has broken international trade rules against subsidizing or dumping goods (i.e., selling below cost), only that the domestic industry was disrupted. Once the International Trade Commission, an independent panel, says that such disruption has occurred, it is up to the president to decide whether to impose remedies. Mr Bush declined to do so in the four Section 421 cases that came to him.

Politically, Mr Obama may have felt he had little choice. The United Steelworkers union filed the complaint in April 2009 and the law required Mr Obama to decide by September 17th 2009. Having promised repeatedly to enforce trade laws more vigorously than Mr Bush, Mr Obama presumably felt he needed to do something. The economic benefits to those who lobbied for protection, however, are minuscule. Domestic manufacturers have largely abandoned the low-end tyre market. The tariffs, which drop from 35% in the first year to 25% in the third, will mostly divert supply to Mexico, India, Indonesia and Brazil, says Tom Prusa, a Rutgers economist who has done work for tyre companies.

China also bears some blame. American negotiators were ready to withhold the tariffs if China made concessions, but to no avail. Mr Obama's defenders note that China would not have gained entry to the WTO without the 'safeguard' provisions, which bought political support among its trading partners. And voters and Congress might be less likely to support future trade agreements if the safeguards in existing agreements are never used.

Still, Mr Obama's imposition of tariffs will tempt more industries and unions to seek similar relief, and he will have to decide whether this decision is a template or an exception. Other countries, fearing a wave of diverted Chinese imports, could copy America's action. After Mr Bush raised steel tariffs in 2002, half a dozen other countries followed. Under the terms on which China entered the WTO, others can impose safeguards simply because America has. The European Union, however, would struggle to master enough support among its member states.

China itself faces a delicate balancing act. On September 15th 2009 more than 300 of the Communist Party's top officials held a four-day annual meeting in Beijing where, among other things, they were expected to decide whether to give President Hu's presumed successor, Vice-President Xi Jinping, a further boost by making him a deputy commander-in-chief of the armed forces. Succession politics could be complicated by high-level disputes over how to respond to the Americans.

But nor can he let Mr Obama entirely off the hook. Having announced an investigation into America's alleged dumping, it will be hard to back away. Indeed, the spat will awaken unpleasant memories of the controversy over China's accession to the WTO. China agreed to the safeguards clause in 2001 with gritted teeth, in part because its reformists saw WTO entry as a useful tool for encouraging market-oriented reforms. China's prime minister at the time, Zhu Rongji, was subjected to

harsh criticism from conservatives at home for pressing so hard for WTO entry. Times are more difficult now than they were back then, so expect a few more fireworks.

Source: 'Playing with fire; The tyre wars.' *The Economist* [US] 19 September 2009: © 2009 The Economist Newspaper Ltd. Biz/ed Custom Journals. Web. 2 February 2010. <http://find.galegroup.com/gps/start.do?prodId=IPS&userGroupName=bized>. © 2009 The Economist Newspaper Ltd.

buying as much olive oil as they want from abroad, the supply of olive oil is no longer perfectly elastic at the world price. Instead, as long as the price of olive oil in Isoland is above the world price, the licence holders import as much as they are permitted, and the total supply of olive oil in Isoland equals the domestic supply plus the quota amount. That is, the supply curve above the world price is shifted to the right by exactly the amount of the quota. (The supply curve below the world price does not shift because, in this case, importing is not profitable for the licence holders.)

The price of olive oil in Isoland adjusts to balance supply (domestic plus imported) and demand. As the figure shows, the quota causes the price of olive oil to rise above the world price. The domestic quantity demanded falls from Q_1^D to Q_2^D, and the domestic quantity supplied rises from Q_1^S to Q_2^S. Not surprisingly, the import quota reduces olive oil imports.

Now consider the gains and losses from the quota. Because the quota raises the domestic price above the world price, domestic sellers are better off, and domestic buyers are worse off. In addition, the licence holders are better off because they make a profit from buying at the world price and selling at the higher domestic price. To measure these gains and losses, we look at the changes in consumer surplus, producer surplus and licence-holder surplus.

Before the government imposes the quota, the domestic price equals the world price. Consumer surplus, the area between the demand curve and the world price, is area $A + B + C + D + E' + E'' + F$. Producer surplus, the area between the supply curve and the world price, is area G. The surplus of licence holders equals zero because there are no licences. Total surplus, the sum of consumer, producer and licence-holder surplus, is area $A + B + C + D + E' + E'' + F + G$.

After the government imposes the import quota and issues the licences, the domestic price exceeds the world price. Domestic consumers get surplus equal to area $A + B$, and domestic producers get surplus equal to area $C + G$. The licence holders make a profit on each unit imported equal to the difference between the Isolandian price of olive oil and the world price. Their surplus equals this price differential times the quantity of imports. Thus, it equals the area of the rectangle $E' + E''$. Total surplus with the quota is the area $A + B + C + E' + E'' + G$.

To see how total welfare changes with the imposition of the quota, we add the change in consumer surplus (which is negative), the change in producer surplus (positive) and the change in licence-holder surplus (positive). We find that total surplus in the market decreases by the area $D + F$. This area represents the deadweight loss of the import quota.

"You drive a Japanese car, drink French wine, eat Chinese food, own an American computer and holiday in Mexico. How can you be AGAINST free trade?!"

This analysis should seem somewhat familiar. Indeed, if you compare the analysis of import quotas in Figure 9.7 with the analysis of tariffs in Figure 9.6, you will see that they are essentially identical. Both tariffs and import quotas raise the domestic price of the good, reduce the welfare of domestic consumers, increase the welfare of domestic producers and cause deadweight losses. There is only one difference between these two types of trade restriction: a tariff raises revenue for the government (area E in Figure 9.6), whereas an import quota creates surplus for licence holders (area E' + E'' in Figure 9.7).

Tariffs and import quotas can be made to look even more similar. Suppose that the government tries to capture the licence-holder surplus for itself by charging a fee for the licences. A licence to sell 1 tonne of olive oil is worth exactly the difference between the Isolandian price of olive oil and the world price, and the government can set the licence fee as high as this price differential. If the government does this, the licence fee for imports works exactly like a tariff: consumer surplus, producer surplus and government revenue are exactly the same under the two policies.

In practice, however, countries that restrict trade with import quotas rarely do so by selling the import licences. For example, in 1991 the European Union reached an agreement with Japan to 'voluntarily' limit the sale of Japanese cars in member countries of the EU. In this case, the Japanese government allocates the import licences to Japanese firms, and the surplus from these licences (area E' + E'') accrues to those firms. This kind of import quota is, from the standpoint of the welfare of the European Union, strictly worse than an EU tariff on imported cars. Both a tariff and an import quota raise prices, restrict trade and cause deadweight losses, but at least the tariff produces revenue for the European Union rather than for Japanese auto companies. It is perhaps not surprising, therefore, that this arrangement was terminated at the end of 1999.

Although in our analysis so far import quotas and tariffs appear to cause similar deadweight losses, a quota can potentially cause an even larger deadweight loss, depending on the mechanism used to allocate the import licences. Suppose that when Isoland imposes a quota, everyone understands that the licences will go to those who spend the most resources lobbying the Isolandian government. In this case, there is an implicit licence fee – the cost of lobbying. The revenues from this fee, however, rather than being collected by the government, are spent on lobbying expenses. The deadweight losses from this type of quota include not only the losses from overproduction (area D) and underconsumption (area F) but also whatever part of the licence-holder surplus (area E' + E'') is wasted on the cost of lobbying.

The Lessons for Trade Policy

The team of Isolandian economists can now write to the new president:

Dear Madam President,

You asked us three questions about opening up trade. After much hard work, we have the answers.

Question: If the government allowed Isolandians to import and export olive oil, what would happen to the price of olive oil and the quantity of olive oil sold in the domestic olive oil market?

Answer: Once trade is allowed, the Isolandian price of olive oil would be driven to equal the price prevailing around the world.

If the world price is now higher than the Isolandian price, our price would rise. The higher price would reduce the amount of olive oil Isolandians consume and raise the amount of olive oil that Isolandians produce. Isoland

Public Choice Theory

There is a branch of economics called public choice theory which looks at the gains and losses associated with lobbying processes like that described in our analysis so far. One of the key concepts of public choice theory is rent seeking. Rent seeking refers to cases where resources are allocated to provide rents (returns) for individuals or groups and where those rents have negative social value.

The following example highlights the issue in relation to arguments for restrictions on imports, relating to labour.

Migrant Workers

The expansion of the EU in 2004 led to the possibility of an increase in the number of workers with free access to enter all EU countries. In the UK, there was much written about immigration into the UK from the new members of the EU. In particular, the number of workers coming into the UK from Poland received widespread press coverage.

Many Polish workers legitimately working in the UK brought with them a high level of skills, motivation, work ethic and expertise. There were plenty of employers willing to testify to the benefits these workers brought to the UK economy. There were some, however, who have expressed deep concern that the flood of migrant workers to the UK was damaging. The argument put forward was that these workers were taking jobs that could be done by UK workers and that they were taking these jobs because they are prepared to work for substantially less than UK workers would be.

In 2007 Bulgaria and Romania became part of the EU. There were fears that the migration seen from Polish workers would be repeated and as a result the government negotiated restrictions on the number of migrant workers who could come to the UK.

In this case, the rents are the wages paid to UK-based workers who get

some preference over migrant workers who are now subject to a 'quota'. The costs are that the job concerned could be done by someone from Bulgaria (for example) at a lower wage, as well as to a higher quality with a subsequent benefit to society. The benefits to society as a whole of having migrant workers are subsumed amidst the fear of the effect of the flooding of the labour market with migrant workers.

The public choice theorist would be looking to judge empirically the effects of rent seeking in this case to determine the deadweight loss of the policy decision. The investigation would focus on whether the policy to raise the income of an individual or group (such as domestic-based workers in the UK) and the amount of resources that would be needed to raise that income in comparison to the losses gained by others in society would have an overall negative social impact or not.

---

would, therefore, become an olive oil exporter. This occurs because, in this case, Isoland would have a comparative advantage in producing olive oil.

Conversely, if the world price is now lower than the Isolandian price, our price would fall. The lower price would raise the amount of olive oil that Isolandians consume and lower the amount of olive oil that Isolandians produce. Isoland would, therefore, become an olive oil importer. This occurs because, in this case, other countries would have a comparative advantage in producing olive oil.

Question: Who would gain from free trade in olive oil and who would lose, and would the gains exceed the losses?

Answer: The answer depends on whether the price rises or falls when trade is allowed. If the price rises, producers of olive oil gain and consumers of olive oil lose. If the price falls, consumers gain and producers lose. In both cases, the gains are larger than the losses. Thus, free trade raises the total welfare of Isolandians.

Question: Should a tariff or an import quota be part of the new trade policy?

Answer: A tariff, like most taxes, has deadweight losses: the revenue raised would be smaller than the losses to the buyers and sellers. In this case, the deadweight losses occur because the tariff would move the economy closer to our current no-trade equilibrium. An import quota works much like a tariff and would cause similar deadweight losses. The best policy, from the standpoint of economic efficiency, would be to allow trade without a tariff or an import quota.

We hope you find these answers helpful as you decide on your new policy.

Your obedient servants,

Isolandian economics team

Quick Quiz Draw the supply and demand curve for wool suits in the country of Autarka. When trade is allowed, the price of a suit falls from 300 to 200 grams of gold. In your diagram, what is the change in consumer surplus, the change in producer surplus and the change in total surplus? How would a tariff on suit imports alter these effects?

FYI

Other Benefits of International Trade

Our conclusions so far have been based on the standard analysis of international trade. As we have seen, there are winners and losers when a nation opens itself up to trade, but the gains to the winners exceed the losses of the losers. Yet the case for free trade can be made even stronger. There are several other economic benefits of trade beyond those emphasized in the standard analysis. Here, in a nutshell, are some of these other benefits:

- *Increased variety of goods.* Goods produced in different countries are not exactly the same. German beer, for instance, is not the same as American beer. Free trade gives consumers in all countries greater variety from which to choose.
- *Lower unit costs through economies of scale.* Some goods can be produced at low unit or average cost only if they are produced in large

quantities – a phenomenon called *economies of scale.* A firm in a small country cannot take full advantage of economies of scale if it can sell only in a small domestic market. Free trade gives firms access to larger world markets and allows them to realize economies of scale more fully.
- *Increased competition.* A company shielded from foreign competitors is more likely to have market power, which in turn gives it the ability to raise prices above competitive levels. This is a type of market failure. Opening up trade fosters competition and gives the invisible hand a better chance to work its magic.
- *Enhanced flow of ideas.* The transfer of technological advances around the world is often thought to be linked to international trade in the goods that embody those advances. The best way for a poor, agricultural nation to

learn about the computer revolution, for instance, is to buy some computers from abroad, rather than trying to make them domestically.
- *Generates economic growth.* We have seen in Chapter 3 how gains from trade can benefit all countries involved. For poor countries, the increase in output can be a trigger to generating economic growth which may also bring an improvement in the standard of living for its citizens.

Thus, free international trade increases variety for consumers, allows firms to take advantage of economies of scale, makes markets more competitive, facilitates the spread of technology and helps generate economic growth. If the Isolandian economists thought these effects were important, their advice to their president would be even more forceful.

THE ARGUMENTS FOR RESTRICTING TRADE

The letter from the economics team persuades the new president of Isoland to consider opening up trade in olive oil. She notes that the domestic price is now high compared to the world price. Free trade would, therefore, cause the price of olive oil to fall and hurt domestic olive oil producers. Before implementing the new policy, she asks Isolandian olive oil companies to comment on the economists' advice.

Not surprisingly, the olive oil companies are opposed to free trade in olive oil. They believe that the government should protect the domestic olive oil industry from foreign competition. Let's consider some of the arguments they might give to support their position and how the economics team would respond.

The Jobs Argument

Opponents of free trade often argue that trade with other countries destroys domestic jobs. In our example, free trade in olive oil would cause the price of olive oil to fall, reducing the quantity of olive oil produced in Isoland and thus reducing employment in the Isolandian olive oil industry. Some Isolandian olive oil workers would lose their jobs.

Yet free trade creates jobs at the same time that it destroys them. When Isolandians buy olive oil from other countries, those countries obtain the resources to buy other goods from Isoland. Isolandian workers would move from the olive oil industry to those industries in which Isoland has a comparative advantage. Although the transition may impose hardship on some workers in the short run, it allows Isolandians as a whole to enjoy a higher standard of living.

Opponents of trade are often sceptical that trade creates jobs. They might respond that *everything* can be produced more cheaply abroad. Under free trade, they might argue, Isolandians could not be profitably employed in any industry. As Chapter 3 explains, however, the gains from trade are based on comparative advantage, not absolute advantage. Even if one country is better than another country at producing everything, each country can still gain from trading with the other. Workers in each country will eventually find jobs in the industry in which that country has a comparative advantage.

The National Security Argument

When an industry is threatened with competition from other countries, opponents of free trade often argue that the industry is vital for national security. Free trade would allow Isoland to become dependent on foreign countries to supply vital resources. If a war later broke out, Isoland might be unable to produce enough to defend itself and remain self-sufficient.

Economists acknowledge that protecting key industries may be appropriate when there are legitimate concerns over national security. Yet they fear that this argument may be used too quickly by producers eager to gain at consumers' expense. Certainly, it is tempting for those in an industry to exaggerate their role in national defence to obtain protection from foreign competition.

The Infant Industry Argument

New industries sometimes argue for temporary trade restrictions to help them get started. After a period of protection, the argument goes, these industries will mature and be able to compete with foreign competitors. Similarly, older industries sometimes argue that they need protection to help them adjust to new conditions. In 2002, for example, when US President George Bush imposed steep tariffs on the import of steel from the European Union, he argued that the industry needed protection in order to be able to afford to pay the pensions and health care costs of its retired workers and while it was going through a period of adjustment in terms of making its production more efficient in order to be able to cope with intense foreign competition.

Economists are often sceptical about such claims. The primary reason is that the infant industry argument is difficult to implement in practice. To apply protection successfully, the government would need to decide which industries will eventually be profitable and decide whether the benefits of establishing these industries exceed the costs to consumers of protection. Yet 'picking winners' is extraordinarily difficult. It is made even more difficult by the political process, which often awards protection to those industries that are politically powerful. And once a powerful industry is protected from foreign competition, the 'temporary' policy is hard to remove.

In addition, many economists are sceptical about the infant industry argument even in principle. Suppose, for instance, that the Isolandian olive oil industry is young and unable to compete profitably against foreign rivals. Yet there is reason to believe that the industry can be profitable in the long run. In this case, the owners of the firms should be willing to incur temporary losses to obtain the eventual profits. Protection is not necessary for an industry to grow. Firms in various industries – such as many internet firms today – incur temporary losses in the hope of growing and becoming profitable in the future. And many of them succeed, even without protection from foreign competition.

The Unfair Competition Argument

A common argument is that free trade is desirable only if all countries play by the same rules. If firms in different countries are subject to different laws and regulations, then it is unfair (the argument goes) to expect the firms to compete in the international marketplace. For instance, suppose that the government of Neighbourland subsidizes its olive oil industry by giving olive oil companies large tax breaks. The Isolandian olive oil industry might argue that it should be protected from this foreign competition because Neighbourland is not competing fairly.

Would it, in fact, hurt Isoland to buy olive oil from another country at a subsidized price? Certainly, Isolandian olive oil producers would suffer, but Isolandian olive oil consumers would benefit from the low price. Moreover, the case for free trade is no different: the gains of the consumers from buying at the low price would exceed the losses of the producers. Neighbourland's subsidy to its olive oil industry may be a bad policy, but it is the taxpayers of Neighbourland who bear the burden. Isoland can benefit from the opportunity to buy olive oil at a subsidized price.

The Protection as a Bargaining Chip Argument

Another argument for trade restrictions concerns the strategy of bargaining. Many policy makers claim to support free trade but, at the same time, argue that trade restrictions can be useful when we bargain with our trading partners. They claim that the threat of a trade restriction can help remove a trade restriction already imposed by a foreign government. For example, Isoland might threaten to impose a tariff on olive oil unless Neighbourland removes its tariff on wheat. If Neighbourland responds to this threat by removing its tariff, the result can be freer trade.

The problem with this bargaining strategy is that the threat may not work. If it doesn't work, the country has a difficult choice. It can carry out its threat and implement the trade restriction, which would reduce its own economic welfare. Or it can back down from its threat, which would cause it to lose prestige in international affairs. Faced with this choice, the country would probably wish that it had never made the threat in the first place.

IN THE NEWS

Economics is a dynamic subject and accepted wisdoms can always be questioned. The belief that free trade makes everyone better off is widely accepted but, as with any theory, needs to be supported by observation and evidence. What happens if observation reveals something contrary to the accepted wisdom?

Economists Rethink Free Trade

It's no wholesale repudiation, to be sure, but something momentous is happening as doubts begin to creep in.

Many ordinary householders have long been suspicious of free trade, seeing it as a destroyer of good-paying jobs. Most economists, though, have told a different story. For them, free trade has been the great unmitigated good, the force that drives a country to shed unproductive industries, focus on what it does best, and create new, higher-skilled jobs that offer better pay than those that are lost. This support of free trade by the academic establishment is a big reason why global leaders are keen to be associated with a free-trade agenda. The experts they consult have always told them that free trade was the best route to ever higher living standards.

But something momentous is happening inside the church of free trade: doubts are creeping in. We're not talking wholesale, dramatic repudiation of the theory. Economists are, however, noting that their ideas can't explain the disturbing stagnation in income that much of the middle class is experiencing. They also fear a protectionist backlash unless more is done to help those who are losing out. 'Previously, you just had extremists making extravagant claims against trade,' says Gary C. Hufbauer, a senior fellow at the Peterson Institute for International Economics. 'Now there are broader questions being raised that would not have been asked 10 or 15 years ago.'

So global leaders may be consulting on trade with experts who feel a lot less confident of the old certainties than they did just a few years ago. From Alan S. Blinder, a former vice-chairman of the Federal Reserve and member of the Council of Economic Advisers in the Clinton Administration, to Dartmouth's Matthew J. Slaughter, an international economist who served on President George W. Bush's CEA, many in the profession are re-evaluating the impact of globalization. They have studied the growth of low-wage work abroad and seen how high-speed tele-communications make it possible to handle more jobs offshore. Now they fear these factors are more menacing than they first thought.

No one is suggesting that trade is bad for countries overall. According to estimates by the Peterson Institute and others, trade and investment liberalization over the past decades have added $500 billion to $1 trillion to annual income in the US, for example.

Yet concern is rising that the gains from free trade may increasingly be going to a small group at the top. For the vast majority of Americans, Dartmouth's Slaughter points out, income growth has all but disappeared in recent years. And it's not just the low-skilled who are getting slammed. Inflation-adjusted earnings have fallen in every educational category other than the 4% who hold doctorates or professional degrees. Such numbers, Slaughter argues, suggest the share of Americans who aren't included in the gains from

trade may be very big. '[That's] a very important change from earlier generations, and it should give pause to people who say they know what's going on,' he says.

Blinder warns the pain may just be starting. Millions of service jobs in the developed world could face competition from workers in India and other low-wage nations. Many of the newly vulnerable will be in skilled fields, such as accounting or research – jobs many global companies will be able to move offshore in ever greater numbers. 'It will be a messy process of adjustment, with a lot of victims along the way,' Blinder says.

In an interview with the *Financial Times* in 2008, Hillary Clinton agreed with economist Paul A. Samuelson's argument that traditional notions of comparative advantage may no longer apply. 'The question of whether spreading globalization and information technology are strengthening or hollowing out our middle class may be the most paramount economic issue of our time,' her chief economic adviser, Gene Sperling, recently wrote. Barack Obama's adviser, the University of Chicago's Austan D. Goolsbee, is not convinced free trade is the culprit behind the squeeze on incomes. But he believes many workers aren't sharing in the gains from open markets and fears a political blowback unless something is done.

What to do? Blinder argues for a big expansion of unemployment insurance and a major overhaul of programmes which are put in place to retrain manufacturing workers whose jobs disappear. More vocational training and wage insurance, which would partially reimburse displaced workers who take new jobs at lower pay, also figure in his proposals.

That's not enough, says Slaughter. He sees a need for some form of income redistribution to spread the gains from free trade to more workers. In a controversial article Slaughter co-wrote in the summer of 2007 for *Foreign Affairs*, he proposed 'A New Deal for Globalization' in which payroll taxes for workers earning below the national median income level would be eliminated. It's one more sign of how far the trade debate has moved.

by Jane Sasseen

Source: Adapted from: http://www.businessweek.com/magazine/content/08_06/b4070032762393.htm Accessed 2 February 2010.

CASE STUDY

Trade Agreements and the World Trade Organization

A country can take one of two approaches to achieving free trade. It can take a *unilateral* approach and remove its trade restrictions on its own. This is the approach that the United Kingdom took in the 19th century and that Chile and South Korea have taken in recent years. Alternatively, a country can take a *multilateral* approach and reduce its trade restrictions while other countries do the same. In other words, it can bargain with its trading partners in an attempt to reduce trade restrictions around the world.

Perhaps the most important example of the multilateral approach is the European Union (EU), which at the time of writing has a total membership of 27 with three candidate countries who have applied to join (Croatia, Turkey and the Former Yugoslav Republic of Macedonia). The EU is an example of a **customs union**. A customs union is a group of countries that agree not to impose any restrictions at all on trade between their own economies, but to impose the same restrictions as one another on goods imported from outside the group.

Two other examples of the multilateral approach are the North American Free Trade Agreement (NAFTA) – which in 1993 lowered trade barriers among the United States, Mexico and Canada – and the General Agreement on Tariffs and Trade (GATT), which is a continuing series of negotiations among many of the world's countries with the goal of promoting free trade. The United States helped to found GATT after World War II in response to the high tariffs imposed during the Great Depression of the 1930s. Many economists believe that the high tariffs contributed to the economic hardship during that period. GATT has successfully reduced the average tariff among member countries from about 40 per cent after World War II to about 5 per cent today.

The rules established under GATT are now enforced by an international institution called the World Trade Organization (WTO). The WTO was established in 1995 and has its headquarters in Geneva, Switzerland. As of February 2010 148 countries have joined the organization, accounting for about 98 per cent of world trade. Around 30 other nations are negotiating membership to the WTO. The functions of the WTO are to administer trade agreements, provide a forum for negotiations and handle disputes that arise among member countries.

customs union
a group of countries that agree not to impose any restrictions at all on trade between their own economies, but to impose the same restrictions as one another on goods imported from countries outside the group

What are the pros and cons of the multilateral approach to free trade? One advantage is that the multilateral approach has the potential to result in freer trade than a unilateral approach because it can reduce trade restrictions abroad as well as at home. If international negotiations fail, however, the result could be more restricted trade than under a unilateral approach.

In addition, the multilateral approach may have a political advantage. In most markets, producers are fewer and better organized than consumers – and thus wield greater political influence. Reducing the Isolandian tariff on olive oil, for example, may be politically difficult if considered by itself. The olive oil companies would oppose free trade, and the users of olive oil who would benefit are so numerous that organizing their support would be difficult. Yet suppose that Neighbourland promises to reduce its tariff on wheat at the same time that Isoland reduces its tariff on olive oil. In this case, the Isolandian wheat farmers, who are also politically powerful, would back the agreement. Thus, the multilateral approach to free trade can sometimes win political support when a unilateral reduction cannot.

Quick Quiz The textile industry of Autarka advocates a ban on the import of wool suits. Describe five arguments its lobbyists might make. Give a response to each of these arguments.

CONCLUSION

Economists and the general public often disagree about free trade. In particular, economists are usually opposed to trade restrictions while the general public often wants to see restrictions on trade in order to 'protect' the domestic economy from 'cut-throat' foreign competition.

To understand better the economists' view of trade, let's continue our parable. Suppose that the country of Isoland ignores the advice of its economics team and decides not to allow free trade in olive oil. The country remains in the equilibrium without international trade.

Then, one day, some Isolandian inventor discovers a new way to make olive oil at very low cost. The process is quite mysterious, however, and the inventor insists on keeping it a secret. What is odd is that the inventor doesn't need any workers or fields to make olive oil. The only input he requires is wheat.

The inventor is hailed as a genius. Because olive oil is used in so many products, the invention lowers the cost of many goods and allows all Isolandians to enjoy a higher standard of living. Workers who had previously produced olive oil do suffer when their factories close, but eventually they find work in other industries. Some become farmers and grow the wheat that the inventor turns into olive oil. Others enter new industries that emerge as a result of higher Isolandian living standards. Everyone understands that the displacement of these workers is an inevitable part of progress.

After several years, a newspaper reporter decides to investigate this mysterious new olive oil process. She sneaks into the inventor's factory and learns that the inventor is a fraud. The inventor has not been making olive oil at all. Instead, he has been smuggling wheat abroad in exchange for olive oil from other countries. The only thing that the inventor had discovered was the gains from international trade.

When the truth is revealed, the government shuts down the inventor's operation. The price of olive oil rises and workers return to jobs in olive oil factories. Living standards in Isoland fall back to their former levels. The inventor is jailed and held up to public ridicule. After all, he was no inventor. He was just an economist.

SUMMARY

- The effects of free trade can be determined by comparing the domestic price without trade to the world price. A low domestic price indicates that the country has a comparative advantage in producing the good and that the country will become an exporter. A high domestic price indicates that the rest of the world has a comparative advantage in producing the good and that the country will become an importer.

- When a country allows trade and becomes an exporter of a good, producers of the good are better off, and consumers of the good are worse off. When a country allows trade and becomes an importer of a good, consumers are better off, and producers are worse off. In both cases, the gains from trade exceed the losses.

- A tariff – a tax on imports – moves a market closer to the equilibrium that would exist without trade and, therefore,

reduces the gains from trade. Although domestic producers are better off and the government raises revenue, the losses to consumers exceed these gains.

- An import quota – a limit on imports – has effects that are similar to those of a tariff. Under a quota, however, the holders of the import licences receive the revenue that the government would collect with a tariff.

- There are various arguments for restricting trade: protecting jobs, defending national security, helping infant industries, preventing unfair competition and responding to foreign trade restrictions. Although some of these arguments have some merit in some cases, economists believe that free trade is usually the better policy.

KEY CONCEPTS

world price, p. 176
tariff, p. 181

import quota, p. 183
customs union, p. 192

QUESTIONS FOR REVIEW

1. What does the domestic price that prevails without international trade tell us about a nation's comparative advantage?

2. When does a country become an exporter of a good? An importer?

3. Draw the supply and demand diagram for an importing country. What is consumer surplus and producer surplus before trade is allowed? What is consumer surplus and producer surplus with free trade? What is the change in total surplus?

4. Describe what a tariff is, and describe its economic effects.

5. What is an import quota? Compare its economic effects with those of a tariff.

6. List five arguments often given to support trade restrictions. How do economists respond to these arguments?

7. What is the difference between the unilateral and multilateral approaches to achieving free trade? Give an example of each.

PROBLEMS AND APPLICATIONS

1. France represents a small part of the world apple market.
   a. Draw a diagram depicting the equilibrium in the French apple market without international trade. Identify the equilibrium price, equilibrium quantity, consumer surplus and producer surplus.
   b. Suppose that the world apple price is below the French price before trade, and that the French apple market is now opened to trade. Identify the new equilibrium price, quantity consumed, quantity produced domestically and quantity imported. Also show the change in the surplus of domestic consumers and producers. Has domestic total surplus increased or decreased?

2. The world price of wine is below the price that would prevail in France in the absence of trade.
   a. Assuming that French imports of wine are a small part of total world wine production, draw a graph for the French market for wine under free trade. Identify consumer surplus, producer surplus and total surplus in an appropriate table.
   b. Now suppose that an outbreak of phyloxera (a sap sucking insect which damages grape vines) in California and South America destroys much of the grape harvest there. What effect does this shock have on the world price of wine? Using your graph and table from part (a), show the effect on consumer surplus, producer surplus and total surplus in France. Who are the winners and losers? Is France better or worse off?

3. The world price of cotton is below the no-trade price in country A and above the no-trade price in country B. Using supply and demand diagrams and welfare tables such as those in the chapter, show the gains from trade in each country. Compare your results for the two countries.

4. Suppose that European Union countries impose a common tariff on imported cars to protect the European car industry from foreign competition. Assuming that Europe is a price taker in the world car market, show on a diagram: the change in the quantity of imports, the loss to European consumers, the gain to European car manufacturers, government revenue and the deadweight loss associated with the tariff. The loss to consumers can be decomposed into three pieces: a transfer to domestic producers, a transfer to the government and a deadweight loss. Use your diagram to identify these three pieces.

5. Write a brief essay advocating or criticizing each of the following policy positions.
   a. The government should not allow imports if foreign firms are selling below their costs of production (a phenomenon called 'dumping').
   b. The government should temporarily stop the import of goods for which the domestic industry is new and struggling to survive.
   c. The government should not allow imports from countries with weaker environmental regulations than ours.

6. Suppose that a technological advance in Japan lowers the world price of televisions.
   a. Assume Switzerland is an importer of televisions and there are no trade restrictions. How does the technological advance affect the welfare of Swiss consumers and Swiss producers? What happens to total surplus in Switzerland?
   b. Now suppose that Switzerland has a quota on television imports. How does the Japanese technological advance affect the welfare of Swiss consumers, Swiss producers and the holders of import licences?

7. When the government of Tradeland decides to impose an import quota on foreign cars, three proposals are suggested: (1) Sell the import licences in an auction. (2) Distribute the licences randomly in a lottery. (3) Let people wait in line and distribute the licences on a first-come, first-served basis. Compare the effects of these policies. Which policy do you think has the largest deadweight losses? Which policy has the smallest deadweight losses? Why? (Hint: the government's other ways of raising tax revenue themselves all cause deadweight losses.)

8. (This question is challenging.) Consider a small country that exports steel. Suppose that a 'pro-trade' government decides to subsidize the export of steel by paying a certain amount for each tonne sold abroad. How does this export subsidy affect the domestic price of steel, the quantity of steel produced, the quantity of steel consumed and the quantity of steel exported? How does it affect consumer surplus, producer surplus, government revenue and total surplus? (Hint: the analysis of an export subsidy is similar to the analysis of a tariff.)

9. Examine a trade dispute or trade agreement that has been in the news lately. In this case, who do you think are the winners and losers from free trade? Which group has more political clout? Note: a good place to look for this information is the website of the World Trade Organization (http://www.wto.org).

For further resources, visit
www.cengage.com/mankiw_taylor2

4

THE ECONOMICS OF THE
PUBLIC SECTOR

10 EXTERNALITIES

Firms that make and sell paper also create, as a by-product of the manufacturing process, a chemical called dioxin. Scientists believe that once dioxin enters the environment it raises the population's risk of cancer, birth defects and other health problems.

Is the production and release of dioxin a problem for society? In Chapters 4 to 9 we examined how markets allocate scarce resources with the forces of supply and demand, and we saw that the equilibrium of supply and demand is typically an efficient allocation of resources. To use Adam Smith's famous metaphor, the 'invisible hand' of the marketplace leads self-interested buyers and sellers in a market to maximize the total benefit that society derives from that market. This insight is the basis for one of the *Ten Principles of Economics* in Chapter 1: markets are usually a good way to organize economic activity. Should we conclude, therefore, that the invisible hand prevents firms in the paper market from emitting too much dioxin?

Markets do many things well, but they do not do everything well. In this chapter we begin our study of another one of the *Ten Principles of Economics:* governments can sometimes improve market outcomes. We examine why markets sometimes fail to allocate resources efficiently, how government policies can potentially improve the market's allocation and what kinds of policies are likely to work best.

The market failures examined in this chapter fall under a general category called *externalities.* An externality arises when a person engages in an activity that influences the well-being of a bystander (a third party) who neither pays nor

© BURAK PEKAKCAN / ISTOCK

receives any compensation for that effect. If the impact on the bystander is adverse, it is called a *negative externality*; if it is beneficial, it is called a *positive externality*.

We have seen how the operation of markets is based on millions of decisions being made by individuals and groups. The invisible hand means that individuals and groups make decisions which are designed to maximize their individual or group welfare. In making these decisions there will be private costs and private benefits. In making a car journey, for example, a person incurs various private costs such as the fuel used in the journey, the wear and tear (depreciation) on the car, the contribution of the vehicle tax and insurance costs related to the journey that the individual has to pay. In using their car the individual also gains a number of private benefits; convenience, warmth, the pleasure of driving, listening to music on the radio, not to mention getting to a destination relatively quickly. However, in making the decision to make the journey the individual may not take into consideration the cost (or benefit) to society that is imposed as a result of that decision. An extra car on the road contributes to congestion, road wear and tear; there are the emissions that the car gives off, the noise pollution and the increased risk of accident which may cause injury or even death to a third party. There may also be some social benefits of the decision; using a car means that there is an extra seat available for someone else to use on public transport, for example.

These social costs are not taken into consideration by the individual as they get into their car. They are costs which have to be borne by a third party. The cost of repairing damaged roads, the cost of dealing with accident and injury, delays caused as a result of congestion, the effects and costs of dealing with pollution and so on, all have to be borne by others – often the taxpayer. Equally, any social benefits arising from the decision are gained by those not party to the initial decision without them having to pay for the benefit derived.

In the presence of externalities, society's interest in a market outcome extends beyond the well-being of buyers and sellers who participate in the market; it also includes the well-being of bystanders who are affected indirectly. Because buyers and sellers neglect the external effects of their actions when deciding how much to demand or supply, the market equilibrium is not efficient when there are externalities. That is, the equilibrium fails to maximize the total benefit to society as a whole. The release of dioxin into the environment, for instance, is a negative externality. Self-interested paper firms will not consider the full cost of the pollution they create and, therefore, will emit too much pollution unless the government prevents or discourages them from doing so.

Externalities come in many varieties, as do the policy responses that try to deal with the market failure. Here are some examples:

- The exhaust from cars is a negative externality because it creates smog that other people have to breathe. Drivers do not take into consideration this externality and so tend to drive too much thus increasing pollution. The government attempts to solve this problem by setting emission standards for cars. It also taxes petrol in order to reduce the amount that people drive.
- Restored historic buildings convey a positive externality because people who walk or drive by them can enjoy their beauty and the sense of history that these buildings provide. Building owners do not get the full benefit of restoration and, therefore, tend to discard older buildings too quickly. Many national governments respond to this problem by regulating the destruction of historic buildings and by providing tax incentives to owners who restore them.
- Barking dogs create a negative externality because neighbours are disturbed by the noise. Dog owners do not bear the full cost of the noise and, therefore, tend to take too few precautions to prevent their dogs from barking. The government may address this problem by making it illegal to 'disturb the peace'.

- Research into new technologies provides a positive externality because it creates knowledge that other people can use. Because inventors cannot capture the full benefits of their inventions, they tend to devote too few resources to research. The government addresses this problem partially through the patent system, which gives inventors an exclusive use over their inventions for a period of time.
- A programme of vaccination against a flu virus protects those who receive it from the risk of contracting the virus. Those who are not vaccinated, however, may receive some benefit too because the prevalence of the virus is lower and so there is a reduced risk that they will contract flu. Health services also benefit because they do not have to devote resources to treating those with flu. Governments encourage flu vaccinations because there are positive benefits to society as a whole.

In each of these cases, some decision maker fails to take account of the external effects of his or her behaviour. The government responds by trying to influence this behaviour to protect the interests of bystanders.

EXTERNALITIES AND MARKET INEFFICIENCY

In this section we use the tools from Chapter 7 to examine how externalities affect economic well-being. The analysis shows precisely why externalities cause markets to allocate resources inefficiently. Later in the chapter we examine various ways in which private actors and public policy makers may remedy this type of market failure.

Welfare Economics: A Recap

We begin by recalling the key lessons of welfare economics from Chapter 7. To make our analysis concrete, we will consider a specific market – the market for aluminium. Figure 10.1 shows the supply and demand curves in the market for aluminium.

As you should recall from Chapter 7, the supply and demand curves contain important information about costs and benefits. The demand curve for aluminium reflects the value of aluminium to consumers, as measured by the prices they are willing to pay. At any given quantity, the height of the demand curve shows the willingness to pay of the marginal buyer. In other words, it shows the value to the consumer of the last unit of aluminium bought. Similarly, the supply curve reflects the costs of producing aluminium. At any given quantity, the height of the supply curve shows the cost of the marginal seller. In other words, it shows the cost to the producer of the last unit of aluminium sold.

In the absence of government intervention, the price adjusts to balance the supply and demand for aluminium. The quantity produced and consumed in the market equilibrium, shown as Q_{MARKET} in Figure 10.1, is efficient in the sense that it maximizes the sum of producer and consumer surplus. That is, the market allocates resources in a way that maximizes the total value to the consumers who buy and use aluminium minus the total costs to the producers who make and sell aluminium.

Negative Externalities

Now let's suppose that aluminium factories emit pollution: for each unit of aluminium produced, a certain amount of a pollutant enters the atmosphere. This

FIGURE 10.1

The Market for Aluminium

The demand curve reflects the value to buyers, and the supply curve reflects the costs of sellers. The equilibrium quantity, Q$_{MARKET}$, maximizes the total value to buyers minus the total costs of sellers. In the absence of externalities, therefore, the market equilibrium is efficient.

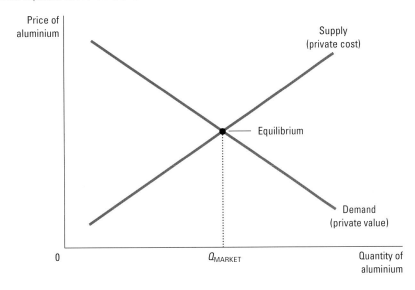

pollutant may pose a health risk for those who breathe the air, it is a negative externality. There is a cost involved in dealing with the effects of the pollutant which may be the health care that those affected have to receive. This cost is not taken into consideration by producers of aluminium who only consider the private costs of production. How does this externality affect the efficiency of the market outcome?

Because of the externality, the cost to *society* of producing aluminium is larger than the cost to the aluminium producers. For each unit of aluminium produced, the *social (or external) cost* includes the private costs of the aluminium producers plus the costs to those bystanders affected adversely by the pollution. Figure 10.2 shows the social cost of producing aluminium. The social cost curve is above the supply curve because it takes into account the external costs imposed on society by aluminium producers. At every price the social cost is higher than the private cost so we can say that the social cost curve is the sum of the private costs and the social or external cost. The difference between these two curves reflects the social or external cost of the pollution emitted.

What quantity of aluminium should be produced? To answer this question, we once again consider what a benevolent social planner would do. The planner wants to maximize the total surplus derived from the market – the value to consumers of aluminium minus the cost of producing aluminium. The planner understands, however, that the cost of producing aluminium includes the external costs of the pollution.

The planner would choose the level of aluminium production at which the demand curve crosses the social cost curve. This intersection determines the optimal amount of aluminium from the standpoint of society as a whole. Below this

"I've been nominated 'Industrialist of the Year' and the Department of Environment are going to prosecute me for pollution."

FIGURE 10.2

Pollution and the Social Optimum

In the presence of a negative externality, such as pollution, the social cost of the good exceeds the private cost. The optimal quantity, $Q_{OPTIMUM}$, is therefore smaller than the equilibrium quantity, Q_{MARKET}.

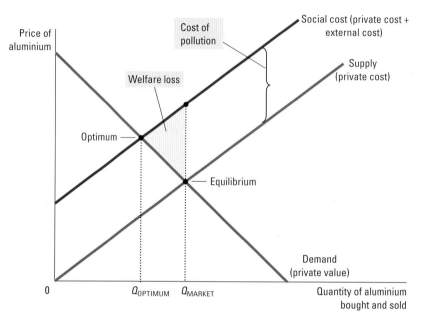

level of production, the value of the aluminium to consumers (as measured by the height of the demand curve) exceeds the social cost of producing it (as measured by the height of the social cost curve). The planner does not produce more than this level because the social cost of producing additional aluminium exceeds the value to consumers.

Note that the equilibrium quantity of aluminium, Q_{MARKET}, is larger than the socially optimal quantity, $Q_{OPTIMUM}$. The reason for this inefficiency is that the market equilibrium reflects only the private costs of production. In the market equilibrium, the marginal consumer values aluminium at less than the social cost of producing it. That is, at Q_{MARKET} the demand curve lies below the social cost curve. Thus, reducing aluminium production and consumption below the market equilibrium level raises total economic well-being. We can measure changes in well-being by the welfare loss associated with different market outcomes. We measure the difference in the value placed on each marginal unit of production of aluminium between $Q_{OPTIMUM}$ and Q_{MARKET} by consumers as shown by the shaded triangle in Figure 10.2.

How can the social planner achieve the optimal outcome? The answer is to somehow force the decision maker to take into consideration some or all of the social costs of the decision. In our example, one way to do this would be to tax aluminium producers for each tonne of aluminium sold. The tax would shift the supply curve for aluminium upward by the size of the tax. If the tax accurately reflected the social cost of the pollution released into the atmosphere, the new supply curve would coincide with the social cost curve. In the new market equilibrium, aluminium producers would produce the socially optimal quantity of aluminium.

The use of such a tax is called **internalizing an externality** because it gives buyers and sellers in the market an incentive to take account of the external effects of their actions. Aluminium producers would, in essence, take the costs of pollution into account when deciding how much aluminium to supply because the tax would make them pay for these external costs. The policy is based on one of the *Ten Principles of Economics:* people respond to incentives. Later in this chapter we consider other ways in which policy makers can deal with externalities.

internalizing an externality
altering incentives so that people take account of the external effects of their actions

Positive Externalities

Although some activities impose costs on third parties, others yield benefits. For example, consider education. Education yields positive externalities because a more educated population leads to improved productivity and increases the potential for economic growth, which benefits everyone. Notice that the productivity benefit of education is not necessarily an externality: the consumer of education reaps most of the benefit in the form of higher wages. But if some of the productivity benefits of education spill over and benefit other people, as is the case if economic growth is stimulated, then this effect would count as a positive externality as well.

The analysis of positive externalities is similar to the analysis of negative externalities. As Figure 10.3 shows, the demand curve does not reflect the value to society of the good. The value placed on an activity such as education is valued less by consumers than the total value to society. Because the social value (or external benefit) is greater than the private value, the social value curve lies

FIGURE 10.3

Education and the Social Optimum

In the presence of a positive externality, the social value of the good exceeds the private value. The optimal quantity, $Q_{OPTIMUM}$, is therefore larger than the equilibrium quantity, Q_{MARKET}.

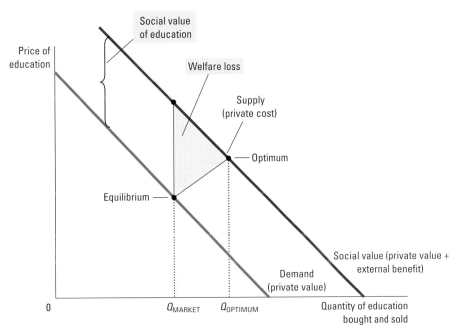

above the demand curve. The social value curve is the private value plus the external benefit to society at each price. At every price the benefit to society is greater than the private benefit, hence the social value curve lies to the right of the private benefit curve. The optimal quantity is found where the social value curve and the supply curve (which represents costs) intersect. Hence, the socially optimal quantity is greater than the quantity determined by the private market.

Once again, the government can correct the market failure by inducing market participants to internalize the externality. The appropriate response in the case of positive externalities is exactly the opposite to the case of negative externalities. To move the market equilibrium closer to the social optimum, a positive externality requires a subsidy. In fact, that is exactly the policy many governments follow by heavily subsidizing education.

To summarize: negative externalities lead markets to produce a larger quantity than is socially desirable. Positive externalities lead markets to produce a smaller quantity than is socially desirable. To remedy the problem, the government can internalize the externality by taxing goods that have negative externalities and subsidizing goods that have positive externalities.

CASE STUDY

Technology Spillovers and Industrial Policy

Consider the market for industrial robots. Robots are at the frontier of a rapidly changing technology. Whenever a firm builds a robot, there is some chance that it will discover a new and better design. This new design will benefit not only this firm but society as a whole because the design will enter society's pool of technological knowledge. This type of positive externality is called a *technology spillover.*

In this case, the government can internalize the externality by subsidizing the production of robots. If the government paid firms a subsidy for each robot produced, the supply curve would shift down by the amount of the subsidy, and this shift would increase the equilibrium quantity of robots. To ensure that the market equilibrium equals the social optimum, the subsidy should equal the value of the technology spillover.

How large are technology spillovers, and what do they imply for public policy? This is an important question because technological progress is the key to why living standards rise over time. Yet it is also a difficult question on which economists often disagree.

Some economists believe that technology spillovers are pervasive and that the government should encourage those industries that yield the largest spillovers. For instance, these economists argue that if making computer chips yields greater spillovers than making fish and chips, then the government should use the tax laws to encourage the production of computer chips relative to the production of fish and chips. Government intervention in the economy that aims to promote technology-enhancing industries is sometimes called *industrial policy.*

In the debate over climate change, some argue that a better way forward for society is to focus efforts on developing new technologies that will reduce our reliance on carbon-based technologies. (Technology, by the way, is defined as the application of knowledge to solve practical problems.) Governments throughout Europe and in the US are providing incentives for the development of so-called 'green technologies'. Some claim that development in this area could bring similar change and benefits to those of the information technology revolution which has taken place over the last 30 years. Key areas of green technology relate to energy production and efficiency, construction, green chemistry (using technologies that reduce or eliminate the use or production of substances that are hazardous or present long-term dangers) and green nanotechnology.

This latter technology involves the use of materials at a minute scale and may also incorporate green chemistry. One area where nanotechnology is being developed is the food industry. The technology could lead to more efficient use of pesticides and fertilizers, improving the safety and viability of genetic engineering, dealing with plant and animal pathogens, enhancing food flavours, removing pathogens from food, increasing output and productivity, improving the safety and efficiency of food packaging, and improving the way humans and animals absorb nutrients. The benefits of this technology are being promoted to the developing world, where there are still millions of people who have to suffer starvation and malnutrition, as well as the developed world.

Other economists are sceptical about industrial policy. Even if technology spillovers are common, the success of an industrial policy requires that the government be able to measure the size of the spillovers from different markets. This measurement problem is difficult at best. Moreover, without precise measurements, the political system may end up subsidizing those industries with the most political clout (remember public choice theory referred to in Chapter 9), rather than those that yield the largest positive externalities.

Another way to deal with technology spillovers is patent protection. The patent laws protect the rights of inventors by giving them exclusive use of their inventions for a period of time. When a firm makes a technological breakthrough, it can patent the idea and capture much of the economic benefit for itself. The patent is said to internalize the externality by giving the firm a **property right** over its invention. If other firms want to use the new technology, they have to obtain permission from the inventing firm and pay it some royalty. Thus, the patent system gives firms a greater incentive to engage in research and other activities that advance technology.

property rights
the exclusive right of an individual, group or organization to determine how a resource is used

Quick Quiz Give an example of a negative externality and a positive externality • Explain why market outcomes are inefficient in the presence of externalities.

PRIVATE SOLUTIONS TO EXTERNALITIES

We have discussed why externalities lead markets to allocate resources inefficiently, but have mentioned only briefly how this inefficiency can be remedied. In practice, both private actors and public policy makers respond to externalities in various ways. All of the remedies share the goal of moving the allocation of resources closer to the social optimum. In this section we examine private solutions.

The Types of Private Solution

Although externalities tend to cause markets to be inefficient, government action is not always needed to solve the problem. In some circumstances, people can develop private solutions.

IN THE NEWS

The concept of externalities has a large range of applications. The models developed in previous chapters relating to the measurement of well-being can be applied to debate a number of perceived problems in society including some issues that arouse a great deal of moral fervour / or anger. This article looks at one of these controversial issues.

Prostitution

In the UK in 2005, a debate at a conference of the nursing profession centred on problems in Liverpool caused by prostitution that have impacts on health and social care needs. The consequences of the existence of prostitution are of direct relevance to nurses not only in the UK but in many parts of Europe, particularly for those who work in major cities. The response of different countries to prostitution allows economists to analyse the externalities, both positive and negative and the associated changes in well-being associated with the practice. The UK government produced a consultation document on prostitution called *Paying the Price* in 2004. The document recognized that the law on prostitution in the UK was 'outdated, confusing and ineffective'. It looked at the possibilities for establishing managed zones for prostitutes to work in and for establishing legalized brothels.

Different laws relating to the practice exist in different European countries and even if it is illegal, governments have to accept that it goes on and that there are social and economic costs that exist. There is evidence that more liberal policies towards prostitution have been suc-

cessful in The Netherlands, Australia and Germany. By amending legislation, the social costs could be accounted for more effectively and in addition the welfare of those who work in the industry could be more closely monitored and improved.

Some of the problems faced by those who work as prostitutes and the wider implications of this industry raise very important issues. These include drug abuse, child exploitation, crime, and health problems such as sexually transmitted diseases. For those who live near 'red light districts' there are also problems; they have to put up with the girls on the streets and their clients as well as the hangers on in the industry – the pimps and drug dealers who tend to be involved. Would more relaxed laws on prostitution lead to more working girls (and men) being prepared to seek help and advice as a result of removing the fear of prosecution?

Legalizing prostitution, for example, might lead to the externalities being internalized. This means that the external costs (and benefits) of a problem would now be accounted for in decision-making. A prostitute who freely goes to a health clinic for regular check-ups and health advice (because they do not have to fear prosecution)

may contribute to the reduction in sexually transmitted diseases which society (the taxpayer in this case) has to pay for through treatment via publicly funded health services. Taking the industry out of the twilight world of criminality would also enable the authorities to monitor what goes on, help reduce the incentives to criminal activity, including drug abuse and child exploitation, have brothels that were subject to minimum standards and regulations and so benefit those who wish to sell and buy these services, as well as releasing public resources such as policing and justice to deal with other criminal activity.

Of course, the problem is that the very idea of selling sex is something that arouses moral indignation. For the economist the job is to try and measure the costs and benefits of different policy options and present these to the policy makers for decision.

Sometimes, the problem of externalities is solved with moral codes and social sanctions. Consider, for instance, why most people do not litter. Although there are laws against littering, these laws are not vigorously enforced. Most people do not litter just because it is the wrong thing to do. Advertising and parental guidance help us to distinguish what society accepts as a norm for behaviour. This moral injunction tells us to take account of how our actions affect other people. In economic terms, it tells us to internalize externalities.

Another private solution to externalities is charities, many of which are established to deal with externalities. For example, Greenpeace, whose goal is to protect the environment, is a non-profit organization funded with private donations. As another example, colleges and universities sometimes receive gifts from alumni, corporations and foundations in part because education has positive externalities for society.

The private market can often solve the problem of externalities by relying on the self-interest of the relevant parties. Sometimes the solution takes the form of integrating different types of business. For example, consider an apple grower and a beekeeper who are located next to each other. Each business confers a positive externality on the other: by pollinating the flowers on the trees, the bees help the orchard produce apples. At the same time, the bees use the nectar they get from the apple trees to produce honey. Nevertheless, when the apple grower is deciding how many trees to plant and the beekeeper is deciding how many bees to keep, they neglect the positive externality. As a result, the apple grower plants too few trees and the beekeeper keeps too few bees. These externalities could be internalized if the beekeeper bought the apple orchard or if the apple grower bought the beehives: both activities would then take place within the same firm, and this single firm could choose the optimal number of trees and bees. Internalizing externalities is one reason that some firms are involved in different types of business.

Another way for the private market to deal with external effects is for the interested parties to enter into a contract. In the foregoing example, a contract between the apple grower and the beekeeper can solve the problem of too few trees and too few bees. The contract can specify the number of trees, the number of bees, and perhaps a payment from one party to the other. By setting the right number of trees and bees, the contract can solve the inefficiency that normally arises from these externalities and make both parties better off. Joint ventures and partnering are good examples of where such contracts can generate positive externalities and improve efficiency.

The Coase Theorem

How effective is the private market in dealing with externalities? A famous result, called the **Coase theorem**, after British economist Ronald Coase, suggests that it can be very effective in some circumstances. According to the Coase theorem, if private parties can bargain *without cost* over the allocation of resources, then the private market will always solve the problem of externalities and allocate resources efficiently.

To see how the Coase theorem works, consider an example. Suppose that Sofie owns a dog (a corgi, in fact) named Brandy. Brandy barks and disturbs Lucas, Sofie's neighbour. Sofie gets a benefit from owning the dog, but the dog confers a negative externality on Lucas. Should Sofie be forced to send Brandy to the dogs' home, or should Lucas have to suffer sleepless nights because of Brandy's barking?

Consider first what outcome is socially efficient. A social planner, considering the two alternatives, would compare the benefit that Sofie gets from the dog to the cost that Lucas bears from the barking. If the benefit exceeds the cost, it is efficient for Sofie to keep the dog and for Lucas to live with the barking. Yet if the cost exceeds the benefit, then Sofie should get rid of the dog.

According to the Coase theorem, the private market will reach the efficient outcome on its own. How? Lucas can simply offer to pay Sofie to get rid of the

Coase theorem
the proposition that if private parties can bargain without cost over the allocation of resources, they can solve the problem of externalities on their own

dog. Sofie will accept the deal if the amount of money Lucas offers is greater than the benefit of keeping the dog.

By bargaining over the price, Sofie and Lucas can always reach the efficient outcome. For instance, suppose that Sofie gets a €500 benefit from the dog and Lucas bears an €800 cost from the barking. In this case, Lucas can offer Sofie €600 to get rid of the dog, and Sofie will gladly accept. Both parties are better off than they were before, and the efficient outcome is reached.

It is possible, of course, that Lucas would not be willing to offer any price that Sofie would accept. For instance, suppose that Sofie gets a €1 000 benefit from the dog and Lucas bears an €800 cost from the barking. In this case, Sofie would turn down any offer below €1 000, while Lucas would not offer any amount above €800. Therefore, Sofie ends up keeping the dog. Given these costs and benefits, however, this outcome is efficient.

So far, we have assumed that Sofie has the legal right to keep a barking dog. In other words, we have assumed that Sofie can keep Brandy unless Lucas pays her enough to induce her to give up the dog voluntarily. How different would the outcome be, on the other hand, if Lucas had the legal right to peace and quiet?

According to the Coase theorem, the initial distribution of rights does not matter for the market's ability to reach the efficient outcome. For instance, suppose that Lucas can legally compel Sofie to get rid of the corgi. Although having this right works to Lucas's advantage, it probably will not change the outcome. In this case, Sofie can offer to pay Lucas to allow her to keep the dog. If the benefit of the dog to Sofie exceeds the cost of the barking to Lucas, then Sofie and Lucas will strike a bargain in which Sofie keeps the dog.

Although Sofie and Lucas can reach the efficient outcome regardless of how rights are initially distributed, the distribution of rights is not irrelevant: it determines the distribution of economic well-being. Whether Sofie has the right to a barking dog or Lucas the right to peace and quiet determines who pays whom in the final bargain. But, in either case, the two parties can bargain with each other and solve the externality problem. Sofie will end up keeping the dog only if the benefit exceeds the cost.

To sum up: the Coase theorem says that private economic actors can solve the problem of externalities among themselves. Whatever the initial distribution of rights, the interested parties can always reach a bargain in which everyone is better off and the outcome is efficient.

CASE STUDY

Chewing Gum

Walk down the streets of most towns and cities in Europe, look at the pavements and you will notice lots of black blobs on the floor. This is the remnants of chewing gum, which has been spat out and trodden into the flagstones and tarmac that form our walkways. Local government authorities have long complained about the cost of cleaning up the remains of chewing gum. This is an example of a social cost, a negative externality. One local authority in London points out that cleaning up chewing gum costs them in excess of £100 000 a year. Larger councils in metropolitan areas of the UK experience costs at least twice that amount. It is not only the cost of removing the gum; there is also the effect on energy use. Steam cleaning is a method employed to get rid of gum, but the cost of energy to generate the steam is also significant. In many cases, as with the black blobs, the problem becomes almost impossible to eradicate without very expensive treatments and they remain as a testament to our bad habits.

Whilst it is accepted as a social cost, coming up with a solution does not seem to be easy. One of the issues is who should be responsible for the cost and for solving the problem – should this be an example of the 'polluter pays' principle? In which case, who is the polluter: the chewing gum manufacturer or the individual who uses the chewing gum and then disposes of it in a way that reduces social value?

The industry has been investigating the problem and attempting to develop a gum that is both biodegradable and less sticky. Part of the production process and a key to the success of the gum industry has been the fact that it is stretchy, retains its properties in all conditions and has a long shelf life. Gum is made from synthetic rubber and has various sweeteners and flavourings added. Any change to the product would require significant research and investment by the industry.

Some argue that there is not enough incentive for firms to take research and development seriously and in such cases other strategies need to be adopted. One suggestion is to levy a tax on chewing gum to cover the cost of cleaning it up – 1p per packet has been suggested, but in Ireland a figure of 7p has been reported to be under consideration.

Other suggestions have been spot fines for people who do not dispose of chewing gum properly; educating the public to dispose of gum more responsibly; coating the pavements with a non-stick substance; and having gum boards where users can stick their gum. In one town in southern England a clean-up campaign was followed by the erection of a number of these gum boards – each one collected 1 600 pieces of gum every week and resulted in a lower reported incidence of gum litter on the streets.

In the United States a more radical solution was suggested by one irate commentator. Mark Frauenfelder noted that an industrial chewing gum removal machine was being marketed at $8 000. Frauenfelder noted that this seemed rather steep and that shopping mall and theme park owners could 'simply purchase a gun for less than $100 and shoot the morons who spit their gum on the ground'!

Why Private Solutions Do Not Always Work

Despite the appealing logic of the Coase theorem, private actors on their own often fail to resolve the problems caused by externalities. The Coase theorem applies only when the interested parties have no trouble reaching and enforcing an agreement. In the world, however, bargaining does not always work, even when a mutually beneficial agreement is possible.

Sometimes the interested parties fail to solve an externality problem because of **transaction costs**, the costs that parties incur in the process of agreeing to and following through on a bargain. In our example, imagine that Sofie and Lucas speak different languages so that, to reach an agreement, they will need to hire a translator. If the benefit of solving the barking problem is less than the cost of the translator, Sofie and Lucas might choose to leave the problem unsolved. In more realistic examples, the transaction costs are the expenses not of translators but of the lawyers required to draft and enforce contracts.

At other times bargaining simply breaks down. The recurrence of wars and labour strikes shows that reaching agreement can be difficult and that failing to reach agreement can be costly. The problem is often that each party tries to hold out for a better deal. For example, suppose that Sofie gets a €500 benefit from the dog, and Lucas bears an €800 cost from the barking. Although it is efficient for

transaction costs
the costs that parties incur in the process of agreeing and following through on a bargain

Lucas to pay Sofie to get rid of the dog, there are many prices that could lead to this outcome. Sofie might demand €750, and Lucas might offer only €550. As they haggle over the price, the inefficient outcome with the barking dog persists.

Reaching an efficient bargain is especially difficult when the number of interested parties is large because coordinating everyone is costly. For example, consider a factory that pollutes the water of a nearby lake. The pollution confers a negative externality on the local fishermen. According to the Coase theorem, if the pollution is inefficient, then the factory and the fishermen could reach a bargain in which the fishermen pay the factory not to pollute. If there are many fishermen, however, trying to coordinate them all to bargain with the factory may be almost impossible.

There are two other key reasons why reaching an efficient bargain may not arise: asymmetric information and the assumption of rational behaviour. An example of the former is that Sofie and Lucas may not have perfect knowledge of the costs and benefits to each other of the barking dog. In such situations it becomes very difficult to negotiate an efficient outcome. Both parties have imperfect information about the situation of the other and so incentives may be distorted. Lucas, for example, might exaggerate the cost to him of the barking dog whilst Sofie does the same with regard to the benefits she gets from keeping her dog. The situation is further complicated by the existence of *free riders*. Lucas may not be the only person in the neighbourhood suffering from the barking dog but others may not live directly next to Sofie. These other 'victims' can benefit from any agreement that Sofie and Lucas arrive at but do not pay any of the costs of solving the problem. If Lucas is aware of this then why should he pay the full amount to solve the problem when others will also benefit but not contribute? If all victims think the same way then the problem will remain unsolved and there will be an inefficient outcome.

As regards the assumption of rational behaviour, we assumed that an efficient outcome could be found if Lucas offered €600 for Sofie to get rid of the dog. If Sofie were able to put a price on the value of the dog to her and this was €500, then it would be irrational for her not to accept the money to get rid of the dog. The money could be used to secure something which gave greater value to her than the ownership of the dog. Of course, in real life such rational behaviour may be clouded by all sorts of behavioural and psychological influences that Sofie may not be able to value. The guilt she may feel in getting rid of the dog, the reactions of her friends and family, the sentimental value of the dog to her and so on.

When private bargaining does not work, the government can sometimes play a role. The government is an institution designed for collective action. In the polluting factory example above, the government can act on behalf of the fishermen, even when it is impractical for the fishermen to act for themselves. In the next section, we examine how the government can try to remedy the problem of externalities.

Quick Quiz Give an example of a private solution to an externality. • What is the Coase theorem? • Why are private economic actors sometimes unable to solve the problems caused by an externality?

PUBLIC POLICIES TOWARDS EXTERNALITIES

When an externality causes a market to reach an inefficient allocation of resources, the government can respond in one of two ways. *Command-and-control policies* regulate behaviour directly. *Market-based policies* provide incentives so that private decision makers will choose to solve the problem on their own.

Regulation

The government can remedy an externality by making certain behaviours either required or forbidden. For example, it is a crime in any European country to dump poisonous chemicals into the water supply. In this case, the external costs to society far exceed the benefits to the polluter. The government therefore institutes a command-and-control policy that prohibits this act altogether.

In most cases of pollution, however, the situation is not this simple. Despite the stated goals of some environmentalists, it would be impossible to prohibit all polluting activity. For example, virtually all forms of transport – even the horse – produce some undesirable polluting by-products. But it would not be sensible for the government to ban all transport. Thus, instead of trying to eradicate pollution altogether, society has to weigh the costs and benefits to decide the kinds and quantities of pollution it will allow.

Environmental regulations can take many forms. Sometimes the government may dictate a maximum level of pollution that a factory may emit. Other times the government requires that firms adopt a particular technology to reduce emissions. In all cases, to design good rules, the government regulators need to know the details about specific industries and about the alternative technologies that those industries could adopt. This information is often difficult for government regulators to obtain.

Pigovian Taxes and Subsidies

Instead of regulating behaviour in response to an externality, the government can use market-based policies to align private incentives with social efficiency. For instance, as we saw earlier, the government can internalize the externality by taxing activities that have negative externalities and subsidizing activities that have positive externalities. Taxes enacted to correct the effects of negative externalities are called **Pigovian taxes**, after the English economist Arthur Pigou (1877–1959), an early advocate of their use.

Pigovian tax
a tax enacted to correct the effects of a negative externality

Economists usually prefer Pigovian taxes over regulations as a way to deal with pollution because such taxes can reduce pollution at a lower cost to society. To see why, let us consider an example.

Suppose that two factories – a paper mill and a steel mill – are each dumping 500 tonnes of effluent into a river each year. The government decides that it wants to reduce the amount of pollution. It considers two solutions:

- *Regulation*. The government could tell each factory to reduce its pollution to 300 tonnes of effluent per year.
- *Pigovian tax*. The government could levy a tax on each factory of €50 000 for each tonne of effluent it emits.

The regulation would dictate a level of pollution, whereas the tax would give factory owners an economic incentive to reduce pollution. Which solution do you think is better?

Most economists would prefer the tax. They would first point out that a tax is just as effective as a regulation in reducing the overall level of pollution. The government can achieve whatever level of pollution it wants by setting the tax at the appropriate level. The higher the tax, the larger the reduction in pollution.

Indeed, if the tax is high enough, the factories will close down altogether, reducing pollution to zero.

The reason why economists would prefer the tax is that it reduces pollution more efficiently. The regulation requires each factory to reduce pollution by the same amount, but an equal reduction is not necessarily the least expensive way to clean up the water. It is possible that the paper mill can reduce pollution at lower cost than the steel mill. If so, the paper mill would respond to the tax by reducing pollution substantially to avoid the tax, whereas the steel mill would respond by reducing pollution less and paying the tax.

In essence, the Pigovian tax places a price on the right to pollute. Just as markets allocate goods to those buyers who value them most highly, a Pigovian tax allocates pollution to those factories that face the highest cost of reducing it. Whatever the level of pollution the government chooses, it can achieve this goal at the lowest total cost using a tax.

Economists also argue that Pigovian taxes are better for the environment. Under the command-and-control policy of regulation, the factories have no reason to reduce emission further once they have reached the target of 300 tonnes of effluent. By contrast, the tax gives the factories an incentive to develop cleaner technologies, because a cleaner technology would reduce the amount of tax the factory has to pay.

Pigovian taxes are unlike most other taxes. As we discussed in Chapter 8, most taxes distort incentives and move the allocation of resources away from the social optimum. The reduction in economic well-being – that is, in consumer and producer surplus – exceeds the amount of revenue the government raises, resulting in a deadweight loss. By contrast, when externalities are present, society also cares about the well-being of the bystanders who are affected. Pigovian taxes correct incentives for the presence of externalities and thereby move the allocation of resources closer to the social optimum. Thus, while Pigovian taxes raise revenue for the government, they also enhance economic efficiency.

CASE STUDY

Why Is Petrol Taxed so Heavily?

Petrol tax: payable 24 hours a day.

In European countries, petrol is among the most heavily taxed goods in the economy. In the United Kingdom, for instance, more than three-quarters of what motorists pay for petrol is tax; in Norway it is over 70 per cent, in the Netherlands over 60 per cent, and in Germany and Sweden around 65 per cent.

Why is this tax so common? One possible answer is that tax on petrol is a Pigovian tax aimed at correcting three negative externalities associated with driving:

- *Congestion.* If you have ever been stuck in bumper-to-bumper traffic, you have probably wished that there were fewer cars on the road. A petrol tax keeps congestion down by encouraging people to take public transport, participate in carpools and live closer to work.
- *Accidents.* Whenever a person buys a large car or 4x4 vehicle like a Range Rover, he makes himself safer, but he puts his neighbours at risk. Statistical research has shown that a person driving a typical car is much more likely to die if hit by a 4x4 vehicle than if hit by another car. The petrol tax is an indirect way of making people pay when their large, petrol-thirsty vehicles impose risk on others, which in turn makes them take account of this risk when choosing what vehicle to purchase.

- *Pollution.* The burning of fossil fuels such as petrol increases carbon emissions which, it is argued, are contributing to global warming. Experts disagree about how dangerous this threat is, but there is no doubt that the petrol tax reduces the risk by reducing the use of petrol.

So the tax on petrol, rather than causing deadweight losses like most taxes, actually makes the economy work better. It means less traffic congestion, safer roads and a cleaner environment.

Tradable Pollution Permits

Returning to our example of the paper mill and the steel mill, let us suppose that, despite the advice of its economists, the government adopts the regulation and requires each factory to reduce its pollution to 300 tonnes of effluent per year. Then one day, after the regulation is in place and both mills have complied, the two firms go to the government with a proposal. The steel mill wants to increase its emission of effluent by 100 tonnes. The paper mill has agreed to reduce its emission by the same amount if the steel mill pays it €5 million. Should the government allow the two factories to make this deal?

From the standpoint of economic efficiency, allowing the deal is good policy. The deal must make the owners of the two factories better off, because they are voluntarily agreeing to it. Moreover, the deal does not have any external effects because the total amount of pollution remains the same. Thus, social welfare is enhanced by allowing the paper mill to sell its right to pollute to the steel mill.

The same logic applies to any voluntary transfer of the right to pollute from one firm to another. If the government allows firms to make these deals, it will, in essence, have created a new scarce resource: pollution permits. A market to trade these permits will eventually develop, and that market will be governed by the forces of supply and demand. The invisible hand will ensure that this new market efficiently allocates the right to pollute. The firms that can reduce pollution only at high cost will be willing to pay the most for the pollution permits. The firms that can reduce pollution at low cost will prefer to sell whatever permits they have.

One advantage of allowing a market for pollution permits is that the initial allocation of pollution permits among firms does not matter from the standpoint of economic efficiency. The logic behind this conclusion is similar to that behind the Coase theorem. Those firms that can reduce pollution most easily would be willing to sell whatever permits they get, and those firms that can reduce pollution only at high cost would be willing to buy whatever permits they need. As long as there is a free market for the pollution rights, the final allocation will be efficient whatever the initial allocation.

Although reducing pollution using pollution permits may seem quite different from using Pigovian taxes, in fact the two policies have much in common. In both cases, firms pay for their pollution. With Pigovian taxes, polluting firms must pay a tax to the government. With pollution permits, polluting firms must pay to buy the permit. (Even firms that already own permits must pay to pollute: the opportunity cost of polluting is what they could have received by selling their permits on the open market.) Both Pigovian taxes and pollution permits internalize the externality of pollution by making it costly for firms to pollute.

The similarity of the two policies can be seen by considering the market for pollution. Both panels in Figure 10.4 show the demand curve for the right to pollute. This curve shows that the lower the price of polluting, the more firms will choose to pollute. In panel (a) the government uses a Pigovian tax to set a price for pollution. In this case, the supply curve for pollution rights is perfectly elastic

FIGURE 10.4

The Equivalence of Pigovian Taxes and Pollution Permits

In panel (a) the government sets a price on pollution by levying a Pigovian tax, and the demand curve determines the quantity of pollution. In panel (b) the government limits the quantity of pollution by limiting the number of pollution permits, and the demand curve determines the price of pollution. The price and quantity of pollution are the same in the two cases.

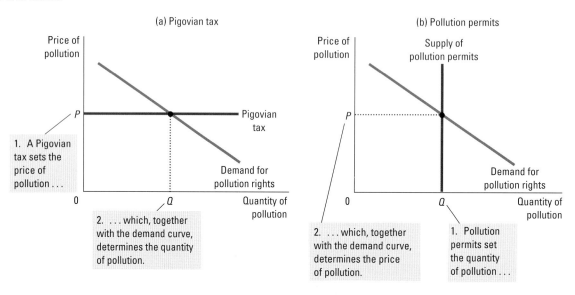

(because firms can pollute as much as they want by paying the tax), and the position of the demand curve determines the quantity of pollution. In panel (b) the government sets a quantity of pollution by issuing pollution permits. In this case, the supply curve for pollution rights is perfectly inelastic (because the quantity of pollution is fixed by the number of permits), and the position of the demand curve determines the price of pollution. Hence, for any given demand curve for pollution, the government can achieve any point on the demand curve either by setting a price with a Pigovian tax or by setting a quantity with pollution permits.

In some circumstances, however, selling pollution permits may be better than levying a Pigovian tax. Suppose the government wants no more than 600 tonnes of effluent to be dumped into the river. But, because the government does not know the demand curve for pollution, it is not sure what size tax would achieve that goal. In this case, it can simply auction off 600 pollution permits. The auction price would yield the appropriate size of the Pigovian tax.

The idea of the government auctioning off the right to pollute may at first sound like a creature of some economist's imagination. And, in fact, that is how the idea began. But a number of governments around the world – in particular the US government – have used such a system as a way to control pollution. In 2002, European Union environment ministers unanimously agreed to set up a market to trade pollution permits for carbon dioxide (CO_2), the main so-called greenhouse gas of concern. Pollution permits, like Pigovian taxes, are increasingly being viewed as a cost-effective way to keep the environment clean.

PUBLIC/PRIVATE POLICIES TOWARDS EXTERNALITIES

Property Rights

In some cases, private solutions to externalities can occur but need some form of legal back-up to be able to work. One such example is the establishment of property rights. In order for any economy to work efficiently, a system of property rights has to be established and understood. This is not as easy as it sounds, however. Property rights grant the exclusive right of an individual, group or organization to determine how a resource is used. The basic theory is this. If you decided to throw a brick through the window of my house I would be well within my rights to expect legal redress. The reason is that you have caused damage to my property and provided I can prove it was you who caused the damage and that I am the legal owner of the house, I can expect compensation, under the law, to put right the damage. This may include replacing the window pane and for any emotional trauma I have experienced.

With things such as rivers, streams, land and air it is less easy to establish who are the legal owners. If some system could be devised whereby the ownership of property could be established then those that cause damage to that property can be brought to book! Extending property rights, therefore, might be one area where externalities can be internalized. For example, if property rights over the air that we breathe can be extended, then any firm polluting that air (in whatever way, noise, smell, smoke, etc.) could face prosecution for doing so. The threat of prosecution is sufficient to act as an incentive to find ways of not polluting the air.

Extension of property rights also means that the owner of the property (which can be intellectual as well as physical) can also exercise the right to sell or share that property if they so wish at some mutually agreeable price. Extending property rights allows individuals, groups and organizations to be able to arrive at efficient solutions. If, for example, an individual was assigned property rights for the air 1 kilometre above their property, then if a nearby factory wanted to pollute that air they would have to enter into negotiations with the houseowner to do so at some mutually agreeable price. The resulting right to pollute could also be sold to another party. A more developed system of property rights can, therefore, improve well-being and it has been identified as playing a crucial role in good governance, particularly relevant for developing countries to be able to attract the sort of inward investment that will help their economies to grow.

There are problems with extending property rights, however. How do we apportion rights to such things as air, the seas, rivers and land? The cost of establishing property rights and getting international agreement on what they entail is considerable and may counteract the social benefits they might provide. If property rights were extended to the volume of air 1 km above a person's property, imagine the complexity of the negotiations that would have to be carried out with any business nearby, or airlines and the military for the right to share that air! Property owners may also have insufficient knowledge about their rights and exactly what they mean; it is also not a costless exercise to prove that property rights have been violated.

In the music industry the complexities of property rights have been the subject of debate and countless lawsuits in recent years. It not only relates to the issues of file sharing, pirating, copying CDs for personal use and downloading but also to the artists themselves and the rights to the music that they have written and performed. Intellectual property law is an incredibly complex area and different countries interpret property rights in different ways making any international agreement even more difficult. Despite the complexities, there have been efforts

IN THE NEWS

The increasing concern over levels of global carbon emissions has prompted governments around the world to look at so-called 'cap and trade' schemes. Markets to trade carbon emission permits have sprung up but whilst the theory may be relatively straighforward, the practice may introduce a number of imperfections that may not result in a socially desirable outcome being reached.

Carbon Trading Permits

The European Union has prided itself on being a leader in setting up carbon trading through the European Trading Scheme (ETS). The EU sets limits on the amount of carbon certain large industries like steel, cement and power generation are allowed to emit over a period of time. Permits are then issued to these industries and they have to work to meet their allowance. If they manage to reduce their carbon emissions below their permitted levels then they can sell the excess permits to others who may have had more difficulty meeting their targets.

Whilst such methods are, in theory, possible solutions to the problem of this type of pollution, the practice has seen different outcomes. The EU was accused of reducing the effectiveness of the system by *giving* permits to industry rather than auctioning them off. As a result there was a surplus of permits on the market and their price dropped. The effectiveness of the emissions trading scheme in reducing carbon emissions and acting as an incentive to producers to find more socially efficient ways of operating was called into question. The end of 2007 brought in the next phase of the scheme and it was hoped that the EU would learn the lessons from its mistakes.

The new limits, set to cover the period between 2008 and 2012, planned to tighten the amount of carbon pollu-

tion that can be emitted. In 2007 emissions of carbon were up by 1 per cent. However, the amount of carbon emitted was below targets set by the EU; 1.88 billion tonnes as against a target of 1.90 billion tonnes. It seems that France and Germany had been successful in having emissions below target levels whilst the UK, Spain and Italy were producing above their target levels. The overall figures, however, imply that tougher limits are required and that there would be a surplus of permits on the market, driving down prices.

The new targets set by the EU sought to reduce emissions by 9 per cent between 2008 and 2012. In addition, lessons from the first phase were learned and there was a larger number of permits that had to be bought by industry rather than being given to them. The new targets initially had some effect. The price of permits on the market began to rise. Since the beginning of 2008, when the new targets came into operation, permits were trading above €20 per tonne and analysts were expecting the price to rise further as the year progressed.

However, the recession in 2008 changed things. The global downturn led to a reduction in output and so firms were better able to meet their carbon emission limits. This also meant they were able to sell their permits and so the market saw a significant rise in the supply of permits which

pushed down prices from a high of €30 to around €12 per permit. The Climate Change Summit, held in December 2009 in Copenhagen, was supposed to deliver a global agreement on carbon emissions and analysts were anticipating the market for carbon permits to rise significantly as a result of an announcement cutting carbon emissions. The failure to reach any binding agreement at the summit kept the market depressed and by early February 2010, prices were hovering at around €13 per permit.

At this level, the price of a permit does not present a sufficient incentive for firms to invest in technology to reduce carbon emissions. For firms to be prepared to incur the costs of investing in new technologies, the price of carbon permits must be high enough to give an incentive to divert resources to developing more efficient production methods and other technologies such as carbon capture and storage. If the cost of such investment is above the level a firm has to pay for a permit then there is no incentive to invest. Analysts have suggested that prices of permits need to be between €30 and €50 each to begin to have any effect on such investment; at these levels the opportunity cost of buying more permits to emit carbon starts to become too high. The market, it seems, has some way to go before it begins to deliver the social benefits hoped for.

to extend property rights to help bring social benefits. In many parts of Europe, property rights over public spaces such as national parks, rivers and seas have meant that environmental laws can be established and enforced and this has led to an improvement in well-being for millions who are able to use these spaces, enjoy cleaner rivers and exploit the resources of the sea.

Objections to the Economic Analysis of Pollution

Some environmentalists argue that it is in some sense morally wrong to allow anyone to pollute the environment in return for paying a fee. Clean air and clean water, they argue, are fundamental human rights that should not be debased by considering them in economic terms. How can you put a price on clean air and clean water? The environment is so important, they claim, that we should protect it as much as possible, regardless of the cost.

Economists have little sympathy with this type of argument. To economists, good environmental policy begins by acknowledging the first of the *Ten Principles of Economics* in Chapter 1: people face trade-offs. Certainly, clean air and clean water have value. But their value must be compared to their opportunity cost – that is, to what one must give up to obtain them. Eliminating all pollution is impossible. Trying to eliminate all pollution would reverse many of the technological advances that allow us to enjoy a high standard of living. Few people would be willing to accept poor nutrition, inadequate medical care or shoddy housing to make the environment as clean as possible.

Economists argue that some environmental activists hurt their own cause by not thinking in economic terms. A clean environment is a good like other goods. Like all normal goods, it has a positive income elasticity: rich countries can afford a cleaner environment than poor ones and, therefore, usually have more rigorous environmental protection. In addition, like most other goods, clean air and water obey the law of demand: the lower the price of environmental protection, the more the public will want. The economic approach of using pollution permits and Pigovian taxes reduces the cost of environmental protection and should, therefore, increase the public's demand for a clean environment.

> **Quick Quiz** A glue factory and a steel mill emit smoke containing a chemical that is harmful if inhaled in large amounts. Describe three ways the town government might respond to this externality. What are the pros and cons of each of your solutions?

CONCLUSION

The invisible hand is powerful but not omnipotent. A market's equilibrium maximizes the sum of producer and consumer surplus. When the buyers and sellers in the market are the only interested parties, this outcome is efficient from the standpoint of society as a whole. But when there are external effects, such as pollution, evaluating a market outcome requires taking into account the well-being of third parties as well. In this case, the invisible hand of the marketplace may fail to allocate resources efficiently.

In some cases, people can solve the problem of externalities on their own. The Coase theorem suggests that the interested parties can bargain among themselves and agree on an efficient solution. Sometimes, however, an efficient outcome cannot be reached, perhaps because the large number of interested parties makes bargaining difficult.

When people cannot solve the problem of externalities privately, the government often steps in. Yet, even now, society should not abandon market forces entirely. Rather, the government can address the problem by requiring decision makers to bear the full costs of their actions. Pigovian taxes on emissions and pollution permits, for instance, are designed to internalize the externality of pollution. Increasingly, they are being seen as effective policies for those interested in protecting the environment. Market forces, properly redirected, are often the best remedy for market failure.

SUMMARY

- When a transaction between a buyer and seller directly affects a third party, the effect is called an externality. Negative externalities, such as pollution, cause the socially optimal quantity in a market to be less than the equilibrium quantity. Positive externalities, such as technology spillovers, cause the socially optimal quantity to be greater than the equilibrium quantity.

- Those affected by externalities can sometimes solve the problem privately. For instance, when one business confers an externality on another business, the two businesses can internalize the externality by merging. Alternatively, the interested parties can solve the problem by negotiating a contract. According to the Coase theorem, if people can bargain without cost, then they can

always reach an agreement in which resources are allocated efficiently. In many cases, however, reaching a bargain among the many interested parties is difficult, so the Coase theorem does not apply.

- When private parties cannot adequately deal with external effects, such as pollution, the government often steps in. Sometimes the government prevents socially inefficient activity by regulating behaviour. At other times it internalizes an externality using Pigovian taxes. Another public policy is to issue permits. For instance, the government could protect the environment by issuing a limited number of pollution permits. The end result of this policy is largely the same as imposing Pigovian taxes on polluters.

KEY CONCEPTS

internalizing an externality, p. 203
property right, p. 205

Coase theorem, p. 207
transaction costs, p. 209

Pigovian taxes, p. 211

QUESTIONS FOR REVIEW

1. Give an example of a negative externality and an example of a positive externality.

2. Use a supply and demand diagram to explain the effect of a negative externality in production.

3. In what way does the patent system help society solve an externality problem?

4. List some of the ways that the problems caused by externalities can be solved without government intervention.

5. Imagine that you are a non-smoker sharing a room with a smoker. According to the Coase theorem, what determines whether your roommate smokes in the room? Is this outcome efficient? How do you and your roommate reach this solution?

6. What are Pigovian taxes? Why do economists prefer them over regulations as a way to protect the environment from pollution?

PROBLEMS AND APPLICATIONS

1. Do you agree with the following statements? Why or why not?
   a. 'The benefits of Pigovian taxes as a way to reduce pollution have to be weighed against the deadweight losses that these taxes cause.'
   b. 'When deciding whether to levy a Pigovian tax on consumers or producers, the government should be careful to levy the tax on the side of the market generating the externality.'

2. Consider the market for fire extinguishers.
   a. Why might fire extinguishers exhibit positive externalities?
   b. Draw a graph of the market for fire extinguishers, labelling the demand curve, the social value curve, the supply curve and the social cost curve.
   c. Indicate the market equilibrium level of output and the efficient level of output. Give an intuitive explanation for why these quantities differ.
   d. If the external benefit is €10 per extinguisher, describe a government policy that would result in the efficient outcome.

3. In many countries, contributions to charitable organizations are deductible from income tax. In what way does this government policy encourage private solutions to externalities?

4. Mick loves playing rock music at high volume. Luciano loves opera and hates rock music. Unfortunately, they are next-door neighbours in an apartment building with paper-thin walls.
   a. What is the externality here?
   b. What command-and-control policy might the landlord impose? Could such a policy lead to an inefficient outcome?
   c. Suppose the landlord lets the tenants do whatever they want. According to the Coase theorem, how might Mick and Luciano reach an efficient outcome on their own? What might prevent them from reaching an efficient outcome?

5. It is rumoured that the Swiss government subsidizes cattle farming, and that the subsidy is larger in areas with more tourist attractions. Can you think of a reason why this policy might be efficient?

6. Greater consumption of alcohol leads to more motor vehicle accidents and, thus, imposes costs on people who do not drink and drive.
   a. Illustrate the market for alcohol, labelling the demand curve, the social value curve, the supply curve, the social cost curve, the market equilibrium level of output and the efficient level of output.
   b. On your graph, shade the area corresponding to the deadweight loss of the market equilibrium. (Hint: the deadweight loss occurs because some units of alcohol are consumed for which the social cost exceeds the social value.) Explain.

7. Many observers believe that the levels of pollution in our economy are too high.
   a. If society wishes to reduce overall pollution by a certain amount, why is it efficient to have different amounts of reduction at different firms?
   b. Command-and-control approaches often rely on uniform reductions among firms. Why are these approaches generally unable to target the firms that should undertake bigger reductions?
   c. Economists argue that appropriate Pigovian taxes or tradable pollution rights will result in efficient pollution reduction. How do these approaches target the firms that should undertake bigger reductions?

8. The Pristine River (or the 'Blue Pristine', as it is affectionately known) has two polluting firms on its banks. European Industrial and Creative Chemicals each dump 100 tonnes of effluent into the river each year. The cost of reducing effluent emissions per tonne equals €10 for European Industrial and €100 for Creative. The government wants to reduce overall pollution from 200 tonnes to 50 tonnes per year.
   a. If the government knew the cost of reduction for each firm, what reductions would it impose to reach its overall goal? What would be the cost to each firm and the total cost to the firms together?
   b. In a more typical situation, the government would not know the cost of pollution reduction at each firm. If the government decided to reach its overall goal by imposing uniform reductions on the firms, calculate the reduction made by each firm, the cost to each firm and the total cost to the firms together.
   c. Compare the total cost of pollution reduction in parts (a) and (b). If the government does not know the cost of reduction for each firm, is there still some way for it to reduce pollution to 50 tonnes at the total cost you calculated in part (a)? Explain.

9. 'A fine is a tax for doing something wrong. A tax is a fine for doing something right.' Discuss.

10. Figure 10.4 shows that for any given demand curve for the right to pollute, the government can achieve the same

outcome either by setting a price with a Pigovian tax or by setting a quantity with pollution permits. Suppose there is a sharp improvement in the technology for controlling pollution.

a. Using graphs similar to those in Figure 10.4, illustrate the effect of this development on the demand for pollution rights.

b. What is the effect on the price and quantity of pollution under each regulatory system? Explain.

11. Suppose that the government decides to issue tradable permits for a certain form of pollution.

a. Does it matter for economic efficiency whether the government distributes or auctions the permits? Does it matter in any other ways?

b. If the government chooses to distribute the permits, does the allocation of permits among firms matter for efficiency? Does it matter in any other ways?

12. Some people argue that the primary cause of global warming is carbon dioxide, which enters the atmosphere in varying amounts from different countries but is distributed equally around globe within a year. In order to solve this problem, some economists have argued that carbon dioxide emissions should be reduced in countries where the costs are least, with the countries that bear that burden being compensated by the rest of the world.

a. Why is international cooperation necessary to reach an efficient outcome?

b. Is it possible to devise a compensation scheme such that all countries would be better off than under a system of uniform emission reductions? Explain.

13. Some people object to market-based policies to reduce pollution, claiming that they place a monetary value on cleaning our air and water. Economists reply that society *implicitly* places a monetary value on environmental clean-up even under command-and-control policies. Discuss why this is true.

14. (This problem is challenging.) There are three industrial firms in Eurovia.

Firm	Initial pollution level	Cost of reducing pollution by 1 unit
A	70 units	€20
B	80	25
C	50	10

The government wants to reduce pollution to 120 units, it gives each firm 40 tradable pollution permits.

a. Who sells permits and how many do they sell? Who buys permits and how many do they buy? Briefly explain why the sellers and buyers are each willing to do so. What is the total cost of pollution reduction in this situation?

b. How much higher would the costs of pollution reduction be if the permits could not be traded?

For further resources, visit
www.cengage.com/mankiw_taylor2

11 PUBLIC GOODS AND COMMON RESOURCES

An old song lyric maintains that 'the best things in life are free.' A moment's thought reveals a long list of goods that the songwriter could have had in mind. Nature provides some of them, such as rivers, mountains, beaches, lakes and oceans. The government provides others, such as playgrounds, parks and parades. In each case, people do not pay a fee when they choose to enjoy the benefit of the good.

Free goods provide a special challenge for economic analysis. Most goods in our economy are allocated in markets, where buyers pay for what they receive and sellers are paid for what they provide. For these goods, prices are the signals that guide the decisions of buyers and sellers. When goods are available free of charge, however, the market forces that normally allocate resources in our economy are absent.

In this chapter we examine the problems that arise for goods without market prices. Our analysis will shed light on one of the *Ten Principles of Economics* in Chapter 1: governments can sometimes improve market outcomes. When a good does not have a price attached to it, private markets cannot ensure that the good is produced and consumed in the proper amounts. In such cases, government policy can potentially remedy the market failure and raise economic well-being.

THE DIFFERENT KINDS OF GOODS

How well do markets work in providing the goods that people want? The answer to this question depends on the good being considered. As we discussed in Chapter 7, we can rely on the market to provide the efficient number of ice cream cornets: the price of ice cream cornets adjusts to balance supply and demand, and this equilibrium maximizes the sum of producer and consumer surplus. Yet, as we discussed in Chapter 10, we cannot rely on the market to prevent aluminium manufacturers from polluting the air we breathe: buyers and sellers in a market typically do not take account of the external effects of their decisions. Thus, markets work well when the good is ice cream, but they work badly when the good is clean air.

In thinking about the various goods in the economy, it is useful to group them according to two characteristics:

excludability
the property of a good whereby a person can be prevented from using it when they do not pay for it

- Is the good **excludable**? Can people who do not pay for the use of a good be prevented from using the good?

rivalry
the property of a good whereby one person's use diminishes other people's use

- Is the good **rival**? Does one person's use of the good diminish another person's ability to use it?

Using these two characteristics, Figure 11.1 divides goods into four categories:

private goods
goods that are both excludable and rival

1. **Private goods** are both excludable and rival. Consider an ice cream cornet, for example. An ice cream cornet is excludable because it is possible to prevent someone from eating an ice cream cornet – you just don't give it to him. An ice cream cornet is rival because if one person eats an ice cream cornet, another person cannot eat the same cornet. Most goods in the economy are private goods like ice cream cornets. When we analysed supply and demand in Chapters 4, 5 and 6 and the efficiency of markets in Chapters 7, 8 and 9, we implicitly assumed that goods were both excludable and rival.

public goods
goods that are neither excludable nor rival

2. **Public goods** are neither excludable nor rival. That is, people cannot be prevented from using a public good, and one person's use of a public good does not reduce another person's ability to use it. For example, a country's national

FIGURE 11.1

Four Types of Goods

Goods can be grouped into four categories according to two questions: (1) Is the good excludable? That is, can people be prevented from using it? (2) Is the good rival? That is, does one person's use of the good diminish other people's use of it? This diagram gives examples of goods in each of the four categories.

		Rival?	
		Yes	No
Excludable?	Yes	Private goods • Ice cream cornets • Clothing • Congested toll roads	Natural monopolies • The fire service • Cable TV • Uncongested toll roads
	No	Common resources • Fish in the ocean • The environment • Congested non-toll roads	Public goods • Flood-control dams • National defence • Uncongested non-toll roads

defence system: it protects all of the country's citizens equally and the fact that one person is being defended does not affect whether or not another citizen is defended.

3. **Common resources** are rival but not excludable. For example, fish in the ocean are a rival good: when one person catches fish, there are fewer fish for the next person to catch. Yet these fish are not an excludable good because, given the vast size of an ocean, it is difficult to stop fishermen from taking fish out of it when, for example, they have not paid for a licence to do so.

4. When a good is excludable but not rival, it is an example of a *natural monopoly.* For instance, consider fire protection in a small town. It is easy to exclude people from using this good: the fire service can just let their house burn down. Yet fire protection is not rival. Firefighters spend much of their time waiting for a fire, so protecting an extra house is unlikely to reduce the protection available to others. In other words, once a town has paid for the fire service, the additional cost of protecting one more house is small. In Chapter 15 we give a more complete definition of natural monopolies and study them in some detail.

common resources
goods that are rival but not excludable

In this chapter we examine goods that are not excludable and, therefore, are available to everyone free of charge: public goods and common resources. As we will see, this topic is closely related to the study of externalities. For both public goods and common resources, externalities arise because something of value has no price attached to it. If one person were to provide a public good, such as a national defence system, other people would be better off, and yet they could not be charged for this benefit. Similarly, when one person uses a common resource, such as the fish in the ocean, other people are worse off, and yet they are not compensated for this loss. Because of these external effects, private decisions about consumption and production can lead to an inefficient allocation of resources, and government intervention can potentially raise economic well-being.

Quick Quiz Define *public goods* and *common resources,* and give an example of each.

PUBLIC GOODS

To understand how public goods differ from other goods and what problems they present for society, let's consider an example: a fireworks display. This good is not excludable because it is impossible to prevent someone from seeing fireworks, and it is not rival because one person's enjoyment of fireworks does not reduce anyone else's enjoyment of them.

The Free Rider Problem

The citizens of a small Spanish town, Hereza, like seeing fireworks on 6 January when Spain celebrates Epiphany. Each of the town's 500 residents places a €10 value on the experience. The cost of putting on a fireworks display is €1 000. Because the €5 000 of benefits exceed the €1 000 of costs, it is efficient for Hereza residents to have a fireworks display on 6 January.

Would the private market produce the efficient outcome? Probably not. Imagine that Conchita, a Hereza entrepreneur, decided to put on a fireworks display.

Conchita would surely have trouble selling tickets to the event because her potential customers would quickly figure out that they could see the fireworks even without a ticket. Because fireworks are not excludable, people have an incentive to be free riders. A **free rider** is a person who receives the benefit of a good but avoids paying for it.

One way to view this market failure is that it arises because of an externality. If Conchita did put on the fireworks display, she would confer an external benefit on those who saw the display without paying for it. When deciding whether to put on the display, Conchita ignores these external benefits. Even though a fireworks display is socially desirable, it is not privately profitable. As a result, Conchita makes the socially inefficient decision not to put on the display.

Although the private market fails to supply the fireworks display demanded by Hereza residents, the solution to Hereza's problem is obvious: the local government can sponsor a 12th Night celebration. The town council raises revenue by levying taxes on property in the area (in Spain these local property taxes are known as *Impuesto sobre Bienes Inmuebles* (IBI)). Suppose that the council uses this mechanism so as to raise on average an extra €2 from every resident of Hereza and then uses the resulting revenue to hire Conchita to produce the fireworks. Everyone in Hereza is better off by €8 – the €10 in value from the fireworks minus the €2 tax bill. Conchita can help Hereza reach the efficient outcome as a public employee even though she could not do so as a private entrepreneur.

The story of Hereza is simplified, but it is also realistic. In fact, many local councils in Spain do pay for fireworks for festivals, as do local councils in the United Kingdom on 5 November; local governments in France pay for fireworks on 14 July (Bastille Day) and many local governments in the USA pay for fireworks on 4 July (Independence Day). Moreover, the story shows a general lesson about public goods: because public goods are not excludable, the free rider problem prevents the private market from supplying them. The government, however, can potentially remedy the problem. If the government decides that the total benefits exceed the costs, it can provide the public good and pay for it with tax revenue, making everyone better off.

Some Important Public Goods

There are many examples of public goods. Here we consider three of the most important.

National Defence   The defence of the country from foreign aggressors is a classic example of a public good. Once the country is defended, it is impossible to prevent any single person from enjoying the benefit of this defence. Moreover, when one person enjoys the benefit of national defence, he does not reduce the benefit to anyone else. Thus, national defence is neither excludable nor rival.

National defence is also one of the most expensive public goods. In the UK in 2008 it accounted for about €39 billion of government expenditure – the fourth largest category (behind social security, the National Health Service and education). In France the defence budget was around €32.5 billion, in Germany, €26 billion and in the United States a massive €502 billion! People disagree about whether these amounts are too small or too large, but almost no one doubts that some government spending on national defence is necessary. Even economists who advocate small government agree that the national defence is a public good the government should provide.

Basic Research   The creation of knowledge is a public good. If a mathematician proves a new theorem, the theorem enters the general pool of knowledge that anyone can use without charge. Because knowledge is a public good,

*"I just thought of a great new idea that will
benefit all mankind. I call it 'TAXES'."*

profit-seeking firms tend to free ride on the knowledge created by others and, as a result, devote too few resources to creating new knowledge.

In evaluating the appropriate policy towards knowledge creation, it is important to distinguish general knowledge from specific, technological knowledge. Specific, technological knowledge, such as the invention of a better battery, can be patented. The inventor thus obtains much of the benefit of his invention, although certainly not all of it. By contrast, a mathematician cannot patent a theorem; such general knowledge is freely available to everyone. In other words, the patent system makes specific, technological knowledge excludable, whereas general knowledge is not excludable.

The government tries to provide the public good of general knowledge in various ways. Government agencies such as the UK's Research Councils subsidize basic research in many academic disciplines, including medicine, mathematics, science and even economics. Some people justify government funding of space exploration programmes – for example by public funding of the European Space Agency (ESA) or the US National Aeronautics and Space Administration (NASA) – on the grounds that it adds to society's pool of knowledge. Certainly, many private goods, including bullet-proof vests and the instant drink Tang, an orange flavoured non-carbonated drink the brand name of which is now owned by Kraft, use materials that were first developed or made popular by scientists and engineers trying to land a man on the moon. Determining the appropriate level of governmental support for these endeavours is difficult because the benefits are hard to measure. Moreover, the politicians who appropriate funds for research usually have little expertise in science and, therefore, are not in the best position to judge what lines of research will produce the largest benefits.

Fighting Poverty Many government expenditure programmes are aimed at helping the poor. These anti-poverty programmes are financed by taxes on families that are financially more successful.

Economists disagree among themselves about what role the government should play in fighting poverty. Here we note one important argument: Advocates of anti-poverty programmes claim that fighting poverty is a public good.

Suppose that everyone prefers to live in a society without poverty. Even if this preference is strong and widespread, fighting poverty is not a 'good' that the private market can provide. No single individual can eliminate poverty because the problem is so large. Moreover, private charity is hard pressed to solve the problem: people who do not donate to charity can free ride on the generosity of others. In this case, taxing the wealthy to raise the living standards of the poor can make everyone better off. The poor are better off because they now enjoy a higher standard of living, and those paying the taxes are better off because they enjoy living in a society with less poverty.

The Difficult Job of Cost–Benefit Analysis

So far we have seen that the government provides public goods because the private market on its own will not produce an efficient quantity. Yet deciding that the government must play a role is only the first step. The government must then determine what kinds of public goods to provide and in what quantities.

Suppose that the government is considering a public project, such as building a new motorway or autobahn. To judge whether to build the motorway, it must compare the total benefits of all those who would use it to the costs of building and maintaining it. To make this decision, the government might hire a team of economists and engineers to conduct a study, called a **cost–benefit analysis**, the goal of which is to estimate the total costs and benefits of the project to society as a whole.

cost–benefit analysis
a study that compares the costs and benefits to society of providing a public good

Cost–benefit analysts have a tough job. Because the motorway will be available to everyone free of charge, there is no price with which to judge the value of the motorway. Simply asking people how much they would value the motorway is not reliable: quantifying benefits is difficult using the results from a questionnaire, and respondents have little incentive to tell the truth. Those who would use the motorway have an incentive to exaggerate the benefit they receive to get the motorway built. Those who would be harmed by the motorway have an incentive to exaggerate the costs to them to prevent the motorway from being built.

The efficient provision of public goods is, therefore, intrinsically more difficult than the efficient provision of private goods. Private goods are provided in the market. Buyers of a private good reveal the value they place on it by the prices they are willing to pay. Sellers reveal their costs by the prices they are willing to accept. By contrast, cost–benefit analysts do not observe any price signals when evaluating whether the government should provide a public good. Their findings on the costs and benefits of public projects are, therefore, rough approximations at best.

CASE STUDY

How Much is a Life Worth?

Ask yourself this question: how much would you say a human life is worth? Or put it another way, how much extra, per year, would you be prepared to pay in taxes to save one additional human life? €10, €10 000, €1 000 000? The question is almost impossible to answer, in part because it is so subjective (a normative proposition) and in part because most of us do not have €1 000 000 or anything like that to make the question feasible.

Imagine that you have been elected to serve as a member of your local town council. The town engineer comes to you with a proposal: the town can spend €10 000 to build and operate a traffic light at the intersection of Main Street (the town's busy main road) and Easy Street (the much quieter, leafy road where the stockbrokers live). At present, there are only signs instructing motorists entering Main Street from Easy Street that they must stop and give way to Main Street traffic. The benefit of the traffic light is increased safety. The engineer estimates, based on data from similar intersections, that the traffic light would reduce the risk of a fatal traffic accident over the lifetime of the traffic light from 1.6 to 1.1 per cent. Should you spend the money for the new light?

To answer this question, you turn to cost–benefit analysis. But you quickly run into an obstacle: the costs and benefits must be measured in the same units if you are to compare them meaningfully. The cost is measured in euros, but the benefit – the possibility of saving a person's life – is not directly monetary. To make your decision, you have to put a monetary value on a human life.

At first, you may be tempted to conclude that a human life is priceless. After all, there is probably no amount of money that you could be paid to voluntarily give up your life or that of a loved one. This suggests that a human life has an infinite monetary value.

For the purposes of cost–benefit analysis, however, this answer leads to nonsensical results. If we truly placed an infinite value on human life, we should be placing traffic lights on every street corner. Similarly, we should all be driving large cars with all the latest safety features, instead of smaller ones with fewer safety features. Yet traffic lights are not at every corner, and people sometimes choose to buy small cars without side-impact air bags or antilock brakes. In both our public and private decisions, we are at times willing to risk our lives to save some money.

Once we have accepted the idea that a person's life does have an implicit monetary value, how can we determine what that value is? One approach, sometimes used by courts to award damages in wrongful death suits, is to look at the total amount of money a person would have earned if he or she had lived. This approach was also used by the US government in deciding what amount of damages to award to the families of people killed in the terrorist attack on the World Trade Center in September 2001. Economists are often critical of this approach. It has the bizarre implication that the life of a retired or disabled person has no value. However, the earnings potential idea has been used as one way of measuring the value of a human life.

Health services across Europe have to find some way of making decisions about who to treat and who not to treat because the demand for health services far outstrips supply. The basis for such a decision can be to put an estimate on the contribution the individual might make to society based on their future earning capacity. Take the example of a patient who is 45. In theory that person has another 20 years of work left in them before the normal retirement age. If the average wage is €25 000 per annum, that means that this individual is worth €500 000 to society. If the treatment therefore costs less than €500 000 it could be argued it is worth treating this individual. One method that has been designed to try to come to terms with this is a unit of measurement of the outcome of treatment called quality-adjusted life years (QALYs). The concept was developed by health economics researchers at the University of York in the UK. A QALY gives a measure of the extra quality of life and the number of years of extra life resulting from a treatment.

To create a scale (the measure of health state) that covers the range of outcomes of a treatment (or intervention as it is called), researchers went from 1, the best possible state of health where all normal functions were at the disposal of the patient, to 0, the worst possible health state. Between these two scales (and it may seem rather bizarre) was 'death' – in other words, an intervention could be carried out that results in the death of the patient.

What could be worse than death? This is very much a normative issue but it may be possible to imagine a state of health that exists where a patient suffers intolerable physical and mental pain. Doctors can cite cases where patients are in a state where quality of life is both terrible and permanent and the patient has no feelings other than continuing pain. In such tragic situations, some might view the quality of life as being worse than being dead.

The researchers drew up the grades within this scale based on responses from patients about their preferences for different states of health. The grades within the scale, therefore, allow the user to be able to calculate the number of QALYs gained from a treatment. If treatment of a condition of a 50-year-old patient restores the person to full health and that person's life expectancy is 76, then the treatment will have resulted in 26 QALYs. If the treatment restores the person to a reasonable state of health but with some disabilities, such as some limitations to walking, breathing, sight, hearing or other problems rated on the scale as 0.75, then the number of QALYs would be 0.75 x 26 = 19.5 QALYs.

Having got some indication of an outcome, the cost of providing that outcome can be identified and as a result some measure of the value for money provided by health care treatment can be identified. Assume that the cost of three treatments is as follows:

- The average cost of a primary hip replacement is €4 160.
- The average cost of a heart transplant is €416 500.
- The average cost of treating a patient with an open lower limb fracture or dislocation is €2 521 per fracture.

Let us assume that the following outcomes outlined in Table 11.2 are possible after treating a 40-year-old patient:

TABLE 11.1

Treatment	Cost per patient	Measure of health state	Additional life expectancy	QALY	Cost per QALY
Hip replacement	€4 160	0.95	15	14.25	€291.92
Heart transplant	€16 500	0.83	10	8.3	€1 987.95
Fracture	€2 521	1.00	35	35	€72.03

Predictably the fracture comes out as providing the best value for money because of the amount of years of 'good health' it provides after treatment. We can also deduce from this that the opportunity cost of treating one person with a heart transplant is 6.8 people that could have been given a hip replacement and achieving the same cost per QALY – in other words the cost per outcome.

This system therefore provides the health professionals with some form of measure of the outcome of treatment, its associated cost, comparisons between hospitals and departments and thus the basis for decision-making.

Another way to value human life is to look at the risks that people are voluntarily willing to take and how much they must be paid for taking them. Mortality risk varies across jobs, for example. Construction workers in high-rise buildings face greater risk of death on the job than office workers do. By comparing wages in risky and less risky occupations, controlling for education, experience and other determinants of wages, economists can get some sense about what value people put on their own lives. Studies using this approach conclude that the value of a human life is about €10 million.

Other models look at the individual's willingness to pay to buy an extra year's worth of life or how much someone would be willing to pay to reduce the risk of death. There are inherent problems with all of these models but the essential basis of each of them is the fundamental concept of a trade-off as outlined in Principle 1 of the *Ten Principles of Economics.*

One economist, Orley Ashenfelter, calculated the value of a human life based on an analysis of the effect of a rise in speed limits on US roads. The rise in the speed limit meant that drivers drove slightly faster. This 'led to' a rise in deaths on the roads by 35 per cent. Ashenfelter then compared this to the data from areas where speed limits had not been changed. People in such areas drove slower.

The trade-off occurs between the numbers of hours saved as a result of faster travel against the lives lost as a result. Ashenfelter found that the saving in time was about 45 million hours whereas the increase in the number of deaths was 360. Dividing the two gives an average of 125 000 hours per life. Multiply this figure by the US average wage and he ended up with the figure of $980 000.

One problem with such calculations is that it might assume that everyone's life is of equal value. Treatment given to a 98-year-old may be valued differently compared to a 25-year-old. The question then arises, where do you draw the line? When does someone become too old to treat? Already there have been cases around Europe where doctors have refused to treat patients who have smoked and drank heavily despite repeated warnings because they feel they have brought the problems onto themselves and that the use of public money to treat such people is misdirected.

The basis of such decision-making, therefore, is to find some way in which human life can be valued and then set the benefits (measured by some agreed monetary value) against the costs of achieving the outcome. If the benefits outweigh the cost this provides the basis for making the decision. We can now return to our original example and respond to the town engineer. The traffic light reduces the risk of fatality by 0.5 percentage points. Thus, the expected benefit from having the traffic light is 0.005 × €10 million, or €50 000. This estimate of the benefit well exceeds the cost of €10 000, so you should approve the project.

Quick Quiz What is the free rider problem? • Why does the free rider problem induce the government to provide public goods? • How should the government decide whether to provide a public good?

COMMON RESOURCES

Common resources, like public goods, are not excludable: they are available free of charge to anyone who wants to use them. Common resources are, however, rival: one person's use of the common resource reduces other people's ability to

IN THE NEWS

Every year in Europe there are train accidents. The nature of such accidents often means that loss of life and serious injury are significant. Such accidents feature strongly in the news when they happen and there is invariably much debate following the accidents about improving safety. One of the key questions facing decision makers and those using (and paying) for train journeys is how much they are prepared to pay to improve safety on the railways and how this can be measured.

The Price of Safety

The catalogue of train accidents which occur in Europe builds every year. Many of these accidents lead to loss of life. In 2006, 23 people died and 10 were injured in north-western Germany when an elevated train, travelling at 200 km/h, crashed near Lathen in Lower Saxony; in August 2008, a EuroCity train travelling from Krakow in Poland to the Czech capital Prague crashed killing 7 people and injuring over 70; in July 2009, 22 people died when a train carrying liquefied petroleum gas derailed in Tuscany and exploded causing damage and injury to neighbouring houses. In December 2009 a large number of people were injured in the Croatian capital of Zagreb when a train crashed into barriers at the city's main railway station. In the UK crashes at Paddington in 1999 killed 31 and injured over 500; in Hatfield in 2000 a train crash killed 4 and injured over 100, in North Yorkshire in 2001 10 died and over 80 were injured, in Berkshire 7 died and over 100 were injured in a crash involving a suspected suicide. In Europe every year an average of 100 people are killed in train accidents. As with airplane accidents, the loss of life and injury when such incidents happen tends to be significant and the event high profile.

One of the outcomes of these accidents is calls for policies and procedures to be put in place to improve passenger safety, something which few people would argue with. In the wake of these accidents emotional friends and relatives call for systems to be implemented which will 'ensure that accidents like this will never happen again'. Politicians are often quick to tap into the emotional grief of the situation by promising to ensure that safety procedures are looked at and implemented to reduce the risk. The question has to be asked, is this a sensible promise to make and can it be supported in terms of cost–benefit analysis? In other words, is it worth spending *any* amount of money to bring the risk down to zero? Relatives of those who have died in such accidents are likely to agree that it is and might say the value of their loved one's life is priceless and that no-one else should have to experience the grief they have.

In looking at whether implementing safety systems would reduce the risk of accident is worthwhile, policy makers may conduct a cost–benefit analysis. There are technical features which can be put in place to help reduce the risk of accident on the railways. Two such systems are Automated Train Protection (ATP) and Train Protection Warning Systems (TPWS). On board computers receive information from sensors on the tracks and signalling systems to warn of potential problems allowing the driver to take action. If the driver does not react to the information then the train will automatically be brought to a halt. These systems will

reduce the risk of accident but at what cost and can the cost of implementing them be justified?

When deciding whether to introduce additional safety measures, policy makers have to consider a number or factors. What is the risk of an event happening which leads to loss of life? How does this risk compare with other modes of transport (important in justifying any proposed expenditure), does the risk identified justify expenditure to reduce that risk? What is the value of the marginal benefit of reducing the risk compared to the marginal cost?

For example, assume that the risk of death on a train journey was put at

1: 100 000 km. In other words, for every 100 000 kilometres you travel on a train there is a chance you may be involved in an accident which results in your death. Would an individual agree that a reduction of the risk to 1: 50 000 km is a good thing?

Any rational person would agree that the lower the risk the better. One way to reduce the risk would be to implement ATP and TPWS systems on every train and throughout the rail network. The cost of doing this would amount to billions of euros. Ultimately this cost is likely to be passed on to the passenger in the form of higher prices. So, how much is an individual passenger willing to pay in extra fare to reduce the risk (which, remember, we assumed every rational person would agree to). Is paying an extra €5 per journey worth it? What about €10, €20, €100? At what point do passengers believe that the extra price they have to pay for the journey outweighs the benefits of the reduced risk?

These decisions are the sort policy makers have to make and economists can help in providing the data upon

which such decisions can be based. Reducing the risk may be desirable but the cost of doing so may be prohibitive. So what is a tolerable risk? In the UK, the Health and Safety Executive (HSE) has devised a tolerability of risk framework (TOR) which was developed in relation to the construction of nuclear power stations, but which can be applied to other situations where risk has to be assessed. This framework was utilized by Professor Andrew Evans, of Imperial College London in a report published by the Royal Academy of Engineering in 2005[1]. The TOR framework ranks risk from 'broadly acceptable' through 'tolerable but must be reduced as low as reasonably practicable' to 'intolerable risk' where the risk cannot be justified. Professor Evans states, 'Individual risk is usually defined as the risk of death per year to a specified or representative individual from a specified activity or hazard.' Tolerable risk for an individual in rail travel is given as 10^{-4} per year. Having established the risk the next stage of a cost–benefit analysis can be undertaken.

Professor Evans notes that calculating these costs and benefits present numerous challenges but must adhere to two principles: '...first, that as far as possible, all costs and benefits, to whomsoever they accrue, should be included; and second, in the context of safety risks, the costs and benefits should be valued as those affected by the risks and costs of reducing them would value them.' Using methods based on these principles, an official value of preventing a fatality is given as £1.31 million (€1.51 million). Implementing automatic train protection was estimated at costing £15 million per prevented fatality (cost per prevented fatality, or CPF). Given that this is significantly higher than the value of preventing a fatality, economists might recommend that such a system was not implemented and that the funds might be better spent elsewhere where the CPF to value ratio is lower and yields a greater benefit than cost. Would you agree?

[1] http://www.raeng.org.uk/news/publications/list/lectures/Lloyds_Safety_Appraisal.pdf

use it. Thus, common resources give rise to a new problem. Once the good is provided, policy makers need to be concerned about how much it is used. This problem is best understood from the classic parable called the **Tragedy of the Commons**.

Tragedy of the Commons
a parable that illustrates why common resources get used more than is desirable from the standpoint of society as a whole

The Tragedy of the Commons

Consider life in a small medieval town. Of the many economic activities that take place in the town, one of the most important is raising sheep. Many of the town's families own flocks of sheep and support themselves by selling the sheep's wool, which is used to make clothing.

As our story begins, the sheep spend much of their time grazing on the land surrounding the town, called the Town Common. No family owns the land. Instead, the town residents own the land collectively, and all the residents are allowed to graze their sheep on it. Collective ownership works well because land is plentiful. As long as everyone can get all the good grazing land they want, the Town Common is not a rival good, and allowing residents' sheep to graze for free causes no problems. Everyone in town is happy.

As the years pass, the population of the town grows, and so does the number of sheep grazing on the Town Common. With a growing number of sheep and a fixed amount of land, the land starts to lose its ability to replenish itself. Eventually, the land is grazed so heavily that it becomes barren. With no grass left on the Town Common, raising sheep is impossible, and the town's once prosperous wool industry disappears and, tragically, many families lose their source of livelihood.

What causes the tragedy? Why do the shepherds allow the sheep population to grow so large that it destroys the Town Common? The reason is that social and private incentives differ. Avoiding the destruction of the grazing land depends on the collective action of the shepherds. If the shepherds acted together, they could reduce the sheep population to a size that the Town Common could support. Yet no single family has an incentive to reduce the size of its own flock because each flock represents only a small part of the problem.

In essence, the Tragedy of the Commons arises because of an externality. When one family's flock grazes on the common land, it reduces the quality of the land available for other families. Because people neglect this negative externality when deciding how many sheep to own, the result is an excessive number of sheep.

If the tragedy had been foreseen, the town could have solved the problem in various ways. It could have regulated the number of sheep in each family's flock, internalized the externality by taxing sheep, or auctioned off a limited number of sheep-grazing permits. That is, the medieval town could have dealt with the problem of overgrazing in the way that modern society deals with the problem of pollution.

In the case of land, however, there is a simpler solution. The town can divide up the land among town families. Each family can enclose its allotment of land with a fence and then protect it from excessive grazing. In this way, the land becomes a private good rather than a common resource. This outcome in fact occurred during the enclosure movement in England in the 17th century.

The Tragedy of the Commons is a story with a general lesson: when one person uses a common resource, he diminishes other people's enjoyment of it. Because of this negative externality, common resources tend to be used excessively. The government can solve the problem by reducing use of the common resource through regulation or taxes. Alternatively, the government can sometimes turn the common resource into a private good.

This lesson has been known for thousands of years. The ancient Greek philosopher Aristotle pointed out the problem with common resources: 'What is common to many is taken least care of, for all men have greater regard for what is their own than for what they possess in common with others.'

Some Important Common Resources

There are many examples of common resources. In almost all cases, the same problem arises as in the Tragedy of the Commons: private decision makers use the common resource too much. Governments often regulate behaviour or impose fees to mitigate the problem of overuse.

Clean Air and Water   As we discussed in Chapter 10, markets do not adequately protect the environment. Pollution is a negative externality that can be remedied with regulations or with Pigovian taxes on polluting activities. One can view this market failure as an example of a common-resource problem. Clean air and clean water are common resources like open grazing land, and excessive pollution is like excessive grazing. Environmental degradation is a modern Tragedy of the Commons.

Congested Roads   Roads can be either public goods or common resources. If a road is not congested, then one person's use does not affect anyone else. In this case, use is not rival, and the road is a public good. Yet if a road is congested, then use of that road yields a negative externality. When one person drives on the road, it becomes more crowded, and other people must drive more slowly. In this case, the road is a common resource.

One way for the government to address the problem of road congestion is to charge drivers a toll. A toll is, in essence, a Pigovian tax on the externality of congestion. Often, as in the case of local roads, tolls are not a practical solution because the cost of collecting them is too high. Nevertheless, tolls are often charged on stretches of motorways in continental Europe and the USA, and occasionally in the UK (on the M6, for example).

Sometimes congestion is a problem only at certain times of day. If a bridge is heavily travelled only during rush hour, for instance, the congestion externality is larger during this time than during other times of day. The efficient way to deal with these externalities is to charge higher tolls during rush hour. This toll would provide an incentive for drivers to alter their schedules and would reduce traffic when congestion is greatest.

Another policy that responds to the problem of road congestion, discussed in a case study in the previous chapter (page 212–213), is the tax on petrol. Petrol is a complementary good to driving: an increase in the price of petrol tends to reduce the quantity of driving demanded. Therefore, a petrol tax reduces road congestion. A petrol tax, however, is an imperfect solution to road congestion. The problem is that the petrol tax affects other decisions besides the amount of driving on congested roads. For example, the petrol tax discourages driving on non-congested roads, even though there is no congestion externality for these roads.

Fish, Whales and Other Wildlife   Many species of animals are common resources. Fish and whales, for instance, have commercial value, and anyone can go to the ocean and catch whatever is available. Each person has little incentive to maintain the species for the next year. Just as excessive grazing can destroy the Town Common, excessive fishing and whaling can destroy commercially valuable marine populations.

The ocean remains one of the least regulated common resources. Two problems prevent an easy solution. First, many countries have access to the oceans, so any solution would require international cooperation among countries that hold different values. Secondly, because the oceans are so vast, enforcing any agreement is difficult. As a result, fishing rights have been a frequent source of international tension among normally friendly countries.

Within the United Kingdom and other European countries, various laws aim to protect fish and other wildlife. For example, the government charges for fishing and hunting licences, and it restricts the lengths of the fishing and hunting seasons. Fishermen are often required to throw back small fish, and hunters can kill only a limited number of animals or shoot certain wild birds such as pheasant or grouse during specified periods of the year. All these laws reduce the use of a common resource and help maintain animal populations.

CASE STUDY

Why the Cow is not Extinct

Throughout history, many species of animals have been threatened with extinction. When Europeans first arrived in North America, more than 60 million buffalo roamed the continent. Yet hunting the buffalo was so popular during the 19th century that by 1900 the animal's population fell to about

"Can the market become my friend too?"

400 before the government stepped in to protect the species. In some African countries today, the elephant faces a similar challenge, as poachers kill the animals for the ivory in their tusks.

Yet not all animals with commercial value face this threat. The cow, for example, is a valuable source of food, but no one worries that the cow will soon be extinct. Indeed, the great demand for beef seems to ensure that the species will continue to thrive.

Why is the commercial value of ivory a threat to the elephant, while the commercial value of beef is a guardian of the cow? The reason is that elephants are a common resource, whereas cows are a private good. Elephants roam freely without any owners. Each poacher has a strong incentive to kill as many elephants as he can find. Because poachers are numerous, each poacher has only a slight incentive to preserve the elephant population. By contrast, cows live on farms that are privately owned. Each farmer takes great effort to maintain the cow population on his farm because he reaps the benefit of these efforts.

Governments have tried to solve the elephant's problem in two ways. Some countries, such as Kenya, Tanzania and Uganda, have made it illegal to kill elephants and sell their ivory. Yet these laws have been hard to enforce, and elephant populations have continued to dwindle. By contrast, other countries, such as Botswana, Malawi, Namibia and Zimbabwe, have made elephants a private good by allowing people to kill elephants, but only those on their own property. Landowners now have an incentive to preserve the species on their own land, and as a result, elephant populations have started to rise. With private ownership and the profit motive now on its side, the African elephant might someday be as safe from extinction as the cow.

Quick Quiz Why do governments try to limit the use of common resources?

CONCLUSION: THE IMPORTANCE OF PROPERTY RIGHTS

In this chapter and the previous one, we have seen there are some 'goods' that the market does not provide adequately. Markets do not ensure that the air we breathe is clean or that our country is defended from foreign aggressors. Instead, societies rely on the government to protect the environment and to provide for the national defence.

Although the problems we considered in these chapters arise in many different markets, they share a common theme. In all cases, the market fails to allocate resources efficiently because *property rights* are not well established. That is, some item of value does not have an owner with the legal authority to control it. For example, although no one doubts that the 'good' of clean air or national defence is valuable, no one has the right to attach a price to it and profit from its use. A factory pollutes too much because no one charges the factory for the pollution it emits. The market does not provide for national defence because no one can charge those who are defended for the benefit they receive.

When the absence of property rights causes a market failure, the government can potentially solve the problem. Sometimes, as in the sale of pollution permits, the solution is for the government to help define property rights and thereby unleash market forces. Other times, as in the restriction on hunting seasons, the solution is for the government to regulate private behaviour. Still other times, as in the provision of national defence, the solution is for the government to supply a good that the market fails to supply. In all cases, if the policy is well planned and well run, it can make the allocation of resources more efficient and thus raise economic well-being.

SUMMARY

- Goods differ in whether they are excludable and whether they are rival. A good is excludable if it is possible to prevent someone from using it. A good is rival if one person's use of the good reduces other people's ability to use the same unit of the good. Markets work best for private goods, which are both excludable and rival. Markets do not work as well for other types of goods.

- Public goods are neither rival nor excludable. Examples of public goods include fireworks displays, national defence and the creation of fundamental knowledge. Because people are not charged for their use of the public good,

they have an incentive to free ride when the good is provided privately. Therefore, governments provide public goods, making their decision about the quantity based on cost–benefit analysis.

- Common resources are rival but not excludable. Examples include common grazing land, clean air and congested roads. Because people are not charged for their use of common resources, they tend to use them excessively. Therefore, governments try to limit the use of common resources.

KEY CONCEPTS

excludability, p. 222
rivalry, p. 222
private goods, p. 222

public goods, p. 222
common resources, p. 223
free rider, p. 224

cost–benefit analysis, p. 226
Tragedy of the Commons, p. 231

QUESTIONS FOR REVIEW

1. Explain what is meant by a good being 'excludable'. Explain what is meant by a good being 'rival'. Is a pizza excludable? Is it rival?

2. Define and give an example of a public good. Can the private market provide this good on its own? Explain.

3. What is cost–benefit analysis of public goods? Why is it important? Why is it hard?

4. Define and give an example of a common resource. Without government intervention, will people use this good too much or too little? Why?

PROBLEMS AND APPLICATIONS

1. The text says that both public goods and common resources involve externalities.
   a. Are the externalities associated with public goods generally positive or negative? Use examples in your

   answer. Is the free market quantity of public goods generally greater or less than the efficient quantity?
   b. Are the externalities associated with common resources generally positive or negative? Use

examples in your answer. Is the free market use of common resources generally greater or less than the efficient use?

2. Think about the goods and services provided by your local government.

    a. Using the classification in Figure 11.1, explain what category each of the following goods falls into:

       • police protection
       • road gritting
       • education
       • rural roads
       • city streets.

    b. Why do you think the government provides items that are not public goods?

3. One of the UK's major broadcasting companies, the British Broadcasting Corporation (BBC) is funded largely by the sale of annual licences. Charles loves watching football matches on TV when the BBC broadcasts them, but he never buys a TV licence.

    a. What name do economists have for Charles?

    b. How can the government solve the problem caused by people like Charles?

    c. Can you think of ways the private market can solve this problem? How does the existence of cable or satellite TV alter the situation?

4. The text states that private firms will not undertake the efficient amount of basic scientific research.

    a. Explain why this is so. In your answer, classify basic research in one of the categories shown in Figure 11.1.

    b. What sort of policy has the United Kingdom adopted in response to this problem?

    c. It is often argued that this policy increases the technological capability of British producers relative to that of foreign firms. Is this argument consistent with your classification of basic research in part (a)? (Hint: can excludability apply to some potential beneficiaries of a public good and not others?)

5. Why is there litter along most major roads but rarely in people's gardens?

6. An *Economist* article (19 March 1994) states: 'In the past decade, most of the rich world's fisheries have been exploited to the point of near-exhaustion.' The article continues with an analysis of the problem and a discussion of possible private and government solutions.

    a. 'Do not blame fishermen for overfishing. They are behaving rationally, as they have always done.' In what sense is 'overfishing' rational for fishermen?

    b. 'A community, held together by ties of obligation and mutual self-interest, can manage a common resource on its own.' Explain how such management can work in principle, and what obstacles it faces in the real world.

    c. 'Until 1976 most world fish stocks were open to all comers, making conservation almost impossible. Then an international agreement extended some aspects of [national] jurisdiction from 12 to 200 miles offshore.' Using the concept of property rights, discuss how this agreement reduces the scope of the problem.

    d. The article notes that many governments come to the aid of suffering fishermen in ways that encourage increased fishing. How do such policies encourage a vicious cycle of overfishing?

    e. 'Only when fishermen believe they are assured a long-term and exclusive right to a fishery are they likely to manage it in the same far-sighted way as good farmers manage their land.' Defend this statement.

    f. What other policies to reduce overfishing might be considered?

7. In a market economy, information about the quality or function of goods and services is a valuable good in its own right. How does the private market provide this information? Can you think of any way in which the government plays a role in providing this information?

8. Do you think the internet is a public good? Why or why not?

9. High-income people are willing to pay more than lower-income people to avoid the risk of death. For example, they are more likely to pay for safety features on cars. Do you think cost–benefit analysts should take this fact into account when evaluating public projects? Consider, for instance, a rich town and a poor town, both of which are considering the installation of a traffic light. Should the rich town use a higher monetary value for a human life in making this decision? Why or why not?

For further resources, visit
www.cengage.com/mankiw_taylor2

12 THE DESIGN OF THE TAX SYSTEM

A l 'Scarface' Capone, the notorious 1920s Chicago gangster and crime boss, was never convicted for his many violent crimes. Yet eventually he did go to jail – for tax evasion. Capone could, quite literally, get away with murder, but he couldn't get away with not paying his taxes. Taxes are inevitable because we as citizens expect the government to provide us with various goods and services. The previous two chapters have started to shed light on one of the *Ten Principles of Economics* from Chapter 1: the government can sometimes improve market outcomes. When the government remedies an externality (such as air pollution), provides a public good (such as national defence) or regulates the use of a common resource (such as fish in a public lake), it can raise economic well-being. Yet the benefits of government come with costs. For the government to perform these and its many other functions, it needs to raise revenue through taxation.

We began our study of taxation in earlier chapters, where we saw how a tax on a good affects supply and demand for that good. In Chapter 6 we saw that a tax reduces the quantity sold in a market, and we examined how the burden of a tax is shared by buyers and sellers, depending on the elasticities of supply and demand. In Chapter 8 we examined how taxes affect economic well-being. We learned that taxes cause deadweight losses: the reduction in consumer and producer surplus resulting from a tax exceeds the revenue raised by the government.

In this chapter we build on these lessons to discuss the design of a tax system. In particular, we consider the fundamental principles of taxation. Most people agree that taxes should impose as small a cost on society as possible and that the burden of taxes should be distributed fairly. That is, the tax system should be both efficient and equitable. As we will see, however, stating these goals is easier than achieving them.

When thinking about the tax system, it is useful to have in mind some basic facts about a particular tax system and so, for illustrative purposes, we'll start with a financial overview of the UK system. We will then provide some outline details of tax systems in other countries as a means of comparison. The website that accompanies this book will feature tax systems for other major European countries.

A FINANCIAL OVERVIEW OF THE UK GOVERNMENT

How much of the nation's income does the government take as taxes? Figure 12.1 shows UK government spending since 1900 as a percentage of GDP. Figure 12.2 shows UK total managed expenditure (spending by central and local government and public enterprises) as a proportion of GDP since 2000. Figure 12.1 shows that, over time, the government has taken a greater role in the economy. In 1910 government spending was about 15 per cent of total income; in the early years of the 21st century it was around 40 per cent. In other words, as the economy's income has grown, the government has grown even more. Perhaps the most striking feature of Figure 12.1, however, is the role of wars. The 20th century

FIGURE 12.1

UK Government Expenditure as a Percentage of GDP

This figure shows the expenditure of the UK government as a percentage of GDP, which measures the total income in the economy. It shows that the government plays a large role in the UK economy and that its role has grown over time.

Source: UK Public Spending (http://www.ukpublicspending.co.uk).

FIGURE 12.2

UK Total Managed Expenditure as a Percentage of GDP

This figure shows the expenditure of the UK government as a percentage of GDP. It shows that government expenditure has risen as a percentage of GDP since 2000 and has risen sharply since 2007.

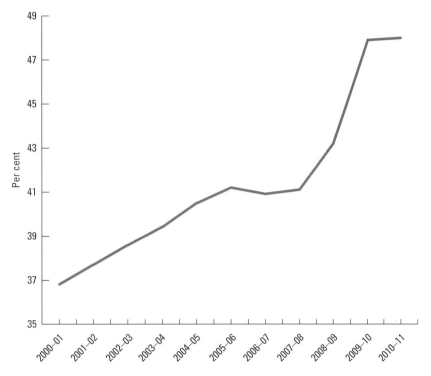

Source: http://www.hm-treasury.gov.uk/d/public_finances_databank.xls accessed 9 February 2010 (Crown Copyright).

began with relatively high spending reflecting the costs of the Boer War. World War I (1914–1918) and World War II (1939–1945) both led to very large increases in public spending. After both of these wars, public spending fell back when hostilities ceased, but to a higher level than before the war. Figure 12.2 shows UK total managed expenditure from 2000 to 2011 (2009–2010 onwards are estimates). It shows how public spending as a proportion of GDP has risen from 36.8 per cent to almost 50 per cent by 2010–2011. Part of the reason for the large rise in expenditure over this period was the recession of 2008–2009. Rising government expenditure was accompanied by falling revenues and so the public deficit widened considerably.

Table 12.1 compares the tax burden for seven major economies – the so-called 'Group of Seven', or G7 – as measured by the total tax revenue as a percentage of the nation's total income in 2008. The overall size of government revenue tells only part of the story, however. Behind the total figures lie thousands of individual decisions about taxes and spending. To understand the government's finances more fully, let's look at how the total breaks down into some broad categories.

Receipts

Table 12.2 shows the sources of UK government revenue in the financial year 2008–09 (in the UK, the tax year or 'fiscal year' runs from the beginning of

TABLE 12.1

Total Tax Revenue as a Percentage of GDP in the G7 Countries, 2008

Italy	43.2%
France	43.1
Germany	36.4
United Kingdom	35.7
Canada	32.2
Japan	28.3 (2007 figure)
United States	26.9

Source: Reproduced with permission from www.oecd.org

TABLE 12.2

Sources of UK Government Revenue, 2008–09

Tax	Amount (billions £)*	Amount per person (£)*	Percentage of receipts (%)
Personal income tax	153.4	2 498	28.25
National Insurance contributions	96.9	1 578	17.84
Value-added tax	78.4	1 277	14.44
Company taxes	66	1 075	12.15
Other indirect taxes	51.7	842	9.25
Council tax	24.4	397	4.49
Capital taxes	18.8	306	3.46
Other taxes and receipts	53.5	871	9.85
Total	543.1	8 845	100%

Source: HM Treasury, and authors' calculations.
*numbers are rounded up

April). (Here we are defining government in a wide sense to include, for example, local government as well as the central government based in London. Taxes are collected by a government agency, Her Majesty's Revenue and Customs.) Total receipts in 2008–09 were £543 billion and in 2009–10 were estimated to be £498 billion[1].

These numbers are so large that they are hard to comprehend. A billion is one thousand million, or 1 with 9 zeros after it (10^9). To appreciate how large a number this is, imagine counting one digit every second. How long would it take to count to one billion? In one year this constant counting would get you to 31 536 000; it would be another 30 years before you reached one billion!

To bring this astronomical figure down to earth, we can divide it by the size of the UK population, estimated at 61.4 million in an ONS report published in August 2009. We then find that the total of taxes levied amounted to around £8 845 for every man, woman and child in the United Kingdom in 2008–09, falling to around £8 111 in 2009–10.

The largest source of revenue for the government is personal income tax. This represents receipts on a tax on individuals' income from all sources: wages from working, interest on savings, dividends from corporations in which the person owns shares, profits from any small businesses he or she operates, and so on. The individual's tax liability (how much he or she owes) is then based on total income for the year.

---

[1]http://www.hm-treasury.gov.uk/d/pbr09_chapter1.pdf

TABLE 12.3

UK Income Tax Bands and Rates, 2010–11

This table shows the marginal tax rates for a UK taxpayer under the age of 65. For 2010–11 the personal allowance was £6475, so that taxable income is any income in excess of this amount. The taxes levied on a taxpayer depend on all the marginal tax rates up to his or her income level. For example, a taxpayer with an income of £34000 pays nothing on the first £6475 of income and 20 per cent of the rest. The 10 per cent band is for income from savings only.

Taxable income	Tax rate
Up to £2440	10%
From £0 to £37400	20
Over £37 401 – £150000	40
Over £150000	50

Source: HM Revenue and Customs. (http://www.hmrc.gov.uk/rates/it.htm)

A person's income tax liability is not simply proportional to their income. Instead, the law requires a more complicated calculation. Taxable income is computed as total income minus a 'personal allowance' – a basic amount of income that is not taxed – and minus certain expenses that policy makers have deemed 'deductible' (such as the costs of operating an office in order to run a small business).

Then the tax liability is calculated from taxable income (income minus personal allowance and deductibles) using a schedule like that shown in Table 12.3 (although the Chancellor of the Exchequer has the power to change this schedule from time to time, and usually does so annually).

This table presents the marginal tax rate – the tax rate applied to each additional amount of income. Because the marginal tax rate rises as income rises, higher income individuals pay a larger percentage of their income in taxes. Note that each tax rate in the table applies only to income within the associated range, not to a person's entire income. For example, in 2009–10, a person with an income of £90000 a year still paid nothing on the first £6475 of income and 20 per cent on the next £30925 before paying 40 per cent on the remainder of income. (We discuss the concept of marginal tax rate more fully later in this chapter.) Note that the UK government introduced a new 50 per cent rate of tax on incomes in excess of £150000 and set an income limit for tax allowance of £100000. Incomes in excess of £100000, therefore, do not qualify for a basic allowance.

Next in importance to the UK government, at around 18 per cent of receipts, are National Insurance contributions. National Insurance contributions, or NICs, are a peculiarity of the UK tax system in that they are part income tax, part payroll tax (a payroll tax is a tax on the wages that a firm pays its workers). NICs work like this: the level of the employee's NICs is based on income, similar to income tax, except that it is usually worked out on weekly rather than annual earnings. The earnings limits and NIC rates for 2010–11 are shown in Table 12.4.

Up to a weekly earned income of £97, nothing is paid. Once a worker earns more than £97 a week, however, he pays 11 per cent of weekly income above £97 and less than £844. On the balance of his weekly earnings in excess of £844 he pays 1 per cent. The payroll tax part of NICs, the employer's NIC, is more straightforward: the employer pays 12.8 per cent of all earnings paid to the employee above £97 a week. These rates will be lower if the worker has 'contracted out' of the state pension scheme (i.e. elected not to receive a state pension).

TABLE 12.4

UK National Insurance Contribution Earnings Limits and Rates, 2010–11

This table shows UK standard rate National Insurance contribution rates in 2010–11. They are worked out on weekly earnings and comprise both an employee's contribution and an employer's contribution. For example, a worker with an income of £950 a week (about £49 400 a year) would pay nothing on the first £97 of weekly income, 11 per cent of what he earned between £97 and £844, and 1 per cent on the remaining £11. In addition, his employer would also have to pay 12.8 per cent of his weekly earnings in excess of £97.

Weekly earnings	Employee's contribution
Up to £97	0%
From £97 to £844	11
Over £844	1

Source: HM Revenue and Customs. http://www.hmrc.gov.uk/rates/nic.htm

NICs are a form of social insurance tax, because a worker's entitlement to certain benefits, such as unemployment benefit and a state pension, depends upon the amount of NICs paid (for this reason they are termed 'contributory' benefits). The revenue from these taxes is paid into a National Insurance fund. A small, fixed proportion of this is allocated to the National Health Service and the remainder is used to fund spending on contributory benefits. However, the link between National Insurance contributions paid and eligibility for benefits is quite weak, and has been getting weaker over time.

Value-added tax, or VAT, comprises about 15 per cent of revenue. VAT is a proportional sales tax, and in the UK is currently levied at three rates; 0 per cent, 5 per cent and 20 per cent of the selling price of a range of goods and services. In November 2008 the government announced that VAT would be temporarily cut from 17.5 per cent to 15 per cent in an attempt to boost consumer spending amidst the recession (at that time VAT was set at 17.5 per cent).

VAT returned to the 17.5 per cent rate on 31 December 2009 and was then increased in January 2011 to 20 per cent. It is called 'value-added' tax because the person producing the good or service is able to deduct any VAT he or she has already paid on goods or services used in producing it before paying the tax bill, so that the tax paid is actually a tax on the value added to the product at each stage of production.

To make this clearer, let's consider an example assuming VAT is set at 20 per cent. Suppose a sculptor wants £800 for a stone sculpture. She will charge £800 plus VAT of £160 (= 20 per cent of £800), or £960 in total. Before paying her VAT bill to HM Revenue and Customs, however, she will deduct from the £160 any VAT she paid in the production of the sculpture. In fact, she bought a block of stone from a local quarry for £200 plus VAT of £40 (= 20 per cent of £200), so she will deduct the £40 VAT she has already paid and send £120 (= £160 – £40) to HM Revenue and Customs. How much VAT will the Revenue and Customs receive in total? They get £40 when the stone is sold to the sculptor; this represents a tax on the value added at this stage of production – digging the stone up from the quarry, where it was worth nothing, and delivering it to the sculptor's studio, where it was worth £200.

Then Revenue and Customs received £120 when the sculptor sold the sculpture. This again represents a tax on the value added at this stage of production: the selling price of £800 minus the cost of marble of £200 equals value added of £600, and 20 per cent of £600 is £120. Adding the £40 the Revenue and Customs received when the block of stone was sold to the sculptor and the £120 they received when the sculptor sold the final sculpture, they have received £160. This is 20 per cent of the total value added in the whole production process – from a value of zero when the stone was in the ground, to £800 when the sculpture was sold (£160 = 20 per cent of £800).

VAT is an example of an **indirect tax**, as opposed to income tax, which is a **direct tax**. A direct tax is levied directly on a person or a company's income or wealth, while an indirect tax is levied on the price of something sold. Other indirect taxes, including taxes on fuel and on cigarettes and alcoholic drinks, account for about 9 per cent of revenue.

After VAT, company taxes are next in importance in terms of the percentage of total tax receipts they represent. These include direct taxes such as local taxes levied on the value of a company's buildings, as well as corporation tax, which is a tax on a company's profits. A corporation is a business that is set up as a separate legal entity. The government taxes each corporation based on its profit – the amount the corporation receives for the goods or services it sells minus the costs of producing those goods or services. Notice that corporate profits are, in essence, taxed twice. They are taxed once by corporation tax when the corporation earns the profits; they are taxed a second time by the individual income tax when the corporation uses its profits to pay dividends to its shareholders.

Council taxes, accounting for about 4.5 per cent of total receipts, are local taxes paid by individuals – in the UK, usually levied on the value of residential property owned – in order to finance local amenities such as refuse collection and local roads.

Capital taxes, accounting for about 3.5 per cent of total tax revenue, are composed of inheritance tax, capital gains tax and stamp duty. Inheritance tax is the tax paid by an individual when he or she inherits money or property. Capital gains tax is paid when an individual makes a profit from investments – for example if he or she buys shares in a company and later sells them at a profit, capital gains tax will be payable on that profit. Stamp duty is a tax levied by the government on capital transactions: for example, when a person buys shares in a company or a house to live in, they will normally be liable to pay a certain percentage of the price as stamp duty. (The term 'stamp duty' is a reminder of years gone by when a government official would have used a rubber stamp on the transaction document as proof that the tax had been paid.)

indirect tax
a tax that is levied on goods and services bought

direct tax
a tax that is levied directly on a person's income

Spending

Table 12.5 shows the spending of the UK government in 2010–11. Total spending in that year was £706.6 billion, or £11 508 per person. This table also shows how the government's spending was divided among major categories.

The largest category in Table 12.5 is social security, which represents transfer payments to the elderly (i.e. pensions) as well as unemployment benefits and other forms of social benefits. (A transfer payment is a government payment not made in exchange for a good or service.) This category is estimated to represent 28 per cent of spending by the UK government in 2010–11.

The second largest category of spending is on the National Health Service. Since 1948, the UK has offered health care to UK residents free at the point of delivery. The term 'free at the point of delivery' is important here. It means that at the time the service is delivered – when you go to see your general practitioner (GP) or you have your appendix taken out in hospital – there is no charge made. At a total cost of £127.2 billion to taxpayers in 2010–11, however, or £2 072 for every man, woman and child in the United Kingdom, it is clear that health care has to be paid for like everything else.

TABLE 12.5

UK Government Spending, 2010–11 (Estimated)

Category	Amount (£ billions)	Amount per person (£)	Percentage of spending %
Social security	197.8	3 221	28
National Health Service	127.2	2 072	18
Education	91.9	1 497	13
Defence	42.4	691	6
Public order and safety	35.3	575	5
Transport	21.2	345	3
Other	190.8	3 107	27
Total	£706.6	£11 508	100%

Source: HM Treasury and authors' calculations.

TABLE 12.6

UK Government Spending as a Percentage of GDP in the Six Main Areas

	1958–59	1978–79	1996–97	2008–09
Social security	6.0%	9.8%	13.1%	11.9%
NHS	3.2	4.4	5.1	7.8
Education	3.3	5.2	4.6	5.7
Defence	6.4	4.5	2.8	2.6
Public order and safety	n/a	1.5	2.0	2.4
Transport	n/a	1.6	1.2	1.5

Source: *A Survey of Public Spending in the UK.* Institute for Fiscal Studies Briefing Note BN43 http://www.ifs.org.uk/bns/bn43.pdf

Next in importance in terms of the amount spent is education, accounting for about £92 billion in 2010–11, or about 13 per cent of total spending. This includes spending on all forms of primary, secondary and higher education, as well as government training programmes.

Expenditure on national defence, weighing in at £42.4 billion, or £691 per person, is the fourth largest individual category. This includes both the salaries of military personnel and purchases of military equipment such as guns, fighter jets and warships.

The fifth category is public order and safety, which includes, for example, the cost of maintaining a police force and a fire service, as well as the criminal justice system. Government spending on transport – for example the cost of maintaining national motorways and the cost of subsidies paid to rail operators for maintaining the rail network – makes up the sixth largest category, at around £21 billion, or some 3 per cent of total spending.

(The category labelled 'other' in Table 12.5 is composed of a range of smaller categories of expenditure, such as environmental protection, housing, culture, science and technology, and agriculture, as well as items such as debt interest.)

In Table 12.6, we show how the main categories of UK government expenditure have changed over time, measured as a percentage of GDP. It is striking how expenditure on social security and the NHS have both increased strongly and steadily over the past four decades, while defence expenditure has shown a steady decline. The decline in defence expenditure is even more marked as a percentage of total government expenditure: as shown in Table 12.5, defence spending in 2010–11 amounted to about 6 per cent of the total, but in the mid-1980s it was about 11 per cent of total government spending. This reflects changing shifts in international political tensions, from the height of the Cold War in the 1960s to its effective end with the collapse of communism in the late 1980s and early 1990s.

The increase in spending on the NHS over time, also evident in Table 12.6, reflects at least three factors: changes in not only the size but also the structure of the population, which means that there is an increasing proportion of elderly people; the general tendency for an increase in demand for health services as countries become richer; and finally the increase in the range of treatable ailments over time as medical science has become more advanced and the use of technology in treatment becomes more prevalent and also more sophisticated.

CASE STUDY

Trade-offs in New Drug Treatments

Humans contracting the cancer, chronic myeloid leukaemia (CML), ten years ago may have faced a very uncertain future. CML is a cancer of the white blood cells in bone marrow, which divide too quickly and do not mature properly to do the work they are supposed to do. When released into the bloodstream, therefore, they increase the risk of the patient suffering infections and in addition they clog up the bone marrow preventing healthy red blood cells and platelets getting out. The prognosis for sufferers was not good, with many having a lifespan from diagnosis of around five years only.

However, a new drug has been developed that helps to block signals in cells that cause them to divide. For some patients with CML, this new drug, called imatinib (with a trade name of Glivec in Europe and Australia) has been available to patients since 2003 following successful trials. Its success means that a number of patients have a far longer lifespan than was previously the case. However, the success of the drug comes at a price for the NHS. The cost of prescribing the drug, which is taken daily by patients in the form of a tablet, is around £19 000 (€22 500) per patient.

Any health authority in the UK having to treat a patient with the drug has to find this money from their available budget. For the patient the drug is literally a life saver and is a far more effective and efficient treatment for their illness, but this is an excellent example of how advances in medicine come at a price that has to be borne by health services and how the budget of the NHS can quickly expand.

Figure 12.3 shows how government spending as a proportion of GDP has changed in the last 30 years. It is worth noting how government spending rises as a proportion of GDP during periods of economic slowdown and fall in periods of stronger growth. There are peaks in the early 1980s, the early 1990s and during the recession of 2008–09.

Total government tax revenue for 2008–09 in Table 12.2 was given as £543.1 billion. However, the amount that government spends may be greater or smaller than that amount. In 2008–09, government spent £620 billion leaving a shortfall of income of around £77 billion. Such a shortfall of receipts compared with spending is called a **budget deficit**. When receipts exceed spending, the government is said to run a **budget surplus**. The government finances a budget deficit by borrowing from the public. When the government runs a budget surplus, it uses the excess receipts to reduce its outstanding debts.

budget deficit
an excess of government spending over government receipts

budget surplus
an excess of government receipts over government spending

FIGURE 12.3

Total Managed Expenditure as a Percentage of GDP

The chart shows changes in total managed expenditure as a percentage of GDP between 1980 and 2010. It shows how government spending is closely linked to the performance of the economy. There are a series of peaks corresponding to periods of recession in the economy.

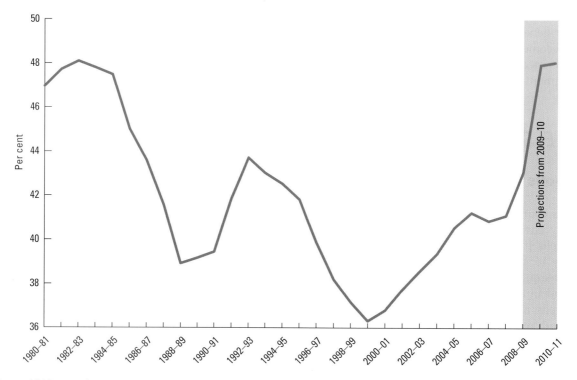

Source: HM Treasury (http://www.hm-treasury.gov.uk/d/public_finances_databank.xls (Crown Copyright)).

Figure 12.4 shows how public sector debt as a percentage of GDP rose sharply in the wake of the recession of 2008–09 and is estimated to rise further until moderating in 2013–14. The impact of recession on the UK economy meant that government tax revenue fell but spending rose (particularly on social security payments). A high proportion of government spending is committed for some years in advance (on ongoing capital projects for example) and as a result the deficit is forecast to get wider.

In the Pre-Budget Report in December 2009, the Chancellor of the Exchequer estimated that the deficit would rise a further £178 billion in 2009–10 before falling back slightly to £174.7 billion in 2010–11. This was based on total managed expenditure being £676 billion against total receipts of £498 billion.

Quick Quiz What are the three most important sources of tax revenue for the UK government? • What are the three most important expenditure categories?

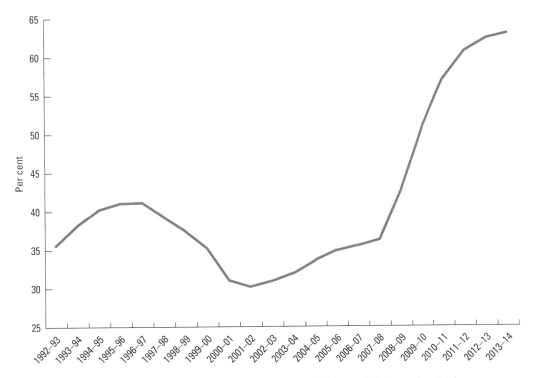

FIGURE 12.4

UK Public Debt as a Percentage of GDP

This figure shows the borrowing of the UK government as a percentage of GDP. It shows that government borrowing rose in the wake of the recession of the early 1990s and then fell back before rising sharply following the recession of 2008–09.

Source: http://www.hm-treasury.gov.uk/d/public_finances_databank.xls accessed 9 February 2010 (Crown Copyright).

TAX SYSTEMS IN OTHER COUNTRIES

Having outlined the tax system in the UK, we will now provide an overview of systems in two other countries. Viewing different tax systems tells us a great deal about the priorities and philosophies that are adopted by other governments with regard to their tax system and allows some comparison of the burden of taxation faced by a country's citizens in relation to others.

South Africa

The main source of tax revenue in South Africa (which has a population of 49.3 million) is income tax. There are a number of taxes levied on individuals and companies that come under the legal definition of income tax. Income tax, therefore, is collected not just from individuals but also from income generated by companies including profit. Income tax is residency based, meaning that if an individual is resident in South Africa they are subject to income tax from all their earnings, both from within South Africa and from without. Non-residents

TABLE 12.7

Income Tax Rates in South Africa

Taxable income (rand)	Rate of tax
0–132 000	18% of each R1
132 000–210 000	R23 760 + 25% of the amount above R132 000
210 000–290 000	R43 260 + 30% of the amount above R210 000
290 001–410 000	R67 260 + 35% of the amount above R290 000
410 001–525 000	R109 260 + 38% of the amount above R410 000
525 001 +	R152 960 + 40% of the amount above R4 525 000

Source: South African Revenue Service.

TABLE 12.8

Turnover Tax Rates for 'Micro-businesses' in South Africa

Taxable turnover (rand)	Rate of tax
0–100 000	0%
100 001–300 000	1%
300 001–500 000	R2 000 + 3% of the amount above R300 000
500 001–750 000	R8 000 + 5% of the amount above R750 000
750 001 +	R20 500 + 7% of the amount above R750 000

Source: South African Revenue Service.

are subject to tax on earnings generated within South Africa. Table 12.7 outlines the tax rates on income.

Corporation tax is one form of income tax levied on companies. In 2008 the government reduced corporation tax from 29 per cent to 28 per cent and there is also a 10 per cent Secondary Tax on Companies (STC) which is payable on net dividends. This was replaced in 2010 by a Dividends Tax. Small businesses are taxed differently: on income up to R54 200 there is a zero rate of tax; a 10 per cent rate on income between R54 201 and R300 000; and on income above R300 000 businesses pay R24 580 plus 28 per cent of the amount over R300 000. So-called 'micro businesses' have to pay a turnover tax levied on their turnover (sales revenue) as outlined in Table 12.8.

Capital gains tax is levied on individuals, companies and trusts at 10 per cent, 14 per cent and 20 per cent respectively. VAT is levied at a rate of 14 per cent on the majority of goods and services (with some exceptions). There are also other taxes on inheritance (called transfer duty), estate duty (at a flat rate of 20 per cent on property), taxes on international air travel, a skills development levy of 1 per cent which is paid by employers on the remuneration paid to employees, and Unemployment Insurance Contributions paid by both employers and employees based on employees' earnings.

TABLE 12.9

South African Government Spending 2008–09

Category	Amount (R billions)	Amount per person (R)	Percentage of spending
General public services	48	974	8.2%
Defence	31	629	5.3
Public order and safety	68	1 340	11.6
Economic affairs	126	2 556	21.5
Environmental protection	5	101	0.8
Housing and community amenities	5	1 318	11.1
Recreation and culture	10	203	1.7
Education	127	2 567	21.7
Social protection	105	2 130	17.9
Total	585	11 827	100%

Source: South Africa Budget 2009; South African Revenue Service.

Total government receipts in 2009–10 were R740.4 billion, with expenditure for the same period at R834.3 billion, giving a budget deficit of R93.9 billion (see Table 12.9 for an analysis of government spending in 2008–09).

Germany

Germany has a population of 82 million. The German tax system has a reputation of being very complex, with legislation around tax involving over 110 laws, 185 forms and some 90 000 policies. It has been reported that administration of the tax system costs €23.7 billion each year, 2.5 per cent of the annual tax yield. In recent years, successive German governments have sought to try and simplify the tax system, the latest reform being in 2008. Being a Federal Republic, taxes are levied by the federal government (*Bund*), the states (*Laender*) and municipalities (*Kommunen*).

For individuals, whether self-employed or in employment, income tax is payable on earnings and if that person is classed as a permanent resident of Germany then they are liable for tax on earnings from overseas as well as from inside Germany. As with South Africa, foreign residents living in Germany are liable for tax on income generated within Germany. Income tax is progressive with rates ranging from 14 per cent to 45 per cent as highlighted in Table 12.10.

In addition to income tax, Germans pay a 5.5 per cent Solidarity Tax, which was levied to help rebuild East Germany after unification of the country in 1991. For many Germans the tax is highly unpopular and it is widely perceived

TABLE 12.10

Income Tax Rates in Germany, 2009

Tax rate (%)	Rate of tax (€)
0	Earnings up to 7 384
14	7 385–52 552
42	52 553–250 400
45	250 401 +

Source: German Federal Ministry of Finance.

TABLE 12.11

Federal Government Spending in Germany, 2009

Category	Amount (€ billions)	Amount per person (€)	Percentage of spending
General public services	54.0	659	17.4%
Health, environment, sport, recreation	1.3	16	0.42
Food, agriculture and forestry water supplies, trade, services	7.4	90	2.4
Economic cooperation and development	6.0	73	1.9
Transport and communications	13.0	158	4.2
Housing, regional planning and local community services	1.9	23	0.6
Commercial enterprises, general real property and capital assets	16.0	195	5.2
Education, training, research and development	15.0	183	4.8
Social security and benefits	153.0	1 866	49.25
General financial management	43.0	524	13.8
Total	310.6	3 783	100%

Source: German Federal Ministry of Finance.

that the tax has not done a great deal to improve conditions in the five eastern states and bring them up to the standards of the rest of the country. If an individual is a member of one of the established churches in Germany 8–9 per cent of their income tax is specified as Church Tax.

Corporation tax in Germany was lowered from 25 per cent to 15 per cent as part of the reforms of company tax which came into force on 1 January 2009. However, a business tax is also payable to municipalities ranging from 14 to 17 per cent. When Solidarity Tax is taken into account, the effective corporate tax rate can be as high as 33 per cent. As part of the tax reforms a flat rate of 25 per cent was levied on income derived from capital investments for individuals.

Value-added tax in Germany is 19 per cent although there are some exceptions, including books, magazines and food which are subject to 7 per cent VAT. Government receipts in 2009 totalled €253.8 billion with expenditure for the same period (see Table 12.11) at €310.6 billion, giving a budget deficit of €56.8 billion.

TAXES AND EFFICIENCY

Now that we have seen how governments raise and spend money, let's consider how one might evaluate tax policy. Obviously, the aim of a tax system is to raise revenue for the government. But there are many ways to raise any given amount of money. In designing a tax system, policy makers have two objectives: efficiency and equity.

One tax system is more efficient than another if it raises the same amount of revenue at a smaller cost to taxpayers and the government. What are the costs of taxes to taxpayers? The most obvious cost is the tax payment itself. This transfer of money from the taxpayer to the government is an inevitable feature of any tax system. Yet taxes also impose two other costs, which well designed tax policy tries to avoid or, at least, minimize:

- The deadweight losses that result when taxes distort the decisions that people make.
- The administrative burdens that taxpayers bear as they comply with the tax laws.

An efficient tax system is one that imposes small deadweight losses and small administrative burdens.

Deadweight Losses

One of the *Ten Principles of Economics* is that people respond to incentives, and this includes incentives provided by the tax system. Taxes have the effect of changing people's behaviour. If the government taxes tea, some people will drink less tea and drink more coffee. If the government taxes housing, some people will change behaviour and look to live in smaller houses and spend more of their income on other things. If the government taxes labour earnings, some people will not see additional work as having the same reward and may decide to work less and enjoy more leisure.

Because taxes have the effect of changing behaviour and distorting incentives, they entail deadweight losses. As we first discussed in Chapter 8, the deadweight loss of a tax is the reduction in economic well-being of taxpayers in excess of the amount of revenue raised by the government. The deadweight loss is the inefficiency that a tax creates as people allocate resources according to the tax incentive rather than the true costs and benefits of the goods and services that they buy and sell.

To recall how taxes cause deadweight losses, consider an example. Suppose that Ian places an €8 value on a pizza, and Dawn places a €6 value on it. If there is no tax on pizza, the price of pizza will reflect the cost of making it (including an element of profit). Let's suppose that the price of pizza is €5, so both Ian and Dawn choose to buy one. Both consumers get some surplus of value over the amount paid. Ian gets consumer surplus of €3, and Dawn gets consumer surplus of €1. Total surplus is €4.

Now suppose that the government levies a €2 tax on pizza and the price of pizza rises to €7. Ian still buys a pizza, but now he has consumer surplus of only €1. Dawn now decides not to buy a pizza because its price is higher than its value to her. The government collects tax revenue of €2 on Ian's pizza. Total consumer surplus has fallen by €3 (from €4 to €1). Because total surplus has fallen by more than the tax revenue, the tax has a deadweight loss. In this case, the deadweight loss is €1.

Notice that the deadweight loss comes not from Ian, the person who pays the tax, but from Dawn, the person who doesn't. The reduction of €2 in Ian's surplus exactly offsets the amount of revenue the government collects. The deadweight loss arises because the tax causes Dawn to alter her behaviour. When the tax raises the price of pizza, Dawn is worse off, and yet there is no offsetting revenue to the government. This reduction in Dawn's welfare is the deadweight loss of the tax.

CASE STUDY

Should Income or Consumption Be Taxed?

When taxes induce people to change their behaviour – such as inducing Dawn to buy less pizza – the taxes cause deadweight losses and make the allocation of resources less efficient. As we have already seen, much government revenue comes from personal income tax. In a case study in Chapter 8 we discussed how this tax discourages people from working as hard as they otherwise might. Another inefficiency caused by this tax is that it discourages people from saving.

Consider a person 25 years old who is considering saving €100. If he puts this money in a savings account that earns 8 per cent and leaves it there, he would have €2 172 when he retires at age 65. Yet if the government taxes one quarter of his interest income each year, the effective interest rate is only 6 per cent. After 40 years of earning 6 per cent, the €100 grows to only €1 029, less than half of what it would have been without taxation. Thus, because interest income is taxed, saving is much less attractive.

Some economists advocate eliminating the current tax system's disincentive towards saving by changing the basis of taxation. Rather than taxing the amount of income that people earn, the government could tax the amount that people spend. Under this proposal, all income that is saved would not be taxed until the saving is later spent. This alternative system, called a consumption tax, would not distort people's saving decisions – but it might lead to distortion of their consumption decisions, depending on how and on what the consumption tax was levied.

Administrative Burden

In the UK, anyone paying (or who should pay) the higher rate of income tax at 40 per cent (in 2010–11, those with taxable income of £37 400 or more) is required to fill in a tax return and send it to HM Revenue and Customs (or file it online). This is a long form that Revenue and Customs use to determine tax liability. If you ask the typical person required to do this for an opinion about the tax system, the opinion is unlikely to be favourable. The administrative burden of any tax system is part of the inefficiency it creates. This burden includes not only the time spent filling out forms but also the time spent throughout the year keeping records for tax purposes and the resources the government has to use to enforce the tax laws.

Many taxpayers – especially those in higher tax brackets – hire accountants or tax lawyers to help them with their taxes. These experts in the complex tax laws fill out the tax forms for their clients and help clients arrange their affairs in a way that reduces the amount of taxes owed. This behaviour is avoidance (optimizing your affairs so that you pay as little tax as possible without breaking the law, which is different from tax evasion – i.e. lying about your affairs in order to reduce the amount of tax paid). Tax avoidance is perfectly legal. Tax evasion is illegal, as Scarface Capone discovered.

Critics of the tax system say that these advisors help their clients avoid taxes by abusing some of the detailed provisions of the tax system (or, as it is sometimes termed, the tax code). These detailed provisions are often dubbed 'loopholes'. In some cases, loopholes are government mistakes: they arise from ambiguities or omissions in the tax laws. More often, they arise because the government has chosen to give special treatment to specific types of behaviour. For example, the UK tax system allows money spent on a personal pension plan to be exempt from income tax, up to a certain limit. This is because the government wants to encourage people to save for their retirement.

The resources devoted to complying with the tax laws are a type of deadweight loss. The government gets only the amount of taxes paid. By contrast, the taxpayer loses not only this amount but also the time and money spent documenting, computing and avoiding taxes.

The administrative burden of the tax system could be reduced by simplifying the tax laws. Yet simplification is often politically difficult. Most people are ready to simplify the tax code by eliminating the loopholes that benefit others, yet few are eager to give up the loopholes that they use. In the end, the complexity of tax law results from the political process as various taxpayers with their own special interests lobby for their causes. This process is called 'rent seeking' and is part of a branch of economics called public choice theory (see Chapter 9). Remember that public choice theory is about the analysis of governmental behaviour, and the behaviour of individuals who interact with government.

Marginal Tax Rates versus Average Tax Rates

When discussing the efficiency and equity of income taxes, economists distinguish between two notions of the tax rate: the average and the marginal. The **average tax rate** is total taxes paid divided by total income. The **marginal tax rate** is the extra taxes paid on an additional unit of income. For example, suppose that the government taxes 20 per cent of the first €50 000 of income and 50 per cent of all income above €50 000. Under this tax, a person who earns €60 000 pays tax of €15 000: 20 per cent of the first €50 000 (0.20 × €50 000 = €10 000) plus 50 per cent of the next €10 000 (0.50 × €10 000 = €5 000). For this person, the average tax rate is €15 000/€60 000, or 25 per cent. But the marginal tax rate is 50 per cent. If the taxpayer earned an additional euro of income, that euro would be subject to the 50 per cent tax rate, so the amount the taxpayer would owe to the government would rise by €0.50.

average tax rate
total taxes paid divided by total income

marginal tax rate
the extra taxes paid on an additional unit of income

The marginal and average tax rates each contain a useful piece of information. If we are trying to gauge the sacrifice made by a taxpayer, the average tax rate is more appropriate because it measures the fraction of income paid in taxes. By contrast, if we are trying to gauge how much the tax system distorts incentives, the marginal tax rate is more meaningful. One of the *Ten Principles of Economics* in Chapter 1 is that rational people think at the margin. A corollary to this principle is that the marginal tax rate measures how much the tax system discourages people from working. If you are thinking of working an extra few hours, the marginal tax rate determines how much the government takes of your additional earnings. It is the marginal tax rate, therefore, that determines the deadweight loss of an income tax.

CASE STUDY

Iceland's Natural Experiment

In the 1980s, Iceland changed its tax system in a way that, as a side effect, provided a natural experiment to show how taxes affect an economy. Before the reform, people paid taxes based on their previous year's income. After the reform, people paid taxes based on their current income. Thus, taxes in 1987 were based on 1986 income, but taxes in 1988 were based on 1988 income.

Income earned in 1987 was never taxed. For this one year of transition, the marginal income tax rate fell to zero. As reported in a December 2001 article in the *American Economic Review*, the citizens of Iceland took advantage of this tax holiday. Total hours worked rose by about 3 per cent in 1987 and then fell back to its normal level in 1988. The production of goods and services in 1987 (as measured by real GDP) was 4 per cent higher than the average of the year before and the year after. This episode confirms one of the *Ten Principles of Economics*: people respond to incentives. The fall in the Icelandic marginal tax rate was for one year only, and this fact surely influenced the response. On the one hand, some people may have put off vacations and worked overtime to take advantage of the temporary incentive. On the other hand, no one would alter career plans and no business would restructure its work environment in response to an incentive that would soon disappear. A permanent change in a marginal tax rate could have either a smaller or a larger incentive effect than a temporary change.

Lump-sum Taxes

lump-sum tax
a tax that is the same amount for every person

Suppose the government imposes a tax of €4 000 on everyone. That is, everyone owes the same amount, regardless of earnings or any actions that a person might take. Such a tax is called a **lump-sum tax**.

A lump-sum tax shows clearly the difference between average and marginal tax rates. For a taxpayer with income of €20 000, the average tax rate of a €4 000 lump-sum tax is 20 per cent; for a taxpayer with income of €40 000, the average tax rate is 10 per cent. For both taxpayers, the marginal tax rate is zero because no tax is owed on an additional unit of income.

A lump-sum tax is the most efficient tax possible. Because a person's decisions do not alter the amount owed, the tax does not distort incentives and, therefore, does not cause deadweight losses. Because everyone can easily compute the amount owed and because there is no benefit to hiring tax lawyers and accountants, the lump-sum tax imposes a minimal administrative burden on taxpayers. If lump-sum taxes are so efficient, why do we rarely observe them in the real world? The reason is that efficiency is only one goal of the tax system. A lump sum tax would take the same amount from the poor and the rich, an outcome most people would view as unfair. To understand the tax systems that we observe, in the next section we consider the other major goal of tax policy – equity.

Quick Quiz What is meant by the efficiency of a tax system? • What can make a tax system inefficient?

TAXES AND EQUITY

In any country, tax policy always generates some of the most heated political debates. The heat is rarely fuelled by questions of efficiency. Instead, it usually arises from disagreements over how the tax burden should be distributed. Of course, if we are to rely on the government to provide some of the goods and services we want, taxes must fall on someone. In this section we consider the equity of a tax system. How should the burden of taxes be divided among the population? How do we evaluate whether a tax system is fair? Everyone agrees that the tax system should be equitable, but there is much disagreement about what equity means and how the equity of a tax system can be judged.

The Benefits Principle

benefits principle
the idea that people should pay taxes based on the benefits they receive from government services

One principle of taxation, called the **benefits principle**, states that people should pay taxes based on the benefits they receive from government services. This principle tries to make public goods similar to private goods. It seems fair that a person who often goes to the cinema pays more in total for cinema tickets than a person who rarely goes. Similarly, a person who gets great benefit from a public good should pay more for it than a person who gets little benefit.

The duty on petrol, for instance, is sometimes justified using the benefits principle, since in some countries, revenues from the tax on petrol are used to build and maintain roads. Because those who buy petrol are the same people who use the roads, this tax might be viewed as a fair way to pay for this government service.

The benefits principle can also be used to argue that wealthy citizens should pay higher taxes than poorer ones. Why? Simply because the wealthy benefit more from public services. Consider, for example, the benefits of police protection from theft. Citizens with much to protect get greater benefit from the police than do those with less to protect. Therefore, according to the benefits principle, the wealthy should contribute more than the poor to the cost of maintaining the police force. The same argument can be used for many other public services, such as fire protection, national defence and the criminal justice system.

It is even possible to use the benefits principle to argue for anti-poverty programmes funded by taxes on the wealthy. As we discussed in Chapter 11, people prefer living in a society without poverty, suggesting that anti-poverty programmes are a public good. If the wealthy place a greater value on this public good than other members of society, perhaps just because the wealthy have more to spend, then, according to the benefits principle, they should be taxed more heavily to pay for these programmes.

The Ability-to-Pay Principle

Another way to evaluate the equity of a tax system is called the **ability-to-pay principle**, which states that taxes should be levied on a person according to how well that person can shoulder the burden. This principle is sometimes justified by the claim that all citizens should make an 'equal sacrifice' to support the government. The magnitude of a person's sacrifice, however, depends not only on the size of his tax payment but also on his income and other circumstances. A €1 000 tax paid by a poor person may require a larger sacrifice than a €10 000 tax paid by a rich one.

The ability-to-pay principle leads to two corollary notions of equity: vertical equity and horizontal equity. **Vertical equity** states that taxpayers with a greater ability to pay taxes should contribute a larger amount. **Horizontal equity** states that taxpayers with similar abilities to pay should contribute the same amount.

Although these notions of equity are widely accepted, applying them to evaluate a tax system is rarely straightforward.

Vertical Equity If taxes are based on ability to pay, then richer taxpayers should pay more than poorer taxpayers. But how much more should the rich pay? Much of the debate over tax policy concerns this question.

Consider the three tax systems in Table 12.12. In each case, taxpayers with higher incomes pay more. Yet the systems differ in how quickly taxes rise with income. The first system is called **a proportional tax** or sometimes a flat tax because all taxpayers pay the same fraction of income. The second system is called **regressive** because high-income taxpayers pay a smaller fraction of their income, even though they pay a larger amount. The third system is called **progressive** because high-income taxpayers pay a larger fraction of their income.

Which of these three tax systems is most fair? Sometimes it is argued that a progressive tax system is fairer because richer people pay more tax and they can afford to do so because they are richer. But richer people will also pay more tax than poorer people under a flat tax system or even under a regressive tax system. In fact, there is no obvious answer, and economic theory does not offer any help in trying to find one. Equity, like beauty, is in the eye of the beholder.

ability-to-pay principle
the idea that taxes should be levied on a person according to how well that person can shoulder the burden

vertical equity
the idea that taxpayers with a greater ability to pay taxes should pay larger amounts

horizontal equity
the idea that taxpayers with similar abilities to pay taxes should pay the same amount

proportional or flat tax
a tax for which high-income and low-income taxpayers pay the same fraction of income

regressive tax
a tax for which high-income taxpayers pay a smaller fraction of their income than do low-income taxpayers

progressive tax
a tax for which high-income taxpayers pay a larger fraction of their income than do low-income taxpayers

TABLE 12.12

Three Tax Systems

Income	Proportional or flat tax		Regressive tax		Progressive tax	
	Amount of tax	Percentage of income	Amount of tax	Percentage of income	Amount of tax	Percentage of income
€50 000	€12 500	25%	€15 000	30%	€10 000	20%
100 000	25 000	25	25 000	25	25 000	25
200 000	50 000	25	40 000	20	60 000	30

Horizontal Equity   If taxes are based on ability to pay, then similar taxpayers should pay similar amounts of taxes. But what determines if two taxpayers are similar? Individuals' circumstances can differ in many ways. To evaluate whether a tax system is horizontally equitable, one must determine which differences are relevant for a person's ability to pay and which differences are not.

Suppose Mr Smith and Ms Jones each have an income of €50 000 a year. Mr Smith is unmarried and has no children, but he has an illness that means that he has to employ someone to be with him while he is at work and getting to and from his place of business. This costs him €20 000 a year. Ms Jones is in good health and is a lone parent with a child aged three. Ms Jones has to pay €15 000 a year for child care while she is at work. Would it be fair for Mr Smith and Ms Jones to pay the same tax because they have the same income? Would it be fairer to give Mr Smith a tax break to help him offset the costs of a caring assistant? Would it be fairer to give Ms Jones a tax break to compensate her for the cost of childcare?

There are no easy answers to these questions.

"... IN SICKNESS OR HEALTH, INFLATION OR DEFLATION, MARRIAGE TAX CREDIT OR DEBIT..."

Tax Incidence and Tax Equity

Tax incidence – the study of who bears the burden of taxes – is central to evaluating tax equity. As we first saw in Chapter 6, the person who bears the burden of a tax is not always the person who gets the tax bill from the government. Because taxes alter supply and demand, they alter equilibrium prices. As a result, they affect people beyond those who, according to statute, actually pay the tax. When evaluating the vertical and horizontal equity of any tax, it is important to take account of these indirect effects.

Many discussions of tax equity ignore the indirect effects of taxes and are based on what economists mockingly call the flypaper theory of tax incidence. According to this theory, the burden of a tax, like a fly on flypaper, sticks wherever it first lands. This assumption, however, is rarely valid.

For example, a person not trained in economics might argue that a tax on expensive fur coats is vertically equitable because most buyers of furs are wealthy. Yet if these buyers can easily substitute other luxuries for furs, then a tax on furs might only reduce the sale of furs. In the end, the burden of the tax will fall more on those who make and sell furs than on those who buy them. Because most workers who make furs are not wealthy, the equity of a fur tax could be quite different from what the flypaper theory indicates.

CASE STUDY

Who Pays Corporation Tax?

Corporation tax provides a good example of the importance of tax incidence for tax policy. Corporation tax is popular among voters. After all, corporations are not people. Voters are always eager to have their taxes reduced and have some impersonal corporation pick up the tab. In a sense, corporation tax appears to be a tax that is imposed on nobody. No wonder it's popular with policy makers also.

Workers pay part of corporation tax.

But before deciding that corporation tax is a good way for the government to raise revenue, we should consider who bears the burden of corporation tax. This is a difficult question on which economists disagree, but one thing is certain: *people pay all taxes*. When the government levies a tax on a corporation, the corporation is more like a tax collector than a taxpayer. The burden of the tax ultimately falls on people – the owners, customers or workers of the corporation.

Many economists believe that workers and customers bear much of the burden of corporation tax. To see why, consider an example. Suppose that the government decides to raise the tax on the income earned by car companies. At first, this tax hurts the owners of the car companies who receive less profit. But, over time, these owners will respond to the tax. Because producing cars is less profitable, they invest less in building new car factories. Instead, they invest their wealth in other ways – for example, by buying larger houses or by building factories in other industries or other countries. With fewer car factories, the supply of cars declines, as does the demand for car workers. Thus, a tax on corporations making cars causes the price of cars to rise and the wages of car workers to fall.

Corporation tax shows how dangerous the flypaper theory of tax incidence can be. Corporation tax is popular in part because it appears to be paid by rich corporations. Yet those who bear the ultimate burden of the tax – the customers and workers of corporations – are often not rich. If the true incidence of corporation tax were more widely known, this tax might be less popular among voters – and policy makers.

Quick Quiz   Explain the benefits principle and the ability-to-pay principle. • What are vertical equity and horizontal equity? • Why is studying tax incidence important for determining the equity of a tax system?

CASE STUDY

Tax Policy – Fair or Foul?

Two years after coming to power in 1997, the then Labour Chancellor of the Exchequer, Gordon Brown, introduced a 10 per cent income tax band. The introduction of the tax was hailed as an incentive to those seeking work to take employment and get off benefits, would help the lower paid and was 'fair'. In 2007, Mr Brown was looking forward to the almost certain possibility that he would become Prime Minister when Tony Blair finally decided to leave office. In his last Budget in this year, Mr Brown announced that the 10p rate of tax was being abolished and that the basic tax rate would be reduced from 22 per cent to 20 per cent. For Mr Brown the move looked to be a popular one; in his Chancellorship he had succeeded in reducing the basic rate from 23 per cent to 20 per cent and analysts viewed the move as a perfect way to start off his impending premiership giving him a large lead over the Conservatives and allowing him to call a quick election to confirm his status as Prime Minister for another five years. Mr Brown, for reasons, ultimately only known to him, decided not to call that election and a year after the announcement of the abolishing of the 10p tax rate he was caught up in a storm of criticism from his own MPs, opposition parties and representatives of the low paid.

Why the furore? Robert Chote from the Institute of Fiscal Studies (IFS) summed the situation up in an article published in April 2008. Under Mr Brown's tax system prior to the announcement, the taxable allowance stood at £5 435; the next £2 230 of tax commanded a 10p rate and the next £32 370 was taxed at 22 per cent. Following the Budget announcement by Mr Brown, the tax allowance stayed at £5 435 and the next £36 000 would be taxed at 20 per cent.

What effect would this have on taxpayers; would it be fairer? Take an example of an individual earning an annual salary of £10 000. Prior to the change this person's tax bill would be:

Tax allowance = £5 435
Taxable income would be £10 000 – £5 435 = £4 565
Of which £2 230 would be taxed at 10 per cent (£223.00)
The remaining £2 335 of taxable income would be taxed at 22 per cent (£513.70)
Total tax paid = £736.70

For an individual earning a salary of £30 000 the situation would be:

Tax allowance = £5 435
Taxable income would be £30 000 – £5 435 = £24 565
Of which £2 230 would be taxed at 10 per cent (£223.00)
The remaining £22 335 of taxable income would be taxed at 22 per cent (£4 913.70)
Total tax paid = £5 136.70

After the 10p rate was abolished and the 20 per cent rate introduced the situation would now be:

On a salary of £10 000:
Tax allowance = £5 435
Taxable income would be £10 000 − £5 435 = £4 565
£4 565 taxed at 20 per cent = £913.00
Total tax paid = £913.00: a net increase in tax paid of £176.30

On a salary of £30 000:
Tax allowance = £5 435
Taxable income would be £30 000 − £5 435 = £24 565
£24 565 taxed at 20 per cent = £4 913.00
Total tax paid = £4 913.00: a net reduction in tax paid of £223.70

Such a simple calculation highlights claims that the abolishing of the 10p rate was hitting the low paid and that the least wealthy people in society were, in effect, subsidizing those who were better off. Chote showed that those on incomes between £5 435 and £19 355 a year would be worse off with those earning £7 755 being the hardest hit with a rise in tax paid of £232.00 a year. Those earning between £19 355 and around £40 000 would gain, however, with someone earning £36 140 benefiting most, being £337 a year better off. The outcry facing Mr Brown, who by now was Prime Minister, and his new Chancellor, Alistair Darling, was significant. The abolishing of the 10p tax was clearly 'unfair' and would hit hardest those it was designed to help; but was it?

This was not the whole story. It seems that the full picture was somehow lost in translation and a party that has been embroiled in accusations of 'spin' clearly did not manage to communicate the big picture very well.

Chote points out that the 2007 Budget was indeed a Budget to help the poor, as claimed by Mr Brown. The abolishing of the 10p tax rate was *one* of the elements of a package that, put together, resulted in winners and losers but led to 'the poorest third of the population emerging as the biggest winners'. Crucial to understanding the issues raised here is being clear about what is meant by 'the poor'. Some people are poor because they are over 65 and have limited income, others because they are single families and have difficulty finding work, others because they are of a particular age with no family but either out of work or in low-paid work, and others because they have low-paid jobs and families to support.

Changes in tax rates are not the only way in which individuals are affected in terms of the tax burden they suffer. In the 2007 Budget, Mr Brown also raised tax allowances for those over 65, increased the child tax credit (a negative tax, in effect, which qualifying individuals can claim if they have a responsibility for at least one child; credits come in the form of a payment from government) and increasing the threshold over which tax credits would not be paid. As a result of these changes, those affected by the abolishing of the 10p tax rate may have lost from that measure but gained from tax credits. Chote pointed out that when all the changes were taken into account the poorest third of the population would have benefited as would the richest third with the remainder being largely unaffected. Any criticism of Mr Brown's tax changes, therefore, might be that he treated different types of poor people differently.

Childless single people under 25 working less than 30 hours a week or who may have relatively high earnings, childless couples and those retiring early are the groups who were likely to lose out as a result of the changes.

The lesson from this case study is that equity and efficiency in the tax system is not as simple as the theory may make it sound. Tax systems in most countries are complex and changes to any system affects different people in different ways. What may look on the surface as a more equitable tax system may in fact have a disproportionate impact on some groups in society who, depending on the 'power' they have, may have problems in getting their plight publicized.

The abolition of the 10p rate caused Mr Brown and Mr Darling considerable problems. The publicity and column inches written on behalf of the 'losers' was such that Mr Darling was forced into announcing measures to compensate those who would lose out from the changes. On 13 May 2008, the government announced that personal tax allowances for 2008–09 would rise by £600 and that there would be a cut in the higher-rate threshold. The cost to the government of these measures was estimated by the IFS at £5.5 billion with £2.6 billion being financed by other tax and spending measures and £2.9 billion from borrowing. The IFS estimated that as a result of the changes, widely reported as a 'climbdown' by the government, 21.3 million families would be better off than before the 13 May announcement but that 900 000 families would still be adversely affected by the cut in the 10p tax rate with around 50 per cent of these being single people under 25.

CONCLUSION: THE TRADE-OFF BETWEEN EQUITY AND EFFICIENCY

Almost everyone agrees that equity and efficiency are the two most important goals of the tax system. But often these two goals conflict. Many proposed changes in the tax laws increase efficiency while reducing equity, or increase equity whilst reducing efficiency. People disagree about tax policy often because they attach different weights to these two goals.

Economics alone cannot determine the best way to balance the goals of efficiency and equity. This issue involves political philosophy as well as economics. But economists do have an important role in the political debate over tax policy: they can shed light on the trade-offs that society faces and can help us avoid policies that sacrifice efficiency without any benefit in terms of equity.

SUMMARY

- Governments raises revenue using various taxes. In many countries, the most important taxes for the government are personal income taxes and social insurance taxes.

- The efficiency of a tax system refers to the costs that it imposes on taxpayers. There are two costs of taxes beyond the transfer of resources from the taxpayer to the government. The first is the distortion in the allocation of resources that arises as taxes alter incentives and behaviour. The second is the administrative burden of complying with the tax laws.

- The equity of a tax system concerns whether the tax burden is distributed fairly among the population.

- According to the benefits principle, it is fair for people to pay taxes based on the benefits they receive from the government. According to the ability-to-pay principle, it is fair for people to pay taxes based on their capability to handle the financial burden. When evaluating the equity of a tax system, it is important to remember a lesson from the study of tax incidence: the distribution of tax burdens is not the same as the distribution of tax bills.

- When considering changes in the tax laws, policy makers often face a trade-off between efficiency and equity. Much of the debate over tax policy arises because people give different weights to these two goals.

KEY CONCEPTS

indirect tax, p. 243
direct tax, p. 243
budget deficit, p. 245
budget surplus, p. 245
average tax rate, p. 253

marginal tax rate, p. 253
lump-sum tax, p. 254
benefits principle, p. 254
ability-to-pay principle, p. 255
vertical equity, p. 255

horizontal equity, p. 255
proportional or flat tax, p. 255
regressive tax, p. 255
progressive tax, p. 255

QUESTIONS FOR REVIEW

1. Over the past century, has the size of government, as measured by tax receipts or government spending, grown more or less slowly than the rest of the economy? (You can find this out for the country you are studying in by using its national statistics service.)

2. What are the two most important sources of revenue for the government?

3. Explain how corporate profits are taxed twice.

4. Why is the burden of a tax to taxpayers greater than the revenue received by the government?

5. Why do some economists advocate taxing consumption rather than income?

6. Give two arguments why wealthy taxpayers should pay more taxes than poor taxpayers.

7. What is the concept of horizontal equity, and why is it hard to apply?

PROBLEMS AND APPLICATIONS

1. Government spending in most industrialized countries has grown as a share of national income over time. What changes in our economy and our society might explain this trend? Do you expect the trend to continue?

2. In a published source or on the internet, find out whether your government had a budget deficit or surplus last year. What do policy makers expect to happen over the next few years?

3. In many industrialized countries, the elderly population is growing more rapidly than the total population. This is partly because of historical movements in the birth rate ('baby booms') and partly due to the fact that people are now living longer on average. Because the elderly are eligible for state retirement pensions, this places an increasing burden on the working age population to pay for those retirement pensions. Discuss the merits of each of the following proposed policies for dealing with this problem. Which do you think would be the best policy or combination of policies? Explain.
   a. Making exempt from income tax any money paid into a private retirement pension fund.

   b. Making exempt from income tax any money paid into a private retirement pension fund so long as the person involved gives up his or her right to a state pension.
   c. Reducing the amount of state retirement pension by 50 per cent.
   d. Raising the minimum age of retirement from 65 to 70 years of age.
   e. Raising the basic rate of income tax.
   f. Raising the higher rate of income tax.
   g. A drive to increase immigration in order to increase the working age population.

4. Suppose you are a typical person in the UK economy. Refer to Tables 12.3 and 12.4 for income tax and employer's National Insurance contribution rates. How much income tax do you pay if you earn £25 000 a year? How much do you pay in National Insurance contributions? Taking both of these taxes into account, what are your average and marginal tax rates? What happens to your total tax bill and to your average and marginal tax rates if your income rises to £40 000?

5. In the UK, value-added tax is levied at the rate of 20 per cent on most goods and services, although it is not levied on a range of items, such as food, books, and water and sewerage systems. Discuss the merits of this policy. Consider the principles of equity and efficiency.

6. VAT is not levied in the UK on children's clothing but it is levied on adult's clothing. Discuss the merits of this distinction, considering both efficiency and equity.

7. Suppose that the tax system had the following features. Explain how individuals' behaviour is affected.
   a. Contributions to charity are tax-deductible.
   b. Sales of beer are taxed.
   c. Realized capital gains are taxed, but accrued gains are not. (When someone owns a share of stock that rises in value, she has an 'accrued' capital gain. If she sells the share, she has a 'realized' gain.)

8. The tax on cigarettes and other smoking products is very high in many countries (in the UK it is over 80 per cent of the selling price) and has been rising over time. Discuss the merits of this policy, considering the principles of equity and efficiency.

9. Categorize each of the following funding schemes as examples of the benefits principle or the ability-to-pay principle.
   a. Visitors to public museums are required to pay an entrance fee.
   b. Local property taxes support primary and secondary schools.
   c. An airport trust fund collects a tax on each plane ticket sold and uses the money to improve airports and the air traffic control system.

10. Any income tax schedule embodies two types of tax rates – average tax rates and marginal tax rates.

a. The average tax rate is defined as total taxes paid divided by income. For the proportional tax system presented in Table 12.12, what are the average tax rates for people earning €50 000, €100 000 and €200 000? What are the corresponding average tax rates in the regressive and progressive tax systems?

b. The marginal tax rate is defined as the extra taxes paid on additional income divided by the increase in income. Calculate the marginal tax rate for the proportional tax system as income rises from €50 000 to €100 000. Calculate the marginal tax rate as income rises from €100 000 to €200 000. Calculate the corresponding marginal tax rates for the regressive and progressive tax systems.

c. Describe the relationship between average tax rates and marginal tax rates for each of these three systems. In general, which rate is relevant for someone deciding whether to accept a job that pays slightly more than her current job? Which rate is relevant for judging the vertical equity of a tax system?

11. As we noted in the text, the employer's contribution element of UK National Insurance contributions (NICs) are effectively a form of income tax. Consider the figures on tax rates and NIC rates given in Tables 12.3 and 12.4. Work out a complete schedule showing the total amount of tax (income tax and employee's NIC combined) payable on income over all ranges.

12. What is the efficiency justification for taxing consumption rather than income? If your country were to adopt a consumption tax, do you think that would make the tax system more or less progressive? Explain.

For further resources, visit
www.cengage.com/mankiw_taylor2

5

FIRM BEHAVIOUR AND THE ORGANIZATION OF INDUSTRY

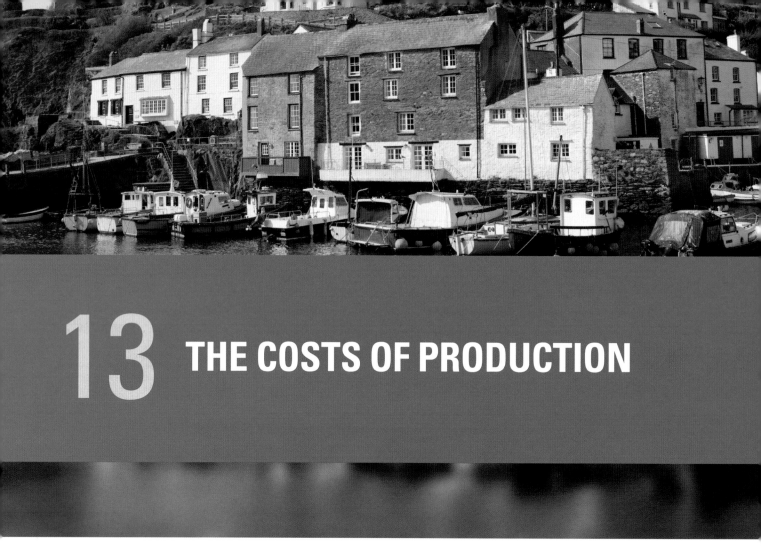

13 THE COSTS OF PRODUCTION

The economy is made up of thousands of firms that produce the goods and services we enjoy every day: Mercedes Benz produces cars, Miele produce kitchen appliances, and Nestlé produces food and drink. Some firms, such as these three, are large; they employ thousands of workers and have thousands of shareholders who share in the firms' profits. Other firms, such as the local hairdresser's shop or pizzeria, are small; they employ only a few workers and may be owned by a single person or family.

In this chapter and the ones that follow, we examine firm behaviour in more detail. This topic will give you a better understanding of what decisions lie behind the supply curve in a market which we introduced in previous chapters. In addition, it will introduce you to a part of economics called *industrial organization* – the study of how firms' decisions regarding prices and quantities depend on the market conditions they face. The town in which you live, for instance, may have several restaurants but only one water supply company. How does this difference in the number of firms affect the prices in these markets and the efficiency of the market outcomes? The field of industrial organization addresses exactly this question.

Before we turn to these issues, however, we need to discuss the costs of production. All firms, from Air France to your local baker's shop, incur costs as they make the goods and services that they sell. As we will see in the coming chapters, a firm's costs are a key determinant of its production and pricing decisions. In this chapter, we define some of the variables that economists use to measure a firm's costs, and we consider the relationships among them. A word of warning: this topic can seem dry and technical. But it provides a crucial foundation for the fascinating topics that follow.

WHAT ARE COSTS?

We begin our discussion of costs at Hungry Horace's Pizza Factory. Horace, the owner of the firm, buys flour, tomatoes, mozzarella cheese, salami and other pizza ingredients. He also buys the mixers and ovens and hires workers to run this equipment. He then sells the resulting pizzas to consumers. By examining some of the issues that Horace faces in his business, we can learn some lessons about costs that apply to all firms in the economy.

Total Revenue, Total Cost and Profit

We begin with the firm's objective. To understand what decisions a firm makes, we must understand what it is trying to do. It is conceivable that Horace started his firm because of an altruistic desire to provide the world with pizza or, perhaps, out of love for the pizza business. More likely, Horace started his business to make money. Economists often use the assumption that the goal of a firm is to maximize profit. Whilst the extent to which this assumption holds in the real world has been questioned, it is a useful starting point for our analysis.

What is a firm's profit? The amount that the firm receives for the sale of its output (pizzas) is called its total revenue, which we introduced in Chapter 5. The amount that the firm pays to buy inputs (flour, mozzarella cheese, workers, ovens, etc.) is called its **total cost**. Horace's profit is the difference between his total revenue and his total cost. **Profit**, therefore, is a firm's total revenue minus its total cost. That is:

$$\text{Profit} = \text{Total revenue} - \text{Total cost}$$

We can express this in the formula:

$$\Pi = \text{TR} - \text{TC}$$

where Π represents profit.

We will assume that Horace's objective is to make his firm's profit as large as possible – in other words, he wants to maximize profit.

To see how a firm goes about maximizing profit, we must consider fully how to measure its total revenue and its total cost. Total revenue is the easy part: it equals the quantity of output the firm produces times the price at which it sells its output. If Horace produces 10 000 pizzas and sells them at €2 a pizza, his total revenue is €20 000. By contrast, the measurement of a firm's total cost is more subtle and open to different interpretations.

> **total cost**
> the market value of the inputs a firm uses in production
>
> **profit**
> total revenue minus total cost

Costs as Opportunity Costs

When measuring costs at Hungry Horace's Pizza Factory, or any other firm, it is important to keep in mind one of the *Ten Principles of Economics* from Chapter 1: the cost of something is what you give up to get it. Recall that the *opportunity cost* of an item refers to all those things that must be forgone to acquire that item. When economists speak of a firm's cost of production, they include the opportunity costs of making its output of goods and services.

A firm's opportunity costs of production are sometimes obvious and sometimes less so. When Horace pays €1 000 for flour, Horace can no longer use that €1 000 to buy something else; he has to sacrifice what else that €1 000 could have purchased. Similarly, when Horace hires workers to make the pizzas, the wages he pays are part of the firm's costs. Because these costs require the firm to pay out some money, they are called **explicit costs**. By contrast, some of a firm's opportunity costs, called **implicit costs,** do not require a cash outlay. Imagine that Horace is skilled with computers and could earn €100 per hour working as a programmer.

> **explicit costs**
> input costs that require an outlay of money by the firm
>
> **implicit costs**
> input costs that do not require an outlay of money by the firm

For every hour that Horace works at his pizza factory, he gives up €100 in income, and this forgone income is also classed as part of his costs by an economist.

This distinction between explicit and implicit costs highlights an important difference between how economists and accountants analyse a business. Economists are interested in studying how firms make production and pricing decisions. Because these decisions are based on both explicit and implicit costs, economists include both when measuring a firm's costs. By contrast, accountants have the job of keeping track of the money that flows into and out of firms. As a result, they measure the explicit costs but often ignore the implicit costs.

The difference between economists and accountants is easy to see in the case of Hungry Horace's Pizza Factory. When Horace gives up the opportunity to earn money as a computer programmer, his accountant will not count this as a cost of his pizza business. Because no money flows out of the business to pay for this cost, it never shows up on the accountant's financial statements. An economist, however, will count the foregone income as a cost because it will affect the decisions that Horace makes in his pizza business. This is an important part of thinking like an economist and was highlighted on page 61 in Chapter 3, 'Should Ingvar Kamprad mow his own lawn?' In Horace's case, if the wage as a computer programmer rose from €100 to €500 per hour, the opportunity cost of running his pizza business might now change his decision-making. The opportunity cost of running the business in terms of what Horace is sacrificing in foregone income has risen. Horace might decide he could earn more by closing the business and switching to computer programming.

The Cost of Capital as an Opportunity Cost

An important implicit cost of almost every business is the opportunity cost of the financial capital that has been invested in the business. As we have already noted, economists and accountants treat costs differently, and this is especially true in their treatment of the cost of capital. Suppose, for instance, that Horace used €300 000 of his savings to buy his pizza factory from the previous owner. If Horace had instead left this money deposited in a savings account that pays an interest rate of 5 per cent, he would have earned €15 000 per year (assuming simple interest). To own his pizza factory, therefore, Horace has given up €15 000 a year in interest income. This forgone €15 000 is an implicit opportunity costs of Horace's business. An economist views the €15 000 in interest income that Horace gives up every year as a cost of his business, even though it is an implicit cost. Horace's accountant, however, will not show this €15 000 as a cost because no money flows out of the business to pay for it.

To explore further the difference between economists and accountants, let's change the example slightly. Suppose now that Horace did not have the entire €300 000 to buy the factory but, instead, used €100 000 of his own savings and borrowed €200 000 from a bank at an interest rate of 5 per cent. Horace's accountant, who only measures explicit costs, will now count the €10 000 interest paid on the bank loan every year as a cost because this amount of money now flows out of the firm. By contrast, according to an economist, the opportunity cost of owning the business is still €15 000. The opportunity cost equals the interest on the bank loan (an explicit cost of €10 000) plus the forgone interest on savings (an implicit cost of €5 000).

Economic Profit versus Accounting Profit

economic profit
total revenue minus total cost, including both explicit and implicit costs

Now let's return to the firm's objective – profit. Because economists and accountants measure costs differently, they also measure profit differently. An economist measures a firm's **economic profit** as the firm's total revenue minus all the

FIGURE 13.1

Economists versus Accountants

Economists include all opportunity costs when analysing a firm, whereas accountants measure only explicit costs. Therefore, economic profit is smaller than accounting profit.

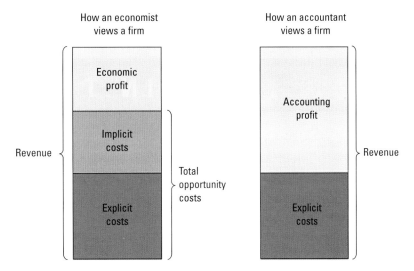

opportunity costs (explicit and implicit) of producing the goods and services sold. An accountant measures the firm's **accounting profit** as the firm's total revenue minus only the firm's explicit costs.

Figure 13.1 summarizes this difference. Notice that because the accountant ignores the implicit costs, accounting profit is usually larger than economic profit. For a business to be profitable from an economist's standpoint, total revenue must cover all the opportunity costs, both explicit and implicit.

accounting profit
total revenue minus total explicit cost

Quick Quiz   Richard Collishaw is a farmer who is also a skilled metal worker. He makes unique garden sculptures that could earn him €40 an hour. One day, he spends 10 hours planting €200 worth of seeds on his farm. What opportunity cost has he incurred? What cost would his accountant measure? If these seeds will yield €400 worth of crops, does Richard earn an accounting profit? Does he earn an economic profit? Would you advise Richard to continue as a farmer or switch to metal working?

PRODUCTION AND COSTS

Firms incur costs when they buy inputs to produce the goods and services that they plan to sell. In this section we examine the link between a firm's production process and its total cost. Once again, we consider Hungry Horace's Pizza Factory.

In the analysis that follows, we make an important simplifying assumption: we assume that the size of Horace's factory is fixed and that Horace can vary

the short run
the period of time in which some factors of production cannot be changed

the long run
the period of time in which all factors of production can be altered

the quantity of pizzas produced only by changing the number of workers. This assumption is realistic in **the short run**, but not in **the long run**. That is, Horace cannot build a larger factory overnight, but he can do so within a year or so. This analysis, therefore, should be viewed as describing the production decisions that Horace faces in the short run. We examine the relationship between costs and time horizon more fully later in the chapter.

IN THE NEWS

Interpreting Profit

Our discussion of the difference between economists' interpretation of profit and that of accountants has important implications. The financial crisis of 2007–09 highlighted ways in which definitions of profit can have serious consequences for banks and ultimately for overall economic stability. This article looks at how these interpretations can cause problems for banks and their investors.

Banking Inquiry May Uncover Ponzi Schemes
By Cormac Butler

To the relief of bank shareholders, not to mention the taxpayer, the Irish Central Bank governor Patrick Honohan is about to focus on what caused the banking crisis. He will identify what encouraged bankers to lend vast sums on speculative loss-making transactions.

People assume that high salaries and bonuses are only paid to bankers and traders who make genuine profits and increase shareholder wealth. Wrong. Poorly devised incentive schemes encourage them to ruin shareholder value. The lending to Irish developers is a case in point.

Many apparently successful financial institutions operate a 'Ponzi' scheme – an investment operation that pays returns to separate investors from their own money or money paid by subsequent investors, rather than from any actual profit earned. In this way shareholders have the illusion of profits, allowing bankers to pay themselves lavish incentives. Named after the

Italian-American fraudster Charles Ponzi who perfected the scam in the 1920s, Ponzis arise because banks exploit what seems a minor – but is in fact a major – accounting flaw.

Irish banks often use 'loss leader' strategies similar to supermarkets. They offer subsidized loans to build customer relationships or increase market share. Once the door is opened, the bank can then sell more lucrative treasury services. In the same way supermarkets may subsidize the cost of bread in the hope of luring customers to more high-margin product lines. Banks can easily hide the subsidy on the loss leader but supermarkets cannot.

Therefore supermarkets will use the strategy sparingly whereas banks will lend recklessly as long as they can show an accounting profit. For almost 20 years, international banks, hungry for large bonuses, have exploited this flaw. Imagine interest rates are expected to be 4 per cent, 5 per cent and 6 per cent over the next three years. A bank borrowing €1 000 000 would have to pay interest of €150 000 over this period. If the bank used the borrowings to buy a bond which paid

Charles Ponzi

interest of 4.6 per cent, the total income from the bond would be only €138 000. There's a shortfall of €12 000, that makes the bond unattractive for the bank's shareholders.

Nevertheless, in the year of purchase, the bank could record an accounting profit of €6 000, from the difference between rates of 4.6 per cent and 4 per cent. Bonuses are often based on just such an accounting profit – yet the banker gets rewarded for destroying shareholder value. Structured product people made millions from the basic accounting flaw above. They developed lethal, leveraged structured products such as 'inverse floaters'. Put simply, with a leverage of say 10, the accounting profit jumps from €6 000 to €60 000 – but the shareholders' loss multiplies to €120 000.

The salespeople learned a lucrative lesson. Many bankers became willing to overpay for dangerous structured products as long as they could record an accounting profit and pay them-

selves bonuses. New accounting rules eventually curtailed 'inverse floater' abuses but – like most badly designed rules – created an even bigger problem. Once the salesmen found bankers were happy to ruin shareholders if they earned a bonus first, they devised complex, lethal securitization portfolios, known now as toxic structured credit products. These produced a high return and therefore, high initial accounting profits.

Yet they were extremely difficult to value. The accounting rules for such risky products are hugely flawed. As the bankers simply didn't care what

they were buying, the salesmen packed hundreds of sub-prime – i.e. dodgy – loans into these overpriced structures and still they flew off the shelves. In the same vein, Irish banks queued up to acquire dodgy loans from property developers without any regard for the fact that these loans were overpriced.

Irish banks offered cheap loans to property developers, knowing that they could create an accounting profit but hide losses.

Source: http://www.irishtimes.com/ newspaper/opinion/2010/0211/1224264198292. html accessed 23 February 2010.

The Production Function

Table 13.1 shows how the quantity of pizzas Horace's factory produces per hour depends on the number of workers. As you see in the first two columns, if there are no workers in the factory Horace produces no pizzas. When there is 1 worker he produces 50 pizzas. When there are 2 workers he produces 90 pizzas, and so on. Figure 13.2 (panel (a)) presents a graph of these two columns of numbers. The number of workers is on the horizontal axis, and the number of pizzas produced is on the vertical axis. This relationship between the quantity of inputs (workers) and quantity of output (pizzas) is called the **production function**.

One of the *Ten Principles of Economics* introduced in Chapter 1 is that rational people think at the margin. As we will see in future chapters, this idea is the key to understanding the decision a firm makes about how many workers to hire and how much output to produce. To take a step toward understanding these decisions, the third column in the table gives the marginal product of a worker. The **marginal product** of any input in the production process is the increase in the quantity of output obtained from one additional unit of that input. When the number of workers goes from 1 to 2, pizza production increases from 50 to 90,

production function
the relationship between quantity of inputs used to make a good and the quantity of output of that good

marginal product
the increase in output that arises from an additional unit of input

TABLE 13.1

A Production Function and Total Cost: Hungry Horace's Pizza Factory

Number of workers	Output (quantity of pizzas produced per hour)	Marginal product of labour	Cost of factory	Cost of workers	Total cost of inputs (cost of factory + cost of workers)
0	0		€30	€0	€30
1	50	50	30	10	40
2	90	40	30	20	50
3	120	30	30	30	60
4	140	20	30	40	70
5	150	10	30	50	80

FIGURE 13.2

Hungry Horace's Production Function

The production function in panel (a) shows the relationship between the number of workers hired and the quantity of output produced. Here the number of workers hired (on the horizontal axis) is from the first column in Table 13.1, and the quantity of output produced (on the vertical axis) is from the second column. The production function gets flatter as the number of workers increases, which reflects diminishing marginal product. The total cost curve in panel (b) shows the relationship between the quantity of output produced and total cost of production. Here the quantity of output produced (on the horizontal axis) is from the second column in Table 13.1, and the total cost (on the vertical axis) is from the sixth column. The total cost curve gets steeper as the quantity of output increases because of diminishing marginal product.

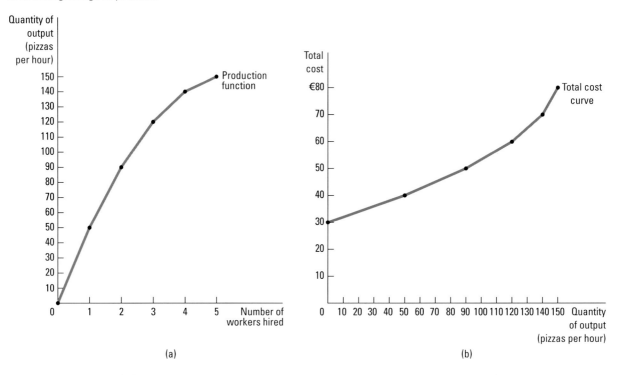

(a)   (b)

so the marginal product of the second worker is 40 pizzas. And when the number of workers goes from 2 to 3, pizza production increases from 90 to 120, so the marginal product of the third worker is 30 pizzas.

Notice that as the number of workers increases, the marginal product declines. The second worker has a marginal product of 40 pizzas, the third worker has a marginal product of 30 pizzas and the fourth worker has a marginal product of 20 pizzas. This property of the production function is called **diminishing marginal product**. At first, when only a few workers are hired, they have easy access to Horace's kitchen equipment. As the number of workers increases, additional workers have to share equipment and work in more crowded conditions. Hence, as more and more workers are hired, each additional worker contributes less to the production of pizzas.

Diminishing marginal product is also apparent in Figure 13.2 (panel (a)). The production function's slope ('rise over run') tells us the change in Horace's output of pizzas ('rise') for each additional input of labour ('run'). That is, the slope of the production function measures the marginal product of a worker. As the number of workers increases, the marginal product declines, and the production function becomes flatter.

diminishing marginal product
the property whereby the marginal product of an input declines as the quantity of the input increases

From the Production Function to the Total Cost Curve

The last three columns of Table 13.1 are reproduced as a graph in Figure 13.2 (panel (b)) to show Horace's cost of producing pizzas. In this example, the cost of operating the factory is €30 per hour and the cost of a worker is €10 per hour. If Horace hires 1 worker, his total cost is €40. If he hires 2 workers, his total cost is €50, and so on. With this information, the table now shows how the number of workers Horace hires is related to the quantity of pizzas he produces and to his total cost of production.

Our goal in the next several chapters is to study firms' production and pricing decisions. For this purpose, the most important relationship in Table 13.1 is between quantity produced (in the second column) and total costs (in the sixth column). Panel (b) of Figure 13.2 graphs these two columns of data with the quantity produced on the horizontal axis and total cost on the vertical axis. This graph is called the *total cost curve.*

Now compare the total cost curve in panel (b) of Figure 13.2 with the production function in panel (a). These two curves are opposite sides of the same coin. The total cost curve gets steeper as the amount produced rises, whereas the production function gets flatter as production rises. These changes in slope occur for the same reason. High production of pizzas means that Horace's kitchen is crowded with many workers. Because the kitchen is crowded, each additional worker adds less to production, reflecting diminishing marginal product. Therefore, the production function is relatively flat. But now turn this logic around: when the kitchen is crowded, producing an additional pizza requires a lot of additional labour and is thus very costly. Therefore, when the quantity produced is large, the total cost curve is relatively steep.

Quick Quiz   If Farmer Schmidt plants no seeds on his farm, he gets no harvest. If he plants 1 bag of seeds he gets 3 tonnes of wheat. If he plants 2 bags he gets 5 tonnes. If he plants 3 bags he gets 6 tonnes. A bag of seeds is priced at €100, and seeds are his only cost. Use these data to graph the farmer's production function and total cost curve. Explain their shapes.

THE VARIOUS MEASURES OF COST

Our analysis of Hungry Horace's Pizza Factory demonstrated how a firm's total cost reflects its production function. From data on a firm's total cost we can derive several related measures of cost which will turn out to be useful when we analyse production and pricing decisions in future chapters. To see how these related measures are derived, we consider the example in Table 13.2 This table presents cost data on Horace's neighbour: Thirsty Virgil's Lemonade Stand.

The first column of the table shows the number of glasses of lemonade that Virgil might produce, ranging from 0 to 10 glasses per hour. The second column shows Virgil's total cost of producing glasses of lemonade. Figure 13.3 plots Virgil's total cost curve. The quantity of lemonade (from the first column) is on the horizontal axis, and total cost (from the second column) is on the vertical axis. Thirsty Virgil's total cost curve has a shape similar to Hungry Horace's. In particular, it becomes steeper as the quantity produced rises, which (as we have discussed) reflects diminishing marginal product.

TABLE 13.2

The Various Measures of Cost: Thirsty Virgil's Lemonade Stand

Quantity of lemonade glasses (per hour)	Total cost	Fixed cost	Variable cost	Average fixed cost	Average variable cost	Average total cost	Marginal cost
0	€3.00	€3.00	€0.00	–	–	–	
1	3.30	3.00	0.30	€3.00	€0.30	€3.30	€0.30
2	3.80	3.00	0.80	1.50	0.40	1.90	0.50
3	4.50	3.00	1.50	1.00	0.50	1.50	0.70
4	5.40	3.00	2.40	0.75	0.60	1.35	0.90
5	6.50	3.00	3.50	0.60	0.70	1.30	1.10
6	7.80	3.00	4.80	0.50	0.80	1.30	1.30
7	9.30	3.00	6.30	0.43	0.90	1.33	1.50
8	11.00	3.00	8.00	0.38	1.00	1.38	1.70
9	12.90	3.00	9.90	0.33	1.10	1.43	1.90
10	15.00	3.00	12.00	0.30	1.20	1.50	2.10

FIGURE 13.3

Thirsty Virgil's Total Cost Curve

Here the quantity of output produced (on the horizontal axis) is from the first column in Table 13.2, and the total cost (on the vertical axis) is from the second column. As in Figure 13.2, the total cost curve gets steeper as the quantity of output increases because of diminishing marginal product.

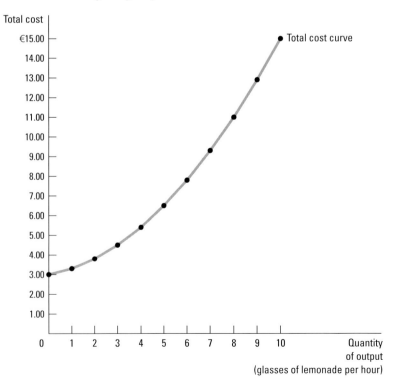

Fixed and Variable Costs

Virgil's total cost can be divided into two types. Some costs, called **fixed costs,** are not determined by the amount of output produced; they can change but not as a result of changes in the amount produced. They are incurred even if the firm produces nothing at all. Virgil's fixed costs include any rent he pays because this cost is the same regardless of how much lemonade Virgil produces. Similarly, if Virgil needs to hire a barman to serve the drinks, regardless of the quantity of lemonade sold, the barman's salary is a fixed cost. The third column in Table 13.2 shows Virgil's fixed cost, which in this example is €3.00.

Some of the firm's costs, called **variable costs,** change as the firm alters the quantity of output produced. Virgil's variable costs include the cost of lemons, sugar, paper cups and straws: the more lemonade Virgil makes, the more of these items he needs to buy. Similarly, if Virgil pays his workers overtime to make more lemonade, the wages of these workers are variable costs. The fourth column of the table shows Virgil's variable cost. The variable cost is 0 if he produces nothing, €0.30 if he produces 1 glass of lemonade, €0.80 if he produces 2 glasses and so on.

A firm's total cost is the sum of fixed and variable costs. In Table 13.2 total cost in the second column equals fixed cost in the third column plus variable cost in the fourth column.

fixed costs
costs that are not determined by the quantity of output produced

variable costs
costs that are dependent on the quantity of output produced

Average and Marginal Cost

As the owner of his firm, Virgil has to decide how much to produce. A key part of this decision is how his costs will vary as he changes the level of production. In making this decision, Virgil might ask his production supervisor the following two questions about the cost of producing lemonade:

• How much does it cost to make the typical glass of lemonade?
• How much does it cost to increase production of lemonade by 1 glass?

Although at first these two questions might seem to have the same answer, they do not. Both answers will turn out to be important for understanding how firms make production decisions.

To find the cost of the typical unit produced, we would divide the firm's total costs by the quantity of output it produces. For example, if the firm produces 2 glasses per hour, its total cost is €3.80, and the cost of the typical glass is €3.80/2, or €1.90. Total cost divided by the quantity of output is called **average total cost**. Because total cost is just the sum of fixed and variable costs, average total cost can be expressed as the sum of average fixed cost and average variable cost. **Average fixed cost** is the fixed cost divided by the quantity of output, and **average variable cost** is the variable cost divided by the quantity of output.

Although average total cost tells us the cost of the typical unit, it does not tell us how much total cost will change as the firm alters its level of production. The last column in Table 13.2 shows the amount that total cost rises when the firm increases production by 1 unit of output. This number is called **marginal cost**. For example, if Virgil increases production from 2 to 3 glasses, total cost rises from €3.80 to €4.50, so the marginal cost of the third glass of lemonade is €4.50 minus €3.80, or €0.70.

It may be helpful to express these definitions mathematically:

average total cost
total cost divided by the quantity of output

average fixed cost
fixed costs divided by the quantity of output

average variable cost
variable costs divided by the quantity of output

marginal cost
the increase in total cost that arises from an extra unit of production

$$\text{Average total cost} = \text{Total cost}/\text{Quantity}$$
$$ATC = TC/Q$$

and

$$\text{Marginal cost} = \text{Change in total cost}/\text{Change in quantity}$$
$$MC = \Delta TC/\Delta Q.$$

Here Δ, the Greek letter delta, represents the change in a variable. These equations show how average total cost and marginal cost are derived from total cost. Average total cost tells us the cost of a typical unit of output if total cost is divided evenly over all the units produced. Marginal cost tells us the increase in total cost that arises from producing an additional unit of output. As we will see more fully in the next chapter, Virgil, our lemonade entrepreneur, will find the concepts of average total cost and marginal cost useful when deciding how much lemonade to produce.

Cost Curves and their Shapes

Just as in previous chapters we found graphs of supply and demand useful when analysing the behaviour of markets, we will find graphs of average and marginal cost useful when analysing the behaviour of firms. Figure 13.4 graphs Virgil's costs using the data from Table 13.2 The horizontal axis measures the quantity the firm produces, and the vertical axis measures marginal and average costs. The graph shows four curves: average total cost (*ATC*), average fixed cost (*AFC*), average variable cost (*AVC*), and marginal cost (*MC*).

FIGURE 13.4

Thirsty Virgil's Average Cost and Marginal Cost Curves

This figure shows the average total cost (ATC), average fixed cost (AFC) average variable cost (AVC) and marginal cost (MC) for Thirsty Virgil's Lemonade Bar. All of these curves are obtained by graphing the data in Table 13.2. These cost curves show three features that are typical of many firms: (1) Marginal cost rises with the quantity of output. (2) The average total cost curve is U-shaped. (3) The marginal cost curve crosses the average total cost curve at the minimum of average total cost.

The cost curves shown here for Thirsty Virgil's Lemonade Bar have some features that are common to the cost curves of many firms in the economy. Let's examine three features in particular: the shape of marginal cost, the shape of average total cost, and the relationship between marginal and average total cost.

Rising Marginal Cost Thirsty Virgil's marginal cost rises with the quantity of output produced. This reflects the property of diminishing marginal product. When Virgil is producing a small quantity of lemonade he has few workers and much of his equipment is not being used. Because he can easily put these idle resources to use, the marginal product of an extra worker is large, and the marginal cost of an extra glass of lemonade is small. By contrast, when Virgil is producing a large quantity of lemonade his stand is crowded with workers and most of his equipment is fully utilized. Virgil can produce more lemonade by adding workers, but these new workers have to work in crowded conditions and may have to wait to use the equipment. Therefore, when the quantity of lemonade being produced is already high, the marginal product of an extra worker is low, and the marginal cost of an extra glass of lemonade is large.

U-Shaped Average Total Cost Thirsty Virgil's average total cost curve takes on a U-shape. To understand why this is so, remember that average total cost is the sum of average fixed cost and average variable cost. Average fixed cost always declines as output rises because the fixed cost does not change as output rises and so gets spread over a larger number of units. Average variable cost typically rises as output increases because of diminishing marginal product. Average total cost reflects the shapes of both average fixed cost and average variable cost. As shown in Figure 13.4 at very low levels of output, such as 1 or 2 glasses per hour, average total cost is high because the fixed cost is spread over only a few units. Average total cost then declines as output increases until the firm's output reaches 5 glasses of lemonade per hour, when average total cost falls to €1.30 per glass. When the firm produces more than 6 glasses, average total cost starts rising again because average variable cost rises substantially. If further units of output were produced the average total cost curve would continue to slope upwards giving the typical U-shape referred to.

The bottom of the U-shape occurs at the quantity that minimizes average total cost. This quantity is sometimes called the **efficient scale** of the firm. For Thirsty Virgil, the efficient scale is 5 or 6 glasses of lemonade. If he produces more or less than this amount, his average total cost rises above the minimum of €1.30.

efficient scale
the quantity of output that minimizes average total cost

The Relationship between Marginal Cost and Average Total Cost If you look at Figure 13.4 (or back at Table 13.2) you will see something that may be surprising at first. Whenever marginal cost is less than average total cost, average total cost is falling. Whenever marginal cost is greater than average total cost, average total cost is rising. This feature of Thirsty Virgil's cost curves is not a coincidence from the particular numbers used in the example: it is true for all firms and is a basic mathematical relationship.

To see why, refer to your understanding of averages and consider what happens to average cost as output goes up by one unit. If the cost of the extra unit is above the average cost of units produced up to that point, then it will tend to pull up the new average cost of a unit. If the new unit actually costs less than the average cost of a unit up to that point, it will tend to drag the new average down. But the price of an extra unit is what economists call marginal cost, so what we have just asserted is tantamount to saying that if marginal cost is less than average cost, average cost will be falling; and if marginal cost is above average cost, average cost will be rising.

This relationship between average total cost and marginal cost has an important corollary: the marginal cost curve crosses the average total cost curve at its minimum. Why? At low levels of output, marginal cost is below average total cost, so average total cost is falling. But after the two curves cross, marginal cost rises above average total cost. For the reason we have just discussed, average total cost must start to rise at this level of output. Hence, at this point of intersection the cost of an additional unit is the same as the average and so the average does not change and the point is the minimum of average total cost. As you will see in the next chapter, this point of minimum average total cost plays a key role in the analysis of competitive firms.

CASE STUDY

Understanding Averages and Marginal Values

When first encountering average and marginal costs, it can be a little confusing so it is often worth thinking about these values in a different context. Sebastien is an up-and-coming basketball player. In the first 18 games of the season Sebastien has scored a total of 306 points. The average points per game (PPG) at this stage of the season, therefore is $306/18 = 17$ points per game. The number of points that Sebastien scores in each successive game is his marginal score. If Sebastien scores 15 points in the 19th game, this is below his average of 17 and his average will fall. If in the next three games he scores 12, 14 and 10 then the marginal points score continues to be below the average and so his average will continue to fall. At the end of the 22nd game he will have scored a total of 357 points and his average will have fallen to 16.2. If in the next four games he scores 20, 18, 22 and 20 points, then each successive game sees his marginal points score being better than his average and so the average will be pulled up. At then end of 26 games, therefore, his total points score will be 437 and his average PPG will have risen to 16.8.

So, if Sebastien marginal points score in each successive game is less than his average, his average will fall but if his marginal points score in each game is more than his average points score then his average will rise. It's the same principle for firms' costs!

Los Angeles Lakers' star player Kobe Bryant scored an average 29.2 points per game (PPG) in the 2009–2010 season, helping the Lakers to win the NBA championship for the second year running.

Typical Cost Curves

In the examples we have studied so far, the firms exhibit diminishing marginal product and, therefore, rising marginal cost at all levels of output. Yet actual firms are often a bit more complicated than this. In many firms, diminishing marginal product does not start to occur immediately after the first worker is hired. Depending on the production process, the second or third worker might have higher marginal product than the first because a team of workers can divide tasks and work more productively than a single worker. Such firms would first experience increasing marginal product for a while before diminishing marginal product sets in.

The table in Figure 13.5 shows the cost data for such a firm, called Berit's Bagel Bin. These data are used in the graphs. Panel (a) shows how total cost *(TC)* depends on the quantity produced, and panel (b) shows average total cost *(ATC)*, average fixed cost *(AFC)*, average variable cost *(AVC)* and marginal cost *(MC)*. In the range of output from 0 to 4 bagels per hour, the firm experiences

Berit's Cost Curves

Many firms, like Berit's Bagel Bin, experience increasing marginal product before diminishing marginal product and, therefore, have cost curves shaped like those in this figure. Panel (a) shows how total cost (TC) depends on the quantity produced. Panel (b) shows how average total cost (ATC), average fixed cost (AFC), average variable cost (AVC) and marginal cost (MC) depend on the quantity produced. These curves are derived by graphing the data from the table. Notice that marginal cost and average variable cost fall for a while before starting to rise.

Quantity of bagels (per hour)	Total cost	Fixed cost	Variable cost	Average fixed cost	Average variable cost	Average total cost	Marginal cost
Q	TC = FC + VC	FC	VC	AFC = FC/Q	AVC = VC/Q	ATC = TC/Q	MC = ΔTC/ΔQ
0	€2.00	€2.00	€0.00	–	–	–	
1	3.00	2.00	1.00	€2.00	€1.00	€3.00	€1.00
2	3.80	2.00	1.80	1.00	0.90	1.90	0.80
3	4.40	2.00	2.40	0.67	0.80	1.47	0.60
4	4.80	2.00	2.80	0.50	0.70	1.20	0.40
5	5.20	2.00	3.20	0.40	0.64	1.04	0.40
6	5.80	2.00	3.80	0.33	0.63	0.96	0.60
7	6.60	2.00	4.60	0.29	0.66	0.95	0.80
8	7.60	2.00	5.60	0.25	0.70	0.95	1.00
9	8.80	2.00	6.80	0.22	0.76	0.98	1.20
10	10.20	2.00	8.20	0.20	0.82	1.02	1.40
11	11.80	2.00	9.80	0.18	0.89	1.07	1.60
12	13.60	2.00	11.60	0.17	0.97	1.14	1.80
13	15.60	2.00	13.60	0.15	1.05	1.20	2.00
14	17.80	2.00	15.80	0.14	1.13	1.27	2.20

(a) Total cost curve

(b) Marginal and average cost curves

increasing marginal product, and the marginal cost curve falls. After 5 bagels per hour, the firm starts to experience diminishing marginal product, and the marginal cost curve starts to rise. This combination of increasing then diminishing marginal product also makes the average variable cost curve U-shaped.

Despite these differences from our previous example, Berit's cost curves share the three properties that are most important to remember:

- Marginal cost eventually rises with the quantity of output.
- The average total cost curve is U-shaped.
- The marginal cost curve crosses the average total cost curve at the minimum of average total cost.

Quick Quiz Suppose BMW's total cost of producing 4 cars is €225 000 and its total cost of producing 5 cars is €250 000. What is the average total cost of producing 5 cars? What is the marginal cost of the fifth car? • Draw the marginal cost curve and the average total cost curve for a typical firm, and explain why these curves cross where they do.

COSTS IN THE SHORT RUN AND IN THE LONG RUN

We noted at the beginning of this chapter that a firm's costs might depend on the time horizon being examined. Let's discuss more precisely why this might be the case.

The Relationship Between Short-Run and Long-Run Average Total Cost

For many firms, the division of total costs between fixed and variable costs depends on the time horizon. Consider, for instance, a car manufacturer, such as Renault. Over a period of only a few months, Renault cannot adjust the number or sizes of its car factories. The only way it can produce additional cars is to hire more workers at the factories it already has. The cost of these factories is, therefore, a fixed cost in the short run. By contrast, over a period of several years, Renault can expand the size of its factories, build new factories or close old ones. Thus, the cost of its factories is a variable cost in the long run.

Because many decisions are fixed in the short run but variable in the long run, a firm's long-run cost curves differ from its short-run cost curves. Figure 13.6 shows an example. The figure presents three short-run average total cost curves representing the cost structures for a small, medium and large factory. It also presents the long-run average total cost curve. As the firm adjusts the size of the factory to the quantity of production, it moves along the long-run curve, and it is adjusting the size of the factory to the quantity of production.

This graph shows how short-run and long-run costs are related. The long-run average total cost curve is a much flatter U-shape than the short-run average total cost curve. In addition, all the short-run curves lie on or above the long-run curve. These properties arise because firms have greater flexibility in the long run. In essence, in the long run, the firm chooses which short-run curve it wants to use. But in the short run, it has to use whatever short-run curve it chose in the past.

The figure shows an example of how a change in production alters costs over different time horizons. When Renault wants to increase production from 1 000 to 1 200 cars per day, it has no choice in the short run but to hire more workers at its existing medium-sized factory. Because of diminishing marginal product, average total cost rises from €10 000 to €12 000 per car. In the long run, however, Renault can expand both the size of the factory and its workforce, and average total cost returns to €10 000.

FIGURE 13.6

Average Total Cost in the Short and Long Runs

Because fixed costs are variable in the long run, the average total cost curve in the short run differs from the average total cost curve in the long run.

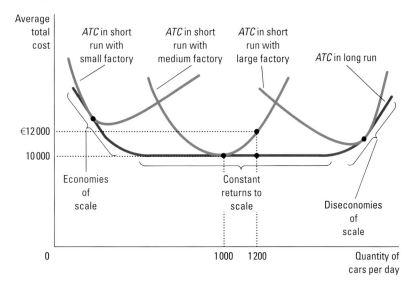

How long does it take for a firm to get to the long run? The answer depends on the firm. It can take a year or longer for a major manufacturing firm, such as a car company, to build a larger factory. By contrast, a person running a newspaper stand might be able to find new premises and expand sales in a matter of weeks or days. There is, therefore, no single answer about how long it takes a firm to adjust its production facilities.

Economies and Diseconomies of Scale

The shape of the long-run average total cost curve conveys important information about the technology for producing a good. When long-run average total cost declines as output increases, there are said to be **economies of scale**. When long-run average total cost rises as output increases, there are said to be **diseconomies of scale**. When long-run average total cost does not vary with the level of output, there are said to be **constant returns to scale**. In this example, Renault has economies of scale at low levels of output, constant returns to scale at intermediate levels of output and diseconomies of scale at high levels of output.

What might cause economies or diseconomies of scale? Economies of scale often arise because higher production levels allow *specialization* among workers and increases the possibility that technology can be used, which permits each worker to become better at his or her assigned tasks. For instance, modern assembly line production may require fewer workers in relation to the technology used but still produce more cars. If Renault were producing only a small quantity of cars, it could not take advantage of this approach and would have higher average total cost. Diseconomies of scale can arise because of *coordination problems* that are inherent in any large organization. The more cars Renault produces, the more stretched the management team becomes, and the less effective the managers become at keeping costs down.

economies of scale
the property whereby long-run average total cost falls as the quantity of output increases

diseconomies of scale
the property whereby long-run average total cost rises as the quantity of output increases

constant returns to scale
the property whereby long-run average total cost stays the same as the quantity of output changes

This analysis shows why long-run average total cost curves are often U-shaped. At low levels of production, the firm benefits from increased size because it can take advantage of greater specialization. Coordination problems, meanwhile, are not yet acute. By contrast, at high levels of production, the benefits of specialization have already been realized, and coordination problems become more severe as the firm grows larger. Thus, long-run average total cost is falling at low levels of production because of increasing specialization and rising at high levels of production because of increasing coordination problems.

CASE STUDY

The Implications of Economies of Scale

Economies of scale are the advantages of large-scale production that result in lower average or unit costs.

Imagine a firm which makes bricks. The current plant has a maximum capacity of 100 000 bricks per week and the total costs are €200 000 per week. The average cost for each brick, therefore, is €2. The firm sets a price of €2.20 per brick giving it a profit margin of €0.20 per brick.

Now imagine that in the long run, the firm expands. It doubles the size of its plant. The total costs, obviously, increase – they are now using more land and putting up more buildings, as well as hiring extra labour and buying more equipment and raw materials. All of this expansion will increase the total cost however, it is not the case that a doubling of capacity will also lead to a doubling of the cost.

Assume TC is now 350 000 per week. The expansion of the plant means that the firm can double its output so its capacity is now 200 000 bricks per week. The proportionate increase in the total costs is less than the proportionate increase in output. Total costs have risen by €150 000 or 75 per cent and total output by 100 per cent, which means that the average cost per brick is now €1.75 per brick.

The firm now faces two scenarios. In Scenario 1, the firm could maintain its price at €2.20 and increase its profit margin on each brick sold from €0.20 to €0.45. Assuming it sells all the bricks it produces its revenue would increase to €440 000 per week.

Scenario 1

Total costs: €350 000 per week

Price per brick: €2.20

Max capacity: 200 000 per week

Max revenue = €440 000 per week

Average cost per brick = €1.75

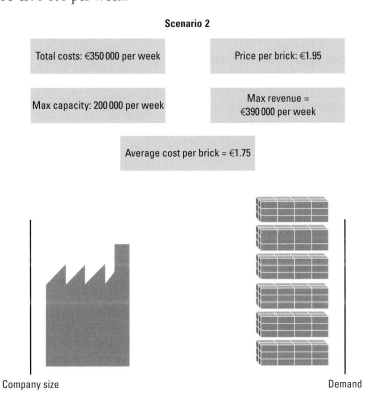

Company size   Demand

In scenario 2, the firm might choose to reduce its price to improve its competitiveness against its rivals. It could maintain its former profit margin of €0.20 and reduce the price to €1.95 improving the chances of increasing its competitive advantage. In this case, if it sells all it produces its revenue would be €390 000 per week.

Scenario 2

Total costs: €350 000 per week

Price per brick: €1.95

Max capacity: 200 000 per week

Max revenue = €390 000 per week

Average cost per brick = €1.75

Company size   Demand

What the firm chooses to do would be dependent on its competitive position. If it played a dominant role in the market it might be able to increase its price and still sell all it produces. If it was in a more competitive market it might not have sold all its capacity in the first place so being able to reduce its price might mean that it can now increase sales against its rivals and increase its total revenue as a result.

Economies of scale, therefore, occur where the proportionate rise in output as a result of the expansion or growth of the firm as defined by a rise in all the factor inputs, is greater that the proportionate rise in costs as a result of the expansion.

Quick Quiz If Airbus produces 9 jets per month, its long-run total cost is €9.0 million per month. If it produces 10 jets per month, its long-run total cost is €9.5 million per month. Does Airbus exhibit economies or diseconomies of scale?

FYI

Lessons From a Pin Factory

'Jack of all trades, master of none.' This well-known adage helps explain why firms sometimes experience economies of scale. A person who tries to do everything usually ends up doing nothing very well. If a firm wants its workers to be as productive as they can be, it is often best to give each a limited task that he or she can master. But this is possible only if a firm employs many workers and produces a large quantity of output.

In his celebrated book *An Inquiry into the Nature and Causes of the Wealth of Nations,* Adam Smith described a visit he made to a pin factory. Smith was impressed by the specialization among the workers and the resulting economies of scale. He wrote:

One man draws out the wire, another straightens it, a third cuts it, a fourth points it, a fifth grinds it at the top for receiving the head; to make the head requires two or three distinct operations; to put it on is a peculiar business; to whiten it is another; it is even a trade by itself to put them into paper.

Smith reported that because of this specialization, the pin factory produced thousands of pins per worker every day. He conjectured that if the workers had chosen to work separately, rather than as a team of specialists, 'they certainly could not each of them make twenty, perhaps not one pin a day.' In other words, because of specialization, a large pin factory could achieve higher

output per worker and lower average cost per pin than a small pin factory.

The specialization that Smith observed in the pin factory is prevalent in the modern economy. If you want to build a house, for instance, you could try to do all the work yourself. But most people turn to a builder, who in turn hires carpenters, plumbers, electricians, painters and many other types of workers. These workers specialize in particular jobs, and this allows them to become better at their jobs than if they were generalists. Indeed, the use of specialization to achieve economies of scale is one reason modern societies are as prosperous as they are.

CONCLUSION

The purpose of this chapter has been to develop some tools that we can use to study how firms make production and pricing decisions. You should now understand what economists mean by the term *costs* and how costs vary with the quantity of output a firm produces. To refresh your memory, Table 13.3 summarizes some of the definitions we have encountered.

TABLE 13.3

The Many Types of Cost: A Summary

Term	Definition	Mathematical description
Explicit costs	Costs that require an outlay of money by the firm	–
Implicit costs	Costs that do not require an outlay of money by the firm	–
Fixed costs	Costs that do not vary with the quantity of output produced	FC
Variable costs	Costs that do vary with the quantity of output produced	VC
Total cost	The market value of all the inputs that a firm uses in production	$TC = FC + VC$
Average fixed cost	Fixed costs divided by the quantity of output	$AFC = FC/Q$
Average variable cost	Variable costs divided by the quantity of output	$AVC = VC/Q$
Average total cost	Total cost divided by the quantity of output	$ATC = TC/Q$
Marginal cost	The increase in total cost that arises from an extra unit of production	$MC = \Delta TC/\Delta Q$

By themselves, of course, a firm's cost curves do not tell us what decisions the firm will make. But they are an important component of that decision, as we will begin to see in the next chapter.

SUMMARY

- One goal of firms is to maximize profit, which equals total revenue minus total cost.

- When analysing a firm's behaviour, it is important to include all the opportunity costs of production. Some of the opportunity costs, such as the wages a firm pays its workers, are explicit. Other opportunity costs, such as the wages the firm owner gives up by working in the firm rather than taking another job, are implicit.

- A firm's costs reflect its production process. A typical firm's production function gets flatter as the quantity of an input increases, displaying the property of diminishing marginal product. As a result, a firm's total cost curve gets steeper as the quantity produced rises.

- A firm's total costs can be divided between fixed costs and variable costs. Fixed costs are costs that are not determined by the quantity of output produced. Variable costs are costs that directly related to the amount produced and so change when the firm alters the quantity of output produced.

- From a firm's total cost, two related measures of cost are derived. Average total cost is total cost divided by the quantity of output. Marginal cost is the amount by which total cost changes if output increases (or decreases) by 1 unit.

- When analysing firm behaviour, it is often useful to graph average total cost and marginal cost. For a typical firm, marginal cost rises with the quantity of output. Average total cost first falls as output increases and then rises as output increases further. The marginal cost curve always crosses the average total cost curve at the minimum of average total cost.

- A firm's costs often depend on the time horizon being considered. In particular, many costs are fixed in the short run but variable in the long run. As a result, when the firm changes its level of production, average total cost may rise more in the short run than in the long run.

KEY CONCEPTS

total cost, p. 265
profit, p. 265
explicit costs, p. 265
implicit costs, p. 265
economic profit, p. 266
accounting profit, p. 267
the short run, p. 268

the long run, p. 268
production function, p. 269
marginal product, p. 269
diminishing marginal product, p. 270
fixed costs, p. 273
variable costs, p. 273
average total cost, p. 273

average fixed cost, p. 273
average variable cost, p. 273
marginal cost, p. 273
efficient scale, p. 275
economies of scale, p. 279
diseconomies of scale, p. 279
constant returns to scale, p. 279

QUESTIONS FOR REVIEW

1. What is the relationship between a firm's total revenue, profit and total cost?

2. Give an example of an opportunity cost that an accountant might not count as a cost. Why would the accountant ignore this cost?

3. What is marginal product, and what does it mean if it is diminishing?

4. Draw a production function that exhibits diminishing marginal product of labour. Draw the associated total cost curve. (In both cases, be sure to label the axes.) Explain the shapes of the two curves you have drawn.

5. Define total cost, average total cost and marginal cost. How are they related?

6. Draw the marginal cost and average total cost curves for a typical firm. Explain why the curves have the shapes that they do and why they cross where they do.

7. How and why does a firm's average total cost curve differ in the short run and in the long run?

8. Define *economies of scale* and explain why they might arise. Define *diseconomies of scale* and explain why they might arise.

PROBLEMS AND APPLICATIONS

1. This chapter discusses many types of costs: opportunity cost, total cost, fixed cost, variable cost, average total cost and marginal cost. Fill in the type of cost that best completes each phrase below:
   a. The true cost of taking some action is its _____.
   b. _____ is falling when marginal cost is below it, and rising when marginal cost is above it.
   c. A cost that does not depend on the quantity produced is a _____ .
   d. In the ice cream industry in the short run, _____ includes the cost of cream and sugar, but not the cost of the factory.
   e. Profits equal total revenue minus _____ .
   f. The cost of producing an extra unit of output is the _____ .

2. Your Aunt Imelda is thinking about opening a pub. She estimates that it would cost €500 000 per year to rent the premises, buy a licence to serve alcohol and to buy in enough Murphy's Irish Stout from the brewery. In addition, she would have to leave her €50 000 per year job as an accountant.
   a. Define opportunity cost.
   b. What is your aunt's opportunity cost of running the pub for a year? If your aunt thought she could sell €510 000 worth of Murphy's in a year, should she open the pub? Explain.

3. Suppose that your university charges you separately for tuition and for room and board.
   a. What is a cost of going to university that is not an opportunity cost?
   b. What is an explicit opportunity cost of going to university?
   c. What is an implicit opportunity cost of going to university?

4. A commercial fisherman notices the following relationship between hours spent fishing and the quantity of fish caught:

Hours	Quantity of fish (in kilograms)
0	0
1	10
2	18
3	24
4	28
5	30

a. What is the marginal product of each hour spent fishing?
b. Use these data to graph the fisherman's production function. Explain its shape.
c. The fisherman has a fixed cost of €10 (his fishing rod). The opportunity cost of his time is €5 per hour. Graph the fisherman's total cost curve. Explain its shape.

5. Clean Sweep is a company that makes brooms and then sells them door-to-door. Here is the relationship between the number of workers and Clean Sweep's output in a given day:

Workers	Output	Marginal product	Total cost	Average total cost	Marginal cost
0	0				
1	20				
2	50				
3	90				
4	120				
5	140				
6	150				
7	155				

a. Fill in the column of marginal product. What pattern do you see? How might you explain it?
b. A worker costs €100 a day, and the firm has fixed costs of €200. Use this information to fill in the column for total cost.
c. Fill in the column for average total cost. (Recall that *ATC = TC/Q.*) What pattern do you see?
d. Now fill in the column for marginal cost. (Recall that *MC = ΔTC/ΔQ.*) What pattern do you see?
e. Compare the column for marginal product and the column for marginal cost. Explain the relationship.
f. Compare the column for average total cost and the column for marginal cost. Explain the relationship.

6. Suppose that you and your roommate have started a bagel delivery service on campus. List some of your fixed costs and describe why they are fixed. List some of your variable costs and describe why they are variable.

7. Consider the following cost information for a pizzeria:

Q (dozens)	Total cost	Variable cost
0	€300	€0
1	350	50
2	390	90
3	420	120
4	450	150
5	490	190
6	540	240

a. What is the pizzeria's fixed cost?
b. Construct a table in which you calculate the marginal cost per dozen pizzas using the information on total cost. Also calculate the marginal cost per dozen pizzas using the information on variable cost. What is the relationship between these sets of numbers? Comment.

8. You are thinking about setting up a lemonade bar. The bar itself costs €200 a week to rent. The ingredients for each cup of lemonade cost €0.50.
a. What is your fixed cost of doing business? What is your variable cost per cup?
b. Construct a table showing your total cost, average total cost and marginal cost for output levels varying from 0 to 100 litres. (Hint: there are 4 cups in a litre.) Draw the three cost curves.

9. Your cousin Vinnie owns a painting company with fixed costs of €200 and the following schedule for variable costs:

Quantity of houses painted per month	1	2	3	4	5	6	7
Variable costs	€10	€20	€40	€80	€160	€320	€640

Calculate average fixed cost, average variable cost and average total cost for each quantity. What is the efficient scale of the painting company?

10. Healthy Harry's Juice Bar has the following cost schedules:

Q (vats)	Variable cost	Total cost
0	€0	€30
1	10	40
2	25	55
3	45	75
4	70	100
5	100	130
6	135	165

a. Calculate average variable cost, average total cost and marginal cost for each quantity.

b. Graph all three curves. What is the relationship between the marginal cost curve and the average total cost curve? Between the marginal cost curve and the average variable cost curve? Explain.

11. Consider the following table of long-run total cost for three different firms:

Quantity	1	2	3	4	5	6	7
Firm A	€60	€70	€80	€90	€100	€110	€120
Firm B	11	24	39	56	75	96	119
Firm C	21	34	49	66	85	106	129

Does each of these firms experience economies of scale or diseconomies of scale?

For further resources, visit
www.cengage.com/mankiw_taylor2

14 FIRMS IN COMPETITIVE MARKETS

If your local petrol station raised the price it charges for petrol by 20 per cent it would see a large drop in the amount of petrol it sold. Its customers would quickly switch to buying their petrol at other petrol stations. By contrast, if your regional water company raised the price of water by 20 per cent, it would see only a small decrease in the amount of water it sold. People might water their lawns less often and buy more water-efficient showers, but they would be hard pressed to reduce water consumption greatly and would be unlikely to find another supplier. The difference between the petrol market and the water market is obvious: there are many firms selling petrol in your area, but there is only one firm selling water. As you might expect, this difference in market structure shapes the pricing and production decisions of the firms that operate in these markets.

In this chapter we examine the behaviour of competitive firms, such as your local petrol station. You may recall that a market is competitive if each buyer and seller is small compared to the size of the market and, therefore, has little ability to influence market prices. By contrast, if a firm can influence the market price of the good it sells, it is said to have *market power*. Later in the book we examine the behaviour of firms with market power, such as your local water company.

Our analysis of competitive firms in this chapter will shed light on the decisions that lie behind the supply curve in a competitive market. Not surprisingly, we will find that a market supply curve is tightly linked to firms' costs of production. (Indeed, this general insight should be familiar to you from our analysis in Chapter 7.) But among a firm's various costs – fixed, variable, average and marginal – which ones are most relevant for its decision about the quantity to supply at any given price? We will see that all these measures of cost play important and interrelated roles.

WHAT IS A COMPETITIVE MARKET?

Our goal in this chapter is to examine how firms make production decisions in competitive markets. As a background for this analysis, we begin by considering what a competitive market is.

The Meaning of Competition

Competition refers to a situation where there are rivals in production who allow the consumer to make a choice. A market in which there is only one supplier has no competition as consumers have no choice but a market where there are many suppliers gives consumers the opportunity of making a choice based on quality, value for money, price and so on. We can summarize the meaning of competition in the following way:

- Where more than one firm offers the same or a similar product there is competition.
- Competition can also manifest itself where substitutes exist: for example, gas and electricity are separate markets but there is the opportunity for consumers to substitute gas cookers for electric ones and so some element of competition exists.
- The closer the degree of substitutability the greater will be the competition that exists.
- Firms may influence the level of competition through the way they build relationships with consumers, encourage purchasing habits, provide levels of customer service and after sales service and so on.

In Chapter 4 we looked at competitive markets. Let us briefly review the lesson on the extreme end of the competitive scale, a *perfectly competitive market*. A competitive market has two characteristics:

- There are many buyers and many sellers in the market.
- The goods offered by the various sellers are largely the same (if identical the goods are described as being 'homogenous'.

As a result of these conditions, the actions of any single buyer or seller in the market have a negligible impact on the market price. Each buyer and seller takes the market price as given.

An example is the market for milk. No single buyer of milk can influence the price of milk because each buyer purchases a small amount relative to the size of the market. Similarly, each seller of milk has limited control over the price because many other sellers are offering milk that is essentially identical. Because each seller can sell all he wants at the going price, he has little reason to charge less, and if he charges more, buyers will go elsewhere. Buyers and sellers in competitive markets must accept the price the market determines and, therefore, are said to be *price takers.*

In addition to the foregoing two conditions for competition, there are two other conditions sometimes thought to characterize perfectly competitive markets:

- Firms can freely enter or exit the market.
- There is a high degree of information available to buyers and sellers in the market.

If, for instance, anyone can decide to start a dairy farm, and if any existing dairy farmer can decide to leave the dairy business, then the dairy industry would satisfy this condition. It should be noted that much of the analysis of competitive firms does not rely on the assumption of free entry and exit because this condition is not necessary for firms to be price takers. But as we will see later in this chapter, entry and exit are often powerful forces shaping the long-run outcome in competitive markets.

The developments in technology now mean that many more people have access to information about firms. Price comparison websites, blogs, review sites and so on mean that it is much easier for consumers to find out about the prices being charged by different firms in a market as well as the sort of service and quality they offer. Firms can also make use of this information and are aware that they are subject to increasing transparency over the way they conduct their business. This can affect their behaviour.

The Revenue of a Competitive Firm

A firm in a competitive market, like most other firms in the economy, tries to maximize profit, which equals total revenue minus total cost. To see how it does this, we first consider the revenue of a competitive firm. To keep matters concrete, let's consider a specific firm: the Grundy Family Dairy Farm.

The Grundy Farm produces a quantity of milk Q and sells each unit at the market price P. The farm's total revenue is $P \times Q$. For example, if a litre of milk sells for €6 and the farm sells 1 000 litres, its total revenue is €6 000.

Because the Grundy Farm is small compared with the world market for milk, it takes the price as given by market conditions. This means, in particular, that the price of milk does not depend on the quantity of output that the Grundy Farm produces and sells. If the Grundys double the amount of milk they produce, the price of milk remains the same, and their total revenue doubles. As a result, total revenue is proportional to the amount of output.

Table 14.1 shows the revenue for the Grundy Family Dairy Farm. The first two columns show the amount of output the farm produces and the price at which it sells its output. The third column is the farm's total revenue. The table assumes that the price of milk is €6 a litre, so total revenue is simply €6 times the number of litres.

TABLE 14.1

Total, Average and Marginal Revenue for a Competitive Firm

Quantity	Price	Total revenue	Average revenue	Marginal revenue
(Q)	(P)	($TR = P \times Q$)	($AR = TR/Q$)	($MR = \Delta TR/\Delta Q$)
1 litre	€6	€6	€6	
2	6	12	6	€6
3	6	18	6	6
4	6	24	6	6
5	6	30	6	6
6	6	36	6	6
7	6	42	6	6
8	6	48	6	6

Just as the concepts of average and marginal were useful in the preceding chapter when analysing costs, they are also useful when analysing revenue. To see what these concepts tell us, consider these two questions:

- How much revenue does the farm receive for the typical litre of milk?
- How much additional revenue does the farm receive if it increases production of milk by 1 litre?

The last two columns in Table 14.1 answer these questions.

average revenue
total revenue divided by the quantity sold

The fourth column in the table shows **average revenue,** which is total revenue (from the third column) divided by the amount of output (from the first column). Average revenue tells us how much revenue a firm receives for the typical unit sold. In Table 14.1, you can see that average revenue equals €6, the price of a litre of milk. This illustrates a general lesson that applies not only to competitive firms but to other firms as well. Total revenue is the price times the quantity ($P \times Q$), and average revenue is total revenue ($P \times Q$) divided by the quantity (Q). Therefore, *for all firms, average revenue equals the price of the good.*

marginal revenue
the change in total revenue from an additional unit sold

The fifth column shows **marginal revenue,** which is the change in total revenue from the sale of each additional unit of output. The sale of one more litre of milk adds €6 to total revenue, therefore the marginal revenue is also €6. In Table 14.1, marginal revenue equals €6, the price of a litre of milk. This result illustrates a lesson that applies only to competitive firms. Total revenue is $P \times Q$, and P is fixed for a competitive firm. Therefore, when Q rises by 1 unit, total revenue rises by P euros. For competitive firms, marginal revenue equals the price of the good.

> **Quick Quiz** When a competitive firm doubles the amount it sells, what happens to the price of its output and its total revenue?

PROFIT MAXIMIZATION AND THE COMPETITIVE FIRM'S SUPPLY CURVE

One goal of a competitive firm is assumed to be maximizing profit, which equals total revenue minus total cost. We have just discussed the firm's revenue, and in the last chapter we discussed the firm's costs. We are now ready to examine how the firm maximizes profit and how that decision leads to its supply curve.

A Simple Example of Profit Maximization

Let's begin our analysis of the firm's supply decision with the example in Table 14.2. In the first column of the table is the number of litres of milk the Grundy Family Dairy Farm produces. The second column shows the farm's total revenue, which is €6 times the number of litres. The third column shows the farm's total cost. Total cost includes fixed costs, which are €3 in this example, and variable costs, which depend on the quantity produced.

The fourth column shows the farm's profit, which is computed by subtracting total cost from total revenue. If the farm produces nothing, it has a loss of €3. If it produces 1 litre, it has a profit of €1. If it produces 2 litres, it has a profit of €4, and so on. To maximize profit, the Grundy Farm chooses the quantity that makes profit as large as possible. In this example, profit is maximized when the farm produces 4 or 5 litres of milk, when the profit is €7.

TABLE 14.2

Profit Maximization: A Numerical Example

Quantity	Total revenue	Total cost	Profit	Marginal revenue	Marginal cost	Change in profit
(Q)	(TR)	(TC)	(TR − TC)	(MR = $\Delta TR/\Delta Q$)	(MC = $\Delta TC/\Delta Q$)	(MR − MC)
0 litres	€0	€3	−€3			
				€6	€2	€4
1	6	5	1			
				6	3	3
2	12	8	4			
				6	4	2
3	18	12	6			
				6	5	1
4	24	17	7			
				6	6	0
5	30	23	7			
				6	7	−1
6	36	30	6			
				6	8	−2
7	42	38	4			
				6	9	−3
8	48	47	1			

There is another way to look at the Grundy Farm's decision: the Grundys can find the profit-maximizing quantity by comparing the marginal revenue and marginal cost from each unit produced. The fifth and sixth columns in Table 14.2 compute marginal revenue and marginal cost from the changes in total revenue and total cost, and the last column shows the change in profit for each additional litre produced. The first litre of milk the farm produces has a marginal revenue of €6 and a marginal cost of €2; hence, producing that litre adds €4 to profit (from −€3 to €1). The second litre produced has a marginal revenue of €6 and a marginal cost of €3, so that litre adds €3 to profit (from €1 to €4). As long as marginal revenue exceeds marginal cost, increasing the quantity produced adds to profit. Since additional production of milk adds to profit it is worth the Grundy Farm producing this extra milk. Once the Grundy Farm has reached 5 litres of milk, however, the situation is very different. The sixth litre would have marginal revenue of €6 and marginal cost of €7, so producing it would reduce profit by €1 (from €7 to €6). It does not make sense for the Grundy Farm to produce the sixth litre and so as a result, the Grundys would not produce beyond 5 litres.

One of the *Ten Principles of Economics* in Chapter 1 is that rational people think at the margin. We now see how the Grundy Family Dairy Farm can apply this principle. If marginal revenue is greater than marginal cost – as it is at 1, 2 or 3 litres – it is worth the Grundys increasing the production of milk; even making a decision to increase production from the third to the fourth litre is worth doing since the MC and MR are the same at this point and as a result the profit level is neither increased nor decreased. If marginal revenue is less than marginal cost – as it is at 5, 6 or 7 litres – the Grundys should decrease production. If the Grundys think at the margin and make incremental adjustments to the level of production, they are naturally led to produce the profit-maximizing quantity.

The Marginal Cost Curve and the Firm's Supply Decision

To extend this analysis of profit maximization, consider the cost curves in Figure 14.1. These cost curves have the three features that, as we discussed in the previous chapter, are thought to describe most firms: the marginal cost curve (MC) is upward sloping; the average total cost curve (ATC) is U-shaped; and the marginal cost curve crosses the average total cost curve at the minimum of average total cost. The figure also shows a horizontal line at the market price (P). The price line is horizontal because the firm is a price taker: the price of the

FIGURE 14.1

Profit Maximization for a Competitive Firm

This figure shows the marginal cost curve (MC), the average total cost curve (ATC) and the average variable cost curve (AVC). It also shows the market price (P), which equals marginal revenue (MR) and average revenue (AR). At the quantity Q_1, marginal revenue MR_1 exceeds marginal cost MC_1, so raising production increases profit. At the quantity Q_2 marginal cost MC_2 is above marginal revenue MR_2, so reducing production increases profit. The profit maximizing quantity Q_{MAX} is found where the horizontal price line intersects the marginal cost curve.

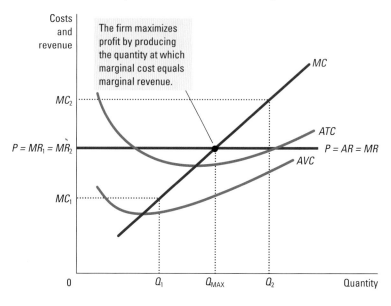

firm's output is the same regardless of the quantity that the firm decides to produce. Keep in mind that, for a competitive firm, the firm's price equals both its average revenue (*AR*) and its marginal revenue (*MR*).

We can use Figure 14.1 to find the quantity of output that maximizes profit. Imagine that the firm is producing at Q_1. At this level of output, marginal revenue is greater than marginal cost. That is, if the firm raised its level of production and sales by 1 unit, the additional revenue (MR_1) would exceed the additional costs (MC_1). Profit, which equals total revenue minus total cost, would increase. Hence, if marginal revenue is greater than marginal cost, as it is at Q_1, the firm can increase profit by increasing production.

A similar argument applies when output is at Q_2. In this case, marginal cost is greater than marginal revenue. If the firm reduced production by 1 unit, the costs saved (MC_2) would exceed the revenue lost (MR_2). Therefore, if marginal revenue is less than marginal cost, as it is at Q_2, the firm can increase profit by reducing production.

Where do these marginal adjustments to level of production end? Regardless of whether the firm begins with production at a low level (such as Q_1) or at a high level (such as Q_2), the firm will eventually adjust production until the quantity produced reaches Q_{MAX}. This analysis shows a general rule for profit maximization: at the profit-maximizing level of output, marginal revenue and marginal cost are exactly equal.

We can now see how the competitive firm decides the quantity of its good to supply to the market. Because a competitive firm is a price taker, its marginal revenue equals the market price. For any given price, the competitive firm's profit-maximizing quantity of output is found by looking at the intersection of

FIGURE 14.2

Marginal Cost as the Competitive Firm's Supply Curve

An increase in the price from P$_1$ to P$_2$ leads to an increase in the firm's profit-maximizing quantity from Q$_1$ to Q$_2$. Because the marginal cost curve shows the quantity supplied by the firm at any given price, it is the firm's supply curve.

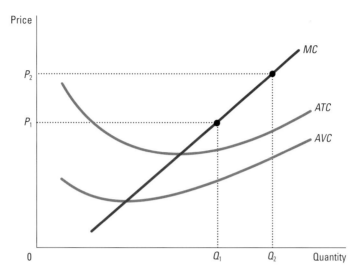

the price with the marginal cost curve. In Figure 14.1, that quantity of output is Q_{MAX}.

Figure 14.2 shows how a competitive firm responds to an increase in the price which may have been caused by a change in global market conditions. Remember that competitive firms are price takers and have to accept the market price for their product. Prices of commodities such as grain, metals, sugar, cotton, coffee, pork bellies, oil and so on are set by organized international markets and so the individual firm has no power to influence price. When the price is P_1, the firm produces quantity Q_1, the quantity that equates marginal cost to the price. Assume that an outbreak of bovine spongiform encephalopathy (BSE) results in the need to slaughter a large proportion of dairy cattle and as a result there is a shortage of milk on the market. When the price rises to P_2, the firm finds that marginal revenue is now higher than marginal cost at the previous level of output, so the firm increases production. The new profit-maximizing quantity is Q_2, at which marginal cost equals the new higher price. In essence, because the firm's marginal cost curve determines the quantity of the good the firm is willing to supply at any price, it is the competitive firm's supply curve.

The Firm's Short-Run Decision to Shut Down

So far we have been analysing the question of how much a competitive firm will produce. In some circumstances, however, the firm will decide to shut down and not produce anything at all.

Here we should distinguish between a temporary shutdown of a firm and the permanent exit of a firm from the market. A *shutdown* refers to a short-run decision not to produce anything during a specific period of time because of current market conditions. *Exit* refers to a long-run decision to leave the market. The short-run and long-run decisions differ because most firms cannot avoid their fixed costs in the short run but can do so in the long run. That is, a firm that shuts down temporarily still has to pay its fixed costs, whereas a firm that exits the market saves both its fixed and its variable costs.

For example, consider the production decision that a farmer faces. The cost of the land is one of the farmer's fixed costs. If the farmer decides not to produce any crops one season, the land lies fallow, and he cannot recover this cost. When making the short-run decision whether to shut down for a season, the fixed cost of land is said to be a *sunk cost.* By contrast, if the farmer decides to leave farming altogether, he can sell the land. When making the long-run decision whether to exit the market, the cost of land is not sunk. (We return to the issue of sunk costs shortly.)

Now let's consider what determines a firm's shutdown decision. If the firm shuts down, it loses all revenue from the sale of its product. At the same time, it saves the variable costs of making its product (but must still pay the fixed costs). Thus, the firm shuts down if the revenue that it would get from producing is less than its variable costs of production; it is simply not worth producing a product which costs more to produce than the revenue generated by its sale. Doing so would reduce profit or make any existing losses even greater.

A little bit of mathematics can make this shutdown criterion more useful. If TR stands for total revenue and VC stands for variable costs, then the firm's decision can be written as:

$$\text{Shut down if } TR < VC$$

The firm shuts down if total revenue is less than variable cost. By dividing both sides of this inequality by the quantity Q, we can write it as:

$$\text{Shut down if } TR/Q < VC/Q$$

Notice that this can be further simplified. TR/Q is total revenue divided by quantity, which is average revenue. As we discussed previously, average revenue for any firm is simply the good's price P. Similarly, VC/Q is average variable cost AVC. Therefore, the firm's shutdown criterion is:

$$\text{Shut down if } P < AVC$$

That is, a firm chooses to shut down if the price of the good is less than the average variable cost of production. This criterion is intuitive: when choosing to produce, the firm compares the price it receives for the typical unit to the average variable cost that it must incur to produce the typical unit. If the price doesn't cover the average variable cost, the firm is better off stopping production altogether. The firm can reopen in the future if conditions change so that price exceeds average variable cost.

We now have a full description of a competitive firm's profit-maximizing strategy. If the firm produces anything, it produces the quantity at which marginal cost equals the price of the good. Yet if the price is less than average variable cost at that quantity, the firm is better off shutting down and not producing anything. These results are illustrated in Figure 14.3. The competitive firm's short-run supply curve is the portion of its marginal cost curve that lies above average variable cost.

Spilt Milk and other Sunk Costs

Sometime in your life you have probably been told, 'Don't cry over spilt milk,' or 'Let bygones be bygones.' These adages hold a deep truth about rational decision making. Economists say that a cost is a **sunk cost** when it has already been committed and cannot be recovered. In a sense, a sunk cost is the opposite of an opportunity cost: an opportunity cost is what you have to give up if you choose to do one thing instead of another, whereas a sunk cost cannot be avoided,

sunk cost
a cost that has already been committed and cannot be recovered

FIGURE 14.3

The Competitive Firm's Short-Run Supply Curve

In the short run, the competitive firm's supply curve is its marginal cost curve (MC) above average variable cost (AVC). If the price falls below average variable cost, the firm is better off shutting down.

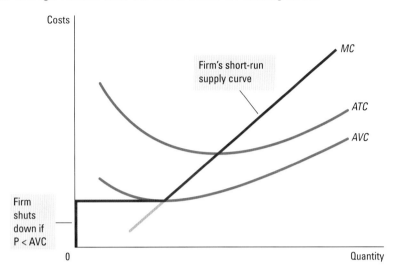

regardless of the choices you make. Because nothing can be done about sunk costs, you can ignore them when making decisions about various aspects of life, including business strategy.

Our analysis of the firm's shutdown decision is one example of the importance of recognizing sunk costs. We assume that the firm cannot recover its fixed costs by temporarily stopping production. As a result, the firm's fixed costs are sunk in the short run, and the firm can safely ignore these costs when deciding how much to produce. The firm's short-run supply curve is the part of the marginal cost curve that lies above average variable cost, and the size of the fixed cost does not matter for this supply decision.

The irrelevance of sunk costs is also important for personal decisions. Imagine, for instance, that you place a €10 value on seeing a newly released film. You buy a ticket for €7, but before entering the cinema you lose the ticket. Should you buy another ticket? Or should you now go home and refuse to pay a total of €14 to see the film? The answer is that you should buy another ticket. The benefit of seeing the film (€10) still exceeds the opportunity cost (the €7 for the second ticket). The €7 you paid for the lost ticket is a sunk cost. As with spilt milk, there is no point in crying about it.

CASE STUDY

Near-empty Restaurants and Off-season Miniature Golf

Have you ever walked into a restaurant for lunch and found it almost empty? Why, you might have asked, does the restaurant even bother to stay open? It might seem that the revenue from the few customers could not possibly cover the cost of running the restaurant.

Staying open can be profitable, even with many tables empty.

In making the decision whether to open for lunch, a restaurant owner must keep in mind the distinction between fixed and variable costs. Many of a restaurant's costs – the rent, kitchen equipment, tables, plates, cutlery and so on – are fixed. Shutting down during lunch would not reduce these costs. In other words, these costs are sunk in the short run. When the owner is deciding whether to serve lunch, only the variable costs – the price of the additional food and the wages of the extra staff – are relevant. The owner shuts down the restaurant at lunchtime only if the revenue from the few lunchtime customers fails to cover the restaurant's variable costs.

An operator of a miniature golf course in a seaside resort faces a similar decision. Because revenue varies substantially from season to season, the firm must decide when to open and when to close. Once again, the fixed costs – the costs of buying the land and building the course – are irrelevant. The miniature golf course should be open for business only during those times of year when its revenue exceeds its variable costs.

The Firm's Long-run Decision to Exit or Enter a Market

The firm's long-run decision to exit the market is similar to its shutdown decision. If the firm exits, it again will lose all revenue from the sale of its product, but now it saves on both fixed and variable costs of production. Thus, the firm exits the market if the revenue it would get from producing is less than its total costs.

We can again make this criterion more useful by writing it mathematically. If TR stands for total revenue and TC stands for total cost, then the firm's criterion can be written as:

$$\text{Exit if } TR < TC$$

The firm exits if total revenue is less than total cost. By dividing both sides of this inequality by quantity Q, we can write it as:

$$\text{Exit if } TR/Q < TC/Q$$

We can simplify this further by noting that TR/Q is average revenue, which equals the price P, and that TC/Q is average total cost ATC. Therefore, the firm's exit criterion is:

$$\text{Exit if } P < ATC$$

That is, a firm chooses to exit if the price of the good is less than the average total cost of production.

A parallel analysis applies to an entrepreneur who is considering starting a firm. The firm will enter the market if such an action would be profitable, which occurs if the price of the good exceeds the average total cost of production. The entry criterion is:

$$\text{Enter if } P > ATC$$

The criterion for entry is exactly the opposite of the criterion for exit.

We can now describe a competitive firm's long-run profit-maximizing strategy. If the firm is in the market, it produces the quantity at which marginal cost equals the price of the good. Yet if the price is less than average total cost at that quantity, the firm chooses to exit (or not enter) the market. These results are illustrated in Figure 14.4. The competitive firm's long-run supply curve is the portion of its marginal cost curve that lies above average total cost.

FIGURE 14.4

The Competitive Firm's Long-Run Supply Curve

In the long run, the competitive firm's supply curve is its marginal cost curve (MC) *above average total cost* (ATC). *If the price falls below average total cost, the firm is better off exiting the market.*

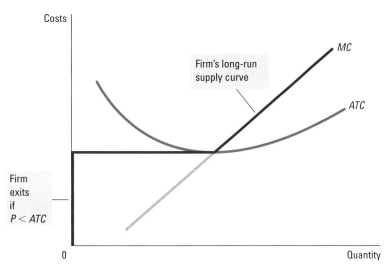

IN THE NEWS

Shutdowns in the Short Run and Long Run

The global economic slowdown of 2008–09 led to many firms having to make difficult decisions about how to respond to falling sales and whether to carry on producing. Many smaller firms were forced to shut down and leave the market but others took different decisions and shut down production operations for a period of time in the hope that economic activity would pick up. This article looks at these two aspects of firms' behaviour.

The economic slowdown left many businesses facing falling sales and thus revenues whilst the opportunity for cutting costs was limited. In the absence of support by the banks due to the credit crunch or only having access to funds at far higher interest rates many firms had to make a painful decision about whether to carry on trading or shut down. Smaller firms tend to face far greater challenges in surviving periods of falling demand than larger firms. Large firms may have large capital assets in the form of buildings, equipment and machinery but in the short run these represent sunk costs and are, therefore, irrelevant to decision-making.

Many smaller firms may be operating at the margin. They are more likely to be in competitive markets and thus have limited opportunities to affect market price and force down supply costs. Many will have been making zero profit and once demand falls and revenue goes down profit levels fall below zero and the firm may have to accept that shut down is the only option and cut its losses; it is better to lose €20 000 than €100 000! In 2008, business failure rates in the UK rose by 30 per cent with 23 879 firms closing over the year. In January 2009, the consultancy and credit checking agency, Experian, reported that 1 418 firms in the UK failed during the month, a 24 per cent fall compared to the same month in 2008. In 2009 the rate of failure continued to slow but the total number of business failures was not expected to peak until 2010.

For larger businesses, the decision may not have been to shut down completely but to cut operations in the short run. An excellent example of this was the motor industry. The European car industry faced a dramatic fall in sales as a result of the recession. In 2010, western European car sales were estimated to be 2.5 million units, a fall of over 60 per cent on the peak of sales in 2007. Particular countries experienced considerable falls in sales. In Iceland car sales fell by 88 per cent in January 2009, in Latvia the fall was 77 per cent and in Ireland, 66 per cent. In Spain car sales fell 41.6 per cent in January 2009 whilst in Italy the fall was 32.6 per cent.

In response to the falling sales a number of the main car manufacturing companies operating in Europe made decisions to shut down production for differing periods from 2008. In the UK,

Honda shut down operations for the four months, February to May 2009; Aston Martin shut down over the holiday period at the end of 2008–2009, Vauxhall shut down for 40 days over the same Christmas and New Year period, and Mini ceased production over February 2009 and for two weeks in August that year.

The situation across the rest of Europe was no different. HIS Global Insight reported that the total lost plant-days in the first quarter of 2009 across Europe as a result of firms shutting down production was 950 which represented 1 368 607 lost production units, around a quarter of total European output. Despite the fact that the European economy seemed to have come out of recession in 2009, the forecasts for 2010 were gloomy. In January 2010 Fiat announced that it was closing its production facilities in Italy for two weeks in February because of poor sales the previous month. General Motors announced that it was going to shut down operations completely at its Antwerp factory in Belgium. The company said that the decision had been taken because it needed to reduce its

capacity by 20 per cent to take account the new market conditions. If it did not shutdown operations at the plant completely its long-term sustainability and the operations at its other European Vauxhall and Opel plants would be compromised, it said.

Whilst the effect on the workers at car manufacturers across Europe was significant with a large number losing their jobs, the total impact on unemployment was less than some analysts had predicted. One of the explanations was that a temporary shutdown of operations might have meant that workers received lower wages but at least they still retained their jobs. For the firms involved, the plant and equipment may be sunk costs but the skills of the workforce represent an investment and those skills would be needed when demand picked up. The cost of making redundancies and then having to recruit new workers in the event of an upturn can be considerable and so it made sense to retain employees, cut costs during the shutdown but save on the costs of having to recruit at a later stage.

Measuring Profit in Our Graph for the Competitive Firm

As we analyse exit and entry, it is useful to be able to analyse the firm's profit in more detail. Recall that profit equals total revenue (TR) minus total cost (TC):

$$\text{Profit} = TR - TC$$

We can rewrite this definition by multiplying and dividing the right-hand side by Q:

$$\text{Profit} = (TR/Q - TC/Q) \times Q$$

But note that TR/Q is average revenue, which is the price P, and TC/Q is average total cost ATC. Therefore:

$$\text{Profit} = (P - ATC) \times Q$$

This way of expressing the firm's profit allows us to measure profit in our graphs.

Panel (a) of Figure 14.5 shows a firm earning positive profit. As we have already discussed, the firm maximizes profit by producing the quantity at which price equals marginal cost. Now look at the shaded rectangle. The height of the rectangle is $P - ATC$, the difference between price and average total cost. The width of the rectangle is Q, the quantity produced. Therefore, the area of the rectangle is $(P - ATC) \times Q$, which is the firm's profit.

FIGURE 14.5

Profit as the Area Between Price and Average Total Cost

The area of the shaded box between price and average total cost represents the firm's profit. The height of this box is price minus average total cost (P − ATC), and the width of the box is the quantity of output (Q). In panel (a), price is above average total cost, so the firm has positive profit. In panel (b), price is less than average total cost, so the firm has losses.

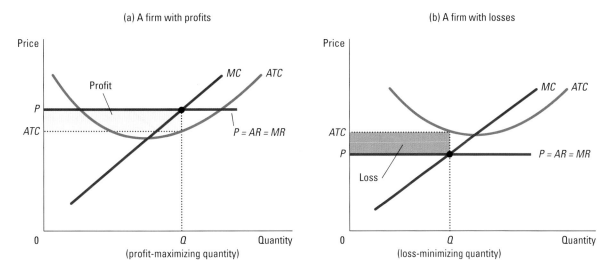

Similarly, panel (b) of this figure shows a firm with losses (negative profit). In this case, maximizing profit means minimizing losses, a task accomplished once again by producing the quantity at which price equals marginal cost. Now consider the shaded rectangle. The height of the rectangle is $ATC − P$, and the width is Q. The area is $(ATC − P) \times Q$, which is the firm's loss. Because a firm in this situation is not making enough revenue to cover its average total cost, the firm would choose to exit the market.

Quick Quiz How does the price faced by a profit-maximizing competitive firm compare to its marginal cost? Explain. • When does a profit-maximizing competitive firm decide to shut down? When does a profit-maximizing competitive firm decide to exit a market?

THE SUPPLY CURVE IN A COMPETITIVE MARKET

Now that we have examined the supply decision of a single firm, we can discuss the supply curve for a market. There are two cases to consider. First, we examine a market with a fixed number of firms. Secondly, we examine a market in which the number of firms can change as old firms exit the market and new firms enter. Both cases are important, for each applies over a specific time horizon. Over short periods of time it is often difficult for firms to enter and exit, so the assumption of a fixed number of firms is appropriate. But over long periods of time, the number of firms can adjust to changing market conditions.

FIGURE 14.6

Market Supply With a Fixed Number of Firms

When the number of firms in the market is fixed, the market supply curve, shown in panel (b), reflects the individual firms' marginal cost curves, shown in panel (a). Here, in a market of 1 000 firms, the quantity of output supplied to the market is 1 000 times the quantity supplied by each firm.

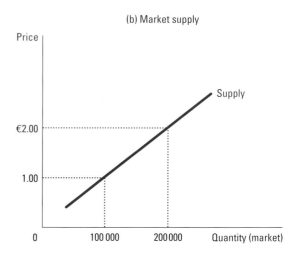

The Short Run: Market Supply with a Fixed Number of Firms

Consider first a market with 1 000 identical firms. For any given price, each firm supplies a quantity of output so that its marginal cost equals the price, as shown in panel (a) of Figure 14.6. That is, as long as price is above average variable cost, each firm's marginal cost curve is its supply curve. The quantity of output supplied to the market equals the sum of the quantities supplied by each of the 1 000 individual firms. Thus, to derive the market supply curve, we add the quantity supplied by each firm in the market. As panel (b) of Figure 14.6 shows, because the firms are identical, the quantity supplied to the market is 1 000 times the quantity supplied by each firm.

The Long Run: Market Supply with Entry and Exit

Now consider what happens if firms are able to enter or exit the market. Let's suppose that everyone has access to the same technology for producing the good and access to the same markets to buy the inputs into production. Therefore, all firms and all potential firms have the same cost curves.

Decisions about entry and exit in a market of this type depend on the incentives facing the owners of existing firms and the entrepreneurs who could start new firms. If firms already in the market are profitable, then new firms will have an incentive to enter the market. This entry will expand the number of firms, increase the quantity of the good supplied, and drive down prices and profits. Conversely, if firms in the market are making losses, then some existing firms will exit the market. Their exit will reduce the number of firms, decrease the quantity of the good supplied, and drive up prices and profits. At the end of this process of entry and exit, firms that remain in the market must be making zero economic profit. Recall that we can write a firm's profits as:

$$\text{Profit} = (P - ATC) \times Q$$

This equation shows that an operating firm has zero profit if and only if the price of the good equals the average total cost of producing that good. If price is above average total cost, profit is positive, which encourages new firms to enter. If price is less than average total cost, profit is negative, which encourages some firms to exit. The process of entry and exit ends only when price and average total cost are driven to equality.

This analysis has a surprising implication. We noted earlier in the chapter that competitive firms produce so that price equals marginal cost. We just noted that free entry and exit forces price to equal average total cost. But if price is to equal both marginal cost and average total cost, these two measures of cost must equal each other. Marginal cost and average total cost are equal, however, only when the firm is operating at the minimum of average total cost. Recall from the preceding chapter that the level of production with lowest average total cost is called the firm's efficient scale. Therefore, the long-run equilibrium of a competitive market with free entry and exit must have firms operating at their efficient scale.

Panel (a) of Figure 14.7 shows a firm in such a long-run equilibrium. In this figure, price P equals marginal cost MC, so the firm is profit-maximizing. Price also equals average total cost ATC, so profits are zero. New firms have no incentive to enter the market, and existing firms have no incentive to leave the market.

From this analysis of firm behaviour, we can determine the long-run supply curve for the market. In a market with free entry and exit, there is only one price consistent with zero profit – the minimum of average total cost. As a result, the long-run market supply curve must be horizontal at this price, as in panel (b) of Figure 14.7. Any price above this level would generate profit, leading to entry

FIGURE 14.7

Market Supply With Entry and Exit

Firms will enter or exit the market until profit is driven to zero. Thus, in the long run, price equals the minimum of average total cost, as shown in panel (a). The number of firms adjusts to ensure that all demand is satisfied at this price. The long-run market supply curve is horizontal at this price, as shown in panel (b).

and an increase in the total quantity supplied. Any price below this level would generate losses, leading to exit and a decrease in the total quantity supplied. Eventually, the number of firms in the market adjusts so that price equals the minimum of average total cost, and there are enough firms to satisfy all the demand at this price.

Why Do Competitive Firms Stay in Business If They Make Zero Profit?

"non-profit-making organization."

At first, it might seem odd that competitive firms earn zero profit in the long run. After all, people start businesses to make a profit. If entry eventually drives profit to zero, there might seem to be little reason to stay in business.

To understand the zero-profit condition more fully, recall that profit equals total revenue minus total cost, and that total cost includes all the opportunity costs of the firm. In particular, total cost includes the opportunity cost of the time and money that the firm owners devote to the business. In the zero-profit equilibrium, the firm's revenue must compensate the owners for the time and money that they expend to keep their business going.

Consider an example. Suppose that a farmer had to invest €1 million to open his farm, which otherwise he could have deposited in a bank to earn €50 000 a year in interest. In addition, he had to give up another job that would have paid him €30 000 a year. Then the farmer's opportunity cost of farming includes both the interest he could have earned and the forgone wages – a total of €80 000. This sum must be calculated as part of the farmer's total costs. In some situations zero profit is referred to as **normal profit** – the minimum amount required to keep factor inputs in their current use. Even if his profit is driven to zero, his revenue from farming compensates him for these opportunity costs.

Keep in mind that accountants and economists measure costs differently. As we discussed in the previous chapter, accountants keep track of explicit costs but usually miss implicit costs. That is, they measure costs that require an outflow of money from the firm, but they fail to include opportunity costs of production that do not involve an outflow of money. As a result, in the zero-profit equilibrium, economic profit is zero, but accounting profit is positive. Our farmer's accountant, for instance, would conclude that the farmer earned an accounting profit of €80 000, which is enough to keep the farmer in business. In the short run as we shall see, profit can be above zero or normal profit which is referred to as **abnormal profit**.

normal profit
the minimum amount required to keep factors of production in their current use

abnormal profit
the profit over and above normal profit

A Shift in Demand in the Short Run and Long Run

Because firms can enter and exit a market in the long run but not in the short run, the response of a market to a change in demand depends on the time horizon. To see this, let's trace the effects of a shift in demand. This analysis will show how a market responds over time, and it will show how entry and exit drive a market to its long-run equilibrium.

Suppose the market for milk begins in long-run equilibrium. Firms are earning zero profit, so price equals the minimum of average total cost. Panel (a) of Figure 14.8 shows the situation. The long-run equilibrium is point A, the quantity sold in the market is Q_1, and the price is P_1.

Now suppose scientists discover that milk has miraculous health benefits. As a result, the demand curve for milk shifts outward from D_1 to D_2, as in panel (b). The short-run equilibrium moves from point A to point B; as a result, the quantity rises from Q_1 to Q_2 and the price rises from P_1 to P_2. All of the existing firms

FIGURE 14.8

An Increase in Demand in the Short Run and Long Run

The market starts in a long-run equilibrium, shown as point A in panel (a). In this equilibrium, each firm makes zero profit, and the price equals the minimum average total cost. Panel (b) shows what happens in the short run when demand rises from D_1 to D_2. The equilibrium goes from point A to point B, price rises from P_1 to P_2, and the quantity sold in the market rises from Q_1 to Q_2. Because price now exceeds average total cost, firms make profits, which over time encourage new firms to enter the market. This entry shifts the short-run supply curve to the right from S_1 to S_2 as shown in panel (c). In the new long-run equilibrium, point C, price has returned to P_1 but the quantity sold has increased to Q_3. Profits are again zero, price is back to the minimum of average total cost, but the market has more firms to satisfy the greater demand.

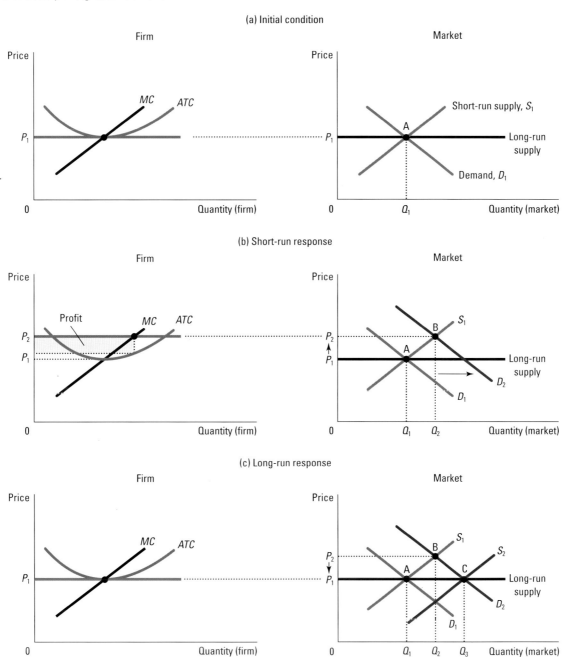

respond to the higher price by raising the amount produced. Because each firm's supply curve reflects its marginal cost curve, how much they each increase production is determined by the marginal cost curve. In the new short-run equilibrium, the price of milk exceeds average total cost, so the firms are making positive profit.

Over time, the profit in this market encourages new firms to enter. Some farmers may switch to milk from other farm products, for example. As the number of firms grows, the short-run supply curve shifts to the right from S_1 to S_2, as in panel (c), and this shift causes the price of milk to fall. Eventually, the price is driven back down to the minimum of average total cost, profits are zero and firms stop entering. Thus, the market reaches a new long-run equilibrium, point C. The price of milk has returned to P_1, but the quantity produced has risen to Q_3. Each firm is again producing at its efficient scale, but because more firms are in the dairy business, the quantity of milk produced and sold is higher.

Why the Long-Run Supply Curve Might Slope Upward

So far we have seen that entry and exit can cause the long-run market supply curve to be horizontal. The essence of our analysis is that there are a large number of potential entrants, each of which faces the same costs. As a result, the long-run market supply curve is horizontal at the minimum of average total cost. When the demand for the good increases, the long-run result is an increase in the number of firms and in the total quantity supplied, without any change in the price.

There are, however, two reasons that the long-run market supply curve might slope upward. The first is that some resources used in production may be available only in limited quantities. For example, consider the market for farm products. Anyone can choose to buy land and start a farm, but the quantity and quality of land is limited. As more people become farmers, the price of farmland is bid up, which raises the costs of all farmers in the market. Thus, an increase in demand for farm products cannot induce an increase in quantity supplied without also inducing a rise in farmers' costs, which in turn means a rise in price. The result is a long-run market supply curve that is upward sloping, even with free entry into farming.

A second reason for an upward sloping supply curve is that firms may have different costs. For example, consider the market for painters. Anyone can enter the market for painting services, but not everyone has the same costs. Costs vary in part because some people work faster than others, use different materials and equipment and because some people have better alternative uses of their time than others. For any given price, those with lower costs are more likely to enter than those with higher costs. To increase the quantity of painting services supplied, additional entrants must be encouraged to enter the market. Because these new entrants have higher costs, the price must rise to make entry profitable for them. Thus, the market supply curve for painting services slopes upward even with free entry into the market.

Notice that if firms have different costs, some firms earn profit even in the long run. In this case, the price in the market reflects the average total cost of the *marginal firm* – the firm that would exit the market if the price were any lower. This firm earns zero profit, but firms with lower costs earn positive profit. Entry does not eliminate this profit because would-be entrants have higher costs than firms already in the market. Higher-cost firms will enter only if the price rises, making the market profitable for them.

Thus, for these two reasons, the long-run supply curve in a market may be upward sloping rather than horizontal, indicating that a higher price is necessary to induce a larger quantity supplied. Nevertheless, the basic lesson about entry and exit remains true. Because firms can enter and exit more easily in the long run than in the short run, the long-run supply curve is typically more elastic than the short-run supply curve.

Quick Quiz In the long run with free entry and exit, is the price in a market equal to marginal cost, average total cost, both, or neither? Explain with a diagram.

CONCLUSION: BEHIND THE SUPPLY CURVE

We have been discussing the behaviour of competitive profit-maximizing firms. You may recall from Chapter 1 that one of the *Ten Principles of Economics* is that rational people think at the margin. This chapter has applied this idea to the competitive firm. Marginal analysis has given us a theory of the supply curve in a competitive market and, as a result, a deeper understanding of market outcomes.

We have learned that when you buy a good from a firm in a competitive market, you can be assured that the price you pay is close to the cost of producing that good. In particular, if firms are competitive and profit-maximizing, the price of a good equals the marginal cost of making that good. In addition, if firms can freely enter and exit the market, the price also equals the lowest possible average total cost of production.

Although we have assumed throughout this chapter that firms are price takers, many of the tools developed here are also useful for studying firms in less competitive markets. In the next chapter we will examine the behaviour of firms with market power. Marginal analysis will again be useful in analysing these firms, but it will have quite different implications.

SUMMARY

- Because a competitive firm is a price taker, its revenue is proportional to the amount of output it produces. The price of the good equals both the firm's average revenue and its marginal revenue.

- To maximize profit, a firm chooses a quantity of output such that marginal revenue equals marginal cost. Because marginal revenue for a competitive firm equals the market price, the firm chooses quantity so that price equals marginal cost. Thus, the firm's marginal cost curve is its supply curve.

- In the short run when a firm cannot recover its fixed costs, the firm will choose to shut down temporarily if the price of the good is less than average variable cost. In the long run when the firm can recover both fixed and variable

costs, it will choose to exit if the price is less than average total cost.

- In a market with free entry and exit, profits are driven to zero in the long run. In this long-run equilibrium, all firms produce at the efficient scale, price equals the minimum of average total cost, and the number of firms adjusts to satisfy the quantity demanded at this price.

- Changes in demand have different effects over different time horizons. In the short run, an increase in demand raises prices and leads to profits, and a decrease in demand lowers prices and leads to losses. But if firms can freely enter and exit the market, then in the long run the number of firms adjusts to drive the market back to the zero-profit equilibrium.

KEY CONCEPTS

average revenue, p. 290
marginal revenue, p. 290

sunk cost, p. 294
normal profit, p. 302

abnormal profit, p. 302

QUESTIONS FOR REVIEW

1. What is meant by a competitive firm?

2. Draw the cost curves for a typical firm. For a given price, explain how the firm chooses the level of output that maximizes profit.

3. Under what conditions will a firm shut down temporarily? Explain.

4. Under what conditions will a firm exit a market? Explain.

5. Does a firm's price equal marginal cost in the short run, in the long run, or both? Explain.

6. Does a firm's price equal the minimum of average total cost in the short run, in the long run, or both? Explain.

7. Are market supply curves typically more elastic in the short run or in the long run? Explain.

PROBLEMS AND APPLICATIONS

1. What are the characteristics of a competitive market? Which of the following drinks do you think is best described by these characteristics? Why aren't the others?
   a. tap water
   b. bottled water
   c. cola
   d. beer.

2. Your flatmate's long hours in the chemistry lab finally paid off – she discovered a secret formula that lets people do an hour's worth of studying in 5 minutes. So far, she's sold 200 doses, and faces the following average total cost schedule:

Q	Average total cost
199	€199
200	200
201	201

   If a new customer offers to pay your flatmate €300 for one dose, should she make one more? Explain.

3. The liquorice industry is competitive. Each firm produces 2 million liquorice bootlaces per year. The bootlaces have an average total cost of €0.20 each, and they sell for €0.30.
   a. What is the marginal cost of a liquorice bootlace?

   b. Is this industry in long-run equilibrium? Why or why not?

4. You go out to the best restaurant in town and order a steak tartar dinner for €40. After eating half of the steak tartar, you realize that you are quite full. Your date wants you to finish your dinner, because you can't take it home and because 'you've already paid for it.' What should you do? Relate your answer to the material in this chapter.

5. Alejandro's lawn-mowing service is a profit-maximizing, competitive firm. Alejandro mows lawns for €27 each. His total cost each day is €280, of which €30 is a fixed cost. He mows 10 lawns a day. What can you say about Alejandro's short-run decision regarding shutdown and his long-run decision regarding exit?

6. Consider total cost and total revenue given in the table below:

Quantity	0	1	2	3	4	5	6	7
Total cost	€8	€9	€10	€11	€13	€19	€27	€37
Total revenue	0	8	16	24	32	40	48	56

   a. Calculate profit for each quantity. How much should the firm produce to maximize profit?

   b. Calculate marginal revenue and marginal cost for each quantity. Graph them. (Hint: put the points between whole numbers. For example, the marginal cost between 2 and 3 should be graphed at 2½.) At what quantity do these curves cross? How does this relate to your answer to part (a)?

c. Can you tell whether this firm is in a competitive industry? If so, can you tell whether the industry is in long-run equilibrium?

7. 'High prices traditionally cause expansion in an industry, eventually bringing an end to high prices and manufacturers' prosperity.' Explain, using appropriate diagrams.

8. Suppose the book-printing industry is competitive and begins in long-run equilibrium.
   a. Draw a diagram describing the typical firm in the industry.
   b. Hi-Tech Printing Company invents a new process that sharply reduces the cost of printing books. What happens to Hi-Tech's profits and the price of books in the short run when Hi-Tech's patent prevents other firms from using the new technology?
   c. What happens in the long run when the patent expires and other firms are free to use the technology?

9. Many small boats are made of fibreglass, which is derived from crude oil. Suppose that the price of oil rises.
   a. Using diagrams, show what happens to the cost curves of an individual boat-making firm and to the market supply curve.
   b. What happens to the profits of boat makers in the short run? What happens to the number of boat makers in the long run?

10. Suppose that the European Union textile industry is competitive, and there is no international trade in textiles. In long-run equilibrium, the price per unit of cloth is €30.
    a. Describe the equilibrium using graphs for the entire market and for an individual producer.
       Now suppose that textile producers in non-EU countries are willing to sell large quantities of cloth in the EU for only €25 per unit.
    b. Assuming that EU textile producers have large fixed costs, what is the short-run effect of these imports on the quantity produced by an individual producer? What is the short-run effect on profits? Illustrate your answer with a graph.
    c. What is the long-run effect on the number of EU firms in the industry?

11. Assume that the gold-mining industry is competitive.
    a. Illustrate a long-run equilibrium using diagrams for the gold market and for a representative gold mine.
    b. Suppose that an increase in jewellery demand induces a surge in the demand for gold. Using your diagrams from part (a), show what happens in the short run to the gold market and to each existing gold mine.
    c. If the demand for gold remains high, what would happen to the price over time? Specifically, would the new long-run equilibrium price be above, below or equal to the short-run equilibrium price in part (b)? Is it possible for the new long-run equilibrium price to be above the original long-run equilibrium price? Explain.

For further resources, visit
www.cengage.com/mankiw_taylor2

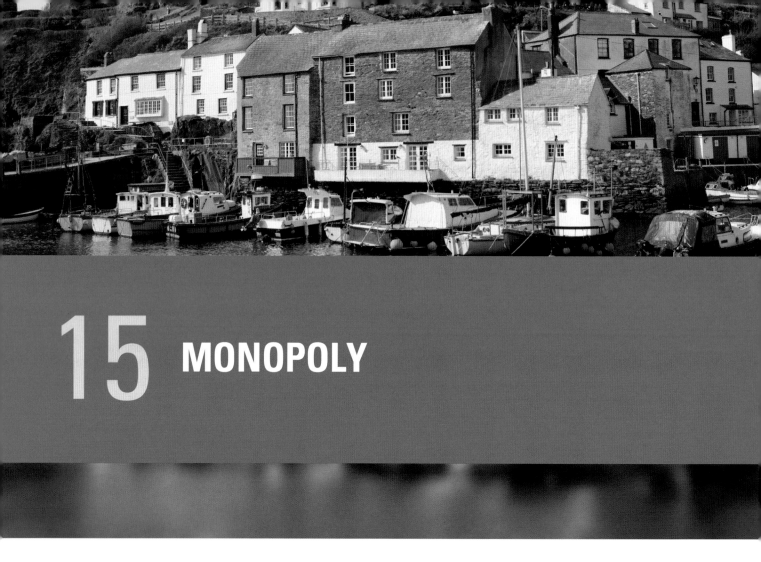

15 MONOPOLY

If you own a personal computer, it probably uses some version of Windows, the operating system sold by the US company, Microsoft Corporation. When Microsoft first designed Windows many years ago, it applied for and received a copyright, first from the US government and then from many of the governments of the world. The copyright gives Microsoft the exclusive right to make and sell copies of the Windows operating system. So if a person wants to buy a copy of Windows, he or she has little choice but to give Microsoft the price that the firm has decided to charge for its product. Windows is the operating system used by over 90 per cent of the PCs in the world (see Figure 15.1). Microsoft is said to have a *monopoly* in the market for Windows.

Microsoft's business decisions are not well described by the model of firm behaviour we developed in the previous chapter. In that chapter we analysed competitive markets in which there are many firms offering essentially identical products, so each firm has little influence over the price it receives. By contrast, a monopoly such as Microsoft has no close competitors and, therefore, can influence the market price of its product. While a competitive firm is a *price taker*, a monopoly firm is a *price maker*.

In this chapter we examine the implications of this market power. We will see that market power alters the relationship between a firm's costs and the price at which it sells its product to the market. A competitive firm takes the price of its output as given by the market and then chooses the quantity it will supply so that price equals marginal cost. By contrast, the price charged by a monopoly exceeds marginal cost. This result is clearly true in the case of Microsoft's Windows. The marginal cost of Windows – the extra cost that Microsoft would

FIGURE 15.1

Computer Operating Systems

A pie chart showing operating system market share; it is clear from the chart that Microsoft's Windows has a majority of the market and can be considered as having considerable monopoly power.

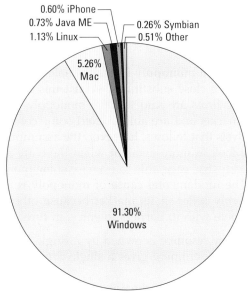

0.60% iPhone
0.73% Java ME — 0.26% Symbian
1.13% Linux — 0.51% Other

5.26% Mac

91.30% Windows

Source: © 2010 http://www.netapplications.com

incur by printing one more copy of the program onto a CD – is only a few euros. The market price of Windows is many times marginal cost.

It is perhaps not surprising that monopolies charge relatively high prices for their products. Customers of monopolies might seem to have little choice but to pay whatever the monopoly charges. But, if so, why is a copy of Windows priced at about €50 and not €500? Or €5 000? The reason, of course, is that if Microsoft set the price that high, fewer people would buy the product. People would buy fewer computers, switch to other operating systems or make illegal copies. Monopolies cannot achieve any level of profit they want because high prices reduce the amount that their customers buy. Although monopolies can control the prices of their goods, their profits are not unlimited.

As we examine the production and pricing decisions of monopolies, we also consider the implications of monopoly for society as a whole. Monopoly firms, like competitive firms, aim to maximize profit. But this goal has very different ramifications for competitive and monopoly firms. As we first saw in Chapter 7, self-interested buyers and sellers in competitive markets are unwittingly led by an invisible hand to promote general economic well-being. By contrast, because monopoly firms are unchecked by competition, the outcome in a market with a monopoly is often not in the best interest of society.

One of the *Ten Principles of Economics* in Chapter 1 is that governments can sometimes improve market outcomes. The analysis in this chapter will shed more light on this principle. As we examine the problems that monopolies raise for society, we will also discuss the various ways in which government policy makers might respond to these problems. The Competition Commission in Europe has been keeping a close eye on Microsoft for some years. Microsoft was accused of preventing fair competition because it bundled its web browser, Internet Explorer (IE), with its Windows operating system (this is known as 'tying'). Companies have complained about the way in which Microsoft allegedly makes it more difficult for other browsers to be interoperable – that is, work within a range of other platforms. The Commission imposed a fine of $1.4 billion in 2008 on Microsoft for breaching EU competition rules. As part of that investigation, the EU insisted that Microsoft made more of its code available to other software manufacturers to ensure greater interoperability. Microsoft had argued that such a move would compromise its security and that the code constituted sensitive commercial information.

WHY MONOPOLIES ARISE

monopoly
a firm that is the sole seller of a product without close substitutes

A firm is a **monopoly** if it is the sole seller of its product and if its product does not have close substitutes. Whilst this is the strict definition of a monopoly, in reality firms are said to have monopoly power if they are a dominant seller in the market and are able to exert some control over the market as a result. In the analysis that follows, however, the assumption is that there is only one seller. We will look in more detail at when there are a small number of dominant firms in an industry, each able to exercise some monopoly power, in Chapter 17.

The fundamental cause of monopoly is *barriers to entry:* a monopoly remains the only seller in its market because other firms cannot enter the market and compete with it. Barriers to entry, in turn, have four main sources:

- A key resource is owned by a single firm.
- The government gives a single firm the exclusive right to produce some good or service.
- The costs of production make a single producer more efficient than a large number of producers.
- A firm is able to gain control of other firms in the market and thus grow in size.

Let's briefly discuss each of these.

Monopoly Resources

The simplest way for a monopoly to arise is for a single firm to own a key resource. For example, consider the market for water in a small town on a remote Scottish island not served by the water company from the mainland. If dozens of town residents on the island have working wells, the competitive model discussed in the preceding chapter describes the behaviour of sellers. As a result, the price of a litre of water is driven to equal the marginal cost of pumping an extra litre. But if there is only one well in town and it is impossible to get water from anywhere else, then the owner of the well has a monopoly on water. Not surprisingly, the monopolist has much greater market power than any single firm in a competitive market. In the case of a necessity like water, the monopolist could command quite a high price, even if the marginal cost is low.

Although exclusive ownership of a key resource is a potential cause of monopoly, in practice monopolies rarely arise for this reason. Actual economies are large, and resources are owned by many people. Indeed, because many goods are traded internationally, the natural scope of their markets is often worldwide. There are, therefore, few examples of firms that own a resource for which there are no close substitutes.

Government-created Monopolies

In many cases, monopolies arise because the government has given one person or firm the exclusive right to sell some good or service. Sometimes the monopoly arises from the sheer political clout of the would-be monopolist. European kings, for example, once granted exclusive business licences to their friends and allies in order to raise money – a highly prized monopoly being the exclusive right to sell and distribute salt in a particular region of Europe. Even today, governments sometimes grant a monopoly (perhaps even to itself) because doing so is viewed to be in the public interest. In Sweden, for example, the retailing of alcoholic beverages is carried out under a state-owned monopoly known as the Systembolaget, because the Swedish government deems it to be in the interests of public health to be able to control directly the sale of alcohol. As a member of the EU, questions have been raised about this policy but Sweden seems keen to maintain its control of alcohol sales. In a recent study commissioned by the Swedish National Institute for Public Health, researchers concluded that if retail alcohol sales were privatized, the net effects on the country would be negative with an increase in alcohol related illness and deaths, fatal accidents, suicides and homicides and a large increase in the number of working days lost to sickness.[1]

The patent and copyright laws are two important examples of how the government creates a monopoly to serve the public interest. When a pharmaceutical company discovers a new drug, it can apply to the government for a patent. If the government deems the drug to be truly original, it approves the patent, which gives the company the exclusive right to manufacture and sell the drug for a fixed number of years – often 20 years. Similarly, when a novelist finishes a book, he can copyright it. The copyright is a government guarantee that no one can print and sell the work without the author's permission. The copyright makes the novelist a monopolist in the sale of his novel.

The effects of patent and copyright laws are easy to see. Because these laws give one producer a monopoly, they lead to higher prices than would occur under competition. But by allowing these monopoly producers to charge higher prices and earn higher profits, the laws also encourage some desirable behaviour. Drug companies are allowed to be monopolists in the drugs they discover in order to encourage research. Authors are allowed to be monopolists in the sale of their books to encourage them to write more and better books.

Thus, the laws governing patents and copyrights have benefits and costs. The benefits of the patent and copyright laws are the increased incentive for creative activity. These benefits are offset, to some extent, by the costs of monopoly pricing, which we examine fully later in this chapter.

Natural Monopolies

An industry is a **natural monopoly** when a single firm can supply a good or service to an entire market at a lower cost than could two or more firms. A natural monopoly arises when there are economies of scale over the relevant range of output. Figure 15.2 shows the average total costs of a firm with economies of scale. In this case, a single firm can produce any amount of output at least cost. That is, for any given amount of output, a larger number of firms leads to less output per firm and higher average total cost.

An example of a natural monopoly is the distribution of water. To provide water to residents of a town, a firm must build a network of pipes throughout the town. If two or more firms were to compete in the provision of this service, each firm would have to pay the fixed cost of building a network. Thus, the average total cost of water is lowest if a single firm serves the entire market.

We saw other examples of natural monopolies when we discussed public goods and common resources in Chapter 11. We noted in passing that some goods in the economy are excludable but not rival. An example is a bridge used

natural monopoly
a monopoly that arises because a single firm can supply a good or service to an entire market at a smaller cost than could two or more firms

[1]Holder, H. (Ed) (2007) *If retail alcohol sales in Sweden were privatized, what would be the potential consequences?* http://www.systembolagetkampanj.se/forskarrapport_en/downloads/Hela_rapporten.pdf

FIGURE 15.2

Economies of Scale as a Cause of Monopoly

When a firm's average total cost curve continually declines, the firm has what is called a natural monopoly. In this case, when production is divided among more firms, each firm produces less, and average total cost rises. As a result, a single firm can produce any given amount at the smallest cost.

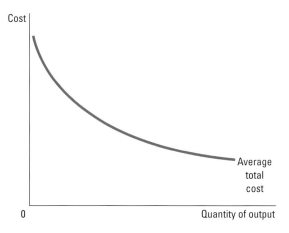

so infrequently that it is never congested. The bridge is excludable because a toll collector can prevent someone from using it. The bridge is not rival because use of the bridge by one person does not diminish the ability of others to use it. Because there is a fixed cost of building the bridge and a negligible marginal cost of additional users, the average total cost of a trip across the bridge (the total cost divided by the number of trips) falls as the number of trips rises. Hence, the bridge is a natural monopoly.

When a firm is a natural monopoly, it is less concerned about new entrants eroding its monopoly power. Normally, a firm has trouble maintaining a monopoly position without ownership of a key resource or protection from the government. The monopolist's profit attracts entrants into the market, and these entrants make the market more competitive. By contrast, entering a market in which another firm has a natural monopoly is unattractive. Would-be entrants know that they cannot achieve the same low costs that the monopolist enjoys because, after entry, each firm would have a smaller piece of the market.

In some cases, the size of the market is one determinant of whether an industry is a natural monopoly. Again, consider a bridge across a river. When the population is small, the bridge may be a natural monopoly. A single bridge can satisfy the entire demand for trips across the river at lowest cost. Yet as the population grows and the bridge becomes congested, satisfying the entire demand may require two or more bridges across the same river. Thus, as a market expands, a natural monopoly can evolve into a competitive market.

External Growth

Many of the largest firms in the world have grown partly through acquisition, merger or takeover of other firms. As they do so, the industry becomes more concentrated; there are fewer firms in the industry. One effect of this is that a firm might be able to develop monopoly power over its rivals and erect barriers to entry to make it harder for new firms to enter. It is for this reason that governments monitor such acquisitions to see if there are implications for competition. In the UK, for example, any merger that gives a firm 25 per cent or more of the market may be investigated to see if the acquisition is in the public interest.

Quick Quiz What are the four reasons that a market might have a monopoly? • Give three examples of monopolies, and explain the reason for each.

HOW MONOPOLIES MAKE PRODUCTION AND PRICING DECISIONS

Now that we know how monopolies arise, we can consider how a monopoly firm decides how much of its product to make and what price to charge for it. The analysis of monopoly behaviour in this section is the starting point for evaluating whether monopolies are desirable and what policies the government might pursue in monopoly markets.

Monopoly versus Competition

The key difference between a competitive firm and a monopoly is the monopoly's ability to influence the price of its output. A competitive firm is small relative to the market in which it operates and, therefore, takes the price of its output as given by market conditions. By contrast, because a monopoly is the sole producer in its market, it can alter the price of its good by adjusting the quantity it supplies to the market.

One way to view this difference between a competitive firm and a monopoly is to consider the demand curve that each firm faces. When we analysed profit maximization by competitive firms in the preceding chapter, we drew the market price as a horizontal line. Because a competitive firm can sell as much or as little as it wants at this price, the competitive firm faces a horizontal demand curve, as in panel (a) of Figure 15.3. In effect, because the competitive firm sells a product with many perfect substitutes (the products of all the other firms in its market), the demand curve that any one firm faces is perfectly elastic.

By contrast, because a monopoly is the sole producer in its market, its demand curve is the market demand curve. Thus, the monopolist's demand curve slopes downward for all the usual reasons, as in panel (b) of Figure 15.3. If the monopolist raises the price of its good, consumers buy less of it. Looked at another way, if the monopolist reduces the quantity of output it sells, the price of its output increases.

The market demand curve provides a constraint on a monopoly's ability to profit from its market power. A monopolist would prefer, if it were possible, to charge a high price and sell a large quantity at that high price. The market demand curve makes that outcome impossible. In particular, the market demand curve describes the combinations of price and quantity that are available to a monopoly firm. By adjusting the quantity produced (or, equivalently, the price charged), the monopolist can choose any point on the demand curve, but it cannot choose a point off the demand curve.

What point on the demand curve will the monopolist choose? As with competitive firms, we assume that the monopolist's goal is to maximize profit.

FIGURE 15.3

Demand Curves for Competitive and Monopoly Firms

Because competitive firms are price takers, they in effect face horizontal demand curves, as in panel (a). Because a monopoly firm is the sole producer in its market, it faces the downward sloping market demand curve, as in panel (b). As a result, the monopoly has to accept a lower price if it wants to sell more output.

Because the firm's profit is total revenue minus total costs, our next task in explaining monopoly behaviour is to examine a monopolist's revenue.

A Monopoly's Revenue

Consider a town with a single producer of water. Table 15.1 shows how the monopoly's revenue might depend on the amount of water produced.

The first two columns show the monopolist's demand schedule. If the monopolist produces just 1 litre of water, it can sell that litre for €1. If it produces 2 litres, it must lower the price to €0.90 in order to sell both litres. And if it produces 3 litres, it must lower the price to €0.80, and so on. If you graphed these two columns of numbers, you would get a typical downward sloping demand curve.

The third column of the table presents the monopolist's *total revenue*. It equals the quantity sold (from the first column) times the price (from the second column). The fourth column computes the firm's *average revenue*, the amount of revenue the firm receives per unit sold. We compute average revenue by taking the number for total revenue in the third column and dividing it by the quantity of output in the first column. As we discussed in the previous chapter, average revenue always equals the price of the good. This is true for monopolists as well as for competitive firms.

The last column of Table 15.1 computes the firm's *marginal revenue*, the amount of revenue that the firm receives for each additional unit of output. We compute marginal revenue by taking the change in total revenue when output increases by 1 unit. For example, when the firm is producing 3 litres of water it receives total revenue of €2.40. Raising production to 4 litres increases total revenue to €2.80. Thus, marginal revenue is €2.80 minus €2.40, or €0.40.

Table 15.1 shows a result that is important for understanding monopoly behaviour: a monopolist's marginal revenue is always less than the price of its good. For example, if the firm raises production of water from 3 to 4 litres, it will increase total revenue by only €0.40, even though it will be able to sell each litre for €0.70. For a monopoly, marginal revenue is lower than price because a monopoly faces a downward sloping demand curve. To increase the amount sold, a monopoly firm must lower the price of its good. Hence, to sell the fourth litre of water, the monopolist must get less revenue for each of the first three litres.

TABLE 15.1

A Monopoly's Total, Average and Marginal Revenue

Quantity of water	Price	Total revenue	Average revenue	Marginal revenue
(Q)	(P)	$(TR = P \times Q)$	$(AR = TR/Q)$	$(MR = \Delta TR/\Delta Q)$
0 litres	€1.1	€0	–	
1	1.0	1.0	€1	€1
2	0.9	1.8	0.9	0.8
3	0.8	2.4	0.8	0.6
4	0.7	2.8	0.7	0.4
5	0.6	3.0	0.6	0.2
6	0.5	3.0	0.5	0
7	0.4	2.8	0.4	−0.2
8	0.3	2.4	0.3	−0.4

Marginal revenue for monopolies is very different from marginal revenue for competitive firms. When a monopoly increases the amount it sells, it has two effects on total revenue ($P \times Q$):

- *The output effect.* More output is sold, so Q is higher, which tends to increase total revenue.
- *The price effect.* The price falls, so P is lower, which tends to decrease total revenue.

Because a competitive firm can sell all it wants at the market price, there is no price effect. When it increases production by 1 unit, it receives the market price for that unit, and it does not receive any less for the units it was already selling. That is, because the competitive firm is a price taker, its marginal revenue equals the price of its good. By contrast, when a monopoly increases production by 1 unit, it must reduce the price it charges for every unit it sells, and this cut in price reduces revenue on the units it was already selling. As a result, a monopoly's marginal revenue is less than its price.

Figure 15.4 graphs the demand curve and the marginal revenue curve for a monopoly firm. (Because the firm's price equals its average revenue, the demand curve is also the average-revenue curve.) These two curves always start at the same point on the vertical axis because the marginal revenue of the first unit sold equals the price of the good. But thereafter, for the reason we just discussed, the monopolist's marginal revenue is less than the price of the good. Thus, a monopoly's marginal revenue curve lies below its demand curve.

You can see in the figure (as well as in Table 15.1) that marginal revenue can even become negative. Marginal revenue is negative when the price effect on revenue is greater than the output effect. In this case, when the firm produces an

FIGURE 15.4

Demand and Marginal Revenue Curves for a Monopoly

The demand curve shows how the quantity affects the price of the good. The marginal revenue curve shows how the firm's revenue changes when the quantity increases by 1 unit. Because the price on all units sold must fall if the monopoly increases production, marginal revenue is always less than the price.

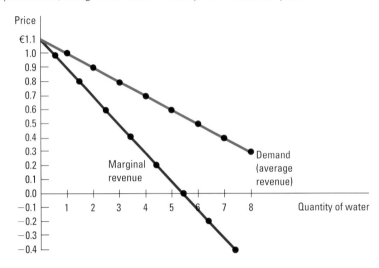

extra unit of output, the price falls by enough to cause the firm's total revenue to decline, even though the firm is selling more units.

Profit Maximization

Now that we have considered the revenue of a monopoly firm, we are ready to examine how such a firm maximizes profit. Recall from Chapter 1 that one of the *Ten Principles of Economics* is that rational people think at the margin. This lesson is as true for monopolists as it is for competitive firms. Here we apply the logic of marginal analysis to the monopolist's decision about how much to produce.

Figure 15.5 graphs the demand curve, the marginal revenue curve and the cost curves for a monopoly firm. All these curves should seem familiar: the demand and marginal revenue curves are like those in Figure 15.4, and the cost curves are like those we encountered in the last two chapters. These curves contain all the information we need to determine the level of output that a profit-maximizing monopolist will choose.

Suppose, first, that the firm is producing at a low level of output, such as Q_1. In this case, marginal cost is less than marginal revenue. If the firm increased production by 1 unit, the additional revenue would exceed the additional costs, and profit would rise. Thus, when marginal cost is less than marginal revenue, the firm can increase profit by producing more units.

A similar argument applies at high levels of output, such as Q_2. In this case, marginal cost is greater than marginal revenue. If the firm reduced production by 1 unit, the costs saved would exceed the revenue lost. Thus, if marginal cost is greater than marginal revenue, the firm can raise profit by reducing production.

In the end, the firm adjusts its level of production until the quantity reaches Q_{MAX}, at which marginal revenue equals marginal cost. Thus, the monopolist's

FIGURE 15.5

Profit Maximization for a Monopoly

A monopoly maximizes profit by choosing the quantity at which marginal revenue equals marginal cost (point A). It then uses the demand curve to find the price that will induce consumers to buy that quantity (point B).

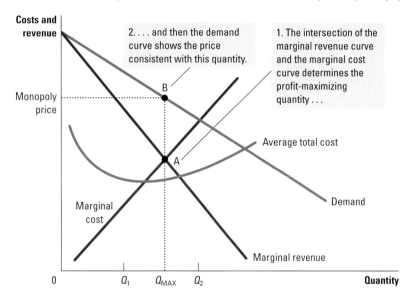

profit-maximizing quantity of output is determined by the intersection of the marginal revenue curve and the marginal cost curve. In Figure 15.5, this intersection occurs at point A.

You might recall from the last chapter that competitive firms also choose the quantity of output at which marginal revenue equals marginal cost. In following this rule for profit maximization, competitive firms and monopolies are alike. But there is also an important difference between these types of firm: the marginal revenue of a competitive firm equals its price, whereas the marginal revenue of a monopoly is less than its price. That is:

$$\text{For a competitive firm : } P = MR = MC$$
$$\text{For a monopoly firm : } P > MR = MC$$

The equality of marginal revenue and marginal cost at the profit-maximizing quantity is the same for both types of firm. What differs is the relationship of the price to marginal revenue and marginal cost.

How does the monopoly find the profit-maximizing price for its product? The demand curve answers this question because the demand curve relates the amount that customers are willing to pay to the quantity sold. Thus, after the monopoly firm chooses the quantity of output that equates marginal revenue and marginal cost, it uses the demand curve to find the price consistent with that quantity. In Figure 15.5, the profit-maximizing price is found at point B.

We can now see a key difference between markets with competitive firms and markets with a monopoly firm: in competitive markets, price equals marginal cost. In monopolized markets, price exceeds marginal cost. As we will see in a moment, this finding is crucial to understanding the social cost of monopoly.

FYI

Why a Monopoly Does Not Have a Supply Curve

You may have noticed that we have analysed the price in a monopoly market using the market demand curve and the firm's cost curves. We have not made any mention of the market supply curve. By contrast, when we analysed prices in competitive markets beginning in Chapter 4, the two most important words were always *supply* and *demand.*

What happened to the supply curve? Although monopoly firms make decisions about what quantity to supply (in the way

described in this chapter), a monopoly does not have a supply curve. A supply curve tells us the quantity that firms choose to supply at any given price. This concept makes sense when we are analysing competitive firms, which are price takers. But a monopoly firm is a price maker, not a price taker. It is not meaningful to ask what such a firm would produce at any price because the firm sets the price at the same time it chooses the quantity to supply.

Indeed, the monopolist's decision about how much to supply is impossible to separate from the demand curve it faces. The shape of the demand curve determines the shape of the marginal revenue curve, which in turn determines the monopolist's profit-maximizing quantity. In a competitive market, supply decisions can be analysed without knowing the demand curve, but that is not true in a monopoly market. Therefore, we never talk about a monopoly's supply curve.

A Monopoly's Profit

How much profit does the monopoly make? To see the monopoly's profit, recall that profit equals total revenue (*TR*) minus total costs (*TC*):

$$\text{Profit} = TR - TC$$

We can rewrite this as:

$$\text{Profit} = (TR/Q - TC/Q) \times Q$$

TR/Q is average revenue, which equals the price *P*, and *TC/Q* is average total cost *ATC*. Therefore:

$$\text{Profit} = (P - ATC) \times Q$$

This equation for profit (which is the same as the profit equation for competitive firms) allows us to measure the monopolist's profit in our graph.

Consider the shaded box in Figure 15.6. The height of the box (the segment BC) is price minus average total cost, $P - ATC$, which is the profit on the typical unit sold. The width of the box (the segment DC) is the quantity sold Q_{MAX}. Therefore, the area of this box is the monopoly firm's total profit.

CASE STUDY

Monopoly Drugs versus Generic Drugs

According to our analysis, prices are determined quite differently in monopolized markets from the way they are in competitive markets. A natural place to test this theory is the market for pharmaceutical drugs, because this market takes on both market structures. When a firm discovers a new drug, patent laws give the firm a monopoly on the sale of that drug. But eventually the

FIGURE 15.6

The Monopolist's Profit

The area of the box BCDE *equals the profit of the monopoly firm. The height of the box* (BC) *is price minus average total cost, which equals profit per unit sold. The width of the box* (DC) *is the number of units sold.*

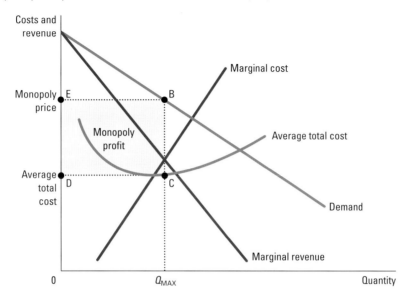

firm's patent runs out, and any company can make and sell the drug. At that time, the market switches from being monopolistic to being competitive.

What should happen to the price of a drug when the patent runs out? Figure 15.7 shows the market for a typical drug. In this figure, the marginal cost of producing the drug is constant. (This is approximately true for many drugs.) During the life of the patent, the monopoly firm maximizes profit by producing the quantity at which marginal revenue equals marginal cost and charging a price well above marginal cost. But when the patent runs out, the profit from making the drug should encourage new firms to enter the market. As the market becomes more competitive, the price should fall to equal marginal cost.

Experience is, in fact, consistent with our theory. When the patent on a drug expires, other companies quickly enter and begin selling so-called generic products that are chemically identical to the former monopolist's brand-name product. And just as our analysis predicts, the price of the competitively produced generic drug is well below the price that the monopolist was charging.

The expiration of a patent, however, does not cause the monopolist to lose all its market power. Some consumers remain loyal to the brand-name drug, perhaps out of fear that the new generic drugs are not actually the same as the drug they have been using for years. As a result, the former monopolist can continue to charge a price somewhat above the price charged by its new competitors.

Quick Quiz   Explain how a monopolist chooses the quantity of output to produce and the price to charge.

FIGURE 15.7

The Market for Drugs

When a patent gives a firm a monopoly over the sale of a drug, the firm charges the monopoly price, which is well above the marginal cost of making the drug. When the patent on a drug runs out, new firms enter the market, making it more competitive. As a result, the price falls from the monopoly price to marginal cost.

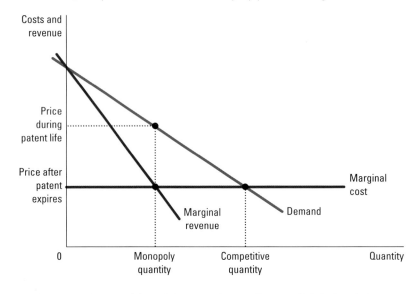

THE WELFARE COST OF MONOPOLY

Is monopoly a good way to organize a market? We have seen that a monopoly, in contrast to a competitive firm, charges a price above marginal cost. From the standpoint of consumers, this high price makes monopoly undesirable. At the same time, however, the monopoly is earning profit from charging this high price. From the standpoint of the owners of the firm, the high price makes monopoly very desirable. Is it possible that the benefits to the firm's owners exceed the costs imposed on consumers, making monopoly desirable from the standpoint of society as a whole?

We can answer this question using the type of analysis we first saw in Chapter 7. As in that chapter, we use total surplus as our measure of economic well-being. Recall that total surplus is the sum of consumer surplus and producer surplus. Consumer surplus is consumers' willingness to pay for a good minus the amount they actually pay for it. Producer surplus is the amount producers receive for a good minus their costs of producing it. In this case, there is a single producer – the monopolist.

You might already be able to guess the result of this analysis. In Chapter 7 we concluded that the equilibrium of supply and demand in a competitive market is not only a natural outcome but a desirable one. In particular, the invisible hand of the market leads to an allocation of resources that makes total surplus as large as it can be. Because a monopoly leads to an allocation of resources different from that in a competitive market, the outcome must, in some way, fail to maximize total economic well-being.

The Deadweight Loss

We begin by considering what the monopoly firm would do if it were run by a benevolent social planner. The social planner cares not only about the profit earned by the firm's owners but also about the benefits received by the firm's consumers. The planner tries to maximize total surplus, which equals producer surplus (profit) plus consumer surplus. Keep in mind that total surplus equals the value of the good to consumers minus the costs of making the good incurred by the monopoly producer.

Figure 15.8 analyses what level of output a benevolent social planner would choose. The demand curve reflects the value of the good to consumers, as measured by their willingness to pay for it. The marginal cost curve reflects the costs of the monopolist. Thus, the socially efficient quantity is found where the demand curve and the marginal cost curve intersect. Below this quantity, the value to consumers exceeds the marginal cost of providing the good, so increasing output would raise total surplus. Above this quantity, the marginal cost exceeds the value to consumers, so decreasing output would raise total surplus.

If the social planner were running the monopoly, the firm could achieve this efficient outcome by charging the price found at the intersection of the demand and marginal cost curves. Thus, like a competitive firm and unlike a profit-maximizing monopoly, a social planner would charge a price equal to marginal

FIGURE 15.8

The Efficient Level of Output

A benevolent social planner who wanted to maximize total surplus in the market would choose the level of output where the demand curve and marginal cost curve intersect. Below this level, the value of the good to the marginal buyer (as reflected in the demand curve) exceeds the marginal cost of making the good. Above this level, the value to the marginal buyer is less than marginal cost.

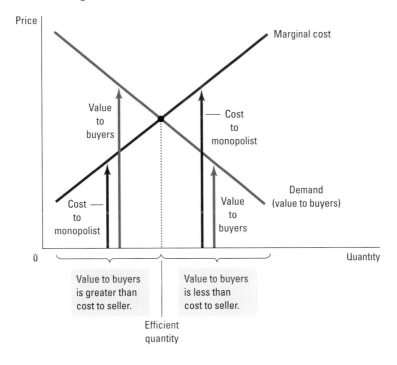

cost. Because this price would give consumers an accurate signal about the cost of producing the good, consumers would buy the efficient quantity.

We can evaluate the welfare effects of monopoly by comparing the level of output that the monopolist chooses to the level of output that a social planner would choose. As we have seen, the monopolist chooses to produce and sell the quantity of output at which the marginal revenue and marginal cost curves intersect; the social planner would choose the quantity at which the demand and marginal cost curves intersect. Figure 15.9 shows the comparison. The monopolist produces less than the socially efficient quantity of output.

We can also view the inefficiency of monopoly in terms of the monopolist's price. Because the market demand curve describes a negative relationship between the price and quantity of the good, a quantity that is inefficiently low is equivalent to a price that is inefficiently high. When a monopolist charges a price above marginal cost, some potential consumers value the good at more than its marginal cost but less than the monopolist's price. These consumers do not end up buying the good. Because the value these consumers place on the good is greater than the cost of providing it to them, this result is inefficient. Thus, monopoly pricing prevents some mutually beneficial trades from taking place.

Just as we measured the inefficiency of taxes with the deadweight loss triangle in Chapter 8, we can similarly measure the inefficiency of monopoly. Figure 15.9 shows the deadweight loss. Recall that the demand curve reflects the value to consumers and the marginal cost curve reflects the costs to the monopoly producer. Thus, the area of the deadweight loss triangle between the demand curve and the marginal cost curve equals the total surplus lost because of monopoly pricing.

The deadweight loss caused by monopoly is similar to the deadweight loss caused by a tax. Indeed, a monopolist is like a private tax collector. As we saw in Chapter 8, a tax on a good places a wedge between consumers' willingness to

FIGURE 15.9

The Inefficiency of Monopoly

Because a monopoly charges a price above marginal cost, not all consumers who value the good at more than its cost buy it. Thus, the quantity produced and sold by a monopoly is below the socially efficient level. The deadweight loss is represented by the area of the triangle between the demand curve (which reflects the value of the good to consumers) and the marginal cost curve (which reflects the costs of the monopoly producer).

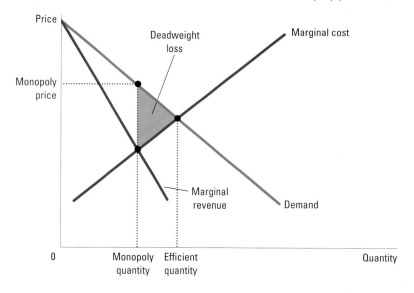

pay (as reflected in the demand curve) and producers' costs (as reflected in the supply curve). Because a monopoly exerts its market power by charging a price above marginal cost, it places a similar wedge. In both cases, the wedge causes the quantity sold to fall short of the social optimum. The difference between the two cases is that the government gets the revenue from a tax, whereas a private firm gets the monopoly profit.

The Monopoly's Profit: A Social Cost?

It is tempting to decry monopolies for 'profiteering' at the expense of the public. And, indeed, a monopoly firm does earn a higher profit by virtue of its market power. According to the economic analysis of monopoly, however, the firm's profit is not in itself necessarily a problem for society.

Welfare in a monopolized market, like all markets, includes the welfare of both consumers and producers. Whenever a consumer pays an extra euro to a producer because of a monopoly price, the consumer is worse off by a euro, and the producer is better off by the same amount. This transfer from the consumers of the good to the owners of the monopoly does not affect the market's total surplus – the sum of consumer and producer surplus. In other words, the monopoly profit itself does not represent a shrinkage in the size of the economic pie; it merely represents a bigger slice for producers and a smaller slice for consumers. Unless consumers are for some reason more deserving than producers – a judgement that goes beyond the realm of economic efficiency – the monopoly profit is not a social problem.

The problem in a monopolized market arises because the firm produces and sells a quantity of output below the level that maximizes total surplus. The deadweight loss measures how much the economic pie shrinks as a result. This inefficiency is connected to the monopoly's high price: consumers buy fewer units when the firm raises its price above marginal cost. But keep in mind that the profit earned on the units that continue to be sold is not the problem. The problem stems from the inefficiently low quantity of output. Put differently, if the high monopoly price did not discourage some consumers from buying the good, it would raise producer surplus by exactly the amount it reduced consumer surplus, leaving total surplus the same as could be achieved by a benevolent social planner.

There is, however, a possible exception to this conclusion. Suppose that a monopoly firm has to incur additional costs to maintain its monopoly position. For example, a firm with a government-created monopoly might need to hire lobbyists to convince lawmakers to continue its monopoly. In this case, the monopoly may use up some of its monopoly profits paying for these additional costs. If so, the social loss from monopoly includes both these costs and the deadweight loss resulting from a price above marginal cost.

Quick Quiz How does a monopolist's quantity of output compare to the quantity of output that maximizes total surplus?

PRICE DISCRIMINATION

So far we have been assuming that the monopoly firm charges the same price to all customers. Yet in many cases firms try to sell the same good to different customers for different prices, even though the costs of producing for the two customers are the same. This practice is called **price discrimination**.

price discrimination
the business practice of selling the same good at different prices to different customers

Before discussing the behaviour of a price-discriminating monopolist, we should note that price discrimination is not possible when a good is sold in a competitive market. In a competitive market, there are many firms selling the same good at the market price. No firm is willing to charge a lower price to any customer because the firm can sell all it wants at the market price. And if any firm tried to charge a higher price to a customer, that customer would buy from another firm. For a firm to price discriminate, it must have some market power.

A Parable about Pricing

To understand why a monopolist would want to price discriminate, let's consider a simple example. Imagine that you are the chief executive officer of Readalot Publishing Company. Readalot's best-selling author has just written her latest novel. To keep things simple, let's imagine that you pay the author a flat €2 million for the exclusive rights to publish the book. Let's also assume – for simplicity – that the cost of printing the book is zero. Readalot's profit, therefore, is the revenue it gets from selling the book minus the €2 million it has paid to the author. Given these assumptions, how would you, as Readalot's CEO, decide what price to charge for the book?

Your first step in setting the price is to estimate what the demand for the book is likely to be. Readalot's marketing department tells you that the book will attract two types of readers. The book will appeal to the author's 100 000 die-hard fans. These fans will be willing to pay as much as €30 for the book. In addition, the book will appeal to about 400 000 less enthusiastic readers who will be willing to pay up to €5 for the book.

What price maximizes Readalot's profit? There are two natural prices to consider: €30 is the highest price Readalot can charge and still get the 100 000 die-hard fans, and €5 is the highest price it can charge and still get the entire market of 500 000 potential readers. It is a matter of simple arithmetic to solve Readalot's problem. At a price of €30, Readalot sells 100 000 copies, has revenue of €3 million, and makes profit of €1 million. At a price of €5, it sells 500 000 copies, has revenue of €2.5 million, and makes profit of €500 000. Thus, Readalot maximizes profit by charging €30 and forgoing the opportunity to sell to the 400 000 less enthusiastic readers.

Notice that Readalot's decision causes a deadweight loss. There are 400 000 readers willing to pay €5 for the book, and the marginal cost of providing it to them is zero. Thus, €2 million of total surplus is lost when Readalot charges the higher price. This deadweight loss is the usual inefficiency that arises whenever a monopolist charges a price above marginal cost.

Now suppose that Readalot's marketing department makes an important discovery: these two groups of readers are in separate markets. All the die-hard fans live in Switzerland and all the other readers live in Turkey. Moreover, it is difficult for readers in one country to buy books in the other. How does this discovery affect Readalot's marketing strategy?

In this case, the company can make even more profit. To the 100 000 Swiss readers, it can charge €30 for the book. To the 400 000 Turkish readers, it can charge €5 for the book (or the Turkish lira equivalent). In this case, revenue is €3 million in Switzerland and €2 million in Turkey, for a total of €5 million. Profit is then €3 million, which is substantially greater than the €1 million the company could earn charging the same €30 price to all customers. Not surprisingly, Readalot chooses to follow this strategy of price discrimination.

Although the story of Readalot Publishing is hypothetical, it describes accurately the business practice of many publishing companies. Textbooks, for example, are often sold at a different price in Europe from in the United States. Even more important is the price differential between hardcover books and paperbacks. When a publisher has a new novel, it initially releases an expensive hardcover edition and later releases a cheaper paperback edition. The difference in price between these two editions far exceeds the difference in printing costs. The publisher's goal is just as in our example. By selling the hardcover to die-hard fans (and libraries) who must have the book as soon as it is published and the paperback to less enthusiastic readers who don't mind waiting, the publisher price discriminates and raises its profit.

The Moral of the Story

Like any parable, the story of Readalot Publishing is stylized. Yet, also like any parable, it teaches some important and general lessons. In this case, there are three lessons to be learned about price discrimination.

The first and most obvious lesson is that price discrimination is a rational strategy for a profit-maximizing monopolist. In other words, by charging different prices to different customers, a monopolist can increase its profit. In essence, a price-discriminating monopolist charges each customer a price closer to his or her willingness to pay than is possible with a single price.

The second lesson is that price discrimination requires the ability to separate customers according to their willingness to pay. In our example, customers were separated geographically. But sometimes monopolists choose other differences, such as age or income, to distinguish among customers. Energy companies are able to discriminate through setting different prices at different times of the day with off-peak usage priced lower than peak time. Similarly, rail companies charge different prices to passengers at certain times of the day with peak travel attracting a much higher price than off-peak travel. Where there is a difference in the price elasticity of demand the monopolist can exploit this and practise price discrimination. Between the hours of 6.00am and 9.30pm on weekday mornings, for example, the price elasticity of demand for rail travel is relatively low whereas between 9.30am and 4.00pm it tends to be relatively high. A higher price can be charged at the peak time but during the off-peak period, the firm may benefit from charging a lower price and encouraging more passengers to travel; the cost of running the train is largely fixed and the marginal cost of carrying an additional passenger is almost zero. Lowering the price, therefore, is a way of utilizing the capacity on the train and adding to profit.

A corollary to this second lesson is that certain market forces can prevent firms from price discriminating. In particular, one such force is *arbitrage,* the process of buying a good in one market at a low price and selling it in another market at a higher price in order to profit from the price difference. In our example, suppose that Swiss bookshops could buy the book in Turkey for €5 and resell it to Swiss readers at a price well below €30. This arbitrage would prevent Readalot from price discriminating because no Swiss resident would buy the book at the higher price. In fact, the increased use of the internet for buying books and other goods through companies like Amazon is likely to affect the ability of companies to price discriminate internationally. Where firms can enforce the division of the market, as in the case of rail fares, it can practise price discrimination. A passenger buying a ticket at off-peak rates is not allowed to travel on a train running during peak periods, and hence arbitrage is circumvented.

The third lesson from our parable is perhaps the most surprising: price discrimination can raise economic welfare. Recall that a deadweight loss arises when Readalot charges a single €30 price, because the 400 000 less enthusiastic readers do not end up with the book, even though they value it at more than its marginal cost of production. By contrast, when Readalot price discriminates, all readers end up with the book, and the outcome is efficient. Thus, price discrimination can eliminate the inefficiency inherent in monopoly pricing.

Note that the increase in welfare from price discrimination shows up as higher producer surplus rather than higher consumer surplus. In our example, consumers are no better off for having bought the book: the price they pay exactly equals the value they place on the book, so they receive no consumer surplus. The entire increase in total surplus from price discrimination accrues to Readalot Publishing in the form of higher profit.

The Analytics of Price Discrimination

Let us consider a little more formally how price discrimination affects economic welfare. We begin by assuming that the monopolist can price discriminate perfectly. *Perfect price discrimination* describes a situation in which the monopolist knows exactly the willingness to pay of each customer and can charge each customer a different price. In this case, the monopolist charges each customer exactly his willingness to pay, and the monopolist gets the entire surplus in every transaction.

Figure 15.10 shows producer and consumer surplus with and without price discrimination. Without price discrimination, the firm charges a single price above marginal cost, as shown in panel (a). Because some potential customers who value the good at more than marginal cost do not buy it at this high price, the monopoly causes a deadweight loss. Yet when a firm can perfectly price discriminate, as shown in panel (b), each customer who values the good at more than marginal cost buys the good and is charged his willingness to pay. All mutually beneficial trades take place, there is no deadweight loss, and the entire

FIGURE 15.10

Welfare With and Without Price Discrimination

Panel (a) shows a monopolist that charges the same price to all customers. Total surplus in this market equals the sum of profit (producer surplus) and consumer surplus. Panel (b) shows a monopolist that can perfectly price discriminate. Because consumer surplus equals zero, total surplus now equals the firm's profit. Comparing these two panels, you can see that perfect price discrimination raises profit, raises total surplus and lowers consumer surplus.

surplus derived from the market goes to the monopoly producer in the form of profit.

In reality, of course, price discrimination is not perfect. Customers do not walk into shops with signs displaying their willingness to pay. Instead, firms price discriminate by dividing customers into groups: young versus old, weekday versus weekend shoppers, Germans versus British, and so on. Unlike those in our parable of Readalot Publishing, customers within each group differ in their willingness to pay for the product, making perfect price discrimination impossible.

How does this imperfect price discrimination affect welfare? The analysis of these pricing schemes is quite complicated, and it turns out that there is no general answer to this question. Compared to the monopoly outcome with a single price, imperfect price discrimination can raise, lower or leave unchanged total surplus in a market. The only certain conclusion is that price discrimination raises the monopoly's profit – otherwise the firm would choose to charge all customers the same price.

Examples of Price Discrimination

Firms use various business strategies aimed at charging different prices to different customers. Now that we understand the economics of price discrimination, let's consider some examples.

Cinema Tickets   Many cinemas charge a lower price for children and senior citizens than for other patrons. This fact is hard to explain in a competitive market. In a competitive market, price equals marginal cost, and the marginal cost of providing a seat for a child or senior citizen is the same as the marginal cost of providing a seat for anyone else. Yet this fact is easily explained if cinemas have some local monopoly power and if children and senior citizens have a lower willingness to pay for a ticket. In this case, cinemas raise their profit by price discriminating.

Airline Prices   Seats on aeroplanes are sold at many different prices. Most airlines charge a lower price for a round-trip ticket between two cities if the traveller stays over a Saturday night. At first this seems odd. Why should it matter to the airline whether a passenger stays over a Saturday night? The reason is that this rule provides a way to separate business travellers and personal travellers. A passenger on a business trip has a high willingness to pay and, most likely, does not want to stay over a Saturday night. By contrast, a passenger travelling for personal reasons has a lower willingness to pay and is more likely to be willing to stay over a Saturday night. Thus, the airlines can successfully price discriminate by charging a lower price for passengers who stay over a Saturday night.

"If we are to reduce prices or leave them the same, may I suggest we raise them first."

Discount Coupons   Many companies offer discount coupons to the public in newspapers and magazines. A buyer simply has to cut out the coupon in order to get €0.50 off his next purchase. Why do companies offer these coupons? Why don't they just cut the price of the product by €0.50?

The answer is that coupons allow companies to price discriminate. Companies know that not all customers are willing to spend the time to cut out coupons. Moreover, the willingness to clip coupons is related to the customer's willingness to pay for the good. A rich and busy executive is unlikely to spend her time cutting discount coupons out of the newspaper, and she is probably willing to pay a higher price for many goods. A person who is unemployed is more likely to clip coupons and has a lower willingness to pay. Thus, by charging a lower price only to those customers who cut out coupons, firms can successfully price discriminate.

Quantity Discounts   So far in our examples of price discrimination the monopolist charges different prices to different customers. Sometimes, however, monopolists price discriminate by charging different prices to the same customer for different units that the customer buys. Traditionally, English bakers would give you an extra cake for nothing if you bought 12. While the quaint custom of the 'baker's dozen' (i.e. 13 for the price of 12) is largely a thing of the past, many firms offer lower prices to customers who buy large quantities. This is a form of price discrimination because the customer effectively pays a higher price for the first unit bought than for last. Quantity discounts are often a successful way of price discriminating because a customer's willingness to pay for an additional unit declines as the customer buys more units.

Quick Quiz   Give two examples of price discrimination. • How does perfect price discrimination affect consumer surplus, producer surplus and total surplus?

PUBLIC POLICY TOWARDS MONOPOLIES

We have seen that monopolies, in contrast to competitive markets, fail to allocate resources efficiently. Monopolies produce less than the socially desirable quantity of output and, as a result, charge prices above marginal cost. Policy makers in the government can respond to the problem of monopoly in one of four ways, by:

- trying to make monopolized industries more competitive
- regulating the behaviour of the monopolies
- turning some private monopolies into public enterprises
- doing nothing at all.

All industrialized countries have some sort of process for legally prohibiting mergers that are against the public interest.

The earliest moves towards using legal remedies to monopoly power were taken in the US in the late 19th and early 20th centuries, forming the basis of legislation that has become known in the US as the anti-trust laws (in the UK and the rest of Europe, anti-trust law and anti-trust policy are more commonly referred to as competition law and competition policy, although usage of both terms is becoming widespread). The first and most important of the US anti-trust laws was the Sherman Anti-trust Act, which the US Congress passed in 1890 to reduce the market power of the large and powerful 'trusts' or companies that were viewed as dominating the economy at the time. The anti-trust laws give the government various ways to promote competition. For example, a proposed merger between two companies which already have substantial market share would be closely examined by the lawyers and economists in the US Department of Justice, who might well decide that the merger would make the industry in question substantially less competitive and, as a result, would reduce the economic well-being of the country as a whole. If so, the Justice Department would challenge the merger in court, and if the judge agreed, the two companies would not be allowed to merge.

Similarly, in Europe, each country has a competition authority. In the UK it is the Competition Commission; in Germany it is the Federal Cartel Office (*Bundeskartellamt*); in 2009 the French Competition Authority began discharging its regulatory powers following reform of competition regulation; and in Italy the Anti-trust

Authority (*Autorità garante della concorrenza e del mercato*) oversees competition issues. National competition authorities such as these cooperate with each other and with the EU Competition Commission through the European Competition Network (ECN). The aim of the network is to coordinate activities and share information to help enforce EU competition law in member states where the opportunities for cross-border business have increased as the EU has developed and expanded.

Whilst each national country can enforce its own competition legislation, these laws have to be in line with overall EU competition legislation. In the UK, for example, the Competition Act 1998 and the Enterprise Act 2002 both deal with competition issues within the UK but cross-border competition cases would be dealt with under EU law. There are well-defined criteria for deciding whether a proposed merger of companies belonging to more than one European Union country is subject to reference exclusively to the European Commission rather than to national authorities, such as the size of the worldwide or European turnover of the companies in question.

Competition legislation covers three main areas.

- Acting against cartels and cases where businesses engage in restrictive business practices which prevent free trade.
- Banning pricing strategies which are anti-competitive such as price fixing, predatory pricing, price gouging and so on, and through behaviour which might lead to a restriction in competition such as the sharing of information or carving up markets between different firms, rigging bids in tender processes or deliberately restricting production to reduce competition. (See Chapter 17 for more on these two areas.)
- Monitoring and supervising acquisitions and joint ventures

The legislation allows competition authorities the right to fine firms who are found guilty of restricting competition, ordering firms to change behaviour and banning proposed acquisitions. The investigation will consider whether the acquisition, regardless of what size company it produces, is in the public interest. This is in recognition of the fact that companies sometimes merge not to reduce competition but to lower costs through more efficient joint production. These benefits from mergers are often called *synergies*.

Clearly, the government must be able to determine which mergers are desirable and which are not. That is, it must be able to measure and compare the social benefit from synergies to the social costs of reduced competition. In the UK, the Director-General of Fair Trading advises the Secretary of State for Business Innovation and Skills (a government minister) on whether or not a particular merger should be referred for investigation by the Competition Commission – an independent body with members from private industry as well as some academic economists – which then reports its conclusions as to whether the proposed merger is in 'the public interest', so that the minister can then rule on whether to allow or prohibit the merger (although the Secretary of State has the power to – and occasionally does – overrule the recommendations of the Competition Commission).

Regulation

Another way in which the government deals with the problem of monopoly is by regulating the behaviour of monopolists. This solution is common in the case of natural monopolies, such as utility companies like water, gas and electricity companies. These companies are not allowed to charge any price they want. Instead, government agencies regulate their prices.

"You've explained why the merger is good for shareholders, investors and suppliers, the only ones you haven't mentioned are the customers."

FIGURE 15.11

Marginal Cost Pricing For a Natural Monopoly

Because a natural monopoly has declining average total cost, marginal cost is less than average total cost. Therefore, if regulators require a natural monopoly to charge a price equal to marginal cost, price will be below average total cost, and the monopoly will lose money.

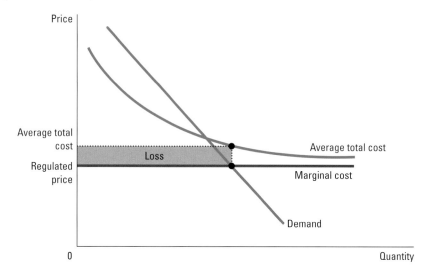

What price should the government set for a natural monopoly? This question is not as easy as it might at first appear. One might conclude that the price should equal the monopolist's marginal cost. If price equals marginal cost, customers will buy the quantity of the monopolist's output that maximizes total surplus, and the allocation of resources will be efficient.

There are, however, two practical problems with marginal-cost pricing as a regulatory system. The first is illustrated in Figure 15.11. Natural monopolies, by definition, have declining average total cost. As we discussed in Chapter 13, when average total cost is declining, marginal cost is less than average total cost. If regulators are to set price equal to marginal cost, that price will be less than the firm's average total cost, and the firm will lose money. Instead of charging such a low price, the monopoly firm would just exit the industry.

Regulators can respond to this problem in various ways, none of which is perfect. One way is to subsidize the monopolist. In essence, the government picks up the losses inherent in marginal-cost pricing. Yet to pay for the subsidy, the government needs to raise money through taxation, which involves its own deadweight losses. Alternatively, the regulators can allow the monopolist to charge a price higher than marginal cost. If the regulated price equals average total cost, the monopolist earns exactly zero economic profit. Yet average-cost pricing leads to deadweight losses, because the monopolist's price no longer reflects the marginal cost of producing the good. In essence, average-cost pricing is like a tax on the good the monopolist is selling.

The second problem with marginal-cost pricing as a regulatory system (and with average-cost pricing as well) is that it gives the monopolist no incentive to reduce costs. Each firm in a competitive market tries to reduce its costs because lower costs mean higher profits. But if a regulated monopolist knows that regulators will reduce prices whenever costs fall, the monopolist will not benefit from lower costs. In practice, regulators deal with this problem by allowing monopolists to keep some of the benefits from lower costs in the form of higher profit, a practice that requires some departure from marginal-cost pricing.

For example, in the UK, utility companies have often been subject to price caps whereby the regulator determines that the real price of the company's product – a kilowatt hour of electricity, for example – should fall by a given number of percentage points each year, reflecting productivity rises. Say, for example, this is 2 per cent. The company would then be allowed to raise its prices each year by the inflation rate *minus* 2 per cent. If the company increases its productivity by, say 4 per cent each year, however (in other words it can produce the same amount of output with 4 per cent less inputs), then in real terms its profits will go up each year. In this way, the system of price caps aims to give natural monopolies the motivation to improve efficiency and productivity that would be supplied by the invisible hand in a competitive market.

Public Ownership

The third policy used by the government to deal with monopoly is public ownership. That is, rather than regulating a natural monopoly that is run by a private firm, the government can run the monopoly itself. An industry owned by the government is called a nationalized industry. This solution is common in many European countries, where the government owns and operates utilities such as the telephone, water and electric companies.

Economists usually prefer private to public ownership of natural monopolies. The key issue is how the ownership of the firm affects the costs of production. Private owners have an incentive to minimize costs as long as they reap part of the benefit in the form of higher profit. If the firm's managers are doing a bad job of keeping costs down, the firm's owners will fire them. By contrast, if the government bureaucrats who run a monopoly do a bad job, the losers are the customers and taxpayers, whose only recourse is the political system. The bureaucrats may become a special interest group and attempt to block cost reducing reforms. Put simply, as a way of ensuring that firms are well run, the voting booth is less reliable than the profit motive.

Doing Nothing

Each of the foregoing policies aimed at reducing the problem of monopoly has drawbacks. As a result, some economists argue that it is often best for the government not to try to remedy the inefficiencies of monopoly pricing. Here is the assessment of economist George Stigler, who won the Nobel Prize for his work in industrial organization, writing in the *Fortune Encyclopedia of Economics:*

> A famous theorem in economics states that a competitive enterprise economy will produce the largest possible income from a given stock of resources. No real economy meets the exact conditions of the theorem, and all real economies will fall short of the ideal economy – a difference called 'market failure.' In my view, however, the degree of 'market failure' for the American economy is much smaller than the 'political failure' arising from the imperfections of economic policies found in real political systems.

As this quotation makes clear, determining the proper role of the government in the economy requires judgements about politics as well as economics.

IN THE NEWS

Monopoly Power and Competition Laws

This article highlights a case where competition authorities are investigating the behaviour of a firm accused of exploiting monopoly power. In this case the firm has a dominant position in the market but is not the only one. Whilst the analysis in this chapter is based on the assumption that there is only one seller in the market, in reality a number of markets have a firm which has a dominant position and can behave as if there is only one seller. In such cases the suspicions of the competition authorities may be aroused.

In February 2010, competition authorities in the European Union (EU) received complaints from three companies, about the search engine giant, Google. The price comparison sites *Foundem*, which is based in the UK and a French search engine site, *ejustice.fr,* claimed that Google is using its dominance in the market to manipulate search results to give more prominence to its own services such as Google Product Search and thus push down competing sites further down the search results. *Ciao! from Bing*, a search engine owned by Microsoft, has filed a complaint with German authorities regarding Google's standard terms and conditions. This was then referred to Brussels and was considered at the same time as the complaints from *Foundem* and *ejustice.fr*.

In the UK, Google has around 90 per cent of the search engine market and globally is estimated to account for over 80 per cent. This, say the complainants, puts Google in a very powerful position. *Foundem* claims that Google uses different algorithms for presenting its own services to that of other sites and as a result is able to create an uneven playing field which raises competition issues. By manipulating search results Google is able to give a greater weighting to its services, for which it receives money, compared to others. *Foundem* was started in 2005 and a spokesperson has said that it encountered problems at an early stage and had its issues with Google resolved in 2009. However, it said that it was acting on behalf of other search firms who may be affected. Microsoft has also commented on the complaint saying that it believes that if there are competition issues as a result of the dominance of one firm over the market then it is right for the EU Commission to investigate. An interesting statement given the dispute between Microsoft and the EU Competition Commission!

Google rejects the claims that it is operating in an anti-competitive manner and has said that it believes it competes fairly in the market. It was notified of the complaints by the Commission and was given time to respond to them. Julia Holtz, a Senior Competition Counsel with Google, presented a robust defence of the company via a corporate blog. In the blog she rather pointedly noted that both *Ciao! from Bing* and *Foundem* have links with Microsoft, the former having been bought by Microsoft in 2008 and the latter as a member of a group called ICOMP, which is partly funded by Microsoft. Holtz says: 'Our algorithms aim to rank first what people are most likely to find useful and we have nothing against vertical search sites.' She went on to say: 'While we will be providing feedback and additional information on these complaints, we are confident that our business operates in the interests of users and partners, as well as in line with European competition law... Though each case raises slightly different issues, the question they ultimately pose is whether Google is doing anything to choke off competition or hurt our users and partners. This is not the case. We always try to listen carefully if someone has a real concern and we work hard to put our users' interests first and to compete fair and square in the market. We believe our business practices reflect those commitments'.

Quick Quiz Describe the ways policy makers can respond to the inefficiencies caused by monopolies. List a potential problem with each of these policy responses.

CONCLUSION: THE PREVALENCE OF MONOPOLY

This chapter has discussed the behaviour of firms that have control over the prices they charge. We have seen that these firms behave very differently from the competitive firms studied in the previous chapter. Table 15.2 summarizes some of the key similarities and differences between competitive and monopoly markets.

From the standpoint of public policy, a crucial result is that monopolists produce less than the socially efficient quantity and charge prices above marginal cost. As a result, they cause deadweight losses. In some cases, these inefficiencies can be mitigated through price discrimination by the monopolist, but at other times they call for policy makers to take an active role.

How prevalent are the problems of monopoly? There are two answers to this question.

In one sense, monopolies are common. Most firms have some control over the prices they charge. They are not forced to charge the market price for their goods, because their goods are not exactly the same as those offered by other firms. A Honda Accord is not the same as a Volkswagen Passat. Ben and Jerry's ice cream is not the same as Wall's. Each of these goods has a downward sloping demand curve, which gives each producer some degree of monopoly power.

Yet firms with substantial monopoly power are quite rare. Few goods are truly unique. Most have substitutes that, even if not exactly the same are very similar. Ben and Jerry can raise the price of their ice cream a little without losing all their sales; but if they raise it very much, sales will fall substantially.

In the end, monopoly power is a matter of degree. It is true that many firms have some monopoly power. It is also true that their monopoly power is usually limited. In these cases, we will not go far wrong assuming that firms operate in competitive markets, even if that is not precisely the case.

TABLE 15.2

Competition versus Monopoly: A Summary Comparison

	Competition	Monopoly
Similarities		
Goal of firms	Maximize profits	Maximize profits
Rule for maximizing	$MR = MC$	$MR = MC$
Can earn economic profits in the short run?	Yes	Yes
Differences		
Number of firms	Many	One
Marginal revenue	$MR = P$	$MR < P$
Price	$P = MC$	$P > MC$
Produces welfare-maximizing level of output?	Yes	No
Entry in long run?	Yes	No
Can earn economic profits in long run?	No	Yes
Price discrimination possible?	No	Yes

SUMMARY

- A monopoly is a firm that is the sole seller in its market. A monopoly arises when a single firm owns a key resource, when the government gives a firm the exclusive right to produce a good, or when a single firm can supply the entire market at a smaller cost than many firms could.

- Because a monopoly is the sole producer in its market, it faces a downward sloping demand curve for its product. When a monopoly increases production by 1 unit, it causes the price of its good to fall, which reduces the amount of revenue earned on all units produced. As a result, a monopoly's marginal revenue is always below the price of its good.

- Like a competitive firm, a monopoly firm maximizes profit by producing the quantity at which marginal revenue equals marginal cost. The monopoly then chooses the price at which that quantity is demanded. Unlike a competitive firm, a monopoly firm's price exceeds its marginal revenue, so its price exceeds marginal cost.

- A monopolist's profit-maximizing level of output is below the level that maximizes the sum of consumer and producer surplus. That is, when the monopoly charges a price above marginal cost, some consumers who value the good more than its cost of production do not buy it. As a result, monopoly causes deadweight losses similar to the deadweight losses caused by taxes.

- Policy makers can respond to the inefficiency of monopoly behaviour in four ways. They can use competition law to try to make the industry more competitive. They can regulate the prices that the monopoly charges. They can turn the monopolist into a government-run enterprise. Or, if the market failure is deemed small compared to the inevitable imperfections of policies, they can do nothing at all.

- Monopolists often can raise their profits by charging different prices for the same good based on a buyer's willingness to pay. This practice of price discrimination can raise economic welfare by getting the good to some consumers who otherwise would not buy it. In the extreme case of perfect price discrimination, the deadweight losses of monopoly are completely eliminated. More generally, when price discrimination is imperfect, it can either raise or lower welfare compared to the outcome with a single monopoly price.

KEY CONCEPTS

monopoly, p. 310   natural monopoly, p. 311   price discrimination, p. 323

QUESTIONS FOR REVIEW

1. Give an example of a government-created monopoly. Is creating this monopoly necessarily bad public policy? Explain.

2. Define natural monopoly. What does the size of a market have to do with whether an industry is a natural monopoly?

3. Why is a monopolist's marginal revenue less than the price of its good? Can marginal revenue ever be negative? Explain.

4. Draw the demand, marginal revenue and marginal cost curves for a monopolist. Show the profit-maximizing level of output. Show the profit-maximizing price.

5. In your diagram from the previous question, show the level of output that maximizes total surplus. Show the deadweight loss from the monopoly. Explain your answer.

6. What gives the government the power to regulate mergers between firms? From the standpoint of the welfare of society, give a good reason and a bad reason that two firms might want to merge.

7. Describe the two problems that arise when regulators tell a natural monopoly that it must set a price equal to marginal cost.

8. Give two examples of price discrimination. In each case, explain why the monopolist chooses to follow this business strategy.

PROBLEMS AND APPLICATIONS

1. A publisher faces the following demand schedule for the next novel of one of its popular authors:

Price (€)	Quantity demanded
€100	0
90	100 000
80	200 000
70	300 000
60	400 000
50	500 000
40	600 000
30	700 000
20	800 000
10	900 000
0	1 000 000

The author is paid €2 million to write the book, and the marginal cost of publishing the book is a constant €10 per book.

a. Compute total revenue, total cost and profit at each quantity. What quantity would a profit-maximizing publisher choose? What price would it charge?

b. Compute marginal revenue. (Recall that $MR = \Delta TR / \Delta Q$.) How does marginal revenue compare to the price? Explain.

c. Graph the marginal revenue, marginal cost and demand curves. At what quantity do the marginal revenue and marginal cost curves cross? What does this signify?

d. In your graph, shade in the deadweight loss. Explain in words what this means.

e. If the author were paid €3 million instead of €2 million to write the book, how would this affect the publisher's decision regarding the price to charge? Explain.

f. Suppose the publisher was not profit-maximizing but was concerned with maximizing economic efficiency. What price would it charge for the book? How much profit would it make at this price?

2. Suppose that a natural monopolist was required by law to charge average total cost. On a diagram, label the price charged and the deadweight loss to society relative to marginal-cost pricing.

3. Consider the delivery of mail. In general, what is the shape of the average total cost curve? How might the shape differ between isolated rural areas and densely populated urban areas? How might the shape have changed over time? Explain.

4. Suppose the Eau de Jeunesse Water Company has a monopoly on bottled water sales in France. If the price of tap water increases, what is the change in Eau de Jeunesse's profit-maximizing levels of output, price and profit? Explain in words and with a graph.

5. A small town is served by many competing supermarkets, which have constant marginal cost.

a. Using a diagram of the market for groceries, show the consumer surplus, producer surplus and total surplus.

b. Now suppose that the independent supermarkets combine into one chain. Using a new diagram, show the new consumer surplus, producer surplus and total surplus. Relative to the competitive market, what is the transfer from consumers to producers? What is the deadweight loss?

6. Guy Rope and his backing group, the Tent Pegs, have just finished recording their latest music CD. Their record company's marketing department determines that the demand for the CD is as follows:

Price (€)	Number of CDs
€24	10 000
22	20 000
20	30 000
18	40 000
16	50 000
14	60 000

The company can produce the CD with no fixed cost and a variable cost of €5 per CD.

a. Find total revenue for quantity equal to 10 000, 20 000 and so on. What is the marginal revenue for each 10 000 increase in the quantity sold?

b. What quantity of CDs would maximize profit? What would the price be? What would the profit be?

c. If you were Guy Rope's agent, what recording fee would you advise Guy to demand from the record company? Why?

7. In 1969 the US government charged IBM with monopolizing the computer market. The government argued (correctly) that a large share of all mainframe computers sold in the United States were produced by IBM. IBM argued (correctly) that a much smaller share of the market for *all* types of computers consisted of IBM products. Based on these facts, do you think that the government should have brought a lawsuit against IBM for violating the US anti-trust laws? Explain.

8. A company is considering building a bridge across a river. The bridge would cost €12 million to build and nothing to maintain. The following table shows the company's anticipated demand over the lifetime of the bridge:

Price per crossing (€)	Number of crossings (in thousands)
€8	0
7	100
6	200
5	300
4	400
3	500
2	600
1	700
0	800

   a. If the company were to build the bridge, what would be its profit-maximizing price? Would that be the efficient level of output? Why or why not?
   b. If the company is interested in maximizing profit, should it build the bridge? What would be its profit or loss?
   c. If the government were to build the bridge, what price should it charge for passengers and vehicles to use the bridge? Explain your answer.
   d. Should the government build the bridge? Explain.

9. The Placebo Drug Company holds a patent on one of its discoveries.
   a. Assuming that the production of the drug involves rising marginal cost, draw a diagram to illustrate Placebo's profit-maximizing price and quantity. Also show Placebo's profits.
   b. Now suppose that the government imposes a tax on each bottle of the drug produced. On a new diagram, illustrate Placebo's new price and quantity. How does each compare to your answer in part (a)?
   c. Although it is not easy to see in your diagrams, the tax reduces Placebo's profit. Explain why this must be true.
   d. Instead of the tax per bottle, suppose that the government imposes a tax on Placebo of €110 000 regardless of how many bottles are produced. How does this tax affect Placebo's price, quantity and profits? Explain.

10. Pablo, Dirk and Franz run the only saloon in town. Pablo wants to sell as many drinks as possible without losing money. Dirk wants the saloon to bring in as much revenue as possible. Franz wants to make the largest possible profits. Using a single diagram of the saloon's demand curve and its cost curves, show the price and quantity combinations favoured by each of the three partners. Explain.

11. The Best Computer Company just developed a new computer chip, on which it immediately acquires a patent.
   a. Draw a diagram that shows the consumer surplus, producer surplus and total surplus in the market for this new chip.
   b. What happens to these three measures of surplus if the firm can perfectly price discriminate? What is the change in deadweight loss? What transfers occur?

12. Explain why a monopolist will always produce a quantity at which the demand curve is elastic. (Hint: if demand is inelastic and the firm raises its price, what happens to total revenue and total costs?)

13. Singer Britney Spears has a monopoly over a scarce resource: herself. She is the only person who can produce a Britney Spears concert. Does this fact imply that the government should regulate the prices of her concerts? Why or why not?

14. Napster, the online file-swapping service, originally allowed people to use the internet to download copies of their favourite songs from other people's computers without cost. In what sense did Napster enhance economic efficiency in the short run? In what sense might Napster have reduced economic efficiency in the long run? Why do you think the courts eventually shut Napster down? Do you think this was the right policy?

15. Many schemes for price discriminating involve some cost. For example, discount coupons take up time and resources from both the buyer and the seller. This question considers the implications of costly price discrimination. To keep things simple, let's assume that our monopolist's production costs are simply proportional to output, so that average total cost and marginal cost are constant and equal to each other.
   a. Draw the cost, demand and marginal revenue curves for the monopolist. Show the price the monopolist would charge without price discrimination.
   b. In your diagram, mark the area equal to the monopolist's profit and call it X. Mark the area equal to consumer surplus and call it Y. Mark the area equal to the deadweight loss and call it Z.
   c. Now suppose that the monopolist can perfectly price discriminate. What is the monopolist's profit? (Give your answer in terms of X, Y and Z.)
   d. What is the change in the monopolist's profit from price discrimination? What is the change in total surplus from price discrimination? Which change is larger? Explain. (Give your answer in terms of X, Y and Z.)
   e. Now suppose that there is some cost of price discrimination. To model this cost, let's assume that the monopolist has to pay a fixed cost C in order to price

discriminate. How would a monopolist make the decision whether to pay this fixed cost? (Give your answer in terms of X, Y, Z and *C*.)

f. How would a benevolent social planner, who cares about total surplus, decide whether the monopolist should price discriminate? (Give your answer in terms of X, Y, Z and *C*.)

g. Compare your answers to parts (e) and (f). How does the monopolist's incentive to price discriminate differ from the social planner's? Is it possible that the monopolist will price discriminate even though it is not socially desirable?

For further resources, visit
www.cengage.com/mankiw_taylor2

16 MONOPOLISTIC COMPETITION

You walk into a bookshop to buy a book to read during your next summer holiday. On the shop's shelves you find the latest blockbuster crime thriller novel, an interesting looking political novel by a new author, a novel about a thirty-something divorcee trying to build a new life, an intellectual literary novel by a French female author, the autobiography of a former prime minister and many other choices. When you pick out a book and buy it, what kind of market are you participating in?

On the one hand, the market for books seems competitive. As you look over the shelves at your bookshop, you find many authors and many publishers vying for your attention. A buyer in this market has thousands of competing products from which to choose. And because many people are willing to put the time and effort into becoming a writer, there are a lot of people wanting to enter the market. Because of this, the book business is not very profitable. For every highly paid novelist, there are hundreds of struggling ones.

On the other hand, the market for books seems monopolistic. Because each book is unique, publishers have some latitude in choosing what price to charge. The sellers in this market are price makers rather than price takers. And, indeed, the price of books greatly exceeds marginal cost. The price of a typical hardcover novel in the UK, for instance, is about £15, whereas the cost of printing one additional copy of the novel is only a few pounds.

monopolistic competition
a market structure in which many firms sell products that are similar but not identical

In this chapter we examine markets that have some features of competition and some features of monopoly. This market structure is called **monopolistic competition**. Monopolistic competition describes a market with the following attributes:

338

- *Many sellers.* There are many firms competing for the same group of customers.
- *Product differentiation.* Each firm produces a product that is at least slightly different from those of other firms. The firm is able to have some control over the extent to which it can differentiate its product from its rivals thus reducing the degree of substitutability and garnering an element of customer or brand loyalty. Thus, rather than being a price taker, each firm faces a downward sloping demand curve.
- *Free entry.* Firms can enter (or exit) the market without restriction. Thus, the number of firms in the market adjusts until economic profits are driven to zero.

Table 16.1 lists examples of the types of market with these attributes.

TABLE 16.1

Examples of Markets which Have Characteristics of Monopolistic Competition

Computer games	Vets
Restaurants	Hotel accommodation
Conference organizers	Air conditioning systems
Wedding planners	Pest control
Plumbing	Removal services
Coach hire	Beauty consultants
Funeral directors	Shop fitters
Fabric manufacturers	Waste disposal
Tailors	Dentists
Music teachers	Children's entertainers
Books	Gas engineers
CDs/DVDs	Steel fabricators
Landscape architects	Driving schools
Environmental consultants	Opticians
Furniture manufacturers	Chimney sweeps

Monopolistic competition is a market structure that lies between the extreme cases of competition and monopoly. Under monopolistic competition, there are many sellers, each of which is small compared to the market. A monopolistically competitive market departs from the perfectly competitive ideal because each of the sellers is able to offer a different product by differentiating it in some way from other suppliers.

COMPETITION WITH DIFFERENTIATED PRODUCTS

To understand monopolistically competitive markets, we first consider the decisions facing an individual firm. We then examine what happens in the long run as firms enter and exit the industry. Next, we compare the equilibrium under monopolistic competition to the equilibrium under perfect competition that we examined in Chapter 14. Finally, we consider whether the outcome in a monopolistically competitive market is desirable from the standpoint of society as a whole.

The Monopolistically Competitive Firm in the Short Run

Each firm in a monopolistically competitive market is, in many ways, like a monopoly. Because its product is different from those offered by other firms, it faces a downward sloping demand curve. (By contrast, remember, a perfectly

FIGURE 16.1

Monopolistic Competitors in the Short Run

Monopolistic competitors, like monopolists, maximize profit by producing the quantity at which marginal revenue equals marginal cost. The firm in panel (a) makes a profit because, at this quantity, price is above average total cost. The firm in panel (b) makes losses because, at this quantity, price is less than average total cost.

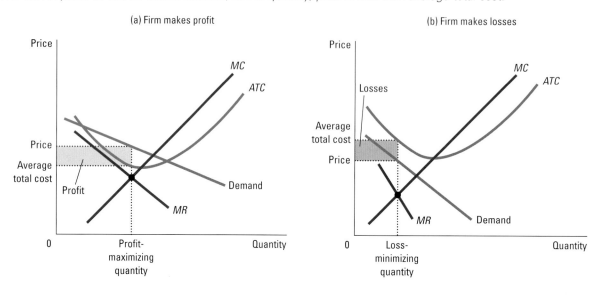

competitive firm faces a horizontal demand curve at the market price.) Thus, the monopolistically competitive firm follows a monopolist's rule for profit maximization: it chooses the quantity at which marginal revenue equals marginal cost and then uses its demand curve to find the price consistent with that quantity.

Figure 16.1 shows the cost, demand and marginal revenue curves for two typical firms, each in a different monopolistically competitive industry. In both panels of this figure, the profit-maximizing quantity is found at the intersection of the marginal revenue and marginal cost curves. The two panels in this figure show different outcomes for the firm's profit. In panel (a), price exceeds average total cost, so the firm makes a profit. In panel (b), price is below average total cost. In this case, the firm is unable to make a positive profit, so the best the firm can do is to minimize its losses.

All this should seem familiar. A monopolistically competitive firm chooses its quantity and price just as a monopoly does. In the short run, these two types of market structure are similar.

The Long-Run Equilibrium

The situations depicted in Figure 16.1 do not last long. When firms are making profits, as in panel (a), new firms have an incentive to enter the market (remember that there is free entry and exit into the market). This entry means that more firms are now offering products for sale in the industry. The increase in supply causes the price received by all firms in the industry to fall. If an existing firm wishes to sell more then it must reduce its price. There are now more substitutes available in the market and so the effect for firms is to shift the demand curve to the left. The effect is that there is an increase in the number of products from

FIGURE 16.2

A Monopolistic Competitor in the Long Run

In a monopolistically competitive market, if firms are making profit, new firms enter and the demand curves for the incumbent firms shift to the left. Similarly, if firms are making losses, old firms exit and the demand curves of the remaining firms shift to the right. Because of these shifts in demand, a monopolistically competitive firm eventually finds itself in the long-run equilibrium shown here. In this long-run equilibrium, price equals average total cost, and the firm earns zero profit.

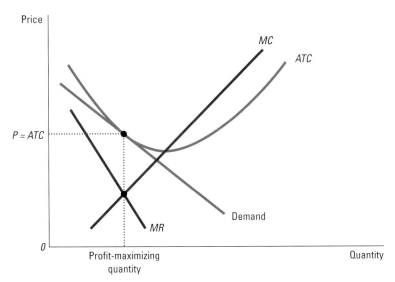

which customers can now choose and, therefore, reduces the demand faced by each firm already in the market. In other words, profit encourages entry, and entry shifts the demand curves faced by the incumbent firms to the left. As the demand for incumbent firms' products falls, these firms experience declining profit.

Conversely, when firms are making losses, as in panel (b), firms in the market have an incentive to exit. As firms exit, the supply will fall and price will rise. There are now fewer substitutes and so customers have fewer products from which to choose. This decrease in the number of firms effectively expands the demand faced by those firms that stay in the market. In other words, losses encourage exit, and exit has the effect of shifting the demand curves of the remaining firms to the right. As the demand for the remaining firms' products rises, these firms experience rising profit (that is, declining losses).

This process of entry and exit continues until the firms in the market are making exactly zero economic profit. Figure 16.2 depicts the long-run equilibrium. Once the market reaches this equilibrium, new firms have no incentive to enter, and existing firms have no incentive to exit.

Notice that the demand curve in this figure just barely touches the average total cost curve. Mathematically, we say the two curves are *tangent* to each other. These two curves must be tangent once entry and exit have driven profit to zero. Because profit per unit sold is the difference between price (found on the demand curve) and average total cost, the maximum profit is zero only if these two curves touch each other without crossing.

To sum up, two characteristics describe the long-run equilibrium in a monopolistically competitive market:

- As in a monopoly market, price exceeds marginal cost. This conclusion arises because profit maximization requires marginal revenue to equal marginal cost and because the downward sloping demand curve makes marginal revenue less than the price.
- As in a competitive market, price equals average total cost. This conclusion arises because free entry and exit drive economic profit to zero.

The second characteristic shows how monopolistic competition differs from monopoly. Because a monopoly is the sole seller of a product without close substitutes, it can earn positive economic profit, even in the long run. By contrast, because there is free entry into a monopolistically competitive market, the economic profit of a firm in this type of market is driven to zero.

Monopolistic versus Perfect Competition

Figure 16.3 compares the long-run equilibrium under monopolistic competition to the long-run equilibrium under perfect competition. (Chapter 14 discussed the equilibrium with perfect competition.) There are two noteworthy differences between monopolistic and perfect competition – excess capacity and the mark-up.

Excess Capacity   As we have just seen, entry and exit drive each firm in a monopolistically competitive market to a point of tangency between its demand and average total cost curves. Panel (a) of Figure 16.3 shows that the quantity of

FIGURE 16.3

Monopolistic versus Perfect Competition

Panel (a) shows the long-run equilibrium in a monopolistically competitive market, and panel (b) shows the long-run equilibrium in a perfectly competitive market. Two differences are notable. (1) The perfectly competitive firm produces at the efficient scale, where average total cost is minimized. By contrast, the monopolistically competitive firm produces at less than the efficient scale. (2) Price equals marginal cost under perfect competition, but price is above marginal cost under monopolistic competition.

output at this point is smaller than the quantity that minimizes average total cost. Thus, under monopolistic competition, firms produce on the downward sloping portion of their average total cost curves. In this way, monopolistic competition contrasts starkly with perfect competition. As panel (b) of Figure 16.3 shows, free entry in competitive markets drives firms to produce at the minimum of average total cost.

The quantity that minimizes average total cost is called the *efficient scale* of the firm. In the long run, perfectly competitive firms produce at the efficient scale, whereas monopolistically competitive firms produce below this level. Firms are said to have *excess capacity* under monopolistic competition. In other words, a monopolistically competitive firm, unlike a perfectly competitive firm, could increase the quantity it produces and lower the average total cost of production.

Mark-up over Marginal Cost A second difference between perfect competition and monopolistic competition is the relationship between price and marginal cost. For a competitive firm, such as that shown in panel (b) of Figure 16.3, price equals marginal cost. For a monopolistically competitive firm, such as that shown in panel (a), price exceeds marginal cost, because the firm always has some market power.

How is this mark-up over marginal cost consistent with free entry and zero profit? The zero-profit condition ensures only that price equals average total cost. It does *not* ensure that price equals marginal cost. Indeed, in the long-run equilibrium, monopolistically competitive firms operate on the declining portion of their average total cost curves, so marginal cost is below average total cost. Thus, for price to equal average total cost, price must be above marginal cost.

In this relationship between price and marginal cost, we see a key behavioural difference between perfect competitors and monopolistic competitors. Imagine that you were to ask a firm the following question: 'Would you like to see another customer come through your door ready to buy from you at your current price?' A perfectly competitive firm would answer that it didn't care. Because price exactly equals marginal cost, the profit from an extra unit sold is zero. By contrast, a monopolistically competitive firm is always eager to get another customer. Because its price exceeds marginal cost, an extra unit sold at the posted price means more profit. According to an old quip, monopolistically competitive markets are those in which sellers send greetings cards to the buyers.

Monopolistic Competition and the Welfare of Society

Is the outcome in a monopolistically competitive market desirable from the standpoint of society as a whole? Can policy makers improve on the market outcome? There are no simple answers to these questions.

One source of inefficiency is the mark-up of price over marginal cost. Because of the mark-up, some consumers who value the good at more than the marginal cost of production (but less than the price) will be deterred from buying it. Thus, a monopolistically competitive market has the normal deadweight loss of monopoly pricing. We first saw this type of inefficiency when we discussed monopoly in Chapter 15.

Although this outcome is clearly undesirable compared to the first-best outcome of price equal to marginal cost, there is no easy way for policy makers to fix the problem. To enforce marginal-cost pricing, policy makers would need to regulate all firms that produce differentiated products. Because such products are so common in the economy, the administrative burden of such regulation would be overwhelming.

Moreover, regulating monopolistic competitors would entail all the problems of regulating natural monopolies. In particular, because monopolistic competitors are making zero profits already, requiring them to lower their prices to equal marginal cost would cause them to make losses. To keep these firms in business, the government would need to help them cover these losses. Rather than raising taxes to pay for these subsidies, policy makers may decide it is better to live with the inefficiency of monopolistic pricing.

Another way in which monopolistic competition may be socially inefficient is that the number of firms in the market may not be the 'ideal' one. That is, there may be too much or too little entry. One way to think about this problem is in terms of the externalities associated with entry. Whenever a new firm considers entering the market with a new product, it considers only the profit it would make. Yet its entry would also have two external effects:

* *The product-variety externality.* Because consumers get some consumer surplus from the introduction of a new product, entry of a new firm conveys a positive externality on consumers.
* *The business-stealing externality.* Because other firms lose customers and profits from the entry of a new competitor, entry of a new firm imposes a negative externality on existing firms.

Thus, in a monopolistically competitive market, there are both positive and negative externalities associated with the entry of new firms. Depending on which externality is larger, a monopolistically competitive market could have either too few or too many products.

Both of these externalities are closely related to the conditions for monopolistic competition. The product-variety externality arises because a new firm would offer a product different from those of the existing firms. The business-stealing externality arises because firms post a price above marginal cost and, therefore, are always eager to sell additional units. Conversely, because perfectly competitive firms produce identical goods and charge a price equal to marginal cost, neither of these externalities exists under perfect competition.

In the end, we can conclude only that monopolistically competitive markets do not have all the desirable welfare properties of perfectly competitive markets. That is, the invisible hand does not ensure that total surplus is maximized under monopolistic competition. Yet because the inefficiencies are subtle, hard to measure and hard to fix, there is no easy way for public policy to improve the market outcome.

Quick Quiz List the three key attributes of monopolistic competition. • Draw and explain a diagram to show the long-run equilibrium in a monopolistically competitive market. How does this equilibrium differ from that in a perfectly competitive market?

ADVERTISING

It is nearly impossible to go through a typical day in a modern economy without being bombarded with advertising. Whether you are reading a newspaper, watching television or driving down the motorway, some firm will try to convince you to buy its product. Such behaviour is a natural feature of monopolistic competition. When firms sell differentiated products and charge prices above marginal cost, each firm has an incentive to advertise in order to attract more buyers to its particular product.

FIGURE 16.4

UK Advertising Spending Share, 2008

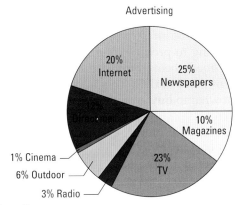

Source: AA's *Quarterly Survey of Advertising Expenditure.*

The amount of advertising varies substantially across products. Firms that sell highly differentiated consumer goods, such as over-the-counter drugs, perfumes, soft drinks, razor blades, breakfast cereals and dog food, typically spend between 10 and 20 per cent of revenue for advertising. Firms that sell industrial products, such as drill presses and communications satellites, typically spend very little on advertising. And firms that sell homogeneous products, such as wheat, peanuts or crude oil, spend nothing at all. In the EU in 2009, spending on online advertising alone was about £14.7 billion.

Advertising takes many forms. Figure 16.4 shows a breakdown of the share of advertising spending in the UK in 2008. Most advertising expenditure in the UK is through newspapers with TV coming a close second. One major change in the way in which firms advertise is the use of the internet. In 2002 around 1 per cent of total advertising spending went on the Internet but this has increased dramatically to 20 per cent by 2008 and is expected to continue to grow.

The Debate over Advertising

Is society wasting the resources it devotes to advertising? Or does advertising serve a valuable purpose? Assessing the social value of advertising is difficult and often generates heated argument among economists. Let's consider both sides of the debate.

The Critique of Advertising   Critics of advertising argue that firms advertise in order to manipulate people's tastes. Much advertising is psychological rather than informational. Consider, for example, the typical television advert for some brand of soft drink. The advert most likely does not tell the viewer about the product's price or quality. Instead, it might show a group of happy people at a party on a beach on a beautiful sunny day. In their hands are cans of the soft drink. The goal of the advert is to convey a subconscious (if not subtle) message: 'You too can have many friends and be happy and beautiful, if only you drink our product.' Critics of advertising argue that such an advert creates a desire that otherwise might not exist.

Critics also argue that advertising impedes competition. Advertising often tries to convince consumers that products are more different than they truly are. By increasing the perception of product differentiation and fostering brand loyalty, advertising makes buyers less concerned with price differences among similar goods. With a less elastic demand curve, each firm charges a larger mark-up over marginal cost.

The Defence of Advertising Defenders of advertising argue that firms use advertising to provide information to customers. Advertising conveys the prices of the goods being offered for sale, the existence of new products and the locations of retail outlets. This information allows customers to make better choices about what to buy and, thus, enhances the ability of markets to allocate resources efficiently.

Defenders also argue that advertising fosters competition. Because advertising allows customers to be more fully informed about all the firms in the market, customers can more easily take advantage of price differences. Thus, each firm has less market power. In addition, advertising allows new firms to enter more easily, because it gives entrants a means to attract customers from existing firms.

CASE STUDY

Advertising – What Does it Really Do?

Ask many people the question 'why do firms advertise?' and they are likely to tell you that it is an attempt by firms to try and increase demand for their products or services. If you consider this view intuitively it might make sense but then ask yourself the question, 'how many times have you seen an advert on the TV and then rushed out to buy the product advertised?' The chances are that this has not (consciously) happened very often at all. So if adverts do not make us rush out to buy products what do they do?

Sutherland and Sylvester (2000)[1] argue that it is largely a myth that adverts are designed to persuade us to buy products or services. They point out the following:

Advertising influences the order in which we evoke or notice the alternatives we consider. This does not feel like persuasion and it is not. It is nevertheless effective. Instead of persuasion and other major effects we should look for 'feathers', or minor effects. These can tip the balance when alternative brands are otherwise equal and, through repetition, can grow imperceptibly by small increments over time.

They liken the effect of advertising to that of watching someone grow up. You know that they are growing but the day-to-day changes in the individual are imperceptible. If you have not seen someone for some time, however, you do tend to notice the difference in their height, shape, features and so on. So it is with many advertising campaigns. The primary aim, they argue, is to generate a series of small effects, which ultimately influence our behaviour and may cause us to view differently the products or the brands that we choose, especially in a crowded marketplace with a large amount of competition.

Exactly how adverts work, therefore, is not easy to quantify. Sutherland and Sylvester suggest that many involved in the advertising industry do not really understand why some adverts seem to work and others don't work anything like as well. It has long been recognized that psychology has a lot to do with advertising. Our understanding of the way the brain works has been revolutionized by the developments afforded by magnetic resonance imaging (MRI) scans. The advertising industry has not been slow in looking at this technology and its potential for improving the focus and efficiency of advertising.

In essence, this technique looks at the response of the brain to different images and messages. Using MRI techniques, the areas of the brain that respond to different stimuli can be identified. The field developed as a result of work carried out by a neuroscientist called Read Montague. Montague is Professor in the Department of Neuroscience at Baylor College of Medicine in Houston, Texas. He gave a group of individuals two colas, Pepsi and Coke, to taste and asked them to state which they preferred. The respondents did not know that the two colas were in fact Pepsi and Coke. The results were 50:50 for the two products.

However, when the experiment was repeated and the respondents were told what they were drinking, around 75% stated that they preferred Coke. Montague found that brain activity in the medial pre-frontal cortex also showed signs of enhanced activity during the exercise. This area of the brain is associated with higher level thinking. Montague posited that the brain was making an association with the images and messages associated with commercials for Coke that respondents had witnessed over the years. He also suggested that such activity might lead to consumers preferring one product to another, even if there was other evidence to suggest that under normal circumstances, they would not have chosen that product.

[1]Sutherland, M. & Sylvester, A.K. (2000) *Advertising and the Mind of the Consumer: What Works, What Doesn't, and Why.* St Leonards, New South Wales, Allen and Unwin.

Advertising as a Signal of Quality

Many types of advertising contain little apparent information about the product being advertised. Consider a firm introducing a new breakfast cereal. A typical advertisement might have some highly paid actor eating the cereal and exclaiming how wonderful it tastes. How much information does the advertisement really provide?

The answer is: more than you might think. Defenders of advertising argue that even advertising that appears to contain little hard information may in fact tell consumers something about product quality. The willingness of the firm to spend a large amount of money on advertising can itself be a *signal* to consumers about the quality of the product being offered.

Consider the problem facing two firms – Nestlé and Kellogg. Each company has just come up with a recipe for a new breakfast cereal, which it would sell for €3 a box. To keep things simple, let's assume that the marginal cost of making cereal is zero, so the €3 is all profit. Each company knows that if it spends €10 million on advertising, it will get 1 million consumers to try its new cereal. And each company knows that if consumers like the cereal, they will buy it not once but many times.

First consider Nestlé's decision. Based on market research, Nestlé knows that its cereal is only mediocre. Although advertising would sell one box to each of 1 million consumers, the consumers would quickly learn that the cereal is not very good and stop buying it. Nestlé decides it is not worth paying €10 million in advertising to get only €3 million in sales. So it does not bother to advertise. It sends its cooks back to the drawing board to find another recipe.

Kellogg, on the other hand, knows that its cereal is great. Each person who tries it will buy a box a month for the next year. Thus, the €10 million in advertising will bring in €36 million in sales. Advertising is profitable here because

Kellogg has a good product that consumers will buy repeatedly. Thus, Kellogg chooses to advertise.

Now that we have considered the behaviour of the two firms, let's consider the behaviour of consumers. We began by asserting that consumers are inclined to try a new cereal that they see advertised. But is this behaviour rational? Should a consumer try a new cereal just because the seller has chosen to advertise it?

In fact, it may be completely rational for consumers to try new products that they see advertised. In our story, consumers decide to try Kellogg's new cereal because Kellogg advertises. Kellogg chooses to advertise because it knows that its cereal is quite good, while Nestlé chooses not to advertise because it knows that its cereal is only mediocre. By its willingness to spend money on advertising, Kellogg signals to consumers the quality of its cereal. Each consumer thinks, quite sensibly, 'Crikey, if the Kellogg Company is willing to spend so much money advertising this new cereal, it must be really good.'

What is most surprising about this theory of advertising is that the content of the advertisement is irrelevant. Kellogg signals the quality of its product by its willingness to spend money on advertising. (This example is used for illustrative purposes only and is not meant to infer that Nestlé deliberately produces inferior products!)

What the advertisements say is not as important as the fact that consumers know ads are expensive. By contrast, cheap advertising cannot be effective at signalling quality to consumers. In our example, if an advertising campaign cost less than €3 million, both Nestlé and Kellogg would use it to market their new cereals. Because both good and mediocre cereals would be advertised, consumers could not infer the quality of a new cereal from the fact that it is advertised. Over time, consumers would learn to ignore such cheap advertising.

This theory can explain why firms pay celebrities large amounts of money to make advertisements that, on the surface, appear to convey no information at all. The information is not in the advertisement's content, but simply in its existence and expense.

Brand Names

branding
the means by which a business creates an identity for itself and highlights the way in which it differs from its rivals

Advertising is closely related to the existence of **branding**. In many markets, there are two types of firms. Some firms sell products with widely recognized brand names, while other firms sell generic substitutes. For example, in a typical supermarket, you can find Pepsi next to less familiar colas, or Kellogg's cornflakes next to the supermarket's own brand of cornflakes, made for it by an unknown firm. Most often, the firm with the famous brand name spends more on advertising and charges a higher price for its product.

Just as there is disagreement about the economics of advertising, there is disagreement about the economics of brand names and branding. Let's consider both sides of the debate.

Critics of brand names argue that branding causes consumers to perceive differences that do not really exist. In many cases, the generic good is almost indistinguishable from the brand-name good. Consumers' willingness to pay more for the brand-name good, these critics assert, is a form of irrationality fostered by advertising. Economist Edward Chamberlin, one of the early developers of the theory of monopolistic competition, concluded from this argument that brand names were bad for the economy. He proposed that the government discourage their use by refusing to enforce the exclusive trademarks that companies use to identify their products.

More recently, economists have defended brand names as a useful way for consumers to ensure that the goods they buy are of high quality. There are two

FYI

Contestable Markets

Most economics textbooks up to the late 1970s covered market structures ranging from perfect competition from one extreme to monopoly at the other. Changes in the way businesses actually operated in the real world meant that there were some gaps between the theory and the observed behaviour of firms. This led to the development of a new theory which was incorporated into the explanation of market structures. The theory of contestable markets was developed by William J. Baumol, John Panzar and Robert Willig in 1982.

The key characteristic of a perfectly contestable market (the benchmark to explain firms' behaviours) was that firms were influenced by the threat of new entrants into a market. We have seen how, in monopolistically competitive markets, despite the fact that each firm has some monopoly control over its product, the ease of entry and exit means that in the long run profits can be competed away as new firms enter the market. This threat of new entrants may make firms behave in a way that departs from what was assumed to be the traditional goal of firms – to maximize profits. The suggestion by Baumol and colleagues was that firms may deliberately limit profits made to discourage new entrants. The other char-

acteristics of a perfectly contestable market are that there are no barriers to entry or exit and no sunk costs. Profits might be limited by what was termed *entry limit pricing*. This refers to a situation where a firm will keep prices lower than they could be in order to deter new entrants. Similarly, firms may also practise *predatory or destroyer pricing* whereby the price is held below average cost for a period to try and force out competitors or prevent new firms from entering the market. Incumbent firms may be in a position to do this because they may have been able to gain some advantages of economies of scale which new entrants may not be able to exploit.

In a contestable market firms may also erect other artificial barriers to prevent entry into the industry by new firms. Such barriers might include operating at over-capacity, which provides the opportunity to flood the market and drive down price in the event of a threat of entry. Firms will also carry out aggressive marketing and branding strategies to 'tighten' up the market or find ways of reducing costs and increasing efficiency to gain competitive advantage. Searching out sources of competitive advantage was a topic written on extensively by Michael Porter, who defined competitive advantage

as being the advantages firms can gain over another which are both distinctive and defensible. These sources are not simply to be found in terms of new product development but through close investigation and analysis of the supply chain, where little changes might make a difference to the cost base of a firm which it can then exploit to its advantage.

Hit-and-run tactics might be evident in a contestable market where firms enter the industry, take the profit and get out quickly (possible because of the freedom of entry and exit). In other cases firms may indulge in what is termed *cream-skimming* – identifying parts of the market that are high in value added and exploiting those markets.

The theory of contestable markets has been widely adopted as a beneficial addition to the theory of the firm and there has been extensive research into its application. There are numerous examples of markets exhibiting contestability characteristics including financial services; airlines, especially flights on domestic routes; the IT industry and in particular internet service providers (ISPs), software and web developers; energy supplies and the postal service.

related arguments. First, brand names provide consumers with *information* which cannot be easily judged in advance of purchase. Second, brand names give firms an *incentive* to meet the needs of consumers, because firms have a financial stake in maintaining the reputation of their brand names. Note that branding does not always equate to high quality. Some firms will happily admit their goods are 'cheap and cheerful' but point out that they provide consumers with value for money. A number of discount stores, for example, expanded during the recession in 2008–09. Firms such as Lidl, Netto, Poundstretcher and Poundland are

"No response - we'll have to use the corporate logo flashcards again"

interested in developing their brand names as much as Armani and Ralph Lauren. Consumers were able to associate the brand name with value for money – important when times are difficult.

To see how these arguments work in practice, consider a famous brand name: Ibis hotels. Imagine that you are driving through an unfamiliar town and you need somewhere to stay for the night. You see a Hotel Ibis and a local hotel next door to it. Which do you choose? The local hotel may in fact offer better accommodation at lower prices, but you have no way of knowing that. In contrast, Hotel Ibis offers a consistent product across many European cities. Its brand name is useful to you as a way of judging the quality of what you are about to buy.

The Ibis brand name also ensures that the company has an incentive to maintain quality. For example, if some customers were to become very ill from bad food served at breakfast at a Hotel Ibis, the news would be disastrous for the company. Ibis would lose much of the valuable reputation that it has built up over the years and, as a result, it would lose sales and profit not just in the hotel that served the bad food but in its many hotels across Europe. By contrast, if some customers were to become ill from bad food served at breakfast in a local hotel, that restaurant might have to close down, but the lost profits would be much smaller. Hence, Ibis has a greater incentive to ensure that its breakfast food is safe.

The debate over brand names thus centres on the question of whether consumers are rational in preferring brand names over generic substitutes. Critics of brand names argue that brand names are the result of an irrational consumer response to advertising. Defenders of brand names argue that consumers have good reason to pay more for brand-name products because they can be more confident in the quality of these products.

Quick Quiz How might advertising make markets less competitive? How might it make markets more competitive? • Give the arguments for and against brand names.

CONCLUSION

Monopolistic competition is true to its name: it is a hybrid of monopoly and competition. Like a monopoly, each monopolistic competitor faces a downward sloping demand curve and, as a result, charges a price above marginal cost. As in a perfectly competitive market, there are many firms, and entry and exit drive the profit of each monopolistic competitor toward zero. Table 16.2 summarizes these lessons.

Because monopolistically competitive firms produce differentiated products, each firm advertises in order to attract customers to its own brand. To some extent, advertising manipulates consumers' tastes, promotes irrational brand loyalty and impedes competition. To a larger extent, advertising provides information, establishes brand names of reliable quality and fosters competition.

The theory of monopolistic competition seems to describe many markets in the economy. It is somewhat disappointing, therefore, that the theory does not yield simple and compelling advice for public policy. From the standpoint of the economic theorist, the allocation of resources in monopolistically competitive markets is not perfect. Yet, from the standpoint of a practical policy maker, there may be little that can be done to improve it.

TABLE 16.2

Monopolistic Competition: Between Perfect Competition and Monopoly

	Market structure		
	Perfect competition	Monopolistic competition	Monopoly
Features that all three market structures share			
Goal of firms	Maximize profits	Maximize profits	Maximize profits
Rule for maximizing	$MR = MC$	$MR = MC$	$MR = MC$
Can earn economic profits in the short run?	Yes	Yes	Yes
Features that monopoly and monopolistic competition share			
Price taker?	Yes	No	No
Price	$P = MC$	$P > MC$	$P > MC$
Produces welfare-maximizing level of output?	Yes	No	No
Features that perfect competition and monopolistic competition share			
Number of firms	Many	Many	One
Entry in long run?	Yes	Yes	No
Can earn economic profits in long run?	No	No	Yes

IN THE NEWS

The debate over the role of advertising and branding is a complex one with few clear cut answers. If firms see an opportunity to be able to differentiate their products from rivals then advertising and branding may be ways that they can reinforce these differences in the minds of consumers. In some cases, firms may specifically choose to focus on developing the brand because it gives them an advantage in what can be a crowded and often unforgiving market place. This article explains one such example which shows that a focus on the brand can have some benefits to both the business and to consumers.

Innis & Gunn

The brewing industry is dominated by a relatively small number or large firms but for many ordinary consumers the market is one which is characterized by brands with few having any idea (or indeed caring) about which major brewer is behind the brand. Competition between brands is intensive and as the industry has become more and more concentrated, the scope for new firms to enter the market has become increasingly difficult. In addition, the industry has faced challenging times over the past few years. In the UK, rising duties on alcohol, the recession, changes in the way that alcoholic drinks are sold not to mention the concern over alcohol abuse have all conspired to cause commercial difficulties for brewers. The British Beer & Pub Association (BB&PA) has published figures showing that in the first half of 2009, an average of 52 pubs a week closed down – 33 per cent more than the equivalent period in 2008 – and 24 000 jobs were lost in the industry over this time. You might not think that this was an industrial climate to launch a new brewing enterprise but the story of Innis & Gunn shows how even within an industry beset by problems there are entrepreneurial opportunities that can be exploited.

The Innis & Gunn brewery is run by Dougal Sharp. His father, Russell Sharp, led a management buyout of the Caledonian brewery in Edinburgh and Dougal became the head brewer, putting his degree in environmental chemistry to use. Caledonian had been working with whisky producer, William Grant & Sons, and had developed a brew that was used to help the production of whisky in oak casks. The brew flavoured the casks prior to the whisky being put in at which point it was supposed to be drained off and discarded. However, Sharp's attention was brought to the fact that this by-product was actually a tasty beer in its own right. After discussion with Grants it was decided to set up a new company to market the by-product – the birth of Innis & Gunn.

Sharp decided that the focus of the new product would be the brand. By building up the brand other factors such as the location of production could be less of a problem. It means, for example, that it is not essential to have a production facility in Scotland, which could be expensive. This opens up the opportunity for the company to outsource production. The key was to build relationships with suppliers and to make sure those suppliers understood the brand. The firm keeps a close eye on the production process and specifies the ingredients used and the maturation process but another Scottish brewery actually produces the beer. Having sorted out the outsourcing of the brewing, Innis & Gunn were then able to plough their limited funds into promoting the brand. The focus on the brand has been deliberate, therefore, and is designed to try and make the beer synonymous with Scotland in the same way that whisky is.

Since 2004 the business has enjoyed growth of 60 per cent per annum on average and the beer sells around half a million cases each year with revenues of around £5 million. Sharp has a target to break the million case mark in the medium term. Its main sales channel in the UK has been supermarkets and off-licences but it is hoped that this can be broadened to include pubs and possibly a draught version of the beer. It has also been successful in export markets which accounts for around 65 per cent of its revenue. It has become the best selling British bottled beer in terms of value and sales in Canada and in early 2010 the company began to turn its attention to the US market. Prior to the decision to target this new market, sales in the US only accounted for 3 per cent of Innis & Gunn's sales but Sharp noted that the total market for the sort of beer the firm is producing makes up 16 per cent of the US beer market – the so called 'craft beer' segment. The company appointed a dedicated marketing and sales team to the US to try and develop the market all based around the promotion of the brand.

The ability of small and medium-sized enterprises (SMEs) to enter mature markets dominated by larger firms is limited. Few are going to be able to set up full production and distribution facilities to compete with those of their bigger rivals – the cost disadvantages are simply too great. By focusing on the brand the firm can instead develop the demand side of the business by encouraging sales outlets and customers of the quality of the product and driving demand as a result. This type of behaviour is one that provides a different business model to the traditional image of a brewer and is another reminder of how the theory of firms is constantly changing as market structures evolve and businesses change to meet new market conditions.

Source: Adapted from Biz/ed 'In the News'. http://www.bized.co.uk/cgi-bin/chron/chron.pl?id=3559

SUMMARY

- A monopolistically competitive market is characterized by three attributes: many firms, differentiated products and free entry.

- The equilibrium in a monopolistically competitive market differs from that in a perfectly competitive market in two related ways. First, each firm in a monopolistically competitive market has excess capacity. That is, it operates on the downward sloping portion of the average total cost curve. Secondly, each firm charges a price above marginal cost.

- Monopolistic competition does not have all the desirable properties of perfect competition. There is the standard deadweight loss of monopoly caused by the mark-up of price over marginal cost. In addition, the number of firms (and thus the variety of products) can be too large or too small. In practice, the ability of policy makers to correct these inefficiencies is limited.

- The product differentiation inherent in monopolistic competition leads to the use of advertising and brand names. Critics of advertising and brand names argue that firms use them to take advantage of consumer irrationality and to reduce competition. Defenders of advertising and brand names argue that firms use them to inform consumers and to compete more vigorously on price and product quality.

KEY CONCEPTS

monopolistic competition, p. 338   branding, p. 348

QUESTIONS FOR REVIEW

1. Describe the three attributes of monopolistic competition. How is monopolistic competition like monopoly? How is it like perfect competition?

2. Draw a diagram depicting a firm in a monopolistically competitive market that is making profits. Now show what happens to this firm as new firms enter the industry.

3. Draw a diagram of the long-run equilibrium in a monopolistically competitive market. How is price related to average total cost? How is price related to marginal cost?

4. Does a monopolistic competitor produce too much or too little output compared to the most efficient level? What

practical considerations make it difficult for policy makers to solve this problem?

5. How might advertising reduce economic well-being? How might advertising increase economic well-being?

6. How might advertising with no apparent informational content in fact convey information to consumers?

7. Explain two benefits that might arise from the existence of brand names.

PROBLEMS AND APPLICATIONS

1. Classify the following markets as perfectly competitive, monopolistic or monopolistically competitive, and explain your answers.
   a. wooden HB pencils
   b. bottled water
   c. copper
   d. local telephone service
   e. strawberry jam
   f. lipstick.

2. What feature of the product being sold distinguishes a monopolistically competitive firm from a monopolistic firm?

3. The chapter states that monopolistically competitive firms could increase the quantity they produce and lower the average total cost of production. Why don't they do so?

4. Sparkle is one firm of many in the market for toothpaste, which is in long-run equilibrium.
   a. Draw a diagram showing Sparkle's demand curve, marginal revenue curve, average total cost curve, and marginal cost curve. Label Sparkle's profit-maximizing output and price.
   b. What is Sparkle's profit? Explain.

   c. On your diagram, show the consumer surplus derived from the purchase of Sparkle toothpaste. Also show the deadweight loss relative to the efficient level of output.
   d. If the government forced Sparkle to produce the efficient level of output, what would happen to the firm? What would happen to Sparkle's customers?

5. Do monopolistically competitive markets typically have the optimal number of products? Explain.

6. The chapter says that monopolistically competitive firms may send greetings cards to their customers. What do they accomplish by this? Explain in words and with a diagram.

7. If you were thinking of entering the ice cream business, would you try to make ice cream that is just like one of the existing (successful) brands? Explain your decision using the ideas of this chapter.

8. Describe three adverts that you have seen on TV. In what ways, if any, were each of these adverts socially useful? In what ways were they socially wasteful? Did the adverts affect the likelihood of your buying the product? Why or why not?

9. For each of the following pairs of firms, explain which firm would be more likely to engage in advertising:
   a. A family-owned farm or a family-owned restaurant.
   b. A manufacturer of forklift trucks or a manufacturer of cars.
   c. A company that invented a very reliable watch or a company that invented a less reliable watch that costs the same amount to make.

10. The makers of *Panadol* pain reliever do a lot of advertising and have very loyal customers. In contrast, the makers of generic paracetamol do no advertising, and their customers shop only for the lowest price. Assume that the marginal costs of *Panadol* and generic paracetamol are the same and constant.
    a. Draw a diagram showing *Panadol*'s demand, marginal revenue and marginal cost curves. Label *Panadol*'s price and mark-up over marginal cost.
    b. Repeat part (a) for a producer of generic paracetamol. How do the diagrams differ? Which company has the bigger mark-up? Explain.
    c. Which company has the bigger incentive for careful quality control? Why?

For further resources, visit
www.cengage.com/mankiw_taylor2

17 OLIGOPOLY

The Europeans love chocolate. The average German eats about 180 62-gram bars of chocolate a year. The Belgians are not far behind at 177 bars, the Swiss around 173 and the British eat around 164 bars per year. There are many firms producing chocolate in Europe including Anthon Berg in Denmark, Camille Bloch, Lindt and Favarger in Switzerland, Guylian and Godiva in Belgium and Hachez in Germany. However, Europeans are likely to find that what they are eating is likely to be made by one of three companies: Cadbury (now owned by US firm Kraft), Mars or Nestlé. These firms dominate the chocolate industry in the European Union. Being so large and dominant they are able to influence the quantity of chocolate bars produced and, given the market demand curve, the price at which chocolate bars are sold.

The previous three chapters discussed three types of market structure. In a competitive market, each firm is so small compared to the market that it cannot influence the price of its product and, therefore, takes the price as given by market conditions. In a monopolized market, a single firm supplies the entire market for a good, and that firm can choose any price and quantity on the market demand curve. In a monopolistic competitive structure, there are many small firms but each is able to differentiate their product in some way and so has some small influence on price.

The European market for chocolate bars fits neither the competitive nor the monopoly model. Competition and monopoly are extreme forms of market structure. Competition occurs when there are many firms in a market offering essentially identical products; monopoly occurs when there is only one firm in a market. It is natural to start the study of industrial organization with these polar cases, for they are the easiest cases to understand. Yet many industries, including the chocolate industry, fall somewhere between these two extremes. Firms in these industries have competitors but, at the same time, do not face so much competition that they are price takers. Economists call this situation *imperfect competition*.

In this chapter we discuss the types of imperfect competition and examine a particular type called *oligopoly*. The essence of an oligopolistic market is that there are only a few sellers. The small number of sellers makes rigorous competition less likely, and it makes strategic interactions among them vitally important. As a result, the actions of any one seller in the market can have a large impact on the profits of all the other sellers. That is, oligopolistic firms are interdependent in a way that competitive firms are not. Our goal in this chapter is to see how this interdependence shapes the firms' behaviour and what problems it raises for public policy.

BETWEEN MONOPOLY AND PERFECT COMPETITION

The cases of perfect competition and monopoly illustrate some important ideas about how markets work. Most markets in the economy, however, include elements of both these cases and, therefore, are not completely described by either of them. The typical firm in the economy faces competition, but the competition is not so rigorous as to make the firm exactly described by the price-taking firm analysed in Chapter 14. The typical firm also has some degree of market power, but its market power is not so great that the firm can be exactly described by the monopoly firm analysed in Chapter 15. In other words, the typical firm in our economy is imperfectly competitive.

There are two types of imperfectly competitive markets. As we saw in Chapter 16, monopolistic competition describes a market structure in which there are many firms selling products that are similar but not identical. An **oligopoly** is a market with only a few sellers, each offering a product similar or identical to the others. One example is the market for chocolate bars. Another is the world market for crude oil: a few countries in the Middle East control much of the world's oil reserves.

Figure 17.1 summarizes the four types of market structure. The first question to ask about any market is how many firms there are. If there is only one firm, the market is a monopoly. If there are only a few firms, the market is an oligopoly. If there are many firms, we need to ask another question: do the firms sell identical or differentiated products? If the many firms sell differentiated products, the market is monopolistically competitive. If the many firms sell identical products, the market is perfectly competitive.

Reality, of course, is never as clear-cut as theory. In some cases you may find it hard to decide what structure best describes a market. There is, for instance, no magic number that separates 'few' from 'many' when counting the number of firms. (Do the approximately dozen companies that now sell cars in Europe make this market an oligopoly or more competitive? The answer is open to debate.) Similarly, there is no sure way to determine when products are differentiated and when they are identical. (Are different brands of milk really the same? Again, the answer is debatable.) When analysing actual markets, economists have to keep in mind the lessons learned from studying all types of market structure and then apply each lesson as it seems appropriate.

oligopoly
competition amongst the few – a market structure in which only a few sellers offer similar or identical products and dominate the market

FIGURE 17.1

The Four Types of Market Structure

Economists who study industrial organization divide markets into four types – monopoly, oligopoly, monopolistic competition and perfect competition.

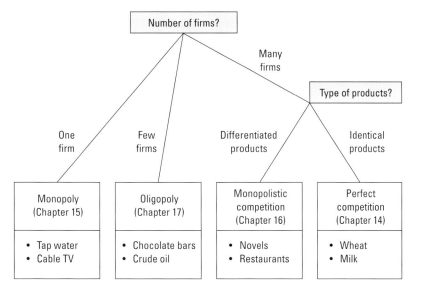

Quick Quiz Define oligopoly and monopolistic competition and give an example of each.

MARKETS WITH ONLY A FEW SELLERS

If a market is dominated by a relatively small number of sellers it is said to be *concentrated*. The *concentration ratio* refers to the proportion of the total market share accounted for by the top *x* number of firms in the industry. For example, a five-firm concentration ratio of 80 per cent means that five firms account for 80 per cent of market share; a three-firm concentration ratio of 72 per cent would indicate that three firms account for 72 per cent of total market sales and so on. There are a number of examples of oligopolistic market structures including brewing, banking, mobile phone networks, the chemical and oil industries, the grocery/supermarket industry, detergents, and entertainment. Note that in each of these industries there might be many sellers in the industry (there are thousands of small independent breweries across Europe, for example) but sales are dominated by a relatively small number of firms. In brewing, the industry is dominated by A-BInBev, Heineken, Carlsberg and SABMiller.

A key feature of oligopoly is the tension that exists between the firms of cooperation and self-interest. The group of oligopolists is best off cooperating and acting like a monopolist – producing a small quantity of output and charging a price above marginal cost. Yet because each oligopolist cares about only its own profit, there are powerful incentives at work that hinder a group of firms from maintaining the monopoly outcome.

A Duopoly Example

To understand the behaviour of oligopolies, let's consider an oligopoly with only two members, called a *duopoly*. Duopoly is the simplest type of oligopoly. Oligopolies with three or more members face the same problems as oligopolies with only two members, so we do not lose much by starting with the case of duopoly.

Imagine a town in which only two residents – Jack and Jill – own wells that produce water safe for drinking. Each Saturday, Jack and Jill decide how many litres of water to pump, bring the water to town, and sell it for whatever price the market will bear. To keep things simple, suppose that Jack and Jill can pump as much water as they want without cost. That is, the marginal cost of water equals zero.

Table 17.1 shows the town's demand schedule for water. The first column shows the total quantity demanded, and the second column shows the price. If the two well owners sell a total of 10 litres of water, water goes for €110 a litre. If they sell a total of 20 litres, the price falls to €100 a litre. And so on. If you graphed these two columns of numbers, you would get a standard downward sloping demand curve.

The last column in Table 17.1 shows the total revenue from the sale of water. It equals the quantity sold times the price. Because there is no cost to pumping water, the total revenue of the two producers equals their total profit.

Let's now consider how the organization of the town's water industry affects the price of water and the quantity of water sold.

Competition, Monopolies and Cartels

Before considering the price and quantity of water that would result from the duopoly of Jack and Jill, let's discuss briefly the two market structures we already understand: competition and monopoly.

TABLE 17.1

The Demand Schedule for Water

Quantity (in litres)	Price	Total revenue (and total profit)
0	€120	€ 0
10	110	1 100
20	100	2 000
30	90	2 700
40	80	3 200
50	70	3 500
60	60	3 600
70	50	3 500
80	40	3 200
90	30	2 700
100	20	2 000
110	10	1 100
120	0	0

Consider first what would happen if the market for water were perfectly competitive. In a competitive market, the production decisions of each firm drive price equal to marginal cost. In the market for water, marginal cost is zero. Thus, under competition, the equilibrium price of water would be zero, and the equilibrium quantity would be 120 litres. The price of water would reflect the cost of producing it, and the efficient quantity of water would be produced and consumed.

Now consider how a monopoly would behave. Table 17.1 shows that total profit is maximized at a quantity of 60 litres and a price of €60 a litre. A profit-maximizing monopolist, therefore, would produce this quantity and charge this price. As is standard for monopolies, price would exceed marginal cost. The result would be inefficient, for the quantity of water produced and consumed would fall short of the socially efficient level of 120 litres.

What outcome should we expect from our duopolists? One possibility is that Jack and Jill get together and agree on the quantity of water to produce and the price to charge for it. Such an agreement among firms over production and price is called **collusion**, and the group of firms acting in unison is called a **cartel**. Once a cartel is formed, the market is in effect served by a monopoly, and we can apply our analysis from Chapter 15. That is, if Jack and Jill were to collude, they would agree on the monopoly outcome because that outcome maximizes the total profit that the producers can get from the market. Our two producers would produce a total of 60 litres, which would be sold at a price of €60 a litre. Once again, price exceeds marginal cost, and the outcome is socially inefficient.

A cartel must agree not only on the total level of production but also on the amount produced by each member. In our case, Jack and Jill must agree how to split between themselves the monopoly production of 60 litres. Each member of the cartel will want a larger share of the market because a larger market share means larger profit. If Jack and Jill agreed to split the market equally, each would produce 30 litres, the price would be €60 a litre and each would get a profit of €1 800.

collusion
an agreement among firms in a market about quantities to produce or prices to charge

cartel
a group of firms acting in unison

The Equilibrium for an Oligopoly

Although oligopolists would like to form cartels and earn monopoly profits, often that is not possible. As we discuss later in this chapter, competition laws prohibit explicit agreements among oligopolists as a matter of public policy. In addition, squabbling among cartel members over how to divide the profit in the market sometimes makes agreement among them impossible. Let's therefore consider what happens if Jack and Jill decide separately how much water to produce.

At first, one might expect Jack and Jill to reach the monopoly outcome on their own, for this outcome maximizes their joint profit. In the absence of a binding agreement, however, the monopoly outcome is unlikely. To see why, imagine that Jack expects Jill to produce only 30 litres (half of the monopoly quantity). Jack would reason as follows:

> I could produce 30 litres as well. In this case, a total of 60 litres of water would be sold at a price of €60 a litre. My profit would be €1 800 (30 litres × €60 a litre). Alternatively, I could produce 40 litres. In this case, a total of 70 litres of water would be sold at a price of €50 a litre. My profit would be €2 000 (40 litres × €50 a litre). Even though total profit in the market would fall, my profit would be higher, because I would have a larger share of the market.

Of course, Jill might reason the same way. If so, Jack and Jill would each bring 40 litres to town. Total sales would be 80 litres, and the price would fall to €40.

Thus, if the duopolists individually pursue their own self-interest when deciding how much to produce, they produce a total quantity greater than the monopoly quantity, charge a price lower than the monopoly price and earn total profit less than the monopoly profit.

Although the logic of self-interest increases the duopoly's output above the monopoly level, it does not push the duopolists to reach the competitive allocation. Consider what happens when each duopolist is producing 40 litres. The price is €40, and each duopolist makes a profit of €1 600. In this case, Jack's self-interested logic leads to a different conclusion:

> Right now my profit is €1 600. Suppose I increase my production to 50 litres. In this case, a total of 90 litres of water would be sold, and the price would be €30 a litre. Then my profit would be only €1 500. Rather than increasing production and driving down the price, I am better off keeping my production at 40 litres.

The outcome in which Jack and Jill each produce 40 litres looks like some sort of equilibrium. In fact, this outcome is called a **Nash equilibrium** (named after economic theorist John Nash, whose life was portrayed in the book, *A Beautiful Mind,* and the film of the same name). A Nash equilibrium is a situation in which economic actors interacting with one another each choose their best strategy given the strategies the others have chosen. In this case, given that Jill is producing 40 litres, the best strategy for Jack is to produce 40 litres. Similarly, given that Jack is producing 40 litres, the best strategy for Jill is to produce 40 litres. Once they reach this Nash equilibrium, neither Jack nor Jill has an incentive to make a different decision.

This example illustrates the tension between cooperation and self-interest. Oligopolists would be better off cooperating and reaching the monopoly outcome. Yet because they pursue their own self-interest, they do not end up reaching the monopoly outcome and maximizing their joint profit. Each oligopolist is tempted to raise production and capture a larger share of the market. As each of them tries to do this, total production rises, and the price falls.

At the same time, self-interest does not drive the market all the way to the competitive outcome. Like monopolists, oligopolists are aware that increases in the amount they produce reduce the price of their product. Therefore, they stop short of following the competitive firm's rule of producing up to the point where price equals marginal cost.

In summary, when firms in an oligopoly individually choose production to maximize profit, they produce a quantity of output greater than the level produced by monopoly and less than the level produced by competition. The oligopoly price is less than the monopoly price but greater than the competitive price (which equals marginal cost).

Nash equilibrium
a situation in which economic actors interacting with one another each choose their best strategy given the strategies that all the other actors have chosen

How the Size of an Oligopoly Affects the Market Outcome

We can use the insights from this analysis of duopoly to discuss how the size of an oligopoly is likely to affect the outcome in a market. Suppose, for instance, that Darby and Joan suddenly discover water sources on their property and join Jack and Jill in the water oligopoly. The demand schedule in Table 17.1 remains the same, but now more producers are available to satisfy this demand. How would an increase in the number of sellers from two to four affect the price and quantity of water in the town?

If the sellers of water could form a cartel, they would once again try to maximize total profit by producing the monopoly quantity and charging the monopoly

F Y I

John Nash – A Beautiful Mind

The story of John Nash was dramatized in the film 'A Beautiful Mind' based on a book of the same name by Sylvia Nasar. Nash entered the world of game theory in the late 1940s and 1950s and gained the Nobel Prize for Economics in 1994 for his contribution to the field. (The scene in the film where Nash 'hits' upon his idea based on him and his friends choosing a girl to date is dramatic licence but an interesting way of presenting the theory all the same!) His work has had an impact on all manner of economic and political situations. It is important to remember that Nash was not an economist – he was a mathematician. In fact, Nash only took one course of economics during his undergraduate studies – a course in International Trade – and that was only to fulfil the degree requirements of the course he was on. Nash's ideas, therefore, are purely in the realm of the application of mathematical ideas to a bargaining problem. The application to economics and other areas has been somewhat broader.

At the heart of Nash's ideas were the mix of both cooperative and non-cooperative games. In the former, there are enforceable agreements between players whilst in the latter there are not. The key thing in both cases is that the players in the game know that they cannot predict with any certainty what the other is going to do (exactly the situation facing firms in an oligopolistic market). Equally, they know what *they* want but are aware that all the other players think as they do. It has been referred to as the 'I think he thinks that I think that he thinks that I think...' scenario.

The solutions that Nash derived were based around this thinking, where each player had to try to put him or herself in the position of others.

The 'equilibrium' position would be where each player makes a decision which represents the best outcome in response to what other players' decisions are. The definition of a Nash equilibrium is a point where no player can improve their position by selecting any other available strategy whilst others are also playing their best option and not changing their strategies. One of the implications of Nash's work is that cooperation may well be the best option in the long term.

Let us take an example.

Assume there are two firms competing with each other for profits in a market. The two firms have three decisions to make with regard to their pricing strategies. They can choose to set their price at either €10, €20 or €30. The matrix showing the profits made at these different prices is shown in Table 17.2 below.

TABLE 17.2

If we look at the situation when each firm decides to set their price at €30, they both make a profit of €60. This, however, is not a Nash equilibrium, since Firm A could improve its position by reducing its price by €10 to €20, whilst B's strategy remains the same (setting price at €30). In this case, A would now gain a profit of €100 rather than €60.

Let's compare this to the situation where both firms set their price at €10. In this case, if Firm A decided to raise their price to €20, they would be worse off if B continued the strategy of charging €10. In such an instance, A would make a loss of 20. The same position applies to firm B. There is no incentive, therefore, for either firm to change their position; the pay-off of zero profit at a price of €10 represents a Nash equilibrium. Any other pricing decision by either firm would lead to one having an incentive to change its price to gain some advantage.

The work of people like John Nash has opened up new insights into human behaviour and the way in which they interact, make decisions and engage in economic bargaining and activity.

price. Just as when there were only two sellers, the members of the cartel would need to agree on production levels for each member and find some way to enforce the agreement. As the cartel grows larger, however, this outcome is less likely. Reaching and enforcing an agreement becomes more difficult as the size of the group increases.

If the oligopolists do not form a cartel – perhaps because competition laws prohibit it – they must each decide on their own how much water to produce. To see how the increase in the number of sellers affects the outcome, consider the decision facing each seller. At any time, each well owner has the option to raise production by 1 litre. In making this decision, the well owner weighs two effects:

- *The output effect*. Because price is above marginal cost, selling one more litre of water at the going price will raise profit.
- *The price effect*. Raising production will increase the total amount sold, which will lower the price of water and lower the profit on all the other litres sold.

If the output effect is larger than the price effect, the well owner will increase production. If the price effect is larger than the output effect, the owner will not raise production. (In fact, in this case, it is profitable to reduce production.) Each oligopolist continues to increase production until these two marginal effects exactly balance, taking the other firms' production as given.

Now consider how the number of firms in the industry affects the marginal analysis of each oligopolist. The larger the number of sellers, the less concerned each seller is about its own impact on the market price. That is, as the oligopoly grows in size, the magnitude of the price effect falls. When the oligopoly grows very large, the price effect disappears altogether, leaving only the output effect. In this extreme case, each firm in the oligopoly increases production as long as price is above marginal cost.

We can now see that a large oligopoly is essentially a group of competitive firms. A competitive firm considers only the output effect when deciding how much to produce: because a competitive firm is a price taker, the price effect is absent. Thus, as the number of sellers in an oligopoly grows larger, an oligopolistic market looks more and more like a competitive market. The price approaches marginal cost, and the quantity produced approaches the socially efficient level.

This analysis of oligopoly offers a new perspective on the effects of international trade. Imagine that Toyota and Honda are the only car manufacturers in Japan, Volkswagen and BMW are the only car manufacturers in Germany, and Citroën and Peugeot are the only car manufacturers in France. If these nations prohibited international trade in cars, each would have a motorcar oligopoly with only two members, and the market outcome would likely depart substantially from the competitive ideal. With international trade, however, the car market is a

IN THE NEWS

Cement Cartels in South Africa

Firms in oligopolistic markets may recognize that finding a way of colluding with rivals will improve their own position. Sometimes price movements may look suspicious but there may be a perfectly reasonable explanation; in other cases, the movements may be exactly what they seem to be – price-fixing by firms.

There have been concerns about competition in the cement industry in Europe for some time but it seems that it is not only Europe that may have problems in this respect. In June 2009, the South African Competition Commission launched raids on the headquarters of a number of cement producers including Pretoria Portland Cement (PPC) Africa's biggest cement producer, Lafarge Industries South Africa, AfriSam Consortium and Natal Portland Cement. The raids were in relation to suspicions of price fixing in the industry.

The Commission noted that despite changes in input prices and the level of demand, the price of cement from producers in South Africa rose broadly in line every six months. The rise in price, in each case, was far above levels implied by the producer price index (PPI), an indicator of the overall input costs in the South African economy. These price rises for cement have averaged at 6 per cent each time making the annual increases around 12 per cent. It is believed that the allegations, if true, had significantly added to infrastructure costs in South Africa. Such projects were particularly sensitive given the investment in infrastructure in preparation for the World Cup finals, which South Africa hosted in 2010.

The investigations were linked to those being conducted in the European Union (EU) and Brazil and centre on price-fixing, the control or limitation of cement extenders (chemicals or other materials added to slurry to increase the yield) and the abuse of its dominant position in the market by PPC. As a result of the raids and the subsequent investigations, PPC admitted that it had taken part in a cartel of cement companies with the aim of fixing prices. In return for this admission and subsequent help with the Commission's investigation, PPC received some leniency in its treatment.

The investigation, along with costs related to a black empowerment deal, meant that PPC had to post a fall in profits for the financial year of 40 per cent. The empowerment deal is part of the South African government's drive to set quotas for businesses to increase the involvement of blacks in ownership, procurement and employment to better reflect the fact that the majority of the population in the country are black.

world market, and the oligopoly in this example has six members. Allowing free trade increases the number of producers from which each consumer can choose, and this increased competition keeps prices closer to marginal cost. Thus, the theory of oligopoly provides another reason, in addition to the theory of comparative advantage discussed in Chapter 3, why all countries can benefit from free trade.

Quick Quiz If the members of an oligopoly could agree on a total quantity to produce, what quantity would they choose? • If the oligopolists do not act together but instead make production decisions individually, do they produce a total quantity more or less than in your answer to the previous question? Why?

GAME THEORY AND THE ECONOMICS OF COOPERATION

As we have seen, oligopolies would like to reach the monopoly outcome, but doing so requires cooperation, which at times is difficult to maintain. In this section we look more closely at the problems people face when cooperation is desirable but difficult. To analyse the economics of cooperation, we need to learn a little about game theory.

game theory
the study of how people behave in strategic situations

Game theory is the study of how people behave in strategic situations. By 'strategic' we mean a situation in which each person, when deciding what actions to take, must consider how others might respond to that action. Because the number of firms in an oligopolistic market is small, each firm must act strategically. Each firm knows that its profit depends not only on how much it produces but also on how much the other firms produce. In making its production decision, each firm in an oligopoly should consider how its decision might affect the production decisions of all the other firms.

Game theory is not necessary for understanding competitive or monopoly markets. In a competitive market, each firm is so small compared to the market that strategic interactions with other firms are not important. In a monopolized market, strategic interactions are absent because the market has only one firm. But, as we will see, game theory is quite useful for understanding the behaviour of oligopolies.

prisoners' dilemma
a particular 'game' between two captured prisoners that illustrates why cooperation is difficult to maintain even when it is mutually beneficial

A particularly important 'game' is called the **prisoners' dilemma**. This game provides insight into the difficulty of maintaining cooperation. Many times in life, people fail to cooperate with one another even when cooperation would make them all better off. An oligopoly is just one example. The story of the prisoners' dilemma contains a general lesson that applies to any group trying to maintain cooperation among its members.

The Prisoners' Dilemma

The prisoners' dilemma is a story about two criminals who have been captured by the police. Let's call them Mr Green and Mr Blue. The police have enough evidence to convict Mr Green and Mr Blue of a relatively minor crime, illegal possession of a handgun, so that each would spend a year in jail. The police also suspect that the two criminals have committed a jewellery robbery together, but they lack hard evidence to convict them of this major crime. The police question Mr Green and Mr Blue in separate rooms, and they offer each of them the following deal:

> Right now we can lock you up for 1 year. If you confess to the jewellery robbery and implicate your partner, however, we'll give you immunity and you can go free. Your partner will get 20 years in jail. But if you both confess to the crime, we won't need your testimony and we can avoid the cost of a trial, so you will each get an intermediate sentence of 8 years.

If Mr Green and Mr Blue, heartless criminals that they are, care only about their own sentences, what would you expect them to do? Would they confess or remain silent? Figure 17.2 shows their choices. Each prisoner has two strategies: confess or remain silent. The sentence each prisoner gets depends on the strategy he or she chooses and the strategy chosen by his or her partner in crime.

Consider first Mr Green's decision. He reasons as follows:

> I don't know what Mr Blue is going to do. If he remains silent, my best strategy is to confess, since then I'll go free rather than spending a year in

FIGURE 17.2

The Prisoners' Dilemma

In this game between two criminals suspected of committing a crime, the sentence that each receives depends both on his decision whether to confess or remain silent and on the decision made by the other.

Mr Green's decision

	Confess	Remain silent
Confess	Mr Green gets 8 years Mr Blue gets 8 years	Mr Green gets 20 years Mr Blue goes free
Remain silent	Mr Green goes free Mr Blue gets 20 years	Mr Green gets 1 year Mr Blue gets 1 year

Mr Blue's decision

jail. If he confesses, my best strategy is still to confess, since then I'll spend 8 years in jail rather than 20. So, regardless of what Mr Blue does, I am better off confessing.

In the language of game theory, a strategy is called a **dominant strategy** if it is the best strategy for a player to follow regardless of the strategies pursued by other players. In this case, confessing is a dominant strategy for Mr Green. He spends less time in jail if he confesses, regardless of whether Mr Blue confesses or remains silent.

dominant strategy
a strategy that is best for a player in a game regardless of the strategies chosen by the other players

Now consider Mr Blue's decision. He faces exactly the same choices as Mr Green, and he reasons in much the same way. Regardless of what Mr Green does, Mr Blue can reduce his time in jail by confessing. In other words, confessing is also a dominant strategy for Mr Blue.

In the end, both Mr Green and Mr Blue confess, and both spend 8 years in jail. Yet, from their standpoint, this is a terrible outcome. If they had *both* remained silent, both of them would have been better off, spending only 1 year in jail on the gun charge. By each pursuing his own interests, the two prisoners together reach an outcome that is worse for each of them.

To see how difficult it is to maintain cooperation, imagine that, before the police captured Mr Green and Mr Blue, the two criminals had made a pact not to confess. Clearly, this agreement would make them both better off *if* they both live up to it, because they would each spend only 1 year in jail. But would the two criminals in fact remain silent, simply because they had agreed to? Once they are being questioned separately, the logic of self-interest takes over and leads them to confess. Cooperation between the two prisoners is difficult to maintain, because cooperation is individually irrational.

Oligopolies as a Prisoner's Dilemma

What does the prisoners' dilemma have to do with markets and imperfect competition? It turns out that the game oligopolists play in trying to reach the

FIGURE 17.3

An Oligopoly Game

In this game between members of an oligopoly, the profit that each earns depends on both its production decision and the production decision of the other oligopolist.

	Saudi Arabia's decision	
	High production	Low production
Iran's decision — High production	Saudi Arabia gets $40 billion Iran gets $40 billion	Saudi Arabia gets $30 billion Iran gets $60 billion
Iran's decision — Low production	Saudi Arabia gets $60 billion Iran gets $30 billion	Saudi Arabia gets $50 billion Iran gets $50 billion

monopoly outcome is similar to the game that the two prisoners play in the prisoners' dilemma.

Consider an oligopoly with two countries, Iran and Saudi Arabia. Both countries sell crude oil. After prolonged negotiation, the countries agree to keep oil production low in order to keep the world price of oil high. After they agree on production levels, each country must decide whether to cooperate and live up to this agreement or to ignore it and produce at a higher level. Figure 17.3 shows how the profits of the two countries depend on the strategies they choose.

Suppose you are the leader of Saudi Arabia. You might reason as follows:

I could keep production low as we agreed, or I could raise my production and sell more oil on world markets. If Iran lives up to the agreement and keeps its production low, then my country earns profit of $60 billion with high production and $50 billion with low production. In this case, Saudi Arabia is better off with high production. If Iran fails to live up to the agreement and produces at a high level, then my country earns $40 billion with high production and $30 billion with low production. Once again, Saudi Arabia is better off with high production. So, regardless of what Iran chooses to do, my country is better off reneging on our agreement and producing at a high level.

Producing at a high level is a dominant strategy for Saudi Arabia. Of course, Iran reasons in exactly the same way, and so both countries produce at a high level. The result is the inferior outcome (from Iran and Saudi Arabia's standpoint) with low profits for each country.

This example illustrates why oligopolies have trouble maintaining monopoly profits. The monopoly outcome is jointly rational for the oligopoly, but each oligopolist has an incentive to cheat. Just as self-interest drives the prisoners in the prisoners' dilemma to confess, self-interest makes it difficult for the oligopoly to maintain the cooperative outcome with low production, high prices and monopoly profits.

IN THE NEWS

Building in Prices?

Throughout the world, competition authorities are increasingly looking at pricing in markets and uncovering examples of price-fixing. Of course, firms engaging in such activity know that it is illegal and so go to great lengths to try and conceal the collusion. This article looks at an example of price-fixing in the construction industry in the UK and how new techniques are being increasingly deployed to uncover secrets that firms may be trying to hide.

For some years the activities of firms in the construction industry have been under some scrutiny but between 2007 and 2009, competition authorities in the UK looked in more detail at allegations of collusion contrary to competition law. In September 2009, competition authorities handed out hefty fines to a number of construction companies who were charged with breaching competition laws. The fines totalled £129.5 million and the companies concerned included Carillion, the Kier Group and Balfour Beatty. The accusations surround a practice known as 'cover pricing' and related to construction projects on a range of public sector works including a school in Derby and a hospital in Nottingham, both in the Midlands. The OFT looked at contracts over a period from 2000 to 2006 worth £200 million in total. The allegations focused on firms operating in general building work, house construction and commercial and industrial construction both in the public and the private sector.

The investigations centred on the way in which firms bid for and acquired contracts. The authorities were particularly interested in the tendering and bidding process for construction projects for cases of bid rigging cartel activity. This includes cases where a group of firms bid for a construction contract. The bids are supposed to be secret and this is meant to provide the

element of competition in the industry. However, there are suggestions that firms were agreeing to carve up the market between themselves. As a result of this they might disclose their intentions to each other so that 'rival' firms would put in bids far higher than the firm who was slated to win the contract. In some cases it is claimed that, because the tender process can be expensive, the 'winning' firm would add on a sum to its bid and use that extra sum is to compensate the 'losers'.

The competition authorities used the latest forensic techniques in their investigation which involved using digital evidence gathering by dissecting files on computers to access information. Firms may have believed that they were able to hide this evidence but these techniques were able to bring to light information that users may have thought was not there. The authorities in the UK also interviewed a number of individuals from the firms concerned. The investigation revealed evidence of bid rigging in thousands of tenders. The total value of these tenders was reported to be around £3 billion.

Many public sector construction projects require companies to be part of an approved list of those allowed to tender. If companies do not tender then they can risk losing their place on this list. In cases where a company may not

want the work, possibly because of capacity limitations, tenders may be put in which are way above the budget guidelines in the knowledge that the company concerned will not win the tender but still show that they are 'interested'. For example, a construction project for a new school might have a guide budget of £15 million. Three companies might put in bids but only one is a serious contender. The other two agree to put in bids which are way above the budget limit: for example, one might put in a tender of £20 million and the other of £22 million. The third puts in a tender of £18 million and wins the contract. Such collusion is against competition law.

The authorities also found that not only had collusion occurred but firms had even raised false invoices to distribute some of the surplus tender to other bidders. In the example above, the winning bidder might raise invoices totalling £500 000 each for the other two who did not win. The outcome is an effective sharing out of contracts amongst companies. The competition authorities said that this historic practice had potentially cost the taxpayer millions of pounds. The reason is that winning bids have been higher than would otherwise be the case under true competitive tendering.

Part of the problem is with the system of the way in which such tenders are operated. The assumption is that each firm operates in isolation and that each firm wants to win the tender it has bid for. Based on these twin assumptions, a firm will always try and submit a bid which is the lowest possible for the job in the hope that it will win and thus the taxpayer gets value for money from the process. Where the flaw in the process occurs is the assumption (and, companies might argue the necessity of bidding to stay on the approved tender list) that every bid is a serious one. The outcome is something that game theorists would not be slow to predict.

Source: Adapted from Biz/ed 'In the News'.

Other Examples of the Prisoners' Dilemma

We have seen how the prisoners' dilemma can be used to understand the problem facing oligopolies. The same logic applies to many other situations as well. Here we consider three examples in which self-interest prevents cooperation and leads to an inferior outcome for the parties involved.

Arms Races   An arms race is much like the prisoners' dilemma. To see this, consider the decisions of two countries – Iran and Israel – about whether to build new weapons or to disarm. Each country prefers to have more arms than the other because a larger arsenal would give it more influence in world affairs. But each country also prefers to live in a world safe from the other country's weapons.

Figure 17.4 shows the deadly game. If Israel chooses to arm, Iran is better off doing the same to prevent the loss of power. If Israel chooses to disarm, Iran is better off arming because doing so would make it more powerful. For each country, arming is a dominant strategy. Thus, each country chooses to continue the arms race, resulting in the inferior outcome in which both countries are at risk.

Advertising   When two firms advertise to attract the same customers, they face a problem similar to the prisoners' dilemma. For example, consider

FIGURE 17.4

An Arms Race Game

In this game between two countries, the safety and power of each country depends on both its decision whether to arm and the decision made by the other country.

Robert J. Aumann and Thomas C. Schelling – Game Theorists who Won the Nobel Prize for Economics

The 2005 Nobel Prize for Economics was awarded to Aumann and Schelling for their work in game theory. Robert J. Aumann was born in Germany in 1930 and has a background in mathematics. His work has been in the field of game theory and specifically the effect of how cooperation can be of benefit as a result of the research he carried out into repeated games. Thomas C. Schelling was born in 1921. His contribution to game theory was set against the backdrop of the Cold War, the tensions between the West and the East and the nuclear arms race. His research on strategies has helped build understanding of conflict and conflict resolution in spheres as diverse as nuclear war and market structure.

Schelling identified two aspects of game theory – non-cooperative game theory and cooperative game theory. Cooperative game theory assumes that there are a set of outcomes or agreements that is known to each player and that each player has preferences over these outcomes. Non-cooperative game theory assumes players have a series of strategies they could use to gain an outcome and that each player has a preference over their desired outcome. The behaviour of firms or individuals might be affected by bargaining which entails some form of conflict of interest but in essence each player will be looking to maximize their returns, whilst knowing at the same time that some agreement is preferable to no agreement at all. In this scenario, how does a player manage to influence the negotiations in order to move towards his or her preferred outcome without upsetting the other players and thus failing to secure

any agreement – an outcome which would be disadvantageous to all concerned, including the player?

Schelling proposed that it might be in the interests of the player to worsen his or her own options in order to gain some sort of concession from another player. Where difficulties arise is if both parties to a conflict make commitments that are seen as being irreversible and incompatible. The result could be stalemate and potential serious conflict. The dispute with Iran over its nuclear programme might be looked at in this light.

In most 'game' situations, the protagonists know something about the position of the other – but not everything. However, if there is any perceived chink in the armour of the other player and this is detected by the other, then there is a potential benefit to follow the hard route. This is why this sort of game is referred to as 'chicken' or 'hawk/dove'. Schelling further included other complications to the analysis by looking at how the strategies of each player would change in light of threats and action. Schelling noted that parties will need to recognize that the costs to them of cheating and gaining some short-term benefit (which may be much greater) is far outweighed by the costs to them in the longer term of the destruction of the trust that results from cheating. The relationships between players will need to be assessed in the context of repeated playing of the game over a period of time.

Aumann's most noted contribution is in the field of long-term cooperation around game theory. We have already seen how, in the prisoners' dilemma, the dominant strategy for Mr Green and Mr Blue was to confess. Aumann asked the

question about what the equilibrium outcome would be if the game were repeated over and over again, with each prisoner trying to maximize the *average* payoff from each game.

In such a situation, Aumann showed that the equilibrium outcome was to cooperate because any cheating on the agreement in the short term would be punishable by a refusal to cooperate at some point in the future – and both players would know this. Any short-term gains, therefore, are outweighed by longer-term losses. Aumann expressed this through what he referred to as a 'supergame' – that is, looking at the collection of repeated games as a whole game in itself. Aumann's work was extended to look at how groups of players might react in such situations. In a cartel, for example, there is always the tendency or incentive for one firm to break the cartel to seek to gain some advantage in the market. Aumann's work suggested that long-term cooperation could be 'enforced' by the many, against the few who might be seeking to defect.

The work was extended in subsequent research to try to take into account the strategies players might adopt in repeated games with incomplete information. This provides an incentive to players to hide, or seek to conceal, information from their rivals. Firms are very keen to keep their costs to themselves! If one player does manage to access information about their rivals and has some form of strategic advantage therefore, what is the best way to utilize this knowledge? If this situation arose, would playing your hand to gain short-term benefit reveal that you did actually know more than you were letting on? For the player who does not have the information they would like, could they discover anything about the player's position by reviewing the strategies and decisions made by that player in the past? Such scenarios are relevant to the world of financial markets where the issue of insider trading is always something that the authorities are keen to stamp out. The number of people with access to privileged information about market moves, business plans and strategies does mean that there is potential for many decisions that could have long-term implications for the markets and the businesses involved.

Aumann and Schelling's work has a great many applications in everyday life. Trade wars, price wars, negotiations over budgets, wage negotiations, discussions about environmental issues, merger discussions, social policy, monetary policy, fiscal policy, the work of the Competition Commission, EU fisheries debates and oligopolies are just some of the major areas where their work can be applied.

Robert J. Aumann (second from right) applauds Thomas C. Schelling as he accepts his Nobel Prize for Economics.

the decisions facing two cigarette companies, Marlboro and Camel. If neither company advertises, the two companies split the market. If both advertise, they again split the market, but profits are lower, since each company must bear the cost of advertising. Yet if one company advertises while the other does not, the one that advertises attracts customers from the other.

Figure 17.5 shows how the profits of the two companies depend on their actions. You can see that advertising is a dominant strategy for each firm. Thus, both firms choose to advertise, even though both firms would be better off if neither firm advertised.

A test of this theory of advertising occurred in many countries during the 1970s and 1980s, when laws were passed in Europe and North America banning cigarette advertisements on television. To the surprise of many observers, cigarette companies did not use their considerable political clout to oppose these bans. When the laws went into effect, cigarette advertising fell and the profits of cigarette companies rose. The television advertising bans did for the cigarette companies what they could not do on their own: they solved the prisoners' dilemma by enforcing the cooperative outcome with low advertising and high profit.

Common Resources In Chapter 11 we saw that people tend to overuse common resources. One can view this problem as an example of the prisoners' dilemma.

Imagine that two oil companies – Shell and BP – own adjacent oil fields. Under the fields is a common pool of oil worth €12 million. Drilling a well to

FIGURE 17.5

An Advertising Game

In this game between firms selling similar products, the profit that each earns depends on both its own advertising decision and the advertising decision of the other firm.

	Marlboro's decision	
Camel's decision	**Advertise**	**Don't advertise**
Advertise	Marlboro gets $3 billion profit Camel gets $3 billion profit	Marlboro gets $2 billion profit Camel gets $5 billion profit
Don't advertise	Marlboro gets $5 billion profit Camel gets $2 billion profit	Marlboro gets $4 billion profit Camel gets $4 billion profit

recover the oil costs €1 million. If each company drills one well, each will get half of the oil and earn a €5 million profit (€6 million in revenue minus €1 million in costs).

Because the pool of oil is a common resource, the companies will not use it efficiently. Suppose that either company could drill a second well. If one company has two of the three wells, that company gets two-thirds of the oil, which yields a profit of €6 million. The other company gets one-third of the oil, for a profit of €3 million. Yet if each company drills a second well, the two companies again split the oil. In this case, each bears the cost of a second well, so profit is only €4 million for each company.

Figure 17.6 shows the game. Drilling two wells is a dominant strategy for each company. Once again, the self-interest of the two players leads them to an inferior outcome.

The Prisoners' Dilemma and the Welfare of Society

The prisoners' dilemma describes many of life's situations, and it shows that cooperation can be difficult to maintain, even when cooperation would make both players in the game better off. Clearly, this lack of cooperation is a problem for those involved in these situations. But is lack of cooperation a problem from the standpoint of society as a whole? The answer depends on the circumstances.

In some cases, the non-cooperative equilibrium is bad for society as well as the players. In the arms race game in Figure 17.4, both Iran and Israel end up at risk. In the common resources game in Figure 17.6, the extra wells dug by Shell and BP are pure waste. In both cases, society would be better off if the two players could reach the cooperative outcome.

By contrast, in the case of oligopolists trying to maintain monopoly profits, lack of cooperation is desirable from the standpoint of society as a whole. The monopoly outcome is good for the oligopolists, but it is bad for the consumers of the product. As we first saw in Chapter 7, the competitive outcome is best for society because it maximizes total surplus. When oligopolists fail to cooperate, the quantity they produce is closer to this optimal level. Put differently, the

Restraint of Trade and Competition Law

One way that policy discourages cooperation is through the common law. Normally, freedom of contract is an essential part of a market economy. Businesses and households use contracts to arrange mutually advantageous trades. In doing this, they rely on the court system to enforce contracts. Yet, for many centuries, courts in Europe and North America have deemed agreements among competitors to reduce quantities and raise prices to be contrary to the public interest. They have therefore refused to enforce such agreements.

Given the long experience of many European countries in tackling abuses of market power, it is perhaps not surprising that competition law is one of the few areas in which the European Union has been able to agree on a common policy. The European Commission can refer directly to the Treaty of Rome to prohibit price-fixing and other restrictive practices such as production limitation, and is especially likely to do so where a restrictive practice affects trade between EU member countries. The EU Competition Commission sets out its role as follows:

> The antitrust area covers two prohibition rules set out in the Treaty on the Functioning of the European Union.
>
> - First, agreements between two or more firms which restrict competition are prohibited by Article 101 of the Treaty, subject to some limited exceptions. This provision covers a wide variety of behaviours. The most obvious example of illegal conduct infringing [the Article] is a cartel between competitors (which may involve price-fixing or market sharing).
> - Second, firms in a dominant position may not abuse that position (Article 102 of the Treaty). This is for example the case for predatory pricing aiming at eliminating competitors from the market.
>
> The Commission is empowered by the Treaty to apply these prohibition rules and enjoys a number of investigative powers to that end (e.g. inspection in business and non business premises, written requests for information, etc). It may also impose fines on undertakings who violate EU antitrust rules. Since 1 May 2004, all national competition authorities are also empowered to apply fully the provisions of the Treaty in order to ensure that competition is not distorted or restricted. National courts may also apply these prohibitions so as to protect the individual rights conferred to citizens by the Treaty.
>
> (Source: http://ec.europa.eu/competition/antitrust/overview_en.html)

Controversies over Competition Policy

Over time, much controversy has centred on the question of what kinds of behaviour competition law should prohibit. Most commentators agree that price-fixing agreements among competing firms should be illegal. Yet competition law has been used to condemn some business practices whose effects are not obvious. Here we consider three examples.

Resale Price Maintenance   One example of a controversial business practice is *resale price maintenance,* also called *fair trade.* Imagine that Superduper Electronics sells DVD players to retail stores for €300. If Superduper requires the retailers to charge customers €350, it is said to engage in resale price maintenance. Any retailer that charged less than €350 would have violated its contract with Superduper.

At first, resale price maintenance might seem anti-competitive and, therefore, detrimental to society. Like an agreement among members of a cartel, it prevents the retailers from competing on price. For this reason, the courts have often viewed resale price maintenance as a violation of competition law.

Yet some economists defend resale price maintenance on two grounds. First, they deny that it is aimed at reducing competition. To the extent that Superduper Electronics has any market power, it can exert that power through the wholesale price, rather than through resale price maintenance. Moreover, Superduper has no incentive to discourage competition among its retailers. Indeed, because a cartel of retailers sells less than a group of competitive retailers, Superduper would be worse off if its retailers were a cartel.

Secondly, economists believe that resale price maintenance has a legitimate goal. Superduper may want its retailers to provide customers with a pleasant showroom and a knowledgeable salesforce. Yet, without resale price maintenance, some customers would take advantage of one store's service to learn about the DVD player's special features and then buy the item at a discount retailer that does not provide this service. To some extent, good service is a public good among the retailers that sell Superduper products. As we discussed in Chapter 11, when one person provides a public good, others are able to enjoy it without paying for it. In this case, discount retailers would free ride on the service provided by other retailers, leading to less service than is desirable. Resale price maintenance is one way for Superduper to solve this free-rider problem.

The example of resale price maintenance illustrates an important principle: business practices that appear to reduce competition may in fact have legitimate purposes. This principle makes the application of competition law all the more difficult. The competition authorities in each EU nation under the European Competition Network are in charge of enforcing these laws must determine what kinds of behaviour public policy should prohibit as impeding competition and reducing economic well-being. Often that job is not easy.

Predatory Pricing   Firms with market power normally use that power to raise prices above the competitive level. But should policy makers ever be concerned that firms with market power might charge prices that are too low? This question is at the heart of a second debate over competition policy.

Imagine that a large airline, call it Tom Airlines, has a monopoly on some route. Then Jerry Express enters and takes 20 per cent of the market, leaving Tom with 80 per cent. In response to this competition, Tom starts slashing its fares. Some anti-trust analysts argue that Tom's move could be anti-competitive: the price cuts may be intended to drive Jerry out of the market so Tom can recapture its monopoly and raise prices again. Such behaviour is called *predatory pricing*.

Although it is common for companies to complain to the relevant authorities that a competitor is pursuing predatory pricing, some economists are sceptical of this argument and believe that predatory pricing is rarely, and perhaps never, a profitable business strategy. Why? For a price war to drive out a rival, prices have to be driven below cost. Yet if Tom starts selling cheap tickets at a loss, it had better be ready to fly more planes, because low fares will attract more customers. Jerry, meanwhile, can respond to Tom's predatory move by cutting back on flights. As a result, Tom ends up bearing more than 80 per cent of the losses, putting Jerry in a good position to survive the price war. As in the old Tom and Jerry cartoons, the predator suffers more than the prey.

Economists continue to debate whether predatory pricing should be a concern for competition policy makers. Various questions remain unresolved. Is predatory pricing ever a profitable business strategy? If so, when? Are the authorities capable of telling which price cuts are competitive and thus good for consumers and which are predatory? There are no simple answers.

Tying   A third example of a controversial business practice is *tying*. Suppose that Makemoney Movies produces two new films – *Spiderman* and *Hamlet*. If

Makemoney offers cinemas the two films together at a single price, rather than separately, the studio is said to be tying its two products.

Some economists have argued that the practice of tying should be banned. Their reasoning is as follows: imagine that *Spiderman* is a blockbuster, whereas *Hamlet* is an unprofitable art film. Then the studio could use the high demand for *Spiderman* to force cinemas to buy *Hamlet*. It seemed that the studio could use tying as a mechanism for expanding its market power.

Other economists are sceptical of this argument. Imagine that cinemas are willing to pay €20 000 for *Spiderman* and nothing for *Hamlet*. Then the most that a cinema would pay for the two films together is €20 000 – the same as it would pay for *Spiderman* by itself. Forcing the cinema to accept a worthless film as part of the deal does not increase the cinema's willingness to pay. Makemoney cannot increase its market power simply by bundling the two films together.

Why, then, does tying exist? One possibility is that it is a form of price discrimination. Suppose there are two cinemas. City Cinema is willing to pay €15 000 for *Spiderman* and €5 000 for *Hamlet*. Country Cinema is just the opposite: it is willing to pay €5 000 for *Spiderman* and €15 000 for *Hamlet*. If Makemoney charges separate prices for the two films, its best strategy is to charge €15 000 for each film, and each cinema chooses to show only one film. Yet if Makemoney offers the two films as a bundle, it can charge each cinema €20 000 for the films. Thus, if different cinemas value the films differently, tying may allow the studio to increase profit by charging a combined price closer to the buyers' total willingness to pay.

Tying remains a controversial business practice. We saw in Chapter 15 how Microsoft had been investigated for 'tying' its internet browser and other software like its Windows Media Player with its Windows operating system and the arguments that the company had put forward in its defence. The argument that tying allows a firm to extend its market power to other goods is not well founded, at least in its simplest form. Yet economists have proposed more elaborate theories for how tying can impede competition. Given our current economic knowledge, it is unclear whether tying has adverse effects for society as a whole.

All the analysis is based on an assumption that rivals may have sufficient information to be able to make a decision and that the decision will be a rational one based on this information. In reality firms do not have perfect information and do not behave rationally. Most firms in oligopolistic markets work very hard to protect sensitive information and only give out what they have to by law. Some information may be given to deliberately obfuscate the situation and hide what their true motives/strategies/tactics are. Economists have tried to include these imperfections into theories. Behavioural economics has become more popular in recent years because it offers some greater insights into the observed behaviour of the real world which often does not conform to the assumptions implied by the assumption of rationality.

Quick Quiz What kind of agreement is illegal for businesses to make?
• Why is competition law controversial?

CONCLUSION

Oligopolies would like to act like monopolies, but self-interest drives them closer to competition. Thus, oligopolies can end up looking either more like monopolies or more like competitive markets, depending on the number of firms in the oligopoly and how cooperative the firms are. The story of the prisoners' dilemma shows why oligopolies can fail to maintain cooperation, even when cooperation is in their best interest.

Policy makers regulate the behaviour of oligopolists through competition law. The proper scope of these laws is the subject of ongoing controversy. Although price fixing among competing firms clearly reduces economic welfare and should be illegal, some business practices that appear to reduce competition may have legitimate if subtle purposes. As a result, policy makers need to be careful when they use the substantial powers of competition law to place limits on firm behaviour.

SUMMARY

- Oligopolists maximize their total profits by forming a cartel and acting like a monopolist. Yet, if oligopolists make decisions about production levels individually, the result is a greater quantity and a lower price than under the monopoly outcome. The larger the number of firms in the oligopoly, the closer the quantity and price will be to the levels that would prevail under competition.

- The prisoners' dilemma shows that self-interest can prevent people from maintaining cooperation, even when

cooperation is in their mutual interest. The logic of the prisoners' dilemma applies in many situations, including arms races, advertising, common-resource problems and oligopolies.

- Policy makers use competition law to prevent oligopolies from engaging in behaviour that reduces competition. The application of these laws can be controversial, because some behaviour that may seem to reduce competition may in fact have legitimate business purposes.

KEY CONCEPTS

oligopoly, p. 356
collusion, p. 359
cartel, p. 359

Nash equilibrium, p. 360
game theory, p. 364
prisoners' dilemma, p. 364

dominant strategy, p. 365

QUESTIONS FOR REVIEW

1. If a group of sellers could form a cartel, what quantity and price would they try to set?

2. Compare the quantity and price of an oligopoly with those of a monopoly.

3. Compare the quantity and price of an oligopoly with those of a competitive market.

4. How does the number of firms in an oligopoly affect the outcome in its market?

5. What is the prisoners' dilemma, and what does it have to do with oligopoly?

6. Give two examples other than oligopoly to show how the prisoners' dilemma helps to explain behaviour.

7. What kinds of behaviour do the competition laws prohibit?

8. What is resale price maintenance, and why is it controversial?

PROBLEMS AND APPLICATIONS

1. *The Economist* (15 November, 2001) reported that 'OPEC has failed to agree immediate production cuts to shore up oil prices. Afraid of losing market share, it wants non-members, who would also benefit from any price support, to cut output as well. So far, they have refused to agree. If oil prices continue to fall, that would provide relief to the beleaguered world economy, but it might wreak havoc on the finances of OPEC members.'
   a. Why do you suppose OPEC was unable to agree on cutting production?
   b. Why do you think oil-producing non-members refused to cut output?

2. A large share of the world supply of diamonds comes from Russia and South Africa. Suppose that the marginal cost of mining diamonds is constant at €1 000 per diamond, and the demand for diamonds is described by the following schedule:

Price (€)	Quantity
€8 000	5 000
7 000	6 000
6 000	7 000
5 000	8 000
4 000	9 000
3 000	10 000
2 000	11 000
1 000	12 000

   a.
   If there were many suppliers of diamonds, what would be the price and quantity?
   b. If there were only one supplier of diamonds, what would be the price and quantity?
   c. If Russia and South Africa formed a cartel, what would be the price and quantity? If the countries split the market evenly, what would be South Africa's production and profit? What would happen to South Africa's profit if it increased its production by 1 000 while Russia stuck to the cartel agreement?
   d. Use your answer to part (c) to explain why cartel agreements are often not successful.

3. This chapter discusses companies that are oligopolists in the market for the goods they sell. Many of the same ideas apply to companies that are oligopolists in the market for the inputs they buy. If sellers who are oligopolists try to increase the price of goods they sell, what is the goal of buyers who are oligopolists?

4. Describe several activities in your life in which game theory could be useful. What is the common link among these activities?

5. Suppose that you and a fellow student are assigned a project on which you will receive one combined grade. You each want to receive a good grade, but you also want to do as little work as possible. The decision box and pay-offs are as follows:

	Your decision	
	Work	**Shirk**
Work (Fellow student's decision)	You get A grade, no fun / Fellow student gets A grade, no fun	You get B grade, fun / Fellow student gets B grade, no fun
Shirk	You get B grade, no fun / Fellow student gets B grade, fun	You get D grade, fun / Fellow student gets D grade, fun

   Assume that having fun is your normal state, but having no fun is as unpleasant as receiving a grade that is two letters lower.
   a. Write out the decision box that combines the letter grade and the amount of fun you have into a single pay-off for each outcome.
   b. If neither you nor your fellow student knows how much work the other person is doing, what is the likely outcome? Does it matter whether you are likely to work with this person again? Explain your answer.

6. The chapter states that the ban on cigarette advertising on television which many countries imposed in the 1970s increased the profits of cigarette companies. Could the ban still be good public policy? Explain your answer.

7. Assume that two airline companies decide to engage in collusive behaviour.
   Let's analyse the game between two such companies. Suppose that each company can charge either a high price for tickets or a low price. If one company charges €100, it earns low profits if the other company charges €100 also, and high profits if the other company charges €200. On the other hand, if the company charges €200, it earns very low profits if the other company charges €100, and medium profits if the other company charges €200 also.
   a. Draw the decision box for this game.
   b. What is the Nash equilibrium in this game? Explain.
   c. Is there an outcome that would be better than the Nash equilibrium for both airlines? How could it be achieved? Who would lose if it were achieved?

8. Farmer Jones and Farmer MacDonald graze their cattle on the same field. If there are 20 cows grazing in the field, each cow produces €4 000 of milk over its lifetime. If there are more cows in the field, then each cow can eat less grass, and its milk production falls. With 30 cows on the field, each produces €3 000 of milk; with 40 cows, each produces €2 000 of milk. Cows cost €1 000 apiece.

   a. Assume that Farmer Jones and Farmer MacDonald can each purchase either 10 or 20 cows, but that neither knows how many the other is buying when she makes her purchase. Calculate the pay-offs of each outcome.

   b. What is the likely outcome of this game? What would be the best outcome? Explain.

   c. There used to be more common fields than there are today. Why? (For more discussion of this topic, reread Chapter 11.)

9. Little Kona is a small coffee company that is considering entering a market dominated by Big Brew. Each company's profit depends on whether Little Kona enters and whether Big Brew sets a high price or a low price:

<table>
<tr><td></td><td></td><td colspan="2" align="center">Big Brew</td></tr>
<tr><td></td><td></td><td align="center">High price</td><td align="center">Low price</td></tr>
<tr><td rowspan="2">Little Kona</td><td>Enter</td><td>Brew makes €3 million
Kona makes €2 million</td><td>Brew makes €1 million
Kona loses €1 million</td></tr>
<tr><td>Don't enter</td><td>Brew makes €7 million
Kona makes zero</td><td>Brew makes €2 million
Kona makes zero</td></tr>
</table>

Big Brew threatens Little Kona by saying, 'If you enter, we're going to set a low price, so you had better stay out.' Do you think Little Kona should believe the threat? Why or why not? What do you think Little Kona should do?

10. Tim and Greg are playing tennis. Every point comes down to whether Greg guesses correctly whether Tim will hit the ball to Greg's left or right. The outcomes are:

<table>
<tr><td></td><td></td><td colspan="2" align="center">Greg guesses</td></tr>
<tr><td></td><td></td><td align="center">Left</td><td align="center">Right</td></tr>
<tr><td rowspan="2">Tim hits</td><td>Left</td><td>Greg wins point
Tim loses point</td><td>Greg loses point
Tim wins point</td></tr>
<tr><td>Right</td><td>Greg loses point
Tim wins point</td><td>Greg wins point
Tim loses point</td></tr>
</table>

   Does either player have a dominant strategy? If Tim chooses a particular strategy (Left or Right) and sticks with it, what will Greg do? So, can you think of a better strategy for Tim to follow?

For further resources, visit
www.cengage.com/mankiw_taylor2

6

THE ECONOMICS
OF LABOUR MARKETS

18 THE MARKETS FOR THE FACTORS OF PRODUCTION

When you finish university, your income will be determined largely by what kind of job you take. If you become a professional economist, you will earn more than if you become a petrol station attendant. This fact is not surprising, but it is not obvious why it is true. No law requires that economists be paid more than petrol station attendants. No ethical principle says that economists are more deserving. If you become an academic economist in a university, you will probably earn less than if you become a banker. What then determines which job will pay you the higher wage?

Your income, of course, is a small piece of a larger economic picture. In 2007 the total income of all EU residents was about €12.371 trillion (€12 371 365 000 000). In 2009 the total income of all UK residents was about £140 000 000 000 (£1.4 trillion).

People earned this income in various ways. Workers earned about two-thirds of it in the form of wages and fringe benefits and about 10 per cent of it is income from self-employment. The rest went to landowners and to the owners of *capital* – the economy's stock of equipment and structures – in the form of rent, profit and interest. What determines how much goes to workers? To landowners? To the owners of capital? Why do some workers earn higher wages than others, some landowners higher rental income than others and some capital owners greater profit than others? Why, in particular, do computer programmers earn more than petrol station attendants?

The answers to these questions, like most in economics, hinge on supply and demand. The supply and demand for labour, land and capital determine the prices paid to workers, landowners and capital owners. To understand why some people have higher incomes than others, therefore, we need to look more deeply at the markets for the services they provide.

This chapter provides the basic theory for the analysis of factor markets. **Factors of production** are the inputs used to produce goods and services. Labour, land and capital are the three most important factors of production. When a computer firm produces a new software program, it uses programmers' time (labour), the physical space on which its offices sit (land), and an office building and computer equipment (capital). Similarly, when a petrol station sells petrol, it uses attendants' time (labour), the physical space (land), and the petrol tanks and pumps (capital).

factors of production
the inputs used to produce goods and services

Although in many ways factor markets resemble the goods markets we have analysed in previous chapters, they are different in one important way: the demand for a factor of production is a *derived demand*. That is, a firm's demand for a factor of production is derived (determined) from its decision to supply a good in another market. The demand for computer programmers is inextricably tied to the supply of computer software, and the demand for petrol station attendants is inextricably tied to the supply of petrol.

The initial analysis will be based on firms operating in a competitive market – both for goods and labour. More will be said on this below but it is also worth remembering that the analysis assumes that labour is free to enter and exit the market and firms are equally free to employ and shed labour at will – in other words people can move into and out of work easily and employers can 'hire and fire' workers when they need to. In reality, of course, there are a number of imperfections in the labour market but our initial analysis serves to act as a benchmark for looking at how labour markets work in reality.

THE DEMAND FOR LABOUR

Labour markets, like other markets in the economy, are governed by the forces of supply and demand. This is illustrated in Figure 18.1. In panel (a) the supply and demand for apples determine the price of apples. In panel (b) the supply and demand for apple pickers determine the price, or wage, of apple pickers.

As we have already noted, labour markets are different from most other markets because labour demand is a derived demand. Most labour services, rather than being final goods ready to be enjoyed by consumers, are inputs into the production of other goods. To understand labour demand, we need to focus on the firms that hire the labour and use it to produce goods for sale. By examining the link between the production of goods and the demand for labour, we gain insight into the determination of equilibrium wages.

The Competitive Profit-maximizing Firm

Let's look at how a typical firm, such as an apple producer, decides the quantity of labour to demand. The firm owns an apple orchard and each week must decide how many apple pickers to hire to harvest its crop. After the firm makes its hiring decision, the workers pick as many apples as they can. The firm then sells the apples, pays the workers, and keeps what is left as profit.

We assume that our firm is *competitive* both in the market for apples (where the firm is a seller) and in the market for apple pickers (where the firm is a buyer). Because there are many other firms selling apples and hiring apple pickers, a single firm has little influence over the price it gets for apples or the wage it pays apple pickers. The firm takes the price and the wage as given by market

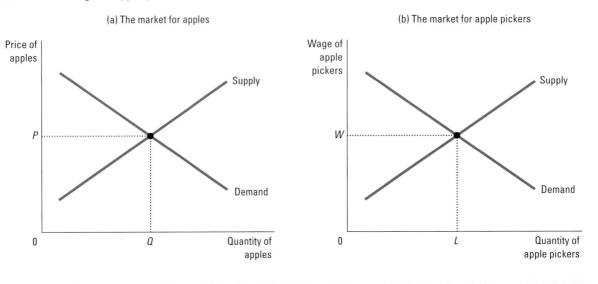

FIGURE 18.1

The Versatility of Supply and Demand

The basic tools of supply and demand apply to goods and to labour services. Panel (a) shows how the supply and demand for apples determine the price of apples. Panel (b) shows how the supply and demand for apple pickers determine the wage of apple pickers.

conditions. It only has to decide how many workers to hire and how many apples to sell.

Secondly, we assume that the firm is *profit-maximizing*. Thus, the firm does not directly care about the number of workers it has or the number of apples it produces. It cares only about profit, which equals the total revenue from the sale of apples minus the total cost of producing them. The firm's supply of apples and its demand for workers are derived from its primary goal of maximizing profit.

The Production Function and the Marginal Product of Labour

To make its hiring decision, the firm must consider how the number of apple pickers affects the quantity of apples it can harvest and sell. Table 18.1 gives a numerical example. In the first column is the number of workers. In the second column is the quantity of apples the workers harvest each week.

These two columns of numbers describe the firm's ability to produce. As we noted in Chapter 13, economists use the term **production function** to describe the relationship between the quantity of the inputs used in production and the quantity of output from production. Here the 'input' is the apple pickers and the 'output' is the apples. The other inputs – the trees themselves, the land, the firm's trucks and tractors, and so on – are held fixed for now. This firm's production function shows that if the firm hires 1 worker, that worker will pick 1 000 kilos of apples per week. If the firm hires 2 workers, the two workers together will pick 1 800 kilos per week, and so on.

Figure 18.2 graphs the data on labour and output presented in Table 18.1. The number of workers is on the horizontal axis, and the amount of output is on the vertical axis. This figure illustrates the production function.

production function
the relationship between the quantity of inputs used to make a good and the quantity of output of that good

TABLE 18.1

How the Competitive Firm Decides How Much Labour to Hire

Labour	Output	Marginal product of labour	Value of the marginal product of labour	Wage	Marginal profit
L (number of workers)	Q (kilos per week)	MPL = ΔQ/ΔL (kilos per week)	VMPL = P × MPL	W	ΔProfit = VMPL − W
0	0				
		1 000	€1 000	€500	€500
1	1 000				
		800	800	500	300
2	1 800				
		600	600	500	100
3	2 400				
		400	400	500	−100
4	2 800				
		200	200	500	−300
5	3 000				

FIGURE 18.2

The Production Function

The production function is the relationship between the inputs into production (apple pickers) and the output from production (apples). As the quantity of the input increases, the production function gets flatter, reflecting the property of diminishing marginal product.

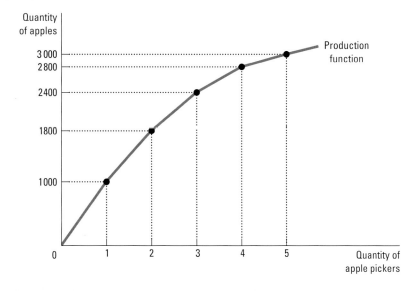

One of the *Ten Principles of Economics* introduced in Chapter 1 is that rational people think at the margin. This idea is the key to understanding how firms decide what quantity of labour to hire. To take a step towards this decision, the third column in Table 18.1 gives the **marginal product of labour**, the increase in the amount of output from an additional unit of labour. When the firm increases the number of workers from 1 to 2, for example, the amount of apples produced rises from 1 000 to 1 800 kilos. Therefore, the marginal product of the second worker is 800 kilos.

marginal product of labour
the increase in the amount of output from an additional unit of labour

Notice that as the number of workers increases, the marginal product of labour declines (remember we are adding more units of a variable factor (labour) to a quantity of fixed factors (land and capital – we are operating in the short run). As you may recall from Chapter 13, this property is called diminishing marginal product. At first, when only a few workers are hired, they pick apples from the best trees in the orchard. As the number of workers increases, additional workers have to pick from the trees with fewer apples. Hence, as more and more workers are hired, each additional worker contributes less to the production of apples. For this reason, the production function in Figure 18.2 becomes flatter as the number of workers rises.

The Value of the Marginal Product and the Demand for Labour

Our profit-maximizing firm is concerned more with money than with apples. As a result, when deciding how many workers to hire, the firm considers how much profit each worker would bring in. Because profit is total revenue minus total cost, the profit from an additional worker is the worker's contribution to revenue minus the worker's wage.

To find the worker's contribution to revenue, we must convert the marginal product of labour (which is measured in kilos of apples) into the *value* of the marginal product (which is measured in euros). We do this using the price of apples. To continue our example, if a kilo of apples sells for €1 and if an additional worker produces 800 kilos of apples, then the worker produces €800 of revenue for the firm.

value of the marginal product
the marginal product of an input times the price of the output

The **value of the marginal product** of any input is the marginal product of that input multiplied by the market price of the output. The fourth column in Table 18.1 shows the value of the marginal product of labour in our example, assuming the price of apples is €1 per kilo. Because the market price is constant for a competitive firm, the value of the marginal product (like the marginal product itself) diminishes as the number of workers rises. Economists sometimes call this column of numbers the firm's *marginal revenue product:* it is the extra revenue the firm gets from hiring an additional unit of a factor of production.

Now consider how many workers the firm will hire. Suppose that the market wage for apple pickers is €500 per week. In this case, as you see in Table 18.1, the first worker that the firm hires is profitable: the first worker yields €1 000 in revenue, or €500 in profit. Similarly, the second worker yields €800 in additional revenue, or €300 in profit. The third worker produces €600 in additional revenue, or €100 in profit. After the third worker, however, hiring workers is unprofitable. The fourth worker would yield only €400 of additional revenue. Because the worker's wage is €500, hiring the fourth worker would mean a €100 reduction in profit. Thus, the firm hires only three workers.

It is instructive to consider the firm's decision graphically. Figure 18.3 graphs the value of the marginal product. This curve slopes downward because the marginal product of labour diminishes as the number of workers rises. The figure also includes a horizontal line at the market wage. To maximize profit, the firm hires workers up to the point where these two curves cross. Below this level of employment, the value of the marginal product exceeds the wage, so hiring another worker would increase profit. Above this level of employment, the value of the marginal product is less than the wage, so the marginal worker is unprofitable. Thus, a competitive, profit-maximizing firm hires workers up to the point where the value of the marginal product of labour equals the wage.

Having explained the profit-maximizing hiring strategy for a competitive firm, we can now offer a theory of labour demand. Recall that a firm's labour demand curve tells us the quantity of labour that a firm demands at any given wage. We

FIGURE 18.3

The Value of the Marginal Product of Labour

This figure shows how the value of the marginal product (the marginal product times the price of the output) depends on the number of workers. The curve slopes downward because of diminishing marginal product. For a competitive, profit-maximizing firm, this value of marginal product curve is also the firm's labour demand curve.

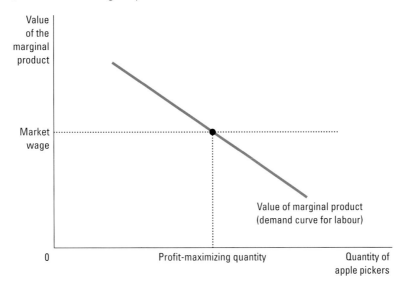

have just seen in Figure 18.3 that the firm makes that decision by choosing the quantity of labour at which the value of the marginal product equals the wage. As a result, the value of marginal product curve is the labour demand curve for a competitive, profit-maximizing firm.

What Causes the Labour Demand Curve to Shift?

The labour demand curve reflects the value of the marginal product of labour. With this insight in mind, let's consider a few of the things that might cause the labour demand curve to shift.

The Output Price   The value of the marginal product is marginal product times the price of the firm's output. Thus, when the output price changes, the value of the marginal product changes, and the labour demand curve shifts. An increase in the price of apples, for instance, raises the value of the marginal product of each worker who picks apples and, therefore, increases labour demand from the firms that supply apples. Conversely, a decrease in the price of apples reduces the value of the marginal product and decreases labour demand.

Technological Change   Between 2000 and 2008, labour productivity per hour worked in the EU 27 increased by 2.94 per cent[1]. Between 1960 and 2008, the amount of output a typical UK worker produced in an hour rose by around 156 per cent[2]. Why? The most important reason is technological progress: scientists and engineers are constantly figuring out new and better ways of doing

---

[1]Source: Eurostat   (http://epp.eurostat.ec.europa.eu/tgm/table.do?tab=table&init=1&language=en&pcode=tsieb040&plugin=0).

[2]Source: Office for National Statistics (http://www.statistics.gov.uk/statbase/TSDdownload2.asp).

FYI

Input Demand and Output Supply: Two Sides of the Same Coin

In Chapter 14 we saw how a competitive, profit-maximizing firm decides how much of its output to sell: it chooses the quantity of output at which the price of the good equals the marginal cost of production. We have just seen how such a firm decides how much labour to hire: it chooses the quantity of labour at which the wage equals the value of the marginal product. Because the production function links the quantity of inputs to the quantity of output, you should not be surprised to learn that the firm's decision about input demand is closely linked to its decision about output supply. In fact, these two decisions are two sides of the same coin.

To see this relationship more fully, let's consider how the marginal product of labour (MPL) and marginal cost (MC) are related. Suppose an additional worker costs €500 and has a marginal product of 50 kilos of apples. In this case, producing 50 more kilos costs

€500; the marginal cost of a kilo is €500/50, or €10. More generally, if W is the wage, and an extra unit of labour produces MPL units of output, then the marginal cost of a unit of output is $MC = W/MPL$.

This analysis shows that diminishing marginal product is closely related to increasing marginal cost. When our apple orchard grows crowded with workers, each additional worker adds less to the production of apples (MPL falls). Similarly, when the apple firm is producing a large quantity of apples, the orchard is already crowded with workers, so it is more costly to produce an additional kilo of apples (MC rises).

Now consider our criterion for profit maximization. We determined earlier that a profit-maximizing firm chooses the quantity of labour so that the value of the marginal product ($P \times MPL$) equals the wage (W). We can write this mathematically as:

$$P \times MPL = W$$

If we divide both sides of this equation by MPL, we obtain:

$$P = W/MPL$$

We just noted that W/MPL equals marginal cost MC. Therefore, we can substitute to obtain:

$$P = MC$$

This equation states that the price of the firm's output is equal to the marginal cost of producing a unit of output. *Thus, when a competitive firm hires labour up to the point at which the value of the marginal product equals the wage, it also produces up to the point at which the price equals marginal cost.* Our analysis of labour demand in this chapter is just another way of looking at the production decision we first saw in Chapter 14.

things. This has profound implications for the labour market. Technological advance raises the marginal product of labour, which in turn increases the demand for labour. Such technological advance explains persistently rising employment in the face of rising wages: even though UK wages (adjusted for inflation) increased by 120 per cent over these four decades, firms nevertheless increased by 17 per cent the amount of labour they employed.

The Supply of other Factors   The quantity available of one factor of production can affect the marginal product of other factors. A fall in the supply of ladders, for instance, will reduce the marginal product of apple pickers and thus the demand for apple pickers. We consider this linkage among the factors of production more fully later in the chapter.

Quick Quiz   Define *marginal product of labour* and *value of the marginal product of labour*. • Describe how a competitive, profit-maximizing firm decides how many workers to hire.

THE SUPPLY OF LABOUR

Having analysed labour demand let's turn to the other side of the market and consider labour supply. Here we discuss briefly and informally the decisions that lie behind the labour supply curve.

The Trade-off between Work and Leisure

One of the *Ten Principles of Economics* in Chapter 1 is that people face trade-offs. Probably no trade-off is more obvious or more important in a person's life than the trade-off between work and leisure. The more hours you spend working, the fewer hours you have to watch TV, socialize with friends or pursue your favourite hobby. The trade-off between labour and leisure lies behind the labour supply curve.

Another of the *Ten Principles of Economics* is that the cost of something is what you give up to get it. What do you give up to get an hour of leisure? You give up an hour of work, which in turn means an hour of wages. Thus, if your wage is €15 per hour, the opportunity cost of an hour of leisure is €15. And when you get a pay rise to €20 per hour, the opportunity cost of enjoying leisure goes up.

The labour supply curve reflects how workers' decisions about the labour–leisure trade-off respond to a change in that opportunity cost. An upward sloping labour supply curve means that an increase in the wage induces workers to increase the quantity of labour they supply. Because time is limited, more hours of work means that workers are enjoying less leisure. That is, workers respond to the increase in the opportunity cost of leisure by taking less of it.

It is worth noting that the labour supply curve need not be upward sloping. Imagine you got that raise from €15 to €20 per hour. The opportunity cost of leisure is now greater, but you are also richer than you were before. You might decide that with your extra wealth you can now afford to enjoy more leisure. That is, at the higher wage, you might choose to work fewer hours. If so, your labour supply curve would slope backwards. In Chapter 21, we discuss this possibility in terms of conflicting effects on your labour supply decision (called the income and substitution effects). For now, we ignore the possibility of backward sloping labour supply and assume that the labour supply curve is upward sloping.

What Causes the Labour Supply Curve to Shift?

The labour supply curve shifts whenever people change the amount they want to work at a given wage. Let's now consider some of the events that might cause such a shift.

Changes in Tastes In 1960, 48.7 per cent of women in the UK were employed at paid jobs or looking for work. By 2005, the proportion had risen to 70 per cent. In the EU27, the employment rate for women rose from 54.4 per cent in 2002 to 58.3 per cent in 2007. There are, of course, many explanations for these developments, but one of them is changing tastes, or attitudes toward work. A generation or two ago, it was the norm for women to stay at home while raising children. Today, family sizes are smaller and more mothers choose to work. The result is an increase in the supply of labour.

Changes in Alternative Opportunities The supply of labour in any one labour market depends on the opportunities available in other labour markets. If the wage earned by pear pickers suddenly rises, some apple pickers may choose to switch occupations. The supply of labour in the market for apple pickers falls.

Immigration Movement of workers from region to region, or country to country, is an obvious and often important source of shifts in labour supply. When immigrants move from one European country to another – from Poland to the UK, for instance – the supply of labour in the United Kingdom increases and the supply of labour in Poland contracts. In fact, much of the policy debate about immigration centres on its effect on labour supply and, thereby, equilibrium in the labour market.

> **Quick Quiz** Who has a greater opportunity cost of enjoying leisure – a petrol station attendant or a brain surgeon? Explain. Can this help explain why doctors work such long hours?

EQUILIBRIUM IN THE LABOUR MARKET

So far we have established two facts about how wages are determined in competitive labour markets:

- The wage adjusts to balance the supply and demand for labour.
- The wage equals the value of the marginal product of labour.

At first, it might seem surprising that the wage can do both these things at once. In fact, there is no real puzzle here, but understanding why there is no puzzle is an important step to understanding wage determination.

Figure 18.4 shows the labour market in equilibrium. The wage and the quantity of labour have adjusted to balance supply and demand. When the market is

FIGURE 18.4

Equilibrium in a Labour Market

Like all prices, the price of labour (the wage) depends on supply and demand. Because the demand curve reflects the value of the marginal product of labour, in equilibrium workers receive the value of their marginal contribution to the production of goods and services.

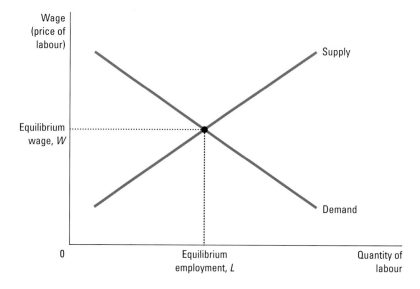

in this equilibrium, each firm has bought as much labour as it finds profitable at the equilibrium wage. That is, each firm has followed the rule for profit maximization: it has hired workers until the value of the marginal product equals the wage. Hence, the wage must equal the value of the marginal product of labour once it has brought supply and demand into equilibrium.

This brings us to an important lesson: any event that changes the supply or demand for labour must change the equilibrium wage and the value of the marginal product by the same amount, because these must always be equal. To see how this works, let's consider some events that shift these curves.

Shifts in Labour Supply

Suppose that immigration increases the number of workers willing to pick apples. As Figure 18.5 shows, the supply of labour shifts to the right from S_1 to S_2. At the initial wage W_1, the quantity of labour supplied now exceeds the quantity demanded. This surplus of labour puts downward pressure on the wage of apple pickers, and the fall in the wage from W_1 to W_2 in turn makes it profitable for firms to hire more workers. As the number of workers employed in each apple orchard rises, the marginal product of a worker falls, and so does the value of the marginal product. In the new equilibrium, both the wage and the value of the marginal product of labour are lower than they were before the influx of new workers.

An episode from Israel illustrates how a shift in labour supply can alter the equilibrium in a labour market. During most of the 1980s, many thousands of Palestinians regularly commuted from their homes in the Israeli-occupied West Bank and Gaza Strip to jobs in Israel, primarily in the construction and

FIGURE 18.5

A Shift in Labour Supply

When labour supply increases from S_1 to S_2, perhaps because of immigration of new workers, the equilibrium wage falls from W_1 to W_2. At this lower wage, firms hire more labour, so employment rises from L_1 to L_2. The change in the wage reflects a change in the value of the marginal product of labour: with more workers, the added output from an extra worker is smaller.

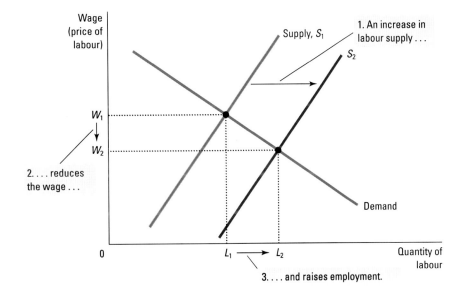

agriculture industries. In 1988, however, political unrest in these occupied areas induced the Israeli government to take steps that, as a by-product, reduced this supply of workers. Curfews were imposed, work permits were checked more thoroughly, and a ban on overnight stays of Palestinians in Israel was enforced more rigorously. The economic impact of these steps was exactly as theory predicts: the number of Palestinians with jobs in Israel fell by half, while those who continued to work in Israel enjoyed wage increases of about 50 per cent. With a reduced number of Palestinian workers in Israel, the value of the marginal product of the remaining workers was much higher.

Shifts in Labour Demand

Now suppose that an increase in the popularity of apples causes their price to rise. This price increase does not change the marginal product of labour for any given number of workers, but it does raise the *value* of the marginal product. With a higher price of apples, hiring more apple pickers is now profitable. As Figure 18.6 shows, when the demand for labour shifts to the right from D_1 to D_2, the equilibrium wage rises from W_1 to W_2, and equilibrium employment rises from L_1 to L_2. Once again, the wage and the value of the marginal product of labour move together.

This analysis shows that prosperity for firms in an industry is often linked to prosperity for workers in that industry. When the price of apples rises, apple producers make greater profit and apple pickers earn higher wages. When the price of apples falls, apple producers earn smaller profit and apple pickers earn lower wages. This lesson is well known to workers in industries with highly volatile prices. Workers in oil fields, for instance, know from experience that their earnings are closely linked to the world price of crude oil.

FIGURE 18.6

A Shift in Labour Demand

When labour demand increases from D_1 *to* D_2, *perhaps because of an increase in the price of the firms' output, the equilibrium wage rises from* W_1 *to* W_2, *and employment rises from* L_1 *to* L_2. *Again, the change in the wage reflects a change in the value of the marginal product of labour: with a higher output price, the added output from an extra worker is more valuable.*

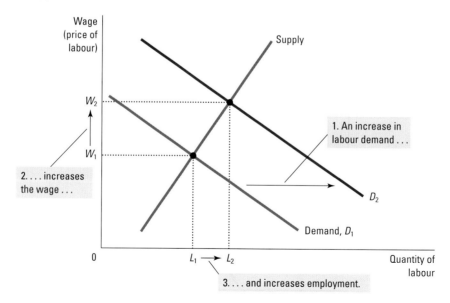

In competitive labour markets, therefore, labour supply and labour demand together determine the equilibrium wage, and shifts in the supply or demand curve for labour cause the equilibrium wage to change. At the same time, profit maximization by the firms that demand labour ensures that the equilibrium wage always equals the value of the marginal product of labour.

CASE STUDY

Productivity and Wages

One of the *Ten Principles of Economics* in Chapter 1 is that our standard of living depends on our ability to produce goods and services. We can now see how this principle works in the market for labour. In particular, our analysis of labour demand shows that wages equal productivity as measured by the value of the marginal product of labour. Put simply, highly productive workers are highly paid, and less productive workers are less highly paid.

This lesson is key to understanding why workers today are better off than workers in previous generations. Panel (a) of Figure 18.7 presents some data on growth in productivity in the UK. From 1961 to 2005, productivity as measured by output per worker grew on average at about 2.03 per cent per year. Real wages (that is, wages adjusted for inflation) grew at almost the same rate: 2.0 per cent per year. With a growth rate of close to 2.0 per cent per year, productivity and real wages double about every 35 years.

Table 18.2 shows the rates of growth for the ten-year periods from 1950 to 2000. Notice that from 1971 to 1980 growth in productivity, at 1.80 per cent per year, was slow compared with the period before 1970. Over the period 1990–2000, productivity growth picked up slightly but was still less than in the 1950s and 1960s. There is a similar pattern in productivity growth in the US. The cause of the productivity slowdown in the 1970s is not well understood, but the link between productivity and real wages is exactly as standard theory predicts. The slowdown in productivity growth from 2.7 to 1.8 per cent per year coincided with a slowdown in real wage growth from around 3.0 to 1.5 per cent per year over the period 1973–95, and the growth in productivity over the more recent period of about 1.6 per cent was also reflected in a similar growth rate of real wages of 1.7 per cent per annum. Both theory and history confirm the close connection between productivity and real wages.

In more recent times productivity in the UK fell dramatically as shown in panel (b) of Figure 18.7 This was mainly caused by the financial crisis and the subsequent recession. There is also another reason for the fall in productivity that has been a feature of the recession that occurred. A number of large employers, especially car manufacturers, had long periods where they suspended production. Rather than making workers redundant, however, firms retained staff but paid them a proportion of their normal wage. Many workers were pleased to retain their job even though their wages fell and firms avoided heavy costs in redundancy pay, shutting down factories and having to recruit new labour when the upturn in business eventually occurred. Economists have to be aware, therefore, of new types of behaviour by firms and how this might change theory.

Growth in productivity is measured here as the annualized rate of change in output per worker. Growth in real wages is measured as the annualized change in average wages deflated by the Retail Prices Index. These productivity data measure average productivity – the quantity of output divided by the quantity of labour – rather than marginal productivity, but average and marginal productivity are thought to move closely together.

FIGURE 18.7

UK Labour Productivity, 1961–2005

(a) Annual labour productivity growth, 1961–2005

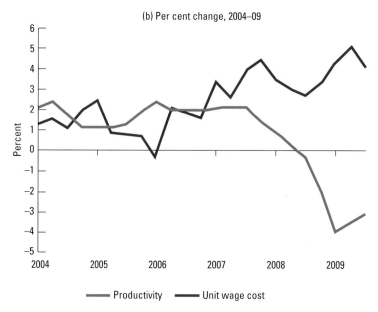

(b) Per cent change, 2004–09

Productivity ——— Unit wage cost

Source: http://www.statistics.gov.uk/cci/nugget.asp?id=133

TABLE 18.2

Annual Growth in UK Productivity, 1951–2000 (%)

1951–1960	2.3
1961–1970	2.7
1971–1980	1.8
1981–1990	2.0
1991–2000	2.1

Monopsony

On the preceding pages, we built our analysis of the labour market with the tools of supply and demand. In doing so, we assumed that the labour market was competitive. That is, we assumed that there were many buyers of labour and many sellers of labour, so each buyer or seller had a negligible effect on the wage.

Yet imagine the labour market in a small town dominated by a single large employer. That employer can exert a large influence on the going wage, and it may well use that market power to alter the outcome. Such a market in which there is a single buyer is called a *monopsony*.

A monopsony (a market with one buyer) is in many ways similar to a monopoly (a market with one seller).

Recall from Chapter 15 that a monopoly firm produces less of the good than would a competitive firm: by reducing the quantity offered for sale, the monopoly firm moves along the product's demand curve, raising the price and also its profits. Similarly, a monopsony firm in a labour market hires fewer workers than would a competitive firm: by reducing the number of jobs available, the monopsony firm moves along the labour supply curve, reducing the wage it pays and raising its profits. Thus, both monopolists and monopsonists reduce economic activity in a market below the socially optimal level. In both cases, the existence of market power distorts the outcome and causes deadweight losses.

This book does not present the formal model of monopsony because, in the real world, monopsonies are rare although on a small scale, a number of towns in parts of Europe may be highly dependent on a major employer – a motor vehicle manufacturer, a steel works or chocolate manufacturer, for example. In such situations, the analysis may have to be amended to take into consideration the effect that monopoly power of the employer has on the local labour market. In most labour markets, however, workers have many possible employers, and firms compete with one another to attract workers. In this case, the model of supply and demand is the best one to use.

Quick Quiz How does immigration of workers affect labour supply, labour demand, the marginal product of labour and the equilibrium wage?

THE OTHER FACTORS OF PRODUCTION: LAND AND CAPITAL

We have seen how firms decide how much labour to hire and how these decisions determine workers' wages. At the same time that firms are hiring workers, they are also deciding about other inputs to production. For example, our apple-producing firm might have to choose the size of its apple orchard and the number of ladders to make available to its apple pickers. We can think of the firm's factors of production as falling into three categories: labour, land and capital.

Economists use the term **capital** to refer to the stock of equipment and structures used for production – they are not used for their own sake but for what they can contribute to production. The economy's capital represents the accumulation of goods produced in the past that are being used in the present to produce new goods and services. For our apple firm, the capital stock includes the ladders used to climb the trees, the baskets that are used to collect the picked apples, trucks used to transport the apples, the buildings used to store the apples, and even the trees themselves.

capital
the equipment and structures used to produce goods and services

Equilibrium in the Markets for Land and Capital

What determines how much the owners of land and capital earn for their contribution to the production process? Before answering this question, we need to distinguish between two prices: the purchase price and the rental price. The *purchase price* of land or capital is the price a person pays to own that factor of production indefinitely. The *rental price* is the price a person pays to use that factor for a limited period of time. It is important to keep this distinction in mind because, as we will see, these prices are determined by somewhat different economic forces.

Having defined these terms, we can now apply the theory of factor demand that we developed for the labour market to the markets for land and capital. The wage is, after all, simply the rental price of labour. Therefore, much of what we have learned about wage determination applies also to the rental prices of land and capital. As Figure 18.8 illustrates, the rental price of land, shown in panel (a), and the rental price of capital, shown in panel (b), are determined by supply and demand. Moreover, the demand for land and capital is determined just like the demand for labour. That is, when our apple-producing firm is deciding how much land and how many ladders to rent, it follows the same logic as when deciding how many workers to hire. For both land and capital, the firm increases the quantity hired until the value of the factor's marginal product equals the factor's price. Thus, the demand curve for each factor reflects the marginal productivity of that factor.

We can now explain how much income goes to labour, how much goes to landowners and how much goes to the owners of capital. As long as the firms using the factors of production are competitive and profit-maximizing, each factor's rental price must equal the value of the marginal product for that factor: labour, land and capital each earn the value of their marginal contribution to the production process.

FIGURE 18.8

The Markets for Land and Capital

Supply and demand determine the compensation paid to the owners of land, as shown in panel (a), and the compensation paid to the owners of capital, as shown in panel (b). The demand for each factor, in turn, depends on the value of the marginal product of that factor.

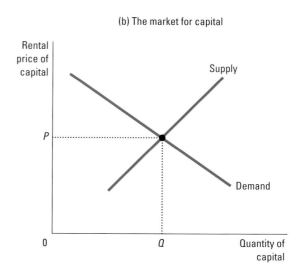

Now consider the purchase price of land and capital. The rental price and the purchase price are obviously related: buyers are willing to pay more for a piece of land or capital if it produces a valuable stream of rental income. And, as we have just seen, the equilibrium rental income at any point in time equals the value of that factor's marginal product. Therefore, the equilibrium purchase price of a piece of land or capital depends on both the current value of the marginal product and the value of the marginal product expected to prevail in the future.

Linkages Among the Factors of Production

We have seen that the price paid to any factor of production – labour, land, or capital – equals the value of the marginal product of that factor. The marginal product of any factor, in turn, depends on the quantity of that factor that is available. Because of diminishing marginal product, a factor in abundant supply has a low marginal product and thus a low price, and a factor in scarce supply has a high marginal product and a high price. As a result, when the supply of a factor falls, its equilibrium factor price rises.

When the supply of any factor changes, however, the effects are not limited to the market for that factor. In most situations, factors of production are used

FYI

What is Capital Income?

Labour income is an easy concept to understand: it is the wages and salaries that workers get from their employers. The income earned by capital, however, is less obvious.

In our analysis, we have been implicitly assuming that households own the economy's stock of capital – equipment, machinery, computers, warehouses and so forth – and rent it to the firms that use it. Capital income, in this case, is the rent that households receive for the use of their capital. This assumption simplified our analysis of how capital owners are compensated, but it is not entirely realistic. In fact, firms usually own the capital they use and, therefore, they receive the earnings from this capital.

These earnings from capital, however, eventually get paid to households. Some of the earnings are paid in the

form of interest to those households who have lent money to firms (anyone who has savings in a financial institution, who pays into a pension fund or an insurance policy is indirectly actually lending money to businesses!). Bondholders and bank depositors are two examples of recipients of interest. Thus, when you receive interest on your bank account, that income is part of the economy's capital income.

In addition, some of the earnings from capital are paid to households in the form of dividends. Dividends are payments by a firm to the firm's shareholders. A shareholder is a person who has bought a share in the ownership of the firm and, therefore, is entitled to share in the firm's profits. (This is usually called an equity or, quite simply, a share.)

A firm does not have to pay out all of its earnings to households in the form

of interest and dividends. Instead, it can retain some earnings within the firm and use these earnings to buy additional capital. Although these retained earnings do not get paid to the firm's shareholders, the shareholders benefit from them nonetheless. Because retained earnings increase the amount of capital the firm owns, they tend to increase future earnings and, thereby, the value of the firm's equities.

These institutional details are interesting and important, but they do not alter our conclusion about the income earned by the owners of capital. Capital is paid according to the value of its marginal product, regardless of whether this income gets transmitted to households in the form of interest or dividends or whether it is kept within firms as retained earnings.

together in a way that makes the productivity of each factor dependent on the quantities of the other factors available to be used in the production process. As a result, a change in the supply of any one factor alters the earnings of all the factors.

For example, suppose one night lightning strikes the storehouse in which are kept the ladders that the apple pickers use to pick apples from the orchards, and many of the ladders are destroyed in the ensuing fire. What happens to the earnings of the various factors of production? Most obviously, the supply of ladders falls and, therefore, the equilibrium rental price of ladders rises. Those owners who were lucky enough to avoid damage to their ladders now earn a higher return when they rent out their ladders to the firms that produce apples.

Yet the effects of this event do not stop at the ladder market. Because there are fewer ladders with which to work, the workers who pick apples have a smaller marginal product. Thus, the reduction in the supply of ladders reduces the demand for the labour of apple pickers, and this causes the equilibrium wage to fall.

This story shows a general lesson: an event that changes the supply of any factor of production can alter the earnings of all the factors. The change in earnings of any factor can be found by analysing the impact of the event on the value of the marginal product of that factor.

CASE STUDY

The Economics of the Black Death

Workers who survived the plague were lucky in more ways than one.

In 14th-century Europe, the bubonic plague wiped out about one-third of the population within a few years. This event, called the *Black Death*, provides a grisly natural experiment to test the theory of factor markets that we have just developed. Consider the effects of the Black Death on those who were lucky enough to survive. What do you think happened to the wages earned by workers and the rents earned by landowners?

To answer this question, let's examine the effects of a reduced population on the marginal product of labour and the marginal product of land. With a smaller supply of workers, the marginal product of labour rises. (This is simply diminishing marginal product working in reverse.) Thus, we would expect the Black Death to raise wages.

Because land and labour are used together in production, a smaller supply of workers also affects the market for land, the other major factor of production in medieval Europe. With fewer workers available to farm the land, an additional unit of land produced less additional output. In other words, the marginal product of land fell. Thus, we would expect the Black Death to lower rents.

In fact, both predictions are consistent with the historical evidence. Wages approximately doubled during this period, and rents declined 50 per cent or more. The Black Death led to economic prosperity for the peasant classes and reduced incomes for the landed classes.

Quick Quiz What determines the income of the owners of land and capital? • How would an increase in the quantity of capital affect the incomes of those who already own capital? How would it affect the incomes of workers?

IN THE NEWS

The recession of 2008–09 had a major impact on productivity levels in many European countries, in the US and the Far East. The decline in productivity in different countries is important because it can not only affect standards of living but also international competitiveness. This article looks at the early evidence of changes in productivity at the start of the recession.

Labour Productivity, the Recession and Standards of Living

Europe suffered a slowdown in labour productivity growth in 2007 as measured by growth in output per hour worked, as the business cycle passed its peak and structural reform remained sluggish. The latest annual productivity report from The Conference Board, the international business membership and research organization, shows output per hour worked rose by 1.4 per cent across the 27 European Union states in 2007, down from 1.7 per cent the previous year. It is expected to slow further, to 1.3 per cent, in 2008 in the EU27, and even to 1 per cent in the 'old' 15 member EU. For the second year running, however, Europe performed better than the US, where productivity rose by just 1.1 per cent.

The disappointing European average was the result of weak productivity growth in a number of major economies, including Germany (1 per cent), France (0.6 per cent), Italy (1 per cent) and Spain (0.6 per cent). But it masked some impressive performances, most notably in the UK where productivity rose by 2.9 per cent, making it the top performer among the EU15. Recession concerns and the credit crunch cloud the US economic outlook for 2008, but US productivity growth is expected to accelerate to 1.7 per cent in 2009, while Japan's rate is forecast to pick up to 1.9 per cent.

Despite better European performance in the past two years, the US

maintains its productivity edge over the longer term. Innovation is more deeply embedded in the business process in the United States, particularly in service industries. Large investments in information and communications technology (ICT) have gone together with rapid increases in efficiency, which are not found in Europe and Japan. However, Irish labour productivity has been boosted because of the overwhelming dominance of US companies in the Irish economy.

Despite the slow increase in US labour productivity, the level of GDP per hour worked is still among the highest in the advanced economies. In 2007, output per hour worked was US$52.10 – very close to the levels of France, The Netherlands, and Austria, and only significantly behind two smaller economies: Norway ($70.10) and Luxembourg ($70.30). An illustration of the choices that can be made where high levels of labour productivity coincide with low unemployment is provided by Austria and the US. Austria has higher output per worker than the US and similar levels of employment, but its employees work 15 per cent fewer hours a year reducing its GDP per person to 15 per cent below US levels.

Meanwhile, in emerging economies, productivity growth continued to accelerate, topping 8 per cent in the BRIC (Brazil, Russia, India, China) countries on average in 2007, accelerating from 7.5 per cent between 2000 and 2005. There were large differences between the individual economies, however,

with China notching up 10.6 per cent growth while Brazil managed just 1.9 per cent. Productivity levels in emerging economies are still very low at between 10 per cent and 40 per cent of the US level. However, as the wage gaps are generally even larger, the labour cost per unit of output provides a cost competitiveness advantage to emerging economies which for manufacturing can be as low as 20 per cent of the US level.

The report warns that advanced economies will need to raise annual productivity growth to well above 2 per cent over the next two decades to maintain current living standards. Given the limits to labour force growth almost everywhere, the onus will be on technology and innovation to drive the growth process. Indeed, one of the most significant changes is the emphasis on innovation-related spending in the emerging world. While expenditure on research and development (R&D) and investment in information and communication technology in emerging economies are still at less than half of the level in advanced economies, the spending gap is narrowing. This reflects a commitment to compete on the basis of innovation capacity not just cost.

Source: http://www.finfacts.com/ irelandbusinessnews/publish/ article_1012338.shtml and http://www .conference-board.org/pdf_free/ Productivity2008Briefing.pdf

CONCLUSION

The theory developed in this chapter is called the *neoclassical theory of distribution*. According to the neoclassical theory, the amount paid to each factor of production depends on the supply and demand for that factor. The demand, in turn, depends on that particular factor's marginal productivity. In equilibrium, each factor of production earns the value of its marginal contribution to the production of goods and services.

The neoclassical theory of distribution is widely accepted. Most economists begin with the neoclassical theory when trying to explain how an economy's income is distributed among the economy's various members. In the following two chapters, we consider the distribution of income in more detail. As you will see, the neoclassical theory provides the framework for this discussion.

Even at this point you can use the theory to answer the question that began this chapter: why are computer programmers paid more than petrol station attendants? It is because programmers can produce a good of greater market value than can a petrol station attendant. People are willing to pay dearly for a good computer game, but they are willing to pay little to have their petrol pumped and their windscreen washed. The wages of these workers reflect the market prices of the goods they produce. If people suddenly got tired of using computers and decided to spend more time driving, the prices of these goods would change, and so would the equilibrium wages of these two groups of workers.

SUMMARY

- The economy's income is distributed in the markets for the factors of production. The three most important factors of production are labour, land and capital.

- The demand for factors, such as labour, is a derived demand that comes from firms that use the factors to produce goods and services. Competitive, profit-maximizing firms hire each factor up to the point at which the value of the marginal product of the factor equals its price.

- The supply of labour arises from individuals' trade-off between work and leisure. An upward sloping labour supply curve means that people respond to an increase in the wage by enjoying less leisure and working more hours.

- The price paid to each factor adjusts to balance the supply and demand for that factor. Because factor demand reflects the value of the marginal product of that factor, in equilibrium each factor is compensated according to its marginal contribution to the production of goods and services.

- Because factors of production are used together, the marginal product of any one factor depends on the quantities of all factors that are available. As a result, a change in the supply of one factor alters the equilibrium earnings of all the factors.

KEY CONCEPTS

factors of production, p. 383
production function, p. 384

marginal product of labour, p. 385
value of the marginal product, p. 386

capital, p. 395

QUESTIONS FOR REVIEW

1. Explain how a firm's production function is related to its marginal product of labour, how a firm's marginal product of labour is related to the value of its marginal product and how a firm's value of marginal product is related to its demand for labour.

2. Give two examples of events that could shift the demand for labour.

3. Give two examples of events that could shift the supply of labour.

4. Explain how the wage can adjust to balance the supply and demand for labour while simultaneously equalling the value of the marginal product of labour.

5. If the population of Norway suddenly grew because of a large immigration, what would you expect to happen to wages? What would happen to the rents earned by the owners of land and capital?

PROBLEMS AND APPLICATIONS

1. Suppose that the government proposes a new law aimed at reducing heath care costs: all citizens are to be required to eat one apple daily.
   a. How would this apple-a-day law affect the demand and equilibrium price of apples?
   b. How would the law affect the marginal product and the value of the marginal product of apple pickers?
   c. How would the law affect the demand and equilibrium wage for apple pickers?

2. Show the effect of each of the following events on the market for labour in the computer manufacturing industry.
   a. The government buys personal computers for all university students.
   b. More university students graduate in engineering and computer science.
   c. Computer firms build new manufacturing factories.

3. Your enterprising uncle opens a sandwich shop that employs 7 people. The employees are paid €6 per hour and a sandwich sells for €13. If your uncle is maximizing his profit, what is the value of the marginal product of the last worker he hired? What is that worker's marginal product?

4. Imagine a firm that hires two types of workers – some with computer skills and some without. If technology advances so that computers become more useful to the firm, what happens to the marginal product of the two types? What happens to equilibrium wages? Explain, using appropriate diagrams.

5. Suppose a harsh winter in Normandy destroys part of the French apple crop.
   a. Explain what happens to the price of apples and the marginal product of apple pickers as a result of the freeze. Can you say what happens to the demand for apple pickers? Why or why not?
   b. Suppose the price of apples doubles and the marginal product falls by 30 per cent. What happens to the equilibrium wage of apple pickers?
   c. Suppose the price of apples rises by 30 per cent and the marginal product falls by 50 per cent. What happens to the equilibrium wage of apple pickers?

6. In recent years, the United Kingdom has experienced a significant inflow of capital in the form of direct investment, especially from the Far East. For example, both Honda and Nissan have built car plants in the United Kingdom.
   a. Using a diagram of the UK capital market, show the effect of this inflow on the rental price of capital in the United Kingdom and on the quantity of capital in use.
   b. Using a diagram of the UK labour market, show the effect of the capital inflow on the average wage paid to UK workers.

7. Suppose that labour is the only input used by a perfectly competitive firm that can hire workers for €150 per day. The firm's production function is as follows:

Days of labour	Units of output
0	0
1	7
2	13
3	19
4	25
5	28
6	29

Each unit of output sells for €110. Plot the firm's demand for labour. How many days of labour should the firm hire? Show this point on your graph.

8. (This question is challenging.) This chapter has assumed that labour is supplied by individual workers acting competitively. In some markets, however, the supply of labour is determined by a union of workers.

   a. Explain why the situation faced by a labour union may resemble the situation faced by a monopoly firm.

   b. The goal of a monopoly firm is to maximize profits. Is there an analogous goal for labour unions?

   c. Now extend the analogy between monopoly firms and unions. How do you suppose that the wage set by a union compares to the wage in a competitive market? How do you suppose employment differs in the two cases?

   d. What other goals might unions have that make unions different from monopoly firms?

For further resources, visit
www.cengage.com/mankiw_taylor2

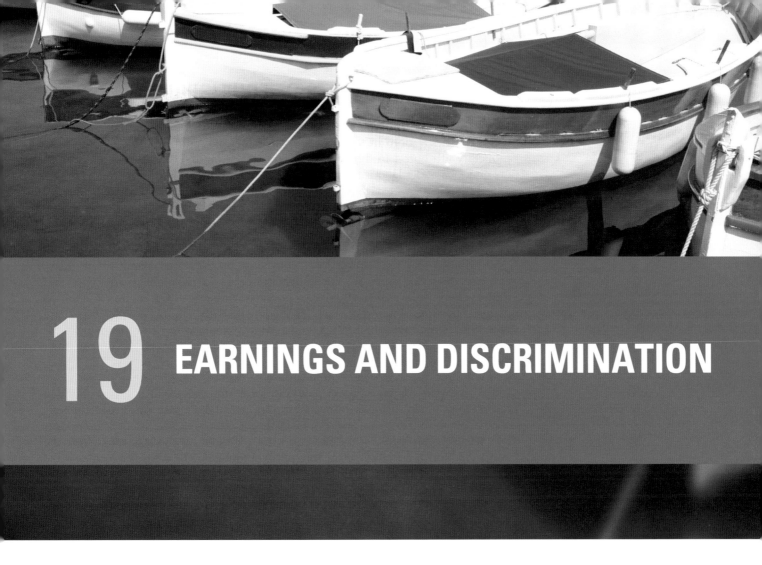

19 EARNINGS AND DISCRIMINATION

In the United Kingdom today, a successful barrister will earn in excess of £200 000 a year, a typical doctor in general practice about £118 000, an experienced secondary school teacher around £35 000 and a bus driver with over ten years experience around £23 000. In Switzerland a long-haul airline pilot with 20 years experience can expect to earn around €157 000 whilst an outsourcing manager is paid around €80 000 and a sales associate around €45 000. These examples illustrate the large differences in earnings that are so common in a modern economy. The differences explain why some people live in large houses, drive expensive cars and go on holiday to exotic places, while other people live in small houses or apartments, take the bus and seldom go abroad for a holiday.

Why do earnings vary so much from person to person? Chapter 18, which developed the basic neoclassical theory of the labour market, offers an answer to this question. There we saw that wages are governed by labour supply and labour demand. Labour demand, in turn, reflects the marginal productivity of labour. In equilibrium, each worker is paid the value of his or her marginal contribution to the economy's production of goods and services.

This theory of the labour market, though widely accepted by economists, is only the beginning of the story. To understand the wide variation in earnings that we observe, we must go beyond this general framework and examine more precisely what determines the supply and demand for different types of labour. That is our goal in this chapter.

SOME DETERMINANTS OF EQUILIBRIUM WAGES

Workers differ from one another in many ways. Jobs also have differing characteristics – both in terms of the wage they pay and in terms of their non-monetary attributes. In this section we consider how the characteristics of workers and jobs affect labour supply, labour demand and equilibrium wages.

Compensating Differentials

When a worker is deciding whether to take a job, the wage is only one of many job attributes that the worker takes into account. Some jobs require few skills, and are 'easy' and safe; others might require considerable skill, experience and may be very dull, whilst others can be very dangerous. The 'better' the job as gauged by these non-monetary characteristics, the more people there are who are willing (and able) to do the job at any given wage. In other words, the supply of labour for jobs requiring few skills or no experience is greater than the supply of labour for highly skilled, and dangerous jobs. As a result, 'good' jobs will tend to have lower equilibrium wages than 'bad' jobs.

For example, imagine you are looking for a summer job at a seaside holiday resort. Two kinds of jobs are available. You can take a job hiring out sunbeds on the beach, or you can take one as a refuse collector. The sunbed attendants take leisurely strolls along the beach during the day and check to make sure the holidaymakers have paid for the hire of their sunbeds. The refuse collectors wake up before dawn to drive dirty, noisy lorries around town to pick up rubbish from households and firms. Which job would you want? Most people would prefer the beach job if the wages were the same. To induce people to become refuse collectors, the town has to offer higher wages to refuse collectors than to sunbed attendants.

compensating differential
a difference in wages that arises to offset the non-monetary characteristics of different jobs

Economists use the term **compensating differential** to refer to a difference in wages that arises from non-monetary characteristics of different jobs. Compensating differentials are prevalent in the economy. Here are some examples:

- Workers who maintain and repair major roads such as motorways, are paid more than other public sector workers who repair roads in towns and cities. This is because the danger level of working on major roads is much higher, not to mention the fact that they often have to work unsociable hours (when drivers are not using the motorways).
- Workers who work night shifts at factories and in other forms of employment such as 24-hour retail outlets are paid more than similar workers who work day shifts. The higher wage compensates them for having to work at night and sleep during the day, a lifestyle that most people find undesirable (and disorientating!).
- University lecturers and professors are on average paid less than lawyers and doctors, who have similar levels of education. Lecturers' lower wages compensate them for the great intellectual and personal satisfaction that their jobs offer. (Indeed, teaching economics is so much fun that it is surprising that economics professors get paid anything at all!)

We're hoping to employ a workaholic for whom job-satisfaction is reward enough.

Human Capital

As we discussed in the previous chapter, the word *capital* usually refers to the economy's stock of equipment and structures. The capital stock includes the farmer's tractor, the manufacturer's factory and the teacher's laptop. The essence of capital is that it is a factor of production that itself has been produced.

There is another type of capital that, while less tangible than physical capital, is just as important to the economy's production. **Human capital** is the accumulation of investments in people. The most important type of human capital is education. Like all forms of capital, education represents an expenditure of resources at one point in time to raise productivity in the future. But, unlike an investment in other forms of capital, an investment in education is tied to a specific person, and this linkage is what makes it human capital.

human capital
the accumulation of investments in people, such as education and on-the-job training

Not surprisingly, workers with more human capital on average earn more than those with less human capital. University graduates in Europe and North America, for example, earn almost twice as much as those workers who end their education after secondary school. This large difference tends to be even larger in less developed countries, where educated workers are in scarce supply.

It is easy to see why education raises wages from the perspective of supply and demand. Firms – the demanders of labour – are willing to pay more for the highly educated because highly educated workers have higher marginal products. Workers – the suppliers of labour – are willing to pay the cost of becoming educated only if there is a reward for doing so. In essence, the difference in wages between highly educated workers and less educated workers may be considered a compensating differential for the cost of becoming educated.

Ability, Effort and Chance

Why do football players in the top European leagues such as the English Premiership or the Spanish *La Liga* get paid more than those in the minor leagues? Certainly, the higher wage is not a compensating differential. Playing in the major leagues is associated with more glamour and prestige as well as the, often considerably, higher wages. The major leagues do not necessarily require more years of schooling or more experience. To a large extent, players in the major leagues earn more just because they have greater natural ability.

Natural ability is important for workers in all occupations. Because of heredity and upbringing, people differ in their physical and mental attributes. Some people have physical and mental strength whereas others have less of both. Some people are able to solve complex problems, others less so. Some people are outgoing, others awkward in social situations. These and many other personal characteristics determine how productive workers are and, therefore, play a role in determining the wages they earn.

Closely related to ability is effort. Some people are prepared to put in long hours and considerable effort into their work whereas others are content to do what they are required to do and no more. We should not be surprised to find that those who put in more effort may be more productive and earn higher wages. To some extent, firms reward workers directly by paying people on the basis of what they produce. Salespeople, for instance, are often paid based on a percentage of the sales they make. At other times, greater effort is rewarded less directly in the form of a higher annual salary or a bonus.

Chance also plays a role in determining wages. If a person attended college to learn how to repair televisions with vacuum tubes and then found this skill made obsolete by the invention of solid-state electronics, he or she would end up earning a low wage compared to others with similar years of training. The low wage of this worker is due to chance – a phenomenon that economists recognize but do not shed much light on.

How important are ability, effort and chance in determining wages? It is hard to say, because ability, effort and chance are hard to measure. But indirect evidence suggests that they are very important. When labour economists study wages, they relate a worker's wage to those variables that can be measured – years of schooling, years of experience, age and job characteristics. Although all of these measured variables affect a worker's wage as theory predicts, they account for less than half of the variation in wages in our economy. Because so much of the variation in wages is left unexplained, omitted variables, including ability, effort and chance, must play an important role.

CASE STUDY

The Benefits of Beauty

People differ in many ways. One difference is in how attractive they are. Indeed, the idea of beauty is something that is not simply personal – the so-called 'golden ratio' plays a part in our perception of beauty. Those people whose faces and bodies conform most closely to the proportions outlined in the golden ratio are generally seen as being 'beautiful'! Both females and males generally agree that Brad Pitt is a handsome man. In part for this reason, his films attract large audiences. Not surprisingly, the large audiences mean a large income for Mr Pitt.

How prevalent are the economic benefits of beauty? Labour economists Daniel Hamermesh and Jeff Biddle tried to answer this question in a study published in the December 1994 issue of the *American Economic Review.* Hamermesh and Biddle examined data from surveys of individuals in the United States and Canada. The interviewers who conducted the survey were asked to rate each respondent's physical appearance. Hamermesh and Biddle then examined how much the wages of the respondents depended on the standard determinants – education, experience and so on – and how much they depended on physical appearance.

The researchers found that beauty pays. People who are deemed to be more attractive than average earn 5 per cent more than people of average looks. People of average looks earn 5 to 10 per cent more than people considered less attractive than average. Similar results were found for men and women.

What explains these differences in wages? There are several ways to interpret the 'beauty premium.'

One interpretation is that good looks are themselves a type of innate ability determining productivity and wages. Some people are born with the attributes of a film star; other people are not. Good looks are useful in any job in which workers present themselves to the public – such as acting, sales and waiting on tables. In this case, an attractive worker is more valuable to the firm than an unattractive worker. The firm's willingness to pay more to attractive workers reflects its customers' preferences.

A second interpretation is that reported beauty is an indirect measure of other types of ability. How attractive a person appears depends on more than just heredity. It also depends on dress, hairstyle, personal demeanour and other attributes that a person can control. Perhaps a person who successfully projects an attractive image in a survey interview is more likely to be an intelligent person who succeeds at other tasks as well.

A third interpretation is that the beauty premium is a type of discrimination, a topic to which we return later.

Brad Pitt: good looks pay.

An Alternative View of Education: Signalling

Earlier we discussed the human capital view of education, according to which schooling raises workers' wages because it makes them more productive.

Although this view is widely accepted, some economists have proposed an alternative theory, which emphasizes that firms use educational attainment as a way of sorting between high-ability and low-ability workers. According to this alternative view, when people earn a university degree, for instance, they do not become more productive, but they do *signal* their high ability to prospective employers. Because it is easier for high-ability people to earn a university degree than it is for low-ability people, more high-ability people get college degrees. As a result, it is rational for firms to interpret a college degree as a signal of ability.

The signalling theory of education is similar to the signalling theory of advertising discussed in Chapter 16. In the signalling theory of advertising, the advertisement itself contains no real information, but the firm signals the quality of its product to consumers by its willingness to spend money on advertising. In the signalling theory of education, schooling has no real productivity benefit, but the worker signals his innate productivity to employers by his willingness to spend years at school. In both cases, an action is being taken not for its intrinsic benefit but because the willingness to take that action conveys private information to someone observing it.

Thus, we now have two views of education: the human capital theory and the signalling theory. Both views can explain why more educated workers tend to earn more than less educated workers. According to the human capital view, education makes workers more productive; according to the signalling view, education is correlated with natural ability. But the two views have radically different predictions for the effects of policies that aim to increase educational attainment. According to the human capital view, increasing educational levels for all workers would raise all workers' productivity and thereby their wages. According to the signalling view, education does not enhance productivity, so raising all workers' educational levels would not affect wages.

Most likely, the truth lies somewhere between these two extremes. The benefits to education are probably a combination of the productivity enhancing effects of human capital and the productivity revealing effects of signalling. The open question is the relative size of these two effects.

The Superstar Phenomenon

Although most actors earn little and often take jobs as waiters to support themselves, Julia Roberts earns millions of pounds for each film she makes. Similarly, while most people who play tennis do it for free as a hobby, Roger Federer earns millions on the professional circuit. Julia Roberts and Roger Federer are superstars in their fields, and their great public appeal is reflected in astronomical incomes.

Why do Julia Roberts and Roger Federer earn so much? It is not surprising that there are differences in incomes within occupations. Good carpenters earn more than mediocre carpenters, and good plumbers earn more than mediocre plumbers. People vary in ability and effort, and these differences lead to differences in income. Yet the best carpenters and plumbers do not earn the many millions that are common among the best actors and athletes. What explains the difference? To understand the tremendous incomes of Julia Roberts and Roger Federer, we must examine the special features of the markets in which they sell their services. Superstars arise in markets that have two characteristics:

- Every customer in the market wants to enjoy the good supplied by the best producer.
- The good is produced with a technology that makes it possible for the best producer to supply every customer at low cost.

Julia Roberts: popularity + technology = superstar.

strike
the organized withdrawal of labour from a firm by a union

efficiency wages
above-equilibrium wages paid by firms in order to increase worker productivity

the level that would prevail without a union, perhaps because they can threaten to withhold labour from the firm by calling a **strike**. Studies suggest that union workers earn about 10 to 20 per cent more than similar non-union workers.

A third reason for above-equilibrium wages is suggested by the theory of **efficiency wages**. This theory holds that a firm can find it profitable to pay high wages because doing so increases the productivity of its workers. In particular, high wages may reduce worker turnover (hiring and training new workers is an expensive business), increase worker effort, and raise the quality of workers who apply for jobs at the firm. In addition, a firm may feel it has to offer high wages in order to attract and keep the best people – this has been an argument put forward by the banking sector in response to plans by governments in Europe to tax bankers' earning in the wake of the financial crisis. If this theory is correct, then some firms may choose to pay their workers more than they would normally earn.

Above-equilibrium wages, whether caused by minimum wage laws, unions or efficiency wages, have similar effects on the labour market. In particular, pushing a wage above the equilibrium level raises the quantity of labour supplied and reduces the quantity of labour demanded. The result is a surplus of labour, or unemployment. The study of unemployment and the public policies aimed to deal with it is usually considered a topic within macroeconomics, so it goes beyond the scope of this book. But it would be a mistake to ignore these issues completely when analysing earnings. Although most wage differences can be understood while maintaining the assumption of equilibrium in the labour market, above-equilibrium wages play a role in some cases.

Quick Quiz Define *compensating differential* and give an example.
• Give two reasons why more educated workers earn more than less educated workers.

THE ECONOMICS OF DISCRIMINATION

discrimination
the offering of different opportunities to similar individuals who differ only by race, ethnic group, sex, age or other personal characteristics

Another source of differences in wages is discrimination. **Discrimination** occurs when the marketplace offers different opportunities to similar individuals who differ only by race, ethnic group, sex, age or other personal characteristics. Discrimination reflects some people's prejudice against certain groups in society. Although discrimination is an emotionally charged topic that often generates heated debate, economists try to study the topic objectively in order to separate myth from reality.

Measuring Labour Market Discrimination

How much does discrimination in labour markets affect the earnings of different groups of workers? This question is important, but answering it is not easy.

There is no doubt that different groups of workers earn substantially different wages. An interesting and particularly striking example of this is in the average amount of money earned by people belonging to different ethnic groups in the United States, as Table 19.2 demonstrates.

The situation in the UK and parts of Europe is not dissimilar. A report published in 2010 by the National Equality Panel[1] showed that inequalities in incomes and earnings are 'high' in Britain compared with other industrialized

[1]Hills, J et al. (2010). *An anatomy of economic inequality in the UK.* http://sticerd.lse.ac.uk/dps/case/cr/CASEreport60.pdf

TABLE 19.2

US Median Annual Earnings by Race and Sex

	White	Black	Percentage by which earnings are lower for black workers
Men	$41 982	$32 976	21%
Women	$32 173	$29 680	8%
Percentage by which earnings are lower for women workers	23%	10%	

Note: Earnings data are for the year 2005 and apply to full-time, year-round workers aged 14 and over.
Source: US Bureau of the Census.

countries, and considering figures from 30 years ago. Women, for example, earn 21 per cent less in terms of median hourly pay for all employees and 13 per cent less than men for those working full time. The Report also found that people from non-white ethnic backgrounds are paid less than white British men. Pakistani and Bangladeshi Muslim men and Black African Christian men earn between 13 and 21 per cent less than white British Christian men. Chinese men are one of the highest paid groups in Britain but they are paid 11 per cent less than would be expected given their qualifications. Women from nearly all ethno-religious backgrounds have pay which is anything between a quarter and a third less than their white British Christian male counterparts even with the same qualifications age and in the same occupation, according to the report.

In Germany women earned around 24 per cent less than men in 2009 compared with the European Union average of 18 per cent. Of the 27 member countries of the EU, only in Estonia, the Czech Republic, Austria and The Netherlands is there a higher gender gap in pay in favour of men. Pay differentials between men and women across Europe have hardly changed over the past 15 years according to the European Commission.

Taken at face value, these differentials look like evidence that US, UK and European employers discriminate against those from ethnic minorities and women. Yet there is a potential problem with this inference. Even in a labour market free of discrimination, different people have different wages. People differ in the amount of human capital they have and in the kinds of work they are able and willing to do. The wage differences we observe in the economy are, to some extent, attributable to the determinants of equilibrium wages we discussed in the preceding section. Simply observing differences in wages among broad groups – whites and blacks, men and women – does not prove that employers discriminate.

Consider, for example, the role of human capital. Whether an individual has a degree can account for some of these differences and as we have seen above, the type of degree can also have an impact. White male workers in the United States are about 75 per cent more likely to have a university degree than blacks. Thus, at least some of the difference between the wages of American whites and the wages of American blacks can be traced to differences in educational attainment. Moreover, human capital may be more important in explaining wage differentials than measures of years of schooling suggest. Historically, state schools in predominantly black areas of the United States have been of lower quality – as measured by expenditure, class size and so on – than state schools in predominantly white areas. Similarly, for many years, American schools – in common with European schools – directed girls away from science and mathematics courses, even though these subjects may have had greater value in the marketplace than some of the alternatives. If we could measure the quality as well as the quantity of education, the differences in human capital among these groups would seem even larger. The Federal Bureau of Statistics in Germany points out that gender pay differences in Germany may be due to a number of factors including differences in educational attainment, a high proportion of women work in part-time occupations (69 per cent of employed mothers in 2009) and the type of employment they go into; many of the jobs women enter tend to be low-skill, low-paid jobs.

Human capital acquired in the form of job experience can also help explain wage differences. In particular, women tend to have less job experience on average than men. One reason is that female labour force participation has increased in industrialized economies over the past several decades. Because of this historic change, in both Europe and North America, the average female worker today is younger than the average male worker. In addition, women are more likely to interrupt their careers to raise children. For both reasons, the experience of the average female worker is less than the experience of the average male worker.

Yet another source of wage differences is compensating differentials. Men and women do not always choose the same type of work, and this fact may help explain some of the earnings differential between men and women. For example, women are more likely to be personal assistants or receptionists and men are more likely to be lorry drivers. (Some people would argue that women get 'ushered' into these types of jobs because of stereotypes, but that is not the point here.) The relative wages of personal assistants, receptionists and lorry drivers depend in part on the working conditions of each job. Because these non-monetary aspects are hard to measure, it is difficult to gauge the practical importance of compensating differentials in explaining the wage differences that we observe.

In the end, the study of wage differences among groups does not establish any clear conclusion about the prevalence of discrimination in labour markets. Most economists believe that some of the observed wage differentials are attributable to discrimination, but there is no consensus about how much. The only conclusion about which economists are in consensus is a negative one: because the differences in average wages among groups in part reflect differences in human capital and job characteristics, they do not by themselves say anything about how much discrimination there is in the labour market.

Of course, differences in human capital among groups of workers may themselves reflect discrimination. The less rigorous curriculums historically offered to female students, for instance, can be considered a discriminatory practice. Similarly, the inferior schools historically available to black American students may be traced to prejudice on the part of city councils and school boards. But this kind of discrimination occurs long before the worker enters the labour market. In this case, the disease is political, even if the symptom is economic.

Discrimination by Employers

Let's now turn from measurement to the economic forces that lie behind discrimination in labour markets. If one group in society receives a lower wage than another group, even after controlling for human capital and job characteristics, who is to blame for this differential?

The answer is not obvious. It might seem natural to blame employers for discriminatory wage differences. After all, employers make the hiring decisions that determine labour demand and wages. If some groups of workers earn lower wages than they should, then it seems that employers are responsible. Yet many economists are sceptical of this easy answer. They believe that competitive, market economies provide a natural antidote to employer discrimination. That antidote is called the profit motive.

Imagine an economy in which workers are differentiated by their hair colour. Blondes and brunettes have the same skills, experience and work ethic. Yet, because of discrimination, employers prefer not to hire workers with blonde hair. Thus, the demand for blondes is lower than it otherwise would be. As a result, blondes earn a lower wage than brunettes.

How long can this wage differential persist? In this economy, there is an easy way for a firm to beat out its competitors: it can hire blonde workers. By hiring blondes, a firm pays lower wages and thus has lower costs than firms that hire brunettes. Over time, more and more 'blonde' firms enter the market to take advantage of this cost advantage. The existing 'brunette' firms have higher costs and, therefore, begin to lose money when faced with the new competitors. These losses induce the brunette firms to go out of business. Eventually, the entry of blonde firms and the exit of brunette firms cause the demand for blonde workers to rise and the demand for brunette workers to fall. This process continues until the wage differential disappears.

Put simply, business owners who care only about making money are at an advantage when competing against those who also care about discriminating. As a result, firms that do not discriminate tend to replace those that do. In this way, competitive markets have a natural remedy for employer discrimination.

CASE STUDY

Becker's 'Employer Taste' Model

As you might expect by now, economists have spent some time looking at the economics of discrimination. One important piece of research into this area is from Nobel Prize winner Gary Becker from the University of Chicago, who in 1971 revised his earlier 1957 work on the economics of discrimination. The basis of the employer taste model is that (for whatever reason) some employees will resist working with other employees, possibly because of gender or race. People may, therefore, have a 'taste' for only working with certain groups of people. Those outside this accepted group may end up being disadvantaged as a result.

Assume that a UK firm, which grows asparagus, hires workers to cut the spears. It has a choice of employing locals or migrant workers. Local people have a prejudice against migrant workers for some reason. Our analysis of a competitive firm assumes that workers will be employed up to the point at which the wage equals the marginal revenue product of labour. Assume that both local and migrant workers have the same level of productivity. If the firm has to employ workers at a going wage (which is above the minimum wage) then it may choose not to employ workers from the disadvantaged group because of the preferences of its core workforce. If, however, the firm is able to pay workers from the disadvantaged group lower wages then it faces a trade-off. There is an incentive for it to increase profits by employing these 'disadvantaged' workers – the migrant workers from Europe. If migrant workers were prepared to work for the minimum wage then the firm could lower its costs and increase profit as a result.

A discriminatory firm might employ some migrant workers but would pay these workers a lower wage to avoid upsetting their local workers. This is the 'employer taste' model – discrimination will exist because employers do not employ labour from certain genders, race, etc. unless the workers are prepared to accept lower wages. This discrimination may continue whilst there is some limit to the competition in the labour market – in this case it might be that all firms are prepared to act in the same way.

However, if there were other asparagus farms in the area who were not discriminatory then they might choose to hire all workers at the minimum wage which would increase its overall profits. Such a firm would also employ more workers (remember that the lower the wage rate the more workers a firm is willing to employ). There could be an influx of migrant workers to the area who are willing to take advantage of the jobs available. These non-discriminatory firms could not only produce more output but at a lower wage cost per unit and so make more profit possibly driving out the discriminatory firm from the industry.

In the UK, such a situation has manifested itself in recent years. The extension of membership of the EU in 2004 led to an increase in the number of migrant workers from countries such as Poland, Lithuania and the Czech Republic coming to Britain to find work. Many of these workers appeared willing to take on jobs that paid relatively low wages, such as cutting asparagus spears. In Cambridgeshire in the south-east of England, a large number found work on the farms in the region picking and packing fruit and vegetables. In the town of Wisbech, for example, there are over 2 000 'local' people who are unemployed but there have been around 9 000 migrant workers who have secured jobs in the area – mostly in jobs where the wages are traditionally low.

The sensitivity of the situation in Wisbech with some of the local unemployed blaming migrant workers for their lack of work is difficult. Some employers have been accused of exploiting migrant labour by paying them low wages but some counter that they are paying at least the minimum wage and that they find migrant workers not only willing to work for lower pay but also that their productivity levels are relatively high compared with some 'local' labour. In this case not only are migrant workers prepared to work for lower wages but their marginal product is higher at each price (wage). Some farmers claim that 'local' workers are not prepared to do the sort of work that is available and believe that it is too low paid. It seems that regardless of discrimination, employers are more concerned with getting value for money from their employees and are prepared to put profit before discrimination.

Discrimination by Customers and Governments

Although the profit motive is a strong force acting to eliminate discriminatory wage differentials, there are limits to its corrective abilities. Here we consider two of the most important limits: *customer preferences* and *government policies.*

To see how customer preferences for discrimination can affect wages, consider again our imaginary economy with blondes and brunettes. Suppose that restaurant owners discriminate against blondes when hiring waiters. As a result, blonde waiters earn lower wages than brunette waiters. In this case, a restaurant could open up with blonde waiters and charge lower prices. If customers only cared about the quality and price of their meals, the discriminatory firms would be driven out of business, and the wage differential would disappear.

On the other hand, it is possible that customers prefer being served by brunette waiters. If this preference for discrimination is strong, the entry of blonde restaurants need not succeed in eliminating the wage differential between brunettes and blondes. That is, if customers have discriminatory preferences, a competitive market is consistent with a discriminatory wage differential. An economy with such discrimination would contain two types of restaurants. Blonde restaurants hire blondes, have lower costs and charge lower prices. Brunette restaurants hire brunettes, have higher costs and charge higher prices. Customers who did not care about the hair colour of their waiters would be attracted to the lower prices at the blonde restaurants. Bigoted customers would go to the brunette restaurants. They would pay for their discriminatory preference in the form of higher prices.

Another way for discrimination to persist in competitive markets is for the government to mandate discriminatory practices. If, for instance, the government passed a law stating that blondes could wash dishes in restaurants but could not work as waiters, then a wage differential could persist in a competitive market. The example of segregated buses in the United States in the 1950s and 1960s is one example of government-mandated discrimination. More recently, before South Africa abandoned its system of apartheid, blacks were prohibited from working in some jobs. Discriminatory governments pass such laws to suppress the normal equalizing force of free and competitive markets.

To sum up: competitive markets contain a natural remedy for employer discrimination. The entry into the market of firms that care only about profit tends to eliminate discriminatory wage differentials. These wage differentials persist in competitive markets only when customers are willing to pay to maintain the discriminatory practice or when the government mandates it.

Quick Quiz   Why is it hard to establish whether a group of workers is being discriminated against? • Explain how profit-maximizing firms tend to eliminate discriminatory wage differentials. • How might a discriminatory wage differential persist?

CONCLUSION

In competitive markets, workers earn a wage equal to the value of their marginal contribution to the production of goods and services. There are, however, many things that affect the value of the marginal product. Firms pay more for workers who are more talented, more diligent, more experienced and more educated because these workers are more productive. Firms pay less to those workers against whom customers discriminate because these workers contribute less to revenue.

The theory of the labour market we have developed in the last two chapters explains why some workers earn higher wages than other workers. The theory does not say that the resulting distribution of income is equal, fair or desirable in any way. That is the topic we take up in Chapter 20.

SUMMARY

- Workers earn different wages for many reasons. To some extent, wage differentials compensate workers for job attributes. Other things equal, workers in hard, unpleasant jobs get paid more than workers in easy, pleasant jobs.

- Workers with more human capital get paid more than workers with less human capital. The return to accumulating human capital is high and has increased over the past two decades.

- Although years of education, experience and job characteristics affect earnings as theory predicts, there is much variation in earnings that cannot be explained by things

that economists can measure. The unexplained variation in earnings is largely attributable to natural ability, effort and chance.

- Some economists have suggested that more educated workers earn higher wages not because education raises productivity but because workers with high natural ability use education as a way to signal their high ability to employers. If this signalling theory is correct, then increasing the educational attainment of all workers would not raise the overall level of wages.

- Wages are sometimes pushed above the level that brings supply and demand into balance. Three reasons for above-equilibrium wages are minimum wage laws, unions and efficiency wages.

- Some differences in earnings are attributable to discrimination on the basis of race, sex or other factors. Measuring the amount of discrimination is difficult, however, because one must correct for differences in human capital and job characteristics.

- Competitive markets tend to limit the impact of discrimination on wages. If the wages of a group of workers are lower than those of another group for reasons not related to marginal productivity, then non-discriminatory firms will be more profitable than discriminatory firms. Profit-maximizing behaviour, therefore, can reduce discriminatory wage differentials. Discrimination persists in competitive markets, however, if customers are willing to pay more to discriminatory firms or if the government passes laws requiring firms to discriminate.

KEY CONCEPTS

compensating differential, p. 404
human capital, p. 405

union, p. 409
strike, p. 410

efficiency wages, p. 410
discrimination, p. 410

QUESTIONS FOR REVIEW

1. Why do coal miners get paid more than other workers with similar amounts of education?

2. In what sense is education a type of capital?

3. How might education raise a worker's wage without raising the worker's productivity?

4. What conditions lead to economic superstars? Would you expect to see superstars in dentistry? In music? Explain.

5. Give three reasons why a worker's wage might be above the level that balances supply and demand.

6. What difficulties arise in deciding whether a group of workers has a lower wage because of discrimination?

7. Do the forces of economic competition tend to exacerbate or ameliorate discrimination on the basis of race?

8. Give an example of how discrimination might persist in a competitive market.

PROBLEMS AND APPLICATIONS

1. University students sometimes work as summer interns for private firms or the government. Many of these positions pay little or nothing.
   a. What is the opportunity cost of taking such a job?
   b. Explain why students are willing to take these jobs.
   c. If you were to compare the earnings later in life of workers who had worked as interns and those who had taken summer jobs that paid more, what would you expect to find?

2. As explained in Chapter 6, a minimum wage law distorts the market for low-wage labour. To reduce this distortion,

some economists advocate a two-tiered minimum wage system, with a regular minimum wage for adult workers and a lower, 'sub-minimum' wage for teenage workers. Give two reasons why a single minimum wage might distort the labour market for teenage workers more than it would the market for adult workers.

3. A basic finding of labour economics is that workers who have more experience in the labour force are paid more than workers who have less experience (holding constant the amount of formal education). Why might this be so? Some studies have also found that experience at the

same job (called 'job tenure') has an extra positive influence on wages. Explain.

4. At some universities, economics lecturers receive higher salaries than lecturers in some other fields.
   a. Why might this be true?
   b. Some other universities have a policy of paying equal salaries to lecturers in all fields. At some of these, economics lecturers have lighter teaching loads than lecturers in some other fields. What role do the differences in teaching loads play?

5. Hannah works for Joachim, whom she hates because of his snobbish attitude. Yet when she looks for other jobs, the best she can do is find a job paying €15 000 less than her current salary. Should she take the job? Analyse Hannah's situation from an economic point of view.

6. Imagine that someone were to offer you a choice: you could spend four years studying at the world's best university, but you would have to keep your attendance there a secret. Or you could be awarded an official degree from the world's best university, but you couldn't actually attend (although no one need ever know this). Which choice do you think would enhance your future earnings more? What does your answer say about the debate over signalling versus human capital in the role of education?

7. When recording devices were first invented almost 100 years ago, musicians could suddenly supply their music to large audiences at low cost. How do you suppose this development affected the income of the best musicians? How do you suppose it affected the income of average musicians?

8. When Alan Greenspan (former chairman of the US Federal Reserve) ran an economic consulting firm in the 1960s, he hired primarily female economists. He once told *The New York Times,* 'I always valued men and women equally, and I found that because others did not, good women economists were cheaper than men.' Is Greenspan's behaviour profit-maximizing? Is it admirable or despicable? If more employers were like Greenspan, what would happen to the wage differential between men and women? Why might other economic consulting firms at the time not have followed Greenspan's business strategy?

9. Research into discrimination in US sport found that attendance at some US sports was higher when clubs had a higher proportion of white players than black players and that this may have something to do with the fact that black players earned less than white players. Customer discrimination in sports, therefore, seems to have an important effect on players' earnings. Note that this is possible because sports fans know the players' characteristics, including their race. Why is this knowledge important for the existence of discrimination? Give some specific examples of industries where customer discrimination is and is not likely to influence wages.

10. Suppose that all young women were channelled into careers as secretaries, nurses and teachers; at the same time, young men were encouraged to consider these three careers and many others as well.
    a. Draw a diagram showing the combined labour market for secretaries, nurses and teachers. Draw a diagram showing the combined labour market for all other fields. In which market is the wage higher? Do men or women receive higher wages on average?
    b. Now suppose that society changed and encouraged both young women and young men to consider a wide range of careers. Over time, what effect would this change have on the wages in the two markets you illustrated in part (a)? What effect would the change have on the average wages of men and women?

11. This chapter considers the economics of discrimination by employers, customers and governments. Now consider discrimination by workers. Suppose that some brunette workers did not like working with blonde workers. Do you think this worker discrimination could explain lower wages for blonde workers? If such a wage differential existed, what would a profit-maximizing entrepreneur do? If there were many such entrepreneurs, what would happen over time?

 For further resources, visit www.cengage.com/mankiw_taylor2

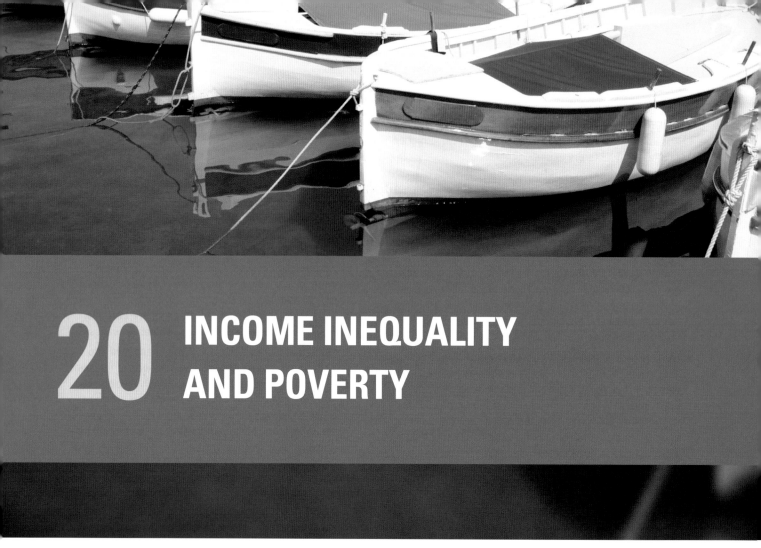

20 INCOME INEQUALITY AND POVERTY

'The only difference between the rich and other people,' Mary Colum once said to Ernest Hemingway, 'is that the rich have more money.' This may be so but the statement leaves many questions unanswered. The gap between rich and poor is a fascinating and important topic of study – for the very rich, the comfortably rich, for the struggling poor, and indeed for all members of a modern economy. If Hemingway had studied economics, he might have used this reply: 'Yes, but why are they so rich while others are not so rich?'

From the previous two chapters you should have some understanding about why different people have different incomes. A person's earnings depend on the supply and demand for that person's labour, which in turn depend on natural ability, human capital, compensating differentials, discrimination and so on. Labour earnings as measured by employee contributions make up about 53 per cent of total income in the UK economy, around 50 per cent in the Netherlands, 51 per cent in Germany, 56 per cent in Sweden and 48 per cent in the eurozone as a whole[1]. The factors that determine wages are also largely responsible for determining how an economy's total income is distributed among the various members of society. In other words, they determine who is rich and who is poor.

In this chapter we discuss the distribution of income – a topic that raises some fundamental questions about the role of economic policy. One of the *Ten Principles of Economics* in Chapter 1 is that governments can sometimes improve market outcomes. This possibility is particularly important when considering the

---

[1]Source: Compensation of employees as a proportion of GDP (income approach), http://stats.oecd.org/Index.aspx

distribution of income. The invisible hand of the marketplace acts to allocate resources efficiently, but it does not necessarily ensure that resources are allocated fairly. As a result, many economists – though not all – believe that the government should redistribute income to achieve greater equality. In doing so, however, the government runs into another of the *Ten Principles of Economics:* people face trade-offs. When the government enacts policies to make the distribution of income more equitable, it distorts incentives, alters behaviour and makes the allocation of resources less efficient.

Our discussion of the distribution of income proceeds in three steps. Firstly, we assess how much inequality there is in our society. Secondly, we consider some different views about what role the government should play in altering the distribution of income. Thirdly, we discuss various public policies aimed at helping society's poorest members.

THE MEASUREMENT OF INEQUALITY

We begin our study of the distribution of income by addressing four questions of measurement:

- How much inequality is there in our society?
- How many people live in poverty?
- What problems arise in measuring the amount of inequality?
- How often do people move among income classes?

These measurement questions are the natural starting point from which to discuss public policies aimed at changing the distribution of income.

European Income Inequality

Imagine that you lined up all the families in the economy according to their annual income. Then you divided the families into groups: the bottom 10 per cent, the next 20 per cent and so on until we got to the top 10 per cent. Table 20.1 shows the income ranges for each of these groups in the United Kingdom in 2008. It also shows the cut-off for the bottom 10 per cent and the top 10 per cent. You can use this table to find where your family lies in the income distribution.

"And this is for keeping wages down."

For examining differences in the income distribution over time, economists find it useful to present the income data as in Table 20.2. This table shows the share of total income that each group of families received. In 2008 the bottom fifth of all families received 7.1 per cent of all income, and the top fifth of all families received 43.1 per cent of all income. In other words, even though the top and bottom fifths include the same number of families, the top fifth has over six times as much income as the bottom fifth.

TABLE 20.1

The Distribution of Annual Family Income in the United Kingdom, 2008

10% have income less than:	£ 9 932
30% have income less than:	£15 132
50% have income less than:	£20 436
70% have income less than:	£27 196
90% have income less than:	£41 912

Source: Institute for Fiscal Studies. DWP http://sticerd.lse.ac.uk/dps/case/cr/CASEreport60.pdf

TABLE 20.2

Income Inequality in the United Kingdom

Year	Bottom fifth	Second fifth	Middle fifth	Fourth fifth	Top fifth
2008	7.1%	12.0%	16.1%	21.7%	43.1%
2002	7.5	12.0	16.0	22.0	42.0
1990	7.5	12.0	16.5	22.5	41.5
1979	10.0	14.0	18.0	23.0	35.0

Source: UK Department for Work and Pensions and Department of Social Security: http://research.dwp.gov.uk/asd/hbai/hbai2008/pdf_files/full_hbai09.pdf

Table 20.2 also shows the distribution of income in 1979, 1990 and 2002. The distribution has been quite stable over the period 1990–2008. But comparing the distributions in these years with the distribution in 1979, we can see that UK income inequality increased over the 1980s: the top fifth increased its share by about 7 per cent over that decade and every other fifth decreased its share of total disposable income. In fact, the poorer a group was in relative terms, the more they contributed to the richest group's increased share, with the bottom fifth reducing its share of the total from 10 per cent to 7.1 per cent and the next fifth from 14 to 12 per cent.

In Chapter 19 we discussed some explanations for this recent rise in inequality. Increases in international trade with low-wage countries and changes in technology have tended to reduce the demand for unskilled labour and raise the demand for skilled labour. As a result, the wages of unskilled workers have fallen relative to the wages of skilled workers, and this change in relative wages has increased inequality in family incomes.

How does the amount of inequality in the UK compare with that in the rest of Europe? Data from the European Union Community Statistics on Income and Living Conditions initially compiled in 2005 and revised in 2008, show considerable differences in income inequality between countries in the EU. One immediate point to notice is that average incomes vary, with those countries that used to be part of the Soviet Bloc having the lowest average incomes. Luxembourg has an average income of €29 153, around 5.5 times that of Lithuania (€5 304). Portugal, Greece and Spain all have average incomes between €10 000 and €15 000 whereas the original members of the EU such as France, Italy, Belgium and the Netherlands have average incomes between €15 000 and €20 000. Figure 20.1 shows the income distributions of the countries of the EU. The data bars are marked to show the proportions of each decile (where the population has been divided into ten equal parts). It can be seen that countries like Luxembourg, Italy and Ireland have average incomes in the ninth and tenth deciles, much higher than those of the bottom deciles.

If we look at the wider world, Figure 20.2 compares inequality in 12 countries. The inequality measure is the ratio of the income received by the richest tenth of the population to the income of the poorest tenth. The most equality is found in Japan where the top tenth receives 4.5 times as much income as the bottom tenth. The least equality is found in Brazil, where the top group receives 51.3 times as much income as the bottom group. Although all countries have significant disparities between rich and poor, the degree of inequality varies substantially throughout the world.

Problems in Measuring Inequality

Although data on the income distribution give us some idea about the degree of inequality in our society, interpreting these data is not as straightforward as it

FIGURE 20.1

The Income Distributions of the Countries of the European Union (euros, PPP)

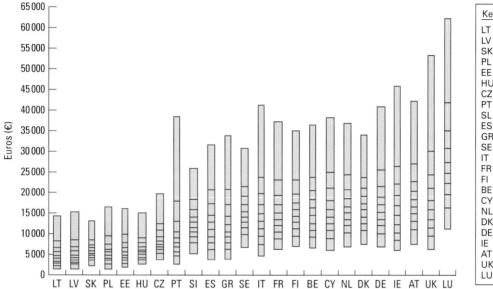

Note: The bottom of the data bars represents the first decile, the top represents the tenth decile and the marks in between show the average incomes of the individual deciles. This data is based on purchasing power parity (PPP).

Source: EU-SILC (2005), recalculations from the 2008 March data release.

might first appear. The data are based on households' annual incomes. What people care about, however, is not their incomes but their ability to maintain a good standard of living. For various reasons, data on the income distribution give an incomplete picture of inequality in living standards. We examine these reasons below.

The Economic Life Cycle Incomes vary predictably over people's lives. A young worker, especially one still engaged in full-time study, has a low income. Income rises as the worker gains maturity and experience, peaks at around age 50, and then falls sharply when the worker retires at around age 65. This regular pattern of income variation is called the **life cycle**.

Because people can borrow and save to smooth out life cycle changes in income, their standard of living in any year depends more on lifetime income than on that year's income. The young often borrow, perhaps to go to university or to buy a house, and then repay these loans later when their incomes rise. People have their highest saving rates when they are middle-aged. Because people can save in anticipation of retirement, the large declines in incomes at retirement need not lead to similar declines in standard of living.

This normal life cycle pattern causes inequality in the distribution of annual income, but it does not represent true inequality in living standards. To gauge the inequality of living standards in our society, the distribution of lifetime incomes is more relevant than the distribution of annual incomes. Unfortunately, data on lifetime incomes are not readily available. When looking at any data on inequality, however, it is important to keep the life cycle in mind. Because a

life cycle
the regular pattern of income variation over a person's life

FIGURE 20.2

Inequality Around the World

This figure shows a measure of inequality: the income (or expenditure) that goes to the richest 10 per cent of the population divided by the income (or expenditure) that goes to the poorest 10 per cent. Among these nations, Japan and Germany have the most equal distribution of economic well-being while South Africa and Brazil have the least equal.

person's lifetime income smoothes out the highs and lows of the life cycle, lifetime incomes are surely more equally distributed across the population than are annual incomes.

Transitory Versus Permanent Income   Incomes vary over people's lives not only because of predictable life cycle variation but also because of random and transitory forces. One year a frost kills off the Normandy apple crop and Normandy apple growers see their incomes fall temporarily. At the same time, the Normandy frost drives up the price of apples and English apple growers see their incomes temporarily rise. The next year the reverse might happen.

Just as people can borrow and lend to smooth out life cycle variation in income, they can also borrow and lend to smooth out transitory variation in income. When English apple growers experience a good year, they would be foolish to spend all of their additional income. Instead, they save some of it, knowing that their good fortune is unlikely to persist. Similarly, the Normandy apple growers respond to their temporarily low incomes by drawing down their savings or by borrowing. To the extent that a family saves and borrows to buffer itself from transitory changes in income, these changes do not affect its standard of living. A family's ability to buy goods and services depends largely on its **permanent income**, which is its normal, or average, income.

permanent income
a person's normal income

To gauge inequality of living standards, the distribution of permanent income is more relevant than the distribution of annual income. Although permanent income is hard to measure, it is an important concept. Because permanent income excludes transitory changes in income, permanent income is more equally distributed than is current income.

Economic Mobility

People sometimes speak of 'the rich' and 'the poor' as if these groups consisted of the same families year after year. In fact, this is not at all the case. Economic mobility, the movement of people among income classes, is quite substantial in European and North American economies. Movements up the income ladder can be due to good luck or hard work, and movements down the ladder can be due to bad luck or laziness. Some of this mobility reflects transitory variation in income, while some reflects more persistent changes in income.

Because economic mobility is so great, poverty is a long-term problem for relatively few families. Because it is likely that the temporarily poor and the persistently poor face different problems, policies that aim to combat poverty need to distinguish between these groups.

Another way to gauge economic mobility is the persistence of economic success from generation to generation. Economists who have studied this topic find substantial mobility. If a father earns 20 per cent above his generation's average income, his son will most likely earn 8 per cent above his generation's average income. There is almost no correlation between the income of a grandfather and the income of a grandson. There is much truth to the old saying, 'From shirtsleeves to shirtsleeves in three generations.'

The Poverty Rate

A commonly used gauge of the distribution of income is the poverty rate. The **poverty rate** is the percentage of the population whose family income falls below an absolute level called the **poverty line**. Poverty is a relative concept – one person's poverty is another person's wealthy. A millionaire is wealthy compared to someone earning €50 000 a year but is poor compared to a billionaire! For this reason economists distinguish between absolute and relative poverty. **Absolute poverty** is when individuals do not have access to the basic requirements of life – food, shelter and clothing. **Relative poverty** occurs when individuals are excluded from being able to take part in what are considered the normal, acceptable standards of living in a society.

To get some idea of levels of poverty across different countries, therefore, similar measures have to be used. In Europe the measure for defining the poverty line is set at 60 per cent of the median income. If measuring across Europe, this income has to be equivalized and is called the equivalized household income. If the median income is €20 000 then any family earning less than €12 000 a year would be classed as living in poverty. In the UK there are over 12 million families classed as living in poverty. Figure 20.3 shows poverty rates across European countries in 2000 and 2004. The poverty rate in countries like France, the UK, Germany and Portugal has fallen between these two years but in many countries it has risen. Once again we see the former Soviet states faring badly with the Czech Republic, Hungary, Estonia, Latvia and Poland all seeing an increase in the poverty rate. These latter three countries had poverty rates in excess of 20 per cent in 2004. The recession is likely to have made things worse for many countries as a result of widespread job losses across Europe.

Looking at the poverty rate in addition to other data on inequality is important. We might observe that average incomes have risen over time but not everyone is able to share in the increased prosperity that has occurred. Understanding something of why some people get left behind is crucial to developing policies to support people to help them gain a better standard of living.

poverty rate
the percentage of the population whose family income falls below an absolute level called the poverty line

poverty line
an absolute level of income set by the government below which a family is deemed to be in poverty. In the UK and Europe this is measured by earnings less than 60 per cent of median income

absolute poverty
a level of poverty where an individual does not have access to the basic of life – food, clothing and shelter

relative poverty
a situation where an individual is not able to access what would be considered acceptable standards of living in society

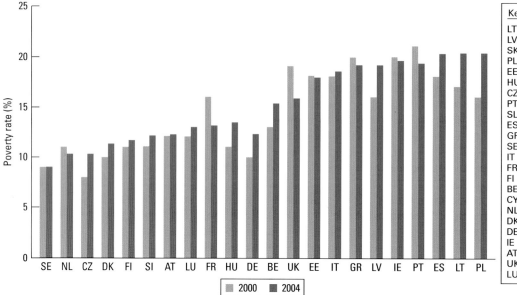

FIGURE 20.3

Poverty rates across European countries in 2000 and 2004

Key
LT Lithuania
LV Latvia
SK Slovakia
PL Poland
EE Estonia
HU Hungary
CZ Czech Republic
PT Portugal
SL Slovenia
ES Spain
GR Greece
SE Sweden
IT Italy
FR France
FI Finland
BE Belgium
CY Cyprus
NL Netherlands
DK Denmark
DE Germany
IE Ireland
AT Austria
UK United Kingdom
LU Luxembourg

Note: countries are ranked according to year 2004.

Source: ECHP (2000) and EU-SILC (2005) recalculations from the 2008 March data release.

THE POLITICAL PHILOSOPHY OF REDISTRIBUTING INCOME

We have just seen how the economy's income is distributed and have considered some of the problems in interpreting measured inequality. This discussion was *positive* in the sense that it merely described the world as it is. We now turn to the *normative* question facing policy makers: What *should* the government do about economic inequality?

This question is not just about economics. Economic analysis alone cannot tell us whether policy makers *should* try to make our society more egalitarian. Our views on this question are, to a large extent, a matter of political philosophy. Yet because the government's role in redistributing income is central to so many debates over economic policy, here we digress from economic science to consider a bit of political philosophy.

Utilitarianism

utilitarianism
the political philosophy according to which the government should choose policies to maximize the total utility of everyone in society

utility
a measure of happiness or satisfaction

A prominent school of thought in political philosophy is **utilitarianism**. The founders of utilitarianism were the British philosophers Jeremy Bentham (1748–1832) and John Stuart Mill (1806–1873). To a large extent, the goal of utilitarians is to apply the logic of individual decision-making to questions concerning morality and public policy.

The starting point of utilitarianism is the notion of **utility** – the level of happiness or satisfaction that a person receives from his or her circumstances. Utility is a measure of well-being and, according to utilitarians, is the ultimate objective of all public and private actions. The proper goal of the government, they claim, is to maximize the sum of utility of everyone in society.

The utilitarian case for redistributing income is based on the assumption of *diminishing marginal utility.* It seems reasonable that an extra euro of income to a poor person provides that person with more additional utility than does an extra euro to a rich person. In other words, as a person's income rises, the extra well-being derived from an additional euro of income falls. This plausible assumption, together with the utilitarian goal of maximizing total utility, implies that the government should try to achieve a more equal distribution of income.

The argument is simple. Imagine that Dieter and Ernst are the same, except that Dieter earns €80 000 and Ernst earns €20 000. In this case, taking a euro from Dieter to pay Ernst will reduce Dieter's utility and raise Ernst's utility. But, because of diminishing marginal utility, Dieter's utility falls by less than Ernst's utility rises. Thus, this redistribution of income raises total utility, which is the utilitarian's objective.

At first, this utilitarian argument might seem to imply that the government should continue to redistribute income until everyone in society has exactly the same income. Indeed, that would be the case if the total amount of income – €100 000 in our example – were fixed. But, in fact, it is not. Utilitarians reject complete equalization of incomes because they accept one of the *Ten Principles of Economics* presented in Chapter 1: people respond to incentives.

To take from Dieter to pay Ernst, the government must pursue policies that redistribute income, such as the income tax and welfare systems that operate in all industrialized countries. Under these policies, people with high incomes pay high taxes, and people with low incomes receive income transfers. Yet, as we saw in Chapter 8, taxes distort incentives and cause deadweight losses. If the government takes away additional income a person might earn through higher income taxes or reduced transfers, both Dieter and Ernst have less incentive to work hard. As they work less, society's income falls, and so does total utility. The utilitarian government has to balance the gains from greater equality against the losses from distorted incentives. To maximize total utility, therefore, the government stops short of making society fully egalitarian.

A famous parable sheds light on the utilitarian's logic. Imagine that Dieter and Ernst are thirsty travellers trapped at different places in the desert. Dieter's oasis has much water; Ernst's has little. If the government could transfer water from one oasis to the other without cost, it would maximize total utility from water by equalizing the amount in the two places. But suppose that the government has only a leaky bucket. As it tries to move water from one place to the other, some of the water is lost in transit. In this case, a utilitarian government might still try to move some water from Dieter to Ernst, depending on how thirsty Ernst is and how leaky the bucket is. But, with only a leaky bucket at its disposal, a utilitarian government will not try to reach complete equality.

Liberalism

A second way of thinking about inequality might be called **liberalism**. Philosopher John Rawls develops this view in his book *A Theory of Justice.* This book was first published in 1971, and it quickly became a classic in political philosophy.

Rawls begins with the premise that a society's institutions, laws and policies should be just. He then takes up the natural question: how can we, the members of society, ever agree on what justice means? It might seem that every person's point of view is inevitably based on his or her particular circumstances – whether he or she is talented or less talented, diligent or lazy, educated or less educated, born to a wealthy family or a poor one. Could we ever *objectively* determine what a just society would be?

liberalism
the political philosophy according to which the government should choose policies deemed to be just, as evaluated by an impartial observer behind a 'veil of ignorance'

To answer this question, Rawls proposes the following thought experiment. Imagine that before any of us is born, we all get together for a meeting to design the rules that govern society. At this point, we are all ignorant about the station in life each of us will end up filling. In Rawls's words, we are sitting in an 'original position' behind a 'veil of ignorance'. In this original position, Rawls argues, we can choose a just set of rules for society because we must consider how those rules will affect every person. As Rawls puts it, 'Since all are similarly situated and no one is able to design principles to favour his particular conditions, the principles of justice are the result of fair agreement or bargain.' Designing public policies and institutions in this way allows us to be objective about what policies are just.

Rawls then considers what public policy designed behind this veil of ignorance would try to achieve. In particular, he considers what income distribution a person would consider fair if that person did not know whether he or she would end up at the top, bottom or middle of the distribution. Rawls argues that a person in the original position would be especially concerned about the possibility of being at the *bottom* of the income distribution. In designing public policies, therefore, we should aim to raise the welfare of the worst-off person in society. That is, rather than maximizing the sum of everyone's utility, as a utilitarian would do, Rawls would maximize the minimum utility. Rawls's rule is called the **maximin criterion**.

Because the maximin criterion emphasizes the least fortunate person in society, it justifies public policies aimed at equalizing the distribution of income. By transferring income from the rich to the poor, society raises the well-being of the least fortunate. The maximin criterion would not, however, lead to a completely egalitarian society. If the government promised to equalize incomes completely, people would have no incentive to work hard, society's total income would fall substantially and the least fortunate person would be worse off. Thus, the maximin criterion still allows disparities in income, because such disparities can improve incentives and thereby raise society's ability to help the poor. Nonetheless, because Rawls's philosophy puts weight on only the least fortunate members of society, it calls for more income redistribution than does utilitarianism.

Rawls's views are controversial, but the thought experiment he proposes has much appeal. In particular, this thought experiment allows us to consider the redistribution of income as a form of *social insurance*. That is, from the perspective of the original position behind the veil of ignorance, income redistribution is like an insurance policy. Homeowners buy fire insurance to protect themselves from the risk of their housing burning down. Similarly, when we as a society choose policies that tax the rich to supplement the incomes of the poor, we are all insuring ourselves against the possibility that we might have been a member of a poor family. Because people dislike risk, we should be happy to have been born into a society that provides us this insurance.

It is not at all clear, however, that rational people behind the veil of ignorance would truly be so averse to risk as to follow the maximin criterion. Indeed, because a person in the original position might end up anywhere in the distribution of outcomes, he or she might treat all possible outcomes equally when designing public policies. In this case, the best policy behind the veil of ignorance would be to maximize the average utility of members of society, and the resulting notion of justice would be more utilitarian than Rawlsian.

Libertarianism

A third view of inequality is called **libertarianism**. The two views we have considered so far – utilitarianism and liberalism – both view the total income of society as a shared resource that a social planner can freely redistribute to achieve some social goal. By contrast, libertarians argue that society itself earns no income – only individual members of society earn income. According to lib-

maximin criterion
the claim that the government should aim to maximize the well-being of the worst-off person in society

libertarianism
the political philosophy according to which the government should punish crimes and enforce voluntary agreements but not redistribute income

ertarians, the government should not take from some individuals and give to others in order to achieve any particular distribution of income.

For instance, philosopher Robert Nozick writes the following in his famous 1974 book *Anarchy, State, and Utopia*:

> We are not in the position of children who have been given portions of pie by someone who now makes last minute adjustments to rectify careless cutting. There is no *central* distribution, no person or group entitled to control all the resources, jointly deciding how they are to be doled out. What each person gets, he gets from others who give to him in exchange for something, or as a gift. In a free society, diverse persons control different resources, and new holdings arise out of the voluntary exchanges and actions of persons.

Whereas utilitarians and liberals try to judge what amount of inequality is desirable in a society, Nozick denies the validity of this very question.

The libertarian alternative to evaluating economic *outcomes* is to evaluate the *process* by which these outcomes arise. When the distribution of income is achieved unfairly – for instance, when one person steals from another – the government has the right and duty to remedy the problem. But, as long as the process determining the distribution of income is just, the resulting distribution is fair, no matter how unequal.

Nozick criticizes Rawls's liberalism by drawing an analogy between the distribution of income in society and the distribution of marks awarded to students taking a course of study. Suppose you were asked to judge the fairness of the marks awarded in the economics course you are now taking. Would you imagine yourself behind a veil of ignorance and choose a marks distribution without knowing the talents and efforts of each student? Or would you ensure that the process of assigning marks to students is fair without regard for whether the resulting distribution is equal or unequal? For the case of course marks at least, the libertarian emphasis on process over outcomes is compelling.

Libertarians conclude that equality of opportunities is more important than equality of incomes. They believe that the government should enforce individual rights to ensure that everyone has the same opportunity to use his or her talents and achieve success. Once these rules of the game are established, the government has no reason to alter the resulting distribution of income.

Libertarian Paternalism

We finally introduce a relatively new concept linked to these philosophies put forward by University of Chicago economists, Richard H. Thaler and Cass R. Sunstein[2]. Libertarian paternalism recognizes that people should be free to choose but that 'choice architects' (the government in the case of making decisions about rectifying inequality) have a legitimate role in trying to influence people's behaviour in order to make their lives longer, healthier and better – improving their utility. Thaler and Sunstein question whether specific policy moves are the best way of changing behaviour to improve utility and whether 'nudges' could achieve the end result whilst retaining the freedom of people to make choices. Nudges relate to details that might often seem insignificant but when paid attention to, can influence the choices people make to 'nudge' them in the direction of improving their own and society's welfare. Their work covers diverse areas but includes savings for pensions and social security systems, both of which have an impact on inequality in society.

---

[2]Thaler, R. H. & Sunstein C. R. (2009) *Nudge: Improving decisions about health, wealth and happiness.* London, Penguin.

Quick Quiz Franz earns more than Paloma. Someone proposes taxing Franz in order to supplement Paloma's income. How would a utilitarian, a liberal and a libertarian evaluate this proposal?

Policies to Reduce Poverty

As we have just seen, political philosophers and economists hold various views about what role the government should take in altering the distribution of income. Political debate among the larger population of voters reflects a similar disagreement. Despite these continuing debates, however, most people believe that, at the very least, the government should try to help those most in need. According to a popular metaphor, the government should provide a 'safety net' to prevent any citizen from falling too far.

Poverty is one of the most difficult problems that policy makers face. Poor families are more likely than the overall population to experience homelessness, drug dependency, domestic violence, health problems, teenage pregnancy, illiteracy, unemployment and low educational attainment. Members of poor families are both more likely to commit crimes and more likely to be victims of crimes. Although it is hard to separate the causes of poverty from the effects, there is no doubt that poverty is associated with various economic and social ills.

Suppose that you were a policy maker in the government, and your goal was to reduce the number of people living in poverty. How would you achieve this goal? Here we consider some of the policy options that you might consider. Although each of these options does help some people escape poverty, none of them is perfect, and deciding upon the best combination is not easy.

Minimum Wage Laws

Laws setting a minimum wage that employers can pay workers are a perennial source of debate. Advocates view the minimum wage as a way of helping the working poor without any cost to the government. Critics view it as hurting those it is intended to help.

The minimum wage is easily understood using the tools of supply and demand, as we first saw in Chapter 6. For workers with low levels of skill and experience, a high minimum wage forces the wage above the level that balances supply and demand. It therefore raises the cost of labour to firms and reduces the quantity of labour that those firms demand. The result is higher unemployment among those groups of workers affected by the minimum wage. Although those workers who remain employed benefit from a higher wage, those who might have been employed at a lower wage are worse off.

The magnitude of these effects depends crucially on the elasticity of demand. Advocates of a high minimum wage argue that the demand for unskilled labour is relatively inelastic, so that a high minimum wage depresses employment only slightly. Critics of the minimum wage argue that labour demand is more elastic, especially in the long run when firms can adjust employment and production more fully. They also note that many minimum wage workers are teenagers from middle-income families, so that a high minimum wage is imperfectly targeted as a policy for helping the poor.

The effects are also dependent on the degree of substitutability between workers in different industries – the ease with which workers can transfer from one industry to another. Minimum wage laws affect all businesses in all industries in different ways; some industries are not affected greatly by minimum wage laws because they already pay in excess of the minimum wage and so labour market equilibrium is not affected in that particular market. In low-paid industries, such as cleaning, hotel and catering and restaurants, for example, all employers are affected in the same way if they have to increase pay to meet minimum wage laws. As a result no one employer can necessarily gain any advantage over another by paying workers lower wages and thus having lower costs. Whilst minimum wage laws are a contentious issue, it is also a highly complex one requiring detailed analysis and an understanding that the labour market is not simply an amorphous 'one'; it consists of many smaller markets each of which has a varying influence on other markets.

Social Security

One way to raise the living standards of the poor is for the government of a country to supplement their incomes. The primary way in which the government does this is through **social security**. This is a broad term that generally encompasses various government benefits. In the UK, for example, Income Support is paid mainly to poor people who are either lone parents and carers, or incapable of work, or else disabled, tax credits are payments made to those in work and with families but who receive low incomes and have to care for children, while Jobseeker's Allowance is paid to unemployed people who are able and willing to work but temporarily cannot find a job.

> **social security**
> government benefits that supplement the incomes of the needy

A common criticism of the social security system is that it may create bad incentives. For example, since a single mother may lose Income Support if she were married to a man who was in work, the Income Support programme may encourage families to break up or encourage illegitimate births. However, governments may introduce other mechanisms to create good incentives. Tax credits, for example, are designed to encourage family members to take paid work in the belief that a person in work, albeit on a low income, is in a better position than one who does not take a job.

How severe are these potential problems with the benefit system? No one knows for sure. Proponents of the benefit system point out that being a poor, single mother is a difficult existence at best, and they are sceptical that many people would be encouraged to pursue such a life if it were not thrust upon them. Moreover, if it can be proved that a person is incapable of work or is disabled, it seems cruel and ridiculous to argue that this is because of the benefits they are receiving. It is often easy, however, for the popular press to portray examples of those who abuse the system; it is important that, as a budding economist, you ask appropriate questions and try to distinguish between fact and opinion in such cases.

Negative Income Tax

Whenever the government chooses a system to collect taxes, it affects the distribution of income. This is clearly true in the case of a progressive income tax, whereby high-income families pay a larger percentage of their income in taxes than do low-income families. Many economists have advocated supplementing the income of the poor using a **negative income tax**. According to this policy, every family would report its income to the government. High-income families would pay a tax based on their incomes. Low-income families would receive a subsidy. In other words, they would 'pay' a 'negative tax'.

> **negative income tax**
> a tax system that collects revenue from high-income households and gives transfers to low-income households

For example, suppose the government used the following formula to compute a family's tax liability:

$$\text{Taxes due} = (1/3 \text{ of income}) - €10\,000$$

In this case, a family that earned €60 000 would pay €10 000 in taxes, and a family that earned €90 000 would pay €20 000 in taxes. A family that earned €30 000 would owe nothing. And a family that earned €15 000 would 'owe' –€5 000. In other words, the government would send this family a cheque for €5 000.

Under a negative income tax, poor families would receive financial assistance without having to demonstrate need. The only qualification required to receive assistance would be a low income. Depending on one's point of view, this feature can be either an advantage or a disadvantage. On the one hand, a negative income tax does not encourage illegitimate births and the break-up of families, as critics of the welfare system believe current policy does. On the other hand, a negative income tax would subsidize those who are simply lazy and, in some people's eyes, undeserving of government support.

In-Kind Transfers

Another way to help the poor is to provide them directly with some of the goods and services they need to raise their living standards. For example, charities provide the needy with food, shelter and toys at Christmas. Governments in some countries give poor families vouchers that can be used to buy food or clothing in shops; the shops then redeem the vouchers for money. In the UK, poor people may qualify for free school meals for their children and medical benefits such as free prescriptions, dental treatment and eyesight tests.

in-kind transfers
transfers to the poor given in the form of goods and services rather than cash

Is it better to help the poor with these **in-kind transfers** or with direct cash payments? There is no clear answer.

Advocates of in-kind transfers argue that such transfers ensure that the poor get what they need most. Among the poorest members of society, alcohol and drug addiction is more common than it is in society as a whole. By providing the poor with food and shelter rather than cash, society can be more confident that it is not helping to support such addictions.

Advocates of cash payments, on the other hand, argue that in-kind transfers are inefficient and disrespectful. The government does not know what goods and services the poor need most. Many of the poor are ordinary people down on their luck. Despite their misfortune, they are in the best position to decide how to raise their own living standards. Rather than giving the poor in-kind transfers of goods and services that they may not want, it may be better to give them cash and allow them to buy what they think they need most.

Anti-poverty Policies and Work Incentives

Many policies aimed at helping the poor can have the unintended effect of discouraging the poor from escaping poverty on their own. To see why, consider the following example. Suppose that a family needs an income of €10 000 to maintain a reasonable standard of living. And suppose that, out of concern for the poor, the government promises to guarantee every family that income. Whatever a family earns, the government makes up the difference between that income and €10 000. What effect would you expect this policy to have?

The incentive effects of this policy are obvious: any person who would earn under €10 000 by working has no incentive to find and keep a job. For every euro that the person would earn, the government would reduce the income supplement by one euro. In effect, the government taxes 100 per cent of additional earnings. An effective marginal tax rate of 100 per cent is surely a policy with a large deadweight loss.

The adverse effects of this high effective tax rate can persist over time. A person discouraged from working loses the on-the-job training that a job might offer. In addition, his or her children miss the lessons learned by observing a parent with a full-time job, and this may adversely affect their own ability to find and hold a job.

Although the anti-poverty policy we have been discussing is hypothetical, it is not as unrealistic as it might first appear. In the UK, for example, Income Support

IN THE NEWS

One of the interesting things about economics is that there are diverse views about important issues like poverty that may sometimes raise uncomfortable questions which need to be considered. Appreciating different perspectives is an important part of the economist's toolbox. These two articles are examples of perspectives on poverty, specifically child poverty. The first presents an overview of issues facing policy makers (and shoppers in Europe) on the use of children in Bangladesh to manufacture goods sold in Western markets. The second offers a perspective on ways to help children escape poverty. You should aim to try and understand the perspectives being put forward in each case and ask yourself if an appreciation of these perspectives enables us to arrive at policy decisions which may be more effective in helping improve welfare than those that already exist.

1. Perspectives on Poverty

Many consumers in the developed world are able to go into retail stores and buy clothes at prices that, if time was taken to think about it, are quite remarkable. Access to cheap clothing has become something many almost take for granted. There have been some reports about high profile firms exploiting labour in countries like Bangladesh. These companies tend to respond to these reports swiftly to try and reassure consumers that they do all they can to ensure that ethical guidelines are being adhered to in the factories where their products are manufactured.

Most consumers are probably aware of the ethical issues surrounding the availability of cheap clothing. Most, if asked, would probably not condone the use of child labour and most would also say that wages ought to be fair and working conditions adequate for people who produce the clothes. The problem, of course, is that if steps were taken to improve wages and working conditions then the cost of producing the clothes would increase and the price to consumers is also likely to rise. The question is, to what extent would consumers be willing to pay more for their clothing to ensure improved pay and working conditions for workers in countries like

Bangladesh and thus help raise them out of poverty?

There is also another side to the story. In the developed world it is relatively easy to sit back and complain about poor wages and conditions in a country like Bangladesh and deplore the fact that children are used in manufacturing. In the 19th century, children were widely used in industry throughout Europe, often in appalling conditions and subject to considerable danger. Few children had access to education. In Bangladesh today, the situation is much the same. Education is provided by the state for children between the ages of 6 and 10 but there are reports that only half of the children in this age group attend school. Access to education outside this free provision requires payment and many families in Bangladesh cannot afford to educate their children.

Instead, many children have jobs which help to supplement the family income. There was a law, passed in 2006, which is meant to guarantee a fixed salary, holiday entitlement, access to education and compensation in the event of accident. The extent to which this law is observed is open to some debate. The result is that many children will work long hours in difficult

conditions and have to forsake education. One of the problems facing Bangladesh in changing the attitudes to this is that many families rely on the incomes of children in the family to help them survive. For consumers in the developed world, the stories of exploitation, danger, hardship and abuse – both physical and sexual – may seem too difficult to accept but for many families in Bangladesh these conditions are a fact of life.

The reports of children working for low wages and in poor conditions raise important questions about the nature of poverty and how to deal with it. What is right and moral may be to prevent children working below a certain age (that, of course, is a subjective opinion) but to achieve this the cycle of poverty needs to be broken. In so doing, children will not have to work to supplement income and if access to education can be widened then this may help future generations. As in 19th century Britain, the process may be a long one before conditions improve for millions in Bangladesh and attitudes will have to change not only in countries like Bangladesh but also in the developed world.

Source: Adapted from http://www.bized.co.uk/cgi-bin/chron/chron.pl?id=3370

2. Economic Truths of Child Labour

Every high street offers us items created by people whose poverty we can barely imagine. The tea in our cups was plucked by some young woman earning pennies in Sri Lanka. Our coffee has similar origins.

Now we are learning that fashionable trainers were crafted by children in grim circumstances in Laos or the Philippines. The International Labour Organization (ILO), an arm of the United Nations, published a report outlining these horrors and urging steps the world should take to suppress child labour. It says that one in six children is at work between their 6th and 17th birthdays. The occurrence of child labour seems a good barometer of local poverty. The ILO's arguments are more than moral outrage – they also say that children are of less economic value without decent schooling.

I don't contest the good intentions of these arguments. I'm sure I'd be pained if I saw children in workshops in Cambodia or Somalia. Yet for the ILO's economic literacy, I give low marks: suppressing child labour would only deepen misery. In its foggy way, the ILO argues parents should be paid the equivalent of their child's market value, replacing the income forfeited if the child attends school instead. It is ambiguous where this money would come from but presumably through taxation of the population – i.e. the parents.

It is easy for us to 'tut' about child labour from our capitalist affluence. If you live in the deeply impoverished nations where markets have been suppressed or deformed, your only asset is your ability to work, and that of your children. Sometimes I find people assume children did nothing more than picnic and play happily until the evil capitalists forced them into the textile mills and down the mines after the Industrial Revolution. The truth is that child labour was the reality of life in all rural economies long before Dickens got on the case of the child chimney sweeps.

It was the rise in capitalism that permitted the extended years of leisure we call education. Working in the newly emerging factories was regarded as a far better option than slaving in the fields – linen was more profitable than turnips. Child labour is not the invention of modern 'globalization'. All farming has always used children. Scotland's school summer holidays exist not so everyone can fly down to the Spanish Costas, but so that children can help with the harvest. To learn rural skills was the reality of education in most of human history. In more urban areas the young would learn other appropriate skills.

I believe that working in scruffy factories in Manila or Nairobi is an opportunity for the people involved. Making fashion garments or chic trainers for eventual sale on Princes Street [*the main shopping area in Edinburgh, the capital of Scotland*] offers far greater benevolence than the humbugging of overseas aid. Aid is famously described as a device by which the poor people in the West fund the rich in the Third World. But free trade in shirts transfers money from the rich of the West to the poor of the East.

US democratic presidential candidates shout at each other about child labour as a malignancy [*something that is evil in nature and has the characteristic of uncontrolled growth*] caused by globalization. Our own politicians are apprehensive about 'asylum seekers', the new euphemism for immigration. Do people try to flock Westwards because of our crazy policies? Or do they look for a solution to the economic problems they have in their own country?

The biggest single preventable cause of poverty is the European Union's agricultural policies. Affluence could spread across the planet if we opened our markets to non-EU foodstuffs. I remain baffled why no Scottish politician campaigns to cut the price of our groceries. Would it not be popular?

I'm not advocating sending any child into dangerous or degrading roles, but I do believe every school could allow pupils to widen their knowledge and experience by participating in local commercial life. It could be fun. It could be life-changing. Many of Scotland's young are held captive in schools that bore and alienate them. All that we seem to accept is newspaper paper rounds and there is even talk in Brussels of banning them. Participating in your community's shops, say, can only widen experience. With regard to student jobs as a degradation, it ought to be part of growing up.

As the economies of Asia accelerate, the number of children working tumbles, as parents prefer to buy education. They know the educated child should earn more and so help the extended family. Self-interest must be a better guide than abstract good intentions from the ILO's office block in Geneva. Next time you are exploring the ever-cheaper wares in your favourite shops, look at the origin labels. The people who produce these items are richer than they would be without production lines nearer their homes.

A pernicious [*having the quality of destroying or being destructive*] argument

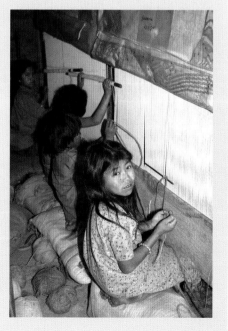

is that children working stop adults earning full wages. This is precisely the economic dunce speak that used to argue a woman's place is in the home. Adam Smith argued that a poor man's poverty can be his asset; he can trade or work his way up. The Third World's great advantage is their relative cheapness. Muddled, if kindly, thinking wants to suppress this. Rich countries should welcome the new nations joining the markets. Child labour will evaporate as prosperity spreads. In the meantime, Scottish pupils might find a day's work far more educational than torture by chalkboard.

Source: Adapted from John Blundell, the Director General of the Institute of Economic Affairs (IEA) (http://www.iea.org.uk). The article originally appeared in *The Scotsman* newspaper on 23 February 2004.

and Housing Benefit (a subsidy to a poor family's rent or mortgage interest payments) are benefits aimed at helping the poor and are tied to family income. As a family's income rises, the family becomes ineligible for these benefits. When all benefits being received are taken together, it is common for families to face effective marginal tax rates that are very high. Sometimes the effective marginal tax rates even exceed 100 per cent, so that poor families are worse off when they earn more: they are caught in a 'poverty trap'. By trying to help the poor, the government discourages those families from working. According to critics of anti-poverty policies, these social security benefits alter work attitudes and create a 'culture of poverty'.

It might seem that there is an easy solution to this problem: reduce benefits to poor families more gradually as their incomes rise. For example, if a poor family loses €0.30 of benefits for every extra €1 it earns, then it faces an effective marginal tax rate of 30 per cent. Although this effective tax reduces work effort to some extent, it does not eliminate the incentive to work completely.

The problem with this solution is that it greatly increases the cost of the social security system. The more gradual the phase-out, the more families are eligible for some level of benefits – and the more the social security system costs. Thus, policy makers face a trade-off between burdening the poor with high effective marginal tax rates and burdening taxpayers with a costly anti-poverty programme.

There are various other ways to try to reduce the work disincentive of anti-poverty programmes, such as stopping or reducing benefits to people who have not found a job within a reasonable period of time or who have turned down job offers for no good reason. In the UK, this kind of reasoning underpins the structure of the benefits paid to the unemployed: unemployed people may be eligible to receive a benefit called Jobseeker's Allowance. To receive the allowance, however, the claimant must be capable of starting work immediately and of actively taking steps to find a job such as attending interviews, writing applications or seeking job information. They must also have a current 'jobseeker's agreement' with the Employment Service, which includes such information as hours available for work, the desired job and any steps that the claimant is willing to take to find work (such as moving to a different town). They must be prepared to work up to 40 hours a week and have a reasonable prospect of finding work (i.e. not place too many restrictions on the type of work they are willing to undertake). If a claimant refuses to take up a job offer without good reason, they may be denied further payments of Jobseeker's Allowance. People aged 18–24 who have been unemployed and claiming Jobseeker's Allowance for six months or more are required to participate in a government scheme designed to get them into work (which includes, for example, a personal advisor on suitable job opportunities) called the New Deal for Young Persons. Those aged 25 or over must participate in a similar programme, called the New Deal 25-Plus programme, if they have been unemployed and claiming Jobseeker's Allowance for 18 months.

Quick Quiz List three policies aimed at helping the poor, and discuss the pros and cons of each.

CONCLUSION

People have long reflected on the distribution of income in society. Plato, the ancient Greek philosopher, concluded that in an ideal society the income of the richest person would be no more than four times the income of the poorest person. Although the measurement of inequality is difficult, it is clear that our society has much more inequality than Plato recommended.

One of the *Ten Principles of Economics* discussed in Chapter 1 is that governments can sometimes improve market outcomes. There is little consensus, however, about how this principle should be applied to the distribution of income. Philosophers and policy makers today do not agree on how much income inequality is desirable, or even whether public policy should aim to alter the distribution of income. Much of public debate reflects this disagreement. Whenever taxes are raised, for instance, politicians argue over how much of the tax hike should fall on the rich, people from the middle-income group, and the poor.

Another of the *Ten Principles of Economics* is that people face trade-offs. This principle is important to keep in mind when thinking about economic inequality. Policies that penalize the successful and reward the unsuccessful reduce the incentive to succeed. Thus, policy makers face a trade-off between equality and efficiency. The more equally the pie is divided, the smaller the pie becomes. This is the one lesson concerning the distribution of income about which almost everyone agrees.

SUMMARY

- Data on the distribution of income show wide disparity in industrialized economies.

- Because in-kind transfers, the economic life cycle, transitory income and economic mobility are so important for understanding variation in income, it is difficult to gauge the degree of inequality in our society using data on the distribution of income in a single year. When these other factors are taken into account, they tend to suggest that economic well-being is more equally distributed than is annual income.

- Political philosophers differ in their views about the role of government in altering the distribution of income. Utilitarians (such as John Stuart Mill) would choose the distribution of income to maximize the sum of utility of everyone in society. Liberals (such as John Rawls) would determine the distribution of income as if we were behind a 'veil of ignorance' that prevented us from knowing our own stations in life. Libertarians (such as Robert Nozick) would have the government enforce individual rights to ensure a fair process but then not be concerned about inequality in the resulting distribution of income.

- Various policies aim to help the poor – minimum wage laws, social security, negative income taxes and in-kind transfers. Although each of these policies helps some families escape poverty, they also have unintended side effects. Because financial assistance declines as income rises, the poor often face effective marginal tax rates that are very high. Such high effective tax rates discourage poor families from escaping poverty on their own.

KEY CONCEPTS

life cycle, p. 421
permanent income, p. 422
poverty rate, p. 423
poverty line, p. 423
absolute poverty, p. 423

relative poverty, p. 423
utilitarianism, p. 424
utility, p. 424
liberalism, p. 425
maximin criterion, p. 426

libertarianism, p. 426
social security, p. 429
negative income tax, p. 429
in-kind transfers, p. 430

QUESTIONS FOR REVIEW

1. How does the extent of income inequality in your country compare to that of other nations around the world?

2. What groups in the population are most likely to live in poverty?

3. When gauging the amount of inequality, why do transitory and life cycle variations in income cause difficulties?

4. How would a utilitarian, a liberal and a libertarian determine how much income inequality is permissible?

5. What are the pros and cons of in-kind (rather than cash) transfers to the poor?

6. Describe how anti-poverty programmes can discourage the poor from working. How might you reduce this disincentive? What are the disadvantages with your proposed policy?

PROBLEMS AND APPLICATIONS

1. Table 20.2 shows that income inequality in the United Kingdom has increased during the past 20 years. Some factors contributing to this increase were discussed in Chapter 19. What are they?

2. Economists often view life cycle variation in income as one form of transitory variation in income around people's lifetime, or permanent, income. In this sense, how does your current income compare to your permanent income? Do you think your current income accurately reflects your standard of living?

3. The chapter discusses the importance of economic mobility.
   a. What policies might the government pursue to increase economic mobility *within* a generation?
   b. What policies might the government pursue to increase economic mobility *across* generations?
   c. Do you think we should reduce spending on social security benefits in order to increase spending on government programmes that enhance economic mobility? What are some of the advantages and disadvantages of doing so?

4. Consider two communities. In one community, ten families have incomes of €100 each and ten families have incomes of €20 each. In the other community, ten families have incomes of €200 each and ten families have incomes of €22 each.
   a. In which community is the distribution of income more unequal? In which community is the problem of poverty likely to be worse?
   b. Which distribution of income would Rawls prefer? Explain.
   c. Which distribution of income do you prefer? Explain.

5. The chapter uses the analogy of a 'leaky bucket' to explain one constraint on the redistribution of income.
   a. What elements of your country's system for redistributing income create the leaks in the bucket? Be specific.
   b. Do you think that people with left-wing political views believe that the bucket used for redistributing income is more or less leaky than it is believed to be by people with more right-wing political views? How does that belief affect their views about the amount of income redistribution that the government should undertake?

6. Suppose there are two possible income distributions in a society of ten people. In the first distribution, nine people would have incomes of €30 000 and one person would have an income of €10 000. In the second distribution, all ten people would have incomes of €25 000.
   a. If the society had the first income distribution, what would be the utilitarian argument for redistributing income?
   b. Which income distribution would Rawls consider more equitable? Explain.
   c. Which income distribution would Nozick consider more equitable? Explain.

7. Suppose that a family's tax liability equalled its income multiplied by one-half, minus €10 000. Under this system, some families would pay taxes to the government, and some families would receive money from the government through a 'negative income tax'.
   a. Consider families with pre-tax incomes of €0, €10 000, €20 000, €30 000, and €40 000. Make a table showing pre-tax income, taxes paid to the government or

money received from the government, and after-tax income for each family.

b. What is the marginal tax rate in this system (i.e. out of every €1 of extra income, how much is paid in tax)? What is the maximum amount of income at which a family *receives* money from the government?

c. Now suppose that the tax schedule is changed, so that a family's tax liability equals its income multiplied by one-quarter, minus €10 000. What is the marginal tax rate in this new system? What is the maximum amount of income at which a family receives money from the government?

d. What is the main advantage of each of the tax schedules discussed here?

8. John and Jeremy are utilitarians. John believes that labour supply is highly elastic, whereas Jeremy believes that labour supply is quite inelastic. How do you suppose their views about income redistribution differ?

9. Do you agree or disagree with each of the following statements? What do your views imply for public policies, such as taxes on inheritance?

a. 'Every parent has the right to work hard and save in order to give his or her children a better life.'

b. 'No child should be disadvantaged by the sloth or bad luck of his or her parents.'

For further resources, visit
www.cengage.com/mankiw_taylor2

7

TOPICS FOR
FURTHER STUDY

21 THE THEORY OF CONSUMER CHOICE

When you walk into a shop, you are confronted with thousands of goods that you might buy. Of course, because your financial resources are limited, you cannot buy everything that you want. The assumption is, therefore, that you consider the prices of the various goods being offered for sale and buy a bundle of goods that, given your resources, best suits your needs and desires.

In this chapter we develop the theory that describes how consumers make decisions about what to buy. So far throughout this book we have summarized consumers' decisions with the demand curve. As we discussed in Chapters 4 through to 7, the demand curve for a good reflects consumers' willingness to pay for it. When the price of a good rises, consumers are willing to pay for fewer units, so the quantity demanded falls. We now look more deeply at the decisions that lie behind the demand curve. The theory of consumer choice presented in this chapter provides a more complete understanding of demand, just as the theory of the competitive firm in Chapter 14 provides a more complete understanding of supply. We will look at the traditional analysis of consumer behaviour and also introduce some ideas that have arisen as a result of more recent research in psychology, which is increasingly being looked at with interest by economists.

One of the *Ten Principles of Economics* discussed in Chapter 1 is that people face trade-offs. The theory of consumer choice examines the trade-offs that people face in their role as consumers. When a consumer buys more of one good, he can afford less of other goods. When he spends more time enjoying leisure and less time working, he has lower income and can afford less consumption. When he spends more of his income in the present and saves less of it, he must accept a lower level of consumption in the future. The theory of consumer choice examines how consumers facing these trade-offs make decisions and how they respond to changes in their environment.

After developing the basic theory of consumer choice, we apply it to three questions about household decisions. In particular, we ask:

- Do all demand curves slope downward?
- How do wages affect labour supply?
- How do interest rates affect household saving?

At first, these questions might seem unrelated. But, as we will see, we can use the theory of consumer choice to address each of them.

THE BUDGET CONSTRAINT: WHAT THE CONSUMER CAN AFFORD

Most people would like to increase the quantity or quality of the goods they consume – to take longer holidays, drive fancier cars or eat at better restaurants. People consume less than they desire because their spending is *constrained*, or limited, by their income. We begin our study of consumer choice by examining this link between income and spending.

To keep things simple, we use a model which examines the decisions facing a consumer who buys only two goods: cola and pizza. Of course, real people buy thousands of different kinds of goods. Yet using this model greatly simplifies the problem without altering the basic insights about consumer choice.

We first consider how the consumer's income constrains the amount he spends on cola and pizza. Suppose that the consumer has an income of €1 000 per month and that he spends his entire income each month on cola and pizza. The price of a litre of cola is €2 and the price of a pizza is €10.

The table in Figure 21.1 shows some of the many combinations of Cola and pizza that the consumer can buy. The first line in the table shows that if the consumer spends all his income on pizza, he can eat 100 pizzas during the month, but he would not be able to buy any cola at all. The second line shows another possible consumption bundle: 90 pizzas and 50 litres of cola. And so on. Each consumption bundle in the table costs exactly €1 000.

The graph in Figure 21.1 illustrates the consumption bundles that the consumer can choose. The vertical axis measures the number of litres of cola, and the horizontal axis measures the number of pizzas. Three points are marked on this figure. At point A, the consumer buys no cola and consumes 100 pizzas. At point B, the consumer buys no pizza and consumes 500 litres of cola. At point C, the consumer buys 50 pizzas and 250 litres of cola. Point C, which is exactly at the middle of the line from A to B, is the point at which the consumer spends an equal amount (€500) on cola and pizza. Of course, these are only three of the many combinations of cola and pizza that the consumer can choose. All the points on the line from A to B are possible. This line, called the **budget constraint**, shows the consumption bundles that the consumer can afford. In this case, it shows the trade-off between cola and pizza that the consumer faces.

budget constraint
the limit on the consumption bundles that a consumer can afford

The slope of the budget constraint measures the rate at which the consumer can trade one good for the other. Recall from the appendix to Chapter 2 that the slope between two points is calculated as the change in the vertical distance divided by the change in the horizontal distance ('rise over run'). From point A to point B, the vertical distance is 500 litres, and the horizontal distance is

FIGURE 21.1

The Consumer's Budget Constraint

The budget constraint shows the various bundles of goods that the consumer can afford for a given income. Here the consumer buys bundles of cola and pizza. The table and graph show what the consumer can afford if his income is €1 000, the price of cola is €2 and the price of pizza is €10.

Litres of cola	Number of pizzas	Spending on cola	Spending on pizza	Total spending
0	100	€0	€1 000	€1 000
50	90	100	900	1 000
100	80	200	800	1 000
150	70	300	700	1 000
200	60	400	600	1 000
250	50	500	500	1 000
300	40	600	400	1 000
350	30	700	300	1 000
400	20	800	200	1 000
450	10	900	100	1 000
500	0	1 000	0	1 000

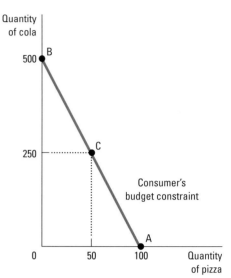

100 pizzas. Because the budget constraint slopes downward, the slope is a negative number – this reflects the fact that to get one extra pizza, the consumer has to *reduce* his consumption of cola by five litres. In fact, the slope of the budget constraint (ignoring the minus sign) equals the *relative price* of the two goods – the price of one good compared to the price of the other. A pizza costs 5 times as much as a litre of cola, so the opportunity cost of a pizza is 5 litres of cola. The budget constraint's slope of 5 reflects the trade-off the market is offering the consumer: 1 pizza for 5 litres of cola.

> **Quick Quiz** Draw the budget constraint for a person with income of €1 000 if the price of cola is €5 and the price of pizza is €10. What is the slope of this budget constraint?

PREFERENCES: WHAT THE CONSUMER WANTS

Our goal in this chapter is to see how consumers make choices. There are two key assumptions that are made about consumers. One is that they have limited incomes but unlimited wants and the second is that they prefer to have more than less. These basic assumptions allow us to investigate behaviour in relation to how a consumer allocates limited income among different preferences. The budget constraint is one piece of the analysis: it shows what combination of goods the consumer can afford given his income and the prices of the goods. The consumer's choices, however, depend not only on his budget constraint but also on his preferences regarding the two goods. Therefore, the consumer's preferences are the next piece of our analysis.

Representing Preferences with Indifference Curves

The consumer's preferences allow him to choose among different bundles of cola and pizza. If you offer the consumer two different bundles, he chooses the bundle that best suits his tastes. If the two bundles suit his tastes equally well, we say that the consumer is *indifferent* between the two bundles.

Just as we have represented the consumer's budget constraint graphically, we can also represent his preferences graphically. We do this with indifference curves. An **indifference curve** shows the bundles of consumption that make the consumer equally happy. In this case, the indifference curves show the combinations of cola and pizza with which the consumer is equally satisfied.

Figure 21.2 shows two of the consumer's many indifference curves. The consumer is indifferent among combinations A, B and C, because they are all on the same curve. Not surprisingly, if the consumer's consumption of pizza is reduced, say from point A to point B, consumption of cola must increase to keep him equally happy. If consumption of pizza is reduced again, from point B to point C, the amount of cola consumed must increase yet again.

The slope at any point on an indifference curve equals the rate at which the consumer is willing to substitute one good for the other. This rate is called the **marginal rate of substitution** (*MRS*). In this case, the marginal rate of substitution measures how much cola the consumer requires in order to be compensated for a one-unit reduction in pizza consumption. Notice that because the indifference curves are not straight lines, the marginal rate of substitution is not the same at all points on a given indifference curve. The rate at which a consumer is willing to trade one good for the other depends on the amounts of the goods he is already consuming. That is, the rate at which a consumer is willing to trade pizza for cola depends on whether he is hungrier or thirstier, which in turn depends on how much pizza and cola he has.

The consumer is equally happy at all points on any given indifference curve, but he prefers some indifference curves to others. We assume that consumers would rather have more of a good than less of it. Because he prefers more consumption to less, higher indifference curves are preferred to lower ones. In Figure 21.2, any point on curve I_2 is preferred to any point on curve I_1.

indifference curve
a curve that shows consumption bundles that give the consumer the same level of satisfaction

marginal rate of substitution
the rate at which a consumer is willing to trade one good for another

FIGURE 21.2

The Consumer's Preferences

The consumer's preferences are represented with indifference curves, which show the combinations of cola and pizza that make the consumer equally satisfied. Because the consumer prefers more of a good, points on a higher indifference curve (I_2 here) are preferred to points on a lower indifference curve (I_1). The marginal rate of substitution (MRS) shows the rate at which the consumer is willing to trade cola for pizza.

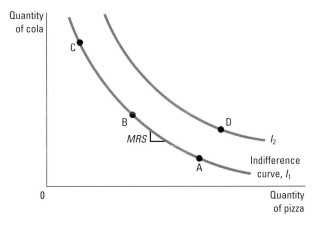

A consumer's set of indifference curves gives a complete ranking of the consumer's preferences. That is, we can use the indifference curves to rank any two bundles of goods. For example, the indifference curves tell us that point D is preferred to point A because point D is on a higher indifference curve than point A. (That conclusion may be obvious, however, because point D offers the consumer both more pizza and more cola.) The indifference curves also tell us that point D is preferred to point C because point D is on a higher indifference curve. Even though point D has less cola than point C, it has more than enough extra pizza to make the consumer prefer it. By seeing which point is on the higher indifference curve, we can use the set of indifference curves to rank any combinations of cola and pizza.

Four Properties of Indifference Curves

Because indifference curves represent a consumer's preferences, they have certain properties that reflect those preferences. Here we consider four properties that describe most indifference curves:

- *Property 1: Higher indifference curves are preferred to lower ones.* Consumers usually prefer more of something to less of it. This preference for greater quantities is reflected in the indifference curves. As Figure 21.2 shows, higher indifference curves represent larger quantities of goods than lower indifference curves. Thus, the consumer prefers being on higher indifference curves.
- *Property 2: Indifference curves are downward sloping.* The slope of an indifference curve reflects the rate at which the consumer is willing to substitute one good for the other. In most cases, the consumer likes both goods. Therefore, if the quantity of one good is reduced, the quantity of the other good must increase in order for the consumer to be equally happy. For this reason, most indifference curves slope downward.
- *Property 3: Indifference curves do not cross.* To see why this is true, suppose that two indifference curves did cross, as in Figure 21.3. Then, because point A is

FIGURE 21.3

The Impossibility of Intersecting Indifference Curves

A situation like this can never happen. According to these indifference curves, the consumer would be equally satisfied at points A, B and C, even though point C has more of both goods than point A.

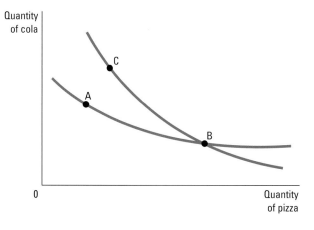

on the same indifference curve as point B, the two points would make the consumer equally happy. In addition, because point B is on the same indifference curve as point C, these two points would make the consumer equally happy. But these conclusions imply that points A and C would also make the consumer equally happy, even though point C has more of both goods. This contradicts our assumption that the consumer always prefers more of both goods to less. This is called the *'axiom of transitivity'* – given any three baskets of goods, if A is preferred to B and B to C then A must be preferred to C. Thus, indifference curves cannot cross.

- *Property 4: Indifference curves are bowed inward.* The slope of an indifference curve is the marginal rate of substitution – the rate at which the consumer is willing to trade off one good for the other. The marginal rate of substitution (*MRS*) usually depends on the amount of each good the consumer is currently consuming. In particular, because people are more willing to trade away goods that they have in abundance and less willing to trade away goods of which they have little, the indifference curves are bowed inward. As an example, consider Figure 21.4. At point A, because the consumer has a lot of cola and only a little pizza, he is very hungry but not very thirsty. To induce the consumer to give up 1 pizza, the consumer has to be given 6 litres of cola: the marginal rate of substitution is 6 litres per pizza. By contrast, at point B, the consumer has little cola and a lot of pizza, so he is very thirsty but not very hungry. At this point, he would be willing to give up 1 pizza to get 1 litre of cola: the marginal rate of substitution is 1 litre per pizza. Thus, the bowed shape of the indifference curve reflects the consumer's greater willingness to give up a good that he already has in large quantity.

FIGURE 21.4

Bowed Indifference Curves

Indifference curves are usually bowed inward. This shape implies that the marginal rate of substitution (MRS) depends on the quantity of the two goods the consumer is consuming. At point A, the consumer has little pizza and much cola, so he requires a lot of extra cola to induce him to give up one of the pizzas: the marginal rate of substitution is 6 litres of cola per pizza. At point B, the consumer has much pizza and little cola, so he requires only a little extra cola to induce him to give up one of the pizzas: the marginal rate of substitution is 1 litre of cola per pizza.

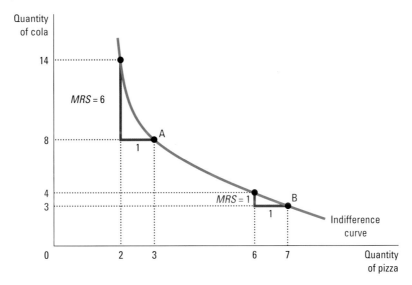

Two Extreme Examples of Indifference Curves

The shape of an indifference curve tells us about the consumer's willingness to trade one good for the other. When the goods are easy to substitute for each other, the indifference curves are less bowed; when the goods are hard to substitute, the indifference curves are very bowed. To see why this is true, let's consider the extreme cases.

Perfect Substitutes Suppose that someone offered you bundles of 50 cent coins and 10 cent coins. How would you rank the different bundles?

Most probably, you would care only about the total monetary value of each bundle. If so, you would judge a bundle based on the number of 50 cent coins plus five times the number of 10 cent coins. In other words, you would always be willing to trade 1 50 cent coin for 5 10 cent coins, regardless of the number of coins in either bundle. Your marginal rate of substitution between 10 cent coins and 50 cent coins would be a fixed number: 5.

We can represent your preferences over 50 cent coins and 10 cent coins with the indifference curves in panel (a) of Figure 21.5. Because the marginal rate of substitution is constant, the indifference curves are straight lines. In this extreme case of straight indifference curves, we say that the two goods are **perfect substitutes**.

perfect substitutes
two goods with straight-line indifference curves

Perfect Complements Suppose now that someone offered you bundles of shoes. Some of the shoes fit your left foot, others your right foot. How would you rank these different bundles?

In this case, you might care only about the number of pairs of shoes. In other words, you would judge a bundle based on the number of pairs you could assemble from it. A bundle of 5 left shoes and 7 right shoes yields only 5 pairs. Getting 1 more right shoe has no value if there is no left shoe to go with it.

FIGURE 21.5

Perfect Substitutes and Perfect Complements

When two goods are easily substitutable, such as 50 cent and 10 cent coins, the indifference curves are straight lines, as shown in panel (a). When two goods are strongly complementary, such as left shoes and right shoes, the indifference curves are right angles, as shown in panel (b).

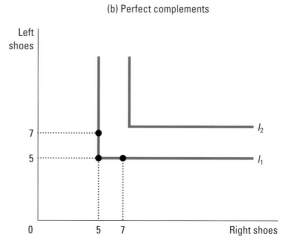

We can represent your preferences for right and left shoes with the indifference curves in panel (b) of Figure 21.5. In this case, a bundle with 5 left shoes and 5 right shoes is just as good as a bundle with 5 left shoes and 7 right shoes. It is also just as good as a bundle with 7 left shoes and 5 right shoes. The indifference curves, therefore, are right angles. In this extreme case of right-angle indifference curves, we say that the two goods are **perfect complements**.

In the real world, of course, most goods are neither perfect substitutes (like coins of different denominations) nor perfect complements (like right shoes and left shoes). More typically, the indifference curves are bowed inward, but not so bowed as to become right angles.

perfect complements
two goods with right-angle
indifference curves

Quick Quiz Draw some indifference curves for cola and pizza. Explain the four properties of these indifference curves.

OPTIMIZATION: WHAT THE CONSUMER CHOOSES

The goal of this chapter is to understand how a consumer makes choices. We have the two pieces necessary for this analysis: the consumer's budget constraint and the consumer's preferences. Now we put these two pieces together and consider the consumer's decision about what to buy.

The Consumer's Optimal Choices

Consider once again our cola and pizza example. The consumer would like to end up with the best possible combination of cola and pizza – that is, the combination on the highest possible indifference curve. But the consumer must also end up on or below his budget constraint, which measures the total resources available to him.

Figure 21.6 shows the consumer's budget constraint and three of his many indifference curves. The highest indifference curve that the consumer can reach (I_2 in the figure) is the one that just barely touches the budget constraint. The point at which this indifference curve and the budget constraint touch is called the *optimum*. The consumer would prefer point A, but he cannot afford that point because it lies above his budget constraint. The consumer can afford point B, but that point is on a lower indifference curve and, therefore, provides the consumer less satisfaction. The optimum represents the best combination of consumption of cola and pizza available to the consumer.

Notice that, at the optimum, the slope of the indifference curve equals the slope of the budget constraint. We say that the indifference curve is *tangent* to the budget constraint. The slope of the indifference curve is the marginal rate of substitution between cola and pizza, and the slope of the budget constraint is the relative price of cola and pizza. Thus, the consumer chooses consumption of the two goods so that the marginal rate of substitution equals the relative price.

In Chapter 7 we saw how market prices reflect the marginal value that consumers place on goods. This analysis of consumer choice shows the same result in another way. In making his consumption choices, the consumer takes as given the relative price of the two goods and then chooses an optimum at which his marginal rate of substitution equals this relative price. The relative price is the rate at which the *market* is willing to trade one good for the other, whereas the marginal rate of substitution is the rate at which the *consumer* is willing to

FIGURE 21.6

The Consumer's Optimum

The consumer chooses the point on his budget constraint that lies on the highest indifference curve. At this point, called the optimum, the marginal rate of substitution equals the relative price of the two goods. Here the highest indifference curve the consumer can reach is I₂. The consumer prefers point A, which lies on indifference curve I₃, but the consumer cannot afford this bundle of cola and pizza. In contrast, point B is affordable, but because it lies on a lower indifference curve, the consumer does not prefer it.

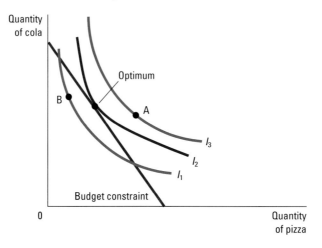

trade one good for the other. At the consumer's optimum, the consumer's valuation of the two goods (as measured by the marginal rate of substitution) equals the market's valuation (as measured by the relative price). As a result of this consumer optimization, market prices of different goods reflect the value that consumers place on those goods.

How Changes in Income Affect the Consumer's Choices

Now that we have seen how the consumer makes the consumption decision, let's examine how consumption responds to changes in income. To be specific, suppose that income increases. With higher income, the consumer can afford more of both goods. The increase in income, therefore, shifts the budget constraint outward, as in Figure 21.7. Because the relative price of the two goods has not changed, the slope of the new budget constraint is the same as the slope of the initial budget constraint. That is, an increase in income leads to a parallel shift in the budget constraint.

The expanded budget constraint allows the consumer to choose a better combination of cola and pizza. In other words, the consumer can now reach a higher indifference curve. Given the shift in the budget constraint and the consumer's preferences as represented by his indifference curves, the consumer's optimum moves from the point labelled 'initial optimum' to the point labelled 'new optimum'.

Notice that in Figure 21.7 the consumer chooses to consume more cola and more pizza. Although the logic of the model does not require increased consumption of both goods in response to increased income, this situation is the most common one. As you may recall from Chapter 4, if a consumer wants

FYI

Utility: An Alternative Way to Describe Preferences and Optimization

We have used indifference curves to represent the consumer's preferences. Another common way to represent preferences is with the concept of *utility*. Utility is an abstract measure of the satisfaction or happiness that a consumer receives from a bundle of goods. Economists say that a consumer prefers one bundle of goods to another if the first provides more utility than the second.

Indifference curves and utility are closely related. Because the consumer prefers points on higher indifference curves, bundles of goods on higher indifference curves provide higher utility. Because the consumer is equally happy with all points on the same indifference curve, all these bundles provide the same utility. You can think of an indifference curve as an 'equal-utility' curve.

The *marginal utility* of any good is the increase in utility that the consumer gets from an additional unit of that good. Most goods are assumed to exhibit *diminishing marginal utility*: the more of the good the consumer already has, the lower the marginal utility provided by an extra unit of that good. Think about it from the point of view of drinking when you are thirsty. If you are very thirsty the value placed on the consumption of the first drink offered is very high (let's give it a value out of 10 – it might, therefore be

10/10). If you are then offered a second drink, it might also give you some utility but chances are the rating you give it will not be as high as the first drink which served to quench that raging thirst (say 9/10). The offer of a third drink might now start to be a little too much. Your thirst has been quenched and whilst you might still drink it the utility ranking is now only 6/10. Each additional drink adds to *total* utility but the *addition* to total utility (marginal utility) is declining.

The marginal rate of substitution between two goods depends on their marginal utilities. For example, if the marginal utility of good X is twice the marginal utility of good Y, then a person would need 2 units of good Y to compensate for losing 1 unit of good X, and the marginal rate of substitution equals 2. More generally, the marginal rate of substitution (and thus the slope of the indifference curve) equals the marginal utility of one good divided by the marginal utility of the other good.

Utility analysis provides another way to describe consumer optimization. Recall that at the consumer's optimum, the marginal rate of substitution equals the ratio of prices. That is:

$$MRS = P_X/P_Y$$

Because the marginal rate of substitution equals the ratio of marginal

utilities, we can write this condition for optimization as:

$$MU_X/MU_Y = P_X/P_Y$$

Now rearrange this expression to become:

$$MU_X/P_X = MU_Y/P_Y$$

This equation has a simple interpretation: at the optimum, the marginal utility per euro spent on good X equals the marginal utility per euro spent on good Y. Why? If this equality did not hold, the consumer could increase utility by changing behaviour, switching spending from the good that provided lower marginal utility per euro and more on the good that provided higher marginal utility per euro. This would be the rational thing to do.

When economists discuss the theory of consumer choice, they might express the theory using different words. One economist might say that the goal of the consumer is to maximize utility. Another economist might say that the goal of the consumer is to end up on the highest possible indifference curve. The first economist would conclude that, at the consumer's optimum, the marginal utility per euro is the same for all goods, whereas the second would conclude that the indifference curve is tangent to the budget constraint. In essence, these are two ways of saying the same thing.

more of a good when his income rises, economists call it a normal good. The indifference curves in Figure 21.7 are drawn under the assumption that both cola and pizza are normal goods.

Figure 21.8 shows an example in which an increase in income induces the consumer to buy more pizza but less cola. If a consumer buys less of a good when his income rises, economists call it an inferior good. Figure 21.8 is drawn under the assumption that pizza is a normal good and cola is an inferior good.

FIGURE 21.7

An Increase in Income

When the consumer's income rises, the budget constraint shifts out. If both goods are normal goods, the consumer responds to the increase in income by buying more of both of them. Here the consumer buys more pizza and more cola.

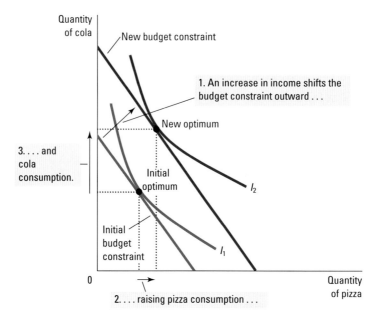

FIGURE 21.8

An Inferior Good

A good is an inferior good if the consumer buys less of it when his income rises. Here cola is an inferior good: when the consumer's income increases and the budget constraint shifts outward, the consumer buys more pizza but less cola.

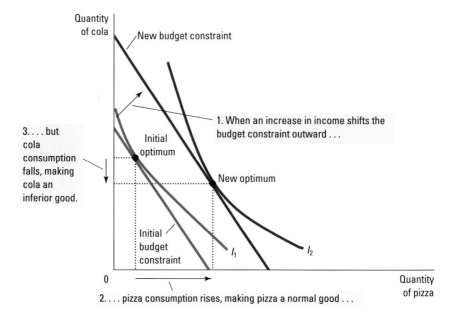

Although most goods are normal goods, there are some inferior goods in the world. One example is bus rides. High-income consumers are more likely to own cars and less likely to ride the bus than low-income consumers. Bus rides, therefore, are an inferior good.

How Changes in Prices Affect the Consumer's Choices

Let's now use this model of consumer choice to consider how a change in the price of one of the goods alters the consumer's choices. Suppose, in particular, that the price of cola falls from €2 to €1 a litre. It is no surprise that the lower price expands the consumer's set of buying opportunities. In other words, a fall in the price of any good causes the budget constraint to pivot. With his available income of €1 000 the consumer can now buy twice as many litres of cola than before but the same amount of pizza. Figure 21.9 shows that point A in the figure stays the same (100 pizzas). Yet if the consumer spends his entire income of €1 000 on cola, he can now buy 1 000 rather than only 500 litres. Thus, the end point of the budget constraint pivots outwards from point B to point D.

Notice that in this case the pivoting of the budget constraint changes its slope. (This differs from what happened previously when prices stayed the same but the consumer's income changed.) As we have discussed, the slope of the budget constraint reflects the relative price of cola and pizza. Because the price of cola has fallen to €1 from €2, while the price of pizza has remained €10, the consumer can now trade a pizza for 10 rather than 5 litres of cola. As a result, the new budget constraint is more steeply sloped.

FIGURE 21.9

A Change in Price

When the price of cola falls, the consumer's budget constraint shifts outward and changes slope. The consumer moves from the initial optimum to the new optimum, which changes his purchases of both cola and pizza. In this case, the quantity of cola consumed rises and the quantity of pizza consumed falls.

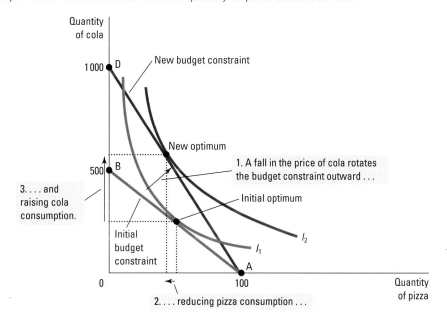

How such a change in the budget constraint alters the consumption of both goods depends on the consumer's preferences. For the indifference curves drawn in this figure, the consumer buys more cola and less pizza.

Income and Substitution Effects

The impact of a change in the price of a good on consumption can be decomposed into two effects: an **income effect** and a **substitution effect**. To see what these two effects are, consider how our consumer might respond when he learns that the price of cola has fallen. He might reason in the following ways:

'Great news! Now that cola is cheaper, my income has greater purchasing power – my income now buys me more. I am, *in effect*, richer than I was. Because I am richer, I can buy both more cola and more pizza.' (This is the income effect.)

'Now that the price of cola has fallen, I get more litres of cola for every pizza that I give up. Because pizza is now *relatively* more expensive, I should buy less pizza and more cola.' (This is the substitution effect.)

Which statement do you find more compelling?

In fact, both of these statements make sense. The decrease in the price of cola makes the consumer better off. If cola and pizza are both normal goods, the consumer will want to spread this improvement in his purchasing power over both goods. This income effect tends to make the consumer buy more pizza and more cola. Yet, at the same time, consumption of cola has become less expensive relative to consumption of pizza. This substitution effect tends to make the consumer choose more cola and less pizza.

Now consider the end result of these two effects. The consumer certainly buys more cola, because the income and substitution effects both act to raise purchases of cola. But it is ambiguous whether the consumer buys more pizza, because the income and substitution effects work in opposite directions. This conclusion is summarized in Table 21.1.

We can interpret the income and substitution effects using indifference curves. The income effect is the change in consumption that results from the movement to a higher indifference curve. The substitution effect is the change in consumption that results from being at a point on an indifference curve with a different marginal rate of substitution.

Figure 21.10 shows graphically how to decompose the change in the consumer's decision into the income effect and the substitution effect. When the price of cola falls, the consumer moves from the initial optimum, point A, to the new

TABLE 21.1

Income and Substitution Effects When the Price of Cola Falls

Good	Income effect	Substitution effect	Total effect
Cola	Consumer is richer, so he buys more cola.	Cola is relatively cheaper, so consumer buys more cola.	Income and substitution effects act in same direction, so consumer buys more cola.
Pizza	Consumer is richer, so he buys more pizza.	Pizza is relatively more expensive, so consumer buys less pizza.	Income and substitution effects act in opposite directions, so the total effect on pizza consumption is ambiguous.

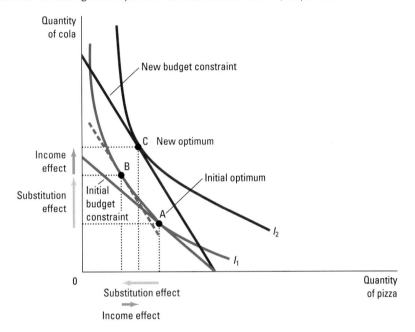

FIGURE 21.10

Income and Substitution Effects

The effect of a change in price can be broken down into an income effect and a substitution effect. The substitution effect – the movement along an indifference curve to a point with a different marginal rate of substitution – is shown here as the change from point A to point B along indifference curve I_1. The income effect – the shift to a higher indifference curve – is shown here as the change from point B on indifference curve I_1 to point C on indifference curve I_2.

optimum, point C. We can view this change as occurring in two steps. First, the consumer moves *along* the initial indifference curve I_1 from point A to point B. The consumer is equally happy at these two points, but at point B the marginal rate of substitution reflects the new relative price. (The dashed line through point B reflects the new relative price by being parallel to the new budget constraint.) Next, the consumer *shifts* to the higher indifference curve I_2 by moving from point B to point C. Even though point B and point C are on different indifference curves, they have the same marginal rate of substitution. That is, the slope of the indifference curve I_1 at point B equals the slope of the indifference curve I_2 at point C.

Although the consumer never actually chooses point B, this hypothetical point is useful to clarify the two effects that determine the consumer's decision. Notice that the change from point A to point B represents a pure change in the marginal rate of substitution without any change in the consumer's welfare. Similarly, the change from point B to point C represents a pure change in welfare without any change in the marginal rate of substitution. Thus, the movement from A to B shows the substitution effect, and the movement from B to C shows the income effect.

Deriving the Demand Curve

We have just seen how changes in the price of a good alter the consumer's budget constraint and, therefore, the quantities of the two goods that he chooses to buy. The demand curve for any good reflects these consumption decisions. Recall that a demand curve shows the quantity demanded of a good for any given price. We can view a consumer's demand curve as a summary of the optimal decisions that arise from his budget constraint and indifference curves.

For example, Figure 21.11 considers the demand for cola. Panel (a) shows that when the price of a litre falls from €2 to €1, the consumer's budget constraint shifts outward. Because of both income and substitution effects, the consumer increases his purchases of cola from 250 to 750 litres. Panel (b) shows the demand curve that results from this consumer's decisions. In this way, the theory of consumer choice provides the theoretical foundation for the consumer's demand curve, which we first introduced in Chapter 4.

Although it is comforting to know that the demand curve arises naturally from the theory of consumer choice, this exercise by itself does not justify developing the theory. There is no need for a rigorous, analytic framework just to establish that people respond to changes in prices. The theory of consumer choice is, however, very useful. As we see in the next section, we can use the theory to delve more deeply into the determinants of household behaviour.

FIGURE 21.11

Deriving the Demand Curve

Panel (a) shows that when the price of cola falls from €2 to €1, the consumer's optimum moves from point A to point B, and the quantity of cola consumed rises from 250 to 750 litres. The demand curve in panel (b) reflects this relationship between the price and the quantity demanded.

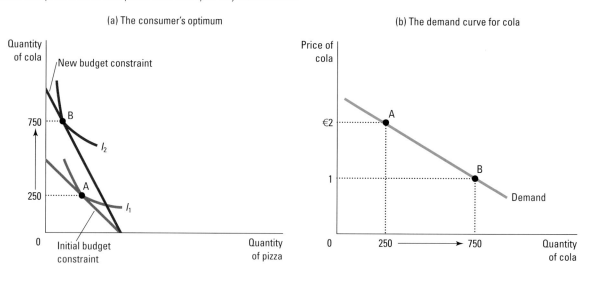

Quick Quiz Draw a budget constraint and indifference curves for cola and pizza. Show what happens to the budget constraint and the consumer's optimum when the price of pizza rises. In your diagram, decompose the change into an income effect and a substitution effect.

THREE APPLICATIONS

Now that we have developed the basic theory of consumer choice, let's use it to shed light on three questions about how the economy works. These three questions might at first seem unrelated. But because each question involves household decision-making, we can address it with the model of consumer behaviour we have just developed.

Do All Demand Curves Slope Downward?

Normally, when the price of a good rises, people buy less of it. Chapter 4 called this usual behaviour the *law of demand.* This law is reflected in the downward slope of the demand curve.

As a matter of economic theory, however, demand curves can sometimes slope upward. In other words, consumers can sometimes violate the law of demand and buy *more* of a good when the price rises. To see how this can happen, consider Figure 21.12. In this example, the consumer buys two goods – meat and potatoes. Initially, the consumer's budget constraint is the line from point A to point B. The optimum is point C. When the price of potatoes rises, the budget constraint shifts inward and is now the line from point A to point D. The optimum is now point E. Notice that a rise in the price of potatoes has led the consumer to buy a larger quantity of potatoes.

Why is the consumer responding in a seemingly perverse way? The reason is that potatoes here are a strongly inferior good. When the price of potatoes rises,

FIGURE 21.12

A Giffen Good

In this example, when the price of potatoes rises, the consumer's optimum shifts from point C to point E. In this case, the consumer responds to a higher price of potatoes by buying less meat and more potatoes.

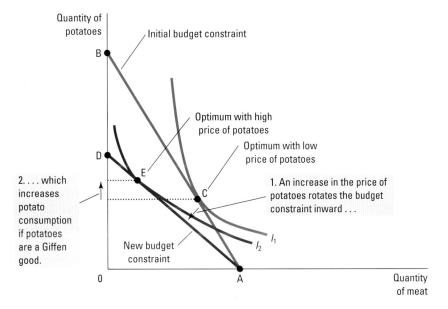

Giffen good
a good for which an increase in the price raises the quantity demanded

the consumer is poorer. The income effect makes the consumer want to buy less meat and more potatoes. At the same time, because the potatoes have become more expensive relative to meat, the substitution effect makes the consumer want to buy more meat and less potatoes. In this particular case, however, the income effect is so strong that it exceeds the substitution effect. In the end, the consumer responds to the higher price of potatoes by buying less meat and more potatoes.

Economists use the term **Giffen good** to describe a good that violates the law of demand. (The term is named after the British economist Robert Giffen, who first noted this possibility.) In this example, potatoes are a Giffen good. Giffen goods are inferior goods for which the income effect dominates the substitution effect. Therefore, they have demand curves that slope upward.

Economists disagree about whether any Giffen good has ever been discovered. Some historians suggest that potatoes were in fact a Giffen good during the Irish potato famine of the 19th century. Potatoes were such a large part of people's diet (historians estimate that the average working man might eat up to fourteen pounds of potatoes a day) that when the price of potatoes rose, it had a large income effect. People responded to their reduced living standard by cutting back on the luxury of meat and buying more of the staple food of potatoes. Thus, it is argued that a higher price of potatoes actually raised the quantity of potatoes demanded.

Whether or not this historical account is true, it is safe to say that Giffen goods are very rare. Some economists, (for example, Dwyer and Lindsey, 1984 and Rosen, 1999) have claimed that a legend has built up around Robert Giffen and that the evidence does not support his idea. Others have suggested that rice and wheat in parts of China might exhibit Giffen qualities. The theory of consumer choice does allow demand curves to slope upward. Yet such occurrences are so unusual that the law of demand is as reliable a law as any in economics.[1,2,3]

How Do Wages Affect Labour Supply?

So far we have used the theory of consumer choice to analyse how a person decides how to allocate his income between two goods. We can use the same theory to analyse how a person decides to allocate his time between work and leisure.

Consider the decision facing Cristina, a freelance software designer. Cristina is awake for 100 hours per week. She spends some of this time enjoying leisure – riding her horse, watching television, studying economics and so on. She spends the rest of this time developing software at her computer. For every hour she spends developing software, she earns €50, which she spends on consumption goods. Thus, her wage (€50) reflects the trade-off Cristina faces between leisure and consumption. For every hour of leisure she gives up, she works one more hour and gets €50 of consumption.

Figure 21.13 shows Cristina's budget constraint. If she spends all 100 hours enjoying leisure, she has no consumption. If she spends all 100 hours working, she earns a weekly consumption of €5 000 but has no time for leisure. If she works a normal 40-hour week, she enjoys 60 hours of leisure and has weekly consumption of €2 000.

Figure 21.13 uses indifference curves to represent Cristina's preferences for consumption and leisure. Here consumption and leisure are the two 'goods' between which Cristina is choosing. Because Cristina always prefers more leisure

---

[1]Dwyer, G.P. & Lindsay, C.M. (1984) 'Robert Giffen and the Irish Potato'. In *The American Economic Review*, **74**:188–192.

[2]Jensen, R & Miller, N. (2008) 'Giffen Behavior and Subsistence Consumption'. In *American Economic Review*, **97**:1553–1577.

[3]Rosen, S. (1999) 'Potato Paradoxes'. In *The Journal of Political Economy*, **107**:294–213.

FIGURE 21.13

The Work–Leisure Decision

This figure shows Cristina's budget constraint for deciding how much to work, her indifference curves for consumption and leisure, and her optimum.

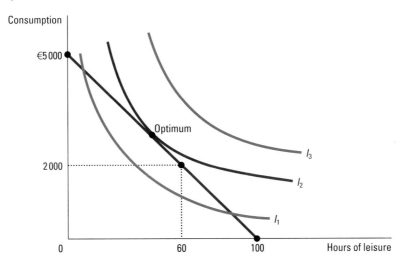

and more consumption, she prefers points on higher indifference curves to points on lower ones. At a wage of €50 per hour, Cristina chooses a combination of consumption and leisure represented by the point labelled 'optimum'. This is the point on the budget constraint that is on the highest possible indifference curve, which is curve I_2.

Now consider what happens when Cristina's wage increases from €50 to €60 per hour. Figure 21.14 shows two possible outcomes. In each case, the budget constraint, shown in the left-hand graph, pivots outward from BC_1 to BC_2. In the process, the budget constraint becomes steeper, reflecting the change in relative price: at the higher wage, Cristina gets more consumption for every hour of leisure that she gives up.

Cristina's preferences, as represented by her indifference curves, determine the resulting responses of consumption and leisure to the higher wage. In both panels, consumption rises. Yet the response of leisure to the change in the wage is different in the two cases. In panel (a), Cristina responds to the higher wage by enjoying less leisure. In panel (b), Cristina responds by enjoying more leisure.

Cristina's decision between leisure and consumption determines her supply of labour because the more leisure she enjoys, the less time she has left to work. In each panel, the right-hand graph in Figure 21.14 shows the labour supply curve implied by Cristina's decision. In panel (a), a higher wage induces Cristina to enjoy less leisure and work more, so the labour supply curve slopes upward. In panel (b), a higher wage induces Cristina to enjoy more leisure and work less, so the labour supply curve slopes 'backward'.

At first, the backward sloping labour supply curve is puzzling. Why would a person respond to a higher wage by working less? The answer comes from considering the income and substitution effects of a higher wage.

Consider first the substitution effect. When Cristina's wage rises, leisure becomes more costly relative to consumption, and this encourages Cristina to substitute consumption for leisure. In other words, the substitution effect induces

An Increase in the Wage

The two panels of this figure show how a person might respond to an increase in the wage. The graphs on the left show the consumer's initial budget constraint BC₁ and new budget constraint BC₂, as well as the consumer's optimal choices over consumption and leisure. The graphs on the right show the resulting labour supply curve. Because hours worked equal total hours available minus hours of leisure, any change in leisure implies an opposite change in the quantity of labour supplied. In panel (a), when the wage rises, consumption rises and leisure falls, resulting in a labour supply curve that slopes upward. In panel (b), when the wage rises, both consumption and leisure rise, resulting in a labour supply curve that slopes backward.

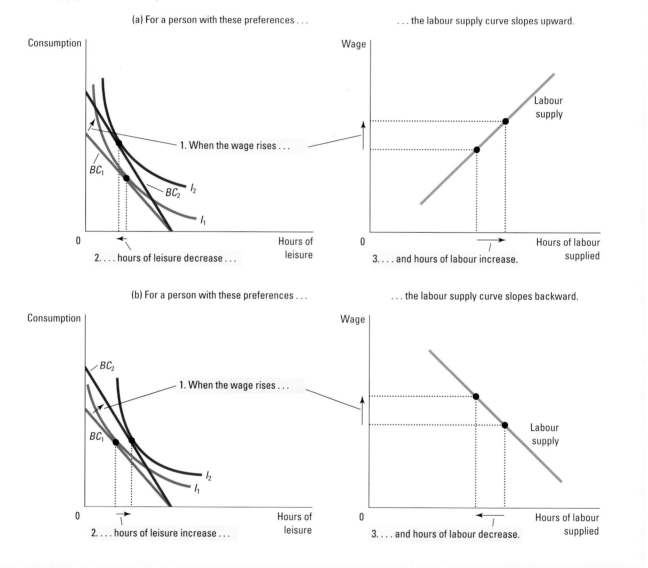

Cristina to work harder in response to higher wages, which tends to make the labour supply curve slope upward.

Now consider the income effect. When Cristina's wage rises, she moves to a higher indifference curve. She is now better off than she was. As long as consumption and leisure are both normal goods, she tends to want to use this increase in well-being to enjoy both higher consumption and greater leisure. In other words, the income effect induces her to work less, which tends to make the labour supply curve slope backward.

In the end, economic theory does not give a clear prediction about whether an increase in the wage induces Cristina to work more or less. If the substitution effect is greater than the income effect for Cristina, she works more. If the income effect is greater than the substitution effect, she works less. The labour supply curve, therefore, could be either upward or backward sloping. This concept has an important application to debates over the effect of tax cuts on work. Some economists argue that cutting taxes encourages people to work more hours because the reward is greater. Such an argument is also used as the basis for supporting an entrepreneurial culture – keep taxes low and this encourages entrepreneurs. Others point out that lower taxes do increase disposable income but workers may now use this higher income to enjoy more leisure and not work additional hours. Having some idea of the relative strength of the income and substitution effects is important in analysing and assessing such policy initiatives.

CASE STUDY

Income Effects on Labour Supply: Historical Trends, Lottery Winners, and the Carnegie Conjecture

The idea of a backward sloping labour supply curve might at first seem like a mere theoretical curiosity, but in fact it is not. Evidence indicates that the labour supply curve, considered over long periods of time, does in fact slope backwards. A hundred years ago many people in Europe and North America worked six days a week. Today five-day working weeks are the norm. At the same time that the length of the working week has been falling, the wage of the typical worker (adjusted for inflation) has been rising.

Here is how economists explain this historical pattern: over time, advances in technology raise workers' productivity and, thereby, the demand for labour. The increase in labour demand raises equilibrium wages. As wages rise, so does the reward for working. Yet rather than responding to this increased incentive by working more, most workers choose to take part of their greater prosperity in the form of more leisure. In other words, the income effect of higher wages dominates the substitution effect.

Further evidence that the income effect on labour supply is strong comes from a very different kind of data: winners of lotteries. Winners of large prizes in the lottery see large increases in their incomes and, as a result, large outward shifts in their budget constraints. Because the winners' wages have not changed, however, the *slopes* of their budget constraints remain the same. There is, therefore, no substitution effect. By examining the behaviour of lottery winners, we can isolate the income effect on labour supply. Nearly all the research on the effects of winning the lottery on labour supply has so far been done in the USA, but the results are striking. Of those winners who win more than $50 000, almost 25 per cent quit working within a year, and another 9 per cent reduce the number of hours they work. Of those winners who win more than $1 million, almost 40 per cent stop working. The income effect on labour supply of winning such a large prize is substantial.

Similar results were found in a study, published in the May 1993 issue of the *Quarterly Journal of Economics*, of how receiving a bequest affects a person's labour supply. The study found that a single person who inherits more than $150 000 is four times as likely to stop working as a single person who inherits less than $25 000. This finding would not have surprised the 19th-century industrialist Andrew Carnegie. Carnegie warned that 'the parent who leaves his son enormous wealth generally deadens the talents and energies of the son, and tempts him to lead a less useful and less worthy life than he otherwise would.' That is, Carnegie viewed the income effect on labour supply to be substantial and, from his paternalistic perspective, regrettable. During his life and at his death, Carnegie gave much of his vast fortune to charity.

How Do Interest Rates Affect Household Saving?

An important decision that every person faces is how much income to consume today and how much to save for the future. We can use the theory of consumer choice to analyse how people make this decision and how the amount they save depends on the interest rate their savings will earn.

Consider the decision facing Emilio, a worker planning ahead for retirement. To keep things simple, let's divide Emilio's life into two periods. In the first period, Emilio is young and working. In the second period, he is old and retired. When young, Emilio earns €100 000. He divides this income between current consumption and saving. When he is old, Emilio will consume what he has saved, including the interest that his savings have earned.

Suppose that the interest rate is 10 per cent. Then for every euro that Emilio saves when young, he can consume €1.10 when old. We can view 'consumption when young' and 'consumption when old' as the two goods that Emilio must choose between. The interest rate determines the relative price of these two goods.

Figure 21.15 shows Emilio's budget constraint. If he saves nothing, he consumes €100 000 when young and nothing when old. If he saves everything, he

FIGURE 21.15

The Consumption–Saving Decision

This figure shows the budget constraint for a person deciding how much to consume in the two periods of his life, the indifference curves representing his preferences, and the optimum.

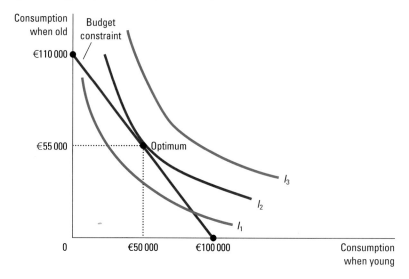

consumes nothing when young and €110 000 when old. The budget constraint shows these and all the intermediate possibilities.

Figure 21.15 uses indifference curves to represent Emilio's preferences for consumption in the two periods. Because Emilio prefers more consumption in both periods, he prefers points on higher indifference curves to points on lower ones. Given his preferences, Emilio chooses the optimal combination of consumption in both periods of life, which is the point on the budget constraint that is on the highest possible indifference curve. At this optimum, Emilio consumes €50 000 when young and €55 000 when old.

Now consider what happens when the interest rate increases from 10 per cent to 20 per cent. Figure 21.16 shows two possible outcomes. In both cases, the budget constraint pivots outward and becomes steeper. At the new higher interest rate, Emilio gets more consumption when old for every euro of consumption that he gives up when young.

The two panels show different preferences for Emilio and the resulting response to the higher interest rate. In both cases, consumption when old rises. Yet the response of consumption when young to the change in the interest rate is different in the two cases. In panel (a), Emilio responds to the higher interest rate by consuming less when young. In panel (b), Emilio responds by consuming more when young.

Emilio's saving, of course, is his income when young minus the amount he consumes when young. In panel (a), consumption when young falls when the interest rate rises, so saving must rise. In panel (b), Emilio consumes more when young, so saving must fall.

FIGURE 21.16

An Increase in the Interest Rate

In both panels, an increase in the interest rate shifts the budget constraint outward. In panel (a), consumption when young falls and consumption when old rises. The result is an increase in saving when young. In panel (b), consumption in both periods rises. The result is a decrease in saving when young.

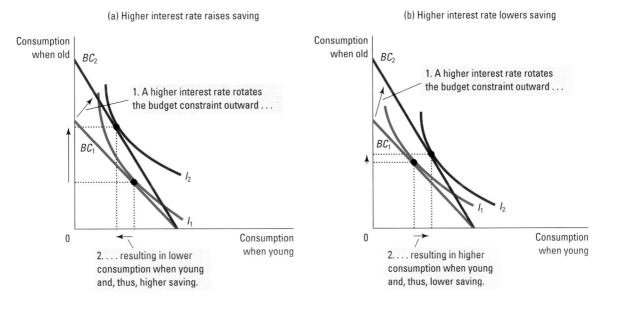

The case shown in panel (b) might at first seem odd: Emilio responds to an increase in the return to saving by saving less. Yet this behaviour is not as peculiar as it might seem. We can understand it by considering the income and substitution effects of a higher interest rate.

Consider first the substitution effect. When the interest rate rises, consumption when old becomes less costly relative to consumption when young. Therefore, the substitution effect induces Emilio to consume more when old and less when young. In other words, the substitution effect induces Emilio to save more.

Now consider the income effect. When the interest rate rises, Emilio moves to a higher indifference curve. He is now better off than he was. As long as consumption in both periods consists of normal goods, he tends to want to use this increase in well-being to enjoy higher consumption in both periods. In other words, the income effect induces him to save less.

The end result, of course, depends on both the income and substitution effects. If the substitution effect of a higher interest rate is greater than the income effect, Emilio saves more. If the income effect is greater than the substitution effect, Emilio saves less. Thus, the theory of consumer choice says that an increase in the interest rate could either encourage or discourage saving.

Although this ambiguous result is interesting from the standpoint of economic theory, it is disappointing from the standpoint of economic policy. It turns out that an important issue in tax policy hinges in part on how saving responds to interest rates. Some economists have advocated reducing the taxation of interest and other capital income, arguing that such a policy change would raise the after-tax interest rate that savers can earn and would thereby encourage people to save more. Other economists have argued that because of offsetting income and substitution effects, such a tax change might not increase saving and could even reduce it. Unfortunately, research has not led to a consensus about how interest rates affect saving. As a result, there remains disagreement among economists about whether changes in tax policy aimed to encourage saving would, in fact, have the intended effect.

Quick Quiz Explain how an increase in the wage can potentially decrease the amount that a person wants to work.

CONCLUSION: DO PEOPLE REALLY THINK THIS WAY?

The theory of consumer choice describes how people make decisions. As we have seen, it has broad applicability. It can explain how a person chooses between cola and pizza, work and leisure, consumption and saving, and so on.

At this point, however, you might be tempted to treat the theory of consumer choice with some scepticism. After all, you are a consumer. You decide what to buy every time you walk into a shop. And you know that you do not decide by writing down budget constraints and indifference curves. Doesn't this knowledge about your own decision-making provide evidence against the theory?

The answer is no. The theory of consumer choice does not try to present a literal account of how people make decisions. It is a model. And, as we first discussed in Chapter 2, models are not intended to be completely realistic.

The best way to view the theory of consumer choice is as a metaphor for how consumers make decisions. No consumer (except an occasional economist) goes through the explicit optimization envisioned in the theory. Yet consumers are aware that their choices are constrained by their financial resources. And, given those constraints, they do the best they can to achieve the highest level of satisfaction. The theory of consumer choice tries to describe this implicit, psychological process in a way that permits explicit, economic analysis. The proof of the pudding is in the eating. And the test of a theory is in its applications. In the last section of this chapter we applied the theory of consumer choice to three practical issues about the economy. If you take more advanced courses in economics, you will see that this theory provides the framework for much additional analysis.

IN THE NEWS

Whilst economists can defend the use of models such as that used in this chapter, they are also aware that new information can also shed light on consumer decision-making. The development of magnetic resonance imaging (MRI) is one example of how economists are able to gain further insights into human behaviour and links with other disciplines, notably psychology, is further extending the frontiers of our understanding.

The Brain and Consumer Choice: Neuroeconomics

Two pieces of research show how the work of psychologists and neuroscientists can help to increase our understanding of the processes involved in decision-making in consumption. In one piece of research, investigators looked at the role played by different areas of the brain in making decisions about investing in financial assets. Researchers also looked at the role of the brain in making purchasing decisions related to preference and price in purchasing chocolate. In both cases, the research was investigating how humans balance out anticipation of the gains and losses that we might get from purchases and whether there was any part of the brain that was associated with being stimulated when faced with the likely gains and losses of a prospective purchase.

The principle behind this investigation was based on the anticipatory effects that occur when faced with a purchasing decision. It is not difficult to

conceptualize on a personal level. Think about when you go into a shop or a store and see something you really like. It might be an expensive purchase and you might know that you should not really be thinking of buying it but the item has really caught your attention and you are debating whether to buy it or not.

On the one hand, you know that the price that is being asked represents a loss – the money you will have to give up is an opportunity cost and means you will have to sacrifice other things that it could also buy you. Equally, you also know that owning this item will provide you with some form of gain – utility. When making the purchasing decision, therefore, you are balancing out these competing forces. The brain plays a role in this; there seems to be two main parts of the brain that are involved in such decisions – the nucleus accumbens and the anterior insular. The nucleus accumbens emits two neuro transmitters – dopamine and serotonin. The former is associated with desire and the latter with inhibition.

The anterior insula is a part of the brain that has some association with emotional experience and conscious feelings. This will include feelings of pain, anger, happiness, disgust, fear and anger.

The research was relatively complex but the main results from their investigations are given below.

- When making decisions on financial instruments, investors tend not to act rationally. These can be called 'risk-seeking mistakes' and 'risk-aversion mistakes'.
- Activity in the nucleus accumbens has an association with risk-seeking mistakes and risky choices.
- Activity in the anterior insula is associated with risk-aversion mistakes and riskless choices.
- Distinct neural circuits associated with anticipatory affect lead to different types of choices.
- Nucleus accumbens activation represents gain prediction.

▶

- Anterior insula activation represents loss prediction.
- Activation of these brain regions can predict decisions to purchase.

In this chapter we looked at a model of consumer behaviour based on a model of rational decision-making – maximizing utility with the constraint of a limited income. However, this might not be the case in reality. The expectations that we might have about a purchase might trigger behavioural or affective (to do with emotions) responses which might influence what we eventually end up buying. The findings might be related to a wide range of decision-making including how we choose to buy insurance and assurance, gambling at casinos, at racing and so on and how we pay for goods and services.

There is a suggestion, for example, that the perceived risk associated with buying goods and services through credit cards is different to that of cash. It has been suggested that we are 'anaesthetized' against the effects of paying. As a result there may be a tendency to overspend when purchasing with credit cards compared to cash. There may also be similar effects going on when people purchase online rather than going to a shop or a store. By understanding how the brain works in this respect, there may be possibilities of building incentives or disincentives to purchase to take account of the way these parts of the brain work.

In making purchasing decisions, we know that there are a number of 'laws' of economics that we might quote. Such 'laws' allow us to be able to make predictions – the very basis of having theories. However, if these laws are based on inaccurate or incomplete knowledge of how humans actually carry out these actions then the model will not be able to be used as a predictive tool.

We assume, for example, that humans are attracted to preferred products (how that preference is gener-

ated is another story). We also assume that consumers prefer lower prices than higher prices and that if a price is deemed 'excessive' then we will avoid purchasing the item. Prices represent a potential gain and a potential loss. However, we might view similar losses and gains in different ways. In some cases we might view a loss as being more important than a gain even if they were of equal magnitude. That contradicts the rational approach that characterizes much of economic theory. If our decision-making is being affected by the activation of these distinct neural circuits then the extent to which they are activated might influence our choice. For example, the research cited examples where men were shown pictures of sports cars and other types of car deemed to be less desirable. Viewing sports cars produced a greater degree of brain activity in the mid-brain. Similar results have been obtained in cases where both men and women are shown preferred rather than less preferred drinks, brands of beer and coffee.

If this is the case, then it might suggest that advertising over a long period

of time might have significant effects in influencing our choices if it has effects on our perceptions of preferred or non-preferred purchases. What is happening is that the perception of loss and gain is being altered in relation to the price that is being charged.

The second piece of research involves the effect on human behaviour of different emotional states and the effect that hormones play in influencing the brain and human behaviour. In a paper presented to a British Psychological Society (BPS) meeting in April 2009, Professor Karen Pine of the University of Hertfordshire outlined her research findings from a study looking at the link between the menstrual cycle in women and purchasing decisions. Professor Pine's study involved 443 women aged 18 to 50. It appeared to show a link between the stage of the menstrual cycle and purchasing decisions. Of the women in the sample, 153 were in the later stages of their menstrual cycle, known as the luteal phase. Of this group, over 60 per cent said that they had indulged in overspending and had bought items on impulse. The spending, in a small number of cases, was way over normal budgets – some women saying that they had overspent by as much as £250. In many cases, the women said that their purchasing decisions at this time were accompanied by feelings of remorse afterwards.

Professor Pine commented, 'The spending behaviour tends to be a reaction to intense emotions. They are feeling stressed or depressed and are more likely to go shopping to cheer themselves up and using it to regulate their emotions.' The study also found that those women with severe pre-menstrual tension (PMT) displayed more extreme examples of this behaviour.

Part of the explanation for this behaviour is that hormonal changes in women at certain times of the menstrual cycle are associated with changes to the part of the brain that is linked to inhibitions and emotions. It has also been suggested that purchasing decisions may be linked to a desire of women to make themselves look more attractive. There has been other research which has suggested that part of female behaviour is driven by the need to demonstrate their fertility – a throwback to very early days when survival of the species depended in part on the ability to reproduce successfully. Around 14 days before the start of ovulation is a time which sees women increase their spending on items that enhance their attractiveness. These items include make-up, high-heeled shoes and jewellery. Professor Pine has said that her findings are supported by other research which shows a so-called 'ornamental effect' linked to stages in the menstrual cycle.

SUMMARY

- A consumer's budget constraint shows the possible combinations of different goods he can buy given his income and the prices of the goods. The slope of the budget constraint equals the relative price of the goods.

- The consumer's indifference curves represent his preferences. An indifference curve shows the various bundles of goods that make the consumer equally happy. Points on higher indifference curves are preferred to points on lower indifference curves. The slope of an indifference curve at any point is the consumer's marginal rate of substitution – the rate at which the consumer is willing to trade one good for the other.

- The consumer optimizes by choosing the point on his budget constraint that lies on the highest indifference curve. At this point, the slope of the indifference curve (the marginal rate of substitution between the goods) equals the slope of the budget constraint (the relative price of the goods).

- When the price of a good falls, the impact on the consumer's choices can be broken down into an income effect and a substitution effect. The income effect is the change in consumption that arises because a lower price makes the consumer better off. The substitution effect is the change in consumption that arises because a price change encourages greater consumption of the good that has become relatively cheaper. The income effect is reflected in the movement from a lower to a higher indifference curve, whereas the substitution effect is reflected by a movement along an indifference curve to a point with a different slope.

- The theory of consumer choice can be applied in many situations. It can explain why demand curves can potentially slope upward, why higher wages could either increase or decrease the quantity of labour supplied, and why higher interest rates could either increase or decrease saving.

KEY CONCEPTS

budget constraint, p. 439
indifference curve, p. 441
marginal rate of substitution, p. 441

perfect substitutes, p. 444
perfect complements, p. 445
income effect, p. 450

substitution effect, p. 450
Giffen good, p. 454

QUESTIONS FOR REVIEW

1. A consumer has income of €3 000. Wine is priced at €3 a glass and cheese is priced at €6 a kilo. Draw the consumer's budget constraint. What is the slope of this budget constraint?

2. Draw a consumer's indifference curves for wine and cheese. Describe and explain four properties of these indifference curves.

3. Pick a point on an indifference curve for wine and cheese and show the marginal rate of substitution. What does the marginal rate of substitution tell us?

4. Show a consumer's budget constraint and indifference curves for wine and cheese. Show the optimal consumption choice. If the price of wine is €3 a glass and the price of cheese is €6 a kilo, what is the marginal rate of substitution at this optimum?

5. A person who consumes wine and cheese gets a rise, so his income increases from €3 000 to €4 000. Show what happens if both wine and cheese are normal goods. Now show what happens if cheese is an inferior good.

6. The price of cheese rises from €6 to €10 a kilo, while the price of wine remains €3 a glass. For a consumer with a constant income of €3 000, show what happens to consumption of wine and cheese. Decompose the change into income and substitution effects.

7. Can an increase in the price of cheese possibly induce a consumer to buy more cheese? Explain.

PROBLEMS AND APPLICATIONS

1. Jacqueline divides her income between coffee and croissants (both of which are normal goods). An early frost in Brazil causes a large increase in the price of coffee in France.
   a. Show how this early frost might affect Jacqueline's budget constraint.
   b. Show how this early frost might affect Jacqueline's optimal consumption bundle assuming that the substitution effect outweighs the income effect for croissants.
   c. Show how this early frost might affect Jacqueline's optimal consumption bundle assuming that the income effect outweighs the substitution effect for croissants.

2. Compare the following two pairs of goods:
   a. Coke and Pepsi
   b. skis and ski bindings.
   In which case do you expect the indifference curves to be fairly straight, and in which case do you expect the indifference curves to be very bowed? In which case will the consumer respond more to a change in the relative price of the two goods?

3. Eric consumes only cheese and bread.
   a. Could cheese and bread both be inferior goods for Eric? Explain.
   b. Suppose that cheese is a normal good for Eric while bread is an inferior good. If the price of cheese falls, what happens to Eric's consumption of bread? What happens to his consumption of cheese? Explain.

4. Oliver buys only lager and kebabs.
   a. In 2009, Oliver earns €100, lager is priced at €2 a litre and kebabs are priced at €4 each. Draw Oliver's budget constraint.
   b. Now suppose that all prices increase by 10 per cent in 2010 and that Oliver's salary increases by 10 per cent as well. Draw Oliver's new budget constraint. How would Oliver's optimal combination of lager and kebabs in 2010 compare to his optimal combination in 2009?

5. Consider your decision about how many hours to work.
   a. Draw your budget constraint assuming that you pay no taxes on your income. On the same diagram, draw another budget constraint assuming that you pay a 15 per cent tax.
   b. Show how the tax might lead to more hours of work, fewer hours or the same number of hours. Explain.

6. Sarah is awake for 100 hours per week. Using one diagram, show Sarah's budget constraints if she earns €6 per hour, €8 per hour and €10 per hour. Now draw indifference curves such that Sarah's labour supply curve is upward sloping when the wage is between €6 and €8 per hour, and backward sloping when the wage is between €8 and €10 per hour.

7. Draw the indifference curve for someone deciding how much to work. Suppose the wage increases. Is it possible that the person's consumption would fall? Is this plausible? Discuss. (Hint: think about income and substitution effects.)

8. Suppose you take a job that pays €30 000 and set some of this income aside in a savings account that pays an annual interest rate of 5 per cent. Use a diagram with a budget constraint and indifference curves to show how your consumption changes in each of the following situations. To keep things simple, assume that you pay no taxes on your income.
   a. Your salary increases to €40 000.
   b. The interest rate on your bank account rises to 8 per cent.

9. As discussed in the text, we can divide an individual's life into two hypothetical periods: 'young' and 'old'. Suppose that the individual earns income only when young and saves some of that income to consume when old. If the interest rate on savings falls, can you tell what happens to consumption when young? Can you tell what happens to consumption when old? Explain.

10. (This problem is challenging.) The welfare system in industrialized countries provides income to some needy families. Typically, the maximum payment goes to families that earn no income; then, as families begin to earn income, the welfare payment declines gradually and eventually disappears. Let's consider the possible effects of a welfare system on a family's labour supply.
   a. Draw a budget constraint for a family assuming that the welfare system did not exist. On the same diagram, draw a budget constraint that reflects the existence of the welfare system.
   b. Adding indifference curves to your diagram, show how the welfare system could reduce the number of hours worked by the family. Explain, with reference to both the income and substitution effects.
   c. Using your diagram from part (b), show the effect of the welfare system on the well-being of the family.

11. (This problem is challenging.) Suppose that an individual incurred no taxes on the first €10 000 she earned and 15 per cent of any income she earned over €10 000. Now suppose that the government is considering two ways to reduce the tax burden: a reduction in the tax rate and an increase in the amount on which no tax is owed.
   a. What effect would a reduction in the tax rate have on the individual's labour supply if she earned €30 000 to start with? Explain in words using the income and substitution effects. You do not need to use a diagram.
   b. What effect would an increase in the amount on which no tax is owed have on the individual's labour supply? Again, explain in words using the income and substitution effects.

12. (This problem is challenging.) Consider a person deciding how much to consume and how much to save for retirement. This person has particular preferences: her lifetime utility depends on the lowest level of consumption during the two periods of her life. That is, Utility = Minimum {consumption when young, consumption when old}
   a. Draw this person's indifference curves. (Hint: recall that indifference curves show the combinations of consumption in the two periods that yield the same level of utility.)
   b. Draw the budget constraint and the optimum.
   c. When the interest rate increases, does this person save more or less? Explain your answer using income and substitution effects.

13. Economist George Stigler once wrote that, according to consumer theory, 'if consumers do not buy less of a commodity when their incomes rise, they will surely buy less when the price of the commodity rises.' Explain this statement using the concepts of income and substitution effects.

For further resources, visit
www.cengage.co.uk/mankiw_taylor2

22 FRONTIERS OF MICROECONOMICS

Economics is a study of the choices that people make and the resulting interactions they have with one another. This study has many facets, as we have seen in the preceding chapters. Yet it would be a mistake to think that all the facets we have seen make up a finished jewel, perfect and unchanging. Like all scientists, economists are always on the lookout for new areas to study and new phenomena to explain. This final chapter on microeconomics offers an assortment of three topics at the discipline's frontier to see how economists are trying to expand their understanding of human behaviour and society.

The first topic is the economics of *asymmetric information*. Many times in life, some people are better informed than others, and this difference in information can affect the choices they make and how they deal with one another. Thinking about this asymmetry can shed light on many aspects of the world, from the market for used cars to the custom of gift giving.

The second topic we examine in this chapter is *political economy*. Throughout this book we have seen many examples where markets fail and government policy can potentially improve matters. But 'potentially' is a needed qualifier: whether this potential is realized depends on how well our political institutions work. The field of political economy applies the tools of economics to understand the functioning of government.

The third topic in this chapter is *behavioural economics*. We have already seen at various times in the book so far, how understanding human behaviour helps to explain economic phenomena. This field brings some of the insights from psychology into the study of economic issues. It offers a view of human behaviour that is more subtle and complex than that found in conventional economic theory, but this view may also be more realistic.

This chapter covers a lot of ground. To do so, it offers not a full helping of these three topics but, instead, a taste of each. One goal is to show a few of the directions economists are heading in their effort to expand knowledge of how the economy works. Another goal is to whet your appetite for more courses in economics.

ASYMMETRIC INFORMATION

'I know something you don't know.' This statement is a common taunt among children, but it also conveys a deep truth about how people sometimes interact with one another. Many times in life, one person knows more about what is going on than another. A difference in access to relevant knowledge is called an *information asymmetry.*

Examples abound. A worker knows more than his employer about how much effort he puts into his job. A seller of a used car knows more than the buyer about the car's condition. The first is an example of a *hidden action,* whereas the second is an example of a *hidden characteristic.* In each case, the party in the dark (the employer, the car buyer) would like to know the relevant information, but the informed party (the worker, the car seller) may have an incentive to conceal it.

Because asymmetric information is so prevalent, economists have devoted much effort in recent decades to studying its effects. And, indeed, the 2001 Nobel Prize in economics was awarded to three economists (George Akerlof, Michael Spence and Joseph Stiglitz) for their pioneering work on this topic. Let's discuss some of the insights that this study has revealed.

Hidden Actions: Principals, Agents and Moral Hazard

Moral hazard is a problem that arises when one person, called the **agent**, is performing some task on behalf of another person, called the **principal**. If the principal cannot perfectly monitor the agent's behaviour, the agent tends to undertake less effort than the principal considers desirable and is not fully responsible for the consequences of their actions. The phrase *moral hazard* refers to the risk, or 'hazard', of inappropriate or otherwise 'immoral' behaviour by the agent.

Moral hazard can lead to *adverse selection.* This means that the market process may end up with 'bad' outcomes because of asymmetric information. Adverse selection is a feature of banking, finance and insurance industries. A bank, for example, may set rules and regulations for its accounts which may lead to some customers, who are not very profitable to the bank, adversely selecting the bank – customers the bank would rather not have. In insurance, the person seeking insurance cover has more information about his or her situation than the insurer. A person who knows they are high risk will look to buy insurance but not necessarily divulge the extent of the risk they pose to the insurance company. How does the insurance company distinguish between its high-risk and low-risk customers? The insurance company would rather take on the low-risk customers than the high-risk ones but high-risk customers adversely select the insurance company. In finance, some investment banks have been accused of putting very risky assets into financial products and clients buying these products did not know the full extent of the risk they were buying – clients were dealing with suppliers who they would have been better off not dealing with. In such a situation, the principal tries various ways to encourage the agent to act more responsibly (such as pricing insurance for high-risk customers higher than for low-risk ones).

moral hazard
the tendency of a person who is imperfectly monitored to engage in dishonest or otherwise undesirable behaviour

agent
a person who is performing an act for another person, called the principal

principal
a person for whom another person, called the agent, is performing some act

The employment relationship is the classic example. The employer is the principal, and the worker is the agent. The moral-hazard problem is the temptation of imperfectly monitored workers to shirk their responsibilities. Employers can respond to this problem in various ways:

- *Better monitoring.* Parents hiring nannies or au pairs have been known to plant hidden video cameras in their homes to record the individual's behaviour when the parents are away. The aim is to catch irresponsible behaviour.
- *High wages.* According to *efficiency wages theories* (discussed in Chapter 19), some employers may choose to pay their workers a wage above the level that equilibrates supply and demand in the labour market. A worker who earns an above-equilibrium wage is less likely to shirk, because if he is caught and fired, he might not be able to find another high-paying job.
- *Delayed payment.* Firms can delay part of a worker's compensation, so if the worker is caught shirking and is fired, he suffers a larger penalty. One example of delayed compensation is the year-end bonus. Similarly, a firm may choose to pay its workers more later in their lives. Thus, the wage increases that workers get as they age may reflect not just the benefits of experience but also a response to moral hazard.

These various mechanisms to reduce the problem of moral hazard need not be used alone. Employers can use a combination of them.

Beyond the workplace, there are many other examples of moral hazard. Individuals with insurance cover, be it fire, motor vehicle or medical insurance, may behave differently as a result of having that cover. A motorist, for example, might drive more recklessly in the knowledge that in the event of an accident the cost will be met primarily by the insurance company. Similarly, families choosing to live near a river may benefit from the scenic views but the increased risk of flooding imposes a cost to the insurance company and the government in the event of a serious flood. The financial crisis of 2007–2009 raised the issue of bankers' bonuses. One argument put forward was that banks were acting recklessly in giving large bonuses to workers which encouraged inappropriate and risky investment. Such behaviour was encouraged because bankers 'knew' that governments would step in to prevent banks from failing.

Many regulations are aimed at addressing the problem: an insurance company may require homeowners to buy smoke detectors or pay higher premiums if there is a history of reckless driving (or even refuse to provide insurance cover to the individual), the government may prohibit building homes on land with high risk of flooding and new regulations may be introduced to curb the behaviour of banks. But the insurance company does not have perfect information about how cautious homeowners are, the government does not have perfect information about the risk that families undertake when choosing where to live and regulators do not know fully the risks that bankers take in investment decisions. As a result, the problem of moral hazard persists.

Hidden Characteristics: Adverse Selection and the Lemons Problem

adverse selection
the tendency for the mix of unobserved attributes to become undesirable from the standpoint of an uninformed party

Adverse selection is a problem that arises in markets where one party knows more about the attributes of a good or service being transacted than the other party does. When this occurs the 'selection' of the good or service may be 'adverse' from the standpoint of the uninformed party to the transaction.

The classic example of adverse selection is the market for used cars. Sellers of used cars know their vehicles' defects while buyers often do not. Because owners of the worst cars are more likely to sell them than are the owners of the best cars, buyers are apprehensive about getting a poor car. If you are unlucky enough to buy a poor car, then we might say that you have bought a 'lemon'. This was the term used by Nobel Prize-winner George Akerlof in his famous research article, 'The Market for Lemons'[1]. His co-prize winners in 2001, Joseph Stiglitz and Michael Spence, also used the term in the context of asymmetric information; it comes from the old-fashioned fruit or gambling machines where three wheels spin and come to rest indicating a picture of a fruit that determines the payout; traditionally, a lemon was bad luck, paying out nothing. As a result of this information asymmetry, many people avoid buying vehicles in the used car market. This lemons problem can explain why a used car only a few weeks old sells for thousands of euros less than a new car of the same type. A buyer of the used car might surmise that the seller is getting rid of the car quickly because the seller knows something about it that the buyer does not.

A second example of adverse selection occurs in the labour market. According to another efficiency wage theory, workers vary in their abilities, and they may know their own abilities better than do the firms that hire them. When a firm cuts the wage it pays, the more talented workers are more likely to quit, knowing they are better able to find other employment. Conversely, a firm may choose to pay an above-equilibrium wage to attract a better mix of workers. Or suppose that a firm is not doing so well and needs to cut the wage bill. It can do this either by reducing wages or by keeping wages where they are and laying off workers at random for a few weeks. If it cuts wages, the very best workers will quit, because they know they will be able to find a better job elsewhere. Of course, the better workers who are randomly selected when the firm chooses instead to impose layoffs may also choose to quit and find a steadier job elsewhere. But in this case only *some* of the best workers quit (since not all of them are laid off because workers were chosen randomly) while if the firms cuts wages, *all* of the best workers will quit.

A third example of adverse selection occurs in markets for insurance. For example, buyers of health insurance know more about their own health problems than do insurance companies. Because people with greater hidden health problems are more likely to buy health insurance than are other people, the price of health insurance reflects the costs of a sicker-than-average person. As a result, people in average health may be discouraged from buying health insurance by the high price.

When markets suffer from adverse selection, the invisible hand does not necessarily work its magic. In the used car market, owners of good cars may choose to keep them rather than sell them at the low price that sceptical buyers are willing to pay. In the labour market, wages may be stuck above the level that balances supply and demand, resulting in unemployment. In insurance markets, buyers with low risk may choose to remain uninsured, because the policies they are offered fail to reflect their true characteristics. Advocates of government-provided health insurance sometimes point to the problem of adverse selection as one reason not to trust the private market to provide the right amount of health insurance on its own.

Signalling to Convey Private Information

Although asymmetric information is sometimes a motivation for public policy, it also motivates some individual behaviour that otherwise might be hard to

---

[1] Akerlof, G. (1970) 'The Market for Lemons: Quality, Uncertainty and the Market Mechanism. *Quarterly Journal of Economics*, **84**:488–500.

signalling
an action taken by an informed party to reveal private information to an uninformed party

explain. Markets respond to problems of asymmetric information in many ways. One of them is **signalling**, which refers to actions taken by an informed party for the sole purpose of credibly revealing his private information.

We have seen examples of signalling in previous chapters. As we saw in Chapter 16, firms may spend money on advertising to signal to potential customers that they have high-quality products. As we saw in Chapter 20, students may earn university degrees in order to signal to potential employers that they are high-ability individuals. Recall that the signalling theory of education contrasts with the human capital theory, which asserts that education increases a person's productivity, rather than merely conveying information about innate talent. These two examples of signalling (advertising, education) may seem very different, but below the surface they are much the same: in both cases, the informed party (the firm, the student) is using the signal to convince the uninformed party (the customer, the employer) that the informed party is offering something of high quality.

What does it take for an action to be an effective signal? Obviously, it must be costly. If a signal were free, everyone would use it, and it would convey no information. For the same reason, there is another requirement: The signal must be less costly, or more beneficial, to the person with the higher-quality product. Otherwise, everyone would have the same incentive to use the signal, and the signal would reveal nothing.

Consider again our two examples. In the advertising case, a firm with a good product reaps a larger benefit from advertising because customers who try the product once are more likely to become repeat customers. Thus, it is rational for the firm with the good product to pay for the cost of the signal (advertising), and it is rational for the customer to use the signal as a piece of information about the product's quality. In the education case, a talented person can get through school more easily than a less talented one. Thus, it is rational for the talented person to pay for the cost of the signal (education), and it is rational for the employer to use the signal as a piece of information about the person's talent.

The world is replete with instances of signalling. Magazine advertisements sometimes include the phrase 'as seen on TV'. Why does a firm selling a product in a magazine choose to stress this fact? One possibility is that the firm is trying to convey its willingness to pay for an expensive signal (a spot on television) in the hope that you will infer that its product is of high quality. For the same reason, graduates of elite universities are always sure to put that fact on their curriculum vitaes.

CASE STUDY

Gifts as Signals

A man is debating what to give his girlfriend for her birthday. 'I know,' he says to himself, 'I'll give her cash. After all, I don't know her tastes as well as she does, and with cash, she can buy anything she wants.' But when he hands her the money, she is offended. Convinced he doesn't really love her, she breaks off the relationship. What's the economics behind this story?

In some ways, gift giving is a strange custom. As the man in our story suggests, people typically know their own preferences better than others do, so we might expect everyone to prefer cash to in-kind transfers. If your employer substituted merchandise for your wages, you would likely object to the means of payment. But your reaction is very different when someone who (you hope) loves you does the same thing.

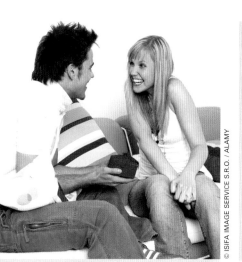

"Now we'll see how much he loves me."

© ISIFA IMAGE SERVICE S.R.O. / ALAMY

One interpretation of gift giving is that it reflects asymmetric information and signalling. The man in our story has private information that the girlfriend would like to know: does he really love her? Choosing a good gift for her is a signal of his love. Certainly, picking out a gift has the right characteristics to be a signal. It is costly (it takes time), and its cost depends on the private information (how much he loves her). If he really loves her, choosing a good gift is easy because he is thinking about her all the time. If he doesn't love her, finding the right gift is more difficult. Thus, giving a gift that suits the girlfriend is one way for him to convey the private information of his love for her. Giving cash shows that he isn't even bothering to try.

An excellent case in point is Valentine's Day. It is a day when millions of women might be expecting to be sent or be given something that extra bit special as a sign of the love and romance felt by their partner. (Of course, it is not only women who might be expecting such gifts but for the purpose of this case study we will make an assumption that a female is expecting a gift from her male partner.) The two parties to the transaction are the female and the male. The woman, it is assumed, is expecting some show of affection and a sign of the love her partner feels for her and this is manifested in some sort of gift. That gift, we will assume, is the traditional red rose. For the man, the whole issue is quite complex.

On the one hand, he will be faced with the certain knowledge that supply and demand will ensure that the price of roses will be high. He could wait for later in the week and pick up some bargains but that might not go down too well. He therefore has to accept that he will have to buy some roses as a sign of his love and affection. The man might know in his own mind just how much he loves the woman. The woman, on the other hand, is going to base the extent of that love and affection, in part, on the size of the bunch of roses that the man will be expected to give her. This is the asymmetric information. She knows that prices of roses will shoot up on Valentine's Day but that's part of the enjoyment. The bigger the bunch of roses the more the man will have spent and this equates directly to the extent of the love and affection he has for her.

The man is now in a quandary. If he buys a large bunch of roses he knows it will set him back anything between €10 and €100 depending on the number and quality and where they are bought from. Buy them from a supermarket and what does that say for your credibility in the romance stakes? Buy them from a florist and you might get more credibility but the price is likely to be much higher. The credibility is the sign sent to your partner that you went out of your way to find the florist and to choose the flowers, all of which signals your devotion.

The man could choose to be clever and just go for the single red rose – very romantic and perhaps great on any other day, but Valentine's Day? It might backfire horribly. He could go for some other flower but that is not really an option. So how many roses are sufficient to send the right signal about his love? 5, 10, 20? It's a tricky decision.

For all you romantic males out there, a word of advice; when you hand over the roses to your partner, look carefully at her face when she first sees them. If there are slight looks of disappointment then you have got the signal wrong. A broad smile and you can be sure you have reduced the degree of asymmetric information. Or you could have them delivered and have to wait until later to find out if your decision-making was right.

The signalling theory of gift giving is consistent with another observation: people care most about the custom when the strength of affection is most in question. Thus, giving cash to a girlfriend or boyfriend is usually a bad move. But when college students receive a cheque from their parents, they are less often offended. The parents' love is less likely to be in doubt, so the recipient probably won't interpret the cash gift as a signal of lack of affection.

Screening to Induce Information Revelation

When an informed party takes actions to reveal his private information, the phenomenon is called signalling. When an uninformed party takes actions to induce the informed party to reveal private information, the phenomenon is called **screening**.

Some screening is common sense. A person buying a used car may ask that it be checked by a car mechanic before the sale. A seller who refuses this request reveals his private information that the car is a lemon. The buyer may decide to offer a lower price or to look for another car.

Other examples of screening are more subtle. For example, consider a firm that sells car insurance. The firm would like to charge a low premium to safe drivers and a high premium to risky drivers. But how can it tell them apart? Drivers know whether they are safe or risky, but the risky ones won't admit to it. A driver's history is one piece of information (which insurance companies in fact use), but because of the intrinsic randomness of car accidents, history is an imperfect indicator of future risks.

The insurance company might be able to sort out the two kinds of drivers by offering different insurance policies that would induce them to separate themselves. One policy would have a high premium and cover the full cost of any accidents that occur. Another policy would have low premiums but would have, say, a €1 000 excess. (That is, the driver would be responsible for the first €1 000 of damage, and the insurance company would cover the remaining risk.) Notice that the excess is more of a burden for risky drivers because they are more likely to have an accident. Thus, with a large enough excess, the low-premium policy with an excess would attract the safe drivers, while the high-premium policy without an excess would attract the risky drivers. Faced with these two policies, the two kinds of drivers would reveal their private information by choosing different insurance policies.

Asymmetric Information and Public Policy

We have examined two kinds of asymmetric information – moral hazard and adverse selection. And we have seen how individuals may respond to the problem with signalling or screening. Now let's consider what the study of asymmetric information suggests about the proper scope of public policy.

The tension between market success and market failure is central in microeconomics. We learned in Chapter 7 that the equilibrium of supply and demand is efficient in the sense that it maximizes the total surplus that society can obtain in a market. Adam Smith's invisible hand seemed to reign supreme. This conclusion was then tempered with the study of externalities (Chapter 10), public goods (Chapter 11), imperfect competition (Chapters 15 through 17) and poverty (Chapter 20). These examples of market failure showed that government can sometimes improve market outcomes.

The study of asymmetric information gives us new reason to be wary of markets. When some people know more than others, the market may fail to put resources to their best use. People with high-quality used cars may have trouble selling them because buyers will be afraid of getting a lemon. People with few health problems may have trouble getting low-cost health insurance because insurance companies lump them together with those who have significant (but hidden) health problems.

Although asymmetric information may call for government action in some cases, three facts complicate the issue. First, as we have seen, the private market can sometimes deal with information asymmetries on its own using a combination of signalling and screening. Secondly, the government rarely has more information than the private parties. Even if the market's allocation of resources is not first-best, it may be second-best. That is, when there are information asymmetries, policy makers may find it hard to improve upon the market's admittedly imperfect outcome. Thirdly, the government is itself an imperfect institution.

> **Quick Quiz** A person who buys a life insurance policy pays a certain amount per year and receives for his family a much larger payment in the event of his death. Would you expect buyers of life insurance to have higher or lower death rates than the average person? How might this be an example of moral hazard? Of adverse selection? How might a life insurance company deal with these problems?

POLITICAL ECONOMY

As we have seen, markets left on their own do not always reach a desirable allocation of resources. When we judge the market's outcome to be either inefficient or inequitable, there may be a role for the government to step in and improve the situation. Yet before we embrace an activist government, we need to consider one more fact: The government is also an imperfect institution. The field of *political economy* (sometimes called the field of *public choice*) applies the methods of economics to study how government works. We have touched upon this concept in Chapters 9, 10 and 12.

The Condorcet Voting Paradox

Most advanced societies rely on democratic principles to set government policy. When a city is deciding between two locations to build a new park, for example, we have a simple way to choose: the majority gets its way. Yet, for most policy issues, the number of possible outcomes far exceeds two. A new park, for instance, could be placed in many possible locations. In this case, as an 18th century French political theorist, the Marquis de Condorcet, famously noted, democracy might run into some problems trying to choose one of the outcomes.

For example, suppose there are three possible outcomes, labelled A, B and C, and there are three voter types with the preferences shown in Table 22.1. The leader of our town council wants to aggregate these individual preferences into preferences for society as a whole. How should he do it?

At first, he might try some pairwise votes (pairwise refers to the process of comparing options in pairs to ascertain which pair is preferred). If he asks voters to choose first between B and C, voter types 1 and 2 will vote for B, giving B the majority. If he then asks voters to choose between A and B, voter types 1 and 3 will vote for A, giving A the majority. Observing that A beats B, and B beats C, the mayor might conclude that A is the voters' clear choice.

But wait: suppose the council leader then asks voters to choose between A and C. In this case, voter types 2 and 3 vote for C, giving C the majority. That is, under pairwise majority voting, A beats B, B beats C, and C beats A. Normally, we expect preferences (as outlined in Chapter 21) to exhibit the axiom of

TABLE 22.1

The Condorcet Paradox

If voters have these preferences over outcomes A, B and C, then in pairwise majority voting, A beats B, B beats C, and C beats A.

	Voter type		
	Type 1	**Type 2**	**Type 3**
Percentage of electorate	35	45	20
First choice	A	B	C
Second choice	B	C	A
Third choice	C	A	B

Condorcet paradox
the failure of majority rule to produce transitive preferences for society

transitivity: if A is preferred to B, and B is preferred to C, then we would expect A to be preferred to C. The **Condorcet paradox** is that democratic outcomes do not always obey this property. Pairwise voting might produce transitive preferences for a society, depending on the pattern of individual preferences, but as our example in the table shows, it cannot be counted on to do so.

One implication of the Condorcet paradox is that the order on which things are voted can affect the result. If the council leader suggests choosing first between A and B and then comparing the winner to C, the town ends up choosing C. But if the voters choose first between B and C and then compare the winner to A, the town ends up with A. And if the voters choose first between A and C and then compare the winner to B, the town ends up with B.

There are two lessons to be learned from the Condorcet paradox. The narrow lesson is that when there are more than two options, setting the agenda (that is, deciding the order in which items are voted) can have a powerful impact on the outcome of a democratic election. The broad lesson is that majority voting by itself does not tell us what outcome a society really wants.

Arrow's Impossibility Theorem

Since political theorists first noticed Condorcet's paradox, they have spent much energy studying voting systems and proposing new ones. For example, as an alternative to pairwise majority voting, the leader of the town council could ask each voter to rank the possible outcomes. For each voter, we could give 1 point for last place, 2 points for second to last, 3 points for third to last and so on. The outcome that receives the most total points wins. With the preferences in Table 22.1, outcome B is the winner. (You can do the arithmetic yourself.) This voting method is called a *Borda count,* after the 18th century French mathematician and political scientist who devised it. It is often used in polls that rank sports teams.

Is there a perfect voting system? Economist Kenneth Arrow (the winner of the 1972 Nobel Prize in Economics) took up this question in his 1951 book *Social Choice and Individual Values.* Arrow started by defining what a perfect voting system would be. He assumes that individuals in society have preferences over the various possible outcomes: A, B, C and so on. He then assumes that society wants a voting scheme to choose among these outcomes that satisfies several properties:

- *Unanimity.* If everyone prefers A to B, then A should beat B.
- *Transitivity.* If A beats B, and B beats C, then A should beat C.
- *Independence of irrelevant alternatives.* The ranking between any two outcomes A and B should not depend on whether some third outcome C is also available.

- *No dictators*. There is no person that always gets his way, regardless of everyone else's preferences.

These all seem like desirable properties for a voting system to have. Yet Arrow proved, mathematically and incontrovertibly, that no voting system can satisfy all of these properties. This amazing result is called **Arrow's impossibility theorem**.

The mathematics needed to prove Arrow's theorem is beyond the scope of this book, but we can get some sense of why the theorem is true from a couple of examples. We have already seen the problem with the method of majority rule. The Condorcet paradox shows that majority rule fails to produce a ranking among the outcomes that always satisfies transitivity.

As another example, the Borda count fails to satisfy the independence of irrelevant alternatives. Recall that, using the preferences in Table 22.1, outcome B wins with a Borda count. But suppose that suddenly C disappears as an alternative. If the Borda count method is applied only to outcomes A and B, then A wins. (Once again, you can do the arithmetic on your own.) Thus, eliminating alternative C changes the ranking between A and B. The reason for this change is that the result of the Borda count depends on the number of points that A and B receive, and the number of points depends on whether the irrelevant alternative, C, is also available.

Arrow's impossibility theorem is a deep and disturbing result. It doesn't say that we should abandon democracy as a form of government. But it does say that, no matter what voting scheme society adopts for aggregating the preferences of its members, in some way it will be flawed as a mechanism for social choice.

Arrow's impossibility theorem a mathematical result showing that, under certain assumed conditions, there is no scheme for aggregating individual preferences into a valid set of social preferences

The Median Voter Is King

Despite Arrow's theorem, voting is how most societies choose their leaders and public policies, often by majority rule. The next step in studying government is to examine how governments run by majority rule work. That is, in a democratic society, who determines what policy is chosen? In some cases, the theory of democratic government yields a surprisingly simple answer.

Let's consider an example. Imagine that society is deciding on how much money to spend on some public good, such as the army or the national parks. Each voter has his own most preferred budget, and he always prefers outcomes closer to his most preferred value to outcomes further away. Thus, we can line up voters from those who prefer the smallest budget to those who prefer the largest. Figure 22.1 is an example. Here there are 100 voters, and the budget size varies from zero to €20 billion. Given these preferences, what outcome would you expect democracy to produce?

According to a famous result called the **median voter theorem**, majority rule will produce the outcome most preferred by the median voter. The *median voter* is the voter exactly in the middle of the distribution. In this example, if you take the line of voters ordered by their preferred budgets and count 50 voters from either end of the line, you will find that the median voter wants a budget of €10 billion. By contrast, the average preferred outcome (calculated by adding the preferred outcomes and dividing by the number of voters) is €9 billion, and the modal outcome (the one preferred by the greatest number of voters) is €15 billion.

The median voter rules the day because his preferred outcome beats any other proposal in a two-way race. In our example, more than half the voters want €10 billion or more, and more than half want €10 billion or less. If someone proposes, say, €8 billion instead of €10 billion, everyone who prefers €10 billion or more will vote with the median voter. Similarly, if someone proposes €12 billion

median voter theorem a mathematical result showing that if voters are choosing a point along a line and each voter wants the point closest to his most preferred point, then majority rule will pick the most preferred point of the median voter

FIGURE 22.1

The Median Voter Theorem: An Example

This bar chart shows how 100 voters' most preferred budget is distributed over five options, ranging from zero to €20 billion. If society makes its choice by majority rule, the median voter (who here prefers €10 billion) determines the outcome.

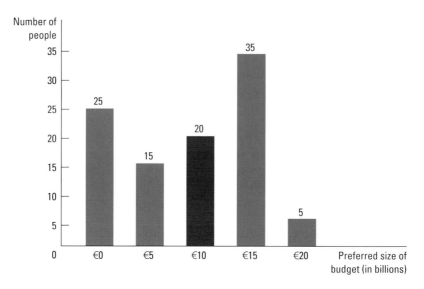

instead of €10 billion, everyone who wants €10 billion or less will vote with the median voter. In either case, the median voter has more than half the voters on his side.

What about the Condorcet voting paradox? It turns out that when the voters are picking a point along a line and each voter aims for his own most preferred point, the Condorcet paradox cannot arise. The median voter's most preferred outcome beats all comers.

One implication of the median voter theorem is that if two political parties are each trying to maximize their chance of election, they will both move their positions toward the median voter. Suppose, for example, that the Red party advocates a budget of €15 billion, while the Blue party advocates a budget of €10 billion. The Red position is more popular in the sense that €15 billion has more proponents than any other single choice. Nonetheless, the Blues get more than 50 per cent of the vote: they will attract the 20 voters who want €10 billion, the 15 voters who want €5 billion and the 25 voters who want zero. If the Reds want to win, they will move their platform toward the median voter. Thus, this theory can explain why the parties in a two-party system (and even in a system where three or four parties dominate the political landscape) are similar to each other: they are both moving towards the median voter.

Another implication of the median voter theorem is that minority views are not given much weight. Imagine that 40 per cent of the population want a lot of money spent on the national parks, and 60 per cent want nothing spent. In this case, the median voter's preference is zero, regardless of the intensity of the minority's view. Such is the logic of democracy. Rather than reaching a compromise that takes into account everyone's preferences, majority rule looks only to the person in the exact middle of the distribution.

Politicians Are People Too

When economists study consumer behaviour, they assume that consumers buy the bundle of goods and services that gives them the greatest level of satisfaction. When economists study firm behaviour, they assume that firms produce the quantity of goods and services that yields the greatest level of profits. What should they assume when they study people involved in the practice of politics?

Politicians also have objectives. It would be nice to assume that political leaders are always looking out for the well-being of society as a whole; that they are aiming for an optimal combination of efficiency and equity. Nice, perhaps, but not realistic. Self-interest is as powerful a motive for political actors as it is for consumers and firm owners. Some politicians are motivated by desire for re-election and are willing to sacrifice the national interest when doing so solidifies their base of voters. Other politicians are motivated by simple greed. If you have any doubt, you should look at the world's poor nations, where corruption and poor governance among government officials is a common impediment to economic development.

This book is not the place to develop a theory of political behaviour. That topic is best left to the political scientists. But when thinking about economic policy, remember that this policy is made not by a benevolent king, but by real people with their own all-too-human desires. Sometimes they are motivated to further the national interest, but sometimes they are motivated by their own political and financial ambitions. We shouldn't be surprised when economic policy fails to resemble the ideals derived in economics textbooks.

Quick Quiz A local district council decides to let the people living in the area vote on how much it should spend on local schools and the resulting student–teacher ratio. A poll finds that 35 per cent of the voters want a ratio of 9:1, 25 per cent want a ratio of 10:1 and 40 per cent want a ratio of 12:1. What outcome would you expect the district to end up with?

BEHAVIOURAL ECONOMICS

Economics is a study of human behaviour, but it is not the only field that can make that claim. The social science of psychology also sheds light on the choices that people make in their lives. The fields of economics and psychology usually proceed independently, in part because they address a different range of questions. But recently a field called *behavioural economics* has emerged in which economists are making use of basic psychological insights. So far in the book we have made reference to a number of instances where behavioural economics has something else to add to our analysis. Let's summarize some of the key insights from behavioural economics here.

People Aren't Always Rational

Economic theory is populated by a particular species of organism, sometimes called *Homo economicus.* Thaler and Sunstein – see Chapter 20 – refer to them as 'econs'. Members of this species are always rational. As managers of firms, they maximize profits. As consumers, they maximize utility (or, equivalently, pick the point on the highest indifference curve). Given the constraints they face, they rationally weigh all the costs and benefits and always choose the best possible course of action.

Real people, however, are *Homo sapiens.* Although in many ways they resemble the rational, calculating people assumed in economic theory, they are far more complex. They can be forgetful, impulsive, confused, emotional and short-sighted. These imperfections of human reasoning are the bread-and-butter of psychologists, but until recently, economists have neglected them.

Herbert Simon, one of the first social scientists to work at the boundary of economics and psychology, suggested that humans should be viewed not as rational maximizers but as *satisficers*. Rather than always choosing the best course of action, they make decisions that are merely good enough. Similarly, other economists have suggested that humans are only 'near rational' or that they exhibit 'bounded rationality'. Bounded rationality is the idea that humans make decisions under the constraints of limited, and sometimes unreliable, information, that they face limits to the amount of information they can process and that they face time constraints in making decisions.

Studies of human decision making have tried to detect systematic mistakes that people make. Here are a few of the findings:

- *People are overconfident.* Imagine that you were asked some numerical questions, such as the number of African countries in the United Nations, the height of the tallest mountain in Europe and so on. Instead of being asked for a single estimate, however, you were asked to give a 90 per cent confidence interval – a range such that you were 90 per cent confident the true number falls within it. When psychologists run experiments like this, they find that most people give ranges that are too small: the true number falls within their intervals far less than 90 per cent of the time. That is, most people are too sure of their own abilities.

- *People give too much weight to a small number of vivid observations.* Imagine that you are thinking about buying a car of brand X. To learn about its reliability, you read *Consumer Reports,* which has surveyed 1 000 owners of car X. Then you run into a friend who owns car X and she tells you that her car is a lemon. How do you treat your friend's observation? If you think rationally, you will realize that she has only increased your sample size from 1 000 to 1 001, which does not provide much new information. In addition, a process called the *reticular activation system* (RAS) works to bring your attention to instances of this car – you will suddenly start to notice more of them. The RAS is an automatic mechanism in the brain that brings relevant information to our attention. Both these effects – your friend's story is so vivid and you have noticed more of these vehicles on the road – mean that you may be tempted to attach a disproportionate weight to them in decision-making.

- *People are reluctant to change their minds.* People tend to interpret evidence to confirm beliefs they already hold. In one study, subjects were asked to read and evaluate a research report on whether capital punishment deters crime. After reading the report, those who initially favoured the death penalty said they were more sure in their view, and those who initially opposed the death penalty also said they were more sure in their view. The two groups interpreted the same evidence in exactly opposite ways.

- *People have a natural tendency to look for examples which confirm their existing view or hypothesis.* Nassim Nicholas Taleb calls this 'naïve empiricism'. People identify, select or observe past instances and quote them as evidence for a viewpoint or hypothesis. For example, every extreme weather event that is reported is selected as evidence of climate change, the fact that the UK enjoyed over a decade of economic growth was evidence that the era of 'boom and bust' had been relegated to the history books or that a rise in the price of petrol of 10 per cent is symptomatic of a broader increase in prices of all goods.

- *People use rules of thumb – heuristics.* When making decisions many people will be influenced by deep-seated rules of thumb or heuristics. There are three main heuristics. *Anchoring* refers to the tendency for people to start with something they are familiar with or know and make decisions or adjustments based on this anchor. Often these anchors are biased and so the adjustment or decision is flawed in some way. The *availability* heuristic refers to cases where decisions are made based on an assessment of the risks of the likelihood of something happening. If examples readily come to mind as a result of excessive media coverage, for example, decisions may be taken with a skewed assessment of the risks. The third heuristic is *representativeness*. In this instance people tend to make judgements by comparing how representative something is to an image or stereotype that they hold. For example we might judge a person with lots of tattoos and piercings in a negative way or we may have an imperfect understanding of patterns as representations of reality, for example, random events. In many European cities perceptions of the prevalence of certain types of crime do not match the facts. People may be more prepared to pay money to buy a lottery ticket if a close friend has just won a reasonable amount of money on the lottery.

Why, you might ask, is economics built on the rationality assumption when psychology and common sense cast doubt on it? One answer is that the assumption, even if not exactly true, is still a good approximation. For example, when we studied the differences between competitive and monopoly firms, the assumption that firms rationally maximize profit yielded many important and valid insights. Recall from Chapter 2 that economic models are not meant to replicate reality but are supposed to show the essence of the problem at hand as an aid to understanding. When actual observed behaviour differs from the model we can analyse this behaviour to explain what is happening, and why, in relation to the 'benchmark' we have in the model.

Another reason that economists so often assume rationality may be that economists are themselves not rational maximizers. Like most people, they are overconfident, and they are reluctant to change their minds. Their choice among alternative theories of human behaviour may exhibit excessive inertia. Moreover, economists may be content with a theory that is not perfect but is good enough. Indeed, the model of rational man may be the theory of choice for a satisficing social scientist.

People Care about Fairness

Another insight about human behaviour is best illustrated with an experiment called the *ultimatum game.* The game works like this: two volunteers (who are otherwise strangers to each other) are told that they are going to play a game and could win a total of €100. Before they play, they learn the rules. The game begins with a flip of a coin, which is used to assign the volunteers to the roles of player A and player B. Player A's job is to propose a division of the €100 prize (in whole euros) between himself and the other player. After player A makes his proposal, player B decides whether to accept or reject it. If he accepts it, both players are paid according to the proposal. If player B rejects the proposal, both players walk away with nothing. In either case, the game then ends.

Before proceeding, stop and think about what you would do in this situation. If you were player A, what division of the €100 would you propose? If you were player B, what proposals would you accept?

Conventional economic theory assumes in this situation that people are rational wealth-maximizers. This assumption leads to a simple prediction: player A should propose that he gets €99 and player B gets €1, and player B should accept the proposal. After all, once the proposal is made, player B is better off accepting it as long as he gets something out of it (remember, people are assumed to act at the margin – a €1 euro gain is better than nothing). Moreover, because player A knows that accepting the proposal is in player B's interest, player A has no reason to offer him more than €1. In the language of game theory (discussed in Chapter 17), the 99–1 split is the Nash equilibrium.

Yet when experimental economists ask real people to play the ultimatum game, the results are very different from this prediction. People in the role of player B usually reject proposals that give them only €1 or a similarly small amount. Knowing this, people in the role of player A usually propose giving player B much more than €1. Some people will offer a 50–50 split, but it is more common for player A to propose giving player B an amount such as €30 or €40, keeping the larger share for himself. In this case, player B usually accepts the proposal.

What's going on here? The natural interpretation is that people are driven in part by some innate sense of fairness. A 99–1 split seems so wildly unfair to many people that they reject it, even to their own detriment. By contrast, a 70–30 split is still unfair, but it is not so unfair that it induces people to abandon their normal self-interest.

Throughout our study of household and firm behaviour, the innate sense of fairness has not played any role. But the results of the ultimatum game suggest that perhaps it should. For example, in Chapters 18 and 19 we discussed how wages were determined by labour supply and labour demand. Some economists have suggested that the perceived fairness of what a firm pays its workers should also enter the picture. Thus, when a firm has an especially profitable year, workers (like player B) may expect to be paid a fair share of the prize, even if the standard equilibrium does not dictate it. The firm (like player A) might well decide to give workers more than the equilibrium wage for fear that the workers might otherwise try to punish the firm with reduced effort, strikes or even vandalism.

To return to the ultimatum game, do you think that a sense of fairness may have its price? If the players were given, say, €1 000 to divide to the nearest hundred, and player A proposed a split of €900 to him and €100 to player B, do you think that player B would be just as likely to reject the proposal as before? What if the prize money were raised to €1 million, to be divided to the nearest €100 000? The answer may depend on the notion of *framing* – behaviour and decision-making will be dependent on the way decision problems or choices are framed.

People Are Inconsistent over Time

Imagine some dreary task, such as doing your laundry or tidying your room. Now consider the following questions:

1. Would you prefer (A) to spend 50 minutes doing the task immediately or (B) to spend 60 minutes doing the task tomorrow?
2. Would you prefer (A) to spend 50 minutes doing the task in 90 days or (B) to spend 60 minutes doing the task in 91 days?

When asked questions like these, many people choose B to question 1 and A to question 2. When looking ahead to the future (as in question 2), they minimize the amount of time spent on the dreary task. But faced with the prospect of doing the task immediately (as in question 1), they choose to put it off.

In some ways, this behaviour is not surprising: everyone procrastinates from time to time. But from the standpoint of the theory of rational humans, it is puzzling. Suppose that, in response to question 2, a person chooses to spend 50 minutes in 90 days. Then, when the 90th day arrives, we allow him to change his mind. In effect, he then faces question 1, so he opts for doing the task the next day. But why should the mere passage of time affect the choices he makes?

Many times in life, people make plans for themselves, but then they fail to follow through. A smoker promises himself that he will quit, but within a few hours of smoking his last cigarette, he craves another and breaks his promise. A person trying to lose weight promises that he will stop eating chocolate bars, but when he gets to the checkout at the supermarket and sees the tempting array of confectionery next to the cash register, the promise is forgotten. In both cases, the desire for instant gratification induces the decision-maker to abandon his own past plans.

Some economists believe that the consumption–saving decision is an important instance where people exhibit this inconsistency over time. For many people, spending provides a type of instant gratification. Saving, like passing up the cigarette or the dessert, requires a sacrifice in the present for a reward in the distant future. And just as many smokers wish they could quit and many overweight individuals wish they ate less, many consumers wish they saved more.

An implication of this inconsistency over time is that people should try to find ways to commit their future selves to following through on their plans. A smoker trying to quit may throw away his cigarettes, and a person on a diet may put a lock on the refrigerator and ask someone else to do the shopping. What can a person who saves too little do? He should find some way to lock up his money before he spends it. Some personal pension plans do exactly that. A worker can agree to have some money taken out of his salary payment before he ever sees it. The money is placed in an account and invested on his behalf by the pension company. When he retires, he can use the money to fund a pension, but the money can only be used before retirement with a penalty. This is one reason why people take out pension plans: they protect people from their own desires for instant gratification. (Thaler and Sunstein have some interesting perspectives on this very topic, one that is of increasing importance in a world where life expectancy is increasing and where the pressure on pensions is rising as a result.)

Quick Quiz   Describe at least three ways in which human decision-making differs from that of the rational individual of conventional economic theory.

IN THE NEWS

In the UK and in Europe, there have been numerous news reports highlighting concerns over the expenses and allowances that elected representatives receive. MEPs and MPs came under heavy criticism for expenses claims made and, in 2009, the British newspapers were full of indignant stories of MPs claiming for moats, duck houses, gardening and even pornographic DVDs! Is moral hazard behind this behaviour?

MPs' and MEPs' Expenses

In May 2009, the British newspaper, *The Daily Telegraph*, published a series of reports on investigations they had carried out over the expenses claimed by members of parliament (MPs). The UK Parliament, like its European equivalent, has rules and regulations governing the claiming of expenses but the revelations seemed to show MPs had been stretching those rules to the very limit. What was revealed shook the confidence in the integrity of MPs and tarnished all, even though many did not abuse the system.

In the UK many MPs need to have a second home in order to carry out their duties in London as opposed to their homes in or around their constituencies. The rules allowed MPs to claim expenses against these second homes but some seemed to have either made claims that might be regarded as fraudulent, such as claiming for mortgage payments when mortgages have been

▶

paid off, whilst others have claimed for repairs to swimming pools, garden work, DVD players, coffee makers, trouser presses and toilet seats, amongst other things. The rules allowed MPs to claim up to £20 000 a year and it has been suggested that MPs have been encouraged to claim the full allowance regardless of whether it is appropriate. The public backlash against MPs was substantial; whilst many could see the necessity of having some sort of expenses system the public did not understand how some MPs could justify, on moral grounds, some of the claims they make, which would certainly not apply to 'ordinary' workers.

In Europe there have been similar concerns. In 2008 a report in *The Times* newspaper suggested that a secret inquiry by the European Parliament showed that the annual parliamentary allowance for all 785 MEPs was being abused to the tune of €100 million. Staff, it was claimed, were making claims for employing fictitious staff,

unqualified family members and receiving bonuses for Christmas far in excess of their annual salary.

One of the problems facing those charged with regulating the behaviour of elected representatives is asymmetric information – the difference in the information available to the public and to MPs. In this case one party, MPs and MEPs, have more and different information to another party, the public. MPs and MEPs have had the privilege of claiming expenses under a set of rules which few outside the two parliaments understood. It was only through freedom of information legislation, for example, that *The Daily Telegraph* was able to get its information and place it in the public domain. MPs and MEPs, therefore, have been protected from risk and as such have behaved in relation to that protection.

Parties that are insulated from risk tend to behave differently as a result. In this case MPs and MEPs have been insulated from the risk that their claims

will be made public and so some have behaved differently than they would if not insulated from risk. This behaviour has been interpreted by the public as being inappropriate and immoral. The agent (MPs and MEPs) may have the incentive to act inappropriately from the viewpoint of the principal (the public). MPs and MEPs have not had to take the consequences and responsibility for their actions and so some may have acted less carefully than they would if those consequences had to be accepted fully by each of them. Any reform to the system, therefore, has to address this fundamental problem and make sure that any new regulatory system addresses the asymmetric information and aligns the interests of MPs and MEPs in legitimately carrying out their duties with what the public see as being fair and equitable.

Source: Adapted from: http://www.bized.co.uk/cgi-bin/chron/chron.pl?id=3361

CONCLUSION

This chapter has examined some of the frontiers of microeconomics. You may have noticed that we have sketched out ideas rather than fully developing them. This is no accident. One reason is that you might study these topics in more detail in advanced courses. Another reason is that these topics remain active areas of research and, therefore, are still being fleshed out.

To see how these topics fit into the broader picture, recall the *Ten Principles of Economics* from Chapter 1. One principle states that markets are usually a good way to organize economic activity. Another principle states that governments can sometimes improve market outcomes. As you study economics, you can more fully appreciate the truth of these principles as well as the caveats that go with them. The study of asymmetric information should make you more wary of market outcomes. The study of political economy should make you more wary of government solutions. And the study of behavioural economics should make you wary of any institution that relies on human decision-making – including both the market and the government.

If there is a unifying theme to these topics, it is that life is messy. Information is imperfect, government is imperfect and people are imperfect. Of course, you knew this long before you started studying economics, but economists need to understand these imperfections as precisely as they can if they are to explain, and perhaps even improve, the world around them.

SUMMARY

- In many economic transactions, information is asymmetric. When there are hidden actions, principals may be concerned that agents suffer from the problem of moral hazard. When there are hidden characteristics, buyers may be concerned about the problem of adverse selection among the sellers. Private markets sometimes deal with asymmetric information with signalling and screening.

- Although government policy can sometimes improve market outcomes, governments are themselves imperfect institutions. The Condorcet paradox shows that majority rule fails to produce transitive preferences for society, and Arrow's impossibility theorem shows that no voting

scheme will be perfect. In many situations, democratic institutions will produce the outcome desired by the median voter, regardless of the preferences of the rest of the electorate. Moreover, the individuals who set government policy may be motivated by self-interest rather than the national interest.

- The study of psychology and economics reveals that human decision-making is more complex than is assumed in conventional economic theory. People are not always rational, they care about the fairness of economic outcomes (even to their own detriment), and they can be inconsistent over time.

KEY CONCEPTS

moral hazard, p. 467
agent, p. 467
principal, p. 467

adverse selection, p. 468
signalling, p. 470
screening, p. 472

Condorcet paradox, p. 474
Arrow's impossibility theorem, p. 475
median voter theorem, p. 475

QUESTIONS FOR REVIEW

1. What is moral hazard? List three things an employer might do to reduce the severity of this problem.

2. What is adverse selection? Give an example of a market in which adverse selection might be a problem.

3. Define *signalling* and *screening*, and give an example of each.

4. What unusual property of voting did Condorcet notice?

5. Explain why majority rule respects the preferences of the median voter rather than the average voter.

6. Describe the ultimatum game. What outcome from this game would conventional economic theory predict? Do experiments confirm this prediction? Explain.

PROBLEMS AND APPLICATIONS

1. Each of the following situations involves moral hazard. In each case, identify the principal and the agent, and explain why there is asymmetric information. How does the action described reduce the problem of moral hazard?
   a. Landlords require tenants to pay security deposits.
   b. Firms compensate top executives with options to buy company shares at a given price in the future.

   c. Car insurance companies offer discounts to customers who install anti-theft devices in their cars.

2. Suppose that the Live-Long-and-Prosper Health Insurance Company charges €5 000 annually for a family insurance policy. The company's president suggests that the company raise the annual price to €6 000 in order to increase its profits. If the firm followed this suggestion,

what economic problem might arise? Would the firm's pool of customers tend to become more or less healthy on average? Would the company's profits necessarily increase?

3. The case study in this chapter describes how a boyfriend can signal to a girlfriend that he loves her by giving an appropriate gift. Do you think saying 'I love you' can also serve as a signal? Why or why not?

4. Some AIDS activists believe that health insurance companies should not be allowed to ask applicants if they are infected with the HIV virus that causes AIDS. Would this rule help or hurt those who are HIV-positive? Would it help or hurt those who are not HIV-positive? Would it exacerbate or mitigate the problem of adverse selection in the market for health insurance? Do you think it would increase or decrease the number of people without health insurance? In your opinion, would this be a good policy?

5. The government is considering two ways to help the needy: giving them cash, or giving them free meals at soup kitchens. Give an argument for giving cash. Give an argument, based on asymmetric information, for why the soup kitchen may be better than the cash handout.

6. Ken walks into a restaurant.
   WAITER: Good afternoon, sir. The specials today are roast lamb and baked trout.
   KEN: I'd like the lamb, please.
   WAITER: I almost forgot. We also have lobster thermidor.
   KEN: In that case, I'll have the trout, please.
   What standard property of decision-making is Ken violating? (Hint: reread the section on Arrow's impossibility theorem.) Is Ken necessarily being irrational? (Hint: what information is revealed by the fact that the chef is able to prepare lobster thermidor?)

7. Why might a political party in a two-party system choose not to move towards the median voter? (Hint: think about abstentions from voting and political contributions.)

8. Two ice cream stands are deciding where to locate along a one-mile beach. Each person sitting on the beach buys exactly one ice cream cone per day from the stand nearest to him. Each ice cream seller wants the maximum number of customers. Where along the beach will the two stands locate?

For further resources, visit
www.cengage.co.uk/mankiw_taylor2

ability-to-pay principle the idea that taxes should be levied on a person according to how well that person can shoulder the burden

abnormal profit the profit over and above normal profit

absolute advantage the comparison among producers of a good according to their productivity

absolute poverty a level of poverty where an individual does not have access to the basic of life – food, clothing and shelter

accounting profit total revenue minus total explicit cost

adverse selection the tendency for the mix of unobserved attributes to become undesirable from the standpoint of an uninformed party

agent a person who is performing an act for another person, called the principal

allocative efficiency a resource allocation where the value of the output by sellers matches the value placed on that output by buyers

Arrow's impossibility theorem a mathematical result showing that, under certain assumed conditions, there is no scheme for aggregating individual preferences into a valid set of social preferences

average fixed cost fixed costs divided by the quantity of output

average revenue total revenue divided by the quantity sold

average tax rate total taxes paid divided by total income

average total cost total cost divided by the quantity of output

average variable cost variable costs divided by the quantity of output

benefits principle the idea that people should pay taxes based on the benefits they receive from government services

branding the means by which a business creates an identity for itself and highlights the way in which it differs from its rivals

budget constraint the limit on the consumption bundles that a consumer can afford

budget deficit an excess of government spending over government receipts

budget surplus an excess of government receipts over government spending

business cycle fluctuations in economic activity, such as employment and production

capital the equipment and structures used to produce goods and services

cartel a group of firms acting in unison

circular-flow diagram a visual model of the economy that shows how money and production inputs and outputs flow through markets among households and firms

Coase theorem the proposition that if private parties can bargain without cost over the allocation of resources, they can solve the problem of externalities on their own

collusion an agreement among firms in a market about quantities to produce or prices to charge

common resources goods that are rival but not excludable

comparative advantage the comparison among producers of a good according to their opportunity cost

compensating differential a difference in wages that arises to offset the non-monetary characteristics of different jobs

competitive market a market in which there are many buyers and many sellers so that each has a negligible impact on the market price

complements two goods for which an increase in the price of one leads to a decrease in the demand for the other (and vice versa).

Condorcet paradox the failure of majority rule to produce transitive preferences for society

constant returns to scale the property whereby long-run average total cost stays the same as the quantity of output changes

consumer surplus a buyer's willingness to pay minus the amount the buyer actually pays

cost the value of everything a seller must give up to produce a good

cost–benefit analysis a study that compares the costs and benefits to society of providing a public good

cross-price elasticity of demand a measure of how much the quantity demanded of one good responds to a change in the price of another good, computed as the percentage change in quantity demanded of the first good divided by the percentage change in the price of the second good

customs union a group of countries that agree not to impose any restrictions at all on trade between their own economies, but to impose the same restrictions as one another on goods imported from countries outside the group

deadweight loss the fall in total surplus that results from a market distortion, such as a tax

demand curve a graph of the relationship between the price of a good and the quantity demanded

demand schedule a table that shows the relationship between the price of a good and the quantity demanded

diminishing marginal product the property whereby the marginal product of an input declines as the quantity of the input increases

direct tax a tax that is levied directly on a person's income

discrimination the offering of different opportunities to similar individuals who differ only by race, ethnic group, sex, age or other personal characteristics

diseconomies of scale the property whereby long-run average total cost rises as the quantity of output increases

dominant strategy a strategy that is best for a player in a game regardless of the strategies chosen by the other players

economic growth the increase in the amount of goods and services in an economy over a period of time

economic profit total revenue minus total cost, including both explicit and implicit costs

economics the study of how society manages its scarce resources

economies of scale the property whereby long-run average total cost falls as the quantity of output increases

economy a word to describe all the economic activity (buying and selling or transactions) that take place in a country or region

efficiency the property of a resource allocation of maximizing the total surplus received by all members of society

efficiency wages above-equilibrium wages paid by firms in order to increase worker productivity

efficient scale the quantity of output that minimizes average total cost

elasticity a measure of the responsiveness of quantity demanded or quantity supplied to one of its determinants

equilibrium a situation in which the price has reached the level where quantity supplied equals quantity demanded

equilibrium price the price that balances quantity supplied and quantity demanded

equilibrium quantity the quantity supplied and the quantity demanded at the equilibrium price

equity the property of distributing economic prosperity fairly among the members of society

excludability the property of a good whereby a person can be prevented from using it when they do not pay for it

explicit costs input costs that require an outlay of money by the firm

exports goods produced domestically and sold abroad

externality the uncompensated impact of one person's actions on the well-being of a bystander (a third party)

factors of production the inputs used to produce goods and services

fixed costs costs that are not determined by the quantity of output produced

free rider a person who receives the benefit of a good but avoids paying for it

game theory the study of how people behave in strategic situations

Giffen good a good for which an increase in the price raises the quantity demanded

gross domestic product per head the market value of all final goods and services produced within a country in a given period of time divided by the population of a country to give a per capita figure

horizontal equity the idea that taxpayers with similar abilities to pay taxes should pay the same amount

human capital the accumulation of investments in people, such as education and on-the-job training

implicit costs input costs that do not require an outlay of money by the firm

import quota a limit on the quantity of a good that can be produced abroad and sold domestically

imports goods produced abroad and purchased for use in the domestic economy

in-kind transfers transfers to the poor given in the form of goods and services rather than cash

income effect the change in consumption that results when a price change moves the consumer to a higher or lower indifference curve

income elasticity of demand a measure of how much the quantity demanded of a good responds to a change in consumers' income, computed as the percentage change in quantity demanded divided by the percentage change in income

indifference curve a curve that shows consumption bundles that give the consumer the same level of satisfaction

indirect tax a tax that is levied on goods and services bought

inferior good a good for which, other things equal, an increase in income leads to a decrease in demand (and vice versa)

inflation an increase in the overall level of prices in the economy

internalizing an externality altering incentives so that people take account of the external effects of their actions

law of demand the claim that, other things equal, the quantity demanded of a good falls when the price of the good rises

law of supply the claim that, other things equal, the quantity supplied of a good rises when the price of the good rises

law of supply and demand the claim that the price of any good adjusts to bring the quantity supplied and the quantity demanded for that good into balance

liberalism the political philosophy according to which the government should choose policies deemed to be just, as evaluated by an impartial observer behind a 'veil of ignorance'

libertarianism the political philosophy according to which the government should punish crimes and enforce voluntary agreements but not redistribute income

life cycle the regular pattern of income variation over a person's life

lump-sum tax a tax that is the same amount for every person

macroeconomics the study of economy-wide phenomena, including inflation, unemployment and economic growth

marginal changes small incremental adjustments to a plan of action

marginal cost the increase in total cost that arises from an extra unit of production

marginal product the increase in output that arises from an additional unit of input

marginal product of labour the increase in the amount of output from an additional unit of labour

marginal rate of substitution the rate at which a consumer is willing to trade one good for another

marginal revenue the change in total revenue from an additional unit sold

marginal tax rate the extra taxes paid on an additional unit of income

market a group of buyers and sellers of a particular good or service

market economy an economy that allocates resources through the decentralized decisions of many firms and households as they interact in markets for goods and services

market failure a situation where scarce resources are not allocated to their most efficient use

market power   the ability of a single economic agent (or small group of agents) to have a substantial influence on market prices

maximin criterion   the claim that the government should aim to maximize the well-being of the worst-off person in society

median voter theorem   a mathematical result showing that if voters are choosing a point along a line and each voter wants the point closest to his most preferred point, then majority rule will pick the most preferred point of the median voter

microeconomics   the study of how households and firms make decisions and how they interact in markets

monopolistic competition   a market structure in which many firms sell products that are similar but not identical

monopoly   a firm that is the sole seller of a product without close substitutes

moral hazard   the tendency of a person who is imperfectly monitored to engage in dishonest or otherwise undesirable behaviour

Nash equilibrium   a situation in which economic actors interacting with one another each choose their best strategy given the strategies that all the other actors have chosen

natural monopoly   a monopoly that arises because a single firm can supply a good or service to an entire market at a smaller cost than could two or more firms

negative income tax   a tax system that collects revenue from high-income households and gives transfers to low-income households

normal good   a good for which, other things equal, an increase in income leads to an increase in demand (and vice versa)

normal profit   the minimum amount required to keep factors of production in their current use

normative statements   claims that attempt to prescribe how the world should be

oligopoly   competition amongst the few – a market structure in which only a few sellers offer similar or identical products and dominate the market

opportunity cost   whatever must be given up to obtain some item – the value of the benefits foregone (sacrificed)

perfect complements   two goods with right-angle indifference curves

perfect substitutes   two goods with straight-line indifference curves

permanent income   a person's normal income

Phillips curve   a curve that shows the short-run trade-off between inflation and unemployment

Pigovian tax   a tax enacted to correct the effects of a negative externality

positive statements   claims that attempt to describe the world as it is

poverty line   an absolute level of income set by the government below which a family is deemed to be in poverty. In the UK and Europe this is measured by earnings less than 60 per cent of median income

poverty rate   the percentage of the population whose family income falls below an absolute level called the poverty line

price ceiling   a legal maximum on the price at which a good can be sold

price discrimination   the business practice of selling the same good at different prices to different customers

price elasticity of demand   a measure of how much the quantity demanded of a good responds to a change in the price of that good, computed as the percentage change in quantity demanded divided by the percentage change in price

price elasticity of supply   a measure of how much the quantity supplied of a good responds to a change in the price of that good, computed as the percentage change in quantity supplied divided by the percentage change in price

price floor   a legal minimum on the price at which a good can be sold

principal   a person for whom another person, called the agent, is performing some act

prisoners' dilemma   a particular 'game' between two captured prisoners that illustrates why cooperation is difficult to maintain even when it is mutually beneficial

private goods   goods that are both excludable and rival

producer surplus   the amount a seller is paid for a good minus the seller's cost

production function   the relationship between quantity of inputs used to make a good and the quantity of output of that good

production possibilities frontier   a graph that shows the combinations of output that the economy can possibly produce given the available factors of production and the available production technology

productivity   the quantity of goods and services produced from each hour of a worker's time

profit   total revenue minus total cost

progressive tax   a tax for which high-income taxpayers pay a larger fraction of their income than do low-income taxpayers

property rights   the exclusive right of an individual, group or organization to determine how a resource is used

proportional or flat tax   a tax for which high-income and low-income taxpayers pay the same fraction of income

public goods   goods that are neither excludable nor rival

quantity demanded   the amount of a good that buyers are willing and able to purchase

quantity supplied   the amount of a good that sellers are willing and able to sell

regressive tax   a tax for which high-income taxpayers pay a smaller fraction of their income than do low-income taxpayers

relative poverty   a situation where an individual is not able to access what would be considered acceptable standards of living in society

rivalry   the property of a good whereby one person's use diminishes other people's use

scarcity   the limited nature of society's resources

screening   an action taken by an uninformed party to induce an informed party to reveal information

shortage   a situation in which quantity demanded is greater than quantity supplied

signalling an action taken by an informed party to reveal private information to an uninformed party

social security government benefits that supplement the incomes of the needy

standard of living refers to the amount of goods and services that can be purchased by the population of a country. Usually measured by the inflation-adjusted (real) income per head of the population

strike the organized withdrawal of labour from a firm by a union

subsidy payment to buyers and sellers to supplement income or lower costs and which thus encourages consumption or provides an advantage to the recipient

substitutes two goods for which an increase in the price of one leads to an increase in the demand for the other

substitution effect the change in consumption that results when a price change moves the consumer along a given indifference curve to a point with a new marginal rate of substitution

sunk cost a cost that has already been committed and cannot be recovered

supply curve a graph of the relationship between the price of a good and the quantity supplied

supply schedule a table that shows the relationship between the price of a good and the quantity supplied

surplus a situation in which quantity supplied is greater than quantity demanded

tariff a tax on goods produced abroad and sold domestically

tax incidence the manner in which the burden of a tax is shared among participants in a market

the long run the period of time in which all factors of production can be altered

the short run the period of time in which some factors of production cannot be changed

total cost the market value of the inputs a firm uses in production

total expenditure the amount paid by buyers, computed as the price of the good times the quantity purchased

total revenue the amount received by sellers of a good, computed as the price of the good times the quantity sold

Tragedy of the Commons a parable that illustrates why common resources get used more than is desirable from the standpoint of society as a whole

transaction costs the costs that parties incur in the process of agreeing and following through on a bargain

union a worker association that bargains with employers over wages and working conditions

utilitarianism the political philosophy according to which the government should choose policies to maximize the total utility of everyone in society

utility a measure of happiness or satisfaction

value of the marginal product the marginal product of an input times the price of the output

variable costs costs that are dependent on the quantity of output produced

vertical equity the idea that taxpayers with a greater ability to pay taxes should pay larger amounts

welfare economics the study of how the allocation of resources affects economic well-being

well-being happiness or satisfaction with life as reported by individuals

willingness to pay the maximum amount that a buyer will pay for a good

world price the price of a good that prevails in the world market for that good

INDEX